FMCG

The Power of Fast-Moving Consumer Goods

D1712909

First Edition Design Publishing

FMCG
The Power of Fast Moving Consumer Goods
Copyright ©2014 Greg Thain and John Bradley

ISBN 978-1622-876-48-8 PRINT PBK
ISBN 978-1622-876-63-1 PRINT HC
ISBN 978-1622-876-47-1 EBOOK

LCCN 2014942766

August 2014

Published and Distributed by
First Edition Design Publishing, Inc.
P.O. Box 20217, Sarasota, FL 34276-3217 USA
www.firsteditiondesignpublishing.com

FMCG

The Power of Fast-Moving Consumer Goods

Greg Thain and John Bradley

Table of Contents

Acknowledgements and Thanks: Greg Thain

This was a large undertaking and we need to thank more than a few people for their help and understanding. First my co-author, John Bradley, who is always fun to work with, either across the Atlantic or from even further afield: I am writing this in the Manila Airport lounge. John's extensive experience of the industry shines through every one of the 500 plus pages. Our editors have also had a major task, so thanks to Tim Bettsworth, but special thanks to John Varnom, who has driven the process to completion over the last few months. John amongst many other achievements was the original marketing director at Virgin,

Ekaterina Safronova and Alexander Utochkin have contributed enormously, with additional data and tireless organization. Individual thanks must also go to Ben Aris, Simon Dunlop, Marat Hasanov, Patrick Cue, Jonathan Tubb, Kim Nicholson, Simon Tyler, Anastasia Lavrenuk, Lionel Thain, Inna Stewart, Adam Duthie, Tic Nica, Dawn Smith, Lumila Belokonova, Leonid Krongauz, Jai Agarwalla, Danny Unger and Martin Cross, all of whom have given us valuable assistance in recent years. We are also very grateful to all the other team players in our offices in Monaco, Manila, Moscow, Shanghai and Dubai.

Finally as always I would thank my family, Katya, Sarah, Nick, Poppy, James and Magnolia.

Acknowledgements and Thanks: John Bradley

I would like to thank Professor Niraj Dawar of the Richard Ivey School of Business for his input and suggestions and especially my wife Audrey for her diligent copy-checking and all-round support.

E-books and Information

This is a new style e-enabled book, allowing twice-yearly updates of all information contained. For updates please see our linked web page at www.Fmcgbook.com.

For information on current books, please see www.storewars.net. Our next publication, **E-Retail Zero Friction in the Digital Universe** is out in July 2014. Please see our linked web page at www.eretailbook.com for further details.

FMCG
The Power of Fast-moving Consumer Goods

FMCG: Dinosaurs or Deciders?

It has become fashionable in some quarters to regard the FMCG category as old hat: a motley crew of yesterday's manufacturers of humdrum products populating the boring centre aisles of yesterday's bricks-and-mortar retail outlets. MBA course attendees want new and they want exciting: Apple, Amazon, Facebook, Google. Yet the biggest four companies in this book, Nestlé, Procter & Gamble, Unilever and PepsiCo, have combined revenues of more than $300 billion - neck and neck with Amazon, Facebook and Google.

OK, so these FMCG companies might still be big, but hasn't all the power shifted to the retailers? Are not the manufacturers a collective spent force? Once again, the numbers say otherwise. Virtually all our 24 companies are enjoying record turnovers and record margins. If power is shifting to the retailers, the cash isn't. And if the cash isn't, the power can't be.

The fact is that the world's largest FMCG companies have never been more successful or more interesting. They still drive the world's advertising industries: where would Google or Facebook be without them? And they have adapted and evolved faster than ever before to remain relevant to consumers in all corners of the globe. FMCG companies are at the forefrontof new retail developments, emerging markets, E-Retailing and online engagement. The Estée Lauder Company founded its online division in 1998 and now has over 340 web and e-Commerce sites, through which sales have grown ten-fold in a decade.

Our Choice of Companies

So how did we arrive at the list of companies profiled in this book? We began with a simple list of FMCG companies ranked by turnover. But we did not stick with this religiously. We decided to exclude three categories: tobacco, beer and spirits. We did so for two main reasons. Firstly, the retail environments in which such products are sold can differ quite dramatically around the world, which lessens the transferability to other product categories or countries of the lessons such companies can teach us. Secondly, particularly for tobacco and beer, a prolonged process of industry consolidation has drastically reduced differentiation.

Scale, and the relentless pursuit of more of it, has become their predominant feature.

A further criterion we used in deciding the final list, and in excluding alcohol and tobacco conglomerates, was a subjective one: any company on our final list could quite conceivably end its days as part of any other. However, whilst it is relatively inconceivable that Nestlé or Unilever might buy SABMiller or Japan Tobacco International, we could easily envisage (ignoring family roadblocks) their acquiring Esteé Lauder, L'Oréal or even Mars Inc. There is also a spread in age: some of the businesses in this book are old, such as Procter & Gamble, which was established in 1837. Others, such as Dean Foods and Reckitt Benckiser, are surprisingly new: both assumed their current forms within the last fifteen years. We have also taken pains to include as many FMCG categories as possible. So we have Dean Foods in the chiller, whilst a couple global giants hold regally forth over on beauty.

How the Book is Organised

The structure of the book is effectively two-fold. We first take an in-depth look at eighteen of the world's largest FMCG businesses, then undertake a less concentrated survey of nine companies based in emerging markets that one day soon might get onto, let alone buy part of, the list. Within the eighteen, there is an almost ten-fold turnover difference between the largest, Nestlé, to the smallest, Esteé Lauder. But all have something to teach us: their differences are as much to do with scope as with capability. Indeed, one of the least impressively performing companies in recent years is Procter & Gamble, now losing out to Colgate in the dental category and to L'Oréal in beauty. Yet P&G are almost twice as big as Colgate and L'Oréal put together.

To understand how this happened, we do not just look at each company's recent performance - we leave that to the investment analysts. We, however, are essentially brand marketers. We look at our chosen companies much more deeply, going right back to their founding and their founding fathers. Despite the prevalence of management consultants sharing best practices and the ubiquity of the MBA case study, we believe each company's performance is as much to do with the strength and uniqueness of its corporate DNA as to how well its senior executives attend to their INSEAD courses.

We are firm believers in the power of institutional knowledge to shape and direct these gigantic businesses. Indeed most companies in this book show a remarkable degree of management continuity. L'Oréal, for example, has had just four CEOs in a century. At Danone, for forty years, there were two, and they were father and son. Itinerant, heroic, parachuted-in CEOs are few and far between at the top of the FMCG food chain.

Sheer Personality

We also start each chapter by looking at how, where, when, why and by whom the company was formed and founded. This is often overlooked by students of business and even by employees in the firms themselves: a quaint bit of historical kitsch irrelevant to the titanic business struggles of today. But the often highly charismatic and driven men and women of the sometimes distant past very frequently bear a wonderfully close relationship with their modern companies' DNA that can still be clearly perceived today. Danone's Daniel Carasso is an excellent example, as certainly is Henkel and, of course, L'Oréal's Eugène Schuller and Estée Lauder, all of whom defined right from the outset the character and strategy of the company and all of whom, were they to walk into head office tomorrow, would feel very much at home right now with what the company was doing and how. Remarkably, the clearest example of this kind of continuity is Mars – only the biggest confectionery company in the world. So, much insight is to be gleaned from quaint historical kitsch after all.

In other businesses, we meet insightful strategists who saw that their existing world was changing, so transformed their businesses to leapfrog the trends. General Mills' James Ford Bell, for example, saw only doom for his regional flour milling company, but reinvented it, revolutionised an industry and created a colossal branded business almost out of nothing.

Competence and Coping

In the second section we look at how each business evolved once it had become established and had developed a core competence or two. In some cases, such as Kellogg's and Heinz, competence was rapidly exploited to create dominant market positions, and then taken international early. In others, as original competences became redundant, it was a case of change them or die. Kimberley-Clark's tariff-driven need to get out of newsprint forced the bet-the-farm commercialisation of their interesting, apparently irrelevant and – at first – highly socially sensitive use of Cellucotton. Henkel's management was almost permanently in crisis mode for forty years, coping with Germany's defeat in the First World War, the French invasion of the Ruhr and their factories based there, the devastation of the Second World War and the post-war Russian theft of almost three quarters of its production capabilities, which were dismantled and shipped off to the Urals. And Nestlé's Swiss head office was surrounded by the Axis powers for years. How management managed has left a permanent imprint. Understanding this imprint means looking at personalities as well as balance sheets.

How Were They Formed and Where Did They Go Next?

The next two sections look at how the modern businesses of today were formed and where they went from the point of formation. And in terms of formation, there were several fronts. For some, it involved the sloughing off of the diversifications that had engulfed many businesses during the 1960s and '70s. Unilever went through trucking, fishing, car dealing, advertising and packaging. General Mills was at one time the world's leading toy company, as it simultaneously solved America's 'What's for supper, Mom?' problem with convenience foods and the Red Lobster and Olive Garden chains. Other businesses reinvented themselves from within: Colgate's George H. Lesch was recalled from their thriving international division to reinvigorate a moribund US organisation. Acquisitions and mergers transformed PepsiCo from serial bankrupt one-hit-wonders into major industry players, while the influx of Phillip Morris tobacco money created new company breed Kraft Foods, formed from the imposed amalgamation of Kraft, General Foods and Nabisco.

All of our chosen companies have, of course, vast international markets. Unilever, Nestlé and Henkel have been regional or global businesses for decades. Nestlé recently celebrated its first hundred years in India, while Unilever has dominated South America for almost as long. In India, Hindustan Lever built the country's leading FMCG business. Kellogg's and Heinz built hugely successful businesses in the U.K. and are so well-established in some of the former British colonies that local customers consider them home-grown.

Of course, the race to conquer the emerging markets of the former Soviet Union, China, India, Indonesia, Brazil, Africa and all the rest is hugely important and hugely influential in shaping policy and progress. And while the stories of Pepsi's Richard Nixon-driven conquest of Russia and Coke's of China are well known, Heinz's steady, even stealthy, accumulation of soy sauce businesses in China and Danone's success with the Aqua brand of water in Indonesia are just as important – in unit terms, Aqua is, in fact, the world's biggest-selling brand of bottled water. International success can also be achieved through collaboration: the Cereal Partners Worldwide relationship which combines General Mills' brands with Nestlé's global reach has been giving Kellogg's a difficult time for many years.

Year by Year

After a quick look at how each company is structured, and how and why their structures have evolved over time – an exercise that convinced us of the inverse relationship between frequency of structural changes and robustness of company strategy – we then look in detail at what each company has done year-by-year over the past decade. Whilst giving a very useful insight into the strategies and activities of the companies, the What Have They Been Doing Recently sections are an excellent way of highlighting changes in momentum, both positive and negative. Procter & Gamble's current malaise was a long time in the making, while the gradual deceleration of the Reckitt Benckiser innovation machine, imperceptible on a quarterly or annual basis, stands out when viewed over a decade. The section also proved to be an excellent device for identifying the severer cases of corporate amnesia, where much-vaunted strategies to transform the business can fade alarmingly when the reality of execution sets in. Take Coke's and Pepsi's hugely expensive acquisitions of their US bottling operations. To get the business back, Coke paid 12 billion times what they originally sold it for. But performance has remained resolutely unchanged at best.

DNA

We then combine all of the above to define what we see as each company's unique DNA, a fascinating exercise in summation intended to highlight the many and varied routes to success that criss-cross the FMCG environment. Some, such as Kimberly-Clark's mastery of absorbency, its marketing of perhaps the world's most embarrassing subject and its subsequent building of consumer trust, are very product specific. Dean Foods' essential make-up rests on the broader managerial skill-set of defining and integrating countless acquisitions, while L'Oréal's is embedded in an ability to think in decades, allied to an unbeatable lead in the science of skin and hair. Sadly, more than one company was, shall we say, genetically challenged: Kellogg's, for example. And one, Kraft/ Mondelēz International, probably still traumatised by continual structural upheaval, may still be fighting to emerge from the consequences.

Now Read On

This book, then, is a comprehensive history of a broad selection of the world's most famous brands, from their humble beginnings to their current exalted status: world leaders and resonating icons of the fast moving consumer goods industry. From smudged pamphlets drafted on kitchen tables to the latest multi-million, multi-platform ad campaign, from backyard experiments with passably dangerous chemicals to global research in pristine laboratories, the book charts in detail the evolution of eighteen household names, whose modern business activities literally define our lives; how they rode the tides of change, built and continue to build their modern empires to establish global structure and reach. **The Power of FMCG** examines the most recent developments in these glittering trajectories. It takes you on a journey through setbacks and astonishing successes, highlighting the key factors that have led to modern pre-eminence, ingenious and often sophisticated brand-building, revealing the DNA of the brands themselves.

As we have indicated, and as you will find in the pages that follow, we analyse how these FMCG giants are responding to emerging markets, their response to the internet and how they have adopted old marketing strategies to this new medium and its very different consumer expectations. It highlights the power that market leaders wield over the global FMCG industry. How PepsiCo, Henkel, Coca-Cola, Colgate Palmolive, Procter and Gamble - to mention just a few – read trends, gather information and monitor technology to best respond to ever-changing, ever-growing, ever more precisely identifiable consumer choice and purchasing power. If you work in retail, FMCG, marketing or consumer goods, this is a must–read book. Consumer marketing and consumer purchases drive our modern world. Every day, the FMCG market leaders expand their reach and increase their dominance. In the global race for consumers and market share, and outside in the world as we know it, here are the giants who have transcended business boundaries to become, in their own right, global financial powers. Here also are some of the emerging contenders. Reports of the demise of FMCG are, we suggest, definitely premature.

Where and When?

The start-dates and locations of our FMCG Companies

Company	Year of Foundation	Place
Coca Cola	1886	Columbus, Georgia, USA
Colgate Palmolive	1806	New York, USA
Danone	1919	Barcelona, Spain
Dean Foods	1925	Franklin Park, Illinois, USA
General Mills	1856	Minneapolis, MN, USA
Heinz	1869	Pittsburgh, Pennsylvania, USA
Henkel	1876	Aachen, Germany
Kellogg's	1906	Battle Creek, Michigan, USA
Kimberly Clark	1872	Neenah, Wisconsin
Kraft	1903	Chicago, Illinois, USA
L'Oréal	1909	Clichy, France
Mars	1911	Tacoma, Washington, USA
Mars Inc	1920	Minneapolis, Minnesota, USA
Nestle	1866	Vevey, Switzerland
Procter & Gamble	1837	Cincinnatti, Ohio, USA
PepsiCo	1902	New Bern, NCa, USA
Colman's	1814	Norwich, England
Reckitt & Sons	1840	Hull, England
Reckitt & Colman	1938	Hull, England
Benckiser	1823	New York, USA
Reckitt Benckiser	1999	Germany
Estée Lauder	1945	New York, USA
Unilever	1823	Rotterdam, Netherlands

Coca-Cola

Where Did They Come From?

By 7th May 1886, the life of 53-year-old druggist John Styth Pemberton had been one of unrelenting failure. His quest to develop a winning patent medicine during his employment at, or part-ownership of, nine different pharmaceutical firms remained unfulfilled. But he was nothing if not indefatigable. The failures of his Extract of Stylinger, Globe Flower Cough Syrup, Triplex Liver Pills and Indian Queen Hair Dye, among many others, had not deterred him from his latest obsession – producing a non-alcoholic version of another of his flops, French Wine of Coca.

Given that French Wine's principle ingredients were alcohol and cocaine, it might seem strange today that all Pemberton wanted to take out was the alcohol. But in those closing years of the century, cocaine was enjoying a brief spell of popular acceptance and had already appeared in other patent medicines such as Dr. Tucker's Specific and Dr. Mitchell's Cola-Bola. Pemberton's latest idea was to remove the mood-depressing alcohol and replace it with an extract of the African kola nut, a second stimulant which would compliment the already stimulating cocaine. So, a day later on May 8th 1886, when Pemberton, his business partner Frank M. Robinson and drug store owner Dr. Joseph Jacobs tasted the first ever glasses of Coca-Cola, it wasn't just what was in the drink that upped their heart-rates and dilated their pupils, it was how it tasted: great. Did they at last have a contender for the American soft drinks market, already decades old, rapidly growing and coining in the cash even then? Who knew? Might their new and as yet unnamed idea conceivably do as well as – hold your breath! - Charles E. Hires' Root Beer? Or even – Heavens above! - Lemon's Superior Sparkling Ginger Ale?

Rather better, as it turns out. Yet had it remained in Pemberton's hands, it would simply have disappeared, let alone changed the world. Christened Coca-Cola by Frank Robinson, the product sold moderately well in the drug stores and soda fountains of Atlanta but was far from making Pemberton either rich or even debt free. When he fell ill the next year, he sold two thirds of his joint-ownership of the company, for the princely sum of $283.2, to the very man who had mixed the first glasses behind the counter of the drug store. The tired and disillusioned Pemberton would almost certainly have taken his drink to the grave.

The lucky new man was Frank Robinson. He'd already come up with the name - and something that looked like Coke's logo today - but he was saddled with a new partner who, a mere drug store counter jockey, had no resources to add anything to the sale and promotion of Coca-Cola. So Robinson approached a prosperous Atlanta drug-store owner and patent medicine manufacturer, Asa Griggs Candler. Candler bought out the jockey and Pemberton's remaining stake for $550, and became the driving force of the new partnership. And here we leave John Pemberton, who died the following year, penniless and in an un-marked plot. His descendants would later try to sue their way back into part-ownership, but to no avail: it had all been legal.

Candler had first fallen for Frank Robinson's impassioned sales pitch because he found that drinking Coca-Cola cured his headaches, which was surely a bless-ing. But not a commercial one. Candler could already see that, for patent medi-cines, the writing was on the wall. The future, Candler realised, lay not in dubi-ous medical claims but the simple act of refreshment. As well as clarity of vision, Candler also brought a nascent business drive and passion. His family, like many affluent Southerners, had been ruined by the Civil War, reduced from comfort to a near poverty which had also put paid to his hopes of studying to be a doctor. And although sales in the initial couple of years were uninspiring - 1,500 gallons of syrup in 1887 rising to only 2,200 in 1889 – the perceptive Asa Candler saw in Coca-Cola a vehicle both to restore his family's lost fortune and – how sweet was this? – one that might ultimately re-conquer the hated North that had taken it all away .

Thus fuelled, his passion for Coca-Cola knew no bounds. And he also really liked the drink: he was convinced that if people knew it like he did, he'd need armed guards on the plant to keep the thirsty hordes at bay. Finally, he succeed-ed in communicating his commitment to the miniscule sales team and took every opportunity to do so, although perhaps one very powerful ally he enlisted for the sales pitch also helped stir the team's blood: his favourite means of ending sales meetings was a rousing rendition of Onward Christian Soldiers.

How Did They Evolve?

Asa Candler realised from the start that there was a two-fold secret to selling a refreshing beverage: make it available to as many customers as possible and make it available where they bought its competitors. This meant soda fountains, locat-ed primarily in drug stores. He beefed up the summertime sales force by hiring cotton buyers, unemployed at that time of year, and sent them far and wide. By 1902 the product was for sale as far away as New England, whilst syrup would soon be manufactured in Chicago, a wholly necessary regionalisation of syrup production as the Pemberton formula didn't have a long shelf life. Robinson and Candler, an experienced druggist in his own right, tinkered endlessly with the recipe until they had something both delicious and amenable to far-flung distribution.

By 1891, syrup sales had rocketed to nearly 20,000 gallons and would double again the next year, despite the beginnings of a press campaign against the evils of cocaine that continued for fifteen years. In response, Candler made the somewhat rash commitment to give up Coca-Cola if cocaine could ever be shown to be addictive. Fortunately, the challenge was never accepted. Meanwhile, the Candler sales and promotion machine, a robust combination of what we'd now call push and pull sales techniques, shifted into gear. The travelling cotton buyers were given a vast armoury of incentives, from any and every kind of branded merchandise, free shipping, stockist rebates and free-trial Coke customer vouchers which they could hand out to anyone who looked interested, all fully-funded by Coca-Cola. Candler also believed strongly in advertising, often spending up to 25% of the now rapidly rising annual income. Within ten years, Coca-Cola would be the single most advertised product in America. Candler paid himself and his staff a pittance. Do these facts – aside from the salaries – begin to ring a few more modern bells?

The next major step was bottling. Candler was at best lukewarm and, once again, Coca-Cola was by no means first on the scene: by the time Pemberton had tasted his first glass in 1886 there were over 500 bottling plants in America, primarily of soda water. But bottling and particularly sealing technology was not what it is now. Product went flat quickly and the glass bottles were prone to exploding without notice. So when, for his approval, Candler was unexpectedly sent the first ever two-dozen case of bottled Coca-Cola by entrepreneur Joseph Biedenharn, he was less than enthusiastic, although he grudgingly acceded to Biedenharn's logic: taking the drink to the people might well be simpler and more effective than taking the people to the drink. A bottle, after all, is easier to ship than a body.

The solution lay in technology. Until the widespread adoption of the Crown Cork bottle top, patented in 1892, the market for bottled carbonated drinks remained small and Candler uninterested, although he did grant a handful of bottling licenses to various small-time operators, probably to forestall their pestering. In 1899, however, he was approached again, this time by two Chattanooga lawyers, Benjamin Franklin Thomas and James Brown Whitehead, who pushed him hard. There were, they argued, almost limitless possibilities for incremental sales via nationwide bottling. Candler was so dubious he granted them what, on the face of it, was the biggest giveaway in business history: the franchise to bottle and sell Coca-Cola everywhere in the United States, apart from the small territories of Biedenharn and others. The lawyers sealed the deal for one US dollar. In due course, and in a very lawyerly fashion, the deal got better yet: Thomas and Whitehead never paid up.

A forever outstanding buck now bought Thomas and Whitehead the rights to set up bottling plants almost anywhere in America, to sell the bottled product to whomsoever they chose at the locked in price of 5 cents and, while simply purchasing simply the syrup form Coca-Cola, to enjoy at no charge – remember that Coke still fully-funded everything – a wealth of promotional materials and nationwide advertising. There was just one problem – capital. Even one bottling plant, let alone the 1,020 that would be in place by 1917, was entirely beyond their means. Indeed, so gloomy did the prospects look for making any money from the license that Whitehead sold half of his share for $5,000.

Their brainwave, which made them fabulously wealthy, was to create entire dynasties of equally wealthy bottling families by dividing up the country and sub-licensing the franchise to large numbers of people who did have the capital, granting them an exclusive territory in perpetuity. Thomas and Whitehead didn't bottle Coca-Cola at all; they simply wholesaled the syrup to people who'd bought the licenses from them. The results? Coca-Cola became absolutely omnipresent in the US and its bottling network persisted for almost all of the company's history. Admittedly, Coca-Cola was not the instant goldmine it very soon became, and many territories changed hands before the system bedded down, but the die was cast, and the pathway to wealth – the six-lane highway to wealth – was truly open..

Of course, Coca-Cola spent hundreds of millions – less a dollar, of course - to buy back bottling many decades later, but this was far from the one-sided deal history and business historians often suggest. As early as 1905, there were 241 Coca-Cola bottling plants, a level, speed and sheer volume of capital investment the parent company could no more have managed than the lawyers. In addition, the bottlers, at least in the early years, added more than just the hard cash they had paid for the licenses and the plant. Most were hard-driven and hard-driving entrepreneurs who injected a raw energy into the system that no mere employee would have been likely to match. While the bottling franchise system made a lot of people wealthy – and all good franchises do - the system also gave Coca-Cola a breadth and depth of national distribution at a speed undreamed-of by other soft drink companies. Everyone did well from the deal.

With no need to worry about a sizeable chunk of the distribution network and, more importantly, no need to raise capital to fund it, the company was free to concentrate on what it did best: driving soda fountain distribution and creating consumer demand for the single, graspable, easily marketable product that was Coca-Cola. The decision by Candler to focus on just one brand was also crucial to the speed in which the brand name spread, although Candler had not always shown such single-mindedness. When he bought his interest in Coca-Cola, his various other companies had manufactured a range of various other drinks. But he cast them all aside. To Candler, Coca-Cola was never just *a* drink, it was *the* drink. Such focus on the product range of one made marketing a much easier proposition: concentrated in content and unprecedented scale.

The early years of the 20th-century saw two crucial changes to building the brand's appeal. In 1902, tired of the endlessly negative press, Candler finally agreed to remove cocaine from the recipe, using spent coca leaves instead. The advertising also shifted its ground and began to focus on a single, key element: refreshment. Consider one nationally advertised 1905 message: Relieves Fatigue and is Indispensible for Business and Professional Men, Students, Wheelmen and Athletes. Or: Relieves Mental and Physical Exhaustion and is the Favourite Drink for Ladies When Thirsty, Weary and Despondent. In 1908, a message that was plastered over 2.5 million square feet of prime advertising real estate plus countless promotional items from clocks to Japanese fans simply proclaimed: Good to the Last Drop. That same year's syrup was a shade less than 2.9 million gallons, a more than three-fold increase in five years. Was this the start of modern copywriting?

Whilst advertising and the relentless programme of opening new soda fountain accounts were the main preoccupations of Coca-Cola head office, the owners of the bottling franchise, Thomas and Whitehead, were creating the bottle, the final piece of brand iconography. They wanted a bottle that would sell Coca-Cola not only full but empty or even broken. They wanted a bottle that could be recognised in the dark. In 1915, a committee made up of Thomas and other key bottlers ran a bottle beauty contest. The winner came from the C.J. Root Company of Indiana, whose designers aimed to mimic the shape of the coca bean but had actually copied that of the cacao bean. Patented by Root in 1915, the most profitable entomological error in history was launched. Sales reached 7.5 million gallons and topped $10 million for the first time.

The brand was in pretty much national distribution, clearly heading for both omnipresence and omnipotence, as per the God of Candler's sales pitch-closing hymn. But it wasn't quite there yet. Sales in the Western US were tiny compared to the brand's southern heartland, so opening more accounts was still the mantra of the company, now under the sole direction of Candler, Frank Robinson having retired in 1914. However, Candler was increasingly distracted by a much less productive activity, lawsuits with copycats. While the company's zeal in chasing down and obliterating any and every threat to the brand's uniqueness was a key factor in its growth, by 1916 Candler was ailing under the strain. His election as mayor of Atlanta was a sort of final straw. He divided his stock between his wife and five children and left them to run things.

At first glance, the family seemed to manage pretty well. The 1916 syrup sales of 9.7 million gallons essentially doubled to 18.7 million in three years. But the sales model, once predominantly consumer pull, had become one of unrelenting stock pressure push. The company's 75,000 soda fountain accounts were being pressured to take more and more syrup. But the company was doing less and less to sell it through. Advertising expenditure, Candle's sacrosanct long-term investment, fell by 6% in 1917.

In September 1919, when the family sold their entire stock to Atlanta financier Ernest Woodruff - a fact Asa Candler, grieving over the recent death of his wife, discovered after the event – it was difficult to escape the conclusion that the family had been goosing the numbers to get a top dollar price, which they did at $25 million. This was a huge purchase at the time, the largest ever in the South, and had required the involvement of some of the wealthiest Wall Street firms of the day. Woodruff was now leveraged up to the eyeballs, a problem enough for any new owner of an unfamiliar business. But his worries paled into insignificance when Samuel Candler Dobbs, the new president, forward-bought vast quantities of sugar in 1920 at 28 cents a pound. The price promptly dropped to two. Woodruff and his wealthy partners were almost bankrupted. Just to stay in business they had to raise another $20 million - almost as much as they had paid in the first place.

Another major woe for the new owners was a major bust-up with the bottlers, provoked by the company's attempt both to increase the syrup price and strike out the in-perpetuity clauses in the franchises. The unsustainability of 18 million gallons a year, a slashed advertising budget and a de-motivated set of bottlers wreaked further havoc; sales stalled in 1920, dropped 15% the next year and a further 3% the year after. Woodruff, not a young man, gave up. In 1923 he stepped down, replacing himself as CEO with his 33-year-old son, Robert W. Woodruff. If he was going to go belly up, he would do so in hands he trusted.

Robert Woodruff was leaving a reasonably successful career in the motor trade for the herculean task of sorting out a company many now believed to have been simply a flash – if a somewhat sustained flash – in an essentially southern pan. But Woodruff Junior brought an astute mind to what could have been an insuperable problem. He immediately realised that Coca-Cola's evident disfunctionality had two roots. Firstly, as Coca Cola was now available in virtually every soda fountain in the country, the sales push model made no sense at all. It had run its course. Constant pressure to buy more Coca-Cola syrup could do nothing at all for sales and great deal to disillusion soda fountain owners with Coca-Cola and drive them into the arms of friendlier competitors. Secondly, the company syrup salesmen and the bottlers' jobbers had begun to compete more for each other's slice of the pie rather than grow the size of the pie itself. To solve these destructive problems, Woodruff would spend most of the 1920s making two major, and crucial, changes, to his style of marketing on the one hand and his business support (in the shape of the bottlers) on the other.

The first major change Woodruff made to his own sales organisation was to decentralise it. Until this point everything had been run out of Atlanta and, as the company's distribution base had multiplied and sales skyrocketed, the Atlanta system had become increasingly unwieldy and unresponsive. So he set up two wholly owned sales corporations, one for Canada (which housed the company's second-largest syrup plant), and one for the US, split into five sales divisions, which themselves were divided again into first sixteen and then twenty sales districts. Then, in 1927, the company held a national sales conference in Atlanta, which Woodruff opened by telling every salesman that he or she was fired, but should report back the next day to learn more. It was what you might call a cultural paradigm shift. In the event, the following morning they all turned up, to hear they were all being offered jobs in the new service department, that they were no longer syrup-pushers but retail sales experts whose only job was to help their accounts sell more Coca-Cola. Woodruff might just have sat back - the company had reached a new sales peak of 22.8 million gallons that year – but he didn't; he was convinced the push model had to go.

Winning the bottlers over was a more nuanced challenge. Bottlers had other options. Although the company discouraged it, many had taken on the bottling of other products to leverage their substantial capital investments. In fact, around one-third of Coca-Cola bottlers' capacity was being used for other brands. Woodruff quickly realised that whilst he could never win total loyalty to the Coca-Cola Company, total loyalty to the Coca-Cola brand might well be a different matter. The first job was to settle the contract disputes, which centred on syrup price and the perpetuity agreement. The first was decided through the courts: syrup price could go up in response to ingredient price. As to perpetuity, Woodruff honoured the original deal: perpetuity would remain in place.

The next task was to give the bottlers the tools they needed to do a better job for Coca-Cola than for its competitors. The six-pack, widely available since the early 1920s, was proving a valuable tool in getting Coca-Cola into the home. But what was really needed was an improvement to impulse buying. Six-pack and soda fountain buyers could have their Coca-Cola cold, whilst idle, on-whim-sales often led to a hot drink or nothing. To ensure cold Cokes for everyone, the company energetically developed the famous top-loading Coca-Cola coolers, first launched in 1929 and distributed to retailers of all kinds for the cost price of $12.50 against a typical retail of $90. Who wouldn't adorn his premises with a deal like that, especially when slipping a Dr. Pepper in there meant that you just lost your fridge? For the first time, bottled sales now exceeded fountain sales. And retailers flocked back to Coke.

With over 1,250 bottlers and over 2,000 jobbers servicing over 900,000 retail outlets, head office could now concentrate on their real responsibility: advertising. And just at the right moment, the next man to overhaul the fortunes of the company would enter stage left. Archie Lee was an ex-newspaper man who had joined Coca's agency D'Arcy in 1920 and almost immediately invested $1,000 in Coca-Cola stock, which gave him a reasonably significant stake in the selling power of his work. It wasn't until 1926 that he was regularly producing ads for Coca-Cola, warming up with some fairly mundane lines such as Nature's Purest and Most Wholesome Drink and The National Family Drink, before hitting the jackpot in 1929 with The Pause That Refreshes, which turned out to be the brand's strapline for the next thirty years. In the first year of airing these four magic words, the company spent half a million dollars pushing them, almost ten times the amount Charles E Hires was spending on the its root beer.

As he moved from an obsession with incremental distribution towards incremental sales per point of distribution, Woodruff was also re-starting the company in the international market. Just as Candler had seen advertising as a sacrosanct investment that would pay back in due course, Woodruff took the same approach internationally. Rapid development of overseas distribution, despite the massive financial and logistical headaches that would come, was a price worth paying. Touchstone for the benefits of going abroad was the company's activities in Canada, where per capita consumption in the principal cities was higher than in the US outside its southern heartland.

Building an export business wasn't simple. Woodruff had travelled to Europe in 1925 to see the retail and competitive landscapes for himself and he saw that much technical work had to be set in train. Syrup (which contained all the sugar) was too expensive to ship, so the company developed a concentrate to which bottlers would now add their own sugar as well as the water and carbon dioxide, even though in some countries this meant tweaking the production process to accommodate beet sugar in place of cane. It worked. By 1930, prompted by

Woodruff's ceaseless urgings, there were over sixty bottlers in twenty-eight countries servicing sales in seventy-six countries - more than double the number four years previously - with virtually all the bottlers being wholly owned by a company subsidiary set up specifically for the purpose.

Even during difficult the 1930s, in the domestic market and internationally, the company maintained its strategies, executing both with a remorseless focus that the concentration on just one brand allowed it to do. Coca-Cola would prove itself not only recession-proof but crash-proof: sales and earnings took a drop for just one year of the Great Depression. 1934 profits of $14 million doubled by 1940, at which point war stepped in. General Dwight Eisenhower in particular, plus the US government, was very good for Coca-Cola. Every soldier, sailor, airman or airwoman, no matter where they served on the globe, should be able to buy a Coke for five cents. As soon as Eisenhower arrived in North Africa, America's first landing on foreign soil, he was cabling the War Office demanding that eight Coca-Cola plants be set up right behind him. The sites of dozens marked across the map the progress of his armies. The emotional value of the brand to America, to Americans and their servicemen everywhere may just have been incalculable.

But then the war ended. And even to the most myopic of company executives, one thing could not be denied: Coca-Cola had a direct competitor. Keep doing the same thing but more so had been a stupendously successful strategy since Woodruff had taken the helm, but after thirty years of unbroken success, any system gets sloppy. Coca-Cola bottlers, many in their third generation of family ownership, had gone the way of the scions of many third generation family-owned businesses, losing their cutting edge as they accumulated expensive ornaments to their life-styles. And so, as wealthy, playboy Coca-Cola bottlers toyed with their expensive lunches, Pepsi bottlers, long denied a seat at the top table, were not just picking up left-overs but starting to remove the plates.

Pepsi executives, having to scrap for every sale, had been far more innovative than their Coca-Cola counterparts, launching a bigger bottle than the Coke 6.5 ounce but one which they sold at the same five cent price. Next to Coke, the Pepsi brand meant value. Meanwhile at Coca-Cola, the 6.5 oz. bottle that had served an estimated 220 billion Cokes had become something of a straitjacket. Timid managers had veered away from launching a new size that could not retain the original shape, while lazy bottlers turned down anything that looked like it might make their lives harder, which meant anything new or different. When an 8% slump in 1954 sales and profits coincided with a Pepsi surge into double digits, both company and indolent bottlers were finally goaded into action. Ten and twelve ounce bottles were catapulted into the marketplace, together with a 26-

ounce guzzler size for America's rapidly growing number of household refrigerators. The bottlers, many of them encountering declining sales for the first time in
their lives, grudgingly got up off their pampered behinds and did some work
pushing the new sizes into stores.

Unfortunately for all concerned, the company's advertising guru, Archie Lee -
so venerated in the company that Woodruff had been best man at his wedding -
had died in 1951. And you could tell. The advertising the company churned out
during the first half of the 1950s had none of his quality. So disappointing was
the work that in 1955 the company switched advertising agencies to McCann
Erikson, who already had a foot in the door: the agency was working for the
company's export division. There is some irony here. Whilst Coca-Cola was still
the undisputed boss in on the international stage, with operations in 105 countries, in its American home market it was now taking its lead from a company
with sales less than a quarter of its own.

McCann Erikson executives convinced the company they had to get into the
trenches and fight the upstart Pepsi head on. New Archie Lee-like advertising
slogans that proclaimed the superiority of Coke were rapidly rolled out: Be Really Refreshed and No Wonder Coke Refreshes Best. So far so OK: but one final
company taboo had also to be confronted. For it wasn't just Pepsi that was doing
well. Soft drinks everywhere were doing well. Coca-Cola was not simply competing with Pepsi-Cola, but with a host of beverage companies with a host of
different brands. And it was coming off worst. Woodruff finally bit the bullet.
The single brand strategy was past its sell-by date.

How Did They Build The Modern Business?

When Coca-Cola purchased the Minute Maid Company in 1960 via an exchange of stock, the story of a brand became the story of a beverage company.
The Minute Maid business had appeared during the Second World War on the
back of its invention of a powdered orange juice process it made for the Army. It
then developed this process into a concentrated frozen orange juice that was by
far the category brand leader. Coca-Cola at first ran its new – and first - acquisition as an essentially stand-alone division, encouraging brand developments such
as Hi-C fruit drinks and even instant coffee and tea. But perhaps the company's
greatest influence on its new acquisition was in its marketing. Coke repositioned
orange juice away from the breakfast-table and out into the world, transforming
it into a beverage to be enjoyed throughout the day. In doing so, of course, it
pitched orange juice as an alternative to Coke, a major mind-shift for the company. Not that it mattered much in practical terms, since there were now so

many alternatives, one more wouldn't make much difference. And it would give them a share in what was a new market for them: something that wasn't a Coke.

Coca-Cola executives now realised that Coca-Cola was the Model T of the beverage industry, good for everyone any time, and only one colour as long as it was very nearly black. But other manufacturers had adopted the General Motors strategy and had been busily segmenting the market. There was no reason, insiders argued, that Coke couldn't do both in tandem. This led to the 1961 launch of Sprite, aimed at a lemon-lime drink market first opened up, and then completely dominated, by Seven-Up, which had been around, mostly unchallenged, since 1929. Seven-Up was big, too: it accounted for a full one-sixth of total industry volume.

And the decision to adopt brand differentiation put new spirit into the former one-brand conglomerate; it now had a hit list and it was hungry in a whole new way. So where next? The answer was something relatively new, the diet drink. But here they must tread carefully. Although diet drinks had been around for at least twenty years, they had been so unpalatable that only the most committed of slimmers would touch them. Once again, however, technology intervened. By 1960, advances in sweeteners created a drink you could swallow not merely without pain but with pleasure, an opportunity first seized by the Royal Crown Company with its Diet Rite Cola which immediately bagged 50% of the diet soda market. Keen to avoid any and all risk of tainting the Coca-Cola brand itself, Tab was launched in 1963 with no reference anywhere on the label to the Coca-Cola Company. In fact, Tab was much more like a private label product a supermarket might produce, which probably accounted for the brand reaching only number three in the diet cola category. However, when Fanta was added to the product range, the company found itself with a brand portfolio broad enough to meet most needs, particularly from company-owned vending machines in which, since more brands always meant more sales, operators were increasingly keen give their customers a choice.

Coca-Cola was now looking in a number of different directions and, in 1964, with the purchase of Duncan Foods, it expanded into the tea and coffee categories. But it was not to be torn away from what had become its latest near-obsession: the development of new soft drink brands. Somewhat fortuitously, and even before the acquisition of Minute Maid, Coke had been working on the use of citrus essences to mask the aftertaste of artificial sweeteners, a technology at the heart of the next launch, Fresca, in 1966. Fresca was a calorie-free, grapefruit-flavoured soft drink targeted at a more discerning adult palate. It was a better bet than Tab, successfully creating a niche in a fairly difficult market. Thus, thanks to brand diversification, in 1967 Coca-Cola still claimed the top spot in the carbonated beverages market. Its 30.4% share was more than double that of upstart Pepsi, which had gone through its own period of apparent mojo-loss. Still more pertinent was that within the market itself, per capita consumption, driven by the baby boomers and lifestyle changes, was heading remorselessly upwards, reaching twenty-six gallons per head per year in the US, and closing in on king coffee which led the way with thirty-eight. Good times ahead whoever you were.

Another key industry change, driven partly by the same demographic and lifestyle trends, was the switch from returnable bottles to non-returnable bottles and cans. Both had been around for at least a decade, primarily in retailer private label offerings (the retailers hadn't wanted to get involved with processing returnables), but hadn't caught on because of the higher retail prices involved. However, the American Can and Steel Institute popularised returnability with a $9 million promotional campaign in the early 1960s, selling the benefits of the casual and the care-free. When you were cruising the strip in your T-Bird, did you really want to bother hoarding your empties? Of course you didn't. And when cans reached a double-digit share of the market, the Glass Containers Manufacturers Institute finally fought back with their own $7 million campaign for the one-way bottle. Coca-Cola was quick to get on board, producing ads pushing the casual image of a trend that clearly signalled modern, and bullying the bottlers to get on the bandwagon. By the end of the decade, 40% of the industry's products came in one-way containers in what had become an irreversible trend.

Modernity was also to be found in Coca-Cola's advertising. Its 1967 campaign kicked off with For the Taste You Never Get Tired Of, itself just a warm up act for the true blockbuster, 1969's It's The Real Thing. Finally Archie Lee's ghost had been laid to rest (or disinterred) and the company had advertising that both equalled Archie's and echoed in the brevity of The Pause That Refreshes. The new and startling campaign prompted the biggest brand overhaul in history, with what the company code-named Project Arden (after the cosmetics brand, Elizabeth Arden). There was to be a new packaging theme that would entail the complete replacement of the now countless items of permanently placed Coca-Cola promotional merchandise, a challenging project since the company had kept no records of where it had all been placed. The changeover consequently took years to complete, which fortunately spread the astronomic cost over several financial years.

So Coca-Cola entered the 1970s in very good shape. During the previous decade, per capita consumption of carbonated soft drinks had increased a whopping 80%, which, with a rising population, had almost doubled industry volume.

Due partly to the expansion of the product range, the Coca-Cola Company had beaten the rest of the market. Sales throughout the 60s increased by 250% and earnings trebled. The company was, by some distance, the world's largest producer of soft drinks, citrus products and, somewhat surprisingly for a so brand-led company, private label instant coffee and tea. In 1970, the company even took a plunge into the water market, although not consumer bottled water, at that time a tiny market for health cranks. It purchased a maker of water-pollution equipment already installed in around half of the non-communist world's water treatment plants. The acquisition would come in especially useful, as continued international expansion was taking Coke into countries where decent water supplies could pose huge problems.

The early 1970s also saw the company getting to grips with a problem that had concerned it for some time, the bottlers, who had returned to their somewhat lethargic ways; the rising market of the 1960s had effectively done most of their work for them. Not that they were ecstatic about the relationship either. They had loyally backed Tab and Fresca and been distinctly underwhelmed by the outcome, especially given the existence of much better-performing brands they could be bottling much more profitably. So the relationship between the company and its bottlers had become fractious.

A particular difficulty for Coke was that the increasing size and geographic reach of the major retailers was now far exceeding the historic bottler territories, compromising supply lines. But changes in the bottler network gave a clue to solving the problem. Closely located regional bottlers had begun to merge, and several were now large enough to attract the interest of the bigger businesses that had begun acquiring franchises from third and fourth generation families keen to cash in their inheritances. Wometco, for example, owned Coke bottling franchises in the US, Canada, the Bahamas and the Dominican Republic. Wouldn't it make perfect sense for Coca-Cola to do the same? It would, and it did. Coca-Cola's $64 million purchase of the Atlanta franchise took the company to ownership of 10% of the US network. But when Twentieth-Century Fox tried to buy a bottler, Coca-Cola saw the real danger: at worst the loss of control of the entire network, and at least the loss of the ability to bend the bottlers to the company's wishes.

So Coca-Cola once again tried to change the bottler agreements to let it adjust the syrup price at will, not just in response to movements in the price of sugar. But the bottlers were no longer family affairs. They were run by huge conglomerates that could pack a punch and they rebelled, exactly what the company had begun to fear. The crunch came in 1978. The big bottlers knew full well that Coca-Cola was making plenty of money on its sugar dealings, so fought the company's proposal aggressively, demanding the right to be supplied not with syrup but with concentrate so they too could buy and profit from the sugar, which many were big enough to do. A deal was finally struck: after a price hike of 24%, the bottlers could buy a concentrate which would go up in price in line with the Consumer Price Index. But the battle scarred the company. They did not like being held to ransom by firms as big and mean as they were. When the right time came along, something would have to be done.

Not that the company didn't have other thngs to worry about. In 1975 their arch rivals launched The Pepsi Challenge. Initially dismissed, it succeeded well enough to eat away at both Coca-Cola's market share and its corporate self-confidence. Pepsi's success was followed by the company's first exit from an overseas market, when the Indian Government's demands to indianise all foreign-owned companies would have obliged Coke to hand over its secret formula, code-named 7-X, to Indian-owned bottlers. They refused point blank and quit India. It wasn't a particularly substantial market – just 1% of global output – but it was an embarrassing slap in the face to this most global of companies. Then Pepsi stole a march by securing the exclusive rights to Russia, although Coca-Cola more than made up for the Indian and Russian disappointments with its Chinese coup, exclusive rights to market cola in China, granted indefinitely.

But despite the China deal and another breakthrough advertising campaign with Mean Joe Green, Coca-Cola in the 1970s was losing ground. In 1979, PepsiCo total sales finally surpassed Coke's. That this was in large part due to PepsiCo's ownership of Frito-Lay rubbed salt into the wound; owner Herman Lay had first offered it to Coca-Cola but they had turned it down. Further bad news arrived beneath the flag of the now ubiquitous Pepsi challenge: sales of Pepsi actually exceeded those of Coke in take-home sales. Coke's overall lead was now totally dependent on its massive lead in vending and food service contracts.

In 1981, the Woodruff era finally came to a close. Roberto Goizueta became chairman and CEO of The Coca-Cola Company and issued in the era of what Goizueta himself christened 'intelligent risk-taking'. Five big moves were made, two of which led to a vigourous re-appraisal of precisely what 'intelligent' meant. The appraisals were later assisted by that most fully-informed of all human analytical procedures, hindsight.

The Acquisition of Columbia Pictures

The levelling off of growth in the soft drinks category already had Coca-Cola's minds turning to greater diversification - the company were already in ocean farming and orange groves - but Goizueta upped the ante in 1982 with the

$750 million acquisition of Columbia Pictures. While the studio was profitable after a run of box office successes, the entertainment business was far more volatile than Coca-Cola had been used to. After something of a rollercoaster ride, the studio's mega-flop, Ishtar, which made back only a quarter of its then vast $55 million budget, convinced Coca-Cola it needed to reduce its exposure to such lunacy. Later in 1987 the company spun off 51% of its entertainment division before selling its remaining stake to Sony in 1989.

Diet Coke

The launch of Diet Coke on August 9th, 1982 was the first brand extension of Coca-Cola in its entire history. While the move was reactive, prompted by the sparkling success of Diet Pepsi (around since 1964) versus the flat sales of Tab, the move was a success, with Diet Coke soon gaining number one status in the diet drinks market before becoming the world's number two selling carbonated soft drink behind Coca-Cola itself. The recipe used for diet Coke was not the original minus sugar and plus sweeteners, but a different one entirely, which convinced the intelligent risk-takers that the Coca-Cola brand could withstand having more variants, so they followed up with Caffeine-Free diet Coca in 1983, Cherry Coca-Cola in 1985 and Diet Cherry Coca a year later.

New Coke

The success of Diet Coke played a crucial role in the ill-fated decision to launch New Coke. While the inexorable success of the Pepsi Challenge was undoubtedly the prompt to look at changing the hallowed recipe, the confidence to actually do it came from the success of the Coke variants, Diet Coke in particular, whose recipe formed the basis of New Coke. Plus, as we have seen, Candler had fiddled around endlessly with the recipe in his early days and had not been shy to remove cocaine when its presence had become both liability and necessity. Maybe the hallowed recipe was just a function of the conservatism of the Woodruff years? Maybe it was. But, as we all know, New Coke proved a classic case study of research only being as good as the questions that are asked. Within three months of its April 23, 1985 launch, Coca-Cola Classic was back on the market and the whole thing was being post-rationalised by traumatised executives as having been a success really because of the anger it had induced in previously passive brand loyalists.

Back to Bottling

As we have seen, before Goizueta took charge, the company had been determined to regain control of its American bottling network and in 1980 had acquired the Coca-Cola Bottling Company of New York for $215 million. Goizueta accelerated this process, acquiring the Associated Coca-Cola Bottling Company in 1982 for $417.5 million. But the big change came in 1986 when the company was approached by the descendants of John T. Lupton (backer of the two Chattanooga dollar-owing lawyers nearly a century ago), to sell Coca-Cola the JTL Corporation, the system's largest single bottler controlling 14% of U.S. output. At the same time these negotiations were running, the second-largest bottling operation, owned by Beatrice Foods, also came onto the market. Coca-Cola couldn't face the thought of these two colossal bottlers being bought by entities unknown, so it borrowed the vast sum of $2.4 billion to purchase them. The two were then combined with Coca-Cola's existing bottling assets to create Coca-Cola Enterprises (CCE), of which the company immediately spun off 51% to pay off their debt, giving CCE the remit of vacuuming up as many other bottlers as it could. After CCE merged with the Johnston Coca-Cola Bottling Group in 1991, keeping mostly Johnston management to run the new entity, CCE had annual revenues of $5 billion a year (half those of the entire Coca-Cola Company) and would soon expand its operations overseas.

Global Sponsorships

As a truly global brand, Coca-Cola was best placed to benefit from the sponsorship opportunities afforded by the massive increase in commercialisation of global events such as the Olympics and the soccer World Cup, which really got going with the 1996 summer Olympics in Coca-Cola's home town of Atlanta.

After Goizueta left in 1997, the focus shifted more towards acquisitions and new product development, bringing into the company portfolio brands such as Powerade - to combat PepsiCo's Gatorade - Dasani - to get a piece of the rapidly growing bottled water market - Barq's Root Beer, Indian brands such as Limca, Maaza and Thums Up - to gain immediate critical mass on the company's return into India - and the 1999 deal to buy the rights for Schweppes, Canada Dry, Crush and Dr. Pepper in 157 countries outside of North America. A major restructuring in 2000 that involved the loss of over 5,000 jobs was the inevitable outcome of an acquisition splurge that had helped expand a brand portfolio into the hundreds. However, the 2002 launch of Vanilla Coke in response to Vanilla

Pepsi confirmed that, when it came to the core cola brands, Coca-Cola was still too much of a follower and not enough of a leader.

How International Are They?

Very. The first sales to Canada and Mexico were recorded in 1897 and the first international bottler - in Panama - was established in 1906. The company entered China in 1927 and reached its 100th country - Sierra Leone - in 1957. Coca-Cola is sold in over 200 countries and is absent only in countries that ban it for political reasons, such as Iran, Syria, Myanmar (Burma), North Korea and Cuba. International unit case volume has exceeded unit case volume in the United States since the 1970s.

How Are They Structured?

The Coca-Cola structure has always been driven by the need to manage four things: brands, syrup/concentrate manufacture, company-owned bottling operations and independent bottler relationships. By the early-mid 2000s, the company structure was essentially split into bottling and non-bottling functions via two operating groups, bottling Investments and corporate. Under corporate, operating groups were divided by different regions, Europe, Eurasia and the Middle East, North America and Asia, Latin America and Africa, all of which had a high degree of local operating autonomy in advertising. Each region also managed many local brands, although global brand equities were managed for the most part by the central, Atlanta-based marketing function. There was also a global customer division to manage the large global customers and a special division to manage the McDonalds relationship alone.

Regionally, the business was split in 2004 as follows:
- Europe, Eurasia & Middle East – 33% of sales and selling129 brands
- North America – 30% of sales and selling 93 brands
- Asia – 21% of sales and selling184 brands
- Latin America – 10% of sales and selling105 brands
- Africa – 5% of sales and selling 86 brands

The company's own fountain operations, together with the finished beverages the company sold such as fruit juices and sports drinks, accounted for around 10% of total volume sales in the year, the remaining 90% going through bottlers with whom the company had one of three relationships. 7% of volume went through bottlers the company owned outright, 25% went through independent bottlers and the remaining 58% went through bottlers in which the company had a non-controlling stake. The largest four of these were:

- CCE. Territories covered were 46 US states, Canada, UK, Belgium, France, Luxembourg, Monaco and the Netherlands. The Coca-Cola Company had a 36% stake
- Almost as big as CCE was Coca-Cola Hellenic Bottling Company SA, whose territory was essentially the rest of Western Europe and all of Eastern Europe including Russia. The company's stake was 24%
- Coca-Cola FEMSA, a Mexican holding company whose territories included around half the population of Mexico, 15% of Brazil, 30% of Argentina, 38% of Guatemala and essentially all of Columbia and the rest of Central America. Coca-Cola had 40% ownership
- Coca-Cola Amatil covered Australia, New Zealand, Indonesia, Fiji, South Korea and Papua New Guinea with the company having 34% ownership

The 2010 acquisition of the North American elements of CCE changed the picture somewhat and led to a three-division structure: Coca Cola International, Coca-Cola America and Bottling Investments Group (BIG). Under Coca-Cola International came the Europe, Pacific, Latin American and Eurasia and Africa regional operations. Coca-Cola Americas was the amalgamation of the acquired parts of CCE with their existing US foodservice business, Minute Maid and the Odwalla juice business. North American supply chain operations and company-owned bottling operations in Philadelphia became a new entity Coca-Cola Refreshments. Coca-Cola North America also dealt with franchise management, a marketing division and an innovation group.

What Have They Been Doing Recently?

2004

The mid-year appointment of E. Neville Isdell as Chairman and CEO brought about a hard dose of reality-checking for the company. Neville, a career company man who had retired in 2001 from running the world's second-largest Coke bottler, was somewhat underwhelmed by what he found on his return. The company's rapid expansion from a handful of brands to around 400 had, perhaps not unexpectedly, led to some degree of lack of focus, as shown in the year's results: a 2% volume increase and 4% top line growth that were, in Neville's words, 'unsatisfactory'. And this was not a one-off. In only three years out of the previous ten had the total revenue growth rate exceeded 3%. In 2004, every single region underperformed against their past five- and ten-year compound average growth rates. While execution was excellent in parts, it was patchy overall. It was clear, Neville thought, that 'a course correction is required'.

The course correction would consist of five key elements:

- Roles and responsibilities needed to be simplified and clarified
- Marketing and innovation would be re-energised with a permanent $350 million to $400 million annual increase
- Best practices would be shared wider and faster
- Innovation focus would be focused on diet and light products
- M&A strategy would seek new, profitable segments of the non-alcoholic beverage industry

It wasn't as if the company had not been innovating. Launches in the year somewhere in the world included diet Coke with Lime (the second-best selling Diet Coca extension), Coca-Cola C2 (a hit in Japan and a miss in the US), Sprite Icy Mint (first launched in China where it helped total sales grow 22%), Fanta Free in Scandinavia, Fanta Naranja Chamoy (a spicy Mexican drink that grew the Fanta brand by 13%) and numerous new Minute Maid lines. But too many areas of the business were either stagnating or, in the case of the German market (down 11% in the year), in deep trouble. The shake-up had been long overdue.

2005

Despite the gargantuan size of the whole Coca-Cola system of company plus bottlers - $80 billion revenue with hundreds of thousands of employees - the Neville effect wasn't long in coming. First up in March had been a restructuring of the regions, creating three new regional entities:

- East, South Asia & Pacific Rim (9% of sales)
- European Union (16% of sales)
- North Asia, Eurasia and the Middle East (16% of sales)

Accompanied by the remaining:

- North America (28% of sales)
- Africa (6% of sales)
- Latin America (25% of sales)

All regions apart from North America reported into the Coca-Cola International Division.

The promised extra $400 million was pumped into marketing and innovation with nearly 400 new products launched in the year, taking the product count to over 2,400 spread across over 400 brands. Despite a host of new launches in carbonated soft beverages - Coca-Cola Zero, Diet Coca Sweetened with Splenda, Sprite Zero / Diet Sprite Zero and a re-launch of Fresca - case volume increased by only 2%, although the 2% increase in regular Coca-Cola volumes was in fact the highest for five years.

The successes behind a total company volume increase of 4% had come from the very places at which Neville had directed his effort, still beverages. Water grew by 17%, helped by the launch of nine new Dasani flavours in the year which, along with more international expansion, grew the Dasani brand by 29%. Sports drinks grew by 23% (with Poweraid now available in 76 countries) and energy drinks, previously almost a nonentity in the company, grew by a massive 200%. Minute Maid chipped in with 11% growth, as did Nestea in the Beverage Partners Worldwide joint venture with Nestlé, which added 23%. As well as global number one in carbonated soft drinks, Coca-Cola was now number one in juice and juice drinks, number two in sports drinks and number three in bottled water.

To restart momentum in the much larger carbonated beverages portfolio, the newly formed marketing, strategy and innovation group in Atlanta began work on a new global campaign, The Coke Side of Life, along with a new digital platform for the brand, iCoke. Long-term partnerships with the International Olympic Committee and FIFA were renewed right through to 2020 and 2022 respectively. Had the corner been turned?

2006

Unit volume again increased by 4%, helped by another 367 additions to a global price list that now included over 2,600 items. After a stellar year in 2005, still beverages grew by another 7%, while the Coca-Cola brand had an excellent year by its standards, growing 3%, with the rest of the sparkling beverages doing slightly better at more than 4%. The heart of the portfolio was in good shape. Coca-Cola, Sprite and Fanta accounted for 56% of total company growth in the year. Even better news was that Coca-Cola Zero, now available in nineteen key markets, was undoubtedly a hit for the company, as was the new global advertising campaign, The Coke Side of Life, launched in over 100 countries. It outperformed the last few years' advertising and one spot got the highest ratings in the company's history.

Within the regions, Africa matched the company growth rate of more than 4%, as did the European Union on existing business, while adding another 2% with the acquisitions of German and Italian water brands. Latin America did one better, growing by 7%, led by the Coca-Cola brand itself across all key markets. The region was also boosted by the acquisition of a major Mexican and Brazilian juice maker. Problem areas were North America where a 1% gain in foodservice and hospitality was wiped out by a 1% decline in retail. The worst case though was East, South Asia and the Pacific Rim, where volumes were down 5%, almost entirely due to a catastrophic double-digit decline in the Philippines, which prompted the company to buy out the bottler and do the job itself.

But undoubted star of the show was the North Asia, Eurasia and Middle East region which grew by 11%, not least because it just happened to be made up of three energetic emerging markets, China, Russia and Turkey. The other key success was the newly formed Bottling Investments Group which ran all the 100%-owned bottlers, growing by 16%, although much of that came from the acquisitions of bottlers in China, South Africa and Philadelphia, a clear sign that the company was keen to increase its full ownership of its bottling system whenever it felt it was being let down by the bottlers.

2007

Momentum in the business was clearly building, with an improved 6% plus increase in case volume. What the company called its Three Cola Strategy - a focus on driving Coca-Cola, Diet Coke and Coca-Cola Zero - was paying dividends, as the combined brand grew by 4%, its biggest increase since 1998. A further key to growth was the continued success of Coca-Cola Zero, the company's most successful new beverage since Diet Coke, now available in 55 countries and already one of Coke's 13 billion $ brands. While much emphasis had been placed on the more exciting areas of still beverages, sparkling drinks still accounted for 80% of company sales, so had to do well for the company as a whole to do well. More good news then was the 8% increase for Sprite and a 5% increase in Fanta.

Within the still beverages part of the portfolio, another 450 new lines had appeared, either through innovation or acquisition, the most notable of the latter being the company's largest ever – that of glacéau, the maker of vitaminwater and smartwater - for $4.1 billion. Also added in the year was the purchase (jointly with the largest Latin American bottler) of Jugos del Valle, which added fifty juice brands in Brazil and Mexico. Latin America was now the largest by-volume region in the company, bigger than North America, where sales of sparkling products declined by 2% in another lacklustre year. CCE needed to pull its socks up.

Elsewhere, the European Union inched ahead by 3%. Africa added more than 10% - almost all in sparkling beverages – with Eurasia at plus 16%, showing what could still be done with the brands in emerging markets. On the bottling investments side, the newly owned Philippines set-up stabilised the business there, while bottlers in the troubled German market were combined into one unit to ensure greater consistency. The company was now starting to take category environmental concerns more seriously, opening the world's largest PET bottle recycling plant as part of a commitment to re-use 100% of its PET packaging in the United States.

The year ended with the announcement of a planned transition in leadership, with E. Neville Idsell planning to handover the CEO reins in July 2008 to long-timer Muhtar Kent, while remaining as chairman for a further nine months. It had been a good innings for Neville.

2008

The global economic problems that hit in the second half of 2008 did little to stem the flow. Unit volume increased by 5% and operating revenue by 11% to reach a shade under $32 billion, a very impressive 46% increase since Neville took the reins in 2004, with the extra billion cases sold the equivalent of a new market the size of Japan. The company could not be faulted for how it had tackled the challenge of a beverage for every need and occasion: there were now nearly 3,000 different offerings (over 750 of which were low- or no-calorie) within nearly 500 brands, another 700-plus new products having been added during 2008 alone, over 200 of them juice products. This meant still beverages had doubled their share of sales from 11% to 22% in the space of eight years and were now delivering nearly 60% of company growth.

The glacéau acquisition had got off to a flying start, increasing its North American case volume by double-digits and launching into five new markets, Australia, Canada, Great Britain, Mexico and New Zealand. Other highlights included the still fizzing Coca-Cola Zero, up 35% in the year as it hit 52 new markets, the highly successful sponsorship of the Beijing Olympics - where the company was found by the Nielsen Company to have been the most recognised and effective sponsor - and the continued success of emerging markets, now contributing over 50% of company sales. While Latin America continued to power ahead by another 8%, the newer emerging markets for the company had been posting impressive, consistent growth numbers:

5 Year CAGR
Brazil+10%
China+19%
Poland+13%
Russia+20%
Turkey+15%

As is the way with these things, the new man at the helm had rearranged the regions as follows:
- Eurasia & Africa (Africa, Middle East, Turkey, Russia, India, CIS states)
- Europe (Western and Eastern Europe up to Russia)
- Pacific (China, Japan, Philippines, Thailand, Australia and all other Pacific countries)
- Unchanged were Latin America (if it ain't broke, don't fix it) and North America (definitely broke, not sure how to fix it).

North America had declined by 1% in the year and its five-year CAGR was a completely underwhelming 0%. In stark contrast to CCE and the remaining independent US bottlers, the performance of the company-owned bottlers could not have been more different, up 14% with 42% of the markets covered experiencing double-digit growth. While many if not most of these markets were emerging and thus had much better dynamics than the US, it cannot have escaped Coca-Cola management's notice that they were building a good track record in running bottlers, and particularly in turning around failures. Coca-Cola itself was now its own second-largest bottler behind CCE.

2009
Despite the fact that even Coca-Cola was not immune to the global economic crisis, with top-line sales falling 3% albeit with a 3% increase in case volume, it still became the latest brand to join the $1 billion club, as the portfolio continued its relentless expansion. There were now over 3,300 products, although Coca-Cola itself was the only one sold in every market with a company presence. Combined with Diet Coke and Coca-Cola Zero (up another 9% in the year) Coca-Cola was a $56 billion global brand at retail, but a brand still not past its peak, at least in some parts of the world. Over the previous twenty years, an extra 5.8 billion cases of the combined Coca-Cola brand had been sold, with almost half of that growth coming from Latin America, primarily Mexico and Brazil. During 2009 alone, the brand had grown double-digit in India, Pakistan and Nigeria, three of the top eight most populated countries on earth. At the other

end of the spectrum, only 5% of the global brand growth over twenty years had come from North America, a paltry average increase of 15,000 cases a year.

Unsurprisingly, trends like these had resulted in somewhat different strategies for developed versus developing markets. In developed markets, the strategy was two-fold: to grow through product enhancements such as added vitamins and/or nutrients - a good example being the newly introduced Burn Energy Shots - while reducing calories and where possible addressing sustainability issues such as packaging and carbon footprint. The second phase in developed markets was the acquisition of brands with higher growth potential, such as the 2007 purchase of glacéau (glacéau smartwater sales grew 33% in the year) and the 2009 investment in the Innocent natural smoothie and juice company.

In developing markets, the strategy was to do what the company had spent most of its existence doing, driving demand and new consumption opportunities, although with a much better-equipped brand toolkit at its disposal than in previous times and markets. Still holding good was the old plan of building capacity ahead of demand; the company and its bottlers were making multi-billion dollar investments in Brazil, China, Mexico and Russia, four countries whose annual sales growth equalled adding a market the size of Germany, the company's sixth-largest!

Within the year, sparkling beverages moved forwards only 1%, although with Coca-Cola up 2%, Coca-Cola Zero up 9% (thanks to launches in another 26 countries), and Sprite up 6%, it seemed the minor and regional brands were the ones suffering most. Still beverages prospered regardless of the economic conditions, with water up 7%, teas 14%, and energy drinks 35%. Regionally, as might have been expected, the sick patients were Europe and moribund North America, which lost 3% volume in sparkling beverages whilst gaining a scant 1% on still. These were tough market conditions for any gain in anything, but in truth, the region had been going nowhere for a long time.

2010

This was the year Coca-Cola Company took the big decision: for the first time, it gained control over its North America bottling route-to-market. The deal was huge, costing a net $1 billion after the sale to CCE of their Norwegian and Swedish bottlers, plus ceding to CCE the right to buy Coca-Cola's 83% stake in their German bottler. While the bottling investments division had by now built up considerable experience, systems and tools in running an integrated system - Coke One - the CEE North American bottling operation was an order of magnitude larger, encompassing 75% of US bottler volume and almost 100% of Canada's. It would be the largest vertical integration in US business history.

The arguments for the acquisition were strong on both the hard and soft side. First and foremost, CCE hadn't been delivering; company volumes in the U.S. had been stagnant for years. On the relationship side, it could be argued that Coca-Cola had fallen into the trap it thought it had avoided when it created CCE in the first place, that of having a bottling partner who was too big and too powerful. The company move into rapid portfolio expansion had exacerbated the inherent tension in the brand owner – bottler relationship. While the brand owner took risks with its revenue by funding R&D and brand advertising, the bottler took risks with its capital by having to gear up for both the new brands and also support the 'opportunity cost' of its delivery assets, carrying yet more new and therefore un-guaranteed Coke brands on its trucks when it could be carrying proven sellers from other companies. And Coca-Colahad indeed inherited with the deal some contracts to bottle and distribute actual rivals: Doctor Pepper and other brands, which it subsequently extended geographically in a 20-year deal that cost the company over $700 million. This was a very a good example of how the need to make the most efficient use of the bottling plants and delivery trucks had now become a Coca-Cola problem.

The inevitable outcome was more tension, which merely added to existing systemic conflicts: just as the bottler wanted higher selling prices and lower concentrate prices, the brand owner wanted precisely the opposite. And these were conflicts that, with someone the size of CEE, would not always resolve themselves in the brand owner's favour. Or, when they did, the brand loyalty on the part of a gigantic bottler constantly courted by other drinks companies might well begin to waver. Coca-Cola decided that the entire US system would be better off without any likelihood of increasing tensions, given the company's explicit strategy of adding yet more beverage brands into the portfolio. It was a big bet, and one the company needed to pay off.

After this big – gigantic - news, it went almost unnoticed that the company enjoyed a very respectable year, growing case volume by 5%, adding another billion cases of shipped product, now up to 25.5 billion cases, and nearly another $5 billion in top line sales. Sparkling beverages increased by 3%, driven almost entirely by growth in Eurasia and Africa of 10%. Russia had its biggest ever increase in sales of the Coca-Cola brand and the ever-dependable Latin America added 4%. Even North America managed to claim a 1% increase, thanks to some additional cross-licensed brands that came with the CCE deal (CCE also bottles some non-Coca-Cola brands in North America). But base business was still flat.

Once again driving company growth was the ever-expanding roster of still beverages, up 10% globally in the year. The new rising star in the company was

Minute Maid Pulpy, the biggest driver of the 21% increase in still sales in the Eurasia and Africa region. Pulpy had been developed and launched in China five years previously to meet local expectations of what a fruit juice should be like and had already been rolled out to another eighteen countries, where consumers fully agreed with the formulation, making the brand the latest member of the $1 billion sales club. Still beverages even increased by 5% in North America, led by double-digit growth for both Powerade and Simply, and now accounted for 24% of company sales, which made the company the world's largest juice and juice-drink operation.

2011

The first full year of the One Coke model operation in North America seemed to have got off to a reasonable start, reporting a 4% growth - the best for years – with sparkling up 3%, although this did include the third party brands. Like-with-like sales of sparkling only inched ahead by 1%, a small improvement over CCE's efforts in the preceding few years but hardly a flying start, given that Coca-Cola Zero had just had its fifth year of double-digit increase. Globally, brand Coca-Cola grew by 3%, as did Fanta, while Sprite did even better at over 5%, all helped by stellar performances such as China, where case volumes increased by 13%, the ninth year out of the last ten the company had grown double-digit. Russia was still growing strongly, increasing sales of the Coca-Cola brand by over 10%. Investment dollars were being poured into these markets: in China, where the company and its bottlers had already invested over $3 billion in the past three years, another $4 billion was committed to the next three. Russia was to receive $3 billion over the next five years, while the Middle East and Africa would get $5 billion over the next ten.

Another 500 products joined the price list, now over 3,500 lines strong and a three-fold increase compared to a decade previously, while the juice drink Del Valle joined the roster of $1 billion brands, the 15th to do so. Since acquiring the parent company, Jugos del Valle, distribution had expanded from two Latin American markets to fifteen and more than doubled sales. Del Valle, along with Minute Maid Pulpy (up another 20%) produced another strong 7%-plus increase in sales of the juices and juice drinks categories.

But the company wasn't just innovating new beverages. The company's new Freestyle fountain dispenser, which could serve over 100 different beverages, was now in more than eighty US markets and the company partnered with Google to test cashless vending machines that dispensed product with a mere wave of a smartphone. On the sustainability front, the new PlantBottle, made partially from plants, was licensed for use by Heinz on their iconic ketchup brand and also helped Dasani return to significant growth. All good stuff. But the big question remained as yet unanswered: had the company done the right thing in buying the CCE North American operation?

What is Their DNA?

For such a gigantic enterprise, Coca-Cola is a remarkably focused company: since they divested themselves of Columbia Pictures, they have done nothing but sell soft drinks, virtually all they did before the purschase. So it is not surprising their DNA is rooted in the dark arts of beverage marketing.

Brand Building

While one would expect all the companies in this book to be highly competent at brand building, all would no doubt aspire to be as good at it as Coca-Cola has been with Coca-Cola itself. It is very easy to take for granted the status of the Coca-Cola brand and its ever-increasing sales, but it is sobering to reflect that most brands invented in the 1800s are now either gone or well past their best. That Coca-Cola continues to scale new heights is not inevitable or due to some locked-in, insuperable entry barriers; as we have seen with the kinds of companies Coca-Cola has been buying, there are very few of those in the beverages category. The brand is as successful as it is solely because the company has made it so. From iconic advertising to the most liked page on Facebook, via the most effective global events sponsorships, the mastery of the science of impulse purchasing and much else, Coca-Cola has and continues to set standards of marketing excellence across the brand management spectrum others can only aim for. They don't really make their money from buying and selling brands, or trading off past glories, they make it by nurturing and growing the world's most valuable brand.

Local Focus

Because of the economics of bottling and canning – it's expensive to ship something that is 99% water over long distances - the company has always had to have a local focus on the operations side. And despite the iconic global campaigns, much of the heavy lifting of creating the sale has always been done at the local level, mostly by the bottler but increasingly by the company, as it has built its expertise in running the bottling side. But even so, it is still a staggering fact that only one of its 500 plus brands – Coca-Cola itself – is sold in all its markets. A select number of brands such as Sprite and Minute Maid are global in all but name, but the vast majority of the company's product range consists of regional or national brands.

Coca-Cola has repeatedly added local and regional brands to the portfolio, usually doing a better job at brand-building that the previous owners. The most striking example of Coca-Cola being as strong local player is in India, where it bought its way back into the market in 1993 by acquiring the leading local cola brand, Thums Up, which was already competing head-on with Pepsi. One would perhaps have expected ham-fitedness of such a global giant, either killing Thums Up outright or at best letting it wither on the vine. But Coca-Cola got behind it, built its equity, and turned this quintessentially Indian brand into the leading sparkling beverage in India.

Optimism

Perhaps the most striking thing about Coca-Cola is in how the company perceives the world around it. Despite size and leading position, it has almost always seen nothing but boundless opportunity to grow both the company and the Coca-Cola brand. There are no complaints about recessions or adverse currency movements or big, nasty, aggressive retailers; factories and workforce are not seen as deadweight costs. Instead the focus is on the 97% of beverages consumed in the world that aren't provided by the Coca-Cola Company. In so doing, there is none of the insular arrogance that can sometimes be associated with American-based companies, more an unquenchable optimism that the future can and will be brighter than the past. It is refreshing.

Summary

The Coca-Cola Company is one of the most written about and best understood packaged goods companies in the world. Apart from the secret formula recently transferred from an Atlanta bank vault to a vault in the Coca-Cola world attraction, there is no secret about what it does and how. The transition from a one-brand to a multi-brand company and then a broadly based beverage company has not been seamless, but it has been a lot more successful than it might have been. The mushrooming of the brand portfolio has not led Coke astray and dented progress of the brand itself: Coca-Cola Zero has been one of the brand success stories of the 21st-century. Acquisitions have been very impressive in terms of consistency too: profitable growth has invariably resulted without diminishing the heart and soul of the business.

Admittedly, given the two-tier nature of the beverages route to market, it is perhaps easier to make beverage acquisitions than it is to acquire fully integrated businesses with countless factories, people and widely differing cultures to be integrated. But that should not diminish what The Coca-Cola Company has achieved. This is now a very different company to the one that thought the maxed-out market for carbonated beverages meant the next step was the movie business, or the one that believed the Pepsi Challenge absolutely demanded the launch New Coke. It is a company that has manoeuvred itself into a very strong position to capture future growth, particularly in emerging markets, while still continuing to build its core, the Coca-Cola brand itself.

But how will the fully integrated business in the US market fare? There are now no indolent bottlers to blame. There is a huge, capital-intensive infrastructure that significantly changes the historical business model and the regional balance of sales and profits. Somewhat perversely, given the scale of opportunity in emerging markets, there is greater dependence on the performance of the US market than there has been for decades. Before the CCE acquisition, the company held around a 30% stake only in the franchise profits of the US market. The 30 is now 80, whilst the stake in CCE's profits in its European markets has shrunk from 35% to zero. Coca-Cola needs to make the US market work.

Colgate Palmolive

Where Did They Come From?

In 1802, Robert Colgate, a British immigrant farmer, closed down a candle and soap-making business he had been running for the previous two years and went back to farming. The same year, his son, William, perhaps fired by a filial zeal to show his father a thing or two, started his own soap business but fared no better, lasting only a year. But William was no quitter. He moved to New York City and spent three years learning the ropes of the soap and candle business before once again setting up on his own in 1806.

After a short partnership with a Francis Smith, terminated in 1812, by 1817 he was advertising that William Colgate and Company . . . Have for Sale on Best Terms a Constant Supply of Soap, Mould and Dipt Candles of the First Quality . . .N.B. The Highest Price Given for Tallow. Business was obviously good: three years later, he opened a second factory in Jersey City to manufacture starch. And he was an early convert to branding, focusing his efforts on his Windsor soap and Pearl Starch. But in truth there was little to distinguish his products from others or to convince the largely self-sufficient American housewife that his soap and starch were any better than she made for herself. In 1857, he died and the business passed to his son. That was the turning point.

Samuel Colgate realised that one the housewife couldn't make herself was a fragrant, perfumed soap and so, by 1866, the company was out of the generic starch business and into perfumed soaps. But Samuel Colgate also saw that the personal soap business was as much about feeling clean and fresh as just getting clean, an insight embodied in Colgate's launch of America's first milled, perfumed soap in 1872, Cashmere Bouquet. A year later the much-neglected arts of oral hygiene had the same treatment when Colgate launching a tooth-paste sold in jars.

But Samuel did not have these markets to himself. The soap and candle business was an easy one to get into - the products could be made on a kitchen counter – and America's rapidly growing towns and cities provided eager markets of housewives without the fields full of pigs to provide the soap and candle raw materials. Hundreds of similar businesses had sprung up, including two the Colgate Empire would eventually devour: Peet Brothers of Kansas City – best-seller Crystal White soap - and the B.J. Johnson Soap Company of Milwaukee who made soap, candles and, somewhat incongruously, cheese.

How Did They Evolve?

At the turn of the 20th century there were hundreds of American soap and toiletry businesses. So how did Colgate and Palmolive emerge (along with Procter & Gamble and Lever Bros) as one of the three soap giants? For two main reasons: firstly by leading not following and secondly by branding; the 2 brands that did it were Colgate toothpaste and Palmolive soap.

Colgate toothpaste's first real breakthrough came in 1890 when the company introduced the collapsible tube, further refined in 1908 with the addition of the ribbon opening to create a tube that would still be familiar in the 1960s. Branded as Colgate Ribbon Dental Cream for Cleaning and Preserving the Teeth and Refreshing the Mouth, Colgate had basically laid out its battleground for the next 100 years. By 1911, Colgate had distributed two million tubes of toothpaste and toothbrushes to schools and sent in hygienists to demonstrate brushing technique. Simply getting more people to brush their teeth has remained a key strategy to this day, although nowadays there is a little more differentiation, with a company price list the size of a small phone book size, 160 different soaps, 625 varieties of perfume and 2,000 other assorted lines. Nonetheless, toothpaste was and remains Colgate's key differentiator.

Meanwhile, over at the B J Johnson Soap Company, Caleb Johnson was having his own brilliant idea: making soap not from animal fats but from oils, specifically palm oil and olive oil. His first came in 1898, a floating soap to ride on the coattails of Procter & Gamble's hugely successful Ivory brand. At the 1909 St. Louis Exposition, however, Caleb discovered some French machinery for making hard-milled soaps, which he immediately purchased, and, from that moment, Palmolive assumed its modern form. The brand's unique formulation sold well, but it was advertising that made the difference. In 1910, Charles Pearce, Johnson's Sales and Advertising Manager signed up with the Lord & Thomas advertising agency: together they would craft a long-running campaign that created a whole new category: luxury soap.

'The luxury-loving Greeks equipped the bath with extravagant accessories – but they lacked PALMOLIVE, the famous modern luxury for toilet, bath and shampoo. True, Palm and Olive oils were the favourite cleansing agents – but obtainable only in their crude natural state. Their scientific combination in the smooth creamy PALMOLIVE lather is a triumph only twentieth century knows how.' Pearce also knew that money for such luxuries was tight, but innovative value-based promotions - buy two, get one free – was his answer. This combination of the best of the ancient with the modern, and at a good price, powered the brand to such heights that in 1917 the B.J. Johnson Company renamed itself the Palmolive Company.

The 1920s saw a great shakedown in the American soap business via merger and takeover mania. While P&G and Lever Brothers were vacuuming up small regional players by the dozen, Palmolive merged with Peet Brothers Company in 1927. A year later they merged again with the Colgate Company to create a $100 million turnover business that was now large enough to fend off any predatory advances P&G or Lever might make. The newly merged company was initially run by Palmolive-Peet's management who, within a year of the merger, were looking at an even bigger deal. Charles Pearce had been seduced by a Wall Street proposal to create nothing less than an industrial behemoth.

The idea was to form a food, drug manufacturers and retailers combine, the first stage of which was to merge Colgate-Palmolive with the Kraft-Phoenix Cheese Company and Hershey Chocolate. The deal was ready to sign by October 1929 and negotiations had been opened with a grocery chain, a meat packer and a canning company. Rumours of the deal sent Colgate stock up 50% and on October 29th it was signed. The merger would have created the largest consumer products company in the world, one of the greatest what could-have-beens in consumer products history. Would have? Could have been? When they returned from a lavish celebratory lunch, the would-be executives had a shock coming. The stock market had crashed, and the deal was off. Colgate-Palmolive stock, which had peaked at 90, bottomed at 7 by 1933, at which point the previously sidelined Colgate family promptly bought back control, installed Bayard Colgate as President, and kicked Charles Pearce upstairs to Chairman.

How International Are They?

In a word, very. Most unusually for an American packaged goods company, international expansion happened very early and would play the key role in defining the modern company. Both Colgate and Palmolive had already been pioneers of international expansion well before the merger. A Colgate Canadian subsidiary was set up in 1913, the same year a Palmolive subsidiary there began exporting Palmolive soap into Britain. During the 1920s, there were healthy exports of Colgate products to Australia, the United Kingdom, Germany and Mexico. Colgate subsidiaries were also set up in several South American countries and a factory established in the U.K. in 1933. Following the 1933 coup by the Colgate family, international development was considerably ramped up, led by the new head of sales and advertising who had spent the previous five years building the company's exports in Europe.

The crucial insight was that businesses which simply exported their products could never compete seriously with indigenous giants - Lever Brothers in the

United Kingdom and Henkel in Germany - because of the cost. What was needed were production facilities in situ and these could best be gained through acquisition. The company acquired Cadmun in France and Binder-Ketels in Germany, plus local operations in Sweden, Italy, Poland and Switzerland. Factories were converted to Palmolive production with only one acquired brand allowed to continue on sale, as Cadmun in France. In 1938, Goodwin & Sons of Manchester, England, one of the few sizeable soap companies to escape Lever Brothers, fell to Palmolive, whose UK production began in October 1939. A year later a German bomb flattened the London Colgate factory. The R.A.F responded by demolishing the Palmolive-Ketel works in Hamburg.

Post-war, Colgate-Palmolive European sales boomed. In Britain, Colgate production had been re-established at the Manchester Palmolive factory and new brands such as Ajax cleanser and Fab detergent, both launched in 1949, quickly became very successful. New factories appeared in France, Italy, Denmark, Switzerland, Spain, Greece, Belgium, Portugal and Ireland. Largely by necessity, overseas subsidiaries often operated with a high level of autonomy, each with their own new products groups, which established early the culture of meeting local needs in the most suitable and profitable ways, although, even as local brands were developed, good advertising ideas were shared across markets, such as Madge the Palmolive Liquid manicurist.

European successes in the 1950s and 60s, largely carrying the company, encouraged Colgate-Palmolive to look further afield. It set up operations in emerging markets such as Malaysia, Thailand and India before they had really started emerging. Unlike in Europe, however, these factories produced only Colgate brands; any potentially competitive local soap makers simply added to the product flow by turning their own capacity over to Palmolive too. By the 1970's, Colgate-Palmolive was well established throughout Europe, Asia, South America and even Africa, a crucial competitive advantage that gave Colgate-Palmolive first mover advantage in dozens of markets that would become increasingly important. As early as 1961, over 50% of sales were coming from outside the United States.

How Did They Build Their Modern Business?

However, Colgate-Palmolive's core U.S. business entered the 1960s in poor shape. The company had made no acquisitions since their original merger, the new product pipeline had been wheezing for decades and the combined forces of P&G and Unilever were taking the core brands of Palmolive soap to the cleaners.

New president George H. Lesch had been appointed from the company's international division in the hope he could transplant some of the foreign success back into the parent company. It was a successful appointment. George's initiatives shaped modern day company: a ramped-up innovation programme, funded by an aggressive and constant pressure on costs. Long before it became fashionable, task forces were set up to look at every aspect of product cost, process and management, engineering out anything that didn't add consumer value. Sacred formulations were changed, suppliers corralled into looking for new compounds and workforces slimmed. Simultaneously, extra resources were poured into consumer research and the core science needed to find breakthrough products. Palmolive washing-up liquid, Cold Power laundry detergent and Ultra Brite toothpaste were just three of the products that emerged to reinvigorate a sagging top line. The reformulation of Colgate toothpaste to include MFP Fluoride boosted sales, as did the adoption in the U.S. of overseas innovations such as fabric conditioner from France and Irish Spring deodorant from Germany. 1961's $500 million sales doubled by 1967.

As the company entered the 1970s, Colgate-Palmolive was doing well everywhere but America, where the product pipeline was steadily failing to produce blockbusters. Management came to what was a quite common conclusion in that era: growth in the U.S was largely maxed out, so further growth could only come from increasingly expensive battles against larger and better funded competitors such as P&G. The 170 year-old company strategy of 'overcoming housewife resistance through advertising', as new Chairman and CEO David R. Foste described it, was played out. Growth would have to come from elsewhere.

Colgate-Palmolive dipped its toe in the waters of diversification in 1971 by acquiring the U.S. rights to sell Wilkinson Sword razors and blades. Next came the acquisition of Kendall & Company, a manufacturer of hospital supplies, bandages, sporting goods and – yes - coatings for oil pipelines. The company ventured further afield in 2003, when it bought the Helena Rubinstein cosmetics business. After cosmetics came sports: the Ram Golf Company, Bancroft Racket Company and Penfold golf balls. The moves certainly boosted sales and earnings. But the core US business continued to languish: every one of these ventures would be sold off within a decade. The one acquisition that would have long-term benefit came in 1976 with the purchase of Riviana Foods, a producer of long-grain rice that had its own subsidiaries in kosher hot dogs, confectionery and, more interestingly, prescription pet foods, in the shape of Hill's Pet Products. The rest of the Riviana Empire would be sold off during the 1980s. But Hill's has been retained to this day.

With the exception of Hill's, the 1980s saw Colgate-Palmolive returning to its core business, re-invigorating its product range through innovation and acquisition while keeping a tight grip on costs. In 1983 the Colgate Total toothbrush was launched, the genesis of a product line that still sells 1.6 billion toothbrushes a year. Two years later came Protex antibacterial soap, now sold in over 50 countries. And in perhaps the company's best-ever acquisition, the Softsoap brand was purchased in 1987, with Vipont Pharmaceutical's oral hygiene products a useful addition two years later. Colgate-Palmolive also realised that, in mature categories such as toothpaste and washing needs, format innovation could be just as powerful as product innovation. Thus they were first to market with gel toothpaste, pump-action dispensers and throw-in pouch laundry detergent.

There were further successful acquisitions in the early 1990s: the Murphy-Phoenix Corporation in 1991 (Murphy's Oil Soap), the Mennen Company a year later (Mennen Speed Stick and Baby Magic) and in 1993 S.C Johnson's liquid soap brands in Europe and Australasia, which together made Colgate the worldwide leader in liquid soap. Colgate Total toothpaste was launched overseas in 1992, although delayed a further five years before American introduction owing to a convoluted FDA approval procedure for its gingivitis-fighting claim. But backed by the company's biggest-ever launch, the brand shot to number one. Colgate toothpaste enjoyed market leadership in the US for the first time.

Colgate-Palmolive was now not only fighting back against P&G in the U.S. but also far outstripping them around the world, and not just because of its far-sighted positioning in those early non-emerging, emerging markets. Early entries into Central Europe and Russia in 1995 and major acquisitions such as Kolynos Oral Care in Latin America were rapidly extending the market share; in Latin America, the oral care market reached a staggering 79%. In what was now a key part of the company's modus operandi, stringent cost-saving measures were initiated not during crises but during periods of relative strength to fund further growth. In 1995, for example, in no sense a problem year, 3,000 employees and 24 factories bit the dust. Hill's Pet Food business also demonstrated its long-term value to the company in 1999. During the first half of the 90s, Hill's – the worldwide leader in therapeutic and wellness pet food – grew at 15% a year and generated margins ten points higher than the company average.

Further progress in oral care market via lines such as Colgate Simply White Gel and Total Plus Whitening, plus the continued growth of Hill's, convinced the company that its future lay more in these two areas than in a toe-to-toe laundry care battle with P&G, where P&G was proportionately much stronger. Consequently, Colgate began to shed its detergent products, selling its Mexican brands to Henkel in 2001 and, in 2003, its European laundry brands to P&G,

cheekily strengthening both Henkel and P&G in each other's home turf. Further laundry care divestments soon followed, the capital from which went to strengthen the European oral care markets through the acquisition of the pharmacy-based oral care business, GABA, whose strong links to tooth care products echoed Colgate's historic presence in the same area. GABA increased Colgate's total European market share from 27% to 33%.

How Are They Structured?

With the conglomerate phase and its attendant turmoil essentially at an end, the structure of Colgate-Palmolive has remained extremely consistent, with little to distract managers from their day jobs of generating growth and cutting costs. The company competes in four core segments with a tightly focused range of key brands: oral care (primarily Colgate brands); personal care (Palmolive, Mennen, Irish Spring, Softsoap); home care (Ajax, Fab detergent, Suavitel fabric softener, Murphy's) and pet nutrition (Hill's Science Diet, Hill's Prescription Diet).

As the company is so global, operating in over 200 countries and generating over 70% of sales from outside North America, it is structured along essentially geographical lines, with oral care, personal care and home care brands organised together in into four regions: North America, Latin America, Europe and Asia/Africa.

That it is one of the very few American companies with South American sales substantially greater than those of North America testifies to the truly global nature of Colgate. The only recent structural change came in 2006 when it was seen that the regional arrangement was too crude: developed was beginning to mix with developing. Consequently, the developing Eastern European markets were moved to the similarly developing Africa/Asia region, whilst the developed Australia/South Pacific moved the other way into developed western European Group. Only Hill's is geographically undifferentiated. Operating as a discrete 5th division of the company, it remains responsible for worldwide sales of its brands, primarily through vets and specialist pet food stores.

What Have They Been Doing Recently?

2004

2004 was a milestone. Sales topped $10 billion for the first time, driven by a 7% sales increase in sales, in turn led largely by volume growth. In a pattern that had become familiar over the years, North America still found growth hard to come by, even though Colgate toothpaste reached a record 35% market share of nearly. Elsewhere volume was more robust, helped not least by Colgate's legendary emerging market strength. On the back of a packaging and advertising relaunch of Total, the company increased its global toothpaste market share by 1.2%, across more than 100 countries, with a record 33% in China and a rapidly rising 17% in Russia.

Emerging market strategy had always focused on increasing category usage through schools education, smaller pack sizes, lower cost formulae, and innovative distribution strategies, all of which propelled to products into tens of millions of small, local stores. In the Philippines, for example, Palmolive Naturals and Aromatherapy shampoo brands in sachet format had added ten points to their shampoo market share in two years. In Central America toothpaste consumption had doubled since 1990. The fact that Colgate held the number one position in toothpaste in 53 of their 67 largest markets meant the onus was on them to build the category.

As it had done often in the past, the developed markets strategy primarily depended on innovation and cost reduction and the innovation pipeline was now unrecognisable. From the limp efforts of the 1970s, it now accounted for fully 40% of the year's sales from lines five or less years old, an impressive number by any standards. New products such as Colgate Max Fresh and Colgate Simply White were complimented by new formats of existing brands. Mennen was extended from stick format to roll-on and aerosol, vindicated by the insight that a significant number of consumers were loyal firstly to the format and only then to the brand. Until now, format alone had kept Mennen out of two-thirds of the global underarm deodorant market.

Despite a record year and the fact that gross margins had increased by 18% over the previous twenty years to a record high of 55.1%, the largest ever cost-reduction programme was announced: true Colgate style. The plan was to move to a truly global supply chain with fewer, bigger, better global and regional manufacturing facilities, business support functions centralised at regional level, and beefed up sales and marketing teams in the individual markets. Over the four-year change program, one third of the factories and 12% of the employees would go.

2005

Volume growth increased sales by nearly $1 billion, with all divisions performing well and record global market shares in both toothpaste and toothbrushes. But the big news was America, with a volume growth of 6.5% after three years in the doldrums. New products like Ajax Ruby Red Grapefruits, Palmolive Oxy

Plus washing-up liquid, Irish Spring MicroClean soap, Softsoap Kitchen Fresh Hands and Softsoap Shea Butter liquid soap exemplified Colgate's skill in extending brands through both line extensions and across categories. Colgate Total, Colgate Luminous and Colgate Max Fresh produced further market share gains.

There is no doubt the company had been progressively sharpening its marketing capabilities and increasing its resources. The innovation pipeline had produced a string of relevant new products and sales teams were doing equally well getting more and more product variants onto the grocery shelves, dominating displays with a sea of bright red branding. Colgate realised that as many as 60% of consumers were making their choices within the store, so it established a wide range of offerings dominating the displays, a feature that classically exploited impulse buying. Scratch and sniff panels on new toothpaste variants and in-store television commercials at Wal-Mart were a further two responses to the need to make the sale at the store level.

Colgate also put great emphasis on building relationships with, and seeking insights from, both dental and veterinarian professionals, the common corporate skill-set linking the oral care and pet care businesses. As well as sending dedicated professional sales teams to visit dentists' and vets' offices to explain the new product science, the expert feedback helped with the development of further initiatives. As an example, a company-organised network of dental hygienists helped refine advertising for the Colgate 360 manual toothbrush. In support, global advertising spend increased by 12% to a record high of almost $1.2 million, a 33% increase in only three years.

With the sale of their North American and South East Asian detergent brands, the move away from detergents continued in both developed and developing markets, which meant goodbye even to long-standing and sustaining brands as Fab and Cold Power. Simultaneously, and on the track of lower costs yet, procurement teams were established in both India and China and plans were finalised to replace five European factories with just one gigantic operation in Poland.

2006

Once again, the Colgate machine was humming. A 7% volume sales increase added almost another $1 billion to the top line, with every division performing well. In good years, strategies always sound cohesive and compelling. Colgate's were no different. They embodied:

- Tight focus on the consumer
- Increased marketing spending
- New ways of communicating

- Building consumption in emerging markets
- A steady stream of innovation

Whilst the first three should be generic to any decent packaged goods business, what was really driving Colgate was the latter two. Excluding Hill's, 80% of sales were now coming from outside North America. Building consumption in emerging markets was a two-stage process. In newly emerging markets such as India and China, it meant reaching the millions of small outlets whose small purchases for the majority of retail sales and Colgate products were now available in 5 million such outlets across the two markets. With that established, the next step is trading the consumer up. Sales in Latin America grew 15% in the year to top $3 billion, driven by a 10% increase in volume, on top of a 16% growth the previous year and with sales growing in every single market. The primary drivers were the company's premium brands: Colgate Total, Colgate Sensitive, Colgate Max Fresh, Colgate 360 toothbrush, Palmolive Nutri-milk and Lady Speedstick.

Clearly, trading-up depended on a steady stream of innovation, which the company was now delivering regularly and across three platforms. Firstly, at the local level, a Global Innovation Fund that allocated resources to selected projects any company employee could submit, 73 of which were selected in 2006. Secondly, innovation projected for the market within three years was sourced from nine category innovation centres located globally but close to the relevant action. The innovation centres' results were evaluated by the company's Global Big Hits process, which were built to identify the best strategic opportunities based on:

- Size of opportunity
- Most incremental potential to reach new consumers
- Which are truly new to the market
- Potential for global expansion

Thirdly, ground-breaking innovation expected to hit the market in 3-5 years would be developed at two new long-term innovation centres, one for oral care and one for Hill's Pet Nutrition. No less important than the processes was the funding, which was garnered from the energetic, constant and aggressive cost-cutting Colgate never failed to conduct. And the new product, once in market, would have its consumer and trade spend tightly managed by the Colgate Business Planning process which set out and evaluated goals both by product and by customer, 18 months ahead of time.

Colgate's willingness, in the years preceding 2006, to divest itself of lower-margin operations with fights on their hands for higher margin, less competitive arenas continued. It sold the Latin American and Canadian bleach brands Javex,

Agua Jane and Nevex and acquired in their place Tom's of Maine, a natural toothpaste business that sold through health and speciality stores.

2007

Business as usual? The top line gained another $1 billion, up 7%. Toothpaste, manual toothbrushes, mouth rinse, bar soaps, shower gels and even lowly fabric conditioners made new global market shares records. In a year when many companies' profits were pushed down by raw materials and energy costs, Colgate, ahead of the game by cutting costs well before the financial crisis struck, was reporting a record margin of 57.3%. With costs under control, there were no raids on the advertising budget to shore up the net margin. That too had increased by 17% to $1.5 billion, another record. The only worry on the horizon was that nearly half of 2007's 12.5% total sales increase had come from positive foreign exchange movements. They, of course, can go down as well as up.

And the innovation pipeline was squeezing out toothpaste. Colgate Total Advanced Clean and Colgate Max Fresh BURST were driving sales and margins, with Colgate Total now accounting for 20% of company toothpaste sales. In body care, breakthrough moisturising technology had been incorporated into the Palmolive and Softsoap ranges, and the Hill's range also benefited from new variants of the Prescription Diet and Science Diet ranges. Body Cleansing became a third new long-term centre of innovation and the company continued to pursue the outside collaboration that had produced the Colgate 360 manual toothbrush with the new Colgate 360 Sonic Power battery toothbrush.

One of the strengths of the Colgate strategy was its fundamentally multi-faceted nature. In addition to blockbuster new products, no opportunity was too small for the company to exploit. Colgate's close contacts with in-store pharmacies revealed that diabetics – frequent visitors – are voracious gatherers of information about their illness. Colgate launched a pharmacy-based information campaign about Colgate Total's ability to fight gingivitis, a prevalent problem for diabetics. And supporting all Colgate's oral-care activities was Bright Smiles, Bright Futures, a 17 year-long campaign which had not only provided health information and samples to over 500 million children in 80 countries, but, brought into stores as in the Carrefour relationship, rolled it out in ten countries during the year. Colgate's grip on the dental professionals, pharmacists and young minds alike gave, and give it still, a clear and tangible strategic advantage.

2008

With an 11% increase in the top line to a new high of $15.3 billion it seemed the global crisis had passed Colgate by. However, while growth before 2007 had been driven almost entirely by volume, that now playing less and less of a part. Of the 11% sales increase, only 4% came from volume. Positive foreign exchange movements delivered half as much, whilst a whopping 5.5% came simply from price increases. In the meantime, costs were increasing, consumer spending was down and Colgate's twin track approach of affordability and trading up could easily be threatened by over-zealous pricing. In Latin America, for example, net selling prices increased by 9.5% in the year, hardly recession-friendly. In the Europe/South Pacific region, prices rose by 5.5% as volume scarcely moved. Hill's prices rose even more, by a full 10.5%. While everyone loves their pets, high-end pet foods are likely to suffer when belts are being tightened.

Ever-reliable, however, the innovation process continued to deliver more winners, some quite extraordinary: Suavitel Magic Moments, for example, a fabric conditioner that was taking Latin America and Europe by storm. Hardly surprising. Its patented technology provided touch-activated fragrance for months after washing. Yet the company continued to reorganise. Dedicated teams of research and development staff focused on each stage of every process: conducting early research; energetically researching innovation inside and outside the company and marrying nascent technology to consumer needs. Colgate also formed an alliance with The Forsyth Institute, the world's leading oral care scientific research organisation and increased the size of the professional sales force that called on dentists'. It also began to seek out academics and other key opinion formers who could issue informed support for the company's products and activities.

2009

It was in 2009 that both and net sales volume increase hit the buffers. Perhaps continued price rises, this year by 6%, had finally had an impact. Nor can adverse currency movements have helped: flat sales, flat volume, and the 6% price rise meant a gross profit margin increase of 2.5%. But that was still a new high: 58.8%. But now, the biggest problem was Hill's Pet Nutrition, at 14% the smallest of the company's five divisions. Here, unit volume actually declined by 7.5%, almost certainly due to the previous year's price increases in response to similar increases in commodity costs. And the rest of the business achieved only 2% growth. Prices were up by an average of 5.5% whilst advertising was down by7%. The heady days of 7% a year suddenly seemed long gone.

But there were occasional highlights. Colgate Wisp, a new portable mini-toothbrush, with a breath-freshening bead for use without water, was targeted at busy young adults and launched via social media and on-campus sampling. It took 5% of the disposable toothbrush market in a year, adding almost the same percentage to the company's total toothbrush share. Colgate Total Enamel Strength, Colgate Sensitive Enamel Protect and Colgate Max White with Mini White Strips made useful progress across several markets. Once again, the company's strategy of endless segmentation with carefully targeted offerings was paying dividends. In Latin America, Colgate's share of the soap bar market, helped by the launch of Palmolive Nutri-Milk, reached a new high of 28%, on top of the company's dominance in oral care. But that 3% volume growth in Latin America came hand-in-hand with prices hikes of 13.5%. How sustainable could that be in the company's biggest region?

2010

Net sales up by a little over 1%; successful innovation; stock on the shelves: price increase roll-backs in selective markets: things were beginning to look a little more sustainable. But in which markets? Greater Asia/Africa increased its sales increased by $350 million, driven by a very impressive 10% increase in volume, primarily in China, Thailand, Philippines, Malaysia, Turkey, Russia and India, where Colgate's share of the rapidly growing toothpaste market reached a record 51.5%. It was just as well. 50% of total sales now came from emerging markets, now vital for the company at a time when the developed markets seemed to be in a never-ending slump.

North America, however, was a marginal exception. Sales volume grew by 3.5% on the back of a 2.5% decrease in prices and the success of another slew of oral care innovations: Colgate Triple Action, Colgate Extra Clean and a relaunched Colgate Total. But the Hill's problem did not go away. Volume declined further by 2, despite price reductions. Worst hit were U.S., Russia, Japan, France and Germany, prompting more price reductions and decreases in pack size, although leavened by innovations such as Hill's Science Diet VetEssentails in Europe and Hill's Science Diet Weight Loss System in the U.S., where, not unlike their owners, 45% of dogs were obese. Other factors kicked in too: the benefits of the restructuring programme begun in 2004 and a second three-year programme, which now brought down worldwide formula costs by 32% and SKUs by 23%. The gross margin rose to 59.1%.

2011

The business was in slightly better shape, posting a 4% volume increase, adding another $1.2 billion to the top line sales to a record $16.7 billion, driven not least by the realisation that cost increases could not permanently be answered simply by price hikes. So, to maintain if not improve competitiveness, Colgate held its prices, even at the cost of 1.5% haircut on the gross margin.

But what 2011 really did reveal was the differing set of challenges in the two halves of Colgate's business: developed and developing markets. In North America, the absolute necessity to promote through price pushed prices down by 3%, but improved volume by 2%. In Europe, the same 3% reduction fared even worse: a 1% increase. The 2010 attention Hill's halted its decline overall; volume was lost in the developed markets of the U.S. and Japan, but counterbalanced by growth in Russia, South Africa and Brazil.

In contrast, the rest of the world looked rosier. The emerging markets, with their large populations and low but rapidly rising core product penetration and consumption, maintained robust GDP growth, which accounted for over half of Colgate's total sales, and powered all the 2011 growth. Sales in Latin America rose by 12%, if more by price increases than by volume. Greater Asia/Africa scored 9.5%, mostly through volume. The two regions added $800 million in sales, as the rest of the company could only cite favourable currency movements as its saviour.

The developed markets' challenge was not a new one, however. The same problems a generation earlier, low GDP growth, flat all-round performance, downward pressure on prices and retailers scrambling to keep their shoppers, all this had prompted a scattergun acquisition spree. So, in June 2011, Colgate purchased the Sanex personal care business from Unilever for $940 million. Unilever had acquired the skin health targeted premium shower gel and deodorant brand as part of its Sara Lee acquisition in 2009 but had been ordered to sell under the European antitrust legislation. As part of the deal, Colgate sold their Columbian detergent brands to Unilever.

What is Their DNA?

Except for the tempestuous conglomerate interlude, the Colgate-Palmolive company has generally been a tightly focused company with few upheavals in structure, direction or management style. With the benefits of this firm base, it has evolved highly distinctive way of doing things, much of it highly effective, of which the three most significant are the company's strength in emerging markets, its relationships with the professionals in its product fields and its ability to control cost.

Emerging Markets.

For a company located in and managed from the USA, Colgate's geographic spread is astounding. Over 50% of total sales come from emerging markets, a figure that increases every year. Even more valuable is a brand strength and brand leadership in the 21st century's fastest growing economies. Colgate-Palmolive has been established in Latin America for 75 years, in Greater Asia for over 50 years, where it has built up dominant market positions. In 2011, in a consumer brand equity survey published by The Economic Times of India, Colgate was ranked as the Most Trusted Brand in the country, not just in toothpaste but also across all product categories. That's an American brand more trusted than home-grown stalwarts such as Britannia Industries, Marico Industries, Tata Beverages and long-term Indian subsidiaries of other globals like Hindustan Unilever and Cadbury India.

Colgate is certainly a virtuoso practitioner of establishing global brands and exploiting global sourcing. It long ago saw and acted on the benefits of changing global products according to local preferences, as it in China with Colgate Plax Fresh Tea mouthwash. Distribution did not stick to expat-friendly big cities but reached out to millions of independent retailers which now account for a staggering one quarter of the company's global sales. Wholesalers are assiduously courted not just with visits and incentives but also with customised, small scale packaging; in China the company offers cases of a mixed dozen products. Colgate employees often spend up to a week in small neighbourhood stores themselves, immersing themselves in the local retailers' world, seeing at first-hand how the storekeeper – his customers' most important product advisor – influences his shoppers buying choices. Such embedding in day-to-day marketplace life gives Colgate-Palmolive a decisive competitive strength in these all-important emerging markets. It is the very antithesis of the stereotypical American company: barging in, ignoring local culture, blindly insisting on doing things the American way.

Relationships with Professionals

A unique feature of oral health is its health professionals, whom we visit on a regular basis in the normal course of caring for our teeth and gums. Bit in between such visits, we ourselves make our own purchasing decisions. A similar set of conditions applies when taking pets to vets Colgate's absolute belief in the power of professional recommendations in driving new product and establishing long-term loyalty has reaped enormous dividends and been backed by considerable resources. The result: Colgate and Hill's are far and away the brands most often recommended by dental and veterinary professionals.

In oral care, Colgate has implemented a 10-point plan to encourage this close relationship, offering guidelines on professional sales, sampling of new products, obtaining dental seals of approvals, having a high visibility at dental conferences, and establishing the annual Colgate Oral Health Month, an education programme which in 2012 provided the opportunity for dental teams to meet, discuss and review how they deliver evidence-based care, treatment and prevention messages to their patients. Hill's Pet Nutrition programme has similarly close ties with the veterinary community.

The relationships are not all one way. Colgate salespeople visit dentists and vets on a regular Basis. Tours are arranged around the company's respective Global Technology Centres for both groups. Insight and information are also in dialogue. Professional input is sought extensively in product and advertising development. In return, it is not unusual for the company to launch new products through dental and veterinary offices; Colgate Sensitive Pro-Relief toothpaste was first launched as a polishing paste in 2009 via meeting of the International Association for Dental Research. The consumer launch followed later in the year, a launch template that was rolled out in 45 countries. Colgate also courts professionals in emerging markets. 77% of dental professionals in Brazil, 81% in India and 85% in China recommend Colgate. Colgate is now the toothpaste most recommended by dentists in 37 countries, a depth of relationship exceptionally hard for a competitor to loosen.

Cost Control.

This might seem an odd choice as virtually every packaged goods company goes through reorganisations, restructurings, downsizing, SKU rationalisations, outsourcings and the like. But most do it in response to some real or perceived crisis. With Colgate, cost reduction is, and has been for many years, simply business as usual. The company has learned how to amalgamate cost-cutting with driving a business, moving far beyond slash and burn approaches and using creativity to find cheaper, better ways to do things.

These steady, on-going funding-the-growth initiatives have usually generated between $300 and $700 million in savings each year, a process aided by the company's early and company-comprehensive embrace of SAP operating systems. Add sweeping changes over manufacturing, logistics and sourcing strategies, while keeping operational sales and marketing structures largely constant, and you generate a steady stream of savings without diverting or disrupting sales and marketing. That Colgate-Palmolive has been able to grow its margin in recent years despite a cost price inflation that has severely affected all packaged goods producers has obviated the need for distracting changes of direction. Colgate-Palmolive is better poised than many to benefit when the recovery comes.

Summary

From that first day in 1928, Colgate-Palmolive has always been the underdog compared P&G and Unilever, at least in terms of size. To have survived and prospered in the face of such competition is testament to both sustained brand strength and sustained management skills. Apart from the one short and aberrational period in its life, and compared to P&G and Unilever, Colgate has remained more tightly focused in terms product categories and more expansive and imaginative in terms of geographical location. In doing so, it has established commanding positions that are the envy of the packaged goods world and without losing too many shirts in the process. Over the past twenty-five years, Colgate-Palmolive's gross margin has grown from the mid 30's to the high 50's. Trading consumers up to premium products, divesting low margin businesses, acquiring high margin ones, developing strong brands that can support premium prices, and always keeping the tightest of grips on costs; those have been its highly successful tricks of the trade.

Given the strength of many of Colgate's global market share positions, it may well now be immune from at least a P&G ambush, for anti-trust reasons at the very least. The company is surely the envy of, if not the western world, then certainly P&G and Unilever. Whether the company can retain this independence in an era when size, brand strength and emerging market exposure are the criteria by which all are judged remains to be seen. Once again, it will almost certainly be the emerging markets that eventually make the difference.

Danone

Where Did They Come From?

In 1905, Daniel Carasso was born in Thessaloníki, Greece, into a Spanish-Jewish family expelled from Spain by the Spanish Inquisition. By 1916, four hundred years later, Isaac Carasso, Daniel's father, decided it was probably safe enough to come back: the family returned to Spain to live there permanently, in Barcelona. In the aftermath of the First World War, however, the city was not a pretty sight. Isaac was appalled by the plight of large numbers of the city's children, suffering and dying from cholera and other intestinal disorders. He determined to do something about it, however little. As we shall see, a humanitarian determination has persisted in Danone to this day: it might well have been the making of the company.

Friends who were doctors had already told Isaac about the beneficial effects of eating yoghurt, a product then virtually unknown outside of the Middle East and Balkans, where it had been consumed for centuries. He had also heard of a parallel development: the then director of the Pasteur Institute in Paris, Ilya Metchnikoff, winner of the 1908 Nobel Prize in medicine for his work on the immune system, was also researching yoghurt. Having analysed countless yoghurts, he had managed to isolate the specific bacteria then use them to ferment yoghourt. Ilya too, interested in how yoghurt achieved its beneficial effects on the digestive system, arranged delivery of the cultures from Paris and began producing his own yoghurt in a small Barcelona shop. Searching for a name for his yoghurt, he plumped for Danone, an affectionate version of his little son's name. It meant 'Big Daniel'.

Danone yoghurt left Isaac with two problems. First, no one in Barcelona had ever heard of it and, second, even if they had, they were deeply disinclined to adapt their eating habits to include yoghurt. It was Isaac's medical connections that came to the rescue. He toured the surgeries of his medical chums, pleading with them to prescribe a dose of yoghurt for any digestive problems they encountered, while he got the product listed in nearby pharmacies. Business, unsurprisingly, was initially very slow, but Isaac persevered and was finally rewarded when local food stores that carried dairy products began asking him for supplies in response to requests from customers who had presumably enjoyed their prescriptions. The product began to move, despite distribution problems: with no refrigerated transport, the yoghurt had to be delivered to shops almost as soon as it was produced, which limited its reach.

In 1923, Isaac sent Daniel to business school in Marseille, France. In something of a full circle, he then went on to study bacteriology to better understand fermentation, ending up at the Pasteur Institute, the source of his father's original cultures. In 1929, Daniel combined his bacteriological and business training to set up Danone in France as a separate company to his father's original in Spain. With his greater commercial acumen and a passion for marketing from his Marseilles business courses, it was obvious to Daniel from the beginning that there was no real future for yoghurt sold as a hand-delivered medicine in pharmacies. But as an appetising and health-giving treat mass production, mass distribution and mass selling techniques made it a very different matter. Daniel believed that yoghurt would have a very wide appeal indeed.

Yoghurt itself was as unknown in 1929 Paris as it had been in 1919 Barcelona, so Daniel's first priority was to develop some advertising, for which he leaned on a friend in the city's biggest advertising agency. The advertising highlighted the beneficial effects of Danone yoghurt, but combined this promise with professional packaging and design, plus distribution across as many food stores as Daniel could persuade to take it. It was a mass-market product waiting to happen.

How Did It Evolve?

The company had been building quite nicely for Daniel until the German invasion of France dislocated first business and then Daniel. His Jewish background convinced him he would be a lot safer moving to America, which he did in 1941, leaving the running of Danone France and Danone Spain to two trusted long-time managers. A year later, in partnership with a Spanish father and son, he purchased a small factory in New York City and began producing again, this time under the name Dannon Milk Products, which Daniel felt Americans would find easier to pronounce.

Given the almost complete unfamiliarity with the product, business once again began slowly. The 200-jars-a-day output was restricted to migrant Turks, Arabs and Greeks who remembered yoghurt from their homelands, plus a handful of health fanatics. Sales as low as $100 a week still made Dannon New York's biggest yoghurt company. In fact, big was very small indeed and the terrible sales turned the product into a national joke. After the war ended, Daniel returned to Paris.

In America, however, it wasn't until 1950 that Dannon finally hit on the idea that would break yoghurt out of its US niche of immigrants and health faddists: put a layer of sweet strawberry conserve in the bottom of the pot and radically change the advertising. 'Doctors recommend it' changed overnight to 'A wonderful snack ... A delicious dessert'. By 1956, Juan Metzger, the junior Spanish partner, knew that they had finally broken through. Bob Hope made a yoghurt joke and nobody laughed.

By 1959, Dannon had annual sales in the United States of $3 million a year and was producing three-quarters of the country's supply of yoghurt, but the company had slipped off Daniel's radar; he was putting all his energies into the French businesses and, to a lesser extent, the Spanish. So when Beatrice Foods turned up with an offer to buy Dannon, the three partners agreed to sell, with Juan Metzger staying on to run Beatrice's new subsidiary. Daniel had taken his eye off the Dannon America ball because Danone France, once up and running again after the war, had been going from strength to strength. But he had learned from the American experience, introducing first fruit-flavoured and then low-fat yoghurts, both of which did wonders for consumer appeal. At least as important was the increasing sophistication of the French retail trade, in which American supermarket-style formats with large chiller displays began to appear to keep pace with French refrigerator sales, which rose from 7% of households in 1954 to 47% a decade later. This retail-to-home chilled infrastructure greatly increased the marketability of Danone yoghurts, before the war an essentially 'consume immediately' item.

In the late 1950s, Danone began building more factories to service the quickly rising demand, locating them around the country to get the best match between milk collection and finished product. However, the rapidly increasing sophistication of the French retail trade was a double-edged sword. Supermarkets had come quite late to the country, only appearing in the late 1950s, but the spread and then evolution of the format was very rapid, with the first Carrefour hypermarket opening in 1963. These large customers baulked at dealing with a plethora of local or regional dairy suppliers and were constantly encouraging Danone to get into other categories, such as *fromage frais*. More worrying to Daniel was the certainty that the same customers were also encouraging other dairy companies to get into yoghurt. The balance of bargaining power was quickly ebbing away from specialist dairy producers to the rapidly growing retailers.

The logical solution to this dilemma was consolidation of the dairy products industry, a process in which Daniel was keen to be predator not prey. So in 1967, Danone merged with the Gervais cheese company. Almost immediately, the newly merged company realised it had barely kept pace despite combining its resources; it could just as easily be held to ransom by the big retailers. Size and diversification were the answers. Gervais-Danone moved into pasta and ready-to-serve meals. Even so, the company was not really up to speed. The forthcoming enlargement of the European Common Market to include the United Kingdom., Ireland and Denmark meant Gervais-Danone needed to be bigger yet to compete effectively. The solution came, not as might have been expected from a competitor, but from one of its suppliers.

BSN was a supplier of glass bottles to Gervais-Danone. BSN itself was the result of a 1966 merger between France's largest manufacturer of flat glass, Glaces de Boussois, and a leading maker of bottles, Souchon-Neuvesel, an interesting company that in 1914 had the inspired idea of buying a 25% stake in the Evian water company. Evian was key buyer of bottles and then became one of France's top baby food companies (more glass bottles). Even though the bottle business was booming - the shift away from large, returnable bottles to small throwaway ones and huge sales growth in water and beer had seen to that - BSN was and Gervais-Danone were facing the same problems, as Common Market expansion big fish in small ponds into small fish in very big ones. Two revolutions sweeping through the glass industry would also sideline BSN's size if not addressed: the switch to throwaway was opening up the market to competitors in cheaper materials such as plastic; in the plate glass business, Pilkington's invention of the float-glass process was making everything else obsolete almost overnight. BSN had done its merger. But like Danone, it still needed size and diversification.

The most logical solution was more consolidation in the packaging industry, so in 1968 BSN launched a takeover bid for one of France's oldest companies, Compagnie de Saint-Gobain, a huge conglomerate with over 150 subsidiaries, largely in the industrial glass and fibreglass markets. Fortunately for BSN, the bid failed, which reminded the BSN Chairman, Antoine Riboud, of a U.S. visit he had made to Illinois Owens, the world's largest glass packaging manufacturer. Riboud remembered that the company strategy had been to diversify from glass into other packaging such as cardboard, metal and plastics. But with glass, sand, the principal raw material, was inexpensive and available in effectively infinite quantities, while the value added by turning it into glass bottles was very substantial. Plastic bottles' principal raw ingredient was petrochemicals, whose price was prone to wild fluctuation and in any event demanded structure and expertise BSN didn't possess. Riboud felt that this sort of diversification was the wrong strategy for BSN

But BSN's stake in Evian got Antoine thinking; there was much more money to be made by filling your own containers than making empty ones for someone else to fill. So, when the opportunity arose in 1970, BSN took over full control of Evian and bought Kronenbourg and the Société Européenne des Brasseries.

Overnight, BSN became the national market leader in the water, beer and baby food categories, all three of which were big buyers of glass bottles: from BSN.

To run its new foods company, BSN brought in Francis Gautier, a packaged goods specialist and previously CEO of Colgate-Palmolive France. Meanwhile, it continued to expand its glass business, buying companies in West Germany, Austria and Belgium. It now enjoyed an almost 50% share of the European flat glass market. But its continuing interest in the glass market, BSN had become a quite different company; it was now a vertically integrated food and beverage company that simply made its own containers – whilst selling them to others, of course.

The problem BSN faced was that there were few container-filling food companies worth buying. The French packaged food industry had not evolved in line with French retailing. It was highly fragmented, essentially made up of thousands of small to medium-sized family-run concerns notable for their long-term lack of innovation and capital. Gervais-Danone was one rare exception. By 1972, it was France's largest food business, turning over two billion francs in the nation's chiller cabinets and grocery aisles, significant exports within the Common Market. Gervais-Danone ticked most of the boxes on BSN's checklist:

- BSN's own food business was too small to compete in the Europe-wide market. Organic growth would be slow or non-existent, so acquisition was the only viable route
- Gervais-Danone was a substantial buyer of glass bottles
- Danone yoghurts and the Gervais cheeses were market leaders
- The company had an international presence
- It was big enough to fulfil BSN's food expansion ambitions in one transaction, obviating the need for a plethora of small purchases

It was a marriage made in some sort of corporate Heaven. In 1973, the two companies merged into BSN-Gervais Danone. Food accounted for 52% of the new company's sales.

The logic of BSN's move was vindicated almost immediately. The 1973 oil crisis, with its surging energy costs and the industrial contraction that followed created tremendous difficulties in its plate and bottled glass businesses driving, the whole company into the red in 1975 for the first and only time in its history. It was only the revenues from the food business that bought the time and provided the resources to restructure its two glass businesses. Both moved into profit by 1979, but not before closing all the existing glass factories and replacing them with five new float-glass plants operating on a license from Pilkington.

The business may have once more been on an even keel, but it was clear that thanks to the licensed Pilkington technology, its processes had diverged so dramatically that there were now no synergies left with the rest of the business. The plate glass business, now modernised, profitable and thus saleable, was disposed of in two tranches, first the businesses outside France, and two years later the remaining French assets. The company was now wholly focused on food. Its glass bottle business essentially became a vertically integrated add-on.

Then the landscape changed yet again. Europe's rapid movements towards a single, fully integrated market prompted BSN-Gervais Danone to consider a major Europe-wide acquisition strategy. With sales still predominantly in one country, and with fully international competitors such as Nestlé and the American giants eyeing up the imminently borderless European market, management realised they would be sitting ducks. Bigger players could easily build unassailable positions in other countries that would both exclude BSN from real competition. Inside France, much greater size resources and scale would also prevail.

European unification sparked another trend, big retail cross border alliances, which had the power to transform BSN-Gervais Danone into what it had been, just another regional supplier in what everyone else recognized as the world's largest single consumer market. To survive and thrive, companies needed to have top brands not simply in a single country but across Europe. So at the end of the 1970s, BSN-Gervais Danone began a series of international expansions, initially targeting southern Europe, where the retailing trade was less concentrated and thus less powerful. The company was very flexible. It would first buy minority stakes on a temporary basis until its own brands, Danone yoghurts in particular, had become established, when BSN would then take over.

For the most part, expansion was focused on sectors in which the company already competed; thus beer brands were bought in Belgium, Spain and Italy, pasta and ready-to-serve brands in Belgium, France, Italy and Spain and .dairy products in Greece, Italy and Spain (where the by then independent Danone SA was partially reacquired in 1992). Mineral water acquisitions in Spain, France (including the Volvic brand) and Italy made BSN-Gervais Danone the world's largest bottler of mineral water. There were new products too: confectionary acquisitions in France and sauce/condiments businesses in France, Italy and the UK, including the iconic HP. There were expansions into frozen ready-to-serve dishes in France, Spain and Italy, and even into the champagne market. The biggest leap was a major expansion into biscuits: the Europe-wide Générale Biscuit Group in1986 and Nabisco's European subsidiaries in 1989. The company duly became the world's second-largest biscuit maker. It also continued to acquire bottling manufacturers.

But the prolonged food acquisitions campaign had also made BSN Europe's third-largest food business. Further, Danone was now not only a Europe-wide yoghurt, it was also an American brand, following the 1982 reacquisition of Dannon from Beatrice Foods. And as shifts away from glass bottles in food packaging made the vertical integration increasingly redundant, parts of the company's glass jar and glass tableware operations had been sold off in 1985.

Then, just as the company paused for breath in its race for scale and reach, a new consumer market opened up right on its doorstep, potentially even larger than the European Economic Community. In 1989, as regime after communist regime crumbled, the whole of the Eastern Bloc flung open its doors. Antoine Riboud immediately galvanised the company around an 'unforeseeable strategic opportunity with practically limitless potential', which contained '400 million people wanting better food'. Dairy foods and biscuits were to lead the charge and the first concrete move, an agreement with an East German dairy to produce Danone fruit yoghurt, came only four months after the fall of the Berlin Wall. Between the collapse and the agreement, company products had been imported through distributors.

Similar Danone joint ventures followed in Czechoslovakia, Hungary, Bulgaria, Poland and Russia. Given the ramshackle distribution systems and inefficient retailers, the company knew it was flying almost blind, but BSN was determined its brands would be known and accepted before completion arrived and before consumers lost their love of all things Western. As it had with previous acquisitions, as soon as products were up and running, BSN took over product quality and distribution – key factors in the yoghurt business – by acquiring their joint venture partners. Biscuits were different. Because they were much better established in the former communist markets thanks to the Eastern Europeans' sweet tooth, the company acquired well-known local brands, Cokoladovny in Czechoslovakia and Bolshevik in Russia, for example, then invested heavily to modernise facilities and finally inserted its own brands into the portfolio gaps.

Eastern Europe early was a key development. As the first man in, huge benefits accrued from the initial appeal of Western brands to millions of consumers with significant money to spend. The process was facilitated by the low costs advertising in the early days of Westernisation and unsophisticated existing retailers, who were falling over themselves to get any Western brand at all onto their shelves. It all added up to a unique opportunity both to shape consumer taste and brand preferences together and to achieve dominance at the point of sale. The Eastern European ventures grew quickly and profitably right from the start.

GREG THAIN & JOHN BRADLEY

With Eastern European expansion came an almost simultaneous move into overseas markets, employing precisely the same logic. The main overseas push began in 1990, when, in a joint venture with India's Britannia Biscuits, RtR Nabisco's Asia-Pacific businesses were acquired along with a 25% stake in Britannia itself, India's largest biscuit company. The company's Asia biscuit presence was further extended in 1992 with joint ventures in China and, in 1995, Indonesia. Similarly, there was a raft of dairy and bottled water joint ventures and acquisitions in a host of Asian and Latin American countries, together with several targeted moves into the likes of Canada, New Zealand and the US.

In addition to all the joint ventures and acquisitions, the company had also found time to extend the core yoghurt product range with the launch, in 1994, of Actimel (DanActive in North America), an innovative pro-biotic yoghurt drink designed to cash in on the rapidly growing health and fitness craze. By 1995, the company's sales outside Europe had almost trebled from their 1989 level, contributing to a doubling of total company sales over the same period to over $16 billion, of which well over half was now coming from outside France.

At this high point, BSN's Chairman and guiding light, Antoine Riboud, retired; his son, Franck Riboud, succeeded him. Franck's first priority was to take a hard look at the company's now somewhat extended product line-up. 25% came from dairy products under the Danone brand name, 20% in pasta and groceries, 14% in biscuits, 9% in beer, 9% in mineral water and 8% in, as it were, glass containers. Franck concluded only three of those categories, dairy, biscuits and water, where it was globally number one or number two, were essentially worth keeping and expanding, via the usual approach of joint ventures leading to full acquisition. Most of the other categories would be sold off when suitable opportunities arose. Not in any sense a fire sale, but a phased retrenchment into three core global categories.

So, in 1997 and 1998, half the grocery products and all the confectionery businesses were disposed of, followed in 1999 by half the glass containers business, followed by the remainder in 2003. In 2000, most of the European beer brands were sold and, in 2002, some European meat businesses and the Chinese beer brands went, leaving just the HP and Lea & Perrins sauces businesses and Bledina, the leading French brand of baby food. While this shedding of the superfluous was going on, and in a growth-side change of tack, a joint venture was set up in 1996 with Coca-Cola Company to sell refrigerated juices and yoghurt drinks in Europe and South America under the Minute Maid and Danone brand names, a deal which gave both companies critical distribution mass in a sector neither had formerly dominated. After Nestlé, Phillip Morris, Unilever, ConAgra, PepsiCo and Coca-Cola, Danone was now the world's seventh-largest food company, number one in dairy and sweet biscuits and number two in bottled water behind Nestlé.

Franck's second move had been to rename the company Danone. The logic, as with the company's past series of expansion moves, was compelling. While the BSN name, which the company had been using since the merger, was widely known in France, with a 93% recognition level, it was almost unknown in markets like Italy and Spain, with recognition levels of just 7% and 4% respectively, despite the company being the leading food producer in both markets. It was also a far from unique name. Spanish and Malaysian banks, a Japanese cable TV channel and an American clothing business all had BSN in their names, plus high awareness factors in their home markets. And BSN in Danone's case was a relic, a leftover from its glass bottle days and without any sort of recognisable logo. In short, in an era when globalisation was pushing company names like Nestlé and Kraft to the fore, it was a pretty hopeless branding device. So the choice of Danone as the replacement was obvious: it was after all by the world's biggest dairy products brand, second only to Coca-Cola for name recognition across Europe, although somewhat fragmented and localised elsewhere. The Danone name and new logo of a boy reaching for a star would be rapidly applied to the company's water and biscuit brands. And Daniel Carasso, the boy in the logo, was still alive to see his dream of rivalling the world's largest food companies become a reality.

It was also a company of big brands: Danone fruit yoghurts, Actimel (which had gone from strength to strength after its 1996 launch), and Danette, a cream dessert developed by the French business unit and rapidly rolled out internationally. Evian and Volvic mineral waters were big global brands, whilst Indonesia's Aqua, with over five billion litres sold a year, was the world's largest brand of bottled water and accounted for over half of Danone's entire water bottling output. Lu biscuits brand was by far the company's biggest, being market leader in Europe. While making big brands bigger was the company's primary focus, along with nurturing a raft of strong local brands, it did not ignore growing trends. In 2001 it acquired 40% of the US organic yoghurt company Stonyfield Farm, taking its usual majority stake two years later. It also developed Sur, an innovative new concept of flavoured waters, for which its Argentinian business was responsible. Sur was rapidly rolled out internationally.

How International Is It?

Before the merger between Danone and Gervais, and apart from the then separately owned Dannon in the US and Danone SA in Spain, Danone had only expanded as far as Belgium and Morocco, while Gervais had set up shop in Belgium and West Germany. But the merger provided both the means and the strategic direction to expand further afield: into Brazil, Mexico and Italy. Diversification had also followed the merger with BSN: the 1978 acquisition of a minority interest in the Belgian brewer Alken, followed a year later by minority stakes in two more beer companies, Mahou in Spain and Wührer in Italy. In 1980, BSN's thirst for beer companies took it into Africa with the purchase of two breweries in Nigeria – one of the largest beer markets in the world. The same year a Japanese joint venture in dairy got BSN into Asia to give it at least a foothold on every continent bar North America.

Dannon had shifted yoghurt from comedians' one-liners to the fastest-growing category in the nation's chillers. By 1967, the company was selling around one-third of the 100 million half-pint cups of yoghurt consumed in the US annually, with flavours spread across ten varieties. The shipping depots in Boston, Detroit, Philadelphia and Washington prompted Dannon's somewhat optimistic claim to be the first company to establish national distribution for a perishable food. Even so, in the highly fragmented, localised US dairy industry, it was market-leading stuff.

As the yoghurt market continued to expand almost exponentially - 1.3 billion containers a year by 1981 - Dannon had maintained its 30% market share and was now truly national. Highly automated plants across the nation were producing fifteen varieties of yoghurt together with a frozen example under the brand name Danny. Throughout this period of dramatic growth, Dannon had been headed by one of the original three founders, Juan Metzger, a natural marketer who had been named Marketer of the Year more than once by the marketing trade press. Juan retired just before BSN bought the company back for $84 million, a price well worth paying to regain control of the brand in a large and fast-growing market.

The first few years of BSN's ownership of Dannon were less than spectacular, with market share slipping to 21% by 1985, albeit in a still strongly growing market. Most of the growth had come historically from expanding distribution across the country, coupled with consumer base far wider that expat Balkanites and dieters. But per capita consumption now seemed to have stagnated. As is so often the case, innovation would now be the key factor. Dannon's success had virtually every dairy in the country launching its own brands of yoghurt. Three new products a year and a doubling of the advertising budget got market share moving in the right direction: 26% by 1986. By 1992, Dannon was selling two million cups of yoghurt a day in a vast range of varieties, flavours and pack sizes. Three years later, market share was up to 37%, right back where it had been two decades before, at 37%, with product provided by two mega-plants in Minster, Ohio and Fort Worth, Texas. The US was now a substantial contributor to Groupe Danone's total sales and profits.

Back in Europe, the 1980s acquisitions had taken the company into just about every Western European market in one or more of its product categories. Further afield, it acquired, in 1984, a minority stake in Pakistan's Continental Biscuits Limited. The post communism dissolution of trade barriers had taken it from East Germany in 1990 to Russia and Poland via Czechoslovakia and Bulgaria in 1995. That same year, the company identified its next targets: India, Indonesia, Malaysia and China for its core categories of fresh dairy products, water and biscuits. And it expanded further into the key Latin American markets of Brazil, Argentina and Mexico.

Danone's approach to China began as usual: joint ventures with leading local players. The biggest, in which Danone held a 51% stake, was in water, with China's leading beverages company, the Hangzhou Wahaha Group. This time, however, the whole enterprise scheme was thwarted by Wahaha's General Manager, Zong Qinhou, who hadn't become China's richest man by selling businesses that were obviously going to be very profitable. The relationship turned sour and ended up in the courts, although by then the company had other Chinese joint ventures in place. Danone, extremely single-minded in turning joint ventures into buy-outs, also failed to get its own way in India. Having bought 25% of India's Britannia Biscuits, it fell out with the controlling family there too. The 25% was sold back. But with its non-core categories disposed of, Danone could concentrate more easily on global reach, as joint ventures emerged in several formerly uncharted markets: Saudi Arabia in 2001, Vietnam in 2006 and Columbia in 2007. Following the company's 2007 acquisition of the baby food company Royal Numico (see below), the balance of overseas business shifted more decisively towards emerging markets: China was Royal Numico's single largest market.

How Is It Structured?

At the merger of BSN-Gervais Danone in 1970, one of the first tasks undertaken by the new general manager of the foods side of the company was to establish divisions based on product sectors. Evian had acquired two French baby food companies in 1965, which were split off from mineral water to form what the company refers to as distinct Product Lines, a practice carried through to today. Another enduring feature of company structure is the fact that fresh dairy has always been local, and always will be while products have an 18- to 21-day shelf life. So the logical management outcome was a highly decentralised approach based on local decision-making and locally run operations. Group coordination was achieved by initiating a strict management by objectives approach with regular overviews at the regional or global level depending on the complexity of the product line. Thus, dairy, with its multitude of business units, joint ventures and local brands would have a strong geographical regional level oversight while waters, a much smaller group of predominantly global and strong national brands, would be managed globally.

So, by 1996, the business had diversified its way to much greater complexity, the organisation was an amalgam of product line and regional structures. Each business unit reported into one of ten business lines: Fresh Dairy Products Europe, Groceries and Fresh & Frozen Ready-to-Serve Meals, Pasta and Canned Foods, Biscuits, Beer, Mineral Water, Glass Containers, Asia-Pacific, Americas & Africa and Exports.

Over the coming years, fresh dairy would generally be managed at the regional level (where sufficient critical mass existed), other product lines run globally, whilst regions without sufficient critical mass would be grouped together. As joint ventures and acquisitions continued to grow the business, the number of country and productline-specific business units increased, whilst the focus strategy was decreasing the number of distinct product lines. The structural outcome was that each key product line – dairy, waters and biscuits – ended up with regional structures of varying complexity. The 2007 sale of biscuits (see next section), plus the acquisition of Royal Numico, thus resulted in four distinct business lines: Fresh Dairy, Waters, Infant Nutrition and Medical Nutrition.

On the R&D side, each business line initially has its own dedicated function, conducting fundamental research which it then passed down to the business units, whose own development departments made the transition from research to production. Some two-thirds of the company's research personnel now worked in the business units.

But this changed in 2000. The three product line R&D teams were combined to form one multidisciplinary centre, the Daniel Carasso Research Center, where activities were refocused on a limited number of key strategic projects which all had nutrition at their heart. So, by 2002, the balance of personnel had shifted, with around 500 working in the centre as against 300 in the business units. Highly decentralised as they were, the business units were also highly innovatory. Danone responded well, fostering a culture of networking, both informally and through more formal 'marketplace' events, where teams from the subsidiaries could compare notes.

Acquisitions were managed separately. A dedicated central business development unit was charged with identifying opportunities relevant to the company's strategic priorities, conducting research and making recommendations to the executive committee, the company's main decision-making body.

What Has It Been Doing Recently?

2004

Focus strategy had enabled Danone to grow organic sales by 5% in 2001, 6% in 2002, 7% in 2003 and - a company record - 7.8% in 2004. The company now had 200 plants in 120 countries. It was number one in the world for dairy, tied number one with Nestlé for waters and world number two for biscuits and the heart of its success was driving growth from powerful market and brand positions. 75% of sales came from markets in which Danone had the lead position. Europe, by far the largest region, accounted for nearly 70% of sales. The Asia-Pacific region was dominated by China, where Danone was market leader in waters and biscuits. The third sales region, Rest of World, was up an impressive 18.6% in the year, and now accounted for 17% of total Danone sales. Here, areas of significant strength were Brazil, Argentina, Mexico, Russia and the US. But also here, the benefits of the Stonyfield Farm acquisition were outweighed by a whopping write-down of the company's interest in DS Waters LP, a 2003 joint venture with the Suntory Group, a home-and-office water delivery business that proved much more difficult to penetrate than Danone had anticipated.

Within dairy, Danone now had an 18% global share and a share of over 25% in its ten most important markets: surging ahead in Latin America, up by 22% on the back of the company's strengths in local adaptation and route-to-market dominance. Following a major country-by-country research programme in 35 markets, Danonino, a children's nutrition enhancement, had been reformulated differently for each market to reflect the differing nutritional issues and was performing particularly well in Argentina and Mexico. The brand reach, with other Danone best-sellers, was also being greatly extended via the placement of Danone-owned fridges in previously unrefrigerated outlets into the less sophisticated sectors of retail trade, with 52,000 in Mexico alone. New products included Danacol, an anti-cholesterol dairy product was launched in a number of European markets. Activia was rolled out in Germany, Canada, Mexico and the Netherlands. Drinkable versions of Activia, Danette and Danonino were launched in France, Spain and Argentina, while the carb diet craze sweeping America was met by Dannon's Light & Fit Carb Control range, launched in January 2004.

In the waters category, skewed much more towards Asia-Pacific (42% of sales) given the predominance of the Wahaha and Aqua brands in China and Indonesia, the year's big news was the rolling-out of functional benefit waters such as Wahaha's G-Vital and the new market extension of Ser flavoured waters, the Argentinian innovation, which after just two years' availability on its home turf had taken water into cola territory by capturing number-two spot in the low-calorie carbonated beverages market,.

But biscuits were facing having a few more challenges. Strategically, Danone had no major global brands. Lu, the company's largest, accounted for 40% of biscuit sales, but predominantly in Western Europe, which meant everywhere was relying on a plethora of well-established local lines such as Bolshevik, launched in Russia in 1855. The biscuit category was characterised by long-standing, local favourites, which served only to fragment one of Danone's key corporate strengths: its global reach. Tactically, the universal rise in importance of the health and nutritional benefits was putting pressure on the R&D first to analyse and then to reformulate countless products to enhance real or perceived health benefits.

2005

With organic sales up another 6.7% and the operating margin inching for-wards despite steep rises in packaging costs - particularly for PET bottles - Da-none was looking unstoppable. The five countries that had been singled out for significant sustained growth – China, Indonesia, Russia, Mexico and the US (for dairy), called the New Frontiers in the company – grew by a combined 18% in the year and now accounted for 25% of total sales.

Across emerging markets in general, Danone's strategy did not simply amount to making its products available to the relatively wealthy through West-ern-style retail outlets, as was the case with many of its competitors. It was also taking steps to reach down the income scale with both product and route-to-market innovation. In South Africa, Danimal had been developed with added iron, zinc and vitamin A, selling for one rand a pack and meeting the nutritional needs of children living in the townships. But with no structured distribution or retail infrastructure to get the product to these consumers, Danone recruited lo-cal unemployed females, daniladies, to sell the product door-to-door, thus gain-ing both distribution and providing much-needed self-employment opportuni-ties. In Bangladesh, the company partnered with a microcredit bank to support a similar idea, while in Indonesia the company financed the purchase of hundreds of push-carts for street sales. Danone's highly decentralised model ably fulfilled its long-term strategy: being first on the block to get high-quality food products to newly emerging consumers. In 2005, 55% of dairy sales came from what it termed 'proximity business': retail outlets outside the large, Western-style supermarkets and hypermarkets. Danone added another 100,000 distribution points through exactly such outlets in the year.

Dairy, in the meantime, had another good year, growing by 7%. Waters had an even better, with an organic growth of 10%, Mexico leading the way with an amazing 42%, driven by the Bonafont brand. The company's nightmare US office-and-home delivery water business was sold off to a venture capital firm. In contrast, the biscuits product line was barely limping along, growing organically by only 1.5%.

While the company was doing well in emerging markets, growing biscuit sales by 30% in Indonesia, 20% in Russia and 9% in China, it was a category where Danone enjoyed few of the advantages it had elsewhere in the portfolio. Weak market positions in the UK and Ireland led to the sell-off of Danone's biscuit businesses in both markets. One big problem for the product line was that the company's main area of focus in R&D – the development of products with distinctive health benefits – was of little relevance in the category. While R&D had a collection of more than 3,000 strains of pro-biotics and was working with the Pasteur Institute to figure out how they interacted with the body, R&D in biscuits was wrestling with the perennial industry problem of producing biscuits with lower levels of fat and sugar that tasted vaguely palatable. In the absence of a solution to this big portfolio problem, smaller ones were addressed. Danone sold its UK and US sauce businesses, a struggling Italian water subsidiary and its last remaining minority interest in beer.

2006

Another year of impressive organic growth, this time up by 9.7%, emphasised the consistency and effectiveness of the Danone business model in dairy and waters, up by 9.2% and 14.8% respectively, although biscuits still trailed: an improved but still modest increase of 3%. The success in dairy was largely due to the continued rollout into new markets of the four power brands, each targeted at a different health benefit:

Activia – aids digestive regularity
Actimel – strengthens the body's natural defences
Vitalinea-Taillefine – aids weight control
Danonino – promotes healthy growth in children

Together, these brands grew by an average of 15%, Activia by a stunning 48% to a combined total of €1.3 billion, joining Actimel as a billion-euro brand. In its first year in the US**Error! Bookmark not defined.**market, Activia - Dan-Active in America - racked up sales of $130 million, making it one of the country's top new grocery products of the year. Elsewhere in dairy, the big news was a joint venture in China with the leading producer of fresh dairy products, Mengniu Dairy Company, which had twenty plants servicing fifteen provinces and would be used to take distribution of Danone products nationwide, a move backed up by the opening of Danone's new research centre in China, tasked with developing product recipes that delivered the key local health and nutrition benefits while tickling local taste buds.

Beverages growth of 14.8% was spurred on more by rolling out new products in existing markets than the dairy strategy of taking existing products to new markets. The Mexican Bonafont brand continued its rapid growth, reaching a billion litres. New Zealand-developed V energy drink was rolled out into Argentina, China and Indonesia, where beverages with a job to do continued as the key growth category. The company also launched its first sugar-free flavoured water into France, Germany and the UK. Biscuits added another 3% but with 80% of sales coming from Europe - 40% from France alone - the sector's inherently low-growth markets still made life difficult. Over several years, these differing growth rates had now had shifted the portfolio balance: 56% to dairy, 28% to beverages and 16% to biscuits.

Strategically, while things seemed to be progressing extremely well, Danone was once again looking to the future, setting itself new and challenging goals. Firstly, chairman and CEO Franck Riboud increased annual growth targets to 6–8% for sales and 7–10% for operating, followed by new goals for international expansion. The company was by now firmly established with strong market shares in approximately 40 countries, which he intended to double within the next few years. Expansion would begin with three to five new countries a year. Ribaud also ditched the usual joint-venture method, arguing that the company now had the resources to enter markets either from scratch or by purchasing small players rather than forming partnerships with market leaders.

The constant quest for new markets, new retail outlets and new consumers also meant that Danone was no longer at the mercy of its largest retailers. Its top-ten worldwide customers (of which six were French) now accounted for just 28% of its total net sales. The largest, Carrefour, accounted for only 8%, in stark contrast to the American market, where it was not unusual for a food manufacturer to put 15–20% of its sales through its top customer. This kind of spread gave

Danone a much greater degree of control of its promotional spend and more power to resist retailer requests for private labels.

2007

The entire history of Danone had been one of big, strategic moves and 2007 saw the biggest yet, the €12.2-billion acquisition of the Dutch infant and medical nutritional company Royal Numico NV and the €3.1 billion sale to Kraft Foods of almost the entire biscuits business. In the words of Franck Riboud, this was a historic year for the company, completing the long-term strategy of transforming a diversified food and beverage company into a focused health-through-food company. So divesting itself of the slow-growing, limited-relevance biscuits businesses in favour of two new product lines with much higher growth rates and profit margins - infant and medical nutrition - was a radical but logical step for Danone to take. Danone had been the first food company to commit itself to make health the main focus of its strategy; biscuits were always going to be a laggard here. Nor was infant nutrition a new category for Danone. It had hung on-to its market-leading French baby food company, and been propelled to number one in Europe and number two worldwide in infant nutrition. Medical nutrition was a new field, but, research-led as it was, it might well suggest products that would transfer to other categories.

Royal Numico had been founded in the late 19th century as a powdered milk business. After World War Two, the focus had switched to baby foods and, after going public in 1981, the company had pursued a Danone-like growth strategy, making numerous acquisitions of leading infant nutrition firms: UK's Cow & Gate, Germany's Pfrimmer and Milupa, Finland's Tutteli and Muksu, Italy's Mellin, and the crown jewel Dumex, the leading brand of baby foods in Asia it bought in 2006. By 2007, the company was active on every continent and generating annual sales of nearly €3 billion.

The medical nutrition side of the business focused mainly on feeding solutions for oncology and Alzheimer's disease patients. The new deal gave Danone four product lines: fresh dairy products with 57% of sales, waters with 21%, baby nutrition with 17%; and medical nutrition with 5%. Growth rates for all four sectors were broadly comparable. It seems almost an afterthought to observe that regular Danone business had also been booming: a 7% sales increase and margins rising for the thirteenth year in a row. This reshaping of the portfolio and the continued good performance encouraged Franck to raise the target sales growth rate up another notch: 8–10% a year, a huge number for a food business. All the company had to do was deliver it.

2008

And in the first year of the new, improved Danone, deliver it did, despite the financial crisis that hit midway through the year. Overall growth came in at 8.8%, one-third volume and two-thirds increased prices. The year had started very well, with growth of nearly 10% in the first half, slowing down to just over 6% in the second half as the recession set in. It was a year of regional contrasts, as many companies discovered. Western markets suffered whilst emerging markets continued almost untouched, although suffering by Danone's standards was only relative, a mere 5% growth in Europe with Asia and South America both up in the mid-teens.

It was also a year of contrasts between the product lines, with baby nutrition leading the way with a very impressive 17%, a bullet expertly dodged in China despite the melamine baby food scandal: Danone's Dumex brand was melamine-free and the swift rollout of a reassurance communication campaign in paid media, on shelf and pack stickers avoided any collateral damage. Medical nutrition took second place in the growth race at +12.7%, completing an excellent first year for the Royal Numico acquisition. Indeed, the category seemed almost immune from the financial crisis, with sales boosted further by the launch of a new compact format for the oral nutrition lines, which packed 200 mls worth of calories and nutrition into a 125 ml serving, ideal for patients with poor appetites. Fresh dairy excelled, growing over 12%, but waters were stormy: just 2% growth, a little more respectable if one excluded the Wahaha joint venture in China, where the relationship had completely broken down. Here, Danone was 'moving on', as Franck succinctly put it.

2009

But not even the Danone growth machine could power through 2009, which saw the biggest downturn for decades: sales for the year up only 3% and well below the pre-crisis target of 8–10%. More interestingly, volume increased almost twice as fast as value, growing by 5.2% in the year, the result of a conscious 2008 strategic decision as the scale of the growing crisis became clear: focus on growing volumes and market share during the tough times, even at the expense of sales value, in order to come out of the recession in a stronger position with a wider consumer base. This, the company argued, was merely adapting the company mission of bringing healthy food to as many people as possible to the new economic circumstances. There would be three components to the new strategy.

First, prices were reviewed market-by-market and reduced not across the board but on a targeted basis – by up to 15% where it the added value of the product was deemed out of line with its affordability in very difficult times. And whilst demand for premium brands such as Actimel and Activia was holding up well - prices were tweaked only slightly - it was with the rest of the product range that affordability had become an issue. If a price cut crippled the margin, the dairy category would quickly develop new, less sophisticated offerings that could set a new price–value relationship. More single-serve versions were launched a correspondingly lower prices, just as new bulk packs brought individual item prices down.

The second element was to maintain or even increase marketing spend, and to adjust both the message and the location. Based on its experience of financial crises in the South American markets, Danone firmly believe that, in tough times, great taste was a more powerful selling message than nutritional benefits, which corresponded to a marketing shift from nutritional reason to feelings: taste, pleasure, fun, humour. The message also came closer to the customer, via point of sale promotions and the point in-store messaging, a combination of lower prices, more single-serve versions and more point of sale push which effectively boosted the level of impulse sales. As an example, the Mexican dairy business which fully implemented this re-set strategy saw a first quarter volume decline of 10% turn into a fourth quarter volume increase of over 13%. Many other Danone markets saw similar, if slightly less spectacular, rebounds – the hugely troubled US market achieving a 9% growth in the fourth quarter. In emerging markets, where there had been much less impact on consumer spending, business growth continued largely as normal, 12% in Indonesia and 7% in China.

With volumes increasing steadily through the year even in sluggish markets, market shares increased in step. Danone ended the year having grown global market share in all four product lines and in 70% of the markets where it operated. Even more impressively, the focus on volume over sales value did not wreck the margins. Aided by a following wind of commodity price decreases, the operating margin increased for the fifteenth year in a row. The strategy re-set, Franck Riboud believed, had reinforced the company's market positions and created a new momentum, with factories achieving record outputs, and leaving him confident of at least a 5% sales increase the next year.

It had been an impressive response to an unexpected economic crisis that had left many other packaged goods companies floundering. One sad note was the death of Daniel Carasso, the founder of the French Danone business. He had made it to 103, a testimony to yoghourt perhaps?

2010

The momentum of the latter part of 2009 carried forward through 2010, when the company averaged nearly 7% sales growth per quarter, with less of a disparity between sales value and sales volume (which grew by 7.6%) than there had been in 2009. Thus, reduced prices from 2009 could be maintained in 2010 as a permanent shift in the price–value relationship rather than as a temporary promotional cut. Once again, the operating margin increased to a new high of 15.2%

Dairy sales increased by 6.5% to slightly under €10 billion, divided almost equally between mature and emerging markets. Half the year's growth in the year came from product innovation, almost all of it developed at the local unit level thanks to Danone's decentralised operating culture, which allowed – as we have noted - local units to develop new products or adapt recipes to meet local taste, nutritional and economic needs, the new product measured by the company's nutripack system to assure a global consistency of quality. The successes this very entrepreneurial model created - a Russian Activia drink, a Scandinavian Activia Pouring Yoghurt or a Bulgarian Activia Breakfast - they were also rolled out not just into the home market but into others where the same market conditions prevailed. This kind of continuous, flexible continuous innovation was crucial to effective competition against private label and local market competitors. The dairy product line also innovated in how it interacted with and reached consumers, launching a series of digital initiatives across multiple markets, including nutritional coaching and competitions to vote on upcoming new flavours. The company extended the concept of Danone Yogurterias: kiosks located in malls, airports and other high-traffic locations, which catered for impulse purchase of yoghurts with customisable toppings.

The dairy group's most significant change came in the Russian market. Here, Danone CIS - number one in the country with a 26% market share and growing strongly - bought Unimilk, the number-three local operator. The purchase not only increased Danone's Russian market share to 40% but also brought three strategic benefits:

- Danone mainly operated in western Russia, while Unimilk's areas of strength were in southern and eastern Russia. Access to Unimilk's 26 modern plants and efficient distribution network meant Danone brands could now go national throughout Russia
- Whilst Danone was focused mostly on supermarkets sales, Unimilk serviced small, independent outlets, still a huge market factor in Russia. Danone brands could now hugely extend their distribution points, opening up more scope for impulse purchase pack sizes.
- Russian Danone was a premium brand, whilst Unimilk's key brands were in more affordable market sectors. Unimilk's leading brand, Prostokvashino, was the largest dairy brand by volume in the country: now

Danone could cover a market covering the entire socio-economic spectrum.

The second significant change in the year for the dairy group was the official ending of the re-set programme; prices were now being allowed to increase, not back to their old levels, but in tune with market movements from their new baseline.

Waters also had a good year, with sales value rising by over 5% and volumes by nearly 8%. The mature markets had returned to growth, largely as a result of Danone's efforts in promoting the health benefits of natural spring water and – to overcome consumer concerns about landfill – the launch of the first 100% recycled PET bottles, rapidly followed by the first PET bottle manufactured partly from sugar-cane waste. In the meantime, emerging markets continued to deliver double-digit growth through a combination of proven-brand extensions: Mexico's Bonafont was rolled out in Brazil, Turkey and Poland, with the company taking a proactive approach in finding and opening up new springs. The two nutrition Product Lines continued as in previous years, both delivering high single-digit increases in sales value and volume.

Reviewing the year, Franck Riboud, described it as a watershed: the last year that sales from established markets would exceed those from the new economies, now 49% of the 2010 total. Danone's key growth markets were what it termed the MICRUB countries: Mexico, Indonesia, China, Russia, the US and Brazil, which were all delivering double-digit growth – a 14% average for the year and 20% in Brazil, Russia and the US – and of a critical mass sufficient to power the whole company. Danone is perhaps alone – and not a little impertinent - in counting the US as an emerging market. Nonetheless, for yoghurt, it ticks both the boxes: a large population and a low but rapidly rising per capita consumption (one-sixth of France and Spain). Danone added to its US presence by buying Yocream, the country's leading brand of frozen yoghurt. The acquisition of Medical Nutrition USA, Inc. also opened up that category stateside.

This meant, of course, that Danone was now pursuing three different regional strategies. In the highly competitive, mature markets of Western Europe, the approach was innovation aimed in health-oriented/well-being food products. In North America, it was developing the size of the product categories through innovation and improved distribution. Emerging countries, where competition came from very low-cost local producers as well as global giants looking to make their presence felt, the strategy was affordability plus availability, which involved not simply product concepts but also production and storage. Danone built a micro-production facility in Bangladesh that cost less than the price of an average house in France and managed the absence of reliable and available factory-to-home refrigeration chains by developing Nutriday yoghurts, stable for three months at room temperature.

2011

With growth in the year of nearly 8% - 3% came from volume and the rest price - Danone sales reached a new high of €19.3 billion, 80% from emerging markets, with Asia growing by 20% and Rest of World by 13%. Europe grew by just 2%, as against 60% of from the six MICRUB markets alone.

In the dairy category, the two main growth engines in previous years, Russia – now the dairy group's single biggest market – and the US both encountered hiccoughs. Russia's eye on the ball was perhaps distracted by the Unimilk merger, whilst the US had been somewhat slow to spot the meteoric rise of the Greek yoghurt, up from 5% of the market in 2009 to 25% in 2011. The US response was the Oikos range, which greatly improved the company's second half-year performance. Elsewhere, Activia, now available in 72 countries, was the big performer. And there remained plenty of innovation at the unit level: new containers in Spain and an Activia Smoothie in Portugal. Also rolled out was a new addition to the brand line up: Densia, fortified with calcium and vitamin D, targeted at improving bone health.

But the year's surprising hero was water, which grew by over 15% and managed to improve its margins despite a 20% increase in packaging costs. Western European markets, helped by a very hot summer, delivered a quarter of the growth; the rest came from emerging markets, two-thirds from the company's range of flavoured and fortified waters such as China's Mizone, Bonafont in Brazil and Aqua in Indonesia. The two nutrition businesses also showed significant growth. Baby nutrition sales increased by 10.7%, a total of more than 50% growth since the 2007 and powered by a rapid internationalisation by Danone, which had taken the brands into seventeen new markets. Medical nutrition grew by 9.4% in the year and 50% since acquisition, again through new market entries but also via the runaway success of the concentrated 125 ml offering, ideal for the elderly, infirm and those suffering poor appetites, which was now rolled out across multiple product lines.

Looking forwards, the next emerging market on the company's radar was India. Danone had had a presence there since its tie-up with Britannia Biscuits, but it had taken a cautious approach to building a presence in other product categories, once again preferring strategic partnerships: it teamed up with Japan's Yakult Honsha Co. to launch a pro-biotic yoghurt into several cities and took a majority stake in Narang Beverages, owners the Himalayan water brand Qua.

Also, and drawing on its micro–factory experience in Bangladesh and Indonesia, Danone set up a similar operations to produce Yum Creamy and Yum Chuski, high-nutrition, low-cost products designed to help poor children with dietary deficiencies. The continuing shift of business towards emerging markets, now employing 60% of the company's staff of 101,000, led to the DanCare programme, a new approach first to attracting and then retaining staff. DanCare was an in-house clinic, designed ensure workers had access to high-quality health care, a preoccupation entirely consistent with a key part of the company's product portfolio.

2012

Sales were up a reasonable 5.45%, and although this was slightly below the historical norm, all seemed well. But beneath the surface lurked some significant issues. The dairy segment – the company's largest with over 50% of sales – was not performing. Sales were only growing in step with price inflation at just over 2%. Volume was actually falling back slightly. The Achilles heel was the southern European countries economic problems: formerly high yoghourt consumers were now struggling to make ends meet. More promising for the company were the US dairy markets, where the company was rapidly catching up with the Greek yoghurt boom through Activia Greek and Oikos Dips. Low per capita consumption markets such as Brazil, Mexico, Russia and China were also beginning to move, the latter two strengthened by new joint ventures.

But the waters were flowing: an increased volume of over 6%, the top-line increase of 10% plus goosed by continuing above-average growth of flavoured aqua-drinks. As with dairy, the company's strategic approach geographically was two-tier approach. In Europe, where top line increases were tough to get given the weakness of the southern European economies, the focus was on to reduce the environmental impact of the company's water brands. Conversely, in the emerging countries, it was all about category and share growth, with key brands such as Bonafont and Mizone rolled out into all markets where new water resources could be acquired.

However, the company's strongest position lay in baby nutrition, where growth of 11.6% was led by the infant formula brands, particularly in the Chinese market, and further supported by a complete restaging of its leading Dumex brand. The North American market was strengthened by the acquisition of Happy Family Organic Superfoods, which, with its strong baby food and infant yoghurt offerings suited Danone perfectly. Organic was by far the fastest-growing part of the US weaning foods market, having doubled its share to over 20%

within three years – a compound average growth rate of 38% compared to the rest of the market's 1%.

The performance of the medical nutritional product group confirmed that Danone actually had a systemic problem with the European region. As sales in China, Turkey and Brazil drove a more than 6% increase overall, European sales declined, like-for-like by over 2%, while Asia grew 12% and the rest of the world by nearly 5%. This, the company decided, was no passing fad but represented a prolonged and possibly permanent downturn in its European businesses, as long as the southern European countries showed no signs of emerging from their near–bankrupt doldrums. And the first half of 2013, the European sales decline accelerated to more than 4% like-for-like, while Russia and North America surged ahead by over 9% and the Rest of World by nearly 16%. Something had to be done.

The answer was announced in December 2012: a severe retrenching of the company's growth goals and supporting cost base. The two-year plan would entail halving the number of country management; Danone would shift to a multi-country management structure. Management functions would be merged and, as company strove simply to maintain existing dairy volume, 900 jobs would be shed. By contrast, it was business as usual in the rest of the world, where all the growth was coming from. Danone struck up one its historical partnership deals by taking a 67% stake in Morocco's largest dairy company, Centrale Laitière du Maroc. And the Indian redoubt was breached: acquisitions were made across all four divisions.

What Is Its DNA?

Danone has an interesting history, with levels of consistency at the very top matched only by other family firms like Mars and Ferrero. The original founder, Daniel Carasso, lived through almost the company's entire history. And from the point that Danone took its modern form after the BSN merger, it has had just two leaders, who just happen to be father and son. This has created an operating style and form based more on individual beliefs and character than best practice promulgated by consultants and imposed by heroic, parachuted-in CEOs. We suggest the following three key features are what make Danone unique:

Health/Well-being

There isn't a serious food company in the world that doesn't have health and well being high on its agenda, but none has been as single-minded as Danone.

Rather than simply bolting acquired or developed healthful alternatives onto existing business, Danone, over a period of ten years, completely reshaped its portfolio with this very end in mind. As a food conglomerate, it was enjoyed profitable and growing products and product lines, but these were sold off over time to give the company a level of strategic focus rare on food companies.

But then Danone is not a typical health food company catering to obsessed niche consumers or trying to persuade consumers to eat rabbit food. Both the dairy and waters Product Lines – 66% of sales – are categories that are designed for all consumers, and recommended for daily consumption – in any quantity - by public health authorities the world over. They both occupy the area of what we might call natural good health, which Danone also sees as inseparable from taste and pleasure. The baby and medical nutrition categories have much tighter target markets but are still aimed at regular consumption. This degree of focus prompted the company to develop its Nutrition and Health Charter in 2009. Here are its fundamentals:

- Adapting products to the needs of consumers in terms of nutritional quality, taste and affordability
- Developing products that have health benefits
- Consumer information presented in a clear and responsible manner
- Promoting healthy lifestyles
- Support for nutrition and health research programmes
- Dialogue with public health authorities, consumer groups and scientists
- Sharing knowledge with the scientific community and health professionals

Many food companies do some or even all of these things in parts of their portfolio. But none do so with the single-mindedness of Danone.

Local/Global

In operational terms, in its embracing of local operational autonomy, Danone is much more like a mid-20th-century international company than a 21st. For local business units to have not just the authority but also the encouragement if not the demand to innovate on global brands, as they see fit and to suit their own market needs, it is a dagger to the heart of global brand managers everywhere. But the beauty of the Danone style is that it can operate indeed this way yet still have global brands that work and originate, from local settings, products with international clout.

The logic of the Danone operational style is unassailable. The dairy category is inherently local in manufacturing terms, thus creating the opportunity to be local in marketing terms too. In waters, while very powerful global brands certainly exist, there are also many local brands whose credibility rests on local springs. Danone is betting that pushing the benefits of mineral water, where provenance can be key, is a better strategy than the Coke/Pepsi model of manufactured bottled water and the Nestlé's de-branding of the local spring in favour of Nestlé global. One key element of this strategy is to create something unique and differentiated, then push it hard. Danone does exactly that.

At a more prosaic level, a key benefit flows from a Danone operational style quite unique among global food companies: speed. Managers nearest the issues have full authority to do something about them. There are no cumbersome layers, no backs to be protected nor agendas second-guessed: if something needs doing, it gets done. With the right mechanisms in place to share and spread successes quickly, it is a very powerful model.

Forward Thinking

Perhaps the most striking thing in the history of Danone is not just that the company made some very big structural and sector participation moves – many companies do that – but the timing of the moves themselves. From the Danone-Gervais merger via the BSN merger, the diversification of the portfolio, the move out of glass, the refocusing of the portfolio, the early moves into Eastern Europe and other emerging markets, the seismic divestment of biscuits coupled with the Royal Numico acquisition, up to the re-set strategy for dairy, none of these was made in extremis. There were no fire sales or desperate measures. All were all made either in anticipation of problems looming or in the expectation opportunities appearing. Even the recent downsizing and consolidation of its European operations was by no means belated, by no means an emergency measure. Quite simply, Danone is the cream on the milk of the world's top food companies without ever having been in a crisis. This is some achievement and, given what looks like an unassailable stability at the top, it all augurs very well indeed well for the company.

Summary

The evolution of Danone from French glass company looking for bottle contents to the world's largest health-through-food company is an impressive story. It is very focused in product range terms – there are just four - four, but very diverse geographically. Russia is its largest market, at 10% of sales, while China, Indonesia, Mexico and Brazil are all in its top ten. The Danone Group is the market leader in the 38 of its biggest countries, with the benefits of a usefully fragmented retail customer base: its top five customers provide only 14% of its sales. Many US-based food businesses are not so lucky, on the hook to that level of sales from just one customer. Few food companies can still see that kind of growth potential in the US. In addition, perhaps the Greek yoghurt phenomenon was useful lesson, and may remain a sharp reminder, that the company cannot be complacent. It is not alone, and needs the speed and creativity its emerging markets are famous for if it is to grasp every opportunity that comes its way. That being said, with the company now structurally geared towards strong product growth in naturally growing emerging markets, the future for Group Danone looks very bright.

Dean Foods

Where Did They Come From?

Milk processing is a tough business. Lots of people buy lots of milk, but they want it fresh and they need it cheap. Milk processing involves a high fixed cost and low margins, usually collecting from farms geographically apart. Profits are very susceptible to relatively small changes in throughput. Milk supplies vary in quantity through the year, with above-average supplies from February to June and below average for the rest of the year. Consumer demand is pretty much the converse: below average early in the year and above average in the last four months. In turn, milk producers attempt to manage this imbalance to their own advantage: converting surplus milk to butter, powder and cheese and, when they are able to increase sales of these items, divert more milk into those products. They thus drive up the price of bulk liquid milk to would-be bottlers. It takes smart strategy to succeed in this world.

Milk processing can also be an invisible business. With annual sales of over $13 billion, more than Heinz and equal to Kellogg's, Dean Foods must be the least well known of the world's big packaged goods companies. Their anonymity is due to two factors: firstly, very little of what they sell is branded Dean's, and secondly: Dean Foods has become the dominant force in the cut-throat but near-anonymous world of America's dairy chiller cabinets.

Origins

As a colossus of the grocery store back wall, the current Dean Foods dates from December 2000, when Suiza Foods, a company only in existence since 1993, bought the long-established Dean Foods and assumed its name. The two companies had become the top two dairy companies in America by following similar strategies. It made sense to come together.

Dean Foods was founded in 1925 by Sam Dean Senior, who worked in a brokerage company trading evaporated milk in Chicago until he started up his own evaporated milk company. Once Dean moved into fresh milk processing in the 1930s, his first field of interest, well, it just evaporated. Nevertheless, Sam Dean had become one of thousands of localised American milk bottlers in the period up to the Second World War. In this tough business, Sam Dean was a relatively small middleman, squeezed between price-conscious retailers always looking for cheaper milk - the price of retail milk was a key driver of 'store foot-fall' for the rapidly growing grocery chains - and farming cooperatives who were always looking to drive up the price of milk. He realised that there were three ways he could improve his own position: building brands of milk would increase his leverage against retailers; developing alternatives to dairy would decrease his reliance on cooperatives; and increasing the scale of his business would enable investment in greater efficiency, by lowering costs, winning more business and increasing profits.

Building the Business

Developing a product range that went beyond liquid milk was the easy part. As early as 1943 Sam had his own R&D lab and their first tangible output was a non-dairy powdered coffee creamer. Four years later he got himself into the ice cream business. Building strong brands and increasing scale was harder. Milk was, and is, a local industry. Being around 87% water and with extremely limited shelf-life, it makes no sense - from transportation costs and product quality reasons - for milk processing to be heavily concentrated in a few vast plants hundreds of miles away from retail customers. Milk processing has thus a much less concentrated industry than, for example, meat packing, or corn milling or soybean processing.

Sam realised that the answer was to go on an acquisition spree. A nationwide milk business could be done; both Kroger and Safeway Inc. had their own national private label operations, Another company, Borden, had approached being national in scope before getting mired in an unproductive series of diversifications. Sam took a more nuanced approach, buying up healthy dairies across the country, which had developed strong local brands for their fresh milk. Dean took costs out by removing supply overlaps, infusing capital to improve processing efficiencies and by having superior marketing, management and R&D expertise that each acquired dairy could utilise.

It was a winning formula. Operating margins almost invariably improved within a year or two of Dean ownership. So popular was the model that for the majority of Dean purchases, it was the dairy owners themselves who made the approach to sell. The acquisitions also brought capabilities into Dean Foods that helped it diversify and build brands. Reiter Dairy in Ohio came with cottage cheese-making facilities while Ryan Milk in Kentucky had aseptic production facilities that enabled life production of long life UHT products. The ice cream unit boomed, supplying over 400 Baskin-Robbins stores. In 1986 Dean diversified into frozen and canned vegetables when it merged with the Larsen Company, third largest in America behind Green Giant and Del Monte.

The acquisition momentum kept on increasing: more dairies and vegetable companies were absorbed. By 1991 Dean's annual sales exceeded $2 billion, around 70% of which was dairy, making Dean Foods a close number two in the national market behind the soon-to-be-floundering Borden. From their 21 dairy processing plants across the country, cost and innovation synergies continued to flow; and the company was able to roll out lines such as frozen yoghurt and lactose-free milk across its dairies much faster than more local players could manage. Alongside the booming dairy business, the vegetable side expanded further with the acquisition of Bird's Eye in 1994.

While the Dean Foods model was proving to be very successful, the dairy industry remained very fragmented: Dean only had 6% of total American milk sales and around the same percentage of the country's dairy plants, so there was plenty of room in the market. This point was noted by Ted Beshears, Chairman of the Milk Industry Foundation and a former manager of milk plants for Southland Corporation (owners of and supplier of milk to 7-11), and entrepreneur, Glenn L. Engles. Beshears and Engles had joined forces in 1988 in the packaged ice business (which was similarly fragmented) to pursue a strategy of gaining scale through acquisition and leveraging economies of scale to improve margin.

In 1993 they switched their attention to the milk market, buying a Puerto Rican dairy, Suiza Dairy. The twist in Beshears and Engles' strategy was the realisation that the critical success factor was the speed in which the company could find, execute, integrate and improve the cost efficiency of dairy acquisitions. While Dean Foods concentrated much of their efforts on building their higher margin vegetable business, Suiza Foods focussed on acquiring as many of the country's best dairies as fast as possible: their sole goal was to win the consolidation battle.

Suiza's need for speed also came from the recognition that industry dynamics were becoming increasingly unfavourable to the milk processor. Per capita milk consumption was in a long-term slow decline, from 29 gallons per person in 1977 to 24 gallons twenty years later. A rising US population alone kept overall market volume stable. Simultaneously, consolidation within the American grocery-retailing industry was reducing the number of potential customers, all vying to increase their share of a static milk market. The inevitable outcomes were a greater downward pressure on the price retailers were willing to pay for fresh milk and an ever increasing demand for private, or own-brand label, which accounted for around two-thirds of total milk sales.

Dean Foods, with their past emphasis on buying strong local milk brands, had a 50/50 split in their sales between branded and private label, but faced the same pressures. At the same time, there was over-capacity within the dairy producing industry. This reduced the leverage of even the big companies such as Dean and Borden, as less efficient independent operators would undercut on price just to stay in business. Suiza's strategy was to approach the better-run dairies and make a similar offer each time: 5 to 7 times EBITDA and insisting that local management stay in place to run the dairy. Once a dairy was bought in a new part of the country, Souza would immediately seek nearby acquisitions to consolidate manufacturing and distribution; the best plants and delivery set-ups would be modernised and inefficient ones closed down. Suiza also aimed to ensure secure sources of fresh milk from the farming industry by forming an alliance with the nation's largest dairy cooperative, Dairy Farmers of America, who took a 33% ownership of Souza and provided capital to help fund the increasingly large acquisitions.

In 1995, after just two years of operation, Suiza had sales of over $1 billion, and they needed all the capital they could get in 1997, making eight acquisitions in the year. Their crowning glory was a $960 million acquisition of Morningstar Group Inc., a move that took Suiza ahead of Dean Foods and also brought nationally recognised dairy and dairy-substitute brands into their portfolio. These included International Delight and Mocha Mix coffee creamers, Second Nature egg substitute and the Lactaid range of lactose-free and lactose-reduced products. By 1999, Suiza had made forty acquisitions; achieved annual sales of nearly $4.5 billion; doubled their share price in four years; and were investing nearly $200 million a year into upgrading facilities and equipment. In 2000, Suiza upped the pace again, buying Southern Foods Group, the country's third-largest milk processor, which operated in eleven states and owned a roster of strong dairy brands, including the liquid dairy arm of the once-mighty Borden. Suiza were now clearly the number one dairy processor and distributor in the country: adding 30 plants, and 5,500 employees, which took their total to over 18,000. Five other acquisitions that year fuelled top line sales to grow by $1.3 billion. Sales of Morningstar brands surged ahead 17% during the acquisition year. Suiza now had the capability to sell and deliver virtually every product in the dairy chiller cabinet to any customer in the United States.

With national scale and scope, Suiza were now an attractive option for other companies to license their brands. In September 2000, they formed a partnership with Hershey to manufacture and sell Hershey-branded dairy products nationally. Suiza also expanded laterally: into the newly emerging soy beverages category by launching their brand Sun Soy. The phenomenal success of Suiza Foods, reaching market leadership with sales approaching $6 billion in only eight years of operation, was recognised when the company was included in the Forbes 2000 Platinum List of the finest companies in America and in Fortune magazine's 2000 list of America's Most Admired Companies. In May 2001, Suiza signed up another major national brand into its licensed brand programme with a deal to launch, manufacture and market P&G's Folger's Jakada, a low fat chilled coffee drink.

While Suiza Foods had been revolutionising the American dairy business, Dean Foods had continued its own acquisition strategy at a more sedate pace and concentrated upon the vegetables side of their business. However, innovation continued on the dairy side when Mayfield Dairy Farms, their Tennessee division, developed a single-serve milk plastic bottle, ideal for sale in school-vending machines, an innovation that was quickly propagated across their other regional companies under the name of Milk Chugs. Dean also focussed on building up a best-in-class Direct Store Delivery (DSD) network for their milk operations, offering retailers a fresher product and allowing their own drivers/salesmen to replenish and merchandise the dairy fixture.

2001 would end with Suiza's biggest deal to date: the acquisition of Dean Foods itself, for $1.5 billion. This created a dairy colossus with more than 90 plants, 30,000 employees, over 6,000 refrigerated delivery routes servicing 150,000 retail customers. This gave the company, which adopted the better-known name of Dean Foods, over 30% of the US liquid milk market. Two-thirds of the combined Suiza/Dean product range was branded - either their own local and regional brands, or well-known national brands licensed from packaged goods companies - and one third of the range was private label. The merged company resolved its arrangement with Dairy Farmers of America by handing over $165 million and six plants where Dean and Suiza had overlapped. The new Dean Foods was now so big it would not struggle to find milk suppliers to supply them.

It now seemed that the mutual dream of Sam Dean, Ted Beshears, and Glenn L. Engles (Chairman and CEO of the newly merged company) had come to fruition. There are very few industries where the middleman is able to even stay in business, let alone build a prominent presence in the value chain between producer and consumer. Taking in tankers of liquid milk at one end of the building and sending out plastic bottles from the other is not much of a value add. However, like the banana industry where branding is located with the middleman, the value add is in collecting, handling and distributing a very time-sensitive product so that it hits stores on a daily basis in optimal condition. Through unprecedented size and scale, the new Dean Foods was now able to do this better and cheaper than anyone else. With such an expensive and efficient milk processing and delivery infrastructure in place, the logic of adding on higher margin, value-added lines, licensed brands and expanding into adjacent categories was unassailable.

Indeed, the strategy of the new company made this logic clear:

- To be their customers' supplier of choice through the widest range of the freshest products delivered direct to store
- To use the mega-merger to further cut costs, with annual cost saving of $120 million targeted by the end of 2004
- To innovate in and drive growth through the added-value branded offerings, such as International Delight coffee creamers, soy and lactose-free products across the dairy fixture, and their licensed brands

Milk was not the only category enhanced by the merger. The combined ice cream operation was the third-largest in the country; with annual sales revenues of nearly $1 billion (a growth of 25% during the previous three years). 2001 also saw an extension for their Baskin-Robbins agreement to be near national in supply. Suiza's Morningstar Foods was also combined with the non-dairy components of Dean Foods - these included their highly successful range of Marie's and Dean's refrigerated dips – to make the largest producer of this category in the country. Dean's vegetable business was set up in a separate operating division, to be hived off as soon as possible.

The management's finely-honed expertise in quickly assimilating acquisitions and getting at the cost synergies was behind an excellent first operational year for this company uniting the two largest dairy operations in the country. Savings were well ahead of target. This enabled significant investment in growth initiatives, the most significant of which was the May 2002 purchase of White Wave, makers of the leading brand in the soy beverage and food sectors, Silk (Dean Foods had held a minority stake in it prior to the merger). The soy category was the darling of the chiller cabinet, increasing by over 30% in the year to $440 million, of which Silk had an overwhelming 80% market share. Further good news on Silk came in the summer when it was listed nationwide by Starbucks as their sole soy beverage.

Also during 2002, licensing rights across all dairy products for another strong brand, Land O'Lakes, was acquired. The company spent $130 million promoting its added-value brands in the year and was rewarded by a 25% volume increase. They promised to increase that spend to $190 million the following year, together with an additional $30 million to promote the by now vast range of regional dairy brands. The Hershey's range of flavoured drinks reached $100 million in annual sales and International Delight sales increased 13%. Total company sales for the year fell just shy of $9 billion, making Dean Foods one of America's largest food companies. It had been a textbook acquisition, so much so that the company was able to keep on making acquisitions into 2003. The logic of continuing to consolidate the milk processing industry still held good, with more dairies being added. In addition, new branded products in adjacent categories were sough. The biggest purchase was the country's leading brand of organic dairy foods, Horizon Organic, in January 2004 - just a month after acquiring the Cremora brand of coffee creamers. The strategic growth brands powered ahead another 27 % in 2003, with Silk growing by more than 40% as it benefited from Dean's advantaged route to market and strong retailer relationships. But Dean was still primarily a fresh milk business. Sales in this category were over $7 billion, spread across forty regional brands and some large private label contracts. The challenge for the company - now their growth by acquisition phase was largely played out - would be to show they had the expertise to grow their share of the chiller cabinet while also growing their sales of milk.

What Have They Been Doing in Recent Years?

2004

2004 was the first year in the new reality of Dean Foods, and it was one in which acquisitions did not play a transformative role in performance. Just one U.S. dairy was bought in the year, and this development was counterbalanced by the company closing eight dairies. The top-line sales increased to over $10 billion with just under $0.7 coming from acquisitions and nearly $1 billion from favourable changes to pricing, volume and mix. Unlike most big companies, increases in reported top-line sales are not necessarily correlated with sales success. By and large, Dean's selling price of fresh milk moves in lockstep with the price of raw milk from the farms. So while the Dean's Dairy Group division saw an increase in net sales of approximately 10%, like-for-like volume was up only 1%, the other 9% being price increases of raw milk passed on by Dean. However, the 1% increase came against a background of a 1% decrease in total market volume, so the company had gained market share.

More encouragingly, the range of branded products had an excellent year, increasing by a total 13% to $1.2 billion, with the company nearly doubling its operating margin in this segment. Silk sales grew 33% on the year, helped by new product variants: Very Vanilla, Enhanced, Unsweetened, Silk Kids and Silk Live. The brand employed a clever segmentation strategy to occupy more shelf space and also make life harder for any aspiring market entrants attracted by the growth rates in this category of goods. Horizon Organic's dairy products sales increased by 24%, helped by the introduction of a range of smoothies, and the Land O'Lakes range did even better, growing by 34%. Organisationally, the company combined all its branded products into one management structure and also prepared to spin off its Speciality Foods Group (which was largely the old Dean vegetable business) to its own shareholders.

2005

The trends of 2004 continued into 2005. The company made only minor changes to its collection of dairies, yet gained more market share in fresh milk and cream – volumes up 2.5% in a flat market. There was another double-digit sales increase in its branded lines - now collectively known as WhiteWave Foods – which was driven by: Silk, up over 20% to a record $337 million; Horizon Organic, up over 44% to a now impressive $273 million; and International Delight, up over 13% to $241 million. The company continued its strategy of bringing in top packaged-goods industry talent with the recruitment of Joe Scalzo to head up the booming WhiteWave Foods segment. Joe had previously been Gillette's Group President, Personal Care and Global Value Chain. WhiteWave's recent consolidation and rapid growth had necessitated a simplification of both the SKU portfolio (reduced by 25% in the year) and the somewhat complicated supply-chain infrastructure. The Speciality Foods Group was successfully spun off, reincarnated as TreeHouse Foods and the Dean Foods Company also divested itself of the Marie's and Dean's dressings and dips brands.

However impressive WhiteWave sales were, structurally Dean Foods was still enormously dependent on its milk business, which brought in 85% of its $10.5 billion sales. Dean's milk processing and delivery employed 25,000 people in 97 manufacturing facilities and 6,500 direct-store-delivery routes, sourcing their milk from more than 11,000 farms. Dean's future success still rested on their being able to use their vast scale and low costs to grow share in a static market which was beset by raw material price fluctuations and increasingly demanding customers.

2006

Once again, the main trends remained the same: another 1% increase in share of the fresh milk/cream market, despite a falling price of raw milk which reduced top-line sales by 1.7%. Dean was now producing 3.3 billion gallons of milk products a year, generating top-line sales of $8.8 billion and an operating income of nearly $700 million. 55% of this business was under company-owned brand names, most now over half a century old, with the remainder retailing under private label brand names.

Despite taking $40 million in sales out of WhiteWaveFoods through SKU rationalisation, sales in the group still increased by over 6%. This was led by Horizon Organic's increase of 24% (giving it a 45% share of the U.S. organic dairy market) and price increases of around 4%. The company was pressing ahead to develop new line extensions such as Plus DHA, which was slated for launch in 2007. In the soymilk sector, Silk, which had lost several SKU's in the cull, increased sales of its continuing lines by 12%; and elsewhere International Delight chipped in with another 7% increase.

With three successful years of Dean Foods' post-acquisition strategy behind it, the company's strategy was proving correct. The stock market concurred, as Dean shares, initially priced at $17 when launched as Suiza in 1992, were trading at $42 by the end of 2006. Things were looking good.

2007

Just when everything seemed peachy, the global economic crisis intervened. 2007 was an exceptionally tough year, despite Dean Foods' top-line sales rocketing ahead by 17%. The problem was that the increase in sales was entirely driven by the rocketing price of raw milk which, in the second half of the year, was 80% higher than the year prior. One outcome of the financial turmoil was a strengthening in the dollar. This dramatically increased foreign demand for US dairy products, and so farmers' cooperatives diverted raw milk supplies into their balancing plants to make as much milk powder and cheese as they could to sell on world markets. This in turn created a shortage of liquid milk, which thus drove up the price. While Dean had agreements in place with most of its customers to increase or decrease the price of their milk on a monthly basis, such were the scale and speed of the raw-material price increases that the company simply couldn't get their own price increases through quickly enough. This knocked almost 4 percentage points off Dean Foods' total gross profit margin for the year, resulting in a 9% drop in operating income.

Even worse, attracted by the growth rate and margins in the organic milk sector, many more farmers had come on-stream. This created a glut of organic milk which coincided with Horizon Organic's competitors initiating a price war. Dean responded by dropping their own prices and increasing marketing investment. While sales volume was protected, in fact growing by 18% on the year, margins were now lower. Despite good years for Silk (up over 8%), International Delight (up over 11%) and Land O'Lakes (up over 13%), WhiteWave's operating income fell by 11%, driven largely by the Horizon Organic issues. The fear was that these would persist.

2007 was a big wake-up call for Dean Foods. The years when consolidation alone would guarantee success were over (although Dean was still buying dairies with another three acquired in the year). In addition, the successes in White-Wave Foods - which had largely come from increasing distribution - were either slowing down or hitting margins issues. Dean had to become as good at improving the efficiency of its existing milk operation as they had been at making and absorbing acquisitions. The company was clearly in a skills transition phase, which it set about testing both by testing, then exploring and internally realigning its business. It focussed DSD on branded fresh milk and ice cream, transferring most of their longer shelf-life products into WhiteWave Foods, whose products were delivered into customers' warehouses. By design, the company was now aligned around routes to market

2008

The high prices of raw milk continued for the majority of 2008 before falling significantly in the last quarter, resulting in the average price for the year being close to the previous year. However, the increased volatility compared to previous years still caused significant profit pressures. Dean Foods' DSD business experienced reduced margins in a market where the company was reliant on big customers. Thus WalMart accounted for 19% of company sales and each of the next four biggest customers contributed another 10%. Overall in the year Dean's DSD liquid milk and ice cream sales increased by 4% to $9.8 billion on a flat volume. Overall, those efficiency measures enacted in 2007 helped to improve company margin by 20 base points.

In the organic milk sector, large increases in organic feed costs drove up the price of raw organic milk. These private label brands chose not to pass on to the consumer, thus constraining the ability of Dean to push up their own prices to fully reflect the cost increases. Despite the volatility in the milk business, further dairy acquisitions were made in the year for an aggregate $96 million, leading to the closure of three ice cream/dairy facilities. The WhiteWave-Morningstar part of the business fared well, increasing sales by a shade under 10% to $2.7 billion. The sales increase came from both volume gains and price increases: Silk sales grew by 10%, Horizon Organic 18% and International Delight by over 9%.

To accelerate the growth of their non-DSD business, the company ramped up its R&D spend to $7.8 million, nearly double the level of two years previously. They also signed a deal with the Hero Group to jointly develop Hero-branded chilled fruit-based beverages in North America.

2009

The hard work looked like it had paid off as the company delivered record profits in total and in each of its business segments. Further efficiencies, from closing four more plants, enabled the DSD arm, now called Fresh Dairy Direct, to grow its volume by 3%. Contradictorily, sales of Fresh Dairy Direct fell by $1.4 billion, but because raw milk prices had tumbled – on average by 36% - the operating profit increased by 9%.

Sales of organic milk were largely flat, which the company attributed to heightened consumer sensitivity to its price premium over regular milk. A range of new products in the year, including Horizon Organic Plus DHA, International-al Delight Coffeehouse Inspirations, Silk Pure Almond and the first output of the Hero partnership, Fruit2day, helped branded sales increase by 9%.

The company portfolio was now reflecting the drive in the previous few years to reduce the dependence on private label and regional branded milk. This was now down to 49% of annual sales. 12% of their business was extended shelf-life dairy products; 8% was accounted for by ice-cream and 6% by soy brands. Inter-estingly, 9% of sales now derived from two regional dairy brands, which had been extended nationally, and so was produced by all the regional dairies. TruMoo chocolate milk was guaranteed free from artificial growth hormones and high fructose corn syrup; and Swiss Premium iced tea was initially developed by their Wengert's Dairy in Pennsylvania to use spare DSD capacity.

The International Dimension

Up to this point in their history, Dean Foods, and before that, the separate Suiza Foods and Dean Foods, had been almost entirely focused upon the USA. In 2000 Suiza had made their first international foray: acquiring a 75% stake in Leche Celta, one of Spain's largest dairy companies, which they later increased to full ownership. The company's Celta brand was the fourth largest in Spain, and also the second largest milk brand in Portugal. Volumes increased by 50% in the first four years of Suiza's ownership, which prompted the company to invest in building a new processing plant in Portugal. A further Spanish acquisition, Tiger foods, followed in May 2004.

The acquisition of Horizon Organic had brought with it Rachel's Organic, a premium UK organic dairy company which held the number one position in organic milk and number two in organic yoghurt. In early 2005, Rachel's was combined with Leche Celta into a new International division. This had a bump-er first year, growing its sales by 38% to $69 million. In 2006, however, the Ibe-rian companies were divested, being adjudged somewhat of a sideshow compared to the potential of Rachel's in the much bigger UK dairy market. The company then made its biggest move to date in building an international presence by acquiring Alpro for $440 million. Alpro was the leading European branded company for soy and plant-based dairy equivalents: it had production facilities in Belgium, the Netherlands. France and the UK, Their product range consisted of two major brands: Alpro, a range of soy milks, margarines, yoghurts, creams and desserts, and Provamel, an organic soy range sold through specialist organic and health outlets.

Alpro had got into soy-based drinks in the 1970s when Philippe Vandemoortele had developed a unique, natural process for making soy milk. His original goal had been to use the drink to help alleviate Third World nutrition deficiencies and he had even begun building a processing plant in Madagascar. However, logistics proved beyond his small company and it was decided to focus on the European market. In 1989 Alpro built Europe's largest UHT soymilk production plant in Belgium and in 1996 took over Sojinal along with its French factory. Alpro's UK factory was built in 2000 and the company acquired the Dutch tofu producer, SoFine Foods, in 2006. Alpro became Dean Foods' European priority, and so divested itself of the much smaller Rachel's UK food service and private label operations. Alpro proved another smooth acquisition with Dean Foods enjoying 8% compound growth in its sales of plant-based products from 2009 to 2011.

2010

Alas, 2009 proved to be a false dawn in the fresh milk category. While oscillations in the price of raw milk were no longer as acute, Dean suffered from the new reality of consumer belt-tightening. As this impacted, Dean Foods' grocery retail customers scrambled to keep up footfall in their stores. They believed a key weapon was the value offered in the milk chiller cabinet, which was primarily achieved via deep discounts on their private, or own-label, milk. Not only was this pain passed back up the supply chain to Dean, but the comparatively better value now offered on private label took share away from Dean's regional brands. Engells believed, quite prudently, that this was the new reality and that Dean's response had to be reducing costs in the milk business as never before. Consequently, 6 facilities, 500 delivery routes, 1,400 staff and $75 million in costs left the business, but not enough to prevent a 30% drop in annual operating income.

Dean Foods' new austerity strategy contained a second part: not to allow the traumas of the milk category to impede the growth of the WhiteWave and Alpro brands. These therefore achieved another record year. The three parts of Dean Foods' business operated very differently, and were at very different stages of their life cycles. Fresh Dairy Direct was commodity-driven with a huge private label component and all about cost reduction. Dean still promoted their local and national brands, supported by the benefit of the DSD system, which enabled them to get milk into stores fresher than most of their competitors. Morningstar Foods, which had been managed within Fresh Dairy Direct, was split out again as it focused mainly on long shelf life products: such as dairy and non-dairy creamers, whipping cream, aerosol cream, whipped toppings, half and half, sour cream and cottage cheese. Most of its sales went into the Foodservice channel or were private label. WhiteWave-Alpro remained brand driven, with the company offering minimal private label, and was all about innovation, investment and growth.

The dairy part of Dean Foods' business had provided the means to buy and then the scope to build brands, but increasingly the future suggested separation. Dean's had brought together three subscale, niche branded businesses. They had now formed them into WhiteWave-Alpro and nearly doubled their sales (up another 8% in 2010) by exploiting Dean Foods' advantaged route to market and strong customer relationships.

2011

In 2011 sales topped $13 billion for the first time and some degree of stability returned to Dean's Fresh Dairy Direct division as cost reductions kicked in. Nevertheless, milk volume declined 1% broadly in line with the market, and the trend in market share towards private label seemed permanent. However, sales in WhiteWave-Alpro grew a healthy 9% through both volume and price increases. All the main brands registered growth in the middle single digits, which was aided by new products such as International Delight multi-serve iced coffee and Silk Fruit & Protein.

In the year, 80% of American homes bought a Dean Foods branded product and, thanks to their foodservice operation, they were named McDonald's 2001 US supplier of the year. After conducting a review of their joint venture with the Hero Group, Dean decided to pull out and wound down their involvement. By the end of the year, Dean had reduced their employee numbers to 24,066, down from a high of nearly 30,000 just after the Suiza-Dean deal. Plainly, efficiency measures were continuing full steam ahead.

2012

At the time of writing, Dean Foods have not published their 2012 results. However, a blockbuster piece of news was Dean's IPO of 13% of the stock in WhiteWave-Alpro, with Dean increasing both the amount of stock offered and the price against market expectations. The offer was the first formal sign that WhiteWave-Alpro, long regarded as the most valuable part of the company, had a very different future from the milk side of the business. Two months later, Dean went a step further. Their Morningstar Foods division was sold to Canada's Saputo Inc. for $1.45 billion. Morningstar had been purchased by Suiza fifteen years previously but now had little in common with the other two components of the business. It was predominantly dairy-based yet did not use the advantaged DSD route to market of Fresh Dairy Direct, and with a mostly foodservice or private-label product range, it would not have sat comfortably within WhiteWave-Alpro. On the other hand, the crown jewel brand of the original Morningstar division, International Delight, was firmly part of the WhiteWave-Alrpo family.

The first three quarters of 2012 were exceptionally strong for WhiteWave-Alpro, with year-on-year sales increasing per quarter by 13%, 11% and 13% respectively. Growth was mostly driven by new coffee creamers and iced coffee lines under the International Delight brand, and the success of Silk Pure Almond. The Alpro sector also grew in the high single digits, aided by its launch of Alpro Almond Milk and Alpro hazelnut drink.

Fresh Dairy Direct had made no dairy acquisitions in the year and divested itself of a large Wisconsin plant in September 2011. This reduced overall volume by around 1.4%. On a like-for-like basis, the company gained market share but saw early volume gains turn to volume losses by the third quarter due to an accelerating decline in the total milk market (down by around 3% on the first three quarters). However, very strong cost controls gave the milk side of the business exceptionally good earnings increases.

Summary

In a world where the balance of power has shifted heavily towards the retailer, Dean Foods is a microcosm of the issues affecting all packaged goods companies. It is also a pointer for companies who come from a more traditional packaged goods background. The milk category is an exceptionally tough business with a commoditised product, a huge private label component and wildly fluctuating input costs. Against that background, Dean Foods became a giant via a well thought through and exceptionally well-executed acquisition strategy that gave it the critical mass to develop an advantaged route to market and low cost base for milk. The scale of their huge milk business, together with the strong customer links inherent in a private-label-dominated category, was then leveraged to expand into better branded sections of the chiller cabinet. Dean Foods demonstrate how very different skill-sets, such as acquisitions, customer relations and brand building, are now all required in order to thrive in today's retail environment.

One thing about Dean Foods is that they don't stand still for very long. The WhiteWave Foods IPO is clearly just the first step in spinning off the entire unit, most likely to Dean Food's existing shareholders. Significantly, Dean's long-time leader, Gregg Engels, has relinquished his CEO position at Dean Foods, and become Chairman and CEO of the now stand-alone WhiteWave Foods. The proceeds from both the IPO and the sale of Morningstar Foods are going to pay down debt. This substantially strengthens Dean Foods' balance sheet, and gives them greater flexibility to make big moves in building Dean and WhiteWave. Dean Foods has shown the benefits of taking the initiative to create their own future. The chances are that they will continue to do so.

General Mills

Where Did They Come From?

There could no better example than General Mills of how understanding a company's past can help illuminate its current challenges. General Mills, formed on 22nd June 1928, was one man's far-sighted response to what market forces had inflicted on the four wheat milling companies who had been the company's original component parts: Washburn Crosby in Minneapolis, the Sperry Flour Company based in San Francisco, the Kell group of mills in Oklahoma and Texas and the Larrowe Milling Company of Detroit. The man was Washburn Crosby's James Ford Bell, who could see that his industry was facing irreversible change. He laid out the two main challenges facing in a confidential report to his fellow directors not too far short of a century ago. What he told them still has parallels today. Here is what he said.

- Products – mainly milled flour and animal feed – were hopelessly over-abundant, which put a downward pressure on prices. Today, apart from a small percentage of genuine 'must-stock' brands, many companies' behave as though their high-price elasticity and low consumer loyalty products can easily be replaced, missed neither on retailers' shelves nor in consumers' homes.

- The retail customer base was increasingly concentrated in the hands of new, powerful anti-manufacturer adversaries: chain stores such as A&P, which promoted its own private label brands at the expense of manufacturers.

- Even its specialist customers – small bakers – were losing out to large and aggressive baking combines. Today, retailers have never been stronger: Wal-Mart's private label business is larger than Procter & Gamble in its entirety.

Increasing costs, combined with the above, were putting an unstoppable squeeze on margins. Manufacturers were finding that retailers and consumers were far from receptive to the passing-on of increased input costs at above-inflation price increases.

Bell was very clear when he told the Washburn Crosby board that 'the hand-writing is on the wall. The process of concentration moves forward. The bargaining power of the buyer is steadily growing. There is no denying its effect on trade

conditions. No legerdemain, no high-pressure sales method, no intensive merchandising practice can restore the old order. The question is how to deal with
it.' How indeed? A question confronting most managers in packaged goods
companies today.

Bell's genius was to see that trying harder with the same business model
wouldn't cut it. Analysing the company's five main sources of business, he could
see nothing but trouble:

- Export was a quarter of the company's sales but was essentially used by
the American wheat milling industry as an outlet for spare capacity, useful only in covering overheads.

- Business with large bakers was substantial, 16% of sales in 1927, but
even less profitable than export, as the large buyers played one milling
company off against another, which Bell thought could only get worse.

- Small baker business with was the largest component of company sales at
30%, but small bakers were losing out to the large baking companies,
another trend Bell was convinced would worsen.

- Household flour sales might make up 25% and might also look very
promising for the future, but it could only be reached through the chain
retailers.

Not a promising outlook overall. And Bell forcefully concluded: 'The methods of the past are not applicable to the present and any attempt to fit them into
a modern setting would be suicidal.' Bell was clearly not a man who hedged his
bets. Today, in the same way, the days when brand manufacturer was king and a
20% ad spend increase in ad spend for a new campaign automatically meant extra listings and display are equally dead.

The answer, Bell proposed, was radical action to address the power imbalance
between wheat miller and retailer: a full-blown merger of like-minded millers,
not locally in the Minneapolis area - antitrust legislation but stop that one - , but
spread across the country, leap-frogging the concentration of retailers that was
still mostly at the regional level. It would also leverage the industry trend towards
large mills – the only ones Bell was interested in joining forces with – which were
growing in number: the overall number of flourmills had halved in just over a
decade. The modern analogy would be the trend towards mergers and acquisitions in packaged goods: P&G bought Gillette not because it wanted to get into
shaving but because Gillette was so big already. In a battle of strength, size matters.

Bell's original and apparently genial proposal was the setting-up of a new
company that would purchase the assets of the selected mills for ten times their

average earnings over the previous five years and allowed each to keep its own board and operate with a large degree of independence. But that was just a smokescreen. Bell knew that the plan would only succeed if the new company became a truly new company, with a truly new way of operating. He was determined that his own company would take the lead.

However, it soon became obvious to Bell that four companies weren't enough: spread nationally they may have been, but they were not national. General Mills' competitors were surely disadvantaged by their smaller scale, but those in the winter wheat-growing areas had the local advantage of much lower distribution costs. General Mills needed such local members too, particularly in the southwest, so, only six months after the company had been formed, it was adding mills in Wichita Falls, Amarillo, Vernon, Waco and El Reno. Sights shifted to California, then beyond. Before long, General Mills had 27 associated operating companies in sixteen states and had become the largest miller in the world.

How Did It Evolve?

The original General Mills can be likened to a decentralised multi-national in the 1970s. It handled the group financial transactions, paid government taxes and arranged appropriate insurance for the company's physical assets. It also acted as central banker to the satellite companies, able to borrow at lower rates than any of its components. And, when group-wide activities made sense, it would coordinate them. Thus, basic research, nutrition programmes on the benefits of wheat, sales assistance to bakers and the like were head office programmes from the beginning. Head office also took care of booking and placing advertising: booking space nationally was cheaper. And each operating company still bought its own wheat, ran its own sales force and was responsible for its own profit and loss. So far, so good, although hardly revolutionary. But - somewhat unusually for a group of managers in a commodity business - Bell and his head office colleagues had a very consumer-centric view of their industry and it would be the implementation of this view that transformed General Mills from a loose association of flour millers into a consumer goods powerhouse to rival anything in America.

At the time of the company's formation, nearly all of its sales had been flour in one guise or another. Back in 1880, Washburn Crosby had entered its best flours in the first International Millers' Exhibition in Cincinnati and had won gold, silver and bronze medals, with the winning flour re-christened Gold Medal flour. Post the merger, it made clear sense for those millers who didn't their own branded flour to adopt into their product ranges, which they did. Gold Medal is still the best-selling brand of flour in America today.

However, Bell was thinking beyond branded bags of flour. 'Our associates,' said Bell, ' can be trusted for products; we in General Mills are selling results rather than products … Our job isn't finished when flour is sold but rather only when it is consumed; consequently, we maintain a continuous drive to get the flour out of the grocer's stock and the baker's bins and off the kitchen shelves to the table in forms appealing to the appetite'. This view, expressed in the early 1930s, was revolutionary in its day and even now might well put many modern companies to shame. The logical consequence, and the making of General Foods, was clear: selling flour and then watching everyone else turn it into something delicious was ridiculous.

In addition to Gold Medal flour, Washburn Crosby also had in its locker a wheat-based product developed in the early 1920s selling as a value-added offering. But it was struggling; its sales had declined by half between 1927 and 1929 and the new company was far from sure that it should keep persevering with a product that by then had been on the market for five years but it was still shifting pitifully small volumes compared to the mountains of Gold Medal flour being sold nationally.

The idea for the product had fallen into Bell's lap in 1921 when he had been buttonholed by the lawyer of a Minneapolis diet crank who was obsessed with the benefits of bran. The lawyer came to the meeting clutching a patent for a process for manufacturing bran flakes, which had been discovered entirely accidentally by his client. The lawyer was looking for a company to commercialise the product and Bell was looking for something he could sell besides bags of flour. Bell signed him up and allocated him space to work up his process, which turned out to be completely useless; his bran flakes crumbled to dust when tumbled around in a package. The crank was politely ushered out of the door and the project forgotten about until picked up again in 1924 by a Washburn Crosby technical expert who tested every strain of commercially available wheat and re-engineered the production process. The result, served up to a delighted Washburn Crosby board, was launched onto the market in late 1924 under a name coined by the wife of the company's New York-based export manager: Wheaties.

Perhaps unsurprisingly for a company more used to the commodity game, the results of competing against cereal goliaths like Kellogg's and Post were uninspiring. Washburn Crosby was only a small, regional company at the time and had little idea how to promote the line. Indeed, its main marketing effort was serendipitous: one of its sales managers had been instrumental in saving Minneapolis's first commercial radio station from going under and had idly suggested to the station manager that it and he could help sell Wheaties. The enterprising manager came up with a brainwave, a commercial based on the tune of a popular hit 'She's a Jazz Baby', but with suitably transformed lyrics:

Have you tried Wheaties?
They're whole wheat with all the bran.
Won't you try Wheaties?
For wheat is the best food of man.

And then the General Mills board met to decide whether Wheaties was really for them. The company's advertising manager pointed out that of the 53,000 cases sold in the past year, , 30,000 had been to the twin cities of Minneapolis and St. Paul, where the ad had been airing for the previous three years. If the ad were extended to more radio stations, he argued, might not these sales be duplicated?

Six weeks later, the company had set up a Packaged Foods division to concentrate on driving national sales of the only two brands the company really possessed: Gold Medal and Wheaties. The male quartet who had sung the ditty, rechristened the Gold Medal Fast Freight, was soon belting the number out coast-to-coast on the newly constituted Columbia Broadcasting System. Wheaties then inaugurated its sponsorship of baseball broadcasting and an ad agency-inspired tagline to go with it: The Breakfast of Champions. In ten years, 1929's 53,000 cases a year had turned into a whopping 4.5 million and Wheaties was the best-selling cereal in the country.

The Packaged Foods division soon latched onto another property that had been languishing within Washburn Crosby since 1921. The company had run a very easy mail-in competition on Gold Medal and over 30,000 responses had flooded into head office, many with additional questions on baking techniques. Here then was an opportunity to build a direct bond with its end-user customers; the company decided that everyone would receive a personalised reply, still better appreciated if signed in a woman's name. The surname of this mythical employee was chosen in honour of a recently deceased company director, William G. Crocker; and the forename Betty for its homely feel. Her signature (still used today) was chosen from examples all female employees had been asked to submit. In 1924, Washburn's infatuation with radio resulted in a half-hour cooking show, The Betty Crocker Cooking School of the Air, which by 1926 was on NBC. Thirteen Betty Crockers gave live cooking demonstrations across the country. In 1930, the company produced the first Betty Crocker cookbook. By

1945, Betty was the second-most-popular woman in America after Eleanor Roosevelt.

All this, of course, was an excellent way to encourage more home-baking, specifically, the company hoped, with Gold Medal flour. But for the company to guarantee its flour was used, Betty had to take a larger role: not just a mouthpiece but also a brand. The chance came with a new idea from another part of the General Mills Empire, the Sperry Company. Carl Smith, a Sperry sales executive, was travelling home to San Francisco on the train one day in November 1930 when, in the dining car, he was delighted to find himself face-to-face with a plate of steaming hot cookies. How on earth could such things have appeared on a train? Smith ventured into the galley where the chef gladly explained how he had blended together a mixture of lard, flour, baking powder and salt before the train left Portland and stored it in an icebox. Now he could take out a portion at a time and make cookies to order. This was a completely novel idea. Housewives everywhere baked everything from scratch. There were no shortcuts. If they didn't have the time, they didn't bake.

Carl took this news to the Sperry head chemist, who immediately set about solving the problems the train chef didn't have to worry about, the biggest of which was shelf life. Any product made commercially would have to stay fresh, in ambient conditions, for weeks rather than for just one frozen train ride. It was not an easy problem to solve. But solution there was: use the then quite rare sesame oil as the fat component, then laminate: layers of fat could be sandwiched between layers of flour, which would keep fat away from the surface and so stop it from turning rancid. .

This was too good an idea for the Sperry Company to keep to itself, especially as it had little experience in, or resources for, brand-building; the General Mills family claimed it, and the Gold Medal and Betty Crocker brand names lent instant credibility to the newly named Bisquick. The appetite of American women to be perfect moms whipping up freshly baked cookies for their kids in the blink of an eye knew no bounds. Within seven months of launch the company had sold half a million cases and made Betty Crocker the perfect vehicle for a whole range of quick-bake mixes made with 100% Gold Medal flour.

General Mills, although still primarily a flour merchant, now had the bit between its teeth. Its next blockbusters would be more breakfast cereal products to hitch to the success of the Wheaties bandwagon. But the cereal, or cereals, had to be different, from Wheaties and from the products of competitors, so the company was naturally interested by the potential of a technology invented by the curator of the herbarium at Columbia University, Professor Alexander Pierce Anderson. The professor had discovered that cornstarch, if placed in a tube and subjected to intense heat, would explosively expand to ten times its original volume. One wonders how many obscure things he did to cornstarch before this particular eureka moment. Whatever, he had conspicuously failed to get rich, having been unable to find a commercial application for his gadget, the 'puffing gun'.

But once the patent on the puffing gun ran out, General Mills was all over it, now using not raw grains but a mixture of cooked grains, pre-seasoned and fortified. The results, after years of refining both recipe and process, were two new breakfast cereals, one of which would become the bedrock of General Mills to this day. The first, Kix, was a corn-based offering and the original sponsor of The Lone Ranger radio serial, but the real winner was made from oats – not a grain readily compatible with more established breakfast cereal production methods – and was christened Cheerioats for its 1941 launch, on the back the snigger-inducing tagline He's Feeling His Cheerioats. Three years later, a writ-wielding competitor claimed sole rights to use of the word 'oats'. OK, the company said, we'll call it Cheerios.

By 1932, sales of flour as a share of business had fallen to 72% and - although actual volume sales were increasing - would continue to decline, down to 55% twenty years later, when packaged foods had become the major focus of growth in the company. General Mills' original role of providing demand for its flour-mills was now firmly in the back seat; it had become a fully-fledged and highly effective packaged goods company with some of the strongest and most enduring brand names in America.

How International Is It?

There can be no doubt that General Mills came late to the international game, understandable in view of the company's origins; after all, its original job was simply to create demand for what came out of flourmills, a mindset kept local because flour milling itself was then a local industry. General Mills' unadventurous first move was to set up abroad, in 1953, a Canadian subsidiary, which was nearer to its Minneapolis headquarters than a large chunk of its US market. True, the conglomerate years had included a handful of overseas purchases - UK's Smith's Crisps, for example - but none of them was of lasting significance.

The company began to take the international opportunity seriously in the post-conglomerate phase, when it was essentially a packaged goods business. In an innovative move, Nestlé and General Mills became joint partners in Cereal Partners Worldwide (CPW), a new venture established in 1990. The idea was to combine into a single cereal company General Mills' expertise in the cereal market and Nestlé's global reach and local market infrastructures, to form a competitor with enough critical mass to take a run at the markets dominated by Kellogg's.

The operation began operations in the UK and southern Europe on 1st June 1990, with a product range soon improved by the purchase of the UK's Shredded Wheat brand, an already successful and established brand that would lead the charge. Overall branding has always been Nestlé domain, a much stronger name outside North America than General Mills. In 1991, the Nesquik brand was added. In 1992, the company expanded into Mexico and Italy, closely followed by Poland, South America and Russia. In 1998, the venture moved into became profit, with equal shares going to the two partners, an arrangement that has continued ever since. By 2008, CPW had become colossal: sales in more than 130 countries topped $3 billion, on the back of more than 50 brands produced in fourteen factories garnering a market share of more than 20%. And perhaps General Mills has the better half of the deal: 50% of an ever-increasing profit – nearly $200 million after tax in 2001 – while Nestlé does most of the work.

Similarly, General Mills partnered with PepsiCo to set up Snack Ventures Europe in 1992, combining PepsiCo brands such as Doritos and Cheetos with General Mills' Bugles and Grainos and then adding to the mix with Snack Ventures' own new products. By 2004, it was Continental Europe's leading snack company, generating sales close to $1 billion. PepsiCo liked this so much, it bought General Mills' share.

But the true General Mills international game-changer came with the 2001 acquisition of Pillsbury. Pillsbury's advantage was first its ownership, for some time, by overseas companies (Britain's Grand Metropolitan and subsequently Diageo) and, second, its acquisition along the way of brands that already had strong international profiles, such as Green Giant and Häagen-Dazs. The Häagen-Dazs brand in particular had been a success around the world, quite often setting up joint ventures with local companies. Its Japanese partnership, for example, made sales of more than $300 million in 2004.

In 1997, Pillsbury had acquired two Hong Kong-based manufacturers, Wanchai Ferry, who made dumplings, and then V. Pearl, a Cantonese dim sum company. This particular Pilsbury connection gave General Mills its first experience of the Chinese market and became the basis of a successful and growing business in this hugely important, exponentially expanding marketplace. General Mills' instantly showed its worth. Its expertise was crucial in developing the local Chinese product ranges into microwaveable formats, which led inexorably to their US launch, a first time move for General Mills.

The international divisions of both companies had been fully integrated by 2004, by which time they were delivering $1.5 billion in sales. The biggest single market was Canada, which had been a strong market for both companies and included virtually all of its big US brands. Outside North America, business was dominated by three global brands: Häagen-Dazs, recently supplemented by the launches of Häagen-Dazs Cream Crisp ice cream sandwiches; Green Giant; and Old El Paso, the leading Mexican food brand in Europe that had been acquired by Pillsbury in 1995. Betty Crocker was well established in Australia. In China, Wanchai Ferry was posting a 36% volume increase on the back of new lines. With operations in fifteen countries and sales in over 100, General Mills was a lot more international that it had been, but as its top overseas international market was Canada it could not be said at that stage to be a properly global company.

By 2012, however, General Mill was well on the way. Total sales rose to $4.2 billion. Asia-Pacific was closing with Canada, both generating close to $1 billion. Crucial in driving the overseas businesses had been the Häagen-Dazs brand, marketed in more than 80 countries and providing a unique presence in markets such as China through more than 160 Häagen-Dazs branded ice cream shops, a concept now expanded to countries such as India and Egypt. The company footprint has been expanded by recent acquisitions such as Yoki in Brazil, and the global brands list augmented by the purchase of a controlling stake in the global Yoplait brand in 2011. And Cereal Partners Worldwide has proved to be a wonderful idea: General Mills cereal brands (branded as Nestlé) sell over 100 countries with, as we have noted, very little effort from, and risk to General Mills.

How Did It Build Its Modern Business?

The transition from the General Mills at the beginning of the 1940s to the General Mills of today looks as though it might have pretty linear. After all, Cheerios is the best-selling breakfast cereal in America. Betty Crocker, now in her eighth pictorial likeness, has her image on dozens of easy recipe products and even Gold Medal is still around. More and more brands were developed, some without any sort of wheat background - Cheerios, for example - to the where the grain mills, no longer organically linked to product at all, were sold; the company seamlessly became a manufacturer and purveyor of brands. And although it did start out that way that is not quite what happened,

The Betty Crocker range had been given a massive shot in the arm in 1948 with the launch of an amazingly good cake mix, Chiffon Cake. General Mills had been approached by the inventor of the recipe who was so confident of his cake idea he charged company executives $5,000 just to watch him bake it – without disclosing to them the ingredients – and for them to sample it from the oven. His recipe was bought on the spot, sum undisclosed, although it will not have come cheap given the cook's demonstration price. And after Betty Crocker Chiffon Cake Mix came Ginger Cake Mix, Crustyquick, Apple Pyequick, Party Cake Mix, Devil's Food Cake Mix and so on ad very nearly infinitum. In the meantime, per capita consumption of flour was falling and so General Mills couldn't waste time in expanding that range.

The launch of the mechanical division in 1940 signalled wider diversification. The division was primarily aimed at the design and manufacture of food preparation equipment, a war-driven initiative that would nonetheless fail in the longer run. The initial interest lay in processing soybeans as a vehicle for expansion into the animal feed market, an idea that led later to the much broader Chemicals division. The post-war consumer boom, driven by rising real incomes and the birth of the supermarket, greatly accelerated brand success. By 1953, the food division alone was generating nearly five times the entire 1930 company profits, a milestone the company celebrated by launching Trix, its first pre-sweetened cereal. The company now had sales of nearly half a billion dollars and controlled one-sixth of the grain-milling capacity of the nation. A year later, as we have noted, the company made its first tentative move abroad by opening a factory in Canada. And the brands were ideally suited for the new medium of television; the company's destiny seemed assured.

Then, in 1962 General Mills appointed a new president, Edwin W. Rawlings, a relative newcomer. Rawlings, perhaps because the electronics and mechanics had diversified far beyond bread-mixing machines (partnering the University of Minnesota in developing a flight recorder, a black box forerunner, for example), saw the company's future reaching far beyond the mundane world of breakfast cereals, flour milling and cake mixes. He first slimmed the company down, selling half the mills, the appliances and animal feeds divisions while bolstering the branded foods side by getting the company into the foodservice sector.

But these were footling changes compared to what was to come. Rawlings embarked on an acquisition spree that would make General Mills the most conglomerated of conglomerates. 1968 purchases of Rainbow Crafts, Parker Bros. and Kenner, makers of Play-Doh, Monopoly and Spirograph, now made General Mills the world's largest toy company. (In 1977, it launched the monumentally successful Star Wars action figures.) In 1969, the company entered specialist retailing via the acquisition of Lacoste and Monet Jewellery brands and the Eddie Bauer sportswear brand two years later. In 1970, the company climbed onto the food chain, buying Red Lobster, a five-outlet franchise it would subsequently take national.

Most outlandish of all was its 1964 designing and building of the submersible that twenty years later would be the first to explore the wreck of the Titanic. There were now thirteen different product categories, along with all the non-grocery-related activities quite enough developments to keep the branded food business rolling and giving it a lasting significance. Then, in 1964, it entered the snack foods business by purchasing Morton Foods. The same year, it launched the Lucky Charms cereal. There was a new snack product, Bugles, in 1966, and the company bought the Tom Huston Peanut Company to bolster the growing snacks business. Two years later, it bought a frozen seafood company.

It had been the mother of all acquisition sprees for General Mills and it did wonders for the top line. Sales in 1976 reached $2.6 billion, having increased a staggering four-fold in the previous seven years. But many of the acquisitions were short-lived. Three-quarters of the 1975 purchases were sold again within five years. Some did work, providing funds for the aggressive support its foods business during the 1970s, with big advertising spends on established brands and a plethora of new products: Hamburger Helper in 1970, Nature Valley granola cereal in 1973 and, in 1977, the interesting purchase of the US rights to the European yoghurt brand Yoplait; Interesting because, in 1977, yoghourt could hardly be given away, unless to its small fan base of the health-obsessed.

The acquisition spree had largely played out by the early 1980s as the focus shifted more to growing organically. Everything on the balance sheet seemed to be performing: Lacoste was a $400 million brand, the success of Red Lobster chain inspired the launch of the Italian-themed Olive Garden concept, the toy division was selling as many Care Bears as it could make and on the food side, Fruit Roll-Ups, Toaster Strudel and Pop Secret popcorn were excellent new products exploiting the company's core expertise.

But the era of conglomerates was coming to an end. Management consultants were preaching focus plus genuine expertise rather than random and disjointed predation. So, in 1985, General Mills began to divest. Toys, fashion and retailing were hived off, with Eddie Bauer and the furniture business not far behind. Fully 25% of sales were ditched, and by the end of the 1980s, General Mills was back to being a food business, although in much better shape than it had been before the spree. Over 90% of the company's food sales came from number one or number two brands and the innovation pipeline was humming: in the late 1980s, at least a quarter of annual sales growth came from new products. The health-fuelled boom in oat bran gave Cheerios a more than 3% jump in market share within a single year.

By 1993, sales had reached $8 billion, two-thirds from packaged goods and the remainder from the booming restaurants division; five Red Lobster outlets had increased to 657 and Olive Garden wasn't far behind with 429 restaurants, although these two restaurant successes were not typical; other themed restaurants - steakhouses, Mexican, health food joints, the Chinese China Coast in 1991 – all failed to take off. However, the rapid growth of the two successful brands was driving profits and powering General Mills to a return on equity of over 40%. But the company was, in effect, running two entirely separate businesses, with vastly different dynamics and little to no synergy. So, in 1995, the restaurants division was spun off as Darden Restaurants Inc. And General Mills returned to its *fons et origo*: a packaged goods company.

That the company had now come back to its roots was precisely encapsulated by what it did next: launch Frosted Cheerios in 1995 and mastermind a PR hoopla around the ageless Betty Crocker's 75th anniversary. A year later, General Mills, still strictly in character, made its largest acquisition yet, buying the cereals and snacks business Ralcorp Holdings Inc., which included brands such as Chex, Chex Mix and Cookie Crisp. This $570m spend, a beefed-up portfolio and a laser-like focus on what was now the company's largest category by meant it could at last seriously challenge long-time foe Kellogg's hegemony in the breakfast cereals market. In 1999, it came within 0.1% of taking the lead..

Nor were convenience foods suffering any neglect. General Mills now owned the Go-GURT range of portable yoghurts, had pioneered Betty Crocker rice and pasta mixes and was marketing yoghurt in a tube. It acquired Lloyd's Barbeque Company, Farmhouse Foods, Gardetto's Bakery and - an inspired early punt onto the organic market - Small Planet Foods. However, and as we have noted, transformed came in 2001 with acquisition of long-time competitor The Pillsbury Company. It too had once been just a miller, with origins almost as old as General Mills'.

The deal was worth an eye-watering $10.5 billion. It almost doubled annual sales from $5.5 billion to $10.5 billion, giving General Mills a renewed level of clout with all the major retailers. It also brought into the company many valuable brand properties: the annual Pillsbury Bake-Off Contest, running since 1949, the Pillsbury Doughboy, who had arrived on the advertising scene in 1965 and the extremely venerable Green Giant brand, acquired by Pillsbury in 1979. In fact, General Mills had first though to sell off Green Giant. It changed its mind. Its near-global Häagen-Dazs licence also sweetened the deal Pillsbury had launched a 50/50 venture with Nestlé two years earlier, giving Nestlé the right to a 99-year licence for the brand in the US and Canada should Pillsbury be sold. Another gem in the Pillsbury portfolio was Old El Paso, which fitted very comfortably into General Mills' portfolio of fast, pre-prepared convenience foods. Above all perhaps, Pillsbury transformed General Mills' international presence.

How Is It Structured?

General Mills has been through four distinct phases: a holding company for flour millers, a milling company with a centralised packaged goods component, an industrial conglomerate and finally, after the Pillsbury acquisition, a packaged goods company.

The original holding company lasted barely eight years, until 1st June 1937, when the subsidiary companies under the holding company umbrella were liquidated and General Mills became an operating company rather than purely an administrative entity. At this point the company had two divisions: Grocery Products and Flour & Feed. By 1953, matters were getting a little more complicated. Flour & Feed was split, making three key divisions along with Grocery Products. The there were four: the chemicals division marking the shift of General Mills into non-foods. As for the conglomerate years, the spree years, they are practically shapeless: following the sale of the chemicals division in 1997, Food Processing, Restaurants, Games and Toys, Fashion and Speciality Retailing all hung out in the same corporate bar, if at separate tables.

- Today the company is back to three main divisions: US Retail, International and Bakeries & Foodservice, a fairly standard arrangement for a US food company. Within the divisions, US Retail ($10.5 billion, 63% of total company) reports seven segments:
- Big G (the breakfast cereals) – $2.4 billion
- Baking Products – $1.8 billion
- Frozen Foods – $1.6 billion
- Snacks – $1.6 billion
- Meals – $1.5 billion
- Yoplait (America's leading brand of yoghurt) – $1.4 billion
- Small Planet Foods and other – $0.2 billion.

On the international side, the company is dived into four regions:
- Europe – $2 billion (almost double the pre-Yoplait purchase level)
- Canada – $1 billion
- Asia-Pacific – $0.8 billion
- Latin America – $0.4 billion.

Bizarrely, Bakeries & Foodservice includes, as well as Foodservice Distributors and Bakeries & National Accounts Restaurants, the small but rapidly growing Convenience Stores. But for route-to-market reasons, CS would fit better strategically in US Retail.

What Has It Been Doing Recently?

2004

With the Pillsbury acquisition fully completed, the new General Mills emerged in 2004 as an $11 billion turnover business, but heavily US-dominated even with the Pillsbury international components: only 14% of sales and 6% of profits came from outside the US, although the joint ventures with Nestlé and PepsiCo added another billion in sales attributable, but not reportable, to General Mills brands.

Within the US, the new company had become a powerful force in grocery. It competed in twelve product categories and at the end of 2004 the company was market leader in seven (yoghurt, frozen vegetables, refrigerated dough, dessert mixes, frozen baked goods, dry dinners and fruits snacks) and running second in the remaining five (ready-to-eat cereals, Mexican products, ready-to-serve soup, microwave popcorn and frozen hot snacks). As with virtually all US-dominated packaged goods companies, there was a dangerously high degree of concentration in the customer base. The top-five US retail customers accounted for 43% of sales; Wal-Mart alone made up 19%

After the endless upheavals of the conglomerate years, the company philosophy was much more steady-as-she-goes. There were four key elements:

- Product innovation
- Channel expansion
- International expansion
- Margin expansion.

So, little to raise the eyebrows here. In the prepared foods business, product innovation is an absolute essential just to stand still, channel expansion makes sense given the concentration of business in a small number of over-influential retailers, whilst international expansion was a strategic necessity: so little of the company's business came from the high-growth, high-potential markets. But margin expansion was tough. The categories involved are highly competitive, which makes price increases a risky proposition. Growth here came mostly from Nature Valley snack bars and Yoplait yoghurt – both far-sighted acquisitions made before either category was showing much promise.

2005

As with most large-scale mergers, the anticipated acceleration in sales growth from the new behemoth proved somewhat illusory, with sales inching up a miserly 2%. The margin expansion goal was missed thanks to increasing commodity price increases and anything salvaged from compensatory price increases had to re-spent on promotion: competitors, particularly Kellogg's, had absorbed the cost increases and kept their prices unchanged. Thus, within the US Retail segment, Big G cereals – the biggest category – suffered volume declines despite a host of new products. Only Yoplait, driven by Yoplait Light and the Progresso reduced-calorie soup brand, showed significant growth. To help keep the year's bottom line respectable, marketing spend reduced by more than $50 million.

With the US-centric Foodservice division flat on the year, the only genuine good news came from the International division, where sales were up by 11% and operating profit by 40%, albeit bother were aided by favourable foreign exchange swings. However, volume was up by 6% in total with the Asia-Pacific region leading the way at more than12%. Here, Wanchai Ferry did more than its fare share, with sales increasing by almost 25%. One major change in business outside North America was the end Snack Ventures Europe. As we noted earlier, PepsiCo so liked the look of its performance it bought out the General Mills 40.5% stake.

2006

Matters improved slightly in 2006 as sales increased by 4%, not least because of over 300 new products launches, although this did involve the restoration of last year's higher marketing spend. But even though overall performance improved, basic trends remained the same: strong growth in the US from the healthier end of the portfolio, with Yoplait, Progresso and Nature Valley sales percentages all growing by double digits, and decline in the bigger and less-trendier cereal and Pillsbury categories.

The International division contributed less to the overall sales increases load – up by just 6% on the year - it was nevertheless instrumental in improving the company's overall margin by adding a full percentage point to operating profit margin. The transformation of General Mills from a North American operator to a global company was still by no means complete. But Pillsbury had accelerated the shift substantially. The company now had 30 plants and 9,000 employees generating nearly $2 billion in non-US sales, half a billion up on the previous three years and a five-fold increase since the year before the merger. Not only were the company's US brands being taken to new markets - Nature Valley bars were launched in Europe and India - but indigenous overseas brands such as

Wanchai Ferry appeared not only in Asian Taiwan but also in European France. Cereal Partners Worldwide made a significant acquisition, buying Australia's Uncle Toby's brand, making that country its second-most-important market after the UK.

2007

New President and CEO Ken Powell now added brand building to the existing list of key drivers, and not before time. Including General Mills' 50% share of the volume sold through Cereal Partners Worldwide, worldwide cereal sales exceeded $3 billion in a category, which absolutely requires committed brand building for long-term success. The Big G range in the US finally returned to growth, if only by just over 2%, and was in any overshadowed by first Canada, which achieved more than 6% and then by Cereal Partners Worldwide at with over 18%, both with the same range. Clearly, General Mills needed to rely less on discounting its cereals and more on improving their relevance. Pointing up this fact, many of the new products launched in the previous year were actually nutritionally improved versions of older major brands. And they were proving successful in attracting new users, which clearly indicated the strategic way forwards. The success of Cascadian Farm organic cereals acquisition made exactly the same point, growing by more than 50% in the year.

So, nutrition became a new lens through which the company began to look at its total global sales, a fact that the new divisions in its portfolio duly reflected:

- Inherently Nutritious Categories – 40% of sales (yoghurt, soy, organic and vegetables, ready-to-eat cereals)
- Better For You Choices – 13% of sales (ready-to-serve soup, snacks)
- Quick and Convenient Options – 47% of sales (refrigerated dough, dinner mixes, dessert mixes, Mexican, ice cream, frozen pizza and snacks)

It was perhaps somewhat generous – even misleading - to include the entire range of ready-to-eat cereals in Inherently Nutritious when it included such offerings as Reese's Puffs and Lucky Charms. While offerings such as Yoplait Light (up another 20% in the year) and Nature Valley were guaranteed to grow, many of the offerings in Quick and Convenient were obviously vulnerable to healthy eating concerns, so new options such as lower-calorie, lower-sugar or lower-fat versions of existing brands were clearly essential.

2008

This was the year that looked as if everything was coming together. Even though the May fiscal year-end temporarily protected the annual performance from the full impact of the global recession, a sales increase of 10% - over $1 billion - was impressive by any standard. Every division in the company grew by at least 5% (Big G, Pillsbury and Meals) and four by double digits (Yoplait, Bakeries & Foodservice, Snack and International). Cheerios, the largest brand in the US cereal market with a 12% share, grew by 8%. The Fibre One cereal brand was successfully extended into snack bars, muffin mixes and yoghurt. Nature Valley granola bars were now sold in 54 countries. And the ever-reliable Wanchai Ferry dumplings grew by another 30% in China as distribution was increased to more cities and regions, an increase which helped General Mills' international division generate over one-third of the total sales and profit growth in the year.

2009

It was 2009 that demonstrated the true resilience of General Mills' business: sales increased another 8% to over $14 billion. The company's first advantage was that it operated in categories that are relatively recession-proof. Home-baking products, for example, positively thrive in tough times. Betty Crocker, Bisquick, Pillsbury refrigerated dough and Gold Medal flour enjoyed absolutely stellar years as more people baked at home. Which leads to the second strength: brands. Of the eleven categories in the US where General Mills competed, it had number-one status in eight and was a strong second in the other three.

The company was also continuing to invest in its brands when the times were tough. Marketing spend increased by 16%, driven by a media spend more than 17% more that the previous year (which had also shown an increase). In addition, investment in the relevance and appeal of the brands by further improvements to nutritional profiles (45% of the entire product range had been improved since 2005) and continued innovation through new lines such as Macaroni Grill dinner mixes also bolstered performance. And although innovation was no longer a huge business strength – only 5% of sales came from new products within the year – those new products had the reputation of reliability – and were. Margins were flat, but were being proactively managed in the face of an overall 9% increase in input costs. The management style – the Holistic Margin Management philosophy – stressed a continual reassessment of every cost, and it worked. Longer-term trends in the food category were also being addressed, with the acquisition of Lärabar, a range of energy bars made with unprocessed ingredients. Pop Secret, the microwavable popcorn, did well too.

The positive performance in the US Retail part of the business (at $10.1 billion and still nearly 70% of total sales) was topped up by an increasingly strong international business, driven by Asia-Pacific and South America, which increased by 16 and 22% respectively, adding 10% across the board. Häagen-Dazs, Old El Paso, Wanchai Ferry and Nature Valley were more well-established core brands building a significant overseas presence. And Cereal Partners Worldwide simply kept on keeping on. It did precisely nothing for the company's visibility. But it did plenty for the bottom line.

2010

Given the previous two years, 2010 was something of a disappointment, with sales growth of only 1%, although a 51-week financial year and the loss of divested lines took 3% off sales. Nevertheless, every operating division achieved growth but bakeries and foodservice, which had a ghastly time – 14% down - as indexed products reduced prices to match falls in the price of wheat. However, the same input cost reductions, plus others across foodstuffs and manufacturing performance, plus those Holistic Margin Management initiatives, added a whopping three points to the year's gross margin, helping to fund a 24% increase in a worldwide advertising spend of over $900 million, a $400 million increase in just three years. Significantly, the biggest marketing spend increases were in digital initiatives such as the company's recipe website, Tablespoon.com, and in its Hispanic marketing platform, Qué Rica Vida, which was successfully building links between General Mills and Latina moms new to America, whose Hispanic consumers were outpacing everyone else with ease. Innovation there was too, once again based on sensible logical extensions to already-strong brands - Yoplait Greek style Yoghurt and Chocolate Cheerios, for example. And there was another well-conceived culturally sensitive co-branding venture, this time using the Good Earth brand to introduce new ideas.

As far as divisions were concerned, international business once again outpaced US retail, although with typical volatility, the company's South American business followed up the previous year's growth with a double-digit decline. In the meantime, China was now a $350 million market for General Mills, largely off the back of Wanchai Ferry (up another 20%) and the Häagen-Dazs cafés. The growing Chinese success story also had a very useful spin-off: it was giving the company confidence in other emerging markets where it had small but growing footholds – India, Brazil and Russia, where once again Häagen-Dazs and Nature Valley were the spearheads into these markets. And whilst Cereal Partners Worldwide had nearly a quarter of the global ready-to-eat cereal market outside of North America, General Mills was perhaps rueing how the deal had panned out in terms of company visibility: its powerhouse cereal brands were helping build the Nestlé brand name and market clout. General Mills operating companies were missing out on the retailer access and leverage.

2011

For the last few years, General Mills has been relying more on price realisation and mix improvements than on organic volume growth to drive top line sales. In tough economic times, retailers, who actually hold the pricing power for major brands, almost inevitably turn to increased levels of discounting to shore up their own market shares. They refuse to accept price increases and they demand higher discounts to fund their own price reductions. General Mills, with its roster of number-one and number-two brands in the US market, is inevitably at the forefront of the pricing battle, which turned out to be the case in 2011, when discounting was widespread. The only real volume momentum in recent years had been in the more niche areas of the portfolio, such as Nature Valley and Small Planet Foods, so without pricing or volume increases much of the portfolio was becalmed. Sales on Big G cereals, Meals and Pillsbury all declined in the year and Yoplait only limped forward 1% owing to the acquisition of the Mountain High all-natural yoghurt business. Even worse, $60 million was slashed from the marketing budget to help make ends meet.

However, outside the US Retail business it was mostly good news. The international division grew by 7%, 6% of which was volume growth in the key brands. Cereal Partners Worldwide posted a 4% gain and the substantial gross margin improvement of the previous year was held on to, albeit helped by a lower-than-average year of increases in input costs. But perhaps the most significant news was on the M&A front, where the company spent $1.2 billion on acquiring a 51% controlling interest in the Yoplait brand from the French farmers' cooperative Sodiaal and a 50% stake in the related company that managed Yoplait's franchise businesses in markets where it did not have a direct presence. The benefits of the acquisition were two-fold. First, General Mills as a North American franchisee for Yoplait had both yoghurt market knowledge and grocery expertise that could be helpful globally. Second, Yoplait, as the world's number-two yoghurt brand behind Danone, would give significant critical mass to General Mills' overseas businesses.

2012

On the face of it, General Mills was back in the groove as sales surged by 12% to reach $16.7 billion. However, at the macro level, all of that 12% increase was accounted for by the Yoplait acquisition: sales in the pre-Yoplait General

Mills business were static. More worryingly, the static outcome was a somewhat manipulated figure - a 3% volume decline counterbalanced by a 3% gain in pricing and mix. Worse, in the US the swings were more extreme. Even the Holistic Margin Management programme was unable to contain massive 10% increase in input costs so these had been largely passed on in price increases, which in turn affected volume despite increases in marketing spend and product innovation. US volume was down by 6% but price and mix added 9%, not enough to prevent a full three percentage points coming off the gross margin. Price increases of this size on leading brands are very risky propositions; they can easily widen the price gap between branded and private label to the point of consumer disloyalty, where the brand premium simply no longer has sufficient value to persuade buyers to part with their cash. And once buyers switch to a private label, there can be no guarantee they will return when and if the price gap narrows.

Within the product categories, innovation such as Peanut Butter Multi-Grain Cheerios and Fibre One 80 Calories kept the cereals ticking over, albeit on reduced volumes. But in the yoghurt category a gathering storm had finally broken on the Yoplait brand. Five years previously, and out of nowhere, the Chobani Greek Yoghurt brand had knocked Yoplait off its perch and become America's leading brand of yoghurt. Despite a rapid launch of Yoplait Greek and the rolling out of Mountain High into more outlets, US yoghurt sales were down a full 5%. This pinpointed a significant chink in General Mills' armour: innovation. The company was excellent at developing new variants of brands or making improvements to existing lines – 65% of sales that year came from products recently changed or improved in some way – but it was weak at real breakthrough innovation, innovation that changed the rules. The company had been built on the breakthrough successes of Bisquick and Cheerios; it had been completely caught out by the phenomenal rise of the Greek yoghurt.

Internationally, matters were somewhat calmer. Yoplait was still performing well, increasing sales by 63%, primarily in Europe, now General Mills' largest international division and generating nearly $1.8 billion out of the $4.2 billion of non-US business. China was now a half-billion-dollar market for the company as Wanchai Ferry continued to grow by double digits. Häagen-Dazs, posting another 30%, was now available in over 80 countries, growing by 16% in the year, and more Old El Paso was sold outside the US than inside. The leviathan that was Cereal Partners Worldwide continued to publicize Nestle and pump money into both company's coffers. In India, General Mills acquired Parampara Foods, an Indian food starters business. The Indian portfolio now boasted Pillsbury Fresh & Multi Grain Atta and dessert mixes, Betty Crocker dessert mixes, Green Giant, Nature Valley and Häagen-Dazs. Oh, and Parampara.

What Is Its DNA?

After such a chequered corporate history - flourmills, Cabbage Patch Dolls, Chocolate Frosted Cheerios, submersible explorers, fashion, Care Bears, restaurant chains to name just a few - it would be surprising if General Mills had built up a set of fixed competencies truly embedded in the business over time and over territory. However, there are two current attributes, which have always been crucial to the company's success. And they can be traced all the way back to the times of the company's great visionary, James Ford Bell.

Convenience Meals

General Mills is clearly in the business of meals and snacks. But whilst ready-to-eat cereals are its biggest category, and it is clearly an expert in the area, the company has no real advantage over the likes of Kellogg's and Post. The same can be said for its ice cream, snack bars and yoghurt, where it is certainly highly competent, but no more so than other global food companies. But the one category that stands out as a point of excellence for General Mills is convenient meals. General Mills has been working on convenience foods for over 40 years, since the launch of Hamburger Helper. The science behind delicious, healthy, quick and easy meals is highly complex and is not easily learnt or replicated. Many companies could have bought Wanchai Ferry and grown the Chinese business through wider Chinese distribution in China; where General Mill added huge incremental value was in re-launching the brand in new convenience formats, such as microwave options that maintain both the product consistency and deliciousness, and in developing shelf-stable versions that can be exported to markets such as the UK and US. Over the last decade, the company has also been very successful in adapting to the trend towards health and wellness in pre-prepared foods.

Making Big Brands Bigger

While this may sound an obvious pre-requisite for any consumer goods business, it is in fact surprisingly rare. Over time, brand portfolios tend to fragment. Old favourites sail into the sunset, as innovation pipelines churn out increasingly niche offerings. The General Mills' portfolio, in contrast, is dominated by a small number of brands, of varying vintages, and almost all are bigger now – much bigger – than they were when they started. Gold Medal flour, Bisquick, Betty Crocker and Cheerios have absolutely maintained their relevance in consumers' minds and their power on retailers' shelves, not least because of an obsessive focus on consumer preference. The company goal is 60% consumer preference, which well over half of its portfolio achieves.

Betty Crocker, the epitome of the interwar consumer society, is as relevant now as she ever was, with her own iPad app chock full of message from the nineteen Betty Crocker test kitchens that churn out 50,000 test recipes a year. Offerings such as Betty Crocker Gluten-Free Dessert Mixes keep the brand relevant, in this case to this century's obsession with constituents, ingredients and allergies. Cheerios is America's best-selling cereal not for the better toys in the box but because the country still loves it and its brand extensions: the weight management offering, Multi-grain Cheerios, and the cholesterol-lowering Honey Nut Cheerios. Indeed, developing relevant brand extensions is a true General Mills' forte, especially when it leverages its technical capabilities into other product sectors; in taking the Fibre One cereal brand into snack bars, muffin mixes and even yoghurt, for example, and the venerable Wheaties brand into snack bars with Wheaties Fuel.

And through inspired acquisitions in the past, the original brand line of brands has been augmented by a limited line-up of equally strong offerings the company has nurtured and grown for decades: Nature Valley, Häagen-Dazs, Yoplait and the host of high-performers brands that came with the Pillsbury acquisition. General Mills has been an excellent brand custodian.

Summary

General Mills has had a more interesting history than most packaged goods companies. From its far-sighted formation to match the growing scale of retailers and its transition to a developer of brands that added value to the output of its flourmills, from its emergence from a somewhat wacky conglomerate period into a focused food business with an impressive range of power brands, General Mills has been one of America's success stories. However, it perhaps can be considered as two distinct companies in one. With over $10 billion in sales in the US plus another billion in Canada and $2 billion in Foodservice and Bakeries, it is a North American powerhouse. Anyone who turns over almost $2 billion with Wal-Mart definitely gets in to see the buyer. But total sales in the rest of the world of just over $4 billion essentially make General Mills a niche player everywhere else. The growth of its Chinese business to $500 million may be laudable but, in the world's second-largest economy, it is based on just two brands – Wanchai Ferry and Häagen-Dazs. Its Indian presence is modest, Brazil the same and Russia tiny.

It is hard to see anything-transformative happening in North America for General Mills, where it has struggled to reach significant volume growth for years. It does operate in a number of categories that are growing healthily, but as it is already number one in the majority, it relies more on natural category growth than internally generated major initiatives. It is not a notably innovative company and has not created any major new categories for some time, nor has it seriously disrupted anyone else's, so it must look abroad. Perhaps the acquisition of Yoplait points the way forward. General Mills needs to become a much bigger player in the rest of the world - and quickly. As developing markets grow at breakneck speed, size will increasingly matter, just as size mattered in the 1920s in the flour-milling business. Its American DNA is readily transferable to the rest of the world, as Wanchai Ferry has demonstrated, so anything is possible. Ironically, General Mills is crying out for a move as far-reaching as the first one James Ford Bell made almost one hundred years ago.

Heinz

Where Did They Come From?

At 5pm on Friday, 17th December 1875, a Pittsburgh food company filed a voluntary petition in bankruptcy. Someone in the company had purchased, ill-advisedly and pre-harvest, an entire season's crop of cucumber and cabbage. It did not work out.

Although the company had been employing 150 people across four cities preparing and selling 300 barrels of sauerkraut, 15,000 barrels of pickles and 50,000 barrels of vinegar, there was no escape. Already its CEO had been arrested twice for apparent (and later disproved) fraud and his parents' house and all the money loaned by relatives appeared to be lost. It would take him nine years to pay off his creditors. And very fortunately, Henry John Heinz was a man not easily deterred: his next business reincarnation would eventually top $11.5 billion sales.

Henry had been launched into the produce business by his mother who tasked him with selling the surplus from the family's garden. By the age of 12, he had bought himself a horse and cart and expanded the garden to three and a half acres to accommodate his best-selling line, which was his mother's prepared horseradish. These he sold in clear glass bottles to showcase the absence of foliage and fillers habitually used by his more established competitors. Henry had already learned two lessons upon which the fortunes of H.J. Heinz & Co. would later flourish: that housewives will pay someone else to do their more difficult kitchen chores, and that a pure product of superior quality, properly packaged and promoted, would sell on its merits.

After a solid grounding in his father's brick business and at Mercantile College, at the age of 25 in 1869, Henry founded the firm of Heinz and Noble with his neighbour, Clarence Noble. They produced and sold bottled pickled food under the Anchor brand name, and naturally their first product was his mother's grated horseradish. Henry was the driving force. His beliefs shaped, and still shape, the modern Heinz business. No doubt resulting from spending his formative years largely in the garden, Henry never lost his fascination with how things grew and how to grow them better. This led to his third idea for a successful food business: to improve the finished product, you must improve it in the ground. So he spent countless hours picking the brains of various government research stations and farmers on how to improve the crops, not just in flavour but from a commercial standpoint: greater yield, earlier maturity and greater consistency.

Yet Heinz, Noble and Company collapsed, apparently due to Clarence Noble's overdose on cucumber and cabbage. Henry was completely undeterred, and two months later set up again, this time with his brother John and cousin Frederick, with the firm of F &J Heinz. Of course, as an un-discharged bankrupt, Henry was not allowed his name over the door but, as manager, he ran the firm nonetheless. One of his earliest decisions was to add, to their range of pickles, the first commercial grade of tomato ketchup to be made available in the USA. Upon this ketchup the fortunes of his new company would rise. Somewhat ironically, the logo for the new company would be the image of a cucumber pickle: whether Henry was cocking a snoot at the bankruptcy authorities, or humbly reminding himself that disaster could always strike, is unclear. In 1888 Henry bought out his brother and cousin and was in sole charge of his destiny.

How Did They Evolve?

Henry Heinz cast a long shadow over the development of the firm. Even as late as 1966 the company had still only had three CEOs; and the three were Henry, his son and grandson. And most of the familiar imagery associated with the company – the octagon-shaped ketchup bottle with its keystone label, neckband and screw top, promoted as one of the 57 Varieties - was in place by the turn of the twentieth century. Henry also bequeathed Heinz's trademark characteristics of salesmanship, initiative and quality. Heinz would be at every food show or country fair, giving away endless free samples backed by a money-back guarantee (unusual for those times). His travellers would sample their products at every sales call and pay the retailer to take down any old Heinz products past their best. But Henry saw that the less ethical companies were giving the entire prepared foods industry a bad name. Heinz products were pure, while it was not unusual for his competitors to be adding dyes, formaldehyde, sawdust and worse.

So Heinz went political. The company worked closely with the main advocate for food quality reform in the US Department of Agriculture. Henry campaigned relentlessly, even sending his son to the White House to give Teddy Roosevelt the hard sell. He finally sealed the deal - via the 1906 Pure Food and Drug Act -when he demonstrated to Roosevelt how adulterants were being used to transform gut-rot whiskey so it could be labelled as 10-year-old malt.

With the force of law behind it, the food industry went on an unprecedented boom, aided by a rapidly growing urban population with rising disposable incomes. Powered by this economic machine, the Heinz business prospered, still run very much on the founder's key principles. These he had enshrined in stained glass windows in his ever-expanding Pittsburgh factory, the most powerful being: 'To do a common thing uncommonly well brings success'. With the other manufacturers having to clean up their act, Heinz had to keep one step ahead in the quality stakes. So Henry's son (and a future Heinz CEO) Howard, who was himself a chemistry major, overcame his father's objections and hired a bacteriologist to lead the systematisation of the company's production processes. Hitherto this had seemed a domain of highly secretive processes amounting to his men dipping their fingers in the mixes rather than reading gauges.

In 1919 Howard succeeded his father as CEO and by 1924 was presiding over a vast, vertically-integrated food empire that relied on 150,000 acres of crops, 25 branch factories, over 100 salting stations, and nearly 800 rail cars. All this was kept busy by nearly 1,500 salesmen out touting for business, including 160 of them overseas, primarily in the UK and Canada. Production processes were vastly improved and in 1931, driven by the impact the Great Depression was having on business, the company saw that its reputation for unimpeachable quality and purity could be used to enter the baby food market. Heinz were far from being the first into the category, but they had the brand strength and the retail coverage that could get distribution for and trial of their first four offerings of strained peas, carrots, mixed vegetables and spinach. This new sector, along with their booming UK business, saw the company through until better economic times returned. In 1936, another trait of the current company was born when Heinz bred its first hybrid tomato seeds to send out to their contracted farmers.

In 1941, the founder's grandson, Henry John Heinz II, became the company's third CEO at the tender age of 33 and, once peacetime production resumed, presided over the next two decades of success as post-war affluence and the baby boom naturally grew their markets for them. But the boom years made Heinz complacent. Many of the key executives had been there for decades and although the company had gone public in 1946, it still ran as a long-established family firm. However, the third-generation family member appeared to have a fraction of the interest in the business as the founder, a common problem for family business dynasties. Whereas the original Henry had kept a diary every day detailing weather and crop growing conditions, Henry Mk II became more interested in travelling the globe, and new Heinz businesses he set up in the Netherlands and Japan were not successful.

The core business was still growing, but becoming increasingly unprofitable. By 1950 it was only making a 2.5% return on sales with matters not improving for another decade or more. The rise of the supermarket format in the US hit Heinz's venerable business model hard. Time-starved chain store branch managers had little time to sample the latest version of Heinz's product range. Food brokers became the industry's preferred means of order-taking and distribution. Margins were continually squeezed as Heinz products regularly played the role of the loss leader for the brash supermarkets. Aside from their highly profitable UK arm (of which more later), the company was barely breaking even; in 1963 over 80% of company profits came from the UK.

While the products were still excellent, the management of the company had failed to move with the times, a fact duly noted by Forbes magazine in a 1964 article, 57 Varieties of Trouble. The company was volume driven, had little awareness of market trends and was losing share to more sophisticated rivals.

How Did They Build Their Modern Business?

Salvation was at hand in the form of the company's fourth CEO, and first non-family member to assume the role: R. Bert Gookin, who had joined the board in 1960. As Vice President for Finance, Gookin persuaded the company to make its first domestic acquisition, of a local fruit-based drinks company. Another similarly underwhelming acquisition followed, but in 1963 Gookin hit the jackpot when he engineered the acquisition of StarKist. Their products, primarily canned tuna and pet-food, were both growing faster than Heinz's traditional area and the company expanded into another boom category – frozen foods - in 1965 when it purchased Ora-Ida foods. These two acquisitions really saved the US Heinz business by giving them time to get their house in order. A year later, Gookin was appointed CEO and was to preside over a remaking of the company.

In a prior role as head of the failing US division, Gookin had hired his Vice-President of Marketing from P&G. This was Heinz's first hiring of an externally trained marketer, but he was soon joined by several of his ex-colleagues. The company realigned itself behind a product management structure - the food service part of the company being separated out organisationally - and the company's marketing was restructured. Gookin next set about the rest of the organisation with a cost-cutting zeal, while simultaneously putting in place the systems and processes of a modern business. The sales force was slashed as the company focused on grocery chain head office buyers. Factories were updated and modernised, improving both quality and costs, and the spending on brand marketing was increased.

One of Gookin's top priorities had been to fix Heinz's ailing US soup business, where they trailed far behind Campbell's. After the ill-fated launches of Happy Soup for children and Great American Soups packaged in red, white and blue, the company switched out of a loss-making branded soup business and embarked on a much more successful private, or own-label soup, strategy. They became the dominant industry supplier, which eventually became the second-largest component of Heinz's US operation.

Despite the success of StarKist and Ora-Ida, Gookin's most significant acquisition came in 1967 when he authorised Heinz UK's partnership with an innovative Irish company, Erin Foods. The value came not so much from Erin's accelerated freeze-drying process, but from its managing director, Tony O'Reilly. A year later Gookin offered O'Reilly, then only 32, the job of managing director of Heinz's booming UK business. He was soon asked to oversee the flagship US operation where he really made his mark. When O'Reilly got there, StarKist was making nearly three-quarters of the US division's profits and most of the growth potential seemed to reside in Ore-Ida. On its traditional product lines, Heinz was shipping over 100 million cases a year and yet barely scraping a profit. Only ketchup and vinegar were market-leading brands.

StarKist had proved an inspired buy. The canned tuna part of the business was successful enough but the jewel in the crown was the pet food side. StarKist's management had got into the cat-food business in the mid-1950s as a way of profitably selling the by-products of tuna processing. StarKist's 9-Lives brand had initially prospered but by the time of the Heinz acquisition it was losing market-share. Heinz's P&G-trained marketers turned to the Leo Burnett advertising agency for help. They came up with Morris the 9-Lives Cat. Morris, who had been rescued from a New England animal shelter, was for a time Heinz's most productive employee, driving up sales to over 20% of the national market and keeping three canneries working flat out.

O'Reilly rapidly reorganised Heinz USA, instilling a much greater level of professionalism and setting the goal of becoming the lowest-cost operator in the industry. However, his greatest success in the role came with Heinz's 1978 acquisitions: of Weight-Watchers International (which ran Weight-Watchers meetings where revenues of $50 million were generated); and of Foodways International who held the license for the manufacture of Weight-Watchers branded frozen meals. The initial attraction had been Foodways, which O'Reilly saw as a good fit with Ora-Ida, but as Heinz learned more of Foodway's relationship with Weight Watchers, it became apparent that this was the real prize. By owning the brand itself, Heinz would have full scope to ride the upcoming health and fitness wave; as a mere licensee it would have been merely a bit-part player.

Another dramatic change, which would be instrumental in driving the revitalisation of the US business, took place over a prolonged period. It even started before Gookin's tenure: this was a complete revolution in the company's flagship tomato ketchup. On their arrival, Gookin's P&G marketing recruits faced the grim news that Heinz Tomato Ketchup's share of the market had slumped to 20%, neck and neck with Del Monte and Hunt's, and was losing money. The key to the coming revolution lay in reducing production costs by switching from making the product from fresh tomatoes, available seasonally, to a Heinz proprietary tomato paste, which would be available all year round. By smoothing the huge peaks and troughs of production, costs could be dramatically reduced. But could it be done without impacting the taste and quality? Yes it could. An unknown Canadian factory employee had made a suggestion: the company should consider the massively efficient evaporators used by the dairy industry to turn surplus liquid milk into milk powder. Once they had proven the process worked, Heinz set about re-engineering around the use of tomato paste and by 1968 was making 50% of its ketchup that way. Protected by patents at every stage of the process, it gave Heinz an advantage in cost and the ability to drive up production volumes, both of which had been limited by the uneconomic nature of the previous process. Advertising spend was ramped up while prices were kept keen. Sales doubled during the second half of the 1960s, and two years later, brand share was a market-leading 34%.

Once Heinz had switched to 100% paste production, the company's agronomists then set about developing tomato hybrids specifically suited to a paste production process. This was really the start of what has become a key part of the Heinz DNA – institutionalising the best tomato expertise. Heinz constantly developed new hybrids to optimise its proprietary processes. Competitors couldn't even use them if they managed to get hold of some from less-than-loyal farmers, as the hybrids didn't reproduce.

A year later, on Gookin's retirement, Tony O'Reilly became the company's fifth CEO. By the time Gookin handed over the CEO baton, he had overseen a transformation of the H.J. Heinz Company, tripled its sales and almost quadrupled its marketing spend as a percentage of sales. Heinz was now capable of moving to the next level. O'Reilly's first priority was to expand the Heinz global footprint.

How International Are They?

Famously, Heinz were given an international dimension by their charismatic founder, Henry, cold-calling on London's prestigious Fortnum & Mason in 1886, and getting a full listing for everything he pitched. The experience taught Henry another of the maxims by which he ran the business: that their field was the world. Having developed the UK business largely himself on his yearly visits and opening a sales office there in 1896, in 1905 Heinz sent his best manager, Charles Hellen, giving him carte blanche to develop as he saw fit.

This latitude would be the making of the business. One of Hellen's first moves was the purchase of a long-established British pickle and sauce manufacturer, Batty and Co. Ltd., giving him a production base and much improved distribution network. Hellen had been relying entirely on products imported from North America - Heinz Baked Beans had first been imported in 1901 - and set about phasing in new Heinz-branded products made locally. This was the first example of the Buy and Build strategy the company would be using 100 years later for new markets. Heinz Salad Cream, launched in 1914, was the company's first brand developed exclusively for the British market. By this time Heinz had also opened small factories in Canada and Spain.

Beans were the making of Heinz's British Empire. Hellen decided to leave behind the upmarket clientele of Fortnum & Mason and focussed his advertising upon working class towns and cities. Heinz Baked Beans became synonymous with good, cheap, nutritious food. Heinz also made a go of its soup business in Britain - Campbell's were slow off the mark entering the market - and was equally successful in canned pasta, salad dressings, ketchup and baby food. In each of these categories Heinz would build a market share of 70% or higher by 1960, and would have so influenced the British palette that they had the world's highest per-capita consumption of baked beans. So successful was this local strategy that, still today, Heinz is regularly voted one of Britain's most favourite brands.

Heinz's success in Britain and Canada naturally led it to look to Australia where a business was established in 1935 and again run with a completely local focus. The company mirrored its UK success, building up commanding positions in baked beans and soup. Although Heinz retained a booming export business, it was 1957 before they ventured abroad again. In what can only be described as an opportunistic rather than strategic expansion policy, Heinz purchased: a Dutch preserves company, built a factory in Venezuela in 1959, a joint-venture in Japan in 1962, an Italian baby-food business in 1963 that would prove a goldmine, a Mexican venture in 1964 that never made a cent, and in 1965 the British arm of the company bought a Portuguese tomato processing company.

The only one of these moves to have lasting significance was the 1963 purchase of the Milan-based Societa del Plasmon, whose business was predominantly baby biscuits, plus an insignificant range of strained baby foods. Heinz installed their latest equipment and processes for making strained baby foods, which, under the highly respected Plasmon brand name, soon became brand leaders in Italy. Baby food in Italy was and is regarded by the consumer as highly complex food bought mainly in pharmacies and thus able to command premium prices and high profit margins. Although Italy has one of the lowest birth rates in the world, it accounted for 25% of total European sales of baby food by the mid-1990s. It was an environment in which Plasmon managed to double its sales between 1987 and 1992, and now is the company's centre of excellence for baby food.

To manage this growing collection of mostly stand-alone businesses, Heinz gradually imposed some degree of head office control and coordination. Yet today Heinz remains more decentralised than most global companies: until 1959, overseas affiliates only had to consult head office for major capital investments and board-level appointments. In 1968, Gookin broke down the company's international division and made each affiliate a profit centre in its own right. An accounting scandal in one affiliate during the 1970s meant that head office's Global Headquarters Group took a much closer interest from that point on, approving and monitoring progress against annual budgets.

When O'Reilly took the helm in 1979, one of his top priorities was to push the Heinz brand much further afield. The realisation that Heinz only marketed its products in countries accounting for 15% of the world's population, and almost none in predicted future growth areas, galvanised the company to look seriously at entering developing markets. Much as they had led the way in setting up in the UK, Heinz was ahead of the curve in its entry into China. In 1984, only four years after China opened itself up to the West, Heinz was invited to manufacture infant cereal to address an endemic shortage of fortified weaning food. Initially the joint venture – agreed and signed in an amazing seven months - was for Heinz to operate only in Guangdong Province, where their new factory opened in June 1986. Being so early into China meant that Heinz had no other western companies to learn from but, conversely, they benefited hugely from first-mover status. They were among the first western companies to advertise on television in China and soon came to grips with the challenges of selling and distributing within the country. Two years later the factory had to be tripled in size and by the mid-1990s, Heinz was selling in 25 cities spread across half the country. It could now be found in Africa, Asia and Eastern Europe, and was setting up in South Korea, Thailand, Botswana, Egypt and, in 1994, India. There Heinz purchased Glaxo's Family Products division, primarily the Complan and Glucon D nutrition brands.

Heinz also did not neglect developed markets. They returned to Spain in 1987 (where they had previously sold an olive business), Greece in 1990 and New Zealand in 1993. Here they acquired, for $300 million, Watties Ltd, the largest food company in Australasia, and with substantial exports into Australia. In 1997 Heinz acquired Poland's leading producer of ketchup, Pudliszki. Weight

Watchers International, under Heinz's management, boomed overseas, generating 40% of its business outside of the United States, particularly as countries took over the brand manufacturing side.

Under O'Reilly, overseas operating divisions became less independent and were encouraged to adopt successes from other markets: for example the UK launched 9-Lives in 1993. But a key part of Heinz's international success lay in catering for local tastes. Thus the flagship Tomato Ketchup brand had significantly different recipes in the major markets: sweeter in the UK, Australia and Venezuela, but spicier in Central Europe.

The O'Reilly Years

It is very rare that a business progresses equally on all fronts. Rather a few runaway successes happen simultaneously. This is what happened for Heinz during the 1980s. The food-service side of the US business - previously something of an orphan once it had been separated out - more than doubled its sales during the decade. So successful had the operation become that Heinz were prompted to make a major acquisition in 1991 of JLFoods for $540 million from its Canadian owner, John Labatt Ltd.

A second gusher of the 1980s was Weight Watchers. The meeting side of the business thrived under Heinz's more entrepreneurial approach. They came up with innovations such as the "At Work" programme, reflecting the fact that the majority of women were now to be found in the workplace.

The food side of the business was a runaway success once Heinz's food scientists got to grips with developing low calorie meals that tasted just as good, if not better than regular ones. An early switch into microwaveable fibreboard trays in 1982 again fitted in with the busier lifestyles of the target market. Despite competition offered by the launch of Stouffer's Lean Cuisine in 1982, Weight Watchers went on to record share growth for 62 successive quarters. Powered by a constant stream of new products, they more than doubled the size of the business. By 1988, they were not only outselling Lean Cuisine but Weight Watchers branded frozen desserts were outselling Sara Lee.

However, the Weight Watchers growth ran out in 1990 and 1991, prompting O'Reilly to carve out a stand-alone company to give the brand the focus it needed to return to growth. The new Weight Watchers Food Company had its own sales, marketing, R&D, finance and some manufacturing functions. 40% of production and back end services such as purchasing and distribution would be handled by other Heinz units, in particular the frozen food division, Ora-Ida. The new management had the remit to challenge and re-invent everything, which they duly did, slashing new product lead times by a factor of six and re-formulating and re-presenting over half its 240 product lines within the first 15 months of operation. The new product range met the need for members to take a more personalised approach, moving away from the prescriptive regime, which had been the basis of the original Weight Watchers. New ranges such as Smart Ones and Personal Cuisine helped modernise the brand and grow sales.

The other big sales success of the 1980s had been the StarKist business. StarKist had expanded into the dog food market with a couple of acquisitions, most notably Jerky Treat in 1979, which trebled its sales within the next two years. The company built on this success, launching Meaty Bone and so creating the indulgent dog treat sector almost single-handedly. The entire product range was booming as the pet category had become one of the fastest-growing in the supermarket.

The tuna side of the business was also humming with the company shipping 40% of America's total consumption aided by having the majority of private label production. With record market shares on all fronts and annual sales approaching $1 billion, it had been a marvellous acquisition that had papered over a lot of the cracks in the mainstream US business.

However, the tuna business was changing. New fishing areas had opened up in the Pacific. This created a glut and the resulting price war exposed Heinz's relative high wage overhead compared to lower cost new entrants. The decision was taken to de-emphasise branded competition in tuna and basically to run a tuna procurement operation to supply the marketing-driven pet food side. Heinz wanted to place bigger bets in pet-food which, as a growth category was far outstripping most other parts of the portfolio. However its profit record had not yet matched its sales success. Three acquisitions were made within the space of nine months to beef up the pet portfolio, doubling the size of the business. In addition to a strong roster of brands, the company was now the largest supplier of private label to the American market.

But Heinz had not been the only company attracted to the pet-food market. Several other packaged goods giants had also either grown or bought their way into it. Pet-foods became a price football within the major retail chains (so much so, specialist pet stores almost exited the battle field to concentrate on high-end products). These retailer-driven price wars eroded margins and forced Heinz to rethink their approach. Despite their recent growth, Heinz were minor players in pet foods, with a portfolio of second-tier brands. As they already had a very well established private label programme, the decision was taken to switch from a consumer to a customer focus (as they had effectively done years earlier with soup).

The premium pet snacks business, which brought much higher margins, maintained its consumer-led strategy but the mainstream pet food business switched over to a private label/fighter brand approach. The results justified the change: volume share, including private label, almost doubled by the mid-1990s, as did the profits.

Heinz emerged from the 1980s in far better shape than they had entered it:

- The US mainstream business had at least started to turn a decent profit
- They had made some highly successful acquisitions
- The company had expanded its footprint globally and margins had increased substantially
- Heinz was widely recognised as a well-run company who were in cost-control, boosting their margins by almost 50%,
- Consumer marketing had become more innovative with the revitalisation of the ketchup business with new lines such as the plastic bottle
- Retail relationships were strong; the company was one of the few brand leaders to successfully incorporate a substantial private label component
- Food service business was booming.

Heinz was now unrecognisable from the sleepy, almost moribund company of the mid-1960s. In 1986 the company was rated one of Dun's Business Month's five best-managed companies and in 1990 O'Reilly was voted Chief Executive of the Year by Chief Executive Magazine. There had been some failures, such as frozen pizzas and frozen cookie dough, and it could be argued that not enough of the growth was coming out of the core Heinz branded products, but it was still an impressive turnaround. By the end of the decade, Heinz' sales had doubled and net profits quadrupled since 1980; market capitalisation having increased ten-fold from when O'Reilly had taken over.

While O'Reilly had benefited from several of the businesses simultaneously performing well, the 1990s began with several of them doing badly. Very few of Heinz's products could genuinely carry a price premium so price wars in pet-food and tuna meant Heinz had to respond; also, gluts in the supply of tomatoes and potatoes – the main ingredient of the Heinz brand and Ida-Ora brand respectively - gave private label the opportunity to widen the price differential with Heinz's leading brands, which put pressure on volumes as value-conscious consumers traded down. New distribution channels such as Club stores were also putting the squeeze on margins.

O'Reilly responded aggressively, convening his top managers from around the world in February 1992 and issuing a challenge to drive through radical change.

Market shares had to be restored and costs had to be slashed. The areas of focus were savings in procurement, reducing overheads, and improving marketing spend efficiency. Heinz was still more like a federation of independent companies rather than a cohesive multi-national so it is unsurprising that cost efficiencies and savings were also to be found by introducing more elements of centralisation. Thus purchasing operations were consolidated with the company seeking a small number of low-cost global suppliers. All the North American Heinz business units moved to one centralised back office for order processing, receivables and related functions. 40% of 1990s marketing budget was diverted from mainstream media and towards in-store activity and price support. Although 1994 sales were no greater than they had been in 1990, Heinz emerged from a two-year period of change with healthier market shares, a healthier bottom line, and a healthier, more aggressive management culture.

The acquisition strategy was also ramped up. JLFoods and Watties had transformed both the food service side and the potential for Heinz in Asia and the Pacific. These were followed up by Heinz acquiring the Farley's brand of baby biscuits in the UK, the All American Gourmet Company, makers of the Budget Gourmet frozen food range, and in March 1995 Heinz paid over $700 million to almost double the size of its pet food business, acquiring Quaker Oats' pet division. This was followed a year later by the acquisition of Earth's Best, a maker of organic baby food. The acquisition surge prompted the company to take a serious look at its structure.

How Are They Structured?

It is fair to say that, by 1997, Heinz was a somewhat convoluted company despite the best efforts of O'Reilly towards centralisation. In the US it had five major business units:

- Heinz USA, the largest affiliate in the company, covered ketchup, baby foods, sauces and condiments; it also had a very substantial private label soup business and a booming food service arm
- Star-Kist Foods, which was spilt into two divisions, Heinz Pet Products and StarKist Seafood (whose consumer business had been boosted by the company going 'dolphin-safe')
- Ora-Ida Foods, the country's largest processor of frozen potatoes to both retail and food service, branded and private label, together with a collection of frozen food brands in a variety of categories
- Weight Watchers International, which ran the meeting side of the business in over twenty countries, fitness facilities and even a publishing arm

- Weight Watchers Food Company, which produced a range of over 250 Weight Watchers by Heinz branded products across frozen, chilled and ambient

Outside the USA, there was barely a food category the company didn't compete in, more often than not under a brand name other than Heinz. In Italy the company made soft drinks, in England canned meats, in Zimbabwe soap, margarine in Korea, maple syrup in Canada and ice cream in New Zealand to mention a few. It was not a streamlined business. In 1997, Heinz embarked on what would seem a never-ending series of restructurings to get cost out and bring more coherence to their structure. They began with the $500 million sale to McCain Foods of the Ora-Ida food service and private label set-up.

O'Reilly passed the CEO baton to Heinz insider, William R. Johnson, who had a track record of simplifying and getting costs out. So Heinz set about closing or selling 25 factories and shedding thousands of staff. The retail side of Ora-Ida was combined with Weight Watchers Foods to create a new unit, the Heinz Frozen Food Company. This was then followed immediately by another downsizing as Heinz planned to close 20 of its remaining 100 factories. In 1999, the company sold Weight Watchers International to a Swiss venture capital firm for $735 million, as it had nothing to do with the running of a modern food business. At around the same time, rumoured merger talks with Bestfoods petered out, leaving Heinz to continue restructuring. The changes would improve Heinz's operating margin by four points up to 18.5% by 2000, better than was being managed by the soon-to-be-merged giants, Unilever and Bestfoods.

Organisationally, the biggest change was to change from a geographic management structure to a category one. Six key categories, accounting for over 80% of the company's sales, became the backbone of the new structure. For the new millennium, Heinz would be globally managed for the first time with the six core categories being:

- Ketchup, Sauces and Condiment
- Food Service
- Infant Feeding
- Tuna
- Quick-serve Meals
- Pet Foods

Heinz also focused its efforts behind its six core markets that generated 80% of company revenue: the USA, UK, Italy, Canada, Australia and New Zealand.

By 2000, although the restructurings had yet to pay off in terms of growth (top-line sales in the year were virtually identical to 1996), within the above categories the company had brands with number one or two positions in more than fifty countries and was generating nearly half its $9.4 billion sales from outside the USA. However, following another spate of acquisitions, products branded as Heinz now accounted for less than one-third of sales. The ketchup business benefitted from the category focus and the increased marketing spend, which was funded by the factory closures. It grew by nearly 10% in the year and reached a healthy 54% share in the USA, with innovations such as the EZ Squirt bottle and green ketchup still in the pipeline. Food service grew by 12.5% in the year to become a $1.6 billion business in its own right.

However, by far the largest organisational change to date, which resulted in the Heinz business of today, came in 2002 when Heinz spun off large parts of its US business and merged them with Del Monte. Thus, the US and Canadian pet foods and pet snacks business, tuna, infant feeding (where Heinz trailed dismally behind Gerber), retail private label soup and gravy, and their College Inn broth business were all hived off. The logic was unassailable. These were businesses that lowered growth rates, margins and had next to no synergy with Heinz's mainstream brands. The move led to the Heinz US business being greatly simplified (SKU count dropped from 13,100 to 7, 300) and leaving it focused on just two key areas: Ketchup, Condiments & Sauces (bolstered by the acquisition of Classico premium pasta sauces), and Frozen Foods (where the company had recently acquired rights to produce products under the TGI Friday brand name). At a stroke the Del Monte deal made Heinz the most internationally diversified US-based food company, reducing its US component to 44% of sales.

Organisationally, the company adopted the by now usual matrix structure of large, global companies: with a category structure for brand management and innovation, and a regional structure for implementation. By 2012, the company would re-focus again around the three main retail categories of Ketchup, Condiments & Sauces, Meals & Snacks, and Infant/Nutrition.

What Have They Been Doing in Recent Years?

2004

With the changes bedded in, the performance of Heinz began to improve. Sales of the remaining parts of the business in 2002 had totalled $7.6 billion, which had grown to $8.4 billion by 2004, with virtually all the growth coming from outside the US, half of it from the UK alone, helped by the earlier acquisition of the market-leading John West tuna brand. The other half of the international growth came mainly from a good acquisition: ABC, the leading soy sauce and juice brand in Indonesia, which was the fourth-most-populous country in the world.

Encouragingly, when looking at performance by category, half of total company growth had come in the core Ketchup, Condiments & Sauces area, helped by the introduction of the upside down ketchup bottle in 14 countries. This powered an 8% annual increase in ketchup volumes. Key emerging trends of health & wellness and Every Day Low Pricing (EDLP) were behind a lot of the company's activities; health & wellness driving its acquisition policy and EDLP its pricing/promotion strategy. The latter was a key reason why dollar sales were static in the US.

Simplification was still high on the agenda with 20% of SKUs being dropped in the year, on top of 20% that had been discontinued in 2003: these savings juiced an 8% increase in marketing spend. Heinz extended its presence in China with the purchase of frozen food company, Shanghai Longfong Foods.

2005

A top-line sales increase of nearly 6% represented good progress, but was heavily dependent on price increases and favourable exchange rates; volume inched upwards by only 1.9%. Sales of the top fifteen power brands, representing nearly two-thirds of total sales, were up over 7%. Overall company performance was dragged down by the remaining third of the business. Ora-Ida potato brands grew by 10% as the company's frozen foods category led the way with 13% annual sales growth. The Food Service division was bolstered by the acquisition of Appetisers, makers of high end frozen hors d'oeuvres. Meanwhile, the European businesses seemed becalmed with flat volumes. The company announced a strategic review of its European operations, sold the struggling HAK brand of prepared vegetables and acquired Britain's iconic HP and Lea & Perrins brands. Looking forwards, more emphasis was going to be placed on Russia, Indonesia, China and India where the company had already established footholds.

Heinz had entered Russia via its baby foods business. It used buckwheat-based products to suit local preferences, and this had helped establish the Heinz brand name. But Russia was also Europe's second-largest market for ketchup so a joint venture was agreed in the year with Petrosoyuz, Russia's leading maker of ketchup, mayonnaise, spreads and margarines. The ABC brand in Indonesia was powering ahead, as was the expanding Heinz portfolio in China. In India, Heinz had been manufacturing ketchup there since 2000 but its business was mostly focused on the nutrition brands purchased from Glaxo. Heinz targeted a 50% sales increase from these developing economies in 2006.

2006

2006 was a better year for Heinz as organic volume increased by nearly 4%, driven by the now healthy North American Consumer Products Division and the Asia Pacific region, both delivering volume increases of around 8%. In North America, Ora-Ida (averaging 10% volume growth a year since 2003) and TGI Fridays were the usual suspects; but ketchup was now humming. A succession of innovations over the previous three years had both grown the category and Heinz's share. There were two basic insights driving the growth. First, that ketchup was a fun product, as shown by the successes of EZ Squirt and coloured ketchups. Then, that, like other fun categories such as confectionery and soft drinks, consumption was elastic if driven by availability. Larger sizes, such as the new Fridge Door Fit bottle, and larger single serve catering packs, were driving increased consumption. Also, in the previous five years Heinz had launched over 25 new varieties of ketchup which accounted for over 40% of their 2006 U.S. ketchup sales. On the back of such growth, the company was able to reduce its retailer investment spend. Infant foods had also finally returned to growth, driven by Plasmon, the fourth-largest brand in Heinz's portfolio, rolling out new lines of baby yoghurts and cheeses.

The Heinz business had been radically re-engineered over the previous three years: the global SKU count had been more than halved from 35,000 down to 16,500; the US Consumer Products division was rated best in class in trade-spend efficiency; and the Heinz Global Innovation and Development centre in Pittsburgh was churning out record numbers of product innovations - over a hundred were lined up for launch in 2007. Heinz had become much more focused, agile and innovative. It had also made further divestments in Europe, selling off the John West tuna business.

2007

For the first time since the hiving off of the non-core US businesses, Heinz sales returned to the $9 billion level. Yet, growth was less than 1%, amid a pattern of sluggish volume. This was not a great short-term return from a hundred-plus new lines, and a $65 million increase in consumer marketing spend to support them. The North American Foods group was still growing at 2.6% but Food service moved backwards, prompting the two to be merged back together as one unit. Most of the good news was coming from overseas: here the Russia, Indonesia, China, India group, now joined by Poland, delivered 30% of the total company annual sales growth. Indonesia's ABC brand was now the world's second-largest brand of soy sauce, distributed to nearly all of Indonesia's 6,000 inhabited islands by a motorbike distribution fleet. In China, Long Fong was on its way to becoming a $100 million brand helped by a slew of new, upmarket dim sum launches. India's Complan brand was growing at 20% annually and Poland's Pudliszki brand had a complete restaging and grew by over 30%. Heinz was also doing well in Australia and Latin America.

Within the categories, the most encouraging trend was the continued growth on global sales of ketchup, up 9%, but Heinz was still suffering from a weak tail of either unbranded or non-Heinz branded lines doing badly, particularly in Europe.

2008

It seemed the investments in marketing and R&D were now paying off as sales jumped 12% - the best performance for fifteen years - to break the $10 billion barrier. There was good news on all fronts. A key driver of growth had been a doubling of the innovation rate from the previous year, Heinz bringing over 200 new lines to market supported by another double-digit increase in consumer marketing. This continued increase in investment and R&D had been made possible by the savings of over $500 million that had flowed from Heinz's simplification strategy since 2003. The company now had fifteen brands generating sales of over $100 million and the emerging markets business grew by 25%, providing 25% of the annual company sales growth while accounting for 13% of sales.

The joint ventures in Russia and China were now wholly owned, allowing Heinz to proceed at a faster pace. In China, Long Fong sales had doubled since its acquisition, as Heinz took the brand to second- and then third-tier cities, and providing small retailers with freezers to stock the brand. In Russia, now the world's second-largest market for ketchup, the Heinz brand was now market leader in Moscow and St. Petersburg, providing a springboard to extend its reach.

Strategically, following a top-level task force (set up the previous year) the company re-oriented itself around a consumer-centric health and wellness axis. Of course, Heinz had been in the health and wellness business ever since Henry Heinz sold his first jar of pure horseradish, so it was a consumer trend heading in Heinz's direction. The company identified four key areas:

- **Lifestyle** (promoting general health and wellness). The Heinz products in this category, such as organic ketchup, Farmers Market products and low fat options, grew by 11% in 2008, but the company did not see itself as naturally advantaged in this area. Work here was focused on developing low salt, sugar- and fat-free versions of existing brands.
- **Children's Nutrition** (Infants, toddlers and children). Here the company was growing faster at over 17%, driven by infant feeding lines in

emerging markets. Brands like Complan were targeted as an illness-related dietary supplement for older people in the west, but in India as a vitamin-enhanced drink for children. The company was investing in a new R&D centre of excellence for this category in Milan, home of the Plasmon brand.

- **Weight Management**. (Enabling/promoting weight reduction, maintenance). Here the jewel in the crown was the Weight Watchers brand, now generating annual sales of $800 million. This was growing relentlessly, driven by the Weight Watchers Smart Ones range, which the company was rapidly expanding. Sales in this area had increased 25% the previous year.
- **Health Management** (Science-influenced foods and beverages). This was really a niche area for the company, mainly based on a couple of gluten-free brands in Italy.

Together, the Heinz brands that fell into these four categories comprised 60% of total sales and were growing at nearly twice the industry rate. The company's acquisition strategy would be to search for companies advantaged in at least one of these four areas.

2009

As Heinz's financial year-end falls in April, their 2009 performance was heavily influenced by the difficult trading conditions in 2008 that followed the financial crash. Unlike many consumer goods companies, Heinz was still able to report another sales increase, albeit marginal at just less than 1%. The stronger US dollar hammered reported sales from overseas where the underlying sales trends were still largely positive: Emerging markets sales grew by nearly 16% excluding currency impacts. The company's greatest marketing success had been its health and wellness-influenced Grown not Made campaign on ketchup. This helped grow global sales by 9%, which in turn contributed to a sales growth of over 13% in the company's top-15 brands. The company also took advantage of the economic conditions to make three significant acquisitions in the year: Benedicta, a French maker of sauces, mayonnaise and dressings, La Bonne Cuisine in New Zealand, which made chilled dips and hummus and Golden Circle, iconic Australian maker of fruit-based foods and beverages.

The new Heinz was a very recession-resilient business, but management recognised that the economic issues represented a sea-change rather than a blip in consumer buying behaviour. Increasingly frugal and thrifty, value-conscious western shoppers were heading into Club stores and Dollar stores, making them the two fastest-growing sales channels in North America. These channels usually demanded tailor-made packs to hit price points, but Heinz were already very well established in them, having had a strong trade marketing focus as the channels had emerged.

2010

Off essentially flat volumes, Heinz delivered a 5% increase in dollar sales. This showed the strength of their brands in being able to withstand commodity-driven price increases in all its markets, and supported by a substantial increase in consumer marketing spend. Innovations were also still being rolled out at the usual pace, with many healthier options of existing brands hitting the shelves. More of the disadvantaged long tail of products was divested during the year as the company transitioned back to its roots of being a ketchup and condiments company that sold a few other things. Ketchup and sauces was now the largest category in the business, delivering virtually all the annual growth.

The recession seemed to have convinced Heinz that perhaps this wasn't the time to completely orientate the company around health and wellness segments: value was now the name of the game. Emerging markets continued their growth trajectory for the company, generating 30% of the sales growth and now 15% of total sales. Sales in the company's Asia/Pacific region topped $2 billion for the first time, a number boosted by the acquisition in the year of China's Foodstar company, the country's leading producer of branded soy sauce and bean curd. Heinz's local focus had realised that they could best introduce their global brands on the back of strong local infrastructures of culturally relevant products, such as soy sauce.

2011

Again off essential flat volumes, Heinz managed to inch its top line ahead by 1.9%. Not bad in recessionary times, but not spectacular either. The year showed the inherent problem in the Heinz portfolio: while progress was made on several of the biggest brands: virtually all the sales growth came in the ketchup and sauces category with Heinz Ketchup growing almost 4% due to innovations such as the PlantBottle - licensed from Coca-Cola - and Heinz Tomato Ketchup with Balsamic Vinegar in the UK, although these were offset by declines elsewhere in the portfolio. The recession was not kind to secondary and tertiary brands, of which Heinz, due to the somewhat scattergun acquisitions during the O'Reilly years, still had more than its fair share. Thus, for every success - TGI Friday's single-serve entrees, Smart Ones breakfast wraps and Classico Light Alfredo Creamy Sauce - there weredeclines: Boston Market in the US and Honig in The

Netherlands. Equally, the Food Service business was hostage to the performance of restaurant foot traffic. But at least the sales growth was coming from the right areas: the big brands - up 3.8% in the year - and emerging markets, where another good year of 12% growth was based on organic growth in the company's key categories of ketchup, condiments and baby food. Their emerging market profile was bolstered by a major acquisition in Brazil of the manufacturer of Quero, a rapidly-growing brand of tomato-based ketchups, sauces and condiments. This was an acquisition in the right product categories where Heinz has genuine advantage and in the right part of the world.

2012

Now it looked as though Heinz was out of the woods, registering a 9% sales increase to over $11.6 billion. But all this was simply masking the same portfolio issues. All the increase came from a favourable sales mix, increased pricing and favourable currency exchange: volume actually declined slightly. In a similar pattern to the previous few years, the areas of good growth continued to grow – ketchup 10% and ketchup and sauces combined by 14%; some areas broke even – infant/nutrition was booming in emerging markets but struggling in developed; and other areas, such as frozen foods and food service, continued to be weak.

Geographically, Heinz' performance is also somewhat schizophrenic. In the previous two years, Heinz top-line sales had increased by slightly over $1.1 billion, 95% of this increase coming from markets other than Heinz's two largest - the USA and UK - which still account for almost half of company sales. By category, Meals and Snacks, which accounts for 38% of total sales, has delivered 16% of the growth in the past two years. Infant Nutrition, 10% of total sales, delivered 6% of the growth. Meanwhile Ketchup and Sauces delivered almost 70% of company growth.

What is Their DNA?

While the company has had a somewhat chequered history, finding itself in virtually every food category in the grocery store at some time or other, we believe the Heinz DNA can be boiled down to three simple components: quality, tomatoes, and global management

Quality

Heinz is one of the world's best-known food brands, with a reputation for quality second to none. Generations of consumers across the globe have trusted

Heinz to feed their precious babies and there can surely be no more compelling demonstration of what it means to trust a company. It is a reputation that simply cannot be bought. Although much of the Heinz portfolio – too much - does not benefit from this (due to the still vast collection of acquired brand names), quality is instilled in their culture and has been since Henry Heinz used clear glass bottles and removed dated product from shelves a century before. In today's no logo world of cynicism and distrust in the motives of large companies, Heinz stands above the fray. No-one can beat Heinz on trustworthiness.

Tomatoes

It is difficult to think of another food company that has an inbuilt, structural advantage in their core raw ingredient. In other food categories many companies claim to purchase only the finest coffee beans, or cocoa beans, or potatoes, and maybe some do. But no one else purchases as many tomatoes, knows them so well, has a history of constantly developing superior hybrids (Heinz has been breeding them since 1936 and has the world's largest database) and has such direct relations with its growers (Heinz can trace 90% of its tomatoes back to the field they were grown in). Quite simply, they have better tomatoes, not just in one year by paying top dollar or getting lucky with climate, but every year, embodied by their proprietary HeinzSeed programme. This trait is not a fad or a whim of an itinerant CEO, it flows straight from the veins of the company founder, Henry J. Heinz. It defines the company. If the company can develop a similar expertise to underpin its rapidly growing soy sauce business in emerging markets, then long-term success will be assured.

Global Management

This might seem a strange choice. There are plenty of companies who do well around the world, but no American food companies do it as well as Heinz. Approximately three-quarters of their sales come from outside the USA. They started very early, setting up a UK business over 100 years ago, and have learned over time the fine art of blending global capability with local preferences. Food, more than any other category, is one where consumers differ locally and, with few exceptions, are reluctant to adopt the preferences of others. Heinz managed the transition from a confederation of stand-alone businesses to one managed globally, along category lines, very well. Their packaging and product innovations are rolled out very rapidly around the world, but always to match the taste preferences and brand personas of the local markets. Nobody does it better! In the food business.

Summary

The Heinz history can be split into four basic parts. While family-managed, the three Heinz Chairmen built a ketchup and condiments empire, developing one of the world's most trusted brand names in the process. Then, the company managed to survive the transition from family-run to manager-run, primarily because of the foresight of the founders in building a highly profitable UK company that was always run by top managerial talent. The third phase was the O'Reilly years, when the company became much broader and much leaner, a better financial performer and with a stock that could be trusted to deliver superior returns. They made some astute acquisitions that caught big waves at the right time, Ora-Ida and Weight-Watchers being two good examples. We believe the company is just entering its fourth phase of getting back to its core of being a ketchup, condiments and sauces company and developing it on a truly global scale.

This being the case, it is not surprising that Heinz has laid out a much more focused strategy than had previously been the case:

- Our predominant focus is on driving continued global growth in Ketchup and Sauces, our largest core category with sales of more than $5 billion.
- We are using our advantaged, well-balanced geographic portfolio, led by our accelerating growth in emerging markets
- We are building and increasingly capitalizing on unique global capabilities and infrastructure to support continued growth and improved productivity.

This can be paraphrased as:

- Sell more ketchup and soy sauce . . .
- . . . In Emerging Markets . . .
- . . . Which is where we will invest . . .
- . . . Developed Market business units need to cut their costs.

And who can really argue with this? Consumer markets are becalmed in the developed world. Heinz's US business is 40% frozen meals and snacks where they have no structural advantage, so it is no surprise they are cutting back, exiting the Boston Market and subsequently the TGI Friday's franchises, closing factories and even downsizing the Long Fong business in China. One might well ask why they stay in the frozen foods business at all. Baby food is a strong category for Heinz in emerging markets, and a good one in which to build and enhance the Heinz brand name. But it is going nowhere for them in developed, as birth rates fall off the chart and competition is fierce (Heinz are global number 3 in prepared baby food).

On the Ketchup and Sauces side, life is currently tough in developed markets due to the economic conditions, so Heinz's innovation is more aimed at new packaging formats to hit lower price points in value-driven channels, such as their 10-ounce ketchup pouch priced at $1. Food service, 30% of US sales, is probably more of a necessary evil than an engine for growth in ketchup.

However, in emerging markets they can barely keep up with demand – Heinz Ketchup began manufacture in Brazil in 2012 – and their soy sauce brands are doing equally as well. Emerging markets account for 7 of the top 10 markets for Ketchup and Sauces, where Heinz is very well positioned. Globally the Ketchup and Sauces category is colossal, valued at $110 billion and is highly fragmented. Heinz, number two globally, have less than 5% share, so the potential is enormous. It is their highest margin business and the only one where they are structurally advantaged. They are developing their expertise base away from Pittsburgh by building innovation centres for ketchups and sauces in Europe with one to follow in Asia.

The time is right for Heinz to get back to doing what their founder set up to do: selling meal-enhancing ketchups, condiments and sauces, but this time to everyone on the planet.

Henkel

Where Did It Come From?

Friedrich Karl Henkel, known throughout his life as Fritz, first developed an interest in industrial chemistry when he joined a paint and varnish firm as a trainee at the age of seventeen. Seven years later, in 1874, he left to set up a chemicals and paint wholesaling business, Henkel & Strebel, where as a wholesaler he would have come into contact with many of the key German chemical industrialists. Only two years later, on 26th September 1876, he left wholesaling, teaming up with the two owners of a factory producing sodium silicate (water-glass) to begin manufacturing a new kind of detergent largely based on the product. The new firm, Henkel & Cie, of Aachen in the Rhineland, took the radical step of actually packaging its new product, in contrast to its competitors who supplied retail outlets in bulk; the retailers ladled or poured out themselves, in the store.

Two years later, having bought out his two partners, Fritz himself developed a new product, Henkel's Bleich-Soda, a bleaching agent made from water-glass and soda, which he launched as Germany's very first branded detergent. But he soon realised that sleepy Aachen was a bit off the beaten track for reaching the burgeoning industrial towns of the Ruhr, so in that same year he relocated to Düsseldorf. Sales of Henkel's Bleich-Soda rocketed and Fritz outgrew his rented factory within a year. So he built his own and linked it directly to the main rail network.

By 1883, Fritz had his own salesmen on the road. But he was struggling to cope with the costs of a dedicated sales force. So, drawing on his wholesaling experience, he decided to spread the fixed costs across a broader product range, and set up as the agent for a range of products: an ultramarine dye, starch, beef extract and a hair pomade. This mixed bag, he reasoned, would pay for the extension of his own brands but could be dropped progressively as and when his own sales grew. The practice of the time was that of roaming sales force, which took initial orders and nothing else. The customer himself had to contact head office for follow-up quantities. Fritz was having none of that. He organised a set of concentrated and well-defined sales districts in which customers were called on with what one supposes must be described as Teutonic regularity. This provided full sales coverage for all his products in 280 towns across the entire country.

Rather than simply using wholesalers, Fritz had adopted this route for product sales, as he was a firm believer in keeping as much of his operation as possible in-house. He also applied this philosophy to the supply of his raw materials, buying the water-glass factory from his former partners and transferring the equipment to Düsseldorf. This was an independent streak that would indelibly shape the future direction of the company, although it threatened to get out of hand when he added Henkel's Thee, Germany's first branded tea, to the product list. The tea was eventually dropped in 1913, although at its high point it had produced more than 10% of sales.

Fritz's own water-glass was not just an ingredient for Henkel's Bleich-Soda but could also be used as raw material for other industrial firms, which turned Fritz's mind to the ever-increasing quantities of waste, primarily potassium, generated by the production process. In 1897, he created a potassium-based fertiliser, which he branded Martellin, which he sold to growers of tobacco, wine-grapes and hops, all products which conformed to the agenda of 19th-century hard-working Germans: sustainability. By the turn of the century, his three top sellers, Henkel's Bleich-Soda, Henkel's Thee and Martellin, plus industrial water-glass, topped one million marks, driven principally by an annual sale of ten million packs of Henkel's Bleich-Soda. This mix of consumer and industrial products would remain a unique feature of the Henkel business model throughout its history.

How Did It Evolve?

Henkel the company stemmed directly from Fritz's enduring interest in chemistry. He was an avid student of everything that was new in chemistry – globally, an early adopter, for example, of the Twitchell process for the hydrolysis of fats into fatty acids, which included the stearic and oleic acids used in detergent manufacture and their by-product, glycerol. But it was Fritz's hiring of chemist Dr Hermann Weber in 1906 that sowed the seeds of his big breakthrough. Dr Weber's task was to research the possible uses of oxygenated salts to act as bleaching agents when combined with soap. Until then, soap powders were just basically pulverised soap. The whiteness of the wash depended entirely on the physical efforts of the housewife. But combine a bleaching agent with the soap and the wash itself would do the work, obviating the need for separate rubbing and bleaching.

Hermann's appointment paid off almost immediately: the very next year there was a product to launch. Looking for a name, Fritz decided to combine elements of its two principal ingredients – perborate and silicate – and came up with Persil, which was launched on 6th June 1907 as the world's first self-acting detergent. Since this saved countless hours of hard, physical graft, it is no surprise that Germany's Hausfrauen fell over themselves to buy what really was a new and life-changing product. Within a year, Fritz had to increase his workforce by 50% and was scouring the world for automated packing machinery to turn out the first year's 4,700 ton production.

By 1909, Fritz was already looking to export his modern-day miracle to other European markets. Whilst a small market like Switzerland could be supplied from his own factory, the much larger French and British markets could not. For France, Fritz concluded a licensing agreement with a local manufacturer, the Société d'Electro Chimie, but in England he was faced with an immovable object: William Lever and the colossal Lever Brothers, already a direct competitor in Germany and the last place Fritz wanted to leave the secrets of his new invention. And Lever was dangerously predatory, busily taking over most of his major rivals. Fritz had no intention of being taken over by anyone, and turned to the highly reputable firm of Joseph Crosfield & Sons Ltd, granting it the patent rights and trademarks of Persil for the United Kingdom and various British, Dutch and Danish colonies. He might have been better off spending time with a decent contracts lawyer, instead of rushing into the new markets as fast as he could. Within ten years, William Lever had bought both Persil licensees, plus the rights to the Persil brand in France, the UK and much of the British Empire. Fritz Henkel would forever regret losing control of a leading detergent brand in some of the world's leading detergent markets.

But this calamity was still ten years away. In the meantime, Fritz was wrestling with the twin challenges of building the Persil brand in Germany as quickly as possible and finding other ways to expand the business. In 1910, the waste product glycerol was turned into profitable us: Henkel built dedicated production facilities that would make him Europe's largest producer of glycerine by the outbreak of the First World War. As glycerine was a key ingredient of dynamite and cordite, business boomed. By 1912, Henkel was churning out nearly 50,000 tons of product a year, of which, only five years after its launch, Persil contributed a massive 40%.

Although Henkel was largely self-sufficient - Fritz's insistence on controlling as much of his supply chain as possible - the outbreak of war, a British Royal Navy blockade and non-negotiable requisitioning by the German military machine did give pause for thought: sooner or later, supplies and raw materials might run out. Glue was deemed most at risk, so the Henkel laboratories, set up in the early 1900s, began experimenting with making adhesives out of their plentiful water-glass. In 1916, the raw materials situation tightened: government controls on the supply of fats meant that Persil had to be reformulated to a war-time, soap-free version. Production of the brand ceased entirely in 1918. The company immediately responded to this setback by launching Sil (No Per), a concentrated detergent and bleach product.

Despite the cataclysmic scale of the First World War, however, the Henkel business remained remarkably unaffected. In 1917, the company was even able to make an acquisition, of the Matthes & Weber soda works, whose principal product it could vertically integrate into Henkel's Bleich-Soda. Rather more difficult to deal with was the French occupation of the Rhineland, which put the main factory behind enemy lines. Henkel's uncompromising solution was to build a new factory in central Germany, even though the company did not need the extra capacity, simply the access to its their main market. However, the increased capacity would prove very useful later on.

By 1920, matters had largely returned to normal. Persil was back on the market in its original formulation and the product range was extended with Ata, a scouring agent designed to launch the company into household cleaning products. The next year, the venerable Henkel's Bleich-Soda was given a friendly makeover by rebranding it as Henko, which heralded something new: an emphasis by Fritz on the importance of branding and advertising. In 1922, a new advertising campaign for Persil featured what would become an iconic German image for the brand, Die Weisse Dame (the White Lady), omnipresent on German advertising hoardings until well into the 1960s.

In 1923, the French occupied of the Ruhr Valley. But this disaster for Germany was a blessing in disguise for Henkel. It forced the company to begin the manufacture of its own glue supplies. Excess product was sold to other glue-deprived companies. There was a ready demand. In fact, there was a ready demand in a high-potential market, particularly with decorators. So the company set about developing specifically targeted products, launching Henkel-Kleister-trocken (dry paste) in 1928 followed by Mala, a cold-water-soluble glue, a year later. Thus began what would become Henkel's largest product category.

A visit to the United States by Fritz's son, Dr Hugo Henkel, introduced another ace to the deck. Henkel junior had become excited about the American use of phosphates for cleaning metal surfaces, so on his return, the laboratories immediately set about developing new products for industrial cleaning, duly launched under the brand name Pedrei. The same technology backed the household cleaner Imi in the first of what would be many crossovers from Henkel's industrial division to consumer side of the business, a combination of branded industrial and branded consumer markets that would become an enduring Henkel trademark. Further good news followed. In 1927, a truce with Lever Bros. on the thorny issue of Persil rights was finally declared: Lever kept the brand for the UK, France and the two countries' colonies while Henkel took the rest of the world. The fortunes of the Persil brand, along with its formulation and variants, now begin to diverge: each company developed Persil as it saw fit.

Henkel, now run by Hugo Henkel, now began both to expand and to acquire. Expansion, through products of its own invention, saw it move into an increasing variety of consumer and industrial markets, whilst series of acquisitions to accelerate the process. Henkel bought floor polish and furniture polish companies, as well other German detergent manufacturers, including the makers of Germany's first synthetic detergent, Fawa. The company was also rapidly developing new ingredients to improve its booming adhesives business and, as was the Henkel way, setting up factories to produce them rather than relying on outside suppliers. And once again, potential disasters turned into hidden benefits. When the National Socialist government put swingeing, impossibly restrictive new conditions on the production and use of fats and oils, Henkel to set up a whaling company and send the company fleet off to the Antarctic. Increasingly tight controls only fostered Henkel creativity. The times were difficult, yet the company made substantial technical breakthroughs on new adhesive compounds. Necessity was truly the mother of invention.

But it could not quite match the next cataclysm. The outbreak of the Second World War saw both Persil and Fawa taken off the market and Henkel's range - by now more than 200 products – was dramatically scaled back and reformulated. But acquisitions could still be made and the company's laboratories still came up with new developments: methods of dealing with detergent-induced irritation in sensitive skin and specific synthetic detergents for coloured fabrics. Company involvement in new uses for cellulose, particularly in adhesives, was also growing very strongly. But the war had its way in some areas. Whilst the company's factories suffered little bomb damage, much more disruptive was the occupation of the main Düsseldorf factory by the Americans and the outright confiscation of Henkel's shiny new detergent factory in the Soviet occupation zone. And when the Third Reich did fall, almost the entire senior management team was interned.

Family members and executives were released in 1947, to the shattering Allied announcement that 70% of Henkel's remaining production capacity was to be dismantled, along with that of more than 900 other German factories. The family called in every favour they could, including some from key industry contacts in the US, managed to get most of their factories off the hit list and, with a mostly intact production and research infrastructure, wasted little time in getting back to business as usual. Perwoll and Lasil, its new synthetic detergents, were launched in 1949, the same year that Procter & Gamble's Tide went national in the US. A year later, Henkel bought itself into hair colourants category and brought back Persil, now enriched with 'optical brighteners'.

In 1950, the company launched a new generation of synthetic resin-based adhesives that signalled the start of a very innovative decade for the adhesives product range, which would launch a multitude of targeted new products based on new technologies. Detergents saw similar progress, side with the launch of Pril dishwashing liquid in 1951, Fa soap in 1954, Dixan in 1957 (formulated for the new drum-style washing machines) and Persil 59 in 1959, the company's first heavy-duty synthetic detergent. As well as developing new products, Henkel was exploiting new promotional styles. It ran West Germany's first-ever television commercial for Persil. It was turning international too, expanding its reach into countries as far afield as Japan and Brazil. And it continued to research: much work was also being done on low-foam surfactants, which set Henkel on the path to industry leadership in the detergents of the future: biodegradables.

How International Are They?

Henkel's remorselessly efficient march to global giant-hood began early: it opened an Austrian sales office in 1886. Three years later, orders were being taken in the Netherlands and Switzerland, soon followed by Italy and the UK. In 1913, the first foreign subsidiary was set up in Switzerland, a smart move: in neutral Switzerland business was conducted there unhindered for the duration of both sets of hostilities. By the end of the 1920s, the company was exporting to almost all European countries as well as Australia and South America. As the export trade grew during the early 1930s, business was sufficiently large for manufacturing subsidiaries to be set up in Norway, the Netherlands and Belgium and by 1937 Henkel owned production facilities in twelve European countries. Unfortunately for Henkel, all were expropriated or nationalised after the Second World War, forcing the company to start again from scratch.

But as early as 1951 the company was sufficiently back on its feet to open its first overseas subsidiary in South Africa. Three years later there was an exclusive trading partner in Japan, the start of a prolonged series of joint ventures in that country culminating in an agreement to market Henkel products with the Japanese Lion Corporation. In 1955, Henkel do Brazil SA was founded; a series of acquisitions there gave Henkel adhesives market leadership. In 1959, a similar story played out in Mexico after the founding of Henkel Mexicana SA. In the 1960s, Turkey and Argentina were added to the list and in 1971 offices were opened in London, Montreal, Athens and Hong Kong, followed by Lagos and

Bangkok a year later. The 1972 Solvite acquisition made Henkel the UK adhesives market leader.

In 1977, there was a step change. Henkel bought General Mills Chemicals, Inc., which had substantial operations in the US, Ireland, Brazil and Japan. Now, foreign acquisition followed foreign acquisition, all in the careful Henkel style, leading to a 1988 entry into the Chinese market in 1988 soon after foreign companies were allowed to enter and an approach Henkel had diplomatically stage-managed by restoring a 747-metre stretch of the Great Wall. The wall building paid off handsomely, as the company now has fifteen subsidiaries and joint ventures in China. Henkel was equally quick off the mark when another wall was not repaired but demolished, moving very swiftly into both Russia and Poland. By 1995, Henkel had seventeen companies in Central and Eastern Europe.

By 2011, 68% of company employees were located outside Western Europe, 55% in emerging markets. Henkel's European region is still the largest, turning over around €8.5 billion. Next in size is North America, with sales of €2.7 billion, then Asia-Pacific at €2.3 billion each, Latin America at just over a billion euros with Africa and Middle East not far behind at €930 million. With 85% of its sales coming from outside Germany, Henkel is the most global of companies.

How Did They Build The Modern Business?

By now the running of the company had passed to the third generation of the Henkel family, normally a risky transition for family-run business. But two sons of Dr Hugo Henkel, Jost Henkel and subsequently his brother Dr Konrad Henkel (Jost died suddenly in 1951 at the age of 52), successfully propelled the business out of the post-war chaos, added a new stability and finally launched the company into a new, expansionist phase that would create a global enterprise. The new intent was signalled in 1960 with the first American acquisition, Standard Chemical Products, Inc., a manufacturer of textile industry chemicals and adhesives, and the 1962 purchase of Henkel's main adhesives competitor in West Germany, Sichel-Werke AG, founded by the inventor of the first ready-to-use decorators' paste. New products such as Dor, an all-purpose cleaner; Somat, for automatic dishwashers; and Saptil, an innovative tube-dispensed stain pre-treatment, ensured the household cleaning businesses kept growing.

Detergents were a different matter. Henkel had had a pre-Tide technology-sharing agreement with P&G, so P&G's late 1950s announcement of its intention to enter the West German market did not go down at all well in Düsseldorf. Henkel broke off the relationship. P&G responded by offering to buy the company, an offer Henkel flatly refused. Both companies limbered up for battle. P&G opened an office in Frankfurt in 1960 and immediately set about looking to buy manufacturing and route-to-market capability. By 1962, Camay and Fairy were being produced under contract; a year later P&G opened its first West German factory.

In the early phase of its market entry, P&G had two distinct advantages over Henkel. First, with a number of breakthrough brands - Crest toothpaste, Crisco shortening, Head & Shoulders shampoo and Lenor fabric conditioner, all of which became very successful in West Germany - it had a greater critical mass in the grocery. Second, it had detergent innovations in the pipeline - Ariel, for example, launched in Germany in 1967 – that were ahead of anything Henkel had. Even so, it wasn't quite all plain sailing. P&G was still a naive enough internationalist not to appreciate crucial local differences, particularly the European preference for low sud-quotient washing machines powders; low sud-quotient next to Tide, anyway. Nevertheless, P&G established itself in West Germany, cementing its permanence with some acquisitions.

So Henkel lost a significant amount of its home market share as the P&G Tide came in. But it did far better than Unilever. When the somewhat sleepy Unilever threat materialised, Henkel responded aggressively, launching a slew of new products: Persil 65, with its temperature-dependent foaming control agent, Dato, for white fabrics, Weisser Riese for heavily soiled white fabrics, Fewamat for automatic washing machines, Henk-o-mat prewash detergent and Fakt, the company's first enzyme-based detergent. Henkel's strategy was to segment the market as much as possible and box Tide in. Unilever's own tide went out; you might say it was taken to the cleaners.

As the competitive dramas played in the foreground, in the background Henkel was laying the groundwork for a longer-term response to P&G's assault on its heartland. A good ten or twenty years ahead of the competition, Henkel set up an ecology department in its Düsseldorf laboratories, focused on finding fully biodegradable surfactants and a replacement for phosphates. And Henkel could also continue to grow its adhesives business virtually unhindered and, in 1969, it made the crucial leap of combining an adhesive innovation with its well-honed consumer marketing skills to create Pritt, the world's first glue stick, almost instantly a standard fixture in every offices and school in Europe.

By acquisition and its own inventiveness, Henkel had also gained a foothold in cosmetics and toiletries sectors, particularly since the launch of Creme 21, a hand cream. So, in 1971, it merged these various elements to create one focused business unit, while still adding to its ever-expanding ranges of household cleaners and detergents. In 1974, the company took another major step, this time into the American market, buying a significant shareholding in the Clorox Company. Clorox produced and marketed some of Henkel's brands in the US, Canada and Puerto Rico in return for access to Henkel's formidable research and development expertise. Henkel was now also by expanding rapidly overseas: in Australia, Guatemala, Venezuela, Indonesia and Jamaica.

The laboratories' search for a phosphate replacement in detergents had also come up trumps with the patenting of the compound Sasil in 1974. Three years later, the company's first low-phosphate brand, Prodixan, completed trials. Sasil trumped anything P&G or Unilever had to offer; it was the engine that regained Henkel's dominant share of the European detergents market. More technological breakthroughs followed: HEDP, a tartar inhibitor which in 1979 propelled Henkel into the toothpaste market in Theramed, Weisser Riese with Sasil had hit the market in the same year.

Meanwhile, in 1980, in America, Henkel bought itself into the automotive supply industry and acquired a maker of adhesives for the household and schools sectors. Back in West Germany, the company re-launched Persil, with Sasil, as a low-phosphate brand, having already won both consumer and retailer approval with two previous brands using the compound. There were also further acquisitions in the German personal care category.

But these imaginative and clearly decisive moves were testing the internal structure of the company. The key issue hinged on ownership. When Fritz had died he had willed a third of his shares in to each of his three sons. The tradition had continued since, with the result that the company now 66 family owners of the company, most of who did not work in the business. It was this diffuse arrangement that was beginning to restrict both the company's access to capital - to fund the increasingly large acquisition and overseas expansion strategies – and its ability to make quick decisions when it had to. So the family decided to take the company public, issuing non-voting preference shares but keeping 100% ownership of the voting ordinary shares. The family, or parts of it, could continue to control the direction of the business – they still own around 80% of the ordinary shares – while being able to fund more ambitious moves. And there was now a far better defined authority structure, a consequence of the flotation.

A sign of the powers came in 1987, when Henkel acquired a minority stake in the US Loctite Corporation, America's leading sealants and adhesives firm. It wasn't that Henkel couldn't now afford a full bid; it was just that it preferred to approach acquisitions cautiously, looking long and hard at all potential purchases, retaining the existing management where possible and avoiding currently unprofitable companies or those with too different an operating cultures. The company was by no means afraid of forming strategic partnerships: they were a low-risk way of evaluating new markets and potential acquisitions. In 1988, the Wall Street Journal described the approach as 'a blend of America's short-term interest on profit and West Germany's long-term emphasis on the future'. The result? Very few, if any, of Henkel's acquisitions came unstuck. The same year revenues exceeded ten billion Deutschmarks for the first time.

With Persil completely phosphate-free by 1987, Henkel published new corporate guidelines which placed environmental protection on an equal footing with profits as company objectives. This was one of the advantages of continuing family control; such commitments could be made without objections from bothersome activist shareholder and financial analysts. This early commitment to environmental protection would be to Henkel's competitive advantage in the future. As early as 1989, all Pritt products were solvent-free and all company detergents sold in West Germany phosphate-free; these were both industry firsts.

In 1990, following the fall of the Berlin Wall, Henkel re-entered the East German market, buying back the factory expropriated in 1946 and fortunately not dismantled or shipped off to the Urals. The main product, the somewhat basic Spee brand, was reformulated then launched nation-wide as a heavy-duty budget detergent. In 1995, and by rather stark contrast, Henkel bought the Schwarzkopf cosmetics and personal care business. Combined with existing assets in those categories, and alongside household cleaning and adhesives, the purchase gave the business a genuine third leg to stand on. A year later, Henkel launched a hostile bid for the 65% of Loctite it didn't already own. The deal was finalised in January 1997 for $1.3 billion, the largest acquisition in Henkel's history and one that catapulted it to global leadership in the category and increased company sales to over twenty billion Deutschmarks.

A year later, the acquisition of the Los Angeles DEP Corporation gave the company a foothold in the US hair care market. It was a move followed almost immediately by a very substantial 50:50 partnership with the Dial Corporation to develop new laundry detergent products sold under Dial's Purex brand and another example of Henkel's extreme flexibility and openness in accessing new markets. In 2000, the two partners bought an 80% stake in one of Mexico's leading detergent manufacturers. 70% of Henkel revenues were now coming from outside Germany.

As Henkel entered the 21st century, it finally took on its current form. It sold off the chemicals division, previously been spun off as a 100% Henkel-owned separate entity. It also continued to spread its global presence, acquiring companies in China and opening the Henkel Loctite Technology Centre Asia Pacific in Yokohama, Japan. It was chosen out of 50 applicants to provide adhesives for the space shuttle, a notable first, and won the approval of the US health authorities for a skin and tissue adhesive now used under licence all over the world. But probably the least-biggest surprise to seasoned Henkel watchers was the announcement in 2003 of the company's intention to acquire the Dial Corporation and thus become a direct rival of P&G on its home turf – an eventuality P&G would have found unthinkable when it first locked horns with Henkel in 1970s West Germany. Was this a case of revenge served cold?

How Is It Structured?

As early as 1919, Fritz Henkel and his three children appointed an eight-strong management committee to run the day-to-day business, and they wasted little time in setting up an up-to-date management structure. Although family owned, Henkel was no personal fiefdom like William Lever's Lever Brothers, nor was it a convoluted bureaucracy as Unilever became

Today the company is structured along product sector rather than geographical lines. There are three distinct branded product sectors: Adhesives – led by the Loctite brand group. With main brands Persil, Purex and Dixan, Laundry and Home Care account for slightly over a quarter of sales. Thirdly comes Beauty Care, growing quickly, with brands like Schwarzkopf, Dial and Syoss. The business does have a fourth division: Henkel Technologies, established in 2001. HT deals in adhesives and sealants, but highly specialised examples, used in such products as cars, books, computers, aircraft, cell phones, shoes and refrigerators. Any one house will have a multitude of Henkel products in it - the owner would never know how many - in addition to those in the bathroom, laundry room, under the sink and in the tool shed.

At the corporate level, and like most German companies, Henkel is run by a triumvirate: the Management Board, responsible for the day-to-day running of the company, the Shareholders' Committee, which meets regularly with the Management Board to discuss strategic direction and the Supervisory Board, a sixteen-member with equal numbers of shareholder and employee representatives who advise and monitor the Management Board in its stewardship of the company. All this is combined, and the family's continuing possession of around 80% of the voting shares, creates a structure that balances the needs and inputs of all the key stakeholder groups.

What Has It Been Doing Recently?

2004

The big event of the year was a transformation of Henkel's position in North America. Several acquisitions effected the change. The largest was Dial, whose Purex brand greatly increased Henkel's share of the US detergents market, added to its range of toiletries and moved the company into air fresheners. The purchase of Advanced Research Laboratories significantly added to Henkel's share of the US hair cosmetics market, and Henkel also exchanged its 29% stake in Clorox for Clorox's household cleaners and insecticides brands in North America and South Korea. With the additional acquisitions of the MAS liquid detergents in Mexico and three American adhesives companies, Henkel's total share of US sales increased from 12% in 2003 to a forecast 25% in 2005. Following this burst of acquisitions, Henkel was now global number three in Laundry and Home Care behind P&G and Unilever, number one in Germany and number two in Europe. In cosmetics/toiletries, Henkel was number one in Germany, number four in Europe and number eight worldwide, while in adhesives Henkel remained a clear global number one.

The acquisitions added 13% to annual sales, reaching €10.6 billion, but underlying organic growth was a rather more sedate 3% increase. The Laundry and Home Care category was juiced up the second half-year with the launches of Bref Power cleaner and Persil Megaperls with ShortWash. Underlying sales of cosmetics/toiletries inched ahead by just under 2%, keeping pace with market growth, the main progress coming from Diadermine, a high-performance skin care range that apparently guarantees a visibly younger-looking skin. A dollop of Diadermine appeared to have rejuvenated sales in the two adhesive products sectors, with underlying growth of over 5% in Consumer and Craftsmen Adhesives, due largely to the innovative Power Pritt and Power Pritt. Henkel Technologies put on 8% across its key sectors of automotive, aerospace, electronics and steel.

Strategically, the company focus was on driving the internationalisation of key brands while nurturing the strong regional and local offerings.

- In laundry and home care, the company's critical markets mass came from its range of heavy-duty detergents supporting its more profitable range of special detergents (for colours, light wash loads etc.), together with the household cleaners range, which provided the highest rate of growth. The plan with the recently acquired air fresheners and insecticides brands was to expand distribution to more Henkel markets.

- Within cosmetics/toiletries, the emphasis was on growing the European businesses organically through innovation and the continued rollout and expansion of the Diadermine brand, while international growth would be achieved primarily through acquisition, providing new markets for Henkel's key international brand, Schwarzkopf.

- In consumer and craftsmen adhesives, the basic strategy was to launch innovative new products in the Craftsmen sector then roll out consumer-friendly versions into the DIY business.

Henkel Technologies focused on providing bespoke products to individual customers.

Obviously, this strategy relied quite heavily on a constant stream of innovation from the 2,800 employees in the company's R&D department who were spending just under 3% of sales per annum. Henkel had adopted a two-tier approach to R&D with Central Research, (consuming 13% of the budget), focused on exploring basic technologies in the fields of biology, chemistry and engineering. Examples of areas being pursued in the year were:

- Increasing efficacy in combating infectious, odour-forming and destructive micro-organisms
- Active ingredients that would noticeably stimulate hair follicles
- Anti-ageing ingredients
- New and better detergent enzymes.

The rest of the R & D budget was spent on the development of go-to-market applications in each of the four product groups. Overall, the company's product range was protected by over 7,600 patents with a further 5,200 pending. Elsewhere, Henkel's Sustainability Report was awarded first place out of 150 German companies evaluated by Capital magazine, news that will surely have cheered up the next round of employees being slated for redundancy as the 'Strong for the Future' restructuring programme, first launched in 2001 and rebranded as Advanced Restructuring Measures, was extended for another year.

2005

Another double-digit sales increase of 13% took sales to within a whisker of €12 billion, once again powered more by acquisitions than underlying growth, which had risen to more than 3.5%. The major acquisitions of the previous year had been seamlessly integrated, with only the Dial food business deemed surplus to requirements, but sales in North America didn't quite reach 25% of the total, clocking in at 23%. With the exception of a Hungarian laundry company, the main 2005 acquisitions were in the adhesives sector, including companies in both India and China.

All regions and product sectors contributed to the growth. Laundry and Home Care returned to positive organic growth at more than 3%, driven by Eastern Europe and Russia in particular, where Henkel was a strong number two, and in other key emerging and developing markets such as India, China, Turkey and Mexico. Henkel gained share in a sluggish European market. The Dial acquisition meant that the company generated more Laundry and Home Care sales in the US than in any other country. Laundry growth tended to be promotionally driven, while Home Care sales were less price-sensitive and driven more by innovation. Within Laundry and Home Care, marketing was conducted on a mostly global basis with distribution managed regionally. Within Europe, grocery chains and drug stores were key distribution channels, whereas outside Europe and North America the company relied mostly on wholesalers and distributors.

Cosmetics and toiletries had a more sluggish year, generating organic growth of just over 1%, almost entirely down to expanding distribution in Eastern Europe. New products such as Poly Color Revital Farbcreme, Taft LYCRA and Fa Yoghurt shower gel all got off to good starts. Henkel's hair salon business, currently number three in the world, was seen as a significant growth opportunity. Within this category, marketing strategies were planned and implemented globally, with distribution handled at a national level through specialist drug stores, multiple grocers and department stores. The salon business was served by a dedicated sales force supported by training and seminars at the 43 Schwarzkopf Academies around the world.

The consumer and craftsmen adhesives business grew organically by 5%, again largely due to big increases in Eastern Europe, a success the company planned to extend to Asia, Latin America and the Middle East led by new lines such as Pritt Easy Start adhesive tape. Distribution for the consumer side was focused on supermarkets, DIY stores and specialist retailers with the Tradesmen operating through specialist retailers. Henkel Technologies relied on direct customer relationships.

Henkel set itself two future goals: to increase the share of business from emerging markets to 30% by 2008 and to increase the share of business from innovation in any three-year period from 25% up to 30%. To help this latter goal, Henkel declared 2006 to be its 'Year of Innovation', expecting all employees to chip in with ideas. In Laundry and Home Care, multifunctional, interdisciplinary, international teams – InnoPower Teams – had been formed for each product sector charged with creating tomorrow's innovations. Meanwhile, next week's innovations were coming from the Central Research Group in areas such as superior bleaching capability and nature-imitating nanotechnological actives for toothpastes to repair sensitive teeth.

2006

The Year of Innovation - 67,000 ideas submitted, more than one for every employee and 20% next-stage approved – was such as success that the scheme was extended to a three-year programme and a Henkel Innovation Trophy was instigated for an open innovation programme. Innovation was also at the heart of a much-improved sales performance. Although reported sales only increased by 6.4% – half the 2005 level – in 2006 there was a neutral effect from acquisitions and disposals, meaning that organic growth had risen to a very healthy 6%, assisted by tailwinds from stronger economies and the ability to push through price increases. There were double-digit sales increases in the targeted markets of Eastern Europe, the Middle East, Africa, Asia-Pacific and Latin America. Within the product sectors, growth was due to the combination of price increases on existing lines and innovations such as Dial for Men, the Pritt Pen Roller and Somat 7, the world's first dishwasher detergent with seven functions,.

Significant events in the year were the acquisition from Gillette of the Right Guard, Soft & Dry and Dry Idea brands, the acquisition of Tunisia's leading hair care company, the expansion of the Shanghai research facility to cover all four product groups and the transition of Henkel's cellular biology research company to work on skin research with the brief of developing an alternative to animal testing.

2007

While sales only advanced by 2.6% to just over €13 billion, underlying sales almost kept pace with the previous year at over 5.8%, where more than 4% was due to volume gains thanks to a dramatic increase of innovation throughout all the product ranges. The most significant change was the reformulation of Persil with a unique active stain remover to mark its centenary, new packaging for the liquid version and new design graphics. The new Persil was part of a 'Best Ever' re-launch of all Henkel's premium detergents in Europe that led to a significant gain in market share, both from competitors and from private label.

Sales in North America were stagnant, as gains in cosmetics and toiletries from the successful integration of Right Guard were wiped out by the dramatic decline in the US automobile industry, which hit sales in Adhesives Technologies hard. The targeted growth regions of Eastern Europe, Africa, the Middle East, Latin America and Asia (except Japan) collectively posted an organic sales increase of over 15%. By now Henkel had 52 production sites around the world,

the largest still in its Düsseldorf home. For large-volume products such as detergents, Henkel's policy was to operate with production sites as close to the markets as possible to minimise transportation costs and the associated environmental impact. With more compact products, such as glue, the strategy was to produce at central, highly automated plants on a regional if not global basis.

The increased emphasis on R&D was visibly bearing fruit, albeit at the level
of expenditure – 2.7% of sales – as had been the case for the past several years.
The corporate research laboratories in Düsseldorf, Darmstadt and Lizuka, Japan
were beavering away in the development of more optimised detergent enzymes
for manufactured through a fermentation 'white biotechnology' process. At the
operational end, the company's Research/Technology Invention Awards went to
projects including a new enzyme for liquid detergents that performed better in
cold washes than anything else on the market and active ingredients that com-
bated the hair ageing process. In addition to the reformulated Persil, other innovations launched in the year included Purex Natural Elements and the new Fa
Natural & Pure body wash, both made from natural ingredients. Henkel's future
goal was to become the clear innovation leader for each category in which it
competed.

2008

In the year the economic crisis really took hold, a sales increase of 8% to over
€14 billion looked amazing at first glance. But a second glance revealed that virtually all of the increase came in the Adhesives Technologies, following the acquisition of National Starch's Adhesives and Electronic Materials businesses for
€3.7 billion, increasing the size of Henkel's division by around one-third. A third
glance redressed the balance, however.

While the top-line sales of both laundry and home care and cosmet-
ics/detergents barely moved, in underlying sales terms they were a much more
impressive at over 3.8% and 4.7% respectively, and gaining market share in both
categories, whilst Adhesive Technologies now shouldering the full impact of the
US automotive's near collapse and losing 3% of its volume. Both laundry and
home care and Adhesive Technologies had introduced significant price increases
in the second half-year in response to surging raw material costs, while cosmetics
and toiletries had ridden the storm, relying more on innovation-driven growth.
The price increases, together with the worsening economic conditions, produced
a slowdown of the company's volume performance, up at the half-year by over
3%, but with volume declines in all three sectors in the second half. Emerging
markets – those ever-trusty performers - again grew by double digits, increasing

the share of company sales from 26% in 2004to 37%. Henkel now enjoyed number-one positions in over 100 country product categories.

Partly in response to the economic slowdown, the year also saw the development of a new strategy, which highlighted three strategic priorities:

- Achieve full business potential
- Focus more on customers
- Strengthen the global team
- In practical terms, the key elements of the strategy were as follows:
- Achieve Full Business Potential
- Optimise the portfolio
- Increase profitability in the mass categories of heavy-duty laundry and hand dishwashing products while driving growth in the profitable speciality categories
- In cosmetics/toiletries, strengthen innovation leadership and expand the Schwarzkopf brand
- Concentrate on top brands
- Increase sales of the top three brands (Schwarzkopf, Persil and Loctite which account for 25% of sales) twice as fast as company average
- Innovation
- Only launch new products if they increase the average gross margin of the product sector concerned and make a positive contribution to sustainable development
- Operational Excellence
- A reduction in the number of production sites in mature markets
- Concentrate on strategic suppliers and on procurement from low-wage countries

Focus More on Customers
- Generate organic growth with key accounts 1.5 times the figure for total Henkel
- Strengthen Global Team
- No specific targets set

As the scale of the unfolding economic crisis became increasingly apparent, an increased focus on the cost base had already begun in February 2008 via Henkel's Global Excellence restructuring programme, on which it spent €500 million in 2008 alone. It had already dissolved the central research division, whose various staff and functions were allocated to one of the three operating business sectors to reduce innovation time-to-market. Research also had to incorporate 500 R&D staff from National Starch and bring get its new, 2007-opened Shanghai facility up to speed. The product innovation venet of the year had been the use the Purex Natural Elements success to introduce a new brand, Terra Activ, with offerings in five product segments.

2009

As expected given 2008's second half downturn, the first half of 2009 was tough. Organic sales were down over 6% against a strong period in the previous year. In the second half-year, Henkel's organic sales almost matched the slow-down level of 2008, pushing total performance for the year down by 3.5%. Overall top-line sales for the year hit just over €13.5 billion, a decline of 3.9% when currency movements and acquisitions/disposals were factored in. The culprit once again was the industrial side of Adhesive Technologies, where widespread and wide-ranging decline in industrial production reduced demand for adhesives and speciality products, and led to a decline in organic sales of over 10%. In contrast, and all things considered, the consumer side was doing very well, growing organic sales in laundry and home care by 2.9%. Cosmetics/toiletries were doing even better, growing by 3.5%. Both sectors achieved record European market shares.

As per the new strategy, growth was largely being achieved in two different ways: by price in detergents to increase margins and by volume in cosmetics/toiletries. In the regions, performance followed the relative weighting of the Adhesives Technologies sector: North American sales decreased organically by 8.6%, Europe/Africa/Middle East were down by 1.9%, Latin America grew by 5%, while Asia-Pacific was anomalous in declining by 5.8%. Gains in cosmetics/detergents were more than wiped out by the company's decision to quit Chinese laundry and home care operations in China, where both P&G and Unilever were already firmly entrenched along and several rapidly growing local players had begun to establish themselves. Henkel compensated for this strategic retreat in South Korea, where it moved into laundry and home care on the back of its acquired position as market leader in the household insecticides category.

Henkel was gaining market share in its consumer categories primarily because of the very strong innovation programme, much accelerated in recent years: sales from new products in laundry and home care and cosmetics/toiletries launched in the previous three years had now reached over 40%. The Western European big news in the year was the launch of ArcticPower Persil, a detergent that required only half the usual dosage and cleaned at full power in water at only 15 degrees Celsius. As a follow-up came the re-launch of Somat 7 as Somat 9. Two new functions had been added: an odour neutraliser and an extra-dry function. In the US, Purex Complete 3-in-1 laundry sheets were a combined detergent/fabric softener with anti-static functionality. Dial Anti-Ox body, with cranberries and antioxidant pearls, was the most successful launch in its category, whilst Right Guard Fast Break was Henkel's extension of its newly-acquired brand. In another first, the Schwarzkopf Essential Color was Henkel's first permanent colourant without ammonia. And as with most of its competitors, Henkel was enthusiastically embracing open innovation by launching a number of special projects with Japan's top universities.

2010

As global trading conditions improved, Henkel bounced back in spectacular style, growing top-line sales by 11% to over €15 billion, underpinned by a 7% organic growth without currency effects and acquisitions/disposals. All three sectors grew, albeit at differing levels: laundry and home care by 1.5% in a shrinking market, cosmetics/toiletries by 4.8%; and Adhesive Technologies by nearly 12% and all three improved their market share. Company sales had again grown by double digits in the targeted emerging markets growth region, more than 19% for the top line and over 12% organically: the region now accounting for 41% of sales, targeted to rise to 45% by 2012. The overall company growth was in fact more than totally due to a volume growth of 8.5%: net prices had declined by 1.5%. Henkel had found, as had many other companies, that price increases taken in the depth of a recession were warmly embraced by consumers.

Within the product sectors, price deflation had been strongest in the laundry and home care category, where much of the 2009 prices had to be rolled back. But an average price drop of 4.2%, had beneficial effects on volume, which increased by nearly 6%, and produced Henkel's largest revenue rise in the Western European region since 2007. Eastern Europe did well thanks to the launch of Persil Gold Plus Cold Active and Africa/Middle East posted a double-digit increase, partly to the expansion of sales in Saudi Arabia. The one disappointment was North America, where tough market and pricing conditions led to significant sales decline. The same pricing/volume and regional sales patterns also applied to the cosmetics/toiletries sector, where average prices declined by 0.9% as volumes rose by nearly 6%, with North America the only region to post a volume decline, although the market share improved. Adhesive Technologies had kept its prices were static and volume increased by nearly 12%, much helped along both led by industrial recoveries and by the launch in the consumer sector of Loctite Power Easy, an odourless, solvent-free instant adhesive that avoided the perennial hospital emergency room filler of instantly glued body parts. And by the end of the year, the integration of the National Starch businesses had also been completed.

The focus on top brands was clearly paying off. The top-ten brands in Laundry and Home Care now accounted for 81% of sector sales while the top-ten in cosmetics/toiletries accounted for 89%, led by Schwarzkopf, the company's largest and fastest-growing brand at €1.8 billion, up from €500 million in 1995.

2011

The change to a more sedate top-line increase of over 3.4% was due more to currency movements than anything else, as underlying organic growth had declined only slightly to a still impressive plus 5.9%. This increase was split almost evenly between volume and price as market conditions eased enough for selective price increases to be pushed through both in laundry and home care, where the 3% growth was split evenly between the two drivers, and particularly in Adhesive Technologies, where nearly two-thirds of the 8.3% organic growth was down to pricing. All cosmetics/toiletries 5.3% growth was volume, reflecting the greater momentum Henkel had enjoyed in this category for some years. Once again, much of the growth came from the emerging markets, up by the usual double digits and mainly thanks to Adhesive Technologies and cosmetics/toiletries. Underlining the company's increasing interest in this region, the construction of Henkel's largest adhesives factory had also begun in Shanghai. Company top ten brands now made up a good 42% of sales which, given these heavily branded and highly recognizable products' better margins, had powered a double-digit increase in company earnings.

In the laundry and home care sector, 41% of sales once again came from innovations or product extensions launched in the previous three years: Persil Black, for example, a detergent especially for black and dark clothes launched in Central Europe, and Somat 9, which had been morphed into Somat 10 thanks to a faster-dissolving 'immediate-active formula'. The results were a strong volume gain in Western Europe, while in Eastern Europe, particularly Russia and Turkey, double digit growth was also accompanied by improved market share. Even the difficult US business rebounded, growing sales and share slightly in a still declining market. Asian organic sales increased only slightly, but they had been hampered by Henkel's exit from the Philippines' market late in the previous year, although the launch of Persil in South Korea undoubtedly more than mediated the loss. Latin America continued to grow strongly. Persil was launched in Mexico. Mega-Caps – water-soluble capsules of concentrated laundry liquid - was newly launched in Western Europe, even as the US got its first taste of Purex crystals.

Cosmetics/toiletries was now up to a 43% innovation rate, impressive by any standards. It was the key reason for the consistent, year-on-year improvements in market share in all the main product categories: hair cosmetics, hair colorants, body care and hair salons, once again with the strongest performance in the emerging markets. Adhesive Technologies' more sedate innovation rate of 30% could be put down to the longer lead times involved in developing its industrial client base's customer-specific solutions.

Overall company R&D investment had settled at a slightly lower level of 2.5% of sales, reflecting the shift in emphasis to open innovation, with developments underway reflecting the continued focus on not just the growth but also sustainability. Good examples here would be the optimisation of the enzyme/stain interaction in low-temperature liquid detergents and glass cleaners surfactants manufactured entirely from renewable raw materials. The company production footprint was also reduced by eight sites during; new, more-efficient factories replacing older sites. Over 50% of company sites reduced both energy and water consumption and waste levels.

Henkel, five times sector leader in the Dow Jones Sustainability Index, already had the clearest, longest-running and most transparent commitment to sustainability among its peers. Yet in 2011 the company launched a new sustainability strategy; it resolved to triple value created relative to ecological footprint by 2030. This was Factor Three. It would mean improving efficiency (through sales increase, footprint reduction or both) by 5–6% a year. Interim goals for the first five years were set: a 10% increase in sales per production unit and a 15% reduction per production unit in water use, energy use and waste production.

2012

The year continued in the vein of 2011. Sales increased by nearly 6%, a performance all the divisions contributed to fairly equally as all gained global market share. The organic sales growth of more than 3.8% was mostly driven by price increases: Henkel again was successful in passing along input cost increases, an ability fuelled by its consistently very high innovation rate. Henkel's regional spread was also a factor in its continued ability to move forwards, declines in the weak southern European markets counterbalanced by growth in Henkel's core northern European markets, leaving Europe at a net break-even position. Very strong emerging markets presence continued as the main engine of growth, double-digit figures in the Middle East, Eastern Europe, Africa, India and China. Overall, emerging markets accounted for 43% of Henkel's global sales and increased by over 9%, 7.8% of which was organic growth.

The year's big news was the unveiling of a new four-year strategy, 2008's having run its course and the business environment having changed considerably in the interim. In looking to the future, the factors Henkel resolved that it must adjust to the increasing consolidation of suppliers and customers, the accelerating importance of the emerging markets, and an increasing dynamism in Henkel's product categories. To achieve the 2016 sales targets of €20 billion, with 50% coming from emerging markets (twelve of its top-twenty countries are in that category), Henkel's strategy contained four strategic imperatives:

- Out-perform
- Globalise
- Simplify
- Inspire

While no sensible company would disagree with any of these, underpinning them were some hard specifics. To out-perform, Henkel now realised the portfolio had to evolve: core categories would receive heavy incremental investment, particularly in R&D, and seven new sites inside the emerging markets themselves. Meanwhile, less-advantaged categories would be scaled back and/or sold. To simplify the business, the number of global suppliers was to be reduced by 40%, while more employees were slated to move out of the divisions into shared service centres, two more of which would be opened in North Africa/the Middle East and China/Japan/South Korea regions. A longer-term goal was to triple the efficiency of the company: in other words, a re-statement of Factor Three. Target year, 2030.

What Is Its DNA?

Henkel is without doubt a unique player in the packaged goods industry. First, German owned and run as it is, it is euro-centric at heart, dominant in the large German market and a key player in the rest of Europe. Second, it has substantial businesses in both branded consumer goods and industrial supplies. While many packaged goods companies have business divisions outside of normal packaged goods (e.g. Heinz' food services business, Coca-Cola's Quick Service Restaurant sales and Kimberley-Clark's hospital supplies and equipment categories), none has them to the same extent as Henkel, 50% of whose sales coming from its mostly industrial Adhesives Technologies sector. But these are current centres of gravity that have shifted over time and will no doubt continue to do so. We believe what really makes the company unique is the following:

Green Innovator

There is barely a company on the planet that does not claim at least some green credentials somewhere within its product range, but Henkel stands alone as a global player who has been, is and will remain completely committed to an innovation programme that constantly seeks to reduce the ecological impact of its products. Strictly speaking, that's the company's only growth strategy. It is succeeding. The impressively high innovation rate and an insistence on launching only products that both improve the profit margin and reduce ecological footprint, more than 40% of the packaged goods ranges are greener every three years and grow profits and market share. By following this strategy Henkel preference shares have averaged a 10% average annual yield since 1985. So if you believe sustainability isn't just a fad but a real sea change in consumer attitudes, Henkel's inbuilt strategic advantage is huge: it has now been measuring all its core competences against this agenda for decades.

Careful Competitor

While the sustainability agenda has proved competitively successful for Henkel, it is not all-powerful. Greener, more-efficient products are useless if the company isn't able to distribute them efficiently and cost-effectively, or if there are entrenched competitors willing to spend anything to protect strong market positions. Perhaps as a consequence, one thing that stands out in Henkel's history is that it has no desire to be absolutely everywhere just for the sake of it. And it very rarely gets into prolonged battles it cannot win:

- Its geographical expansion is weighted towards markets its global competitors tend to underplay: Africa and the Middle East are areas of relative strength for Henkel while Latin America, a Unilever heartland for over 50 years, accounts for only 6% of Henkel's sales
- Rather than get into value-destroying battles of ego and pride, it is not afraid to leave a market if conditions are structurally adverse. Laundry brands, China and the Philippines are key examples here
- Its careful approach to acquisitions has been almost flawless: it takes its time to choose targets and is very flexible in its market entry strategies
- Perhaps the only question that remains to be answered in this regard is its acquisition of Dial in North America. The US Detergents and Home Care categories have been graveyards for the likes of Unilever and Colgate. Whether Henkel can do any better is still an open question

Summary

Henkel now has a $20 billion turnover, split almost equally between its industrially biased Adhesive Technologies and the highly branded home and personal care businesses. Perhaps unsurprisingly, the company mission statement hails it as 'A global leader in brands and technologies'. It defines its values as follows:

- We put our customers at the centre of what we do
- We value, challenge and reward our people
- We drive excellent sustainable financial performance
- We are committed to leadership in sustainability
- We build our future on our family business foundation

One sign of a good strategy is the impossibility of adopting its opposite as an equally viable approach. Against this yardstick, the first two values are generic – no sane company would say otherwise. On sustainable financial performance, all companies would say that. But many chase short-term numbers, something Henkel has never contemplated. But where its values are certainly unique is in the last two: the company is not just committed to sustainability but to leadership in sustainability and in its chosen fields. And it is, at least in stock voting terms, still a family company and hence free to pursue its strategy unhindered by fears of any hostile takeover.

We believe this leadership in sustainability value will indeed sustain both continued growth and continued success for Henkel. It is big enough to benefit from the consolidation of suppliers, manufacturers and customers happening in the world today. It has enough of a platform, particularly in Adhesive Technologies and cosmetics/toiletries, to benefit from the continued rise of emerging markets. It is efficient and well run enough at least to match the ever-growing need for greater operational excellence; the Persil reformulation disasters of the past happened to Unilever, not Henkel. Its least advantageous position, compared to its other two sectors, is laundry and home care. We look forward to its return to the acquisition trail to remedy that defect. And, of course, to making its US business work.

Kellogg's

Where Did It Come From?

In 1855, a pioneer of what would become the Seventh-day Adventist Church accepted an invitation from a group of fervent early believers to move with her family to their hometown of Battle Creek, Michigan. A year later, the Kellogg family also moved to this epicentre of the new church. John and Ann Kellogg eventually had a very large family: eleven children to add to John's six from a previous marriage. They included John Harvey Kellogg, born 1852, and Willie Keith, born 1860. John Senior imposed the strict Adventist diet on his family, forbidding meat, sugar and caffeine. He became a successful Battle Creek businessman, running, amongst other concerns, a broom factory in which both John Harvey and Willie Keith worked after school. Of the two boys, John Harvey eventually graduated from New York's Bellevue hospital in 1975 as a doctor. Willie Keith, or WK as he preferred to be called, worked as a salesman for the family broom company.

In 1876, John Harvey returned home to become medical superintendent at the Western Health Reform Institute hospital run by the church in Battle Creek. As the word 'Reform' implies, it was the belief of the church, and John Harvey in particular, that many patients were in hospital through reasons of their own making. Their reform would result in better health. Something of a man ahead of his time, John Harvey believed that poor diet was at the root of many health problems. He had a particular fixation with constipation, and so imposed a strict diet on patients. They were served only whole grains, fruits, vegetables and other natural foods, and of course meat, sugar and caffeine were verboten.

While John Harvey was cleansing the bowels and souls of the sickly inhabitants of Battle Creek, WK had gone off to Texas to run a broom factory. He returned home when his elder brother offered him a job as business manager at the hospital, by now renamed the Battle Creek sanatorium. Now they were reunited, it would be the less than harmonious relationship between the brothers that would create the Kellogg cereal empire.

John Harvey, who was hard on his patients' diets, was even harder on his staff, in particular WK. He treated WK as his gofer, making him work fifteen-hour days without a single day's holiday. He assigned him a range of tasks, from doing the accounts to cleaning John Harvey's shoes. Meanwhile, John Harvey, fascinated by the ideal of healthy diets, experimented endlessly. He sought to create new foods, which tempted the palettes of his jaded patients, without using the normal taste enhancers of sugar, salt or spices. John Harvey's wife and WK were also enrolled in this difficult task.

The Kellogg brothers were aware that the first breakfast cereal, Granula, was invented in 1863 by James Caleb Jackson. He was also author of The Sexual Organization and Its Healthy Management. Jackson believed the twin evils of constipation and masturbation were intimately linked (a view with which John Harvey had sympathy), and Granula was part of the cure. So the brothers experimented with wheat batter, aiming to develop their own improved version.

As has been the case with the genesis of more than one business empire, the solution would come, not from an inspired flash of genius but through carelessness. A batch of batter was forgotten and went stale. Rather than throw it away, the brothers rolled the dried-out batter into sheets according to their usual process. They were surprised to see that it did not form sheets but broke into small flakes. They decided to bake the flakes to see what they tasted like and, hey presto! Here was a light, healthy and somewhat tasty perfect way for patients to start the day. They named the product Granose Flakes and started feeding the patients.

One patient was a certain Charles W. Post. He toured the brothers' kitchens, and left the sanatorium with a recipe, production process and business idea that would make him a millionaire soon after he founded Post Cereals in 1895. Meanwhile, despite WK's pleas to follow Post's example and commercialise their invention, Granose Flakes was fed only to sanatorium patients. John Harvey relaxed his iron rule to allow the setting up of a mail-order business. Called the Sanitas Food Company, this enabled patients to keep buying Granose Flakes after they had recovered and left the hospital. WK's broom-selling experience came to the fore and in the first year he managed to shift 100,000 lbs of the cereal.

In 1898, aiming to add to the one-product price list, WK developed a similar process, this time making flakes out of corn. WK realised that he needed to use only the inner corn grit to get the texture he wanted and that the flavour would be much improved by adding a little sugar to the corn meal paste. Of course, to John Harvey, adding sugar was a complete non-starter. This added to the tension within their working relations, and especially John Harvey's continued refusal to expand sales beyond the sanatorium alumni. By 1906, WK's seemingly endless supply of filial loyalty finally ran out. He left Sanitas and the sanatorium, taking his recipe for flaked corn with him and, in February 1906, set up the Battle Creek Toasted Corn Flakes Company.

WK piled a third of his working capital into advertising and within a year was selling 2,900 cases a day at a dollar a box profit. Soon after dropping the 'Battle Creek' component of the company name, his fledgling business suffered a near-fatal blow in July 1907 when a stray firework ignited and burnt down his factory. Even as the embers were still glowing, the orders generated by his extravagant advertising campaigns continued to roll in, so WK planned a much larger (and fireproof) factory. WK had struck out on his own, and just in time. By now, another 41 past patients of the sanatorium, and various businessmen with an eye for a quick buck, had followed Charles Post and set up breakfast cereal companies in Battle Creek. All these wannabe cereal millionaires faced several major problems in growing their business.

First-mover Advantage

The market for breakfast cereal barely existed outside of the digestively compliant members of the Battle Creek Seventh-day Adventist Church congregation. The rest of the nation was quite happy starting the day with either stale bread brought back to life by soaking in hot milk and salt, or some kind of oatmeal gruel or porridge. For the fledgling breakfast cereal industry to succeed, it had to change the behaviour of a nation, and someone had to take the lead to do so.

Product Quality

Selling far and wide in the nation's grocery stores meant the product would have to sit in the box for up to several months before being consumed. This was a far cry from cooking in the kitchen one day and feeding to patients the next morning. The shelf-life problem had to be solved if national distribution was the goal.

Winning Shelf Space

Compared to other packaged goods at the time, such as baking soda or soap, breakfast cereals were very bulky and grocery stores were extremely small. They were more like today's convenience stores, carrying only 300 lines or so. They would need a lot of persuading to make room for large boxes of cereal, especially from multiple suppliers. Winning shelf space was critical: this factor alone would ring the death knell for the vast majority of the new cereal companies.

Barriers to Entry

As is self-evident from the fact that 42 cereal companies were operating in Battle Creek alone, it was an industry with next-to-no technical barriers to entry. The cereal category was always going to be one that would demand advertising and lots of it – consumer mind-space would become the only realistic competitive advantage.

The eventual winners in the category would be the ones who best addressed these challenges.

How Did It Evolve?

Kellogg became the world's largest cereal manufacturer because WK realised from the outset that solving the above challenges was critical to success. Anyone, it seemed, could make a reasonable breakfast cereal but only one could build the most successful cereal business, and he made it his mission to do so.

First-mover Advantage

WK realised immediately he had to take the lead in converting people to the idea of eating cereal for breakfast. His timing was to some extent fortuitous. Pasteurised milk was becoming widely available in the major cities, so half his job was being done for him. He gave away product samples as though there was no tomorrow, employing samplers to go door-to-door to demonstrate the ease and convenience of switching o a cereal breakfast. He also spared nothing in advertising the same message. Determined to be the biggest and most impactful advertiser in the cereal business, he had constructed a colossal 106-foot-wide by 80-foot-tall billboard in Times Square requiring 80 tons of steelwork. This he boasted was the world's largest single advertising sign. It was also one of the most effective, increasing his sales in the city fifteen-fold. By 1911, WK was spending a staggering $1 million a year on advertising, dwarfing the investment of his now rapidly dwindling competitors.

Product Quality

Here WK's big breakthrough did not come until 1914. His son, John Leonard Kellogg, came up with the idea, trademarked as Waxtite, of encasing the cereal boxes within an envelope of waxed paper. This sealed the contents from the outside air, thus adding many months to the freshness. This would be one of over 200 patents and trademarks John Leonard would develop in his career in the company. A few years later he solved the more difficult manufacturing challenge of depositing the cereal in a sealed bag inside the box. He also developed a malting process that added more flavour to the Cornflakes.

Winning Shelf Space

Owing to WK's years of experience selling brooms to shopkeepers, he understood this environment very well, better than his competitors. He had a winning combination. WK built consumer demand by aggressive advertising: then, he sent his salesmen into every shop they could find, with an array of incentives to stock his product. As WK's product had a much longer shelf life than his competitors, it was a brave shopkeeper who would refuse to find room for Kellogg's on his shelves.

Barriers to Entry

WK spent a fortune selling the concept of the breakfast cereal category to consumers and shopkeepers alike. However, he was acutely aware that his advertising was in danger of floating all boats in the category. He was already coming under pressure to maintain his trademark on 'Toasted Corn Flakes' (a claim he would ultimately lose in 1922, forcing the Kellogg Company into another company renaming), and too much advertising on one product risked becoming street wallpaper. Early on WK realised a category truth that would continue to this day: breakfast cereals are very responsive to new news. So developing a stream of new products became a company priority. Kellogg's Toasted Rice Flakes had appeared in 1909, soon to be followed by Kellogg's Toasted Wheat Biscuit (demonstrating forcefully to Henry Perky, the inventor of Shredded Wheat, just how low the technical competitive barriers were), Kellogg's Krumbles, Kellogg's 40% Bran Flakes and, in 1916, Kellogg's All-Bran. The dominating use of the Kellogg's name on the box, featuring WK's own signature, was an essential component of building differentiation among cereal brands. In 1910, WK also invented the idea of putting collectibles inside the boxes to increase the pester-power component of brand loyalty, including a set of moving pictures booklets.

While WK was building a cereal empire, John Harvey stopped speaking to his brother. No doubt he saw WK's commercial compromises as a betrayal of family and church principles. John Harvey continued to run the sanatorium along with the Sanitas Food Company. In 1910, he launched the first in a decade-long series of legal battles to prevent WK selling items such as Rice Flakes and Flake Biscuits under the Kellogg name. He claimed prior usage. WK counter-sued on the basis that John Harvey sold under the Sanitas name, not Kellogg. In 1916, the United States Patent Office awarded WK a partial victory by ruling that he had won the right to use the Kellogg name in script form. The matter was finally closed in 1920, when a judge observed that WK had spent millions promoting the Kellogg name; while John Harvey had spent precisely nothing until WK had already popularised the name. Game, set and match to WK.

The same year, the Kellogg Company recorded its first ever-annual loss in the economic slump following the end of the First World War. WK was undeterred. His factory, with fifteen acres of floor space, was capable of producing 30,000 cases of cereal a day, fed by orders from 400 salesmen working out of twenty regional offices nationwide. He just needed to keep converting Americans to the cereal habit. If sales were slow then salesmen did more door-to-door sampling. In 1921, the company launched single servings of its brands: selling them to hospitals, hotels, rail companies and the like. So captive audiences could sample this new kind of breakfast. The same small packets formed the basis of a massive sampling campaign the year after. WK was intent on growing his way out of the slump.

In 1923, John Leonard, much more scientifically minded than his ex-broom-salesman father, came up with the idea of hiring a dietician. It wasn't enough, he reasoned, that Kellogg's cereals were tasty and convenient. They had been invented in the first place for reasons of nutrition and that message was being lost. His first recruit was a dietician at Columbia University, Mary Barber, who established the Home Economics department. In 1924 she issued a leaflet entitled, Food Selection Chart, which was soon approved in Washington to be mailed to home economics teachers across the nation.

Meanwhile, the new product development machine trundled ever onwards. The new brands so generated, where all widely promoted by the company's huge advertising budgets, and filled the expanding shelf space in the emerging supermarkets. In 1925 came the company's first brand targeted at a particular segment, Kellogg's Pep, which was aimed at athletes. Two years later, a blockbuster followed: Kellogg's Rice Krispies. Its famous Snap! Crackle! Pop! slogan soon appeared in the soon-to-be-famous ditty:

Listen to the fairy song of health,
the merry chorus sung by Kellogg's Rice Krispies
as they merrily snap, crackle and pop in a bowl of milk.

If you've never heard food talking,
now is your chance.

The eponymous Leo Burnett-designed cartoon characters appeared in the early 1930s.

The problem of succession loomed large in WK's mind in the mid-1920s. He had booted John Leonard out of the company for the twin crimes of divorcing his wife to marry an employee, and buying an oat-milling factory on the side. WK appointed a succession of non-family members to the President's role but gave them no room to manage. During the Great Depression, he heard that the company was scaling back both on advertising and sampling. So WK intervened to restore the cuts and double the advertising budget. The result was that the company continued to grow through even the hardest of economic times. By the end of the depression, the Kellogg Company was making nearly $6 million a year profit.

The Kellogg Company realised that success came from desire for its products amongst children plus parental approval. Marketing efforts targeted at kids reached new heights when commercial radio became available nationally. Kellogg's sponsored the first network radio programme aimed directly at children, followed by a series of others. The other part of the strategy, parental approval, focused on the nutrition angle. This led to the development of a technique to spray vitamins and minerals onto the cereal during production. The first brand to benefit was Kellogg's Pep, a move reinforced by the company becoming a pioneer regarding the labelling of ingredients on the boxes. The company also sponsored such activities as Admiral Richard E. Byrd's South Pole expedition. Their thinking was: if the cereals were good enough to sustain a group of hardy explorers willing to drag two years' supply across Antarctica, then they would be perceived as good enough for the kids.

The Second World War saw several changes to the Kellogg's business. The company was an enthusiastic contributor to the war effort, not least in allowing its famous home economist, Isabel I. Barber, to take up the post of Food Consultant to the Quartermaster General. There she created all the menus for the army, including rations for combat troops. Kellogg's produced K-rations throughout the war. Regular business did not stand still during the war years. Individual packs of cereals that could be used as the cereal's bowl were developed initially for the army, and have benefited Boy Scout camps ever since. In 1940, the Home Economics department came up with the recipe for Kellogg's Rice Krispies Marshmallow Treats – an invention that would keep on giving half a century later, when the company decided to make and sell the product for itself.

Kellogg's Raisin Bran was launched as the company underwent a major modernisation of its factories, updating its Battle Creek facilities and building several factories across the country. The company even diversified into dog food in 1941 with the launch of Gro-Pup, a dog food so replete with added vitamins and minerals that no meat was required: well worth wagging for, as the ads proclaimed.

After the war, the company embarked on the most expansive era in its history. By 1948, sales had reached $100 million a year. Its factories were modern and highly automated for the time, giving Kellogg a profit margin double that of the typical food company. They enjoyed a dominant share of the market and were well set to benefit from the two factors that would power its business for the next twenty years: the post-war baby boom and the arrival of television advertising. Sadly, WK Kellogg would not live to see much of the new era, passing away in Battle Creek at the age of 91.

In 1951, some twelve million US homes had a television set. Four years later half the homes in the country were tuning in. Kellogg could not have been better positioned: with 85% of its sales coming from ten cereal brands. Its concentrated brand portfolio was fully exploited by the most effective advertising medium the world had ever seen, to produce high profit margins. With its target market, children, getting more numerous by the year, the company launched a raft of new products unashamedly aimed at the young, and backed with prodigious amounts of advertising dollars. The Leo Burnett advertising agency did them proud, developing characters such as Tony the Tiger for the new brand Kellogg's Frosted Flakes, a brand soon joined by Kellogg's Honey Smacks, Kellogg's Sugar Corn Pops, Kellogg's Sugar All-Stars and Kellogg's Cocoa Crispies. Grocery stores, which were in an arms race of their own to build bigger and better stores, fell over themselves to stock anything and everything turned out by the Battle Creek selling machine.

Helped by other additions to the range, such as Kellogg's Special K in 1955 (the first cereal to be fortified with seven vitamins and iron), the company managed to double its sales within a decade. They reached the magic $200 million mark in 1957, the same year another Leo Burnett creation, Cornelius the Rooster, made his debut on the Kellogg's Cornflakes box (it was still the company's best-seller). As the television medium matured, and in an inspired move, Kellogg bought The Huckleberry Hound show and made full use of the likes of Yogi Bear and Boo Boo on their packet. It was a golden era for the company. More new lines, such as Kellogg's Concentrate and Kellogg's OKs, were added to the mix in 1959. OKs' failure turned out to be a blessing in disguise. The equipment installed to make OKs would be utilised during the 1960s to make the more enduring Kellogg's Froot Loops, Kellogg's Apple Jacks and Kellogg's Puffa Puffa

Rice. Kellogg's Bran Buds and Kellogg's Frosted Mini Wheats also joined the line-up.

What would turn out to be one of the more significant moves in the company's history came in 1963, when Post, struggling to compete head-on with Kellogg and General Mills, developed a new breakfast food. It could be warmed in a toaster (which was now a ubiquitous kitchen appliance) and came enclosed in foil to keep it fresh. The product, Country Squares, received a press fanfare but spent many months in test market. This gave Kellogg the chance to head off this threat to its heartland. It developing their version, launched in 1964 under the name Kellogg's Pop-Tarts. Although seen as a reactionary, tactical move at the time, this would turn out to be a major development. Kellogg's Pop-Tarts eventually become the company's single largest brand, growing in volume for every year of its existence. It signalled a shift in direction. Kellogg was no longer a cereal company; it was a breakfast/snack company. This move was accentuated in 1969 when the Kellogg bought Salada Foods, a tea and coffee company.

The International Dimension

Kellogg went international very early for a US-based food company. It opened its first factory in Canada as early as 1914: not least because the main population centres in Ontario were less than half way from its Battle Creek headquarters than the cities on the US eastern seaboard. However, a rival Canadian firm won a legal battle preventing Kellogg from using the Corn Flakes name in Ontario. Kellogg retaliated by purchasing the company for $400,000. Having merged the two businesses, Kellogg based itself in the rival's headquarters.

In the 1920s, Kellogg expanded further afield, using its enlarged Canadian manufacturing base to supply products for export to the United Kingdom and Ireland, the products being proudly advertised as being made in Canada. Building export businesses to other economically well-developed countries was very difficult at that time. Many countries erected trade barriers, as protectionism became the default economic policy of governments. One of the most protective markets was Australia, which imposed a 100% tariff on imported food products in order to protect its fledgling indigenous packaged goods industry. The only realistic avoidance was to build a factory there. This would have the twin benefit of producing tariff-free goods locally and being protected from the competition of foreign imports. So in 1924, Kellogg opened a factory in Sydney. From here, it had a free run to develop the Australian breakfast cereal habit using all the techniques forged in its American business.

In both Australia and the UK, Kellogg would be free from serious competition for decades. This would enable the company to build extremely successful businesses that would also be seen by consumers as being indigenous. As business in the UK continued to grow, the decision was taken to build the company's largest factory to date in Manchester, England. It opened in 1938, to supply not just the UK market but also Continental Europe. Unfortunately however, the outbreak of war put a prolonged hold on the European strategy.

After the war, the company opened its sixth factory just outside Johannesburg in South Africa. Like its UK counterpart, the factory was of sufficient size to export products to nearby countries. The next such regional production hub was built in Mexico in 1951 to supply Central and South America. By this time approximately one-third of total company sales were being generated outside the US. During the late 1950s and throughout the '60s, funded by the booming US business, the company ramped up its international expansion. It aimed at first-mover status in as many developed markets as possible: opening up in Ireland, Sweden, the Netherlands, Denmark, New Zealand, Norway, Venezuela, Columbia, Brazil, Switzerland, Japan, Finland, Spain and Italy.

Each of the overseas businesses was given a high degree of autonomy to develop the breakfast cereal habit as they saw fit given the local breakfast customs. Air travel was then in its infancy, so a trip from Battle Creek to kick the tyres of the Australian operation entailed weeks out of the office. In 1963, the company opened an international technical centre in Europe, which lessened the already slim dependence of the European businesses on Head Office.

One effect of this autonomy was that product ranges differed quite markedly between countries. Each had the R&D capability to develop its own new products, and this proved a benefit in the 1980s when the US business needed a lot of new products, and quickly. While the core brands appeared in all markets, recipes differed slightly to suit local tastes. Advertising slogans such as Snap! Crackle! Pop! Also developed local versions: Piff! Paff! Puff! in Sweden, Knisper! Knasper! Knusper! in Germany, Pim! Pam! Pum! in Mexico, Riks! Raks! Roks! in Finland, Cric! Crac! Croc! in French Canada, Pif! Paf! Pof! in the Netherlands, and Knap! Knaetter! Knak! in South Africa. Kellogg was an early devotee of the principle of acting locally.

All this while, Kellogg's main US competitors had stayed resolutely local, with the exception of small forays into Canada and Mexico. The result was that not only did Kellogg build overwhelming market shares in most of these countries but also international business was proportionately a much larger share of its business than it was for its competitors. This in turn lessened the impact on Kellogg of difficulties in the US market. So successful was the UK business that the company opened a second factory there in 1973. The rate of international expansion slowed down somewhat in the 1980s as the US cereal business, which had been funding all the start-ups, ran into choppy waters for the first time. This limited the most significant international development to a move into South Korea, a market previously supplied by the booming Australian company.

Unfortunately for Kellogg, its free run without serious competition in many of these markets started coming to an end in 1989. General Mills, long jealous of Kellogg's many overseas gold mines, hit on the rather good idea of developing a joint venture with Nestlé, called Cereal Partners Worldwide (CPW). This combined General Mills brands such as Cheerios with the reassurance of Nestlé branding, and the strength of Nestlé's route-to-market capabilities, into many of the markets currently dominated by Kellogg. It turned out that quite a few of the Kellogg overseas subsidiaries had got used to the good life free of a competitive dogfight. CPW began to make significant inroads in Nestlé's stronger markets. This would become a major headache as, by that time, Kellogg held 50% of non-US cereal sales and was generating a third of total company profits overseas.

The CPW threat to Kellogg's affiliates made the company realise it had to re-activate its strategy of being first into up-and-coming markets. So, in 1993, it gained a first Eastern Europe foothold, in Latvia. A year later, a small factory was opened in India, followed by one in Guangzhou, China and then in Thailand. Kellogg now had 29 factories operating in nineteen countries, and supplying nearly 160 countries. However, for all Kellogg's international expansion, its core markets of UK/Ireland, Mexico (where it had implemented a Keebler-style direct store delivery, DSD, system), Canada and Australia/New Zealand accounted for over 80% of its non-US sales; Kellogg had a global footprint but a regional sales base. Following the imposition of the 'Volume to Value' focus on profitable growth, in 2001 most overseas investment was focused on these core markets. At least for a while.

How Did It Build Its Modern Business?

It could be argued the modern company took shape the day the first box of cereal rolled off WK's production line in 1906. Kellogg started as a cereal company and by the late 1960s was the largest one in the world by some considerable margin. While it had aggressive competitors such as General Mills, Post and Quaker, Kellogg was the market leader. It had also expanded overseas while the others had stayed local. But while the company would obviously remain a cereal company to this day, we prefer to date the building of the modern company to the time when it realised the breakfast cereal bonanza of the 1950s and '60s would not continue forever.

The job of building the category had been achieved. Virtually every child in the land ate its products. The cereal market had matured to become a highly expensive dogfight between entrenched competitors. The next challenge was to find other ways to grow. The company had diversified in the past, on an ingredient-processing basis, into dog and other animal feeds, without much success. But its very success in building the packaged goods breakfast market was attracting new competitors who offered something different from the ubiquitous cereals. Pop-Tarts had shown that the company could compete outside of the cereal aisle. So in 1970 it ventured into the freezer section, and bought Fearn International, Inc., specifically so it could acquire an up-and-coming line in Fearn's portfolio, Eggo waffles.

The Kellogg approach to new product development – plenty of it – was soon brought to bear on the Eggo brand with Eggo Blueberry Frozen Waffles, Eggo French Toast and a host of other variants. All these appeared within the first couple of years of Kellogg stewardship. It was good that the company had something to focus on other than cereals; as the category that had seemed would grow forever hit problems in the early 1970s. In 1972, the Federal Trade Commission fired a shot across the bows, accusing Kellogg and its competitors, General Mills and General Foods (who owned the Post brand), of operating a cartel that had overcharged consumers by a collective billion dollars in the previous fifteen years. The FTC also correctly surmised that exceptionally high advertising spends, product proliferation and an overbearing attitude to the retail trade formed highly effective barriers to entry. No one denied this part of the charge – it had been company strategy since day one – but the company counter-argued that it wasn't actually illegal. The price-fixing charge was harder to shake off, but the industry eventually won. However, it was a warning that the cereal category was no longer immune from criticism.

A more harmful salvo would be fired by the American Dental Association, which accused the industry of being less than clear with the paying public as to the sugar content of many of its brands. Kellogg led the fight back; producing arguments to show just how small a percentage of children's daily sugar consumption came from its products. But some mud was bound to stick: they had a host of products sporting the word *sugar* in the brand name, which were promoted ceaselessly on children's television programmes. Sales of sugared cereals declined in 1978 for the first time since they had begun appearing twenty years earlier.

While more new cereal brands were launched, there were no blockbusters. Kellogg was encouraged to put more focus on its Eggo brand, although it was a bit of a loner for the company in the freezer. The company decided it needed an enhanced frozen foods brand portfolio and infrastructure to have the same clout with the frozen foods buyers it was used to having with the cereals buyers. In 1976, it purchased the Mrs. Smith's Pies Company and transferred across the Eggo brand from the Fearn subsidiary to the newly renamed Mrs. Smith's Frozen Food Company. This soon developed new products, launching Kellogg's Diner's Choice range of frozen meals. In 1977, Pure Packed Foods was also acquired to add more oomph to the category.

Coming into the 1980s, it is not clear that Kellogg understood the scale of the challenge now building up for the cereal category. The glory days of the baby boom and a nation glued to television commercials was slowly but inexorably fading. The baby boomers were growing up and, no matter how many new children's brands the company launched or spent on advertising them, baby boomers ate less and less cereal as they grew into adulthood. The 25–49 age group ate half as much cereal per capita as the under-25s. And there were fewer and fewer kids entering the market as the birth rate started contracting. Kellogg had a shrinking target market and, even worse, steadily lost market share: from 43% in 1972 to 36.7% in 1983. Even with annual sales of $2.4 billion and a 28% return on equity, the Kellogg Company was looking every bit a fading star, especially when the company failed in bids to buy Tropicana and (luckily, as it turns out) Crayola Crayons.

That year, 1983, was the turning point. The market stagnation and its own share losses convinced Kellogg it had to aggressively target the 80 million baby boomers who had largely grown out of the Kellogg's child-orientated product range. These people had grown up with Kellogg and had a strong bond with the Kellogg name, but the company was not offering products that appealed to their changed needs. These were people who jogged or worked out at the gym in the mornings. They needed to be persuaded anew that breakfast cereals could be a part of their lifestyle. The company massively ramped up its R&D budget to $20 million – triple the level five years previously – and was soon churning out three varieties of the new Kellogg's Nutri-Grain cereal. Kellogg's Raisin Squares was joined by Kellogg's Apple Cinnamon Squares and Kellogg's Strawberry Squares. Kellogg's Just Right was borrowed from its Australian operation. Kellogg's Mueslix from its German company was launched with a $33 million advertising budget, which was an industry record. Kellogg's Crispix was added. Even old brands joined the party, with Kellogg's All-Bran packaging trumpeting a message from the National Cancer Institute about the benefits of bran in avoiding bowel cancer.

The results of this pivot were impressive. By 1988, consumers aged 25–49 were eating 26% more breakfast cereal than they had been doing five years previously. This helped grow the US cereal category, previously branded as mature, from $3.7 billion to $5.4 billion – a rate of increase three times the average for other grocery categories. Increases accrued to the Kellogg Company, whose US market share was now comfortably north of 40%. Most came at the expense of the smaller competitors. General Foods' Post brand - unable to keep up with the Kellogg onslaught on adults - lost over three share points in the same five-year period. With an R&D budget doubled again to $40 million, Kellogg was launching twice as many new brands than it had in 1983. The majority were aimed at adult consumers. The marketing budget had tripled within five years, up to an eye-watering $865 million – which was 20% of sales. The old brands were not entirely forgotten; a doubling of the ad spend for Kellogg's Frosted Flakes grew sales by 40%. A nostalgia advertising campaign got dads to introduce this brand to their children. Many of the adult brands introduced sold at much higher prices per box than the range of children's cereals. This improved the Kellogg sales mix and thus gross margins, up to 49% from 41% five years previously.

With the cereal business seemingly back on track, attention turned to the remainder of the portfolio. Some hard decisions had to be taken. To date, the company's acquisition record had been lacklustre. To be fair, the company had avoided the wild excesses of the diversification craze that had gripped some of its competitors, but only the Eggo brand could be judged to have added something worthwhile to the Kellogg brand portfolio. Thus, in 1988 its tea business was sold off, followed in 1992 by the now Eggo-less Fearn International. A year later the company said goodbye to Mrs. Smith's Frozen Food brands. Seeking to replicate the Eggo success, another rising breakfast favourite, bagels, was added to the company mix with a 1996 purchase. Lender's produced a range of frozen, refrigerated and fresh bagels. However, this would be a short-lived venture, with Kellogg selling the unit just four years later.

Back in the main portfolio, new trends were reshaping the business once again. In the cereal category Kellogg had completely missed the oat craze of the early 1990s, which worked much to the benefit of General Mills' Cheerios brand. The rise of retailer private label offerings aimed at staples such as the Kellogg's Cornflakes, Frosted Flakes and Rice Krispies brands was hurting the company. The Kellogg market share reached a new low in 1994 of 33.4%, a mere 0.1% ahead of the surging General Mills. The usual company response to such pressure was more new products, more advertising and more price increases. For once these failed to do the trick. Private label prices stayed where they were, which opened up too big a price gap, forcing first General Mills and then Kellogg to roll prices back again.

Kellogg's annual sales were still increasing marginally but were mostly driven by its still booming international division. A new trend benefited Kellogg's Pop-Tarts (now the company's biggest brand) and the newly launched Kellogg's Nutri-Grain snack bars. This was a surging demand for on-the-go snack options that were healthier than chocolate bars. It was at this point that the 1940 recipe for Kellogg's Rice Krispies marshmallow bars made the transition from the back of the cereal box into a new product launched by the company, under the name Kellogg's Rice Krispies Treats. The pressure from private label on its big cereal brands remained inexorable: by 1998, private label market share was estimated to be as high as 20%, mostly having come at the expense of Kellogg brands. The low technical barriers to entry had finally come back to haunt the company. No amount of innovation or advertising was going to stop retailers putting their own products on their shelves.

In 1998, the company embarked on a new direction, cutting its workforce by 25% and entering the functional food category mostly outside of the cereal aisle. They launched Kellogg's Ensemble, a family of foods designed to lower cholesterol. Initially in test market with a planned rollout in late 1999, the brand consisted of seven categories: frozen entrees, bread, dry pasta, ready-to-eat cereal, baked potato crisps, frozen breakfast/dessert mini-loaves and cookies. These were marketed by a newly created division, the Kellogg Ensemble Functional Food Company. The active ingredient in the Ensemble line was psyllium, a soluble fiber proven to reduce cholesterol. Psyllium needed to be consumed in bulk for a person to benefit from its cholesterol-lowering effects: hence the wide product range. It was going to be a tough sell to persuade people to change their entire diets and buy enough of this range.

The CEO appointment of 25-year company veteran Carlos Gutierrez in April 1999 signalled a new change in direction for Kellogg. One of his first acts was to pull the plug on the Ensemble initiative, quickly followed by the offloading of the bagel division. These moves were counterbalanced by the acquisition in late 1999 of Worthington Foods, Inc., a manufacturer of meat alternatives, egg substitutes and other healthy/vegetarian food products. Gutierrez correctly divined that the trend towards healthier eating wasn't going to go away, but that there were better ways to get on the bandwagon than via Ensemble.

Gutierrez had also inherited a company overly focused on the chasing of volume. Any volume at any level of profit: it was a culture developed under the inexorable pressure on sales volume created by the rise of private label. Although it would take a couple of years to address, the re-orientating of the company culture towards the pursuit of profitable volume would be a very important step. Initially, it led to General Mills overtaking Kellogg as the number-one cereal manufacturer. Gutierrez was not too bothered. The foundations were being put in place for a quite different Kellogg Company. In any event, market share cannot be taken to the bank. Kellogg continued its pivot towards more adult-friendly brands, with the launches of Kellogg's Raisin Bran Crunch and Kellogg's Special K Red Berries.

Two very important acquisitions were made in 2000 and 2001. The first, of Kashi Foods, was a recognition that there were newly emerging parts of the cereal market in which Kellogg could not credibly compete under its own name, given its heritage and continued reliance on highly processed sugared cereals. Kashi was a 16-year-old American manufacturer of natural breakfast cereals based around seven whole grains and sesame. Kashi Foods would run completely independently from the mainstream Kellogg cereal business as a stand-alone company. The second major acquisition in 2001, of the Keebler Company, was more transformative. It brought Kellogg a very well established range of cookie and cracker brands, distributed by Keebler's own DSD system. This system got products into stores faster and gave the delivery staff access to shelf merchandising. Kellogg wasted no time in moving its impulse purchase snack lines, such as Kellogg's Rice Krispies Treats and Kellogg's Nutri-Grain Bars, into the Keebler system. Keebler's product innovation team moved to Battle Creek to bolster a newly-created Snacking division. Keebler was by far the largest acquisition in the company's history, costing $4.56 billion, and it completely changed the company's product mix. Breakfast cereals now contributed 53% of sales, 32% from snacks and 15% from other grain-based foods. Keebler was the second-largest cookie and cracker manufacturer in the US, with brands such as Cheez-It, Famous Amos, Plantation, Zoo Animal Crackers, Murray and Keebler. Keebler had been bought in 1974 by the British company United Biscuits, which had all but run it into the ground by 1996. Then a leveraged buyout installed new management who had executed an impressive turnaround. The Cheez-It brand had doubled its volume in five years by the time Kellogg took ownership. Keebler also came with significant overseas operations, which would prove more than useful. Kellogg had a thriving, but geographically limited, international profile.

How Is It Structured?

For the most part of its history, Kellogg has been, organisationally speaking, a very simply structured company. A handful of large cereal businesses operated virtually autonomously until things got a little more complicated, and the company went on the acquisition trail in the 1970s. The Keebler acquisition and the imposition of 'Volume to Value' prompted Gutierrez to simplify the structure into two core divisions: Kellogg North America and Kellogg International. These were subdivided as follows:

- Kellogg North America
- North American Retail Cereal (the main cereal brands plus Kashi, which still runs autonomously)
- North American Retail Snacks (Keebler brands plus Pop-Tarts and Nutri-Grain Bars)
- Frozen and Speciality Channels (Eggo, Morningstar Farms and Worthington in the frozen section plus all products sold through convenience stores, drug stores and vending)
- Kellogg International
- Kellogg Europe (headquartered in the UK)
- Kellogg Latin America (headquartered in Mexico)
- Kellogg Asia Pacific (a broad region also including Africa and the Middle East, run out of Australia)

What Has It Been Doing Recently?

2004

The strategy imposed at the beginning of the 21st century - growing the cereal business, expanding the Snacks business and seeking selected growth opportunities; governed by the twin disciplines of 'Volume to Value' and the symbiotic 'Manage for Cash' (a focus on reducing working capital to pay for fund the growth) - was by now in full swing and delivering impressive results. The low point had been in 2000, when sales had fractionally declined to just over $6 billion. In 2004, sales rose for the fourth consecutive year to reach $9.6 billion, rising a reported 9% in the year itself. The company, however, prefers to focus on what it calls internal growth. This strips out the effect of currency exchange (significant for Kellogg), acquisitions and divestitures, and changes to the number of shipping days in the year. 'Internal growth' showed a more sedate but still good increase of 5% over the previous year. The operating profit was only slightly behind at 4%, the difference reflecting the funding of a double-digit increase in brand-building expenditures.

While both the US and International divisions grew at 5%, the heroes were the US Snacks and Latin America sub-divisions. These grew by 8% and 11%

respectively. The Snacks business benefited from several good innovations. They borrowed the idea of Kellogg's All-Bran Bars from Mexico and launched Cheez-It Twisters, a unique dual-flavoured twisted cracker. Then they ventured into the fruit snacks category. This last innovation made good strategic sense. The category was fast growing, and was sold in the same aisle as the snack bars. Kellogg was a trustworthy name in fruit, given their long experience of launching cereals with fruit inclusions. The company launched in the US, with Disney fruit snacks in the shape of popular Disney characters and Fruit Twistables. These were launched under Froot Loops branding in Canada. Aided by the company's DSD system, the fruit lines quickly established a significant in-store presence and market share.

In Latin America, while doing well in most markets, the greatest growth came from the dominant Mexican market. This was thanks mainly to the Snacks category, which had been launched there in 2003 and was boosted by the 2004introduction of Pop-Tarts. Other significant events were the introduction of reduced-sugar versions of Kellogg's Frosted Flakes and Kellogg's Froot Loops; and the international rollout of the highly successful 'Lose up to 6 lb in 2 weeks' promotion on Kellogg's Special K. This was developed in Venezuela, which had helped drive the brand to be the company's largest globally. Without doubt, the biggest change in the year was the invitation of President Bush to Carlos Gutierrez to serve as Secretary of Commerce in his new administration. The invitation reflected the highly successful turnaround of the Kellogg business. As Gutierrez accepted the invitation, a change of leadership, but not of strategy, resulted.

2005

While the reported sales increase fell from 9% to 6%, the internal growth rate actually inched ahead from 5% to 6%. It was again driven by: the US Snacks business at 7%; Latin America at an impressive 11%; with a helping hand from the US Frozen and Speciality Division. The latter weighed in with an 8% increase, driven by Eggo and the frozen vegetarian food brand Morningstar. The US cereal business inched ahead 2%, gaining market share for the sixth consecutive year in a sluggish market. The European and Asia-Pacific regions both trod water.

In the North American Snacks Division, almost everything did well. Pop-Tarts led, recording its 26th consecutive year of sales growth to reach a staggering 86% share of a somewhat tightly defined toaster pastry category. It was helped by the introduction of yet another new flavour, Cinnamon Roll Pop-Tarts. The DSD-distributed snack bars boomed. Special K bars posted a double-digit increase and the range was extended with the introduction of Oatmeal Raisin All-Bran Bars. The fruit snack business grew again, prompting the company to acquire more manufacturing capability. In Latin America the company still had a mostly free run at the ready-to-eat cereal category and recorded strong share gains in Venezuela, the Caribbean, Columbia and especially the huge Mexican market. Here the company again gained share, to reach 71%.

Elsewhere, the North American Retail Cereal division, which accounted for almost 25% of total company sales, gained 0.4% share on top of a similar gain the previous year. The increase came from the good old strategy of lots of innovation, supported by even more advertising. The successful Kellogg's Raisin Bran Crunch was joined by two new variants, while the Special K brand was broadened with the addition of Special K Fruit and Yoghurt. Meanwhile, the natural and now organic Kashi brand grew by double digits to reach a 2% share of the overall cereal market. This was an excellent achievement in the highly fragmented cereal category. In Asia-Pacific, the only really good news was the three-brand Indian cereal portfolio growing by double digits, albeit from a small base. It would be fair to say that Kellogg was finding it difficult quickly to establish the breakfast cereal habit in both India and China. At least CPW wasn't doing it ahead of them.

2006

Kellogg celebrated its centenary year with a 7% sales increase (both reported and internal) to reach $10.9 billion. Unfortunately, operating profit lagged behind, with a 4% internal growth and a measly 1% reported. This knocked an entire percentage point off the operating profit margin, down to 16.2% - energy, commodity and marketing costs being the causes. With the exception of Asia-Pacific – flat once again – the rest of the business performed well.

The North American Retail Snacks unit was once again the powerhouse of growth. It increased internal sales by 11%. The leaders were Special K Bars, which benefited from new variants, and Go-Tarts, introduced as an on-the-go version of Pop-Tarts. In fruit snacks, a category the company had entered only three years previously, Kellogg had built a 30% market share; and both the cookie and cracker businesses grew, thanks mostly to innovation. The Frozen and Speciality Channels business grew to reach $500 million in sales.

Here, the most notable innovations were the extension of the Kashi cereal brand into frozen entrées and the launch of Eggo Pancakes. The North American cereal business posted a 3% growth and a 0.2% share gain, with many new products launched. The most interesting was Smart Start Healthy Start, a brand with strong cholesterol- and blood pressure-lowering claims; and the introduction of organic versions of Rice Krispies, Raisin Bran and Frosted Mini-Wheats. One benefit of having some very strong cereal businesses overseas was demonstrated with the running across several countries of a "Pirates of the Caribbean" promotion. The high costs could be amortised across markets.

Elsewhere, the European region, under the most competitive pressure from CPW, returned to sales and market share growth, driven by Kellogg's two largest businesses, the UK and France. The Turkish market was targeted, with the formation of a joint venture with a Turkish company to sell co-branded products. A multi-year project was initiated, to reconfigure the company's European manufacturing infrastructure with the goal of making better use of its biggest and most efficient plant in Manchester. Kellogg also was the first company to introduce nutritional labelling on the front of the packages in most European countries. The momentum in Latin American cereals and snacks continued, with a further 8% growth. The troubled Asia-Pacific unit declined slightly, mostly because of problems in Australia, the size of which dominated the performance of the region.

2007

The new strategy implemented in 2000 was continuing to pay off. The company recorded its seventh consecutive year of sales growth, up another 8% on a reported basis to $11.8 billion. But stripping out the currency exchange effects reduced that rate to 5.4%. This broke down into a somewhat sluggish 2.1% volume increase, with another 3.3% coming from pricing and positive mix changes – nice if you can get them and make them stick, but not as dependable as organic growth. To be fair, the company had kept on increasing its advertising, breaking the $1 billion barrier for the first time. More worrying was promotional expenditures, which was a mostly price-related activity. That had by now crept up to nearly 30% of sales – a key factor, along with energy and commodity cost increases, for the operating margin to decline again. The latter was down to 15.9%, despite the more than healthy price increases taken during the year.

Within the divisions, North America grew internally by 5.5%, of which more than two-thirds came from price/mix. Cereals grew by 3%, helped by the usual slew of new products - plus the venerable Rice Krispies brand was kick-started back into life with new lines and a 'Childhood is calling' themed advertising campaign. All-Bran and Kashi also had good years. The Snacks business continued to outperform cereals, posting a 7% increase. This was not least due to the competitive edge provided by the DSD system, which was rated the best in the snack industry by the Advantage Group Performance Monitor. In the Frozen sector, the Kashi brand was extended further into waffles and pizza.

On the international front, a headline sales increase of 12% was predominantly due to currency movements. The underlying growth rate was 5%, with Latin America, as usual, leading the way. It grew by nearly 9%, of which two-thirds was due to volume increases. The Mexican business exceeded Australia to become the company's third-largest operating unit behind the US and the UK, helped by introductions such as All-Bran drinks. Europe was still chugging along, driven by high single-digit increases in Spain and Italy and cereal share gains in the UK and Ireland. The Turkish joint venture was off to a flying start, increasing Kellogg's market share from 2% to 22% in just two years. The Asia-Pacific market continued to be sluggish, reflecting too great a dependence on the Australian and New Zealand markets. There a poor year more than wiped out the benefits of growth in markets such as Korea and Japan, where the company launched its wholesome snacks brands.

The fact was that Kellogg was getting virtually nothing out of the emerging markets boom in that region; the entire Asia-Pacific region was contributing only 5% of company sales and even less in operating profit. Something had to be done. Company acquisitions were still mostly small-scale and North American. Bear Naked, Inc. – a premium granola company – and the Wholesome and Hearty Foods Company – an American vegetarian food manufacturer – were both purchased in the year. Not before time, the company's eye was turning towards emerging markets to look for acquisitions.

A very significant announcement was a global commitment to adjusting how and what the company would market to children under the age of 12. Kellogg had established a global nutrition standard (Nutrient Criteria), which would be applied to all the products marketed to children worldwide. Products that failed the criteria would either be reformulated to comply, or not marketed to children. This was a reflection of the pressure that had been building for some years on companies involved in children's food categories. The days of launching brands like Sugar Smacks and advertising them with popular cartoon characters were long gone.

2008

Everything was looking rosy, with a 9% reported sales increase in a year when the economic crisis was beginning to bite. In fact the going was getting tougher for the company. Of the 9% sales increase, less than 1% came from actual volume growth. Prices had been ramped up, adding 4.5%. Acquisitions added another 1.8%, and a 53-week accounting year chipped in another 1.7%. Ever-increasing cost pressures drove the company margin down even further to 15.2%, not least to promotional expenditures. These now represented a staggering 40% of 2008 net sales. Most if not all of the list price increases was dealt back, as retailers refused to contemplate pushing up in-store prices while their shoppers were feeling the squeeze. Even the Latin American growth machine hit the buffers, with volumes down nearly 3% as prices were pushed up by nearly 7%. It was only a somewhat belated return to growth in the Asia-Pacific region that kept the company in positive growth territory.

Looking to the future, the company made three significant acquisitions in its Asia-Pacific region. In Russia, OJSC Kreker (United Bakers), a manufacturer of commodity cookies, crackers and cereal was acquired; not for its brands but for its six manufacturing facilities and broad distribution network. In China, the company purchased a majority interest in Zhenghang Food Company Ltd ('Navigable Foods'), a manufacturer and distributor of cookies and crackers in the northern and northeast regions of China. Kellogg also bought out one of its longstanding contract manufacturers of crackers, cookies and frozen-dough products in Australia. After these acquisitions, the company now had 32,000 employees and 59 manufacturing facilities in nineteen countries, servicing 180 countries where over 1,500 products were distributed.

2009

In 2009, there was no disguising. All was not well on Planet Kellogg. The company reported a 2% decline in sales. Even the internal growth figure of 3% was more than made up of price increases, as opposed to actual volume growth. Global volume declined by 0.7% and only moved forwards in the Latin American region. On the plus side, operating profit increased by 10% owing to a series of cost savings and productivity initiatives. The latest was the company's 'K-LEAN' (Lean, Efficient, Agile, Network) assault on its manufacturing complexity. Undoubtedly, the global economic slowdown had affected sales performance, but cereal and snacks were two of the most recession-resilient categories, and both were still growing globally. Two-thirds of the company's net sales still came from North America, where a modest cereal volume increase was achieved. Snacks' volumes, previously a big driver of growth for the company, were static. The Frozen and Speciality Channels division declined, as it operated in sectors and channels hit harder by the slowdown.

The company was still doing good things in building for the future. Its main R & D facility, the WK Kellogg Institute for Food and Nutrition Research, was expanded to enable more rapid prototyping across simultaneous project streams. It also continued to invest in an open innovation programme. Media spend was maintained at over $1 billion, in the face of media cost deflation to increase the number of consumer impressions. Advertising and research agencies were consolidated and aligned. Based on a global research study, which showed that adult females shared much the same concerns across different cultures, the Special K 'Moments of Truth' marketing campaign was rolled out globally. This grew the brand in the high double digits. The company was also getting into digital marketing, with many individual brands together with Kelloggnutrition.com. More products, including fruit snacks and Kashi crackers, were added to the DSD system. There was also a lot of brand renovation, following the twin tracks of reducing the 'bad' ingredients such as sugar, sodium and fat, together with increasing the 'good' ingredient. Fibre was added to Froot Loops and Apple Jacks. Clearly, the company was responding to perceived consumer concerns, but a lot of this activity was more good housekeeping than driving growth.

2010

Another sales decline, of 0.6%, was the result of a tonnage volume decline globally of 2.1%. The situation could no longer be remedied by price increases. In fact, there was price deflation in the cereal category in both North America and Europe, as retailers and consumers alike rebelled at prices continually being pushed ahead when real incomes were static at best. A new CEO – John A. Bryant – perhaps helped the soul-searching process as to what was going wrong. Four key factors were identified:

- The old model of innovation and advertising had come unglued somewhat. There had not been enough innovation. All the renovation efforts to improve the nutritional profiles of the core brands had come at the expense of the level of innovation required in tough economic times. Putting more fibre into Froot Loops was a fine, noble and necessary thing, but, in tough times, not many more consumers were going to put their hands in their pockets as a result. The innovation pipeline needed to be refilled, and fast.

- It was not a good year for the VP Manufacturing in North America. The company experienced major supply issues on waffles and then had to institute a product recall, the second largest in the company's history, across some key cereal brands. This was thanks to an odour problem with the package inner liners. The cost of the recall itself was nearly $50 million. The consequential losses were greater, because the recall disrupted the important back-to-school promotions for products unaffected by the odour problem.

- The company was losing share in cereals in too many markets. Although a shortage of innovation was fingered as the culprit, the fact was it had been quite a while since the R&D department had come up with a game-changer. The combination of insufficient innovation and the recall resulted in a 5% decline in the North American cereals business, the company's single largest division. The European cereals did little better.

- While price deflation was a reason for Kellogg's lack of top-line growth, it was something of a disingenuous excuse. The company had been propping up the top-line with above-inflation price increases for a few years and, while it had had to deal with some major cost increases, it had perhaps turned to price increases too readily. Nor had it been early enough and aggressive enough with cost savings.

Just to add to Kellogg's woes, it admitted that it was going to have to re-implement SAP at an additional cost of $70 million. It also took a big write-down on a Chinese factory it had opened a few years previously - business had failed to take off as hoped. The new CEO did what new CEOs do, and reorganised the business segments into the following:

- US Morning Foods Kellogg's cereals, Kashi, Pop-Tarts, Health & Wellness products)
- US Snacks (Cookies, crackers, fruit snacks, cereal bars)
- US Speciality (Foodservice and speciality outlets)
- North America Other (US Frozen and Canada).

The overseas divisions remained unchanged. On the principle that it's never a good thing to work in a business unit with the name 'Other', it would not be surprising to see Kellogg sell its frozen foods portfolio at some stage. The focus was clearly on cereals and snacks.

2011

Kellogg returned to top-line growth in 2011 with reported sales up by 6.5% and internal sales up by 4.5%. This did not herald a return to the heady growth days of the early/mid-2000s. Overall volume was flat, as was operating profit, which had gone nowhere in four years. The company was running fast to stand still and pushing prices ahead despite the price deflation of the previous year. Rather than bleating on about high commodity price inflation, Kellogg needed to accept it as a new fact of life and manage its business accordingly.

Perhaps to make a point to the new CEO, employees in the Other division delivered the best sales increase of all the now seven divisions. They grew the business 7%, of which the majority was volume growth. An increase was always going to follow the previous year's supply problems, but growing the Eggo brand 20% and returning to the historic share high of 70% were impressive achievements. US Morning Foods and Kashi returned to growth with a 5% increase. A strong innovation programme enabled a dialling back on past excessive levels of promotional spending. Sales from new products equalled those of all their competitors' innovations combined, contributing to a global $800 million of sales from products launched in 2011. Share in the US cereal market increased by 0.6% to 33.6%. This was a good improvement but it would have led previous generations of Kellogg managers to fall on their swords. Breakfast snacks did less well overall, growing by 3%. Pop-Tarts as ever did the heavy lifting.

The US Snack category grew sales by 6%, although off flat volumes. Special K Cracker Chips – an idea from the open innovation programme – had an exceptional first year, supported by the ever-reliable Special K and Fibre-Plus snack bars. Overseas volumes declined. Europe was the main culprit, losing 3% of sales volume. The Russian business, in the midst of a transition from an unbranded low-value product range to higher-value Kellogg brands, was starting to show positive signs. Volumes in Latin America returned to growth, albeit marginally, largely as a result of Kellogg's Krave cereal's launch in Mexico. In Asia-Pacific, the bright spots were South Africa and India, which more than made up for a return to sluggishness in the Australian business. President and CEO John A. Bryant and Chairman Jim Jenness declared they were 'not satisfied with this recent performance', although they did not elaborate going how far back. We agree.

2012

A top-line growth of over 7%, to $14.2 billion, suggests that things were improving. However, virtually all that growth was accounted for by Kellogg's major play in the year: the acquisition from Proctor & Gamble of Pringles for $2.7 billion. If Kellogg had owned Pringles for all of 2011, it wouldn't have grown the top line at all. The Pringles deal, while a bit pricey at eleven times earnings, has the potential to be transformative for Kellogg. It tripled the size of its overseas snack business, putting it global number two behind PepsiCo. It also gave the company a commercial and supply chain snack infrastructure in Latin America, Europe and Asia that it hadn't had before.

Meanwhile, back at the ranch, Kellogg had started the year paying the price for continually passing on commodity price increases without sufficient innovation to make the shopper stomach them. US cereal and snack sales were sluggish in the first half-year. The critical UK market did even worse, owing to too many initiatives not performing as expected. This was a major contribution to a decline in total European sales by nearly 4%. Kellogg's inability to add sufficient value to make its price increases digestible drove its gross profit margin down by almost three percentage points over the previous two years. Its big success in the cereal aisle, Krave, gained a full share point in the category, but that came entirely at Kellogg's expense as it only held share. While Pop-Tarts continued its record of sales increases for 30 straight years, Kellogg's sluggish snacks and cookies business was propped up by Special K Cracker Chips and the new Special K Corn Chips.

Elsewhere, the Other segment rode to the rescue once again. Frozen foods posted good increases - the new Thick and Fluffy Eggo waffles and Morningstar Farms plumped up sales. Over in Asia, question marks started to appear around Kellogg's strategy for China. Its newly announced partnership with Singapore-based Wilmar International seemed to be along the lines of General Mills' Cereal Partners Worldwide idea. Kellogg would provide the brands and manufacturing expertise, while Wilmar did the grunt work of scale and route-to-market infrastructure in China. This was the latest of several approaches by Kellogg to the Chinese market, and it was becoming difficult to shake the impression that it had no clear, long-term plan for the market. Overall, the Asia, Australia, South Africa and New Zealand region was only growing in the low single digits – not an impressive level, all things considered.

What Is Its DNA?

Cereals

Notwithstanding the new news of the Pringles deal, Kellogg is first and foremost a breakfast cereal company. It would be unimaginable for the company to divest its cereals business; it was the first thing it sold and pretty much the only thing it sold until the company began to diversify in the 1970s. The concern is that cereal DNA may be a part of the corporate chromosome that doesn't deliver growth in the 21st century. However, it is management's job to make its strengths relevant to changing circumstances.

Global-Local

As discussed above, Kellogg is more of a multi-regional than global company. It has proven itself better than most at sharing ideas across markets, and not just in a 'head office to everywhere else' direction. The relatively high level of autonomy still enjoyed today in the overseas companies has proven to be a significant strength. Perhaps not in the area of meeting local tastes - given the success of CPW in gaining a global market share north of 20% with a range of not very local brands - but certainly in the area of developing and sharing new products and new promotional or advertising campaigns. While this sounds an obvious and easy thing to do, the fact is that most large companies are not very good at it.

It requires the right combination of local autonomy to develop new ideas in different environments, and a not-invented-here management culture that makes managers receptive and willing to proudly copy.

Summary

It could be argued that, while cereals run through Kellogg's veins, either the company is not as good at it as it used to be or it was in the right time at the right place. The fact is that, even today, the vast bulk of its cereals business comes from markets it developed before and soon after the Second World War. Then it had first-mover advantage, sometimes for decades before serious competition turned up. Kellogg has not been particularly adept at either fending off competition, either from CPW or private label, or opening up new markets beyond its core.

Equally, its snacks business (excluding Pringles), while an impressive achievement, has been built largely through happenstance (eg. stealing a march on General Foods with Pop-Tarts) and in morphing its cereal brand equities into snack bars. Pop-Tarts has not been followed up by anything remotely as successful, and there are only a finite number of strong cereal brand equities that can transition into snacks. Pringles will dwarf its existing snack business, which will provide challenges as well as opportunities. Will Pringles make Kellogg a better snack company or will Kellogg make Pringle a better snack brand? The answer to that question in the next few years could well determine the company's fate.

Kimberly-Clark

Where Did They Come From?

On March 26th, 1872, five Wisconsin businessmen pooled $30,000 to buy a paper mill. The initiator of the scheme, Charles Clark, who part-owned a hardware store, had heard a paper mill-owning neighbour boasting of his profits. So he corralled John A. Kimberly, Havilah Babcock, Frank Shattuck and George Whiting to come up with the necessary funds to get in on the act. The neighbour's boasts were seemingly well grounded. In mid-to-late nineteenth-century America, both population and literacy levels were rising fast. These trends fuelled a steep rise in newspaper and magazine circulations, and consequently increased demand for newsprint and finer grades of printing paper. So when the partners opened their first paper mill on the Fox River in Neenah, Wisconsin, a few months later, their prospects seemed promising.

This was a Gilded Age, when virtually all consumer markets were mushrooming. The partners, like many businessmen, knew that success went mostly to the biggest and boldest thinkers. Their mill, at 210 by 88 feet, was large compared too more established set-ups. Only eight years later, having already opened a second mill and substantially upgraded both, the firm was incorporated as Kimberly, Clark & Co. It had a capitalisation of $400,000, a thirteen-fold increase. Clark's neighbour hadn't been exaggerating. By 1892, Kimberley, Clark & Co. had expanded into bond and ledger paper production through a new subsidiary. They were now by far the largest paper company on the Fox River. Their success had come, not from breakthrough innovation or some compelling new feature to their product, but from having a bolder and better-financed expansion strategy than their peers.

In 1893 they were making 55 tons of newsprint a week from one centralised large mill. They converted their other mills to the production of a wide spectrum of products, from cheap rag-based wrapping papers to the best manila grades and bond papers. Further expansion plans were put on hold as the good times in America came to a shuddering halt. During a three-year depression; paper prices dropped by 40%, and radical action was needed just to stay afloat. Wages were cut by 10% and John A. Kimberley organised his competitors into a Paper Makers Association. This cut back production through a coordinated mill shutdown programme across all manufacturers in the region.

By 1895, fifty paper companies had gone bankrupt. Profits at Kimberly, Clark & Co. had plummeted by over 70%, but they survived the crisis due to their aggressive response. As soon as a recovery was half-glimpsed, expansion plans were dusted off and mills were snapped up at rock-bottom prices. The company was now poised to resume its growth strategy, but success in the new century had to be based on more than buying up failed mills. The key differentiator for Kimberly, Clark & Co was to be innovation, driven by a state-of-the-art technical department.

How Did They Evolve?

In 1912, the company set out on a deliberate path of recruiting professional engineers and scientists to set up a properly organised technical department. Its role was primarily to codify the company's quality-testing procedures, which was a common enough practice amongst their competitors. But Kimberly, Clark & Co was to take the concept much further. In 1914 they recruited an Austrian chemistry graduate from the Darmstadt Institute of Pulp and Paper Technology, Ernst Mahler. The need for Kimberly, Clark & Co to innovate was clear. They were one of the country's biggest producers of newsprint, but newsprint prices had never recovered from the low point of 1895, and pulpwood costs were continuing to rise. The killer blow to the newsprint business, which was the mainstay of the company, was the passage of the Underwood Tariff Act in 1913. This opened the country to cheap Canadian imports of newsprint.

All American paper companies were in the same boat and all paddled the same way. They changed over their mills to tariff-protected products, such as paper for books, magazines, wrapping and toilet paper. However, the sudden massive rise in production capacity for those products simply depressed their prices. No one was any better off. Kimberly, Clark & Co managers had seen this coming as early as 1908, but it needed their Austrian paper genius to explore completely different possible products that could be made on their machines. He had to come up with something quickly as the company was already planning to exit newsprint altogether. The answer to their prayers came from a combination of a fact-finding trip to Germany by Mahler and Kimberly in 1914; and the devastation of the American cotton crop by the Boll Weevil. Mahler explored German scientists' latest ideas on bleached groundwood pulp, and also enquired about the possibility of making a cotton wool-type product out of cellulose. This could be an alternative for sanitary-wound dressings. The consensus of opinion was that it was possible, although complicated, to turn tree trunks into ersatz cotton wool. Within a few months of his return, Mahler had mastered the process and had a product: Cellucotton.

The outbreak of war in Europe clearly indicated there might be a demand for such a product. The first samples of Cellucotton wound dressings were ready for testing in hospitals in 1915. The tests were a developer's dream: not only did the product more than meet the required sanitary standards, it proved to be several times more absorbent than cotton. The dressings required changing less frequently, which was a big plus in busy hospitals. Meanwhile, the Boll weevil had decimated the American crop and driven up raw cotton prices. So Cellucotton cost 60% less than raw cotton. This looked to be a winner. Kimberly-Clark contacted the Surgeon-General of the War Department, and gave him a hard sell on the many benefits of Cellucotton wound dressings. The deal was swung when the company patriotically agreed to forgo all profits on supplies sold to the War Department and the Red Cross. By the end of 1917, the company was shipping wound dressings as fast as they could make them.

The end of the war in November 1918 brought matters to a shuddering halt and almost saw the end of Cellucotton. Huge orders were cancelled, forcing the company to immediately shutter one of its two mills devoted to the product. A second was kept going to supply hospitals who had latched onto the product. However, even this outlet disappeared. The Red Cross donated their stocks of wound dressings to hospitals free of charge; and the War Department dumped theirs to jobbers at rock bottom prices.

Cellucotton now seemed a commercial dead duck. Kimberly-Clark's rivals, Scott Paper, had had a similar wartime experience. They had also developed a cellulose derivative, called Zorbik surgical dressings, which, after the war, they dropped completely. They could see no peacetime application for it. Thinking along the same lines, most of the senior management at Kimberly-Clark were keen to get back to the day job of making and selling paper. However, Mahler and Kimberly wanted to give Cellucotton one last go. They met with Walter Luecke, the Chicago representative of Sears Roebuck (to whom the company sold paper for the catalogue) and discussed possible alternative markets. The outcome was that Kimberly-Clark, made Luecke an offer he couldn't refuse: to accept the specific brief of finding markets for Cellucotton.

Luecke reviewed all the correspondence the company had received about Cellucotton from France during the war. He noted letters from nurses who mentioned that the wound dressings also served as very serviceable sanitary napkins. Luecke saw immediately that here was a market of sufficient potential size to make it worthwhile starting up the factory again. But he failed to convince jobbers to buy his Cellucotton and make the napkins. They declared the project hopeless: such a product could never be advertised. Nevertheless, Luecke convinced Mahler and Kimberley to start production again to make a newly-designed sanitary napkin, while he went out to drum up some sales.

This was a classic example of a production-led strategy: 'Here's something we can make, now go and find a market for it'. This should of course have doomed it to failure, especially as the market experts who were consulted wouldn't go anywhere near the idea. But Luecke's background in Sears-Roebuck had given him a good grounding in the art of selling to the American housewife. His first priority was to hire an advertising agency, to come up with a good name and ads that would not offend the delicate sensibilities of the time. In a September 1919 meeting with the agency, they were playing around with the product descriptors. They latched onto its cotton-like texture, and out popped the name, Cotex. This was soon changed to Kotex to make sure it would be pronounced correctly. Later that month a few dozen boxes were shipped to a branch of Woolworth's as a test market.

The problem from the start was how to sell the product. Most women used homemade towelling pads. This involved no embarrassment for buyer or vendor in a sales transaction. The difficulty with Kotex was how to avoid the inherent embarrassment of a transaction for a product that had only one possible use, for an unmentionable topic. The problem was not unlike that faced by condom manufacturers in less enlightened times. Indeed, so big an issue was the embarrassment factor that Walter Luecke got an edict from on high that in no way could the Kimberly-Clark name be associated with such a product. So he set up a subsidiary, the Cellucotton Products Company (CPC), to be the name on the box. Needless to say, nowhere on the box appeared the dreaded term, 'sanitary napkins'.

Perhaps unsurprisingly, Luecke test marketing was not an immediate success. Here was a brand no-one had heard of, that did not mention its function on the package, and was for a use people found too embarrassing to ask for. Shopkeepers were equally embarrassed and kept the product out of sight. When people did find out what it was all about, the company was bombarded with letters strongly objecting to them selling the product at all. However, consumer pressure groups did not have the pulling power they do in today's social media world. Luecke binned the letters and pressed on. He was going to solve the manifold problems of selling Kotex.

Luecke experimented with direct marketing: he sent free samples to women whose addresses he had found in the phone book. That failed - not one contacted the company to take up the offer of regular supplies by mail. Luecke reluctantly concluded that the only viable means of selling Kotex would be through jobbers and wholesalers, backed by a two-pronged advertising campaign. Trade advertising would come first, to establish the wartime and medical credentials for the brand with the retailer. The consumer campaign would follow, again full of medical terms and imagery, with the primary aim of building name recognition. The idea was to reach a point when the customer would simply ask for a box of Kotex, rather than mutter sanitary napkins under her breath. But it was an uphill struggle. Luecke was battling deeply ingrained social taboo.

The turning point is legendary. The president of the company's advertising agency arranged a face-to-face with the editor of the widely read and highly influential Ladies Home Journal. The editor flatly refused to run the Kotex ad. In desperation, the agency president pleaded to show it to the editor's secretary, a white-haired lady in her sixties. If she didn't like the ad, he would accept the editor's judgement. But if she did, then the editor ought to run it. A coin-toss. The editor took the bait. He presumably thought his secretary to be the epitome either of upright, or uptight, American womanhood, and support his editorial policy. Her pronouncement could not have been more emphatic. Not only was Kotex a good thing, and something that women deserved to be told about, but also the Journal had to run the ad. The editor meekly complied.

Was Kotex now off to the races? In 1921, $172,000 was spent on advertising across a range of women's magazines. Few sales resulted, so Luecke's request for a further $200,000 for 1922 occasioned a good degree of boardroom nervousness. Nevertheless, the board bravely bore down on their investment, as the only hope of getting back a penny of what they had put in so far. The missing piece of the sales puzzle fell into place during 1922. The company hit on the idea of making the product a self-service item. This way the embarrassment factor could be avoided. While it may seem an obvious answer today, in 1922 self-service was almost unheard of. Shops were staffed by clerks who went and got what the customer asked for. A few pioneers, such as Clarence Saunders' Piggly Wiggly chain, had been experimenting with self-service stores with just a cashier at the exit. Otherwise, the concept was seen as being very raw, if not downright odd. Not least because it required a host of other, as yet unrealised inventions - such as the shopping cart and pricing guns - to make it function well.

Retailers were now bombarded by trade advertisements encouraging them to place Kotex's box on the counter by the till. The box was now shorn of everything but a large Kotex logo and a medicinal-looking white cross. This was now an integral part of the design. A coin box next to the Kotex would avoid the need for any interaction with store clerks at all. With consumer advertising going full steam ahead, and creating awareness and demand, sales turned the corner. By 1924 the company was converting more mills over to Cellucotton and Kotex

GREG THAIN & JOHN BRADLEY

production. Sales were further improved by Luecke's brainwave: sell the product via vending machines in ladies rest rooms. There he decided to sell singles rather than full boxes. He was not going to upset the retail trade that he had worked so hard to win over.

The corner had been turned but it had been close run. It was based on two remarkable insights. First, that a wound dressing could be adapted to a completely different use. Then, that a handful of throwaway comments from consumers could be a compelling basis for a new product. At the time no one was knocking down the doors of paper companies demanding disposable sanitary towels. Equally, manufacturing-led strategies are not always a bad idea when you have a breakthrough technology, and the ideal application isn't immediately obvious. Scott gave up and lost out on a goldmine. Kimberly-Clark could very easily have given up on the whole idea at several points, but went on to reap enormous benefits from their perseverance. Within five years of Luecke begging for a $200,000 spend on advertising; he was lavishing $3 million on the brand. Kotex was well on the way, not only to creating but owning a new and fast-growing category. Although paper was to be the mainstay of company sales for many years to come, the future of the business was now in the arena of branded packaged goods. This put them into a new realm of direct competition. The success of Kotex attracted a host of competitors, manufacturers and retailers alike. They piled into the market with cheaper versions. CPC responded by reinforcing their high ground position: improving the base product and beginning to segment the market with different pads for different needs. This maintained the value of their price premium. Their advertising featured men in white coats warning darkly of the dangers of; unsafe and unsanitary makeshift methods'.

The game changed in 1926 when Johnson & Johnson entered the fray. They launched Modess and Nupak pads, which, by being thinner, claimed to be less visible under clothing. Kotex responded with a thinner version of their own, rounded and tapered at the ends for even greater invisibility. They hired a fashion model, Lee Miller, who was the first real human used in their ads, to demonstrate the point - wearing a series of swish evening gowns and apparently little else. By 1929, CPC was delivering nearly $2 million profits a year into the parent company.

Meanwhile, the company had been developing the product that would become its next blockbuster, Kleenex Tissues. In true company style, they invented the tissues with an intended use that was completely different to the one that would make the brand famous. The origins of Kleenex go back to 1917, when company researchers developed exceptionally thin sheets of Cellucotton as potential filter linings for gas masks. The Armistice saw the end of that project. It languished for a few years until a bright laboratory assistant observed the rising use of makeup (previously restricted to loose women and in the theatre), and suggested the product might be marketed as something to remove makeup at the end of the day.

In 1923 a project was given the go-ahead to market the already-named Kleenex (which was priced at 65 cents a box of 200 sheets sized 5 by 6 inches) as a cold cream remover. Advertising highlighted the product's close association with Kotex but to disappointing effect. Sales were sluggish. Consumer research revealed the product was too small for its herculean task. So, in 1926, it was upsized to a 9 by 10 inch sheet. This, along with a pop-up box, which left the next tissue standing, was the turning point for the brand. Sales almost doubled in the next two years, to just under $1 million a year.

Then consumer surveys revealed that the sales growth had nothing to do with cold cream removal. 61% of buyers were using the product to blow their noses. Once again, the consumer had done a better job of positioning a product than the CPC marketing department. To their credit, CPC managers immediately latched onto this killer fact. They changed the name from Kleenex Cleansing Tissues to Kleenex Disposable Handkerchiefs. CPC threw a whopping $548,000 behind a new ad campaign in 1930 to announce the news, then doubled the spending for the following year. These were bold moves in the middle of the Great Depression. Wary of the way low price competitors had impacted upon Kotex, CPC initiated the production of lower-priced, private or own-label versions for most of the big retailers.

Throughout the Great Depression, sales of both Kotex and Kleenex continued to grow. Kotex was marketed to the trade as a business builder: every woman who came in to the store to buy them would invariably buy something else just to mask the residual embarrassment factor. The argument was similar to that of stocking condoms in pharmacies: it would have the positive effect of stimulating toothbrush sales by young men who suddenly became dentally aware. Kleenex sales grew simply because it was a breakthrough product. People saw it as far more hygienic than using and reusing fabric handkerchiefs which could spread infection far and wide. No doubt memories of the postwar Spanish Flu pandemic helped to fuel such sentiments. Kleenex sales were to increase seven-fold in the decade. Not only had the brand been repositioned, and then dominated market share, but the brand name became the descriptive noun of the entire category. This was the second time CPC had achieved this rare feat.

However, nothing lasts forever. Kotex experienced a much greater challenge than low-price competitors when in 1932 Earle Haas, a family doctor but working in his garage, developed Tampax tampons. In a story familiar to inventors even today (such as James Dyson), Earle touted his invention around the sanitary napkin manufacturers and was shown the door. Dispirited, he sold out to a Denver businesswoman, Gertrude Tenderich. She was made of sterner stuff. In 1934 Gertrude incorporated the Tampax Sales Corporation, and prepared to battle the big boys. Kimberly-Clark saw that their world had been changed in one fell swoop, yet tried to adapt. Fearful of missing this new market, they immediately developed their own version. This was launched in 1935 under the brand name Fibs. Not a promising start, especially as the company pulled its punches on positioning. Fibs was advertised as an adjunct to Kotex, to be used on the lighter days at the beginning and end of the period, or for hot summer days when wearing a sanitary napkin would be more uncomfortable. Worse, Fibs was flawed. It wasn't as absorbent as Tampax. To their credit, the company did not throw good money after bad and gave up on Fibs. They worked instead to consolidate Kotex's appeal with the very large market of women who were wary of using tampons.

CPC realised that their best chance of long-term success with Kotex was to be the first sanitary protection in a girl's life. Hopefully she would then stick with it until menopause. They were aware that every year, due to the effects of Mother Nature, approximately 2.5% of their loyal consumers would stop using their products forever. The aim was to replace these consumers by another 2.5% who had no experience whatsoever of the category. Their first effort at moulding young female minds had been a booklet they published in 1932. Marjorie May's 12th Birthday was designed primarily as a guide for mothers on raising the topic – a difficult task in those days. In 1940, the company changed tack. They produced 'From One Girl to Another', which replaced the fictional mother-daughter dynamic with a more conversational tone, with the style and language used between young friends.

The next step towards establishing early brand choice was much more ambitious. The Walt Disney Company was hired to make an animated film that would be distributed to high schools across the country, along with mountains of free promotional literature. The Story of Menstruation was very innovative for the time. However, being Disney-made, it was somewhat less than graphic in its depictions of the questionable delights of menstruation awaiting the young audiences. The film also relied on politically correct language rather than using terms in common parlance in high school girls' washrooms.

Encouraged by the success of The Story of Menstruation, CPC commissioned Disney to produce How to Catch a Cold for Kleenex. Costing $150,000 and released in 1951 in full colour, the film would not only be shown for years in schools; but was adopted by NBC as a demonstration of the benefits of colour television and shown nationwide throughout the 1950s. At the end of its run it had been seen by 200 million. This was more people than had seen any of the classic Disney movies to that point, and the airtime didn't cost CPC a penny!

During the 1950s, Kleenex's market share, in a still-growing market, hovered around the 50% mark. Much of the rest consisted of store brands also produced by CPC. But the wolves were circling this increasingly fatted calf. Scott Paper had launched the Scotties brand in 1955, spending heavily to promote its improved softness versus Kleenex. Scotties was unable to break through, gaining less than 10% of the market. However, Kleenex would fare less well when the Death Star of consumer packaged goods companies, Proctor & Gamble, entered the fray in 1960. They launched two dramatically better products: White Cloud toilet paper was bad news for Scott Paper; and Puffs facial tissues was equally disastrous for CPC.

Although CPC had developed two powerhouse brands in Kotex and Kleenex, parent company Kimberly-Clark was still primarily in the pulp and paper business. It was therefore under-equipped to battle the mighty Proctor & Gamble, toe-to-toe on the grocery shelves. By 1965, Kleenex's market share, which peaked a decade earlier at 53%, was down to 32% and with no sign of the floor being reached anytime soon. This trend had not been helped by the parent company devoting much of its time and resources to a series of acquisitions in the commercial paper part of the business. They purchased the Schweitzer Inc. cigarette paper business in 1957 and the American Envelope Company in 1959. As they already had a large industrial products division, developing such areas as new envelope glues and impregnated papers to cover plywood sheets, Kimberly-Clark's R&D resource was diverted from fighting the Proctor & Gamble monolith.

The company added to its troubles during the first half of the 1950s by spending virtually nothing in developing Kotex. This was despite the brand accounting for 35% of company profits. As a consequence, it became vulnerable to competitive attack. Between 1951 and 1957, the brand lost a full ten share points, albeit down to a still dominant 62%. The aggressor was Johnson & Johnson who developed a markedly superior pad, Modess. Kimberly-Clark fought back belatedly but made a serious misstep when they introduced a completely new brand. Fems was targeted at the larger woman, but only achieved a paltry 5% market share, and further diverted precious advertising funds away from Kotex.

To make matters worse, the changing consumer culture of the 1960s saw a slow but inexorable shift in the sanitary protection market from pads to tampons. This was led by the now thriving Tampax. In 1959 Kimberly-Clark started to develop a new tampon and realised they had no new technology with which to trump Tampax on the absorbency front. So they focused their efforts on improving methods of insertion and removal. They resolved to insert the tampon with an attached 'slim inserter' stick in place of Tampax's bulky cardboard applicator and used, for removal, a presumably more reliable knotted double string rather than Tampax's single. These solutions were pushed hard in advertising campaigns and desperate price-cutting tactics were adopted, but the brand failed to make a dent in Tampax.

During the 1960s sales of tampons in America trebled to around a third of the market. Sales of sanitary towels remained static. Kotex had a strong but somewhat precarious share of a static market. This was bad enough but almost a highlight compared to the disaster befalling Kleenex. Procter & Gamble's onslaught caught Kimberly-Clark in a vice, resorting both to hefty price-cutting and increased promotional spending. The only way this could be paid for was by job cuts. Kimberly-Clark seemed set on a strategy of shrinking to greatness through leaner headcount and margins. One glimmer of light came with the 1968 launch of Kleenex Boutique. It featured stylish designs upon oval boxes, and aimed to brighten up the nation's bathroom shelves. Despite lavishing 22% of the entire tissue category's advertising spend on the launch; the outcome was a first year market share of 2%. It rose to 6% the following year, but two-thirds of this came at the expense of the main Kleenex brand.

Kimberly-Clark turned increasingly towards other paper markets, but even that side of the business wasn't going very well after a few ill-judged acquisitions. Between 1957 and 1970, the company's net earnings, as a percentage of sales, declined slowly and inexorably from 8% to a shade over 4%. This was significantly worse than their archrival, Scott Paper. In 1972, earnings dropped again to 3.4%, their worst year since 1934. It looked like the consumer packaged goods side of Kimberly-Clark would turn out to be a glorious but ultimately futile chapter in the history of a commercial paper company that was increasingly shaky anyway. Both their key brands seemed to have a future of decline and despair, and the company was making next to no money elsewhere. Their strategic muddle was illustrated when the company set up K-C Aviation to service planes: they also transformed their executive airplane fleet into a scheduled airline. If you assessed company chances of quintupling its share price in the 1970s, Kimberly-Clark would be least likely. Yet, they did it, and by accomplishing a seemingly impossible feat: vanquishing Procter & Gamble.

How Did They Build The Modern Business?

The turning point for Kimberly-Clark can be traced back to the appointment of Darwin Smith as chairman and CEO in 1971. A bleak future awaited as a paper company with a couple of fading consumer brands. In his in-tray lay a bold plan: essentially to exit many of their pulp and paper businesses and to channel the funds into building resources and capabilities to become a fully-fledged consumer business. Now a packaged goods powerhouse beckoned.

Only hindsight makes this plan look obvious. Selling off a collection of paper mills would provide more funds for the consumer side, but Kimberly-Clark's problem was not simply a lack of funds. At the time, there was little evidence that Kimberly-Clark had the brands, the R&D expertise or the marketing capabilities to do anything different. For a decade or so, they had seemed capable of only an orderly management of declining brands. However, in the absence of a better plan and mindful that the company still had a 40% share of the feminine hygiene market, Darwin gave the go-ahead. Kimberly-Clark began the process by getting out of the coated paper business.

As the business re-orientated itself, there was more bad news. Johnson & Johnson, who now had a 25% share in the sanitary towel market, came out with a game-changer that they test marketed in 1969: the tab-less pad. Until now, Kotex and other pads had to be held in place via sanitary belts or safety pins. This arrangement was disliked by the consumer due to the fiddling around, and satisfactory to Kimberly-Clark who made a healthy profit on the sale of sanitary belts. This revenue stream had deterred the company doing much development work to solve the consumer problem.

Johnson & Johnson's new Stayfree brand, launched nationally in 1971, used an innovative adhesive strip along the bottom of the pad to hold it securely to the underwear - no belts or pins required. As well as being more convenient, it also greatly reduced chaffing. Taken together, the advantages of Stayfree over Kotex were vast. Johnson & Johnson had not only improved a product, they had effectively invented a new category. In fifteen years the market for tabbed pads such as Kotex would disappear. Just to add to the pain, the Stayfree launch coincided almost exactly with the relaxation of the National Association of Broadcasters' ban on the television advertising of tampons and sanitary pads. Stayfree now had the most powerful medium the world had ever seen to ram home its advantages over Kotex.

Kimberly-Clark's sensible strategy at that point was to redesign Kotex as a tab-less pad as quickly as possible and then drown out Stayfree's advertising with their own monster television campaign. Unfortunately, they did neither. They did design a tab-less pad in record time, having it ready only six months after Stayfree, but launched it as a completely new brand under the name of New Freedom. Meanwhile Kotex didn't take to the airwaves to defend its position until 1974, by which time the game was as good as over. New Freedom established itself and steadily gained market share, but could not compensate for the precipitous decline of Kotex - even after the towel was thrown in with a belated redesign to tab-less format in 1975. By then, what was nearly a 60% market share in 1970 had declined to 35% and would eventually bottom out at 15% in the mid-1980s. In 1976, market leadership passed to the ever-growing, newly named Tambrands, who themselves were eclipsed a year later by the Stayfree-inspired Johnson & Johnson. How are the mighty fallen in the midst of battle!

However, this did not mean that Darwin Smith's realignment strategy was a bust. While Kotex was heading for the rocks, the funds from the sales of various paper mills had been partly ploughed into beefing up the R&D function. This was in itself realigned away from paper, glue and laminates towards higher margins, innovative consumer products that used Kimberly-Clark's base Cellucotton technologies. First out of the gate was the launch of the Kotex Lightdays Panty Liner in 1975. This both created a new category and also effectively kept the Kotex brand alive. However, the home run that would really change Kimberly-Clark's fortunes was to come where it was least expected. They took on Procter & Gamble on their home ground; a market they created and completely dominated disposable diapers.

Soon after Proctor & Gamble bought the Charmin Paper Company, a researcher initiated a project to develop a disposable diaper. The result, after three failed test markets, was Pampers, launched in 1961. For reasons best known to themselves, the other paper companies initially gave Proctor & Gamble a free run, As a consequence they missed out on the fastest-growing consumer paper products market of the 1960s (the diaper fillings at that point being cellulose-based). Kimberly-Clark finally began work on their own version in the mid-1960s, using what their designer claimed was a superior folding pattern that better protected against leakage. That would prove somewhat debatable, but the product they test-marketed in 1968, Kimbies, did have an advantage over Pampers: adhesive strips rather than pins.

This advantage did not last long. Pampers redesigned in 1969 so they too used tape, and then the CPC research money for further improvements ran out as the company was hit by the twin disasters befalling Kotex and Kleenex. When Johnson & Johnson brought out a new diaper with fastening tape, Kimbies was all but dead. However, it would be revived by the cash influx coming from the sell-the-mills strategy. The board allocated $17 million to the project to see if something could be salvaged. By 1973 Kimbies was barely on the Proctor & Gamble's radar; but it was a respectable performer in the second-tier of brands, making a modest profit off one billion units.

Until Kimberly-Clark scored another own goal. In this accident-prone phase, the company switched to cheaper glue on the adhesive tabs. The significant loss of adhesion caused anger and anguish for parents across the country. This sounded the death knell for Kimbies which was withdrawn in 1975. The company's launch of Wypall industrial wipers in the same year did little to lift the gloom.

The situation seemed hopeless, but CEO Darwin Smith was buoyed with the funds from selling the mills and with little else to go for anyway. He encouraged one more look at getting into the category, starting from treating the entire history of Kimbies as a learning exercise. A post review of the project identified five main weaknesses:

- The unique folding design had in fact caused more leakages than did Pampers
- The test marketing they had done had been insufficient
- Inadequate product research and engineering
- The glue fiasco had diverted R&D resource at a critical time
- Inadequate market research

Despite this indictment of the Kimberly-Clark marketing and technical departments, Smith channelled all of the proceeds of a 1975 mill sale and even diverted funds from Kotex and Kleenex into a last roll of the dice. He was effectively betting the future of the company that they could beat Procter & Gamble second time around.

The good news was that Procter & Gamble, while not exactly falling asleep at the wheel, did have a few chinks in their armour. Pampers was not a perfect product. They too had glueing problems with the adhesive strips, plus the rectangular shape of the unit inevitably caused bunching between the legs and some leakage. Procter & Gamble had acknowledged this by launching an elasticated, hourglass-shaped diaper in 1976 under the brand name Luvs. They were uncharacteristically hesitant about taking Luvs to a national coverage. Luvs were a super-premium diaper, priced 50% higher than Pampers. Darwin sensed an opening. Procter & Gamble were in effect admitting that Pampers was not the be all and end all of disposable diapers, yet were sluggish in pursuing the opportunity Luvs had identified.

The Kimbies post-mortem had identified three factors where any new brand had to excel to have any chance of succeeding:

- The dryer the baby's bottom for longer, the better
- A reduction in, or elimination of leakage versus Pampers
- An adhesive tape that was reusable several times over without any danger of coming unstuck (something no manufacturer had yet achieved)

Achieve this excellence and consumers had indicated they would pay a substantial premium over Pampers. With an R&D budget four times that allocated to Kimbies, work commenced. The clock was ticking: if Procter & Gamble spent big to establish Luvs on a national footing, the window of opportunity would close.

As well as product issues, there was also a significant retailing issue to be solved. How to get on the shelves? Procter & Gamble had created a must-stock category that was as much a business builder as had been Kotex 50 years earlier. But the product was so bulky, and had such a fast turnover; it had to be allocated a disproportionate amount of shelf space just to keep in stock during the shopping day. Consequently, unlike most other product categories, retailers in even the biggest stores had a huge reluctance to stock any more than the top two brands, and maybe a cheaper private label. Therefore, for any new diaper to succeed, it had at the very least to knock the number two brand out (currently held by Johnson & Johnson). A huge challenge.

By December 1977, Kimberly-Clark was ready to go. As the name communicated, Huggies checked all the boxes – achieving a much tighter fit than Pampers and all but stopping leakage. The Kleenex name was tacked on the front to provide consumer reassurance that their beloved babies' bottoms would be cared for as much as the nation's runny noses. The brand was launched in Wisconsin and Michigan, an area of relative Pampers weakness. It was positioned not as a slightly better Luvs (which was not yet a significant player), but as a much better Pampers. The advertising was cleverly aligned. Huggies were helping mother's battle leakage, rather than taking the credit, as Pampers had been doing. The tagline read: 'Introducing a diaper that helps stop leaking'. This thought would remain communicated, in various expressions, for the next quarter century. Entering at a 30% premium to both Proctor & Gamble and Johnson & Johnson, Kleenex Huggies was racing to occupy and hold the ultra-premium segment identified by Luvs.

Within four years Johnson & Johnson, which was offering nothing better than Pampers, was decimated, and withdrew from the category completely. Proctor & Gamble finally woke up to what was happening and rolled out Luvs nationally, but now they faced the retailing space problem. With Pampers as number one brand and Huggies number two; there was no reason for anyone to find extra shelf space to display Luvs. It had no advantages over Huggies. Proctor & Gamble used all its muscle to replace Huggies with Luvs, and at one point did match market share. Theirs was a push strategy against Huggies' highly effective pull strategy (which was highly appropriate), which meant there would only be one winner.

In 1983 Huggies achieved fully national distribution with a 21% market share and, even worse for Proctor & Gamble, kept gaining ground on Pampers. Huggies was not occupying a super-indulgent niche. It had staked out territory that was becoming the new standard. In 1985 Huggies overtook Pampers to lead the market. The gamble had paid off: Kimberly-Clark was now playing and winning in the big leagues of packaged goods.

The two manufacturers waged a super-absorbency war for the rest of the 1980s. Cellulose padding was replaced by polymers with many times the absorbency. There was no decisive winner. Kimberly-Clark edged ahead with the introduction of Huggies Pull-ups in 1989. This captured a respectable 9% share, as Procter & Gamble were again slow to respond. By the end of the 1980s, Huggies was accounting for the bulk of Kimberly-Clark's sales and profits, along with a sleeper brand launched in 1980. Depend tackled adult incontinence: Kimberly-Clark deftly addressed another sensitive subject on the back of their vast experience regarding menstruation. The company also had fledgling operations in the industrial sector with a variety of wipes, masks and paper-based coveralls, and a small healthcare division.

The company had been successfully realigned behind consumer products - another newcomer was Poise pads (for adult light incontinence), which neatly extended the Kotex Lightdays technology. It had been saved from what would most likely have been a genteel slide into oblivion. Nevertheless, they were, not unlike Tambrands, essentially a one-brand company. As such, they were at risk of unforeseen technological breakthrough killing their golden goose. In a situation not dissimilar to that facing many companies today, they needed a step change in size and breadth. Otherwise, Kimberly-Clark and their Huggies brand were vulnerable to being snapped up by one of the industry goliaths such as Unilever.

The answer lay in a merger with their long-time foe in the paper business, Scott Paper. Scott's consumer division had headed in a different direction to Kimberley-Clark. They had built up strong positions in paper towels, toilet paper, and with Scotties tissues still hanging on as a second-tier value brand. Scott had also been much more aggressive than Kimberly-Clark in expanding internationally. This would provide a quick and cheap way to internationalise the Kimberly-Clark brands. Scott had been America's most profitable paper company in the 1960s, but had fallen on hard times - due mostly to a variety of disastrous acquisitions. By 1991 Scott was losing money. Nevertheless, with sales of $4.7 billion in 1993, it was a major player.

In 1994, Scott appointed Albert J. Dunlap as CEO, and he wasted no time in living up to his nickname of Chainsaw Al. Dunlap slashed every budget in sight, sold every building not deemed completely essential and cut staff numbers by 35%. Next, he began the search for a buyer. Kimberly-Clark was one of twenty-four candidates identified by the investment bankers. The $9.4 billion agreed merger between Kimberly-Clark and Scott in 1995 created a solid number two in consumer paper products behind Procter & Gamble. They had a sales presence in 150 countries and manufacturing operations in 33. To complete the deal, the Scotties brand in the United States had to be sold. Kimberly-Clark laid off 6,000 workers of their own to realise the cost synergies needed to make financial sense.

It took a couple of years to get to grips with this vastly expanded business and repair the damage of Chainsaw Al's slashing of 50% of Scott's R&D budget. By 1999 Kimberly-Clark was turning over $12 billion a year. They introduced new and improved Scott's bathroom tissue products, supported by advertising for the first time in a decade.

The same year, the new company went on the acquisition trail to beef up its healthcare lines of surgical gowns, drapes and disposable face masks. They purchased Ballard Medical Products for $774 million, which added higher-value lines: such as Trach Care, the number one line of respiratory suction catheters; enteral feeding tubes; endoscopy devices and disposable defibrillator pads. This was soon followed by a range of purchases: including Safeskin, a leading maker of disposable gloves for hospitals and scientific institutions; the makers of Italy's second-largest diaper brand; and a Polish tissue business. They also bought, where they could, rights or partnerships to market their brands abroad. Then in November 2004, the company spun off a newly created subsidiary, Neenah Paper. This was specifically created to divest the company of its remaining paper and pulp mills businesses. The transition to packaged goods was now complete, albeit with much enlarged healthcare and professional divisions.

The International Dimension

As with many US companies who transitioned into packaged goods, international expansion was not a priority for a long time. The first port of call was Canada, where the company began selling its products in 1925. They opened a newsprint mill there. They also formed a UK subsidiary to market Kotex and

Kleenex but it was little more than an import office. In 1955, the company took the UK more seriously, yet still shied away from building any overseas factories. They signed up a British contract manufacturer to make Cellucotton under licence, with the products being distributed by a Kimberly-Clark subsidiary. Two years later a new British factory was built in a joint venture with their partner, but was managed by Kimberly-Clark as they gradually took full control of their British outpost. Meanwhile in 1956, Scott Paper had entered into a British joint venture with Bowater Paper Mills, forming Bowater Scott. Their key brand was the highly successful Andrex toilet rolls.

1955 saw Kimberley-Clark venture south of the border into Mexico, buying LA Aurora Paper Company. Renamed Kimberly-Clark de Mexico, it would flourish into one of the country's leading consumer products companies, and used its factories to supply selling operations in Central and South America. In 1957 the British venture was used as a springboard into West Germany, but this three-way joint venture enjoyed limited success. Two years later, a ten-year deal was agreed with South African Pulp and Paper. They would make Cellucotton for Kimberly-Clark, which enabled the company to become a dominant player in that country's sanitary napkin market.

Things then went quiet on the international front until the 1960s when overseas expansion was seen as a major growth opportuannity. The company invested $200 million beefing up its European and Latin American set-ups while also expanding into Australia and the Philippines. During the 1970s, 20% of the company's operating assets were located outside the US, primarily in Europe and Mexico. Unfortunately, Kimberly-Clark's British operation was far less successful than the Bowater-Scott venture and then Mexico became a problem during the 1980s. A devaluation of the Peso decimated profits. In 1984, the Canadian operation was given a shot in the arm with the launch of Huggies, but overall their international expansion had been very limited. Kimberly-Clark lagged far behind Procter & Gamble and Scott Paper despite now having operations in Korea and Japan.

During the late 1980s and early 1990s, the company tried again. They invested over $500 million in Western Europe, launched diapers into Germany via a joint venture and built major new plants in Britain, Korea and Australia. As only second-tier marketing and distribution capabilities existed in those countries, these investments failed to pay back. Tentative ventures into Argentina and China did nothing to change the dynamic. Kimberly-Clark was mostly an also-ran in the rest of the world – a realisation that partly drove the merger with Scott Paper in 1995.

Following the merger, the company used Scott subsidiaries as routes to market for the main Kimberly-Clark brands. They also made acquisitions in Switzerland (serving Germany and Austria), Spain and Portugal. In Taiwan the company bought out the Kimberly-Clark and Scott Paper joint venture partners, and merged the two to form Kimberly-Clark Taiwan into one of the country's biggest consumer goods companies.

Subsequently, the company has focused on expanding its presence in developing and emerging markets, especially the six BRICIT markets: Brazil (entered in 1996, with several subsequent acquisitions); Russia (first factory opened in 2010); India (a joint venture was formed in 1994 between Kimberley-Clark and Hindustan Lever); China (first entered in 1994 and now with four factories); Indonesia (entered in 1991 and now with 800 employees); and Turkey (joint venture established in 1999). Today, slightly under 50% of Kimberley-Clark sales are generated outside the US but less than 30% of operating profit. This reflects a company that is still in development mode in many parts of the world.

How Are They Structured?

The evolution of the company structure has been mostly straightforward. The US market has predominated and there has been a relative lack of a robust acquisition strategy for the larger part of the company's history. The first major change was the re-incorporation of CPC back into the Kimberly-Clark main hierarchy in 1955. Shares in CPC had been sold to managers and employees and needed to be bought back. Following the change, marketing of CPC brands was taken over by the Kimberly-Clark marketing department.

Four years later, there was a major reorganisation aimed to decentralise what had become a cumbersome, top-down structure. Separate divisions were created for Schweitzer cigarette papers, Newsprint, Canadian operations and Consumer Products, with a small International Division tacked onto the latter. The next major change came with the merger with Scott Papers. The structure eventually settled into three divisions: Personal Care; Consumer Tissue; and Business-to-Business. Each of these, to varying degrees, was sold in four regions: United States & Canada, Europe, Asia, Latin America and Other. By 2004, United States, Canada and Europe were consolidated into a North Atlantic Group and by 2006 Business-to-Business had been split into two groups. Professional and Healthcare reflected the increasing size and specialisation of the healthcare business, and had little in common with Scott Towels and Kimberly-Clark industrial wipes.

What Have They Been Doing Recently?

2004

After the November 2004 spinoff of Neenah Paper Inc., Kimberly-Clark had annual sales of just over $15 billion. A consistent record of decent annual growth stretched back to the post-merger period. Innovation was less blockbuster and more incremental: such as Kotex Lightdays; a new folding design for Scottfold washroom dispenser towels; Huggies Convertibles; Goodnights Youth pants; Andrex with Aloe Vera and Kleenex Anti-viral tissues. The Huggies brand was extended laterally into bath and body products, using third-party manufacturers. The company recognised that greater R&D resource was needed to develop more breakthrough innovations. Other highlights included a 35% sales increase for Poise panty-liners and the company gaining number one position in the US in medical products such as face masks and exam gloves.

At this point, 58% of sales were coming from the US. Business was split fairly evenly between the three divisions of Personal Care, Consumer Tissue and Business-to-Business. All regions and divisions were recording growth, with the non-US regions growing at a significantly faster rate. This partly reflected the company's different levels of development - domestic versus overseas - and was also due to significant competitive challenges in the US markets. Of the eight main consumer product categories in which they competed (Diapers, Training/Youth/Swimming pants, Feminine Care, Adult Incontinence Care, Baby Wipes, Facial Tissue, Bathroom Tissue, and Paper Towels), Kimberly-Clark had gained share over the previous two years in only two of them (Adult Incontinence and Bathroom Tissue). This resulted in a need to discount and lower selling prices.

Outside of the US, the European business, although recording level sales for personal care products, was struggling badly. Volume was down 7% and selling prices another 3%. The region was only rescued by a 10% favourable shift in currencies.

2005

The year was dominated by two announcements: a new focused growth strategy, and a major downsizing to pay for it. The growth strategy did not contain any real surprises:

- Strengthen leadership positions in baby and child care, adult care and family care
- Build on regional strengths in feminine care (Americas and parts of Asia)
- Accelerate growth in BRICIT markets

- Extend Professional portfolio into higher margin segments (workplace, safety, do-it-yourself)
- Expand Healthcare globally, adding higher margin products to portfolio

It is hard to argue with any of this, but it was easier said than done. The bill would be met by closing twenty factories and shedding 10% of the workforce. The attractiveness of the BRICIT markets was clear. These markets contained half the world's population, most of the population growth and low but rising penetration of key Kimberley-Clark categories such as disposable diapers. The company was employing a fairly standard, multi-tier strategy in these markets. They offered: a range of low price, affordable products; mid-tier increased performance at good value; and premium priced products for the wealthy. In 2005, company sales grew by 30% in these markets. Elsewhere, the Healthcare strategy towards higher priced, higher margin products was boosted by the acquisition of Microcuff GmbH, for its proprietary endo-tracheal tube technology.

Company sales increased a respectable 5.4% to just under $16 billion, with volume growing 3% and net pricing up by 1%. Matters improved in the problematic US market, as a slew of innovation advanced sales by 4%.

2006

With another 5% sales increase the new growth strategy seemed off to a reasonable start. But, as usual with multi-faceted growth strategies, some things go better and others not so well. Virtually all the volume growth in the year came from the Personal Care and Healthcare divisions. Consumer Tissue moved backwards: a 1% volume decline was probably caused by a 3% increase in net selling prices. On the profit side however, things were not quite so rosy: cost savings of $265 million was more than swallowed up by input cost increases of $385 million.

What were the highlights of the current the growth strategy?

Strengthen leadership positions in baby and childcare, adult care and family care

Things seemed to be on track, with good volume growth in diapers in North America and Europe. The company had significantly reduced the time taken to get a range of incremental innovations to market. In tissues, the Scott brand's sales in the US topped $1 billion - primarily via a strategy of competing in the value segment of the market - and more than $2 billion worldwide.

Accelerate growth in BRICIT markets

Without explanation, this had been promoted from being the number three strategic priority since 2005. Sales were up over 20% in these markets, led by an impressive 35% increase in China thanks to Huggies now being distributed in 40 cities (although the company lagged far behind Pampers in market share). With disposable diaper penetration in the country only reaching 10%, the future looked bright indeed.

Build on regional strengths in feminine care (Americas and parts of Asia)

The mystery attached to this priority having been relegated a place was resolved. News came that their US feminine hygiene business was in the doldrums with continued share losses.

Extend Professional portfolio into higher margin segments (workplace, safety, do-it-yourself)

More bad news. The division was essentially flat, year-on-year: despite bringing Wypall microfiber cloths to market in only eight months, and launching Kimtech Pure clean room wipers for the electronics industry.

Expand Healthcare globally, adding higher margin products to portfolio

A big success story. Global volume grew 7%, led by the company's Sterling brand of exam gloves which, being made from nitrite, were proving to be a very successful, affordable alternative to latex gloves.

2007

Aided by a strong following wind on currencies, Kimberley-Clark had its best year for some time. They recorded a 9% sales increase, of which 6% came from volume, pricing and mix improvements. The stars of the show were the Personal Care division, where a volume increase of 8% contributed to a total sales increase of over 12%; and the non-North Atlantic markets, which delivered $1 billion of the total company growth of $1.5 billion. Highlights in Personal Care included a Huggies turnaround in North America, helped by a $50 million increase in the company's total marketing spend; and growth of 21% in the Developing and Emerging markets. China again led with sales growth exceeding 40%. Since 2004, sales in total Developing and emerging markets had increased 25%, powered by a 50% increase in the BRICIT markets. Elsewhere, Consumer Tissues had a decent year, growing sales by 5% in the difficult North American market.

However, the Healthcare division stuttered as the company withdrew from the latex gloves business.

2008

In a difficult year for all consumer businesses, a sales increase of 6% (up to a new record of $19.4 billion) was not to be sniffed at. Rapidly rising commodity costs meant that the company focused more on achieving price increases (up 4%) than driving volume (up 1%). Within the categories there were quite different dynamics: particularly in North America, where Personal Care sales inched ahead despite significant price increases. Consumer Tissue volumes were much less able to support higher prices, and volumes plummeted 7%. The situation was worse in the price-conscious paper towels category - volumes were down double-digit. In Developing and Emerging markets the same differences in category robustness were evident, but from a much higher baseline. Personal Care sales volumes increased by 10%, despite price increases, but Tissue sales remained flat. The BRICIT markets were again the highlight, as sales advanced another 30%.

The company was still putting cost savings money behind their brands. The marketing budget was again increased, by $95 million. One of the more notable innovations introduced was Kleenex Facial Tissue with Lotion, made using a proprietary technology. This benefited from the largest sampling campaign in the history of the brand. The company's Healthcare division continued its transition away from its heritage. Paper-based disposable items gave way to still disposable but hi-tech medical devices, such as their new enteral feeding tube introducer kit and an expansion of their range of InteguSeal microbial sealants. This part of the portfolio was now becoming quite attractive, but at 7% of total company sales and 8% of operating profits, it was a long way from being a corporate game-changer.

2009

Perhaps 2008 had imbued an over-confidence that price increases could be pushed through relatively painlessly. The company increased prices by an average of 4% in a year when commodity input costs actually decreased and in a year when national economies, particularly the US and Europe, were sluggish to say the least. The outcome was a decline in total volumes of 1.5%, compounded by adverse currency rates. These wiped out the benefit of the price increases and more besides. The vibrant Personal Care category managed to grow volume by 2% and Healthcare had an exceptional year, growing volume 14%. However, fully one-third of this growth was in facemasks due to the H1N1 influenza virus.

Hence it could not be counted on as anything other than a blip. Consumer tissue sales were down another 5% as was the Professional division.

Kimberly-Clark was now more reliant than ever before on the Personal care division for its profits: it accounted for 62% of operating profit compared to 44% of sales. But even within that, it was tough to extract consistent growth from the large US market and the European businesses, with exceptions like the UK and Italy, were something of a problem. In the rest of the world, organic sales of Personal Care products were up 15% as Kimberley-Clark expanded its reach, but few commanding positions were built. General nervousness about prospects was not helped by an end-of-year announcement of another 1,600 job cuts.

2010

Personal are once again effectively carried the business. Volume grew 3%: Health Care again provided the cream with a 7% increase. After several years of price increases and volume declines, it was difficult to escape the conclusion that the Consumer Tissue division was being milked. Its operating margin was half that coming from Personal care and clearly should be improved. The tissue category was much more commoditised than the various personal protection markets in which the company operated. Price increases that the market would not absorb and cutting headcount (another round of sackings and plant closures was to be announced in January 2011) was not looking like a viable long-term strategy for the division. Continued volume declines in a division that accounted for a third of company sales made overall progress difficult to achieve. This was in the absence of breakthrough innovation, and in truth, the company had not managed this since opening up the adult incontinence markets. The core problem was that the merger with Scott, while it had brought international and cost synergy opportunities, had not brought many strong brands into the portfolio. Nor had the R&D department pulled up any trees in the meantime.

2011

Another year and more of the same. Sales increased by 3% to $20.8 billion, with none of the trends changing. Personal Care was still driving volume growth along with the Health Care division, while Consumer Tissue was still putting up prices and losing volume. A change came in the international businesses outside of the North Atlantic. Dollar sales were up an apparently healthy-looking 8%, but volume actually declined by 6%. This was due to aggressive price increases of 7% and some minor divestments and market exits. These international businesses were now not managed regionally, but via a management group, K-C International.

The changing fortunes of the business now led the company to a revision of its growth strategy:

- Grow strong positions in personal care by using our brands and providing innovations
- For Consumer Tissue: bring differentiated, added-value innovations to grow and strengthen our brands; while focusing on net realised revenue, improving mix and reducing costs
- Continue the shift to faster-growing, higher margin segments within the Professional and Health Care divisions
- Drive growth through K-C International by deploying our strong brands and innovation capabilities

The real change from the past was a clear, increased emphasis on innovation. Kimberly-Clark had excelled at incremental innovations, particularly on the Personal Care brands with, for example, Huggies Little Movers Slip-On Diapers. However, in such established categories when facing well-established competitors, that kind of innovation is required just to stand still. It is difficult to think of a Kimberly-Clark major success that could not trace its roots back to Cellucotton, which had been invented during the First World War. Something needed to change in the R&D function. Also, the company's self-set challenge in Consumer Tissue looked more like a wish list than a strategy: more and better innovation while reducing costs and putting prices up. Good luck with that one!

During the previous five years, Kimberly-Clark had increased top-line sales by an average of 2.8% a year, barely keeping up with inflation. Gross Profit had increased by an average of 1.6% a year, due mainly to increases in raw material costs outstripping sales growth. Operating Profit had increased by only 6.7% across the entire five years, due to endless restructuring changes being taken to chase down fixed costs. Kimberly-Clark was beginning to look vulnerable.

2012

At the time of writing, the first three quarters of 2012 showed precious little change from the previous few years. Volumes were up in Personal care and Health care. There was a mixed bag in Professional; and prices were up and volumes down in Consumer Tissue. Geographically, North American sales were sluggish, Europe a mess and K-C International powering ahead. In the first three quarters of the year, K-C International sales were up 9%: including stellar performances in the Chinese, Russian and Brazilian diaper markets.

In many of Kimberly-Clark's European operations, the company had been so late to the market that their diaper business had never really got off the ground despite two decades of effort. As a consequence, the company announced it would be exiting the diaper category in western and central Europe, along with the poorer performing tissue markets in some countries. This involved the sale or closure of five factories, the loss of around 1,400 jobs and a reduction in annual top-line sales of approximately $500 million. This left just a few European strongholds for Kimberly-Clark - UK, Italy, Spain, and Switzerland. These had mostly been developed from the Scott merger or subsequent acquisitions.

What is Their DNA?

A Kimberly-Clark DNA is quite difficult to define. Both Kimberly-Clark and Scott Paper built their businesses by understanding paper and the company still has much expertise in the area with Kleenex, Scott paper towels, Andrex and the like. However, the fact is that the growing parts of their business today have little to do with paper or its derivatives; it's been a long time since Huggies were filled with Cellucotton. Nevertheless, there are interesting spikes of excellence among the spread of Kimberly-Clark's businesses.

Trust

This might seem something of a given. In the world of consumer-packaged goods, every brand is a bond of trust between brand owner and brand consumer. However, Kimberly-Clark operates in areas that both require and engender a very strong bond of trust. We have a much more intimate relationship with many of their products than we do with, say, a can of Coca Cola. Most of the company's large and thriving brands are in the fields of sanitary protection, in-continence protection, diapers and medical devices. We really need to know that these products do what it says on the pack and have been made to the highest standards.

The strength of Kimberly-Clark is that we completely trust their products on and in our bodies, dealing with issues that are a huge problem if the product fails. You cannot get more intimate than that. It is interesting that the parts of the company portfolio that are not doing well are ones that, by and large, do not have the same degree of trust dependence. If a Scott washroom towel doesn't quite dry our hands, we can live with that. If we can't depend on Depend, or an enteral feeding system, that is a deal-breaker.

Embarrassing Subjects

Another corollary of the company's product fields is that, over the decades, they have built up an institutional expertise talking to consumers about difficult or embarrassing subjects. This requires an in-depth body of knowledge on how to do these things well: and to adapt the conversation over time to reflect changing social norms and differing cultures. Kimberly-Clark can be depended upon not to be tone-deaf in dealing with difficult subjects. At the moment, they may not have markedly superior products to the likes of Proctor & Gamble, but they have the capability to have more intimate conversations with consumers. Can they achieve sufficient leverage with this advantage? That is the issue.

Absorbency

If something needs mopping up in the workplace, soaking up from some bodily function, or wiping off something delicate, be it a sore nose or a computer component, Kimberly-Clark has the answer. It makes one wonder if there are other areas in which such expertise could be applied – soaking up oil spills in the Gulf of Mexico, for example.

Summary

Kimberly-Clark is a good example of how understanding the company's history and development can illuminate issues in the business today. The company is built on three major events: the invention and propagation of Cellucotton; the bet-the-farm strategy of selling the mills and taking on Procter & Gamble in diapers; and the merger with Scott's. The first move got a paper company into packaged goods. The second got a struggling packaged goods company into a dynamic set of new and growing categories. The third got the company into a dynamic and growing set of new countries.

However, the latter two came at a price. To compete head on with Proctor & Gamble over a long period of time demands that they be at least matched on R&D resource and sales and marketing umph. This is expensive. Equally, the Scott merger really saddled the business with an increasingly commoditised tissue business they could probably well do without. While the company is turning in decent enough increases in top-line sales, it is the source of the sales growth that is concerning. Too big a part of the portfolio is in volume decline, which, once entrenched, can be very difficult and expensive to stop. The company is chasing after the costs, the latest being named FORCE (Focus On Reducing Costs Everywhere), yet is constantly restructuring as tissue volumes decline further. Consequently, profit performance in recent years has been completely underwhelming. One cannot help thinking that what the company needs is a bold move #4 and to get rid of the tissue business completely. The proceeds could then be spent on really ramping up its international division.

Kraft

Where Did It Come From?

In 1903, you could have filled a medium-sized auditorium with the food industry pioneers whose brands would one day be sold as Kraft. Little did the likes of Oscar F. Mayer, C. W. Post, George Cadbury, Theodor Tobler and countless others realise their own business empires would disappear. Instead, their enterprises would be subsumed under the name of a 29-year-old Chicago cheese pedlar, whose sole asset was a rented cart and only employee was a horse named Paddy.

James Lewis Kraft (known as J.) was an offspring of a Canadian Mennonite family. He moved to Buffalo, New York State, and worked with a cheese company. While running the Chicago branch office, his less-than-reliable partners in Buffalo decided they could do better without him. So, he was left unemployed, with $65 to his name. JL had become well versed in the business, and saw an opening by setting up his own cheese delivery service. Cheese was plagued by poor quality and much waste, so JL was first in line at the wholesalers each morning to purchase the best cheeses. Then, with Paddy pulling his rented cart, he would make the rounds of local grocers.

Having saved them an early-morning trip, he now offered a high-quality product.

Superior quality and service is never a bad business model. Yet, JL struggled to make it viable. He was dismayed to discover, after totting up his December 1903 accounts, a loss of seventeen cents. This was the outcome of early starts and cart driving in all weathers. In 1905, he had the breakthrough idea of wrapping the cheeses and branding them 'Elkhorn'. JL had realised that, as he was the guarantor of quality for his retail customers, this was in fact the primary requirement for a brand: trust. If he delivered already-wrapped cheeses under a wholesaler's or producer's name, he was a mere delivery boy. By choosing only the best cheese, he was able to brand his service – delivering reliably better cheese. This got things moving. JL soon relocated to larger premises, where four of his brothers and joined him, by 1911, the company was advertising Elkhorn cheeses across Chicago.

JL was far from happy. His brand promise was still in the hands of others. If the wholesaler's stock lacked good cheese, JL's choice of the best of a bad lot was not much help to his customers. After all, they were betting their reputations on the quality of cheese JL delivered. 'Not quite as bad as someone else's cheese' was no help to JL, the Elkhorn brand or his customers. So JL spent countless hours experimenting. He aimed to blend cheeses to achieve a regular, dependable taste and consistency. The blend would then be sterilised for an extended shelf life. If he could crack this, it would solve the main problems inherent in the category: inconsistent product and a painfully short shelf life.

Three years of experimentation got him nowhere. No matter which cheeses, temperatures and cooking methods he tried, the result was always the same: the cheese separated into protein and fat. Dismayed, his attention turned to beefing up the cheese wholesaling until the outbreak of World War One cut off imports of European cheeses. Kraft purchased an Illinois creamery to get into the production side and begin domestic manufacturing of Camembert, Brie, Edam and Gouda.

However JL never lost interest in coming up with a consistent sterilised cheese. His big breakthrough came in an experiment when he absentmindedly stirred the hot cheese for fifteen minutes and realised it had not separated. Excitedly, he poured the molten cheese into sterile containers, whereupon it set as it cooled. JL had inadvertently discovered the secret to the process: homogenising the cheese. In August 1915, the product was launched as Elkhorn Kraft Cheese ('The cheese of creamy richness – will keep in any climate'). JL patented his process the next year.

While the breakthrough was good news for the Kraft's, it was bad news for almost everyone else in the cheese industry. Kraft's sterilised cheese was a genuine paradigm-shifting innovation. It brought product consistency and prolonged shelf life to a category beset by quality and freshness issues. Consequently, Kraft incurred the wrath of the cheese barons, Inflammatory press articles describing the product as imitation embalmed and even moonshine cheese. JL had one advantage: people liked his cheese.

It was also a big hit when America entered the war in 1917. The army purchased six million cans of Elkhorn to send to troops in France, which in the process created millions of brand advocates. After the war, Kraft Cheese was being widely advertised in the main magazines of the day; and by 1923, less than a decade after inventing the process, Kraft was the largest cheese company in the world.

How Did It Evolve?

Somewhat surprisingly, since JL had spent almost his entire working life in cheese and it had made him and his brothers wealthy, he did not see Kraft as just a cheese company. In 1922, the company launched a brand of mayonnaise and three years later acquired a maker of French dressing. The company was also a prolific and accomplished advertiser, striving to be at the forefront of this developing art. In 1929, the company sponsored its first radio programme. Kraft was also one of the first to employ a home economist – Marye Dahnke – who, after a solid grounding handing out cheese samples in-store, developed a cheese roadshow. Here, she demonstrated to conservative American housewives that there were more ways to cook with cheese than sandwiches or with macaroni. In 1926, JL stumped up $1,000 for a kitchen, from which Kraft Kitchens was born. Even at this early stage, the future development of Kraft was that of a wide-ranging food company known for its product innovations and its marketing modernity and competence.

Two pivotal events occurred in 1928 that would be at the heart of Kraft's future development. JL's progress beyond being a middleman in the cheese trade was motivated by an obsession with reducing waste. This obsession led directly to the company's next blockbuster. Kraft's cheese factories, acquired in 1914, produced mountains of whey. This was a by-product of the cheese-making process, and JL set his technical experts the task of developing a product to make use of it. The outcome, launched in 1928, was Velveeta, described on the packet as 'The nutritious cheese food that's digestible as milk itself.' The product was more meltable than ordinary cheese and soon became America's leading cooking cheese. With Velveeta, Kraft had hit on an important insight: as long as the product had a nice cheesy taste, consumers valued its utility and practicality irrespective of whether, technically, it was cheese.

This insight would also play a role in the marketing of a brand acquired by Kraft the same year. It merged with the Phoenix Cheese Company of New York. Phenix Cheese had been formed in 1901 with the express purpose of acquiring the world's first cream cheese. This had been invented accidentally in 1872 by an American dairyman, William Lawrence: he subsequently called it Philadelphia. The attraction to Kraft was that Philadelphia was universally agreed to be a great product. Under Phenix, whose owners were investors rather than cheese experts, it had a painfully short shelf life of around two weeks. This severely limited its appeal. Kraft thought it could extend Philadelphia's shelf life, and, almost immediately through process adjustments, it took it to eighteen days. Continuous improvement of the utility and practicality of cheese products had already become a Kraft USP. This attracted the eye of the National Dairy Products Corporation, which acquired Kraft in 1930. National Dairy would run Kraft as an autonomous subsidiary, which left the company expertise in place but backed it up with a greater financial clout than the brothers had been able to muster. With greater financial muscle, Kraft would be able to spend big, behind product innovations coming through the pipeline.

The company's big hit of the 1930s developed in the least auspicious circumstances. The ever-acquisitive JL had bought up a host of regional salad dressing companies, including the makers of Wright's Mayonnaise. Kraft rebranded the latter in 1930 as Kraft Mayonnaise, to launch alongside Kraft Thousand Island Dressing and Kraft French Dressing. In hindsight, the Great Depression was not the best time to launch a series of salad dressings. By the end of 1931, JL's sales team agitated to pull out of mayonnaise: they could hardly give it away. JL, however, was a glass half-full man: 'I appreciate your concern, but we have to move forwards.'

Moving forward for JL meant improving the product. He buttonholed members of the Wright family, who were Kraft's resident experts on mayonnaise. What was needed, said the Wrights, was a hitherto unknown machine that: could automatically measure the ingredients to fine tolerances; blend them to a hitherto unattainable fine emulsion; and run continuously so that one batch was the same as the next. The solution came, improbably, from a class JL ran in his spare time at the local Baptist Church. A new attendee introduced himself to JL as an inventor. JL was taken with Charles Chapman and his latest invention of a combination tea wagon and dishwashing machine. He signed him up on the spot and pronounced to his bemused technical boffins the next day that Charles would be designing their new whipping machine.

While Charles tinkered away in his workshop, Kraft managers realised the new machine, amazingly, not only could do the job but would also be good for making an improved salad dressing. Then someone had the brilliant idea – perhaps thinking of the work that would be involved cleaning this machine between productions of mayonnaise and of dressing – of mixing the two products together. The answer actually tasted delicious, was cheaper than mayonnaise (and thus Depression-friendly) and was christened in honour of Charles' miracle whipping machine, 'Miracle Whip.'

JL was delighted and announced to Kraft's January 1933 sales conference that he had a product that would give the company its best year ever. Reportedly, he was drowned out in catcalls and boos when he unveiled what looked for all the world like another jar of unsellable mayonnaise. You would think by now his staff would have realised that James L. Kraft was tone-deaf to defeatism. He silenced the protests by announcing the brand would be backed by a million dollars of advertising – a colossal sum in the midst of the Depression – and would be launched at the forthcoming World's Fair in Chicago. The product went straight into test market and after just eight weeks the results were judged good enough to go national. By the end of the year, Miracle Whip was outselling all other brands of mayonnaise and salad dressing. If anything demonstrated the drive and verve of the Kraft Company at this stage, it was Miracle Whip.

James L. Kraft would also be at the heart of two other big successes for Kraft in the 1930s. The first was a triumph in the business-to-business market that was almost twenty years in the making. In 1935, JL had heard of a Chicago bakery that made an amazing cheesecake with Philadelphia. So he travelled to try a slice and was so amazed he introduced himself to the owner and offered to help in any way he could. Fourteen years later, the bakery owner finally decided to launch his cheesecake and took JL up on his offer. Kraft technicians, engineers and Marye Dahnke herself were sent to design machinery, processes and the recipe for the newly named Kitchens of Sara Lee Company. Within a few years, Sara Lee was the single largest customer for Philadelphia.

As demonstrated, JL knew a genius and/or a good idea when he saw one and had the skills and determination to back the innovation, overcoming any objections. Without these attributes, it is doubtful that one of the biggest hits in Kraft's entire history would have happened. In the early 1930s, JL received from his sales manager in St Louis a sample picked up from a store. It was a packet of Kraft Grated American Cheese attached to a packet of macaroni by elastic bands. This homemade combo deal was the work of an enterprising St Louis macaroni salesman. JL was all over the idea. He brushed aside his brother's response - that they weren't in the macaroni business and it was hard enough selling cheese - and went straight to Marye Dahnke's kitchens for a second opinion. Marye immediately saw the appeal. It saved the housewife trailing to two different parts of the store. A recipe was quickly developed and, very sportingly, the St Louis macaroni salesman was hired to work on the launch of Kraft Cheese and Macaroni Dinner. The revolutionary 'meal for four in nine minutes' was launched in 1937 as one of the first true convenience foods and cleared a million boxes in its first year.

Following other new ventures in the 1930s included Kraft Caramels in confectionery and Kraft Sandwich Spreads. Kraft was a vibrant, modern, innovative, broadly-based food company, and one the government naturally turned to on the outbreak of the Second World War, The Company would make two main contributions to the war effort: one would improve the nutrition and morale of millions of servicemen and women, the other would save millions of lives.

Kraft was heavily involved in the development of 'K' Rations in 1943. Kraft's existing sterilised cheese, just like everyone else's, did not meet the much different needs of the war. The shelf life and quantities required were far above existing capabilities. The development of a rapidly curing cheese processed at extremely high temperatures became another 'drop everything' project. The result in 1943 was a cheese that took just 24 hours to turn from fresh milk, in at one end of the factory, to, out of the other, tins of cheese that essentially lasted forever. The US Government ordered 100 million pounds of the stuff and the technology would benefit Kraft's production of a wide range of products. Within the next two years, further breakthrough innovations included an industrialised process to make Swiss cheese, and another that extended the shelf life of Philadelphia to several months.

Kraft's second contribution to the war effort came with its involvement in an issue of such importance it would be second only in priority to the Manhattan Project. In 1941, the US Government had been approached by British scientists who had been trying, and failing, to industrialise the production of a potentially wonder antibiotic, penicillin. The British had been able to produce it in minute quantities, enough only to test on mice and one person. The patient, a policeman who had pricked his thumb on a rose thorn and developed a massive infection, had made what seemed like a miraculous recovery until the drug ran out. Then unfortunately he relapsed and died. Penicillin was derived from the Penicillium notatum mould which, as it turned out, was the mould used in the production of Camembert cheese. Kraft employed the free world's leading expert on making Camembert, 'Doc' Stine. JL told Stine to drop everything and solve the problem of growing enough penicillin cultures. The British scientists had only ever been able to make a test tube full.

Stine decided, after encountering the same frustrations as the British, that he needed to find a stronger strain. He isolated hundreds of strains from as many types of Camembert cheese as he could muster. By June 1942 he had made enough penicillin for a ten-person trial. It was so stupendously successful the Government immediately authorised Doc Stine's cultures and process to be industrialised by large pharmaceutical firms. It had been an amazing achievement given that penicillin had been discovered as long ago as 1928 and no one had been able to solve the problem of industrialising it.

After the war, Kraft, which was still a wholly owned, autonomous subsidiary of the National Dairy Products Corporation, changed its name to Kraft Foods Company. This better reflected the broad nature of its product range. Kraft next set about its most ambitious marketing exercise to date: embracing the emerging medium of television. On Wednesday, 7th May 1947, the Kraft Television Theatre became the first commercially sponsored programme on network television. Commercials during the hour-long programme consisted of live cooking demonstrations masterminded by the indefatigable Marye Dahnke. They featured what became known as the 'Kraft Hands' - the demos concentrated entirely on the products and only the hands and wrists of the home economists were in view.

Marye came up with enough recipe ideas for over 650 weekly episodes, and the Kraft Television Theatre would go down in history as one of the most successful sponsorships ever.

The Kraft Television Theatre was the perfect vehicle to promote the next slew of Kraft product innovations. These were aimed at increasing the convenience of cheese, the two most successful being Kraft Cheese Slices and Kraft Cheez Whiz. For once it was not James L. Kraft behind a major innovation, but his brother Norman, who ran the R&D function. Norman would require the same Kraft disregard for naysayers to bring Cheese Slices to market. He first had the idea in the mid-1930s to make cheese slices, instead of making cheese which the grocer or housewife would then slice. In manufacturing terms it was also a lot cheaper, if the technology could be developed, to makes cheese slices rather than slice cheese. The big difference was the saving of labour costs and production difficulties involved in slicing.

By 1941, the product was being test marketed, but the Army's requirements for cheese took up the entire capacity of the factory involved. So the project was shelved until after the war. In 1945, when Norman got things moving again, he encountered the typical sales force reaction. They wanted the easiest sell. Quizzed on value for money, cheese slices versus loaf cheese, he said that sliced would cost six cents a pound more. Cue mass head-shaking, tutting and sucking of air through teeth. He was told to come back when it was the same price per pound. Norman was back in 1947 and Slices was test marketed in Detroit, with disappointing results. Consumers could not tell that the product was sliced: when they could, they did not believe the slices would come apart. After more work and another test market, the company nervously went national in early 1951. They booked a phalanx of demonstration spots on the Kraft Television Theatre. These did the trick and, within a year, Kraft Cheese Slices was the most successful new product in the company's history. James L. Kraft lived to see this success before passing away on 16th February 1953.

While Kraft Cheese Slices was breaking all sales records, next off the production line was another soon-to-be-star of the Kraft Television Theatre's ad breaks. Cheez Whiz was created as an all-purpose cheese sauce. So all-purpose did it become that, when the company did market research to ascertain how consumers were using the product, they came back with over 1,000 different answers. Other launches included: Cracker Barrel in 1954; Kraft Fudgies and the first portion-controlled mayonnaise servings for the food service channel in 1956; Kraft Catalina French Dressing in 1957; and Kraft Jet-Puffed Marshmallows together with whipped cream cheese in 1959. It seemed Kraft had an endless production line of innovations to stay at the forefront of the convenience food revolution.

Kraft also remained at the forefront of other shifts in American society. In 1960, it was the first major player to introduce low-calorie salad dressings. This tapped into a hitherto niche market of hard-core dieters rather than counter any objections to its mainstream offerings. Another big innovation came from the next generation of the Kraft family. G. Howard Kraft, son of JL's brother Charles, solved the company's long-running attempts to extend shelf life of the range of regular cheeses, which could not benefit from sterilisation.

Hitherto, the focus had been on minimising the growth of the naturally-present mould hrough the development of mould-inhibiting wrapping materials. G. Howard's insight was to deny the mould oxygen, so it couldn't grow at all. He replaced air in the package with carbon dioxide. This was absorbed naturally by the cheese, shrinking the wrapper tight around the product. If a wrapper wasn't tight, it meant there was a hole somewhere letting air in. This would be visible to quality control checks. It was a brilliantly simple and effective technology that became the industry standard once Kraft had reaped first-mover benefits.

Its Kraft subsidiary was National Dairy's leading and most successful component. National Dairy took closer interest, first absorbing Kraft into more of a divisional structure and then in 1969 renaming the entire company Kraftco Corporation. In 1976 it was renamed Kraft Inc. With sales of just under $5 billion, mostly coming from Kraft products, it had been one of the best acquisitions in packaged goods history. But the times they were a-changing'.

The days when the majority of American women stayed at home and cooked recipes gleaned from the Kraft Television Theatre were over. More women than ever before were working full-time and home baking was becoming a thing of the past. This was hurting sales of Philadelphia, a product primarily used in baking.

Snacking was all the rage and consumers told Kraft via focus groups that they still liked the taste of Philadelphia and wanted to use it on snacking occasions, but the product simply didn't deliver. Philadelphia cream cheese was too hard to spread; it either broke the crackers or dug holes in slices of bread. The infamous whipping machine was dusted off to aerate the product but that didn't work. The project of making a spreadable Philadelphia was dropped until someone remembered that the huge 50 lb blocks sent to bakeries had a cream dressing mixed in to make it malleable. The same mix was tried in consumer-sized portions but rejected because it didn't taste the same. One tweak to the cheese culture later and Philadelphia Soft Cream Cheese was born. Launched in 1979, it saved the Philadelphia brand from a lingering death.

Kraft's next move was by far its least predictable to date. The changing life-style issues behind the development of Philadelphia Soft Cream Cheese had also slowed the growth of the entire company. Kraft was no longer groundbreaking emergent consumer trends as it had been for its first 40 years. Many Kraft products were now showing their age. Modern, trendy, working moms were more likely to associate the Kraft name with what their mom used to cook. This was also the era when conglomerates were in vogue; why tie yourself to the fate of one particular category when you could buy or merge your way into faster-growing ones? Even so, not many would have predicted that in 1980 Kraft would merge with the industrial firm Dart Industries.

Dart Industries was a $2.4 billion turnover mishmash containing, among other things, a paper cups business, West Bend kitchen appliances, Duracell batteries and, the jewel in its crown, Tupperware. Why would Kraft want to buy Tupperware? That brand was just as dependent on women having the time to attend Tupperware parties as Philadelphia had been on women baking. It was a mystery, known only to the Kraft board.

Added to Kraft's $6.4 billion sales, the newly-merged Dart & Kraft was now the 27th-largest US Company. They had combined sales of more than $9 billion, although each company would be run autonomously. A year later, the company added to its kitchen appliance business by acquiring Kitchen Aid for $460 million. Whether this was all a big distraction for the Kraft division or whether the company had just lost its way matters not. The outcome was that the foods side of Dart & Kraft spent the next few years going nowhere fast. Its $4 billion sales of US consumer foods in 1982 would not be exceeded until 1987. Not only were many brands tired but also the once-innovative marketer had become known as the Dudley Do-Right of the packaged goods industry. Breakthrough innovations were few and far between, the only ones of note being the development of light versions of Philadelphia and Miracle Whip in the early 1980s; and the spending of $35 million to become the first major food company to switch over to tamper-evident packaging.

The trend to eating out was hurting Kraft across the board. The company responded in two ways. In the mid-1980s, it invested heavily in buying up dozens of food distribution companies, becoming the second-largest foodservice company in the United States. It also realised that it needed entry into the one dynamic grocery food category of that time, frozen foods. So, it acquired Tombstone Pizza in 1986, the number-one premium frozen brand in 22 Midwest and West states. Kraft immediately expanded geographically and to speed up new product introductions, such as microwave pizza in 1987. The same year the company spent nearly $300 million for the Budget Gourmet line of frozen entrées: although that would be sold on to Heinz seven years later.

Meanwhile, the core Kraft management culture was getting a long-overdue shake up. There is no doubt that once the five Kraft brothers had retired, the company had lost verve and become staid, risk-averse and inward looking. New president Michael Miles, an ex-Leo Burnett adman who had been recruited from running Kentucky Fried Chicken, was determined to shake things up and bring back some of the company's earlier strengths. The cosy, promote-from-within culture went out of the window. Senior executives were poached from Proctor & Gamble and other top companies, while MBAs were brought in at junior levels. These changes coincided with a belated recognition that the Dart merger had brought no good to Kraft. In 1986, the company was split up. Kraft kept Duracell while the rest was parcelled off as Premark International. So departed the Tupperware unit that had been nothing but trouble for Kraft. The next year Kraft changed its mind about Duracell and sold that off to venture capitalists for $1.8 billion.

Kraft was back to being a food company once again. It would have little enough time as master of its own destiny, because of big changes taking place in the tobacco industry. This is where the Kraft story takes something of a different turn vis a via other companies in this book. Kraft didn't build the modern business: Philip Morris did.

How International Is It?

A business as complex as Kraft Foods consists of hundreds of acquired brands. It is impossible to chart its full international development, so we shall concentrate on the initial international spread of the Kraft brand name and then jump to its post-Nabisco acquisition status.

Kraft's first move outside of the US came as early as 1920. This was in the Kraft brothers' native Canada. They purchased MacLaren's Imperial Cheese Co., which had a factory in downtown Montreal. Canada gave easier access to the British market, which Kraft exploited four years later by opening a sales office in London. Kraft entered the British food market just as it was beginning to develop chain grocery stores. This meant the British population grew up with the Kraft brand, which would join the very select group of US companies, such as Heinz, Kellogg and Ford that were not really seen as being American at all.

Britain also gave ready access to the other main markets of the British Empire including Australia, where its brands came to the attention of the country's largest cheese and butter dealer, Fred Walker. In 1922, Fred had developed what would become Australia's most famous indigenous brand, Vegemite. So he had a strong hand to play when he went to America in 1926 specifically to negotiate

Australian exclusivity to import Kraft products. JL, no mean negotiator himself, talked Fred into a joint venture, which resulted in the creation of the Kraft-Walker Cheese Company. Australia became another country where the Kraft name would be familiar and feel local to generations of consumers.

Kraft's next overseas venture would not fare so well (Velveeta Cheese was launched in Germany in 1937), but in 1950 another Kraft name became a firm favourite of the British. The then revolutionary Kraft Dairylea was launched on a Britain in the midst of post-war austerity and food rationing. Kraft was happy to develop the British and Australian subsidiaries and let them develop their own export trade. It was not aggressive in expanding its overseas markets and did not develop a significant presence on the European mainland until the 1984 acquisition of the Osella cheese business in Italy. By this time overseas sales amounted to around $1.7 billion, dominated by the original three markets of Canada, Britain and Australia.

At the time of the acquisition by Philip Morris, Kraft and General Foods had somewhat similar international profiles.

A comparison of Kraft's and General Foods' international profiles in 1989

Country	Kraft	General Foods
United States	8.5	7.7
Canada	0.7	0.6
Europe	1.3	1.8
Asia-Pacific	0.3	—
Latin America/Rest of World	0.2	0.3

Outside of North America, General Foods' trade was mostly accounted for by Maxwell House, which was Britain's leading brand of instant coffee. However, when the two companies' sales were combined, Kraft General Foods had the highest dollar overseas sales of any American food company. The acquisitions of the coffee and chocolate combine Jacobs Suchard in 1990 and the chocolate firms Wedel in 1991 and Freia Marabou in 1993 substantially increased the company's profile in Continental Europe and South America. There, Suchard's Milka brand was particularly strong.

By 2001, after the Nabisco acquisition, overseas business was accounting for around 25% of total sales. This level had not changed for Kraft since the 1970s. Europe represented about three-quarters of that total, with Latin America and Asia still under-developed when compared to other major food companies. By this point the company had operations in 68 countries. This meant, when combined with export markets, that Philadelphia was sold in 94 countries, making it the world's largest brand of cream cheese. Milka was just behind at 91 countries, followed by Maxwell House at 78 and Ritz Crackers at 49.

Emerging markets were an issue. In 2003, they only accounted for 11% of Kraft's sales despite its 30% share of global packaged foods. Nevertheless, Kraft had begun making baby steps. Philadelphia was launched in Brazil and within six months became the best-selling cream cheese on the market. Also in 2003 its Russian business, anchored by the recently purchased German confectionery firm Stollwerck, grew volume by 14%. However, Kraft could not afford to stand on the emerging markets touchline for much longer.

How Did It Build Its Modern Business?

Philip Morris, for its entire history mostly a cigarette maker, began to diversify in the 1970s along with other tobacco companies. It acquired Miller Brewing and Seven-Up, although neither did particularly well under its ownership. They went searching for better acquisitions, and in 1985, packaged goods food companies fell into the crosshairs of the tobacco giants. R. J. Reynolds acquired Nabisco Brands for $4.9 billion and Philip Morris quickly followed suit by acquiring the sluggish General Foods (the company Post Cereals had developed into) for $5.75 billion.

General Foods was by then a $9 billion turnover company that had acquired along the way brands such as Crystal Light, Jell-O, Kool-Aid, Birds Eye, Oscar Meyer and Maxwell House; in addition to Post Cereals and a large business in frozen vegetables. Philip Morris initially left General Foods to run as before but became increasingly unhappy with its sluggish performance, particularly in coffee and cereals. The company was number three in both categories and losing share. Almost from day one, Philip Morris had been on the lookout for another food company acquisition and Kraft's sale of the unwanted parts of Dart, and then Duracell, suddenly made it a prime candidate. As there was very little overlap between Kraft's and General Food's portfolios, there was unlikely to be any antitrust issues. So in October 1988 it was announced that Philip Morris would acquire Kraft for $13.1 billion. It became the second-largest acquisition in US business history, behind that of Gulf Oil by Chevron. Such was the annual cash surplus generated from the cigarette business that Philip Morris estimated it would pay off the $10 billion of financing debt within five years.

Philip Morris now had a food business with combined sales of over $15 billion; the question was – what to do with it? Owing to the differences in product categories, there were unlikely to be any production efficiencies of note. In addition, while bigger is always better when dealing with retailers, at that time both companies were big enough to be able to negotiate effectively. However, Philip Morris was well aware it was getting not just a roster of big brands and a decent-sized international business but also a better calibre of management in Kraft than it had inherited with General Foods. How best to transplant that expertise? After a year of running the businesses completely independently, the decision was made in 1989 to combine the two companies into one. It was called Kraft General Foods. The initial level of integration was quite light, primarily merging the International and Canadian divisions. The combined company would operate as seven distinct operating units, separated along geographic lines with the US units separated mostly by route to market:

Kraft General Foods' seven operating units and their turnover in 1989

Unit	Turnover ($billion)
General Foods USA	5.1
Kraft USA	4.5
KGF International	3.9 (Kraft plus Maxwell House)
KGF Commercial Products	3.8 (mainy foodservice and 3rd party supply)
Oscar Mayer & Co.	1.3 (recently purchased by General Foods)
KGF Frozen Products	2.1
KGF Canada	1.3

Philip Morris managed the whole thing relatively hands-off. It conducted quarterly performance reviews and bi-annual strategy planning sessions while imposing the (lower) Philip Morris capital expenditure approval limits. In its first year, the focus of Kraft General Foods was to make its numbers head off any more attention from Head Office. It succeeded, by generating over $2 billion in operating income off $23 billion in sales. Although the General Foods USA unit was larger than Kraft USA, it was only half as profitable. This contributed to the decision to give virtually all the top jobs to Kraft people.

The next year a nod was given in the direction of integration by appointing Vice Presidents for Marketing, Sales, Technology and Operations. Nevertheless, the business units still ran mostly autonomously. It was only after five years of largely lacklustre performance by the various US units that Philip Morris bit the bullet and announced a full integration in January 1995, shortly after the announcement that the Foodservice unit was up for sale. Philip Morris had not been happy with the performance of its two acquisitions (which had been added to in Europe by the acquisition of Jacobs Suchard in 1990) and now saw that full integration under the Kraft Foods banner was the best way forward. The merged company would have the largest direct sales force in the US and would be better able to execute cross-category innovations such as Jell-O Yoghurt.

The combined businesses had performed sluggishly in the early to mid-1990s, simply because they were not coming up with many blockbuster new products. Things had started brightly with the 1989 launch of Kraft's Fat Free Miracle Whip and pourable salad dressings and Oscar Mayer's award-winning Lunchables. There was not much following on behind. So the company focused more on acquisitions: bringing in Capri Sun in 1991, Jack's Frozen Pizza Inc. in '92 and Callard & Bowser in '93, along with Nabisco's cold cereal business. The same year the company also sold its ice cream and Birds Eye frozen vegetables businesses.

It would be 1996 before the company had its next big hit. They launched DiGiorno Rising Crust Pizza onto a national market. A genuine breakthrough. James L. Kraft would have been proud of its 'It's Not Delivery. It's DiGiorno' tagline. This was the exception to the rule. Innovations such as Post Cranberry Almond Crunch, special flavour editions of Jell-O, Stove Top Classics, Philadelphia Snack Bars and a microwaveable Kraft Dinner were all well and good, but weren't enough to do more than keep a $20 billion-plus food business ticking over. Kraft Foods' sedate growth coupled with the increasing size and power of the major retailers was shifting the balance of power away from the company. This, along with the usual tobacco cash mountain, persuaded Philip Morris to go for another big food acquisition. In 1999, RJR Nabisco was mired in tobacco-related litigation cases, which were depressing the stock value of the entire enterprise. This prompted the company to divest itself of the tobacco business and rename itself the Nabisco Group Holding Corp. The company's sole asset was an 80.1% share in the Nabisco food business: 19.9% having been placed on the stock market in the mid-1990s. The next year Philip Morris took its chance and acquired Nabisco Holdings for $18.9 billion and, having learnt the lessons from keeping General Foods and Kraft apart for too long, immediately began to merge the two. The next year Philip Morris sold a 16.1% stake in the newly enlarged Kraft Foods. The initial $8.4 billion public offering was the second biggest in US history.

In 2001, Kraft Foods was a gigantic foods business, the largest in North America and the second largest in the world. Only 0.4% of American households did not buy any of the expanded company's products. Thirty-five of its brands had been around for more than 100 years, although that was not necessarily a benefit, while six brands each had revenues of over $1 billion. The integration of Nabisco increased company revenues by 28% to $33.9 billion, around 75% of which came from the US. The volume increase of 3.7% in the first year indicated that management distraction had been avoided this time around.

The combined product portfolios fell into five product categories:

Kraft Foods' five product categories and their turnover in 2001

Product category	Turnover ($billion)
Snacks	10.1
Beverages	6.6
Cheese	6.3
Convenience Meals	5.5
Grocery	5.4

New products generated around $1.1 billion in the year, which, at a little over 3%, showed how far the company was still off the pace on this measure. More encouragingly, volume grew by 11% in Developing Markets, although Latin America and Asia Pacific combined only accounted for around 9% of total sales.

The new business defined its strategy as follows:

- Accelerate growth of core brands – innovation would be focused on four high-growth consumer needs: snacking, beverages, convenience meals, and health and wellness.
- Drive global category leadership – Kraft Foods was now a huge business, so making size count seemed a good idea.
- Optimise the portfolio – slow- or no-growth categories would go (first on the list was the French confectionery business sold to Cadbury), while acquisitions in high-growth categories or countries would be sought.
- Deliver world-class productivity, quality and service – as if any business would say otherwise.
- Build employee and organisational excellence – ditto.

Long on generic statements and the whats, you may think, but rather short on the hows.

But the rate of progress was maintained in 2002 with another 3% volume increase, albeit assisted by the acquisitions of a Turkish snack business and the Australian distributor of Nabisco biscuit brands. New products contributed the remainder with Double Delight Oreo driving the brand to its highest ever US market share of over 14%; Chips Ahoy! Cremewiches; Velveeta Creamy Potatoes; and co-branded efforts across old company lines such as Oreo and Chips Ahoy! Jell-O No Bake pies. Pretty much the only existing lines putting on double-digit growth were the Capri-Sun and Kool-Aid Jammers ready-to-drink beverages and DiGiorno pizzas.

If it was not already clear that adding together two low-growth businesses leaves you with a bigger low-growth business, it became so in 2003. Sales volume increased by a measly 0.7%. This was not the outcome that Philip Morris had expected from its vacuuming-up of three of America's major food businesses. For a management that had predicted a 3% volume growth to deliver only 0.7% meant something had gone badly wrong. The main issue was that unforeseen cost increases in commodities, energy, pensions and medical benefits had been passed on to the consumer as higher prices. The consumer, not unnaturally, had baulked at the prospect of paying more for Kraft's pensions, and gone elsewhere. This drove down volumes and the share in US cheese, cold cuts, coffee, crackers and cookies (only a business as sprawling as Kraft could have at least five product categories all beginning with the same letter). The panic button was hit in September: $200 million was invested in four months to roll back prices and prop up sagging volumes.

But this was not an isolated incident of accountants pushing up prices while the marketing department was out at an agency party. It was symptomatic of a business not delivering growth and having nowhere to turn but pricing when something went wrong. Meaningful innovations were barely trickling out of the pipeline, and the portfolio was unbalanced when compared to the current consumer trends towards health and wellness, on-the-go snacking and hydration. The company was also unbalanced internationally, being too dependent on developed markets such as the United States, the United Kingdom and Australia while its China business was going nowhere. Nettles had to be grasped.

New structures, strategies, investment levels and areas of focus were announced. The company would move to a full-on matrix structure where global category teams would be responsible for category development, global brand management and innovation. A new four-point strategy was unveiled:

- Build superior brand value – a belated recognition that not enough brands had more relevant benefits than the competition, per dollar paid.
- Transform the portfolio – this was now badly out of whack with consumer, customer, retail and demographic trends.
- Expand global scale – emerging markets had to be taken seriously.
- Reduce costs and asset base – in other words, 1–3 were going to be expensive. A major restructuring was announced that would close twenty factories and slash 6,000 jobs

Another announcement was that a further $600 million would be ploughed into shaving down prices and propping up volume during 2004 alone. This would expect to result in volume growth creeping up to 2% (including any acquisitions) – not the best return from $600 million. Kraft Foods, and the people running it, seemed to be on shaky ground.

How Is It Structured?

Even more than with Kraft's international development, it is instructive to consider the evolution of Kraft's management structure before the merger with General Foods and the incorporation of Nabisco.

Immediately prior to being acquired by Philip Morris, Kraft had nine divisions reporting to a Chief Operating Officer: Refrigerator Products, Grocery Products, Frozen Foods, Dairy, Food Ingredients, Food Service, Sales, Operations and Technology, and International. The US-based product groups operated somewhat autonomously, with no over-arching marketing or category management structure. After the Philip Morris acquisition the decision was initially taken not to merge the five US food divisions. This was despite a project team recommending full integration as soon as possible. The latter was put off for another six years, partially because the merger of the two companies in Canada had gone very poorly, particularly in the Sales function. Both companies had vast product ranges: each sales team was very sketchy about the other's portfolio. This led to a tendency for each salesman to promote the portfolio he or she knew best. The situation got so bad that the President of Kraft General Foods Canada was hauled in front of the heads of his seven top customers to be given a severe ear-bashing.

The 1990 mini-restructure was Kraft General Foods' first move to an over-arching marketing function, with links to all the business units. This function would remain largely unchanged even after the full 1995 merger of the US divisions. The year previously, the acquisition of the substantial Jacobs Suchard led to its merger with the much smaller Kraft Europe. This created Kraft Jacobs Suchard as a wholly owned subsidiary of Kraft Foods International.

The next major structural change would come after the disappointing 2003 results highlighted the need for Kraft Foods to catch up with other global packaged goods companies. The setting up of a Global Marketing and Strategy group was not just a rebranding of the previous global marketing function; but a real shift of power away from the business units towards the centre. Category strategy, major innovation projects and global brand management would become defining features of this new function; while still leaving a high degree of autonomy to meet local tastes and nutritional needs – a Kraft strength – with the individual regional and country business units. But Kraft was playing organisational catch-up compared to the likes of Nestlé, Unilever and Heinz.

What Has It Been Doing Recently?

2004

The new strategy and structure were apparently off to a good start with sales up by 5.5% to over $32 billion and volume up by 2.8%. However, fully half of the revenue increase came from favourable currency movements, while the majority of the volume increase was due to the acquisition of Fruit2O, a North American flavoured-water brand. Within the divisions not affected by the acquisition, volume movement was positively arthritic, as Table 10.4 shows:

Volume movement of various Kraft sectors in 2003/04

Division	Volume change 2003/04 (%)
US Convenience meals	+1.5
US Grocery	+0.7
US Snacks & Cereals	+1.4
Europe, Middle East & Africa	−1.3
Latin America & Asia-Pacific	−1.0

However, the company was at the beginning of a strategic transformation so what was more important was the progress being made to reshape Kraft Foods. Here there were promising signs within the now expanded number of strategic thrusts:

Build Superior Consumer Brand Value

Carrying the breakthrough innovation load once again was DiGiorno pizzas, with the introduction of Thin Crispy Crust Pizza and the Rising Crust Microwave Pizza, which cut preparation time down from twenty minutes to five. Cracker Barrel and Kraft Cheese Sticks were good snacking introductions and over 500 lines had improved nutritional profiles. All good stuff but not enough to drive the business forward. More significant was the rollout of Kraft's Consumer Relationship Marketing (CRM) programme. This really was best in class. Kraft.com was the number-one website amongst food companies, while the

What's Cooking and Food&Family quarterly magazines were among the top circulation magazines in Canada and the US.

Build Shopper Demand Through Superior Customer Collaboration

This was a new element to the strategy and long overdue.

Transform the Portfolio

To be fair to Kraft, it was a huge portfolio to transform and there was little it could do in any one year to make much of a difference. To tap into health and wellness trends the company announced collaboration with South Beach Diet, labelling existing products that met the diet's principles while a range of specially formulated lines was in development. Also, the Nabisco 100 Calories Packs and Ritz Chips were big successes in their first year. Elsewhere, the test marketing of the Tassimo hot beverage system in France had been so successful a global rollout was planned for 2005. The company also agreed to sell its sugar confectionery, yoghurt and UK desserts businesses for over $1.5 billion.

Expand Global Scale

While operations in Brazil, Russia, China and Mexico were beefed up, the percentage of operating income coming from overseas was going down rather than up. In 2002, 24% of income came from Kraft International, but this had fallen to 19.4% by 2004. Kraft was still a US-focused business, where its top-five customers accounted for 28% of total company sales; Wal-Mart alone accounted for more of Kraft's sales than did Europe, Middle East & Africa put together.

Drive Out Costs and Under-performing Assets

Thirteen plants were announced for closure. This would still leave the company with 179, so the change was little more than good housekeeping.

Strengthen Employee and Organisational Excellence

The Global Marketing and Category Management Team had spent 2004 getting organised, so we shall look for their influence and effect in the next year.

Act Responsibly

Also new, this element of the strategy covered areas like nutritional labelling, where Kraft led the way to implement clearer information on small pack sizes; healthy eating, where Kraft implemented its 'Sensible Solutions' symbol to highlight better-for-you food options; and advertising to children, where Kraft committed to only advertise Sensible Solutions products to children aged 6–11, phasing out the promotion of non-Sensible Solutions ones.

2005

The new strategy should have shown made impact on growth by now and it had not. Excluding things like the 53rd accounting week and M&A effects, total volume was down by 1%. The bottom line did even worse as the company felt unable to pass on, in increased pricing, of around $800 million of increased commodities' costs. Kraft was held back by private label brands and European hard discounters holding down prices, particularly in Germany. This showed the fundamental fragility of much of the Kraft brand portfolio: it didn't have enough differentiated brands that could stand significant price premiums.

There were bright spots. Sales from new products hit a company high of $1.5 billion, with the South Beach products proving to be mostly incremental. The Crystal Light/Clight brand grew by 12%, reinforcing its position as the US's number-one non-carbonated diet beverage. Also Tang, available in 80 countries, grew by 10% worldwide, while Philadelphia's global sales increased by 7% and the Thin Crust frozen pizza technology delivered $175 million in sales across three brands. The new global Marketing function was making its presence known with new global campaigns for Philadelphia and Maxwell House.

Although the company had over 2,000 people in R&D across five key technology centres (three in the US, one in the UK and one in Germany), the total R&D spend as a percentage of sales was a paltry 1.1%. So it was difficult to view this as a war-winning weapon. It was perhaps also significant that not one of the R&D centres was located in developing markets. There revenues grew by 8%, although it's hard to say the company was thriving. Volume declined in China, Brazil and much of Latin America. This lack of progress was behind a November announcement of a reorganisation of the International businesses into two revised segments: European Union and Developing Markets, Oceania and North Asia.

The final change announced in the year was the addition of three 'guiding principles' to the seven elements of the strategy, these being:

- Put Consumers First, Work Simply

- Act Quickly
- Play to Win

If anything summed up the problems in the company, it was having to put these in writing.

2006

Unsurprisingly, given Kraft's lack of real progress, there was a change at the top in June 2006. An ex-General Foods executive, Irene Rosenfeld, was brought in as CEO from PepsiCo, where she had been successfully running the Frito-Lay unit. She was clearly not impressed with what she found. With volume down by 5% year-on-year (3%, discounting the 2005 53rd accounting week), Irene pulled no punches: 'We recognise that we must fix certain aspects of the business to deliver predictable growth over the long term.' She was spoiled for choice about what to fix first. Again, factoring out the 53rd week issues, the divisions' volume performances in 2006 had been mostly dire:

Volume changes by division in 2006

Division	Volume change year-on-year (%)
North America Beverages	−4.8
North America Cheese & Foodservice	−2.8
North America Convenience Meals	+2.5
North America Grocery	−19.6
North America Snacks & Cereals	−1.4
European Union	+4.0
Developing Markets, Oceania & North Asia	+1.1

While North America Grocery had been affected by the sales of much of the Canadian portfolio and the fruit snacks business, the rest of that portfolio had also performed poorly.

Given such a sorry state of affairs and a new CEO at the helm, you would have bet your house on a new strategy appearing. Irene did not disappoint. While the company clearly had portfolio and regionality issues, the problems were more systemic, as the new strategy made clear:

- Rewire the organisation for growth
- Reinforce a mindset of candour, courage and action throughout the company
- Put operations decisions in the hands of the local-market leaders.

- Reframe the categories
- Broaden the frame of reference for the categories by looking at them through consumers' eyes rather than by production technologies.
- Target premium segments
- Move beyond meal components to meal solutions.
- Exploit the company's sales capabilities
- Leverage the US food industry's largest sales force
- Combine the executional benefits of direct store delivery with the economics of warehouse delivery
- Focus on a select number of developing markets where the company has sufficient scale
- Drive down costs without compromising quality
- Lower overheads as a percentage of sales
- Outsource business processes and shared functions

This was a pretty damning indictment of what had gone before. It recognised that the combining old Kraft (which had just emerged from years of being twinned with a conglomerate) with General Foods and then with Nabisco had successively weakened and diluted the company culture. It was finally time to build a new one, especially as the owner, Altria (the rebranded Philip Morris), cast Kraft Foods adrift, by spinning it off to its shareholders as a separate entity.

2007

Little time was wasted now the company was independent once again in re-shaping the portfolio. In November, the Post Cereals business – almost all its $1.1 billion turnover being North American based – would be merged into Ralcorp Holdings, Inc.. The company's flavoured-water and juice brands were sold. A mere two weeks later, Kraft bought Danone's entire global biscuit business for approximately $7.6 billion. As virtually all the units' $2.8 billion turnover was outside North America, this would make a substantial difference to Kraft's international profile. This profile had not got back to its 1975 level, i.e. accounting for 25% of sales. These changes increased the number of Kraft brands with sales of over $1 billion to nine: Kraft branded cheeses, dinners and dressings, Oscar Mayer, Philadelphia, Maxwell House, Nabisco cookies and crackers, Jacobs coffee, Milka chocolates and Lu biscuits.

Within the year itself, top-line sales increased by an 8.4% that looked healthy enough but in reality owed half of its complexion to currency movements and acquisitions. Organic volume growth was lagging at 1.7%. All the volume growth and more came from overseas. The European Union was up thanks to the previous year's acquisition, from United Biscuits, of the distribution rights for Nabisco brands. Sales picked up across the board in Developing Markets, which was good because volume declined in every one of the North American categories. This was through the combined effect of divestitures, poor sales and the discontinuation of slow-selling lines.

Much groundwork had also been done on the new strategy. Rewiring the organisation for growth had included significant changes to the organisational structure, the senior management team and the incentive systems. The biggest changes were happening within the European Union division. This was moving to a pan-European centralised category management and value chain model where most key strategy and marketing decisions would be taken at the centre; leaving just sales and distribution to be managed locally. The categories were being refocused by use of the 'Growth Diamond'. This concentrated everyone's minds on the four key consumer trends driving growth: Snacking, Quick Meals, Health & Wellness, and Premium. In North America a hybrid sales model of central delivery and direct store delivery was being tested on the biscuit business, and would soon be rolled out across all categories. When it came to driving down costs without compromising quality, $100 million had already been added back into the products to make good incremental quality degradations of the past.

The shareholders of the newly independent Kraft Foods were no doubt hoping these changes would work. An investment of $100 in Kraft shares in 2002 had so far yielded a total shareholder return of minus $4.75. The same $100 invested in Kraft's peer companies over the same period would have almost doubled the stake money. Kraft Foods under Philip Morris's ownership had been far from a success; the independent Kraft Foods needed to do a lot better.

2008

The structural, operational and cultural remaking of Kraft Foods continued apace during 2008. Structurally, there were some significant changes to the make-up of the North American segments as follows:

- US Cheese became a stand-alone unit
- Macaroni & Cheese and other dinner products were moved from US Convenience Foods into US Grocery
- Canada was extracted from each of the segments to operate independently again, and was combined with Foodservice to create a segment that perhaps could be best described as local but different

The combination of these changes and the Danone LU biscuits acquisition meant that there was a distinctly new look to the Kraft business. The most striking observation was the realisation that Kraft was no longer a cheese business that sold some other things, but a snacking and beverage company that also sold cheese:

A breakdown of Kraft's sales by division in 2008

Division	Total sales (%)
Snacks (biscuits, chocolate, salted snacks)	37.7
Beverages (coffee, packaged juice, powdered)	20.1
Cheese	17.7
Convenience Meals (pizza, dinners, lunches, meats)	14.6
Grocery (dressings, condiments, desserts)	9.9

Another notable feature was that the two biggest categories both generated well over 50% of their sales from markets outside of North America; thanks to a series of acquisitions over time. However, Kraft International only generated 23% of company sales because the Cheese, Grocery and Convenience Meals segments had barely been developed beyond North America.

Sales performance again looked good, with the top-line growing by nearly 17% to over $42 billion, but of this increase, the LU biscuit acquisition accounted for 9%, currency 2% and pricing a surprisingly high 7.4% (i.e. $2.6 billion). Not only had all the commodity cost increases of $1.9 billion and incremental marketing spend of $266 million been added into price, but previous years' cost increases had also been piled in. That's a lot of price increase to ask the consumer to swallow, when real incomes in developed markets were static at best.

We believe that profitable volume growth is the true measure of the success of a business. On those counts Kraft hadn't done too well: total volume was down nearly 2% and operating profit down by nearly 4%. These reduced the operating margin from 11% to a paltry 9%. Volumes were down nearly 4% in US Beverages, nearly 7% in US Cheese, slightly up in US Convenience Meals, down by 3.5% in US Grocery and 3% in US Snacks. Outside the US, volume was down by 1% in Europe and up slightly in Developing Markets. Only Canada with its newfound independence managed to grow volume across all retail categories. This was not a thriving business. Volume declines, once allowed to set in, can be very difficult and expensive to halt, let alone recover from. Especially with a recession gathering steam.

2009

This year was largely the same as previous years at Kraft Foods. 'Largely the same' meant more structural change, another strategy change, prices up and volumes down. Blockbuster innovations were a distant memory, DiGiorno frozen pizzas being the last that to make a real difference (and their appearance was far back in 1996).

The latest structural changes involved the disappearance of Kraft International. The business now had three main reporting units: Kraft North America, Kraft Europe and Kraft Developing Markets. Just to keep things interesting, the Central European markets came under the wing of Kraft Developing Markets. This reflected their different stage of development compared to the Western Europe Kraft strongholds. Within Kraft Europe, the Biscuit, Chocolate and Cheese categories became fully independent business units with top and bottom line responsibility. These comprised the entirety of Kraft Europe.

Perhaps of greater importance was the change to the strategy, which had now evolved as follows:

- Focus on growth categories to further transform into a leading snack, confectionery and quick meals company
- Expand footprint in developing markets to benefit from population growth trends
- Expand presence in instant consumptions channels in order to gain share versus grocery channels in the US and European Union
- Enhance margins by improving portfolio mix and reduce costs while investing in quality

It did not take a rocket scientist to work out this was not the strategy of a US-focused cheese company that Kraft had once been. Nor was it the strategy of the Kraft/General Foods/Nabisco Philip Morris creation. It was a strategy for a new company that could perhaps best be paraphrased as 'We need to buy Cadbury', which is what senior management spent most of the second half of the year trying to do.

Such a change in direction was clearly necessary as the current business was essentially going nowhere. 2009 was no different. Volume was basically flat and top-line sales declined by nearly 4% because currency movements knocked off nearly 5% (slightly made up by the follow-on effect of the previous year's price increases adding 2%). The malaise was best illustrated in the US Cheese category, where in 2008 a whopping 14% increase in prices had knocked 7% off volume. This resulted in half the price increases being dealt or rolled back in 2009.

This could not prevent volume falling another 1%. Virtually the only bright spot in the whole US set up was the frozen pizza business, which was up another 13.5% to over $1.5 billion. The irony was, this one shining light was to be sold off to help pay for buying Cadbury.

2010

On 19th January 2010, Kraft Foods announced the terms of its final offer for Cadbury, whose Board recommended acceptance. By early February it was all over, at a cost of around $18.5 billion. Many observers thought the price 'full', if not topside. Cadbury held a 10% global confectionery market share, second only to the recently merged Mars-Wrigley, and held the number one or two position in almost half of the world's largest confectionery markets. Cadbury had only recently come into play as a realistic target for Kraft. It split from the North American beverage unit, Dr Pepper Snapple Group, in 2008, a move that had been prompted by the arrival on the scene of activist shareholder Nelson Peltz. He was also on Irene's case, along with Heinz, Wendy's and others.

Irene approached the Cadbury chairman in August 2009 and, after a short but passionate defence by Cadbury, had triumphed in landing her prize. This made Kraft the world's second-largest food and beverage company with a turnover of $49 billion. Cadbury, which contributed over $9 billion to the top line, was a chocolate and chewing gum company that fitted extremely well with Kraft's existing Suchard-dominated chocolate business. Kraft only had to sell off two small Cadbury units in Poland and Romania for anti-trust reasons. Cadbury added two billion-dollar brands (Cadbury chocolate and Trident gum) to Kraft's existing seven, along with another 30 worth $100 million or more. This expanded Kraft's roster of second-tier brands to over 70.

Perhaps the most important thing Cadbury brought to the party was its international profile. Because of its long history within the old British Empire, Cadbury had built up a dominant position in the Indian market. It had over 70% market share and was long established as one of the country's top packaged goods companies; with exceptionally strong local management and a route to market that covered over a million retail outlets. Cadbury's acquisition of Adams in 2004 had given it exceptionally strong chewing gum businesses in Mexico and Latin America with a solid number-two position in the US. After the Cadbury acquisition, Kraft Foods' developing markets group accounted for nearly a quarter of the company's sales. As Europe added another 17%, the geographic spread of the Kraft business was changing fundamentally. Of Kraft's now global spread of 223 factories, 80% were located outside the US. This is a crucial piece of strategic information for the company to consider as it plans for the future.

Confectionery, now run as a discrete segment, was Kraft's largest, accounting for nearly 28% of sales, with biscuits number two at 22%. The food side of Kraft had been shorn of its growing and profitable frozen pizza business to partially fund Cadbury. DiGiorno, Tombstone and Jack's brands in the US and Delissio in Canada were sold to Nestlé in March 2010 for $3.7 billion. Tombstone and the brands that grew out of it had been one of Kraft's best-ever acquisitions and its departure would put more pressure on the rest of Kraft's US foods businesses to deliver.

Within the year, Kraft actually put up a better performance than of late, growing volume in nearly all its segments. An exception was the distinctly stale cheese unit that lost nearly another 5% of volume – it was not helped by prices going up by 3%. The US grocery unit also declined over 3%, with losses coming in almost all product categories. However, with US beverages and convenience meals both putting on over 3%, there were signs that the more disciplined approach brought in by Irene Rosenfeld was paying dividends. However, her newly expressed revised strategy left no room for doubt where the future lay: '. . . we are seeking to build a global snacks powerhouse with an unrivalled portfolio of brands people love. Our future is centred on three strategies: to delight global snacks consumers, to unleash the power of our Iconic Heritage Brands and to create a performance-driven, values-led organisation'.

2011

The 10.5% increase in sales to $54.4 billion was headlining a wearily familiar tale of mostly flat to declining volumes – up only 0.6%, more than entirely owing to the Cadbury-dominated Kraft Foods developing markets division – and increased prices, up an eye-watering 6% on average. Kraft company policy was to pass on to the consumer any and all increases in input costs with a bit added in on top just for good measure. This is a risky strategy in our view, especially in categories that have a significant private label presence - retailers may not be so keen to follow suit. The riskiness of this approach is compounded by the cutting back of an already ungenerous advertising budget of only 4.4% of sales, down by 0.2% in the year. However, twelve brands each had sales that topped $1 billion (Oreo, Nabisco, LU, Milka, Cadbury, Trident, Jacobs, Maxwell House, Philadelphia, Kraft, Oscar Mayer and Tang).

The highlight of the year was the performance of Kraft Foods in developing markets. It added over $2 billion in sales to jump to 27% of total company sales.

Progress came in all regions, albeit aided by an extra month of Cadbury sales and a 53-week accounting year. Organic volume was up a very healthy 3.9%. Cadbury's developing markets profile had been the primary reason for Kraft buying the British company, so this was an early vindication of the acquisition. Kraft Foods Europe, also heavily strengthened by the Cadbury acquisition, added a further $1.7 billion to the top line with volume up a more sedate 2%, which was still good considering prices had gone up by over 4%.

Back in the US the picture was different. Volume declined across the board even as prices went up. The biggest problem area was in US beverages, where revenues declined over 6% thanks to a major bust-up with Starbucks. According to Kraft, Starbucks unilaterally decided to end their twelve-year-long agreement for Kraft to distribute Starbucks products in grocery stores. Starbucks had offered Kraft $750 million in August 2010 to terminate the partnership, but Kraft had declined and taken the matter to the courts. As things turned nasty, Starbucks alleged that Kraft failed to promote its brands aggressively in stores. Kraft contested this view, as it had extended distribution of Starbucks products from just 4,000 food stores in twelve states to over 40,000 stores in all 50 states and Canada. Annual sales had increased ten-fold to about $500 million a year. The row had been coming for a while as both Kraft and Starbucks had begun competing in the area of the Tassimo coffee system. Starbucks had withdrawn its Starbucks-branded coffee and tea discs for the Tassimo machines (for which Tassimo had exclusivity), prior to launching its own system. Just to add fuel to the fire, Starbucks launched VIA instant coffee and did not distribute through Kraft. The eventual court ruling against Kraft was a big loss that could put at risk its coffee category captaincy status with several big US retailers.

However, this storm in a coffee cup was not going to be Irene's problem much longer. The company announced in August 2011 that it was going to split into two. Irene would pilot the new Global Snacks Business (soon to be named Mondelēz International, Inc.) which would consist of Kraft Foods Europe, Kraft Foods Developing Markets and the North American snacks and confectionery businesses with Tang being thrown in for good measure. The North American Grocery Business (which would retain the Kraft name) would consist of the cheese, beverages, convenience meals and grocery segments along with the Planters nuts and Corn Nuts brands. At this stage there were question marks over European brands like Dairylea and Jacobs coffee, which seemed to fit into neither. Mondelēz would get around $35 billion of the sales and all of the current growth while Kraft was virtually back to where it had been before the Philip Morris acquisition.

While there was little surprise at the splitting of a growing, international snacks and confectionery business from a static, North American cheese, meat and condiments business – it had long been advocated by the ever-present Nelson Peltz – there was some surprise expressed at the timing. Cadbury had not even been fully integrated by this point. But then, Kraft was used to major reorganisations. After all, it had done little else since 1988.

2012

With sales in 2012 of over $18 billion, the newly-reconstituted Kraft Foods Group was easily big enough to win a place in this book in its own right. It was larger than Kellogg's, Heinz, General Mills and Colgate. And, although Mondelēz International claimed to be the one carrying forward the 'values of our legacy organisation', the Kraft Foods Group was very much back to its roots as a US-centric cheese and cooked meats company (the two categories accounting for nearly half of the new company's sales). As such, Kraft Foods Group was in the business of managing big customers: 25% of sales went to Wal-Mart, with another 17% going to its next four biggest customers. But the company did not come out of the demerger completely clean. There was a $650 restructuring programme to oversee, plus the ongoing court battle with Starbucks. Notably, any cash awarded to the company via arbitration would have to be handed over to Mondelēz International.

Of course, the demerger had not magically changed any of the sector, market, or competitive dynamics facing the company. So it was little surprise that sales were down nearly 2%. One cannot help thinking that, after a good year in 2011, the company was paying for decisions taken or deferred to boost the numbers prior to the split. Trade inventory reductions were held to blame for 0.7% of the loss. Within the product sectors, all but one were essentially flat, albeit showing the usual pattern of prices up and volumes down. The outlier was beverages, down by 9%, of which only one-third could be accounted for by the loss of the Starbucks business.

Over on planet Mondelēz International, $35 billion came in sales. Over 80% came from outside North America (45% from developing markets). There was a very different flavour. Operating in the much sexier categories of biscuits (27% of sales), chocolate (another 27%) and gum and candy (15% of sales), and with no customer anywhere accounting for over 10% of total sales (the five largest accounting for only 15%), the company had much more freedom to be creative. Unfortunately, this extra latitude failed to apply to the writers of the company strategy. They, it appeared, were trying for a record: the highest use of generic, management-speak phrases.

Mondelēz International, in case we had forgotten, was a global snacks power-house, on a mission to Create Delicious Moments of Joy. But its five-point strat-egy had a sense of the obvious about it:

- Unleash the Power of Our People (We would love to see just one com-pany set out to 'Restrain and focus our team')
- Transform Snacking (What this actually referred to was the old standby of Make Big Brands Bigger)
- Revolutionize Selling

But although this sounds promising, the strategy eventually spelt out revealed proposals that were a little more prosaic: 'we plan to expand and further develop best-in-class sales and distribution capabilities across our key markets in both developing and developed markets. And:

- Drive Efficiency to Fuel Growth (As everyone does)
- Protect the Well-being of our Planet (As everyone does)

This new company with its new model and new strategy needed to be good because the shareholders' barrel of funds was being scraped deep to create it. Slightly over $1 billion had already been spent on the spin-off. Another near bil-lion was earmarked for the newly announced 2012–2014 restructuring program. Both these were on top of the $1.3 billion already spent integrating Cadbury. While this last programme was claimed to have exceeded its savings targets a year early, one hoped there was enough fat left to pay back the 2012–2014 effort.

After all the hoopla of the spin-off and the countless hours spent crafting The Strategy, it would have been nice to see some early unleashing of the claimed potential. A 2.2% decline in top-line sales was not what the doctor had ordered. To be fair, the company made progress, although more by raising prices than by driving volume growth, but all the gains and more were wiped out by foreign currency movements. Mondelēz International, like many another global compa-ny, treats currency movements its reports as a perfectly acceptable excuse for flat or flattening top-line sales (while often and conveniently glossing over their im-pact when they boost the top line). But the company was deliberately construct-ed as US-based and, although it reports in US dollars, it has over 80% of its sales outside of the US. So currency movements are a fact of life, not an act of God. Buying Mondelēz International shares could effectively become a bet on the movement of the US dollar against a global basket of currencies over time. If the dollar is in for a prolonged good run, Mondelēz International is not.

2012 represented the only year in its existence that Mondelēz International would report the results of a company that operated in over 160 countries, across multiple categories in the three somewhat unhelpful buckets of: developing markets, Europe and North America. For 2013, the company would reorganise itself into five regions: Asia Pacific, Eastern Europe, Middle East & Africa, Europe, Latin America and North America. Whether Mondelēz International would report these new regions for very long became questionable by mid-2013. Nelson Peltz was in the business press, touting a merger between Mondelēz International and PepsiCo, with the soft drinks component being spun off to create what would presumably now be a global snacks super-powerhouse.

What Is Its DNA?

We are going to go out on a limb here and say that Mondelēz International Inc. has not quite found for itself a DNA that is truly distinctive. The sequence of colossal mergers, acquisitions and splits since 1988 has created the most modern of companies: one built and remodelled more by Philip Morris and Wall Street than by a definable management culture, although the Irene Rosenfeld stamp is surely visible. But how much of that stamp is ingrained enough to survive her eventual replacement remains unknown. Mondelēz International is now a cohesive organisation with a clear focus, but, as we noted above, the form and function of its DNA has not yet truly emerged.

Summary

The story of Kraft Foods/Mondelēz International is unique, at least for the companies we have been describing in this book. No other company has been through such a prolonged period of major upheaval. It has been progressively combined and re-combined with other long-established packaged goods giants, each with their own histories, competencies and operating cultures. In many ways, however, we believe this uniqueness will fade over time, not because Kraft will become more like other companies but because other companies will become more like Kraft. As retailers get ever larger and more powerful, and in the absence of a laser-accurate niche focusing, size has become a crucial strategic component for the large FMCG companies. Be big or be unique.

Looking to the future, more mergers, takeovers and splits are inevitable and the Kraft Foods/Mondelēz International experience will provide a valuable pointer as to whether sheer size can generate supplier-strength as well as it can with its retail equivalent. An analysis of the profit of the major FMCG companies worldwide would indicate that only the very largest companies by size are able to maintain the high margins that shareholders demand and expect.

L'Oréal

Where Did They Come From?

Of all the world's top consumer goods businesses, L'Oréal is perhaps still the closest to the vision of its founder. Eugène Schuller was born into very modest circumstances, as the son of a pastry cook. By the age of four, before school, he was buttering tart tins and shelling almonds. These were the beginnings of a life-long, ferocious work habit - clocking 6,000 working hours a year, over 16 hours a day, 365 days a year – that would be the driving force of his business. After finishing school, Eugène entered the Institute for Applied Chemistry in Paris, and paid his way by working nightshift as a pâtissier. He qualified top of his class. An academic career beckoned for the bright, hard-working chemist, and an instructor's post at the Sorbonne initiated what seemed an inevitable rise to a professorship. But he found academia dreary, and left for a job at a maker of chemical products, the Pharmacie Centrale de France. Eugène soon became, first, the head of their research laboratory and then head of chemical services.

In 1905, Eugène's life, and the future global cosmetics industry, changed. He was visited by a hairdresser anxious to pay someone 50 Francs a month to find a safe and reliable hair dye. Eugène eagerly grabbed the project as something to engage his evenings. In those days, cosmetics was a tiny industry in which serious chemists had no interest. It was widely considered to be a frippery used mostly by women of questionable morals. However Eugène found the challenge interesting. Hair dyes at the time were either safe or effective, but never both. Their use could be spotted at a hundred paces. Eugène deconstructed current hair dyes to discover their active and harmful components then, in his kitchen, experimented with new formulae. He would then test out, working at a hairdresser's salon from 8 to 11pm.

By 1907, Eugène had cracked the problem and immediately saw the potential. The hairdresser was bought off and Eugène launched his new hair dye under the brand name Auréole. After selling Auréole to many Parisian hairdressers, in 1909 he founded a company to manufacture and sell the product. Its original name, Société Francaise des Teintures Inoffensives pour Cheveux (literally translated French Society for Inoffensive Tinctures of Hair), later gave way to L'Oréal. To publicise his venture, Eugène contributed articles to a magazine called Coiffure de Paris. This was primarily to get a cheaper (contributor's) rate for advertising, of which he was a prodigious user. Notwithstanding, he was soon sole proprietor and editor, which no doubt helped the magazine's editorial line regarding his product.

The outbreak of the Great War prompted Eugène to enlist in the army. Although he was over age, he persuaded them to admit him as a chemist. Later he was able to transfer to an active posting in the 31st Artillery, rising to the rank of lieutenant and amassing a chestful of medals for valour. While Eugène had been giving the German army the same treatment later doled out to his competitors, the running of L'Oréal was in the hands of his wife. It did very well. The formula for success was already very well established, and top scientists were coming up with products, which offered breakthrough performances at affordable prices. Right from the start, Eugène was clear how he wanted his company to run: it would be based on applying science to the problems of hair care. The rise of Lumière and then Hollywood films was making cosmetics and hair dye more mainstream. Eugène was convinced this growing market could only be conquered by scientifically advanced products.

Soon after returning to the corporate trenches in 1919, revenues ran at 300,000 francs a month. This was largely profit, and Eugène was finding it so easy he got bored. He bankrolled and then principle shareholder of a maker of celluloid combs, before starting another company to enter a bigger celluloid market: movie and still photographic films. He bought out the Lumière film production company. Eugène also dabbled in companies making Bakelite, cellulose acetate and artificial silk. Even as late as 1954 he was still finding time, alongside building L'Oréal, to run a soap company, a paint factory and a magazine.

How Did They Evolve?

By 1920 L'Oréal employed three chemists who, in 1925, came up with his first real blockbuster product, L'Oréal d'Or. This was a hair dye that added golden highlights, which made dyed blonde hair seem natural. However, his business was made by a sea change in women's hairstyles - the Hollywood star-inspired craze for the bob. At first Eugène was appalled by this development. He reasoned that the longer women's hair, the more hair dye they would use. Thus bobs were a disaster. However, the bob required frequent cutting, which drove a massive increase in the number of ladies hair salons. In America they quadrupled during the 1920s. In addition, the bob exposed hair roots a lot more than the previous long styles, so women who dyed their hair needed to touch up the roots much more frequently. Frequent dying was bad for hair, so Eugène immediately set his business to work on devising a ground-breaking bleach. It appeared on the market in 1929 as L'Oréal Blanc. Far from being a disaster, the bob was a goldmine for L'Oréal.

The rise of the perm was another threat. Perms did not accept hair dyes that did not penetrate the hair, as was the then practice. L'Oréal responded in 1929 with what would become a trademark, the patent-protected product. They filed a patent for paradiamines, which formed the basis of fast-penetrating hair colours. The company launched Imédia as a perm-friendly dye. This was an immediate runaway success, popular with hairdressers and clients alike. However, the big worry was that the key ingredient, paraphenylenediamine, was an allergen. Eugène worried tremendously that allergic reactions could kill his business. His products to date had been noted for not causing reactions, so Imédia was launched with a warning advising users to conduct a skin test first. Then, should the worst happen, Imédia advised of the antidote, a rinse of a brine/oxygenated water mix. As it turned out, the demand for perm-friendly dyes far outweighed any consumer worries about a slim chance of a bit of temporary itching. Company revenues in the year exceeded a million francs a month.

The mid-1930s saw the emergence of other strands of the L'Oréal business model that live on to this day. In 1934, the company launched Dop, the first mass market shampoo. For the first but far from last time, L'Oréal would make its science available at affordable prices to as wide a market as possible. A second strand was the importance of keeping the corporate finger on the pulse of consumers' lifestyles: then having products to match new trends and behaviours. When the Front Populaire won the 1936 French elections, L'Oréal was ahead of the game. When Front Populaire enacted a promise to introduce the first paid holiday for French workers, L'Oréal developed and launched Ambre Solaire sun protection oil. By now the company was employing 300 salesmen and was by far the country's most successful hair and skin-care company.

The Second World War did not stop the company's progress, at least on the technical side. In 1942 Eugène developed a mixing tower that embodied a new saponification process. This greatly enhanced the manufacture of soap, and the technology became the industry standard. The company's success during the war became a major problem afterwards. Eugène was branded a collaborator with the Nazi occupiers. It is certainly true that access to raw materials during the war depended entirely on a good relationship with firstly the French Vichy government and then the Nazis. Once the tide of war swung in the Allies favour, Eugène switched horses, but too late to save him from much post-war negative press and vilification.

By this time, another enduring feature of the L'Oréal way was seeded. Firstly André Bettencourt, in 1938, and then François Dalle, in 1941, joined the business. André would marry Eugène's daughter in 1950 and François would go on to succeed Eugène as CEO. There has been only four in the entire company history. Keeping it in the family – both personal and corporate – became a key part of L'Oréal's future success. L'Oréal was also more than ready for the consumer boom of the 1950s. By that time they had more than a hundred chemists and had produced both the first lightening tint (Imélda D, in 1951) and the first colouring shampoo (Colorette, in 1955). The latter was in response to the fashion for more subtlety in hair colouring. In 1954 the company advanced its research capabilities in skin care when they signed technical agreements with Vichy, who were leaders in the field. Vichy's founder, a cosmetologist named Georges Guerin, had discovered the skin healing qualities of Vichy Thermal Spa Water in 1931. He used Vichy Thermal Spa Water to treat a skin wound while staying at the famous spa; and subsequently developed a range of skin products all containing the magic elixir.

In 1957, Eugène Schuller passed away after an immensely busy and productive working life, and the stage was set for 39-year-old new boss, François Dalle, to put in place the final pieces of the jigsaw.

How Did They Build the Modern Business?

Three major changes in François' first four years at the helm reoriented the company. Firstly, in 1957, L'Oréal's hair care products, previously only available at hair salons, were launched onto the consumer market. This dynamic, expanding the science from specialist areas into the mass market, would henceforth be a core part of the company strategy. Secondly, François took the science to a new level by establishing a fundamental research unit. This did not focus on developing products, rather on developing a greater understanding of how skin and hair actually function. This unit, which could manufacture its own molecules, became the company's seedbed. It informed eventual commodities by increasing their efficacy in unique and patent-protected ways. His third move was to focus the company on what it did best – hair and skin care – by selling off the soap business.

After going public on the Paris Stock exchange in 1963 (Eugène's daughter and son-in-law, Liliane and André Bettencourt, retained a majority stake), the company had the financial resources to put in place the next leg of the strategy. While L'Oréal was a successful business, the brand itself, like all good brands, occupied something of a niche. With their research capabilities in basic skin and hair physiology and function, the expertise could be used to enhance any hair and skin brands. It now made complete sense for the company to acquire strong cosmetic brands because it could do a better job developing brands than previous owners. They had superior science capabilities. The L'Oréal laboratories would become the invisible powerhouse behind some of the best-known names in the industry.

The first such major acquisition was of Lancôme in 1964, taking the company into the upscale perfume and make-up sectors in nearly a hundred countries. This was followed a year later by Laboratoires Garnier, a manufacturer of hair care products made with organic ingredients. Acquisitions were not the only growth strategy. In 1964 L'Oréal launched the Kérastase brand, which was a cross between a hair treatment and a spa experience. Distribution was limited to the upper end of hair salons, so staff could be trained to deliver the brand mission of high performance, personalised hair care via an in-salon consultation and ritual treatment. Another brand, Biotherm, was acquired in 1970. That was developed after its founder visited a spa and had the idea of incorporating thermal plankton into skin creams. L'Oréal was now employing 500 scientists, a number that would rise 50% in the next four years. By then it had acquired the mass-market Gemey brand of makeup.

A visit from McKinsey in 1969 resulted in the now sprawling company adopting a divisional structure. The next major change which was to have long lasting ramifications came in 1974. The Bettencourts, fearing that the socialist government might nationalise the company, sold just under half of Liliane's stock to the Swiss food giant, Nestlé. A new French holding company, Gesparal, was formed, owned 51% by Liliane and 49% by Nestlé. This took ownership of her entire L'Oréal stockholding in exchange for about 3% of Nestlé's stock. Clearly, Nestlé could not bring much expertise to such a specialised and scientifically oriented company. But it turned out to be a marriage made in heaven. For Nestlé, it was an excellent investment into a category that was growing faster and had higher profit margins than most of their core businesses. For L'Oréal, it provided a strong immunity against hostile takeover should the family ever decide to bale out. It also protected the company from the short-term demands of the stock market, enabling them to take a longer-term perspective to business strategy than their main competitors.

While L'Oréal continued to make smaller cosmetics acquisitions in the 1970s, it was unable to fully avoid the craze at the time for diversification. In 1973 they took a majority stake in the pharmaceutical company, Synthélabo, and in 1979 bought another pharma company, Metabio-Joullie. They merged the two a year later. Also in the late 1970s, echoing Eugène's earlier policy of buying into magazines used to promote his products; L'Oréal bought substantial strakes in both Marie Claire and Interedi-Cosmopolitan. In one of the new divisions recommended by McKinsey, Parfums et Beauté International, company expertise was applied to Cacharel, a company in which L'Oréal had invested. They developed the first perfume to be launched by Cacharel. L'Oréal soon took control of the perfume arm of Cacharel and Anaïs Anaïs, which was designed to be the first perfume bought by or for teenage girls. This initiative, well away from Lancôme territory, became the world's best-selling perfume and one of the most influential in the history of the category.

1981 saw another significant advance on the scientific side. They opened a new, state-of-the-art dermatological research facility, Laboratoires Dermatalogiques Galderma. This was another tangible benefit from their Nestlé shareholder, a 50:50 joint venture between the two companies. It would become the world's number one dermatology company, generating substantial profits for both parties.

The next main developments illustrated the now unique nature of the company. For the Ambre Solaire brand the company patented an ultra-powerful, anti-UVA ingredient, Mexoril SX. This kept abreast of the changing nature of the sun cream market - away from bronzing to protection. On the skin care side, the launch of L'Oréal Plénitude was a hugely successful example of their strategy: to trickle down scientific advancements from high-end expensive products into mass-market affordable offerings. In 1986 the cycle continued, as the high-end Lancôme brand launched the market's first anti-ageing cream, Niosôme.

Much of the 1980s was spent in the pursuit of one of the world's stellar cosmetics brands that had fallen on hard times. L'Oréal was convinced it could revive Helena Rubinstein whilst benefiting from its attractive stable of brands. Helena Rubinstein, along with Estée Lauder, was one of the Grande Dames who dominated the early cosmetics industry. She had barely arrived in Australia, with hardly a penny to her name, when she started a cosmetics business in 1902. Helena Rubinstein had picked the perfect place. Australia was swimming in the main ingredient of hand cream, lanolin, thanks to the country's 75 million sheep. It was produced as an oil from their fleeces.

By 1908 her success there prompted Helena Rubinstein to move to London and in 1915 she had opened up in New York City. There she was not shy in promoting herself as 'the accepted advisor in beauty matters to Royalty, Aristocracy and the great Artistes of Europe'. American women lapped it up and she had soon more outlets in America than there were Ford dealerships. Helena Rubinstein scored a notable feat in 1928, suggesting we could have done with having Helena around in the financial crash of 2007. She took Lehman Brothers to the cleaners by selling them her business for $7.3 million prior to the Wall Street crash: then bought it back a few years later for $1.5 million. Lehman's hilariously denounced her finesse as 'financially illiterate'.

As the American and then global cosmetics businesses boomed, so did Helena Rubinstein. The US arm of her company grossed $22 million a year, but her death in 1965 at the age of 92 marked a turning point for the company. Her children had inherited neither the business expertise nor chutzpah of their dynamic mother. By 1972 they had had enough and sold out to Colgate-Palmolive for $146 million. Colgate's stewardship was a classic example of the difficulties mass-market companies of the time had in managing upmarket brand franchises. Business went from bad to worse and the company was on the market again by the end of the 1970s. , L'Oréal was sniffing around, but missed out as Helena Rubinstein Inc. was offloaded for a seventh of the purchase price to a private owner. L'Oreal got their first piece of Helena Rubinstein in 1983 when they bought the company's Japanese and South American business units, and a year later they bought 45% of the main business. It was only in 1988 that L'Oréal gained full control of the brand and business they had long coveted.

L'Oréal's rise had been almost seamless. The year it finally bought Helena Rubinstein, L'Oréal became the largest cosmetics company in the world. It was making a profit of over a billion francs a year and made Madame Liliane, the largest individual shareholder, the richest woman in France. Capital magazine calculated her fortune was growing at the staggering rate of 85 million francs a day. But that was just the start. 1988 also marked a 42-year-old, Welsh-born L'Oréal lifer, Lindsay Owen-Jones becoming the company's third CEO. Owen-Jones' governance would make Liliane the richest woman in the world.

Owen-Jones' main thrust in his early years as CEO would be to make the company truly global. This was a process that had started almost immediately after the birth of the company. It would pitch them into direct competition with the packaged goods goliaths, Proctor & Gamble and Unilever.

How International Are They?

As with most Continental European-based companies, international expansion began early, and into adjacent countries. By 1912, L'Oréal was selling its products in Holland, Italy and as far away as Austria. In 1922 the company had opened an agency in Berlin but failed to prosper under its German manageress. She refused to open her accounts books for inspection and was eventually fired to make way for a more trustworthy French L'Oréal employee. Company subsidiaries were established in Italy, Belgium and Denmark during 1936/1937 as business had outgrown the existing distributor arrangements. The latter were used to spread the company name farther afield, and reached the UK, Algeria and even Argentina by the end of the Second World War.

The big international market to crack was the United States. In 1953, using a complex ownership arrangement that was part L'Oréal and part family, a company called Cosmair was established as the sole US licensee for L'Oréal products. The first manager was a long-time employee selected primarily for being half-American. He was not up to the difficult task of penetrating the scale,geographic spread and complexities of the American skin and hair care industries. They were then a niche market. Most of the action was in mainstream cosmetics, a market that grew at 10% a year throughout the 1950s and 1960s.

When Dalle took over as CEO one of his first tasks was to boot out Eugéne's crony and install his own man to run Cosmair. His choice, Jacques Corrèze, was not universally popular, having served a five-year post-war prison term for wartime collaborationist activities. However, he was a better businessman than he had been a patriot. He slowly began to gain distribution for a select few L'Oréal products, in the face of ferocious competition from the American giants of Estée Launder, Helena Rubinstein and the brash Revlon. So difficult was progress that, when Helena Rubinstein died in 1965, Cosmair had only 20 employees and the business was restricted to hair-care products, which were distributed into salons.

Elsewhere, the company was busily gaining a foothold in countries far and wide; Uruguay, Peru, Algeria, Mexico, Canada, Japan, Australia, New Zealand and Hong Kong being added to the list by the mid-1970s. So strongly was the business growing in South America, it set up a multi-division structure there to manage an increasingly complex set of markets. In 1976, the company gained a toehold into the Soviet Union by, first, signing a technical assistance agreement, then setting up a joint venture, Soreal, with the Soviet chemical company, Mosbytchim.

Meanwhile in the US, the Bettencourt-Nestlé share deal meant that Nestlé was now a part owner of Cosmair. It was run successfully during the 1980s by future CEO, Lindsay Owen-Jones. Cosmair had gained a foothold for their L'Oréal, Lancôme, Cacharel and Guy Laroche brands in department stores. With the addition of their salon business, L'Oréal was generating an annual turnover of about $350 million. The size of Cosmair's business doubled in 1984 when, with help from Nestlé, the unit acquired Warner Cosmetics from Warner Communications. This brought into the group a number of strong brands such as Ralph Lauren, Polo and Gloria Vanderbilt. Cosmair's turnover was almost doubled.

In 1985, Biotherm was launched into the US market to add further impetus. Progress was mixed, not least in profits as the company spent 35% of sales on marketing, a full ten points above the industry average. The 1989 launch of Plé-nitude, with a $35 million advertising blitz, also did little for the bottom line. The long-drawn-out acquisition of Helena Rubinstein, with its hugely successful Giorgio Armani men's fragrance brand, gave Cosmair another step change in the size of its US and indeed global operation. The company was now the largest cosmetics firm in the world.

By 1990 Cosmair had a mixed bag of market share positions. In women's fra-grances they trailed badly behind five industry leaders. They had less than half the share of Estée Lauder and Revlon. In the men's fragrance category things, were a lot brighter. Thanks mainly to the acquired Armani and Ralph Lauren brand franchises, Cosmair had nearly a quarter of the market and ranked second only to Unilever. In 1991 Cosmair was turning over $1 billion in sales and was the sixth largest marketer of cosmetics in the United States, employing 3,600 people with a company laboratory located in Clark, New Jersey.

In 2003 Cosmair acquired Redken, a hair care company distributed through salons. This helped make Cosmair America's fourth-largest cosmetics company. Cosmair was now deemed too important to be owned largely by the Liliane Bet-tencourt family and Nestlé. Nestlé owned about 70 percent; Liliane Bettencourt 26 percent; and L'Oréal only four percent. So the unit was purchased by L'Oréal to be a 100% owned subsidiary.

However, the game changer in the US was the acquisition of the mass-market makeup giant, Maybelline, in 1996. This took L'Oréal into the number two slot in US cosmetics, behind Proctor & Gamble. Maybelline was a major leap both financially ($508 million purchase price) and strategically. Maybelline distribut-ed a range of low priced makeup aimed at teenagers, primarily through drug and discount stores. This was the most downmarket sector L'Oréal had yet been in-volved with. They were signalling their intent to spread the benefits of their sci-ence to all sectors and price points in the market. The experience they would gain with Maybelline in the United States would stand them in good stead as they began to extend into markets where affordability was a huge issue.

In 1994, L'Oréal was one of the first foreign companies to obtain authorisa-tion from the Indian government to establish a 100% owned subsidiary. Until this point, government policy had been that no foreign company could own more than 49% of an Indian-based company. This approach saw many major brands, such as Coca Cola, exit the market altogether. In 1997, L'Oréal China was formed as part of a multi-divisional Asian zone structure. The low-priced Maybelline brand was launched a year later to spearhead their charge.

Back in the US, L'Oréal acquired Soft Sheen (a leader in ethnic hair care) in 1998 and Carson in 2000 (a leading beauty products business aimed at the African American sector). These were combined to give L'Oréal a strong ethnic offering. In the US salon sector, the company transformed its position with the acquisition in 2000 of the sector's leading brand, Matrix Essentials. It also cemented an upmarket position by acquiring Kiehl's Since 1851 Inc. Kiehl's distributed its product through a mix of top end department stores, such as Bergdorf Goodman, Neiman Marcus and Sak's Fifth Avenue, together with its own flagship stores. The buy gave L'Oréal a taste for owning retail outlets. Across the other side of the world, in 2001 L'Oréal acquired a 35% share of the Japanese firm, Shu Uemura Cosmetics, Inc. The deal included international rights to the brand outside Japan. Early success in extending the brand to new markets prompted L'Oréal to buy the firm outright in 2004.

By 2003 slightly over 50% of L'Oréal sales derived from their Western European heartland; 28% from the US; and 20% from the rest of the world. Of the company's 50 factories, ten were located in North America, four in South America and eight in Asia. Nearly 50% of the company's output was manufactured outside of Europe. The company was striving to keep enough flexibility to manufacture locally relevant products and formats for the many different markets. With over 500 brands being distributed through more than 400 subsidiaries in 150 countries, L'Oréal had become a truly global company.

How Are They Structured?

Structure is usually the handmaiden of strategy. L'Oréal has had such a consistent strategy over time has resulted in very little internal disruption due to re-organisations. Also, as the business has endured no crises requiring major downsizings, closures or divestments, its restructuring has been mostly organic and reflected the business' growing spread and scope.

The McKinsey-recommended divisional structure from 1969 was tweaked in 1985 when, following all the acquisitions, the Parfum's et Beauté division became unwieldy. It was split into three departments: Lancôme/Piaubert (Piaubert would be sold in 1993); Perfumes; and Active Cosmetics (primarily Vichy, finally acquired in 1980 and soon to be joined by the acquisition of La Roche-Posay). This structure had by 2004 morphed into four divisions, which perhaps more understandable:

- Professional Products - Key brands: L'Oréal Professional; Redken; Matrix, distributed through hair salons
- Consumer Products - Key brands: L'Oréal Paris; Garnier; Maybelline; SoftSheen-Carson, distributed through mass-market channels, including hypermarkets, supermarkets and drug stores

- Luxury Products – Key brands: Lancôme; Biotherm; Helena Rubinstein; Giorgio Armani; Ralph Lauren; Cacharel; Kiehl's Since 1851; Shu Uemura. Perfume, skin care and make-up distributed through specialist channels such as department stores and perfumeries.

- Active Cosmetics – Key brands: Vichy; La Roche-Posey, distributed through pharmacies and dermatologists

The company's dermatology joint venture with Nestlé was managed independently from these four main groups but benefited from access to the L'Oréal research function (which supports all the divisions). Subsequent acquisitions slotted into whichever division represented its core business until 2006. Then the newly acquired Body Shop was set up as a fifth division, due to its unique distribution arrangement of company-owned and franchised stores. By 2009, Kérastase had been added to Professional Products; Yves Saint Laurent and Diesel to Luxury Products, and Innéov and Skinceuticals to Active Cosmetics.

While product development and branding was mostly the domain of the divisions, sales, distribution, local marketing and some local product development was managed along geographical lines: Western Europe; North America; Rest of World, which subdivided into Asia; Latin America, Eastern Europe and Other.

Perhaps the most significant structural change occurred in 2004. The Gasparal Holding Company, which had been set up to facilitate the selling of family shares to Nestlé, was merged with L'Oréal to create a more normalised shareholding arrangement. Previously, the Gasparal principals held most of the voting rights. Nestlé's 49% stake in Gasparal became a 26.4% direct holding in L'Oréal, with Liliane Bettencourt, now aged 82, taking 27.5%. As a takeover had been impossible under the previous arrangements, each party agreed not to increase their shareholdings in L'Oréal during the lifetime of Mdme Bettencourt (still a sprightly 90-year-old at the time of writing.) The deal also cancelled a previous arrangement that gave Nestlé first call on any shares Liliane wanted to sell.

What Have They Been Doing Recently?

1995-2003

By 1995 the company had reached an annual turnover of just over 8 billion Euros. This figure had been boosted, significantly, by the 1990 launch of Lancôme's Trésor, the world's best-selling perfume. Two other enduring blockbusters came in 1996 with the launch of the Garnier Fructus range of affordable hair products. This took the brand global in the mass-market channels, followed by that of Acqua di Giò, which would become the world's best-selling men's fragrance. The same year the company decided to start a process of getting out of everything that did not fit neatly into its structure. It began by merging their 57%-owned Synthélabo pharma unit with Elf Aquitaine's Sanofi. In 2001, the company also sold its stakes in Lanvin and Marie Claire, buying Revlon's Colorama make-up brand the same year. In 2003, the company announced its nineteenth consecutive year of double-digit growth in operating profits, on sales of 14.5 billion euros. Little wonder Liliane was now worth $24 billion, second only to Christy Walton as richest woman in the world.

2004

A solid, if unspectacular 3.6% sales increase was primarily driven by a sluggish European market that accounted for half the company's sales. But L'Oréal was not a company to panic and junk its strategy after a so-so year. The range of 17 brands, most with regional heartlands that had expansion potential, and distribution channels that covered almost the entire market. They provided a good balance of opportunity for growth and security against downturn.

The strategy was clear:

- Innovations on higher-value products that could later be trickled down the range. L'Oréal's ReFinish, Kérastase's Réflection and Innéov Hair Mass, all launched in 2004, were built on breakthroughs from the L'Oréal laboratories that would appear later in other, less expensive brands
- Retail Diversification. The good growth of the Professional Products (up 7.6% like-for-like) and Active Cosmetics (up 165% like-for-like) made up for sluggishness in the main shopping channels. An increase of 70% in the company's internet sales also helped
- Business Segment Strategy. By covering all ends of the market, shifts in consumer spending patterns between price bands would not derail the company. L'Oréal also began opening its own stores for Lancôme and Biotherm
- US Growth. By targeting the US over a long period of time, with aggressive levels of advertising support and strong acquisitions, L'Oréal was still building sales (up 8.1% like-for-like to break the $4 billion barrier) and share in the largest cosmetics market in the world
- Emerging Markets. The host of subsidiaries ten years earlier in markets such as China, India and Eastern Europe was now starting to pay off. Sales in Asia grew 17% and in Eastern Europe by 29% (Vichy, up 37% in Eastern Europe, had become Russia's leading skincare brand and was launched in India in the year.) Sales in China almost doubled through

organic growth – Lancôme grew by 71% - and two acquisitions: Min-nurse, the number three skincare brand, and Yui-Sai, an upmarket de-partment store brand

2005

Given no change to the strategy, trends were pretty much the same, if not a little more pronounced. Overall the sales increase almost doubled to 6.5%, de-spite Western Europe business still being flat. Sales in North America, powered by the runaway success of Garnier Fructus. It was launched there in 2003, and grew by 8.3% like-for-like. Professional Products and Active Cosmetics contin-ued to grow ahead of company average. The Emerging Markets had some spec-tacular successes with Russian Federation up 40%, Mexico 13%, Argentina 22% and China 27% (excluding the impact of the previous year's acquisitions).

2005 was the first year in which two significant shifts in the business crossed key thresholds. Firstly, L'Oréal was no longer a Western European-dominated company. Other regions accounted for over 50% of sales (55% in the second half of the year) and Rest of the World now had more than a quarter of company business. Secondly, L'Oréal was no longer a haircare-dominated company - non-hair-care sales exceeded 50% of the company total for the first time. This was driven largely by skincare sales. These had doubled within five years to account for a quarter of total company sales. However, there was one watchout. Whilst operating profit margins across the product categories were broadly similar, there was no margin impact to the shift towards skincare. Whereas, the geographical shift away from Western Europe did have a margin impact because of the quite substantial differences in profit margins by region (Western Europe 21%, North America 18.3%, Rest of World 13.5%). Improving margins in the growing re-gions was a company priority.

There was still plenty of mileage in the company's growth strategy. The R&D labs continued to fuel product innovation with 2,900 research employees invest-ing €496 million to register a staggering 529 patents (70 of them on packaging developments). The innovations that flowed from this torrent of science were not just targeted at existing key categories. L'Oréal was now putting increased em-phasis on men. In 1990, 4% of European men used a skincare product. By 2003 that had risen to 20%. In Japan, 30% of men under 30% were skincare users, and over 80% in South Korea. Vichy had been ahead of the game, launching Basic Homme in 1986. Now it was time for the big brands to join in. L'Oréal Men Expert was launched into mass-market channels. The other leg of the growth strategy was to launch more of the seventeen brands into more markets. So while Vichy had already built up 1,300 points of sale in China within a year, the Shu Uemura brand was moving in the opposite direction. It was launched on the US west coast. Matrix was expanding from America into markets such as Brazil, India, China and Eastern Europe.

2006

Jean-Paul Agon, only the fourth L'Oréal CEO in almost a century, announced some tweaks to their strategy, as follows:

- Technological innovation an output of the company's productive labs would be at the heart of a new direction for growth. Pro-Xylane was a revolutionary anti-ageing compound for mature skin made using green technology. Seniors were a rapidly increasing percentage of the world population (the number over 50 would multiply 2.5 times by 2050). They visited hair salons more frequently than younger people: and they were more than interested in new products such as Age Recharge by Kérastase. Lancôme, Vichy and La Roche-Posay all launched products containing Pro-Xylane. The R&D budget of 533 million euros was being well spent.
- The creation of major products. This wasn't new either. Jean-Paul just wanted more and bigger ones faster. Not that any CEO would demand fewer, smaller and take as long as you like
- Enhancing the value of the products. Ramping up the technical innovation to get more benefits into more products
- Power brands. See above
- Globalisation of the brands. Geographic expansion saw the opening of subsidiaries in the few remaining new markets such as the Ukraine and Vietnam. Yet the product range still had plenty of mileage: as seen by the launch of Vichy into the US, and Shu Uemura growing by 26% in its US rollout
- Acquisitions. While the company had been a serial acquirer for several decades, the capture of The Body Shop during the year marked a new direction. Opening its first store in India and beginning online shopping in Germany showed the future direction for The Body Shop

Elsewhere, signing licence with Diesel showed L'Oréal was keen to join the industry dogfight for the best names that could be attached to perfumes. In the Active Cosmetics division, the capture of natural, certified organic cosmetics firm Sanflore was a good example of keeping the finger on the pulse of another emerging industry trend.

The sales increase in the year slipped back slightly but as still an above industry average 5.6%. This pushed the company's global market share up from 15% to 15.6%. The US was the laggard, growing only 2.7% due to a downturn in the Professional Products division. This in turn was due to upheavals in the salon distribution channel (distributors rather than company direct calling were the primary route to market), and L'Oréal deciding to cut back its salon network to the better performers. Europe managed a decent 3.8% growth while the Rest of the World powered on by another 12.7%. This was thanks mostly to Latin America and Eastern Europe, where Biotherm was growing at 70% a year in Russia. For the first year, the Rest of the World region was now bigger for L'Oréal than the United States, accounting for over 27% of total sales. More encouraging news was that the operating profit in the Rest of the World increased by a full percentage point. Thanks to a combination of global and local productivity initiatives.

2007

All guns were blazing. L'Oréal sales increased by over 8% to over €17 billion. Every division grew like-for-like by at least 7.5%; business segment perfumes and skincare both grew double digit. Giorgio Armani, Kiehl's and La Roche-Posay all had standout years. Regionally, both Western Europe and North America grew a respectable 4%. These were markets where the number one focus for growth was skincare for seniors. In this category, the over-50's already spent more than double than did the under-40s. In a further development to grasp this opportunity, L'Oréal signed an agreement with Light BioScience, inventors of a photo-modulation technology for skin rejuvenation. Energy Cosmetics, as this emerging sector was called, was a new, non-cosmetic approach to helping ageing skin. L'Oréal had to engage, so their research function set up its own instrumental cosmetics development unit.

Elsewhere, the recently slimmed-down US Professional Products division was strengthened with three acquisitions: the luxury haircare brand PureOlogy and two regional salon distributors, Beauty Alliance and Maly's West. These added both to the product range and route-to-market capabilities. The Body Shop, run as a separate division, delivered a healthy 5.7% like-for-like growth. It switched focus to more company-owned stores (122 of the 161 opened) in new markets (India now had 20 stores and stores opened for the first time in Poland, Czech Republic and Namibia); and using L'Oréal's R&D capabilities (the company opened a new organic and natural cosmetics laboratory specifically to service The Body Shop and Sanoflore).

The Rest of the World region, where the total market for cosmetic products was now as large as Western Europe, delivered a whopping 18% growth. This accounted for more than 60% of the L'Oréal's entire growth. The regional profitability gap problem had not yet been fixed. Yet, for the first time, the company made more operating profit in the Rest of the World region than it did in North America. The high-growth emerging markets of Brazil, Russia, India, Mexico and China had long been identified by L'Oréal. Russia delivered the highest absolute sales growth of any country and Brazil and China were already top five world markets for cosmetics. L'Oréal increased a focus on what it called the Next 12, where it was mostly well established and where tremendous growth rates were displayed. These countries were: Argentina (sales up 37%); Columbia (27%); Czech Republic; Dubai; Indonesia (21%); Philippines; Poland (16%); South Africa; Thailand (22%); Turkey; Ukraine (already the third-largest Eastern European subsidiary, after only three years in existence); and Vietnam, where a subsidiary was established.

2008

The key questions for its centenary year were:
- How well equipped was L'Oréal to cope with the economic crisis
- How did they respond?

How well was L'Oréal equipped for the economic downturn? Obviously, a company with a big exposure to luxury products sold in department stores, and professional products sold in higher end hair salons was going to feel the pinch. Indeed, sales in the Professional Products division were flat in Western Europe and down over 6% in the US. The Luxury Products division fell by 2% in Western Europe and over 7% in the US. However, this was not a global economic crisis but a developed markets one. In the Rest of the World region, sales of Professional Products and Luxury Products were up 15% and 12% respectively.

Even in the developed markets, not all areas of the cosmetics sector were in decline. L'Oréal's long-term acquisitions and innovation strategies had provided a very large business in the mass market, with affordable, advanced technology make-up products. This proved to be recession resilient. Mass-market make-up sales grew 8% in Western Europe. Money may have been tight but girls were still going out of the house looking their best. Their mothers were not going to let their newly regenerated ageing skins start to sag again. Company skincare sales were up over 9% globally. When it came to acne and rosacea, there was no recession at all. In the Galdera dermatology joint venture with Nestlé, sales were up 7% in Western Europe and 18% in the US. So in both geographic and product sector terms, L'Oréal had been well placed indeed to withstand the full impact of the crisis. Total sales were up 2.8% in the year.

How did L'Oréal respond to the downturn? While sales increased, operating profits were down year-on-year for the first time in living memory, albeit only by 3.6%. This is attributable to L'Oréal's response to the crisis. The company, always one for taking the long view, saw the economic crisis as an opportunity to gain advantage over competitors who were more at the mercy of the financial analysts. So advertising and promotional spends were maintained, giving L'Oréal (now the third-largest advertiser in the world) an increased share of voice. The research and development budget was increased by nearly 4% and the department employee count by 6%. The faith was repaid immediately. A 9% increase in the number of patents filed set a new company record of 628. Attention was still paid to costs. Cost of sales and selling, and general and administrative costs came down as part of a policy of "permanent restructuring".

It was a good year to make acquisitions. The biggest was the capture of the Yves Saint Laurent Beauté business. In addition to the iconic Yves Saint Laurent brand, the acquisition also brought into L'Oréal the Boucheron, Stella McCartney, Zegna, Roger & Gallet and Oscar de la Renta brands. These were ready for the inevitable upturn in the luxury market once economic conditions improved. The company also strengthened its American route to market with the acquisition of a third salon distributor, Columbia Beauty Supply. While the year had by no means been plain sailing, the company had weathered the storm better than most and was well poised for the upturn.

2009
The trouble was, however, that the upturn didn't come in 2009. A sales decline of 0.4% was hardly catastrophic, especially given a heavy influence by retail inventory reduction on a massive scale. Like-for-like, the cosmetics divisions combined declined by 1.5%. The Body Shop held steady and the Dermatology JV grew by over 10%. Within the cosmetics divisions, the trends of 2008 continued, but the ebbing economic tide had lowered all boats. Consumer Products Division showed a good 3% gain whereas Professional Products (down 3%) and especially Luxury Products (down 9%) suffered. Total L'Oréal perfume sales were down nearly 15% (excluding acquisitions). Regionally, the Western European markets performed worst (down 6%); North America declined 3% and the growth rate in the Rest of World fell back to an 8% increase.

Action was taken in the poorly performing regions and sectors. For example, the lower-priced Garnier Essentials range, priced at under 5 euros, was extended from its Eastern European markets into Western Europe. This helped the Garnier brand to grow, as did the company's other low-priced, mass-market brand, Maybelline New York. Even the Luxury Products division had to bow to economic reality: it introduced small format perfume bottles and entry-level-priced skincare products. However, there were green shoots in the luxury area. Kiehl's was promoted to pillar brand status as its global rollout drove total sales growth, up by 28%. The newly acquired Yves Saint Laurent brand grew by 17% in the US, driven by new product launches. Lancôme gained market share on the back of new products such as Génifique Youth Activator (protected by seven patents). These bolstered its new positioning as the anti-ageing specialist. And three more US distributors were acquired and merged into the company's SalonCentric distributor brand, which increased market coverage to 80%.

2009 was notable for L'Oréal making official that its primary goal was to re-orient the company decisively towards developing and emerging markets. These "New Markets" now accounted for 33% of group sales, double the level of a decade earlier. They were forecast to exceed 50% within the next ten years. CEO Jean-Paul Agnon set the company the goal of recruiting an extra billion consumers in these markets. This would double the number of men and women using L'Oréal products. As company strategy went forwards, accessibility and affordability would be much more important elements.

There were two new strategic changes to facilitate this shift. First, a further ramping up of R&D capabilities and investment, particularly in areas such as stem cell research. Secondly, a transformation of company culture and structures to increase flexibility. An early example of the benefits of increased flexibility came with a new eyelash product, the Innovative Renewal Lash Serum. The R&D function had managed to decode the life cycle mechanisms of eye lashes. Biological and physical knowledge from the Hair care team was combined with similar contributions from the make-up team to come up with a new hair care product, which would be used in a make-up setting.

2010

As most of the world's economies began a recovery, how well was the new strategy working? Very well it seemed. Sales were up a very impressive 11.6% to just under 20 billion euros. The company's global retail monitoring calculated theirs at $24 billion, well ahead of the cosmetics businesses of Proctor & Gamble ($18.6 billion), Unilever ($15.4 billion) and the more specialised Estée Lauder ($7.4 billion). In the company's drive to recruit a billion new consumers, there was good news. New Markets were now snapping at the heels of the still-becalmed Western Europe region for the title of largest-in-sales. Even better news was that the company's efficiency measures had driven the operating profit margin in New Markets up to 16.9%. This was ahead of North America. Shifting the sales mix to New Markets now would be largely profit neutral, which was good to know in the year China became the company's third-largest market. The company consolidated its three Asian research centres into a new Asian division of R&D to increase the focus on products relevant for Asian skin and hair needs.

The two divisions that had suffered most in the economic crisis had both returned to growth. Professional Products grew by 4%, having added 35,000 salons around the world as customers. Key to the turnaround had been Matrix, pushing its features of easy-to-use products at accessible prices. The brand was up over 18% in New Markets, where it reached well over 60,000 salons. Luxury Products did even better, growing by 7%, due to the growth of Génifique, Kiehl's, Yves Saint Laurent and Lancôme. Kiehl's had now opened 760 sales outlets in 38 countries. It eschewed advertising to focus on product sampling, and doubled sales in three years and grew 66% in the Asia Pacific region in the year.

The heavy lifting of recruiting the extra billion fell to the Consumer Products division, up 5.5% in total and double that in New Markets. But some of the billion had to be found in the old markets, especially at the younger end of the market. Brands like Maybelline were spearheading the drive, with a wide range of affordable yet scientifically advanced innovations. The progress was exemplified by Falsies Mascara, which became the best-selling mascara in North America and Western Europe within a year of being launched. This helped drive the total brand, already the world's best-selling make-up brand, up by 13%.

The Body Shop was beginning to look like one of the company's less inspired moves. Like-for-like sales were still in the doldrums, declining by 1%: it was still in the midst of a strategic reorganisation begun the year before. Growth of 31% in E-commerce sales for the division was the one glimmer of light. Elsewhere: Galderma grew another 16%; L'Oréal's first factory in Russia opened its doors, to service the countries of the old Soviet Union; and the Essie nail care brand was purchased by the North American unit.

2011

A milestone was reached. Sales breached the $20 billion euros barrier, having grown 5%. Sales in New Markets (up nearly 10%) came within 20 million euros of overtaking Western Europe (sales flat again) as the company's largest region. If Eastern Europe hadn't caught a cold, by declining 3% in dismal economic conditions, it would have happened this year rather than next. In the worldwide cosmetics market, New Markets (excluding Japan) accounted for a staggering 87% of worldwide market growth.

The other news was the return from hibernation of the luxury products consumer. This market sector grew by 7.7%. L'Oréal inched further ahead, growing by 8.2% like-for-like. This was the best-performing of the cosmetics divisions and only just behind the ever-buoyant Dermatology JV. Key to the growth, as ever, was breakthrough innovation. Lancôme Visionnaire became the first ever-fundamental skin corrector on the market, ring-fenced by twenty patents. Other luxury successes were the continued expansion of Kiehl's, the extension of the Giorgio Armani brand into female perfume with Acqua di Gioia, and the launch of Loverdose by Diesel. The unit also acquired Clarisonic, the market leader in sonic skincare technology.

The Body Shop finally showed like-for-like growth, moving ahead just over 4%. This was on the back of its 16 online stores and an L'Oréal-driven push to get the brand into travel retail in 44 markets. The High Street part of The Body Shop was still going nowhere fast. The R&D and cost legs of the strategy powered on. R&D spend went up 8% and the annual patent count rose above 600 for the third year in a row. On the cost side, the company strategy, of having production units as close to markets as economically feasible, meant there were now 41 plants. These were well positioned to service the market growth. Productivity per employee had increased by 17% since 2009 and the company was paying no more for its ingredients than it had been in 2008.

What is Their DNA?

L'Oréal is a classic case. Competitors can easily predict what the company will do, but it is extremely difficult to pre-empt them, copy them or stop them doing it. They have built a unique business model with a well-entrenched company culture.

Science

It would not be too much of an exaggeration to describe L'Oréal as a science company with cosmetics factories attached. From the day Eugène Schuller pondered the challenge of conjuring a safe and effective hair dye, L'Oréal has been first and foremost a science company. If Eugène had been approached by a laundress rather than a hairdresser, L'Oréal would probably be giving Proctor & Gamble and Unilever a spanking in detergents rather than cosmetics. Their superior research function has enabled them to grow and develop virtually every brand they have acquired. This includes some apparently tired and past it at the time of purchase. The strategy of cascading scientific benefits down the range to the cheapest products gives them advantage in all parts of the market. Not only do they have better science, they apply it more widely.

Commitment to the centrality of core research into skin and hair has been passionate, prolonged and ongoing. The result is that L'Oréal is unbeatable at their business. No competitor could hope to catch them up and match the annual investment. Their extension into electronic and light technologies is also a guarantee that they will not be outflanked by new technologies. By focusing their research into skin and hair, rather than any specific production technologies, their research has always been solution neutral.

Taking the Long View

Two factors have combined to enable L'Oréal to work on longer timescales than the norm for global consumer packaged goods businesses: consistency of management and of ownership. For a company this size to have only had four CEOs in over a century is remarkable. Those four men have had over 150 years of L'Oréal service between them. Not one itinerant, heroic CEO or Chainsaw Al in sight, to change things around just to show they are there. The course originally steered by Eugène Schuller has been maintained, with appropriate touches on the tiller and updates to reflect a changing world. The commitment and determination to crack the US market in the mid-late 1900s has merely been pivoted towards the new markets.

The share structure of L'Oréal has played a key role in giving the company license to invest early in areas where making a return seems a long way off. The majority of shares are held by two entities, both of which have powerful reasons not to rock the boat, or allow the curse of the predatory, activist shareholder to strike the business. Thus, L'Oréal has been able to invest so much in core research not geared towards any white spaces in the market. They have been able to invest in country- and regional-specific operational set-ups long before sales justified such investment. As a result, they have built up an infrastructure in their New Markets region, which is more than capable of winning L'Oréal their extra billion consumers in the next decade.

Summary

L'Oréal is an exceptional company that has performed exceptional feats with little external fuss or bother. The combination of their scientific capabilities, acquisition strategy and regional expansion has led to consistent success over a long period of time. The only real question looking forwards is what will happen to the ownership structure. Liliane Bettencourt has become unimaginably wealthy by simply letting her father's chosen successors do what they are paid to do. She has little need to sell up. She presumably also has powerful emotional reasons to keep things at L'Oréal pretty much as her father would have approved. However, she will not live forever and the commitment of the next generation to the firm, while often stated, has yet to be tested for real.

Nestlé's motivations are perhaps more hard headed. The returns they have gained on their original investment have far exceeded the return should they have invested the same capital in some part of their own vast empire. The cosmetics market over a long period of time has been faster growing and more profitable than virtually any other consumer goods market. The two companies also have an extremely close relationship, not only in their two joint venture companies but also in sharing main board directors. Would Nestlé like to buy L'Oréal out-right? At the Nestlé 2011 Annual General Meeting, company chairman Peter Brabeck-Letmathe said the issue would be decided in 2014. Then restrictions on either Nestlé or the Bettencourt family selling to outside parties are lifted. Another option to an outright purchase might be for Nestlé and the Bettencourts to take the company private, with Nestlé buying out the independent shareholders.

2014 will be an interesting year for L'Oréal.

Mars

Where Did It Come From?

Mars Inc. is a $33 billion plus business and the world's biggest confectionary company. It owes in existence to a family fight, an everyday event in the tempestuous relationship between a somewhat feckless penny candy seller, Frank Mars, and his irascible, driven and decidedly un-feckless son Forrest.

Franklin Clarence Mars, a childhood victim of a relatively mild bout of polio, spent most of his childhood confined to his parents' house in Hancock, Minnesota, where his mother, in a quest to keep him entertained, taught him everything she knew about making candy. Once Frank had mastered her repertoire, he experimented on his own concoctions and by 1902 was running a wholesale candy firm selling low-quality penny candy in the Minneapolis/St Paul's area. The same year he married Ethel G. Kissack and, despite spending many weeks at a time away from home drumming up sales on the road, found time to father a son, Forrest Edward Mars, in 1904.

Frank's business was not a success. He constantly veered towards bankruptcy, placing tremendous financial strain on a household that for weeks at a time saw no money whatsoever. By 1910, Ethel had had enough and divorced Frank, taking herself and her son to live with her parents in North Battleford, Saskatchewan, a remote Canadian prairie town. Neither mother nor son was too impressed with Frank, who rarely stumped up the alimony and was only ever referred to by Ethel as 'that miserable failure'. But Frank soon got over whatever trauma he felt, married another Ethel, moved to Seattle and set up again, this time as a manufacturer of candy based on the recipes he'd learned as a child.

Within a year, he was bust again, losing everything, including the new family home. Ethel Mk II had more faith in him, although that must have been sorely tested when, in 1914, this time in Tacoma, Washington, his third candy business went bankrupt. As Frank was wont to do, he fled the scene with the perennially optimistic Ethel Mk II in tow, leaving unpaid creditors in his wake. Back in Minneapolis, he sunk his last $400 into yet another candy-making venture. He was a tryer, perhaps a, if not he, vital quality in an entrepreneur. And this time the trying paid off. No doubt much to the surprise of everyone who knew him as nothing but a three-time failure, his newly named company, the Mar-O-Bar Co., hit on a winner, a line he called Victorian Butter Creams, which he got listed in the mighty Woolworths among other outlets. Failure was at long last behind him, and he built up a successful, locally successful, concern. Meanwhile, Forrest thrived at school and in 1922 won a scholarship to the University of California to study mining, a key industry where he had grown up. Understandably strapped for cash given the family circumstances, Forrest, who had clearly inherited his business brains from his mother, created for himself a range of entrepreneurial evening jobs to pay his way through college, with such success that he dropped out of mining to focus on business.

In the summer of 1923, Forrest had taken a job as a travelling salesman for Camel cigarettes. He ended up in Chicago, where he was thrown in jail after illegally covering Chicago's State Street from one end to the other with Camel posters. And who should bail him out but Feckless Frank, who was now living high on the hog thanks to the continued success of his Victorian Butter Creams. The two repaired to a local milk bar and began a heated exchange about business, in particular Frank's business. It was a conversation that created an empire.

Forrest's time selling Camel cigarettes had endeared him to the concept of scale. One, you could sell Camels across the country. Two, the more the company made and sold, the cheaper and more profitable they were to produce, and consequently the more profitable they to sell. So he was somewhat underwhelmed by Frank's little hand-made candy business. Brainstorming about what could be a nationwide success, they came up with the idea of putting the chocolate malted milk drinks they had in front of them into a chocolate bar. Here was something Forrest felt could be sold anywhere and mass-produced cheaply. Frank agreed and soon produced a bar with a malted flavour nougat centre topped with a layer of caramel, encased in a cheap chocolate he named Milky Way. The bars sold as fast as Frank could produce them; in its first year, 1924, the business grossed a staggering $800,000.

It may not seem so today, but the idea of the Milky Way was revolutionary at the time. Until this point, the chocolate bar market consisted almost entirely of bars of chocolate: milk chocolate, dark chocolate, chocolate with nuts in it, but essentially all just chocolate. But nougat, whipped up nougat that was predominantly air, was a lot cheaper than chocolate. Nougat interiors with chocolate coatings still looked like chocolate bars, but, given all that air inside, they could be made much bigger but still sold at the same price. Consequently, the Milky Way looked a very good deal on the counter in comparison to the ubiquitous Hershey.

In September 1924, Forrest returned to Berkeley to resume his mining studies only to realise business was his true calling. The next year, he transferred to Yale, funded by the now wealthy Frank, to study business. He graduated in 1928 and returned to work in Frank's now thriving company. By this time, on Forrest's urging, Frank had relocated Mar-O-Bar Co. to Chicago and by 1929, with a much bigger factory crammed with new equipment, he was churning out twenty million bars of Milky Way a year. The next year, following Forrest's advice to keep things simple, Frank invented the Snickers bar, essentially the Milky Way with nuts and differently flavoured nougat in the caramel. This he followed in 1932 with Three Musketeers, the Milky Way nougat whipped up a bit more and without the caramel layer. All three products could be made on the same equipment and were now covered in excellent chocolate supplied by none other than the Hershey Company. Company sales in 1932 topped $25 million, propelling Mar-O-Bar to America's number one candy maker in the country, albeit in a very fragmented market.

It was at this point that the relationship between father and son, testy at the best of times, seriously deteriorated. Frank kicked Forrest out. Forrest told Frank he could stick his business up his ass. The bone of contention had been expansion plans; Forrest wanted to expand as far and as fast as possible, whereas Frank, perhaps understandably given his past track record, was happy with things just as they were. They struck a deal. Frank gave Forrest $50,000 and the foreign rights to Milky Way and they parted company, never to meet again. Forrest took his wife and young son off to Europe to start his own business. Fifteen months later Frank was dead from a heart attack. This was the acrimonious break between father that signalled not the end of the Mars business but the opposite.

How Did It Evolve?

It might be thought that the Mars Inc. of today grew out of Frank's thriving US business, by now renamed Mars Candies. But in fact its genesis would be in the company Forrest created for himself in the United Kingdom. Forrest, who had never been overly impressed with Frank's attitude to product quality, moved the family to Switzerland in 1933 and took hourly paid jobs on the factory floors of first Jean Tobler and then Nestlé, to learn for himself the secrets of Swiss chocolate-making. When he felt he had learnt enough, he moved the family to Slough in England to set up his own chocolate company. Whilst he put every penny into his small factory, which began with just four employees, his wife Audrey and son Forrest Junior lived in a one-room apartment with no hot water, intermittent heating and very little food. So bad were conditions that Audrey took up her father's offer to ship herself and young Forrest Jnr temporarily back to America, leaving Forrest Snr to concentrate on building the business.

Forrest was canny enough to realise he had to adapt to local circumstances. First of all, his Milky Way recipe was not attuned to the very sweet British tooth, so he tinkered with it. Once he'd got it right – or perfect rather – he was so pleased with the outcome that he rechristened it: the Mars Bar. Second, Forrest knew he was up against an even more powerful foe in Britain than Hershey in the United States: Cadbury Brothers, who bestrode the British chocolate market like a colossus or three. Its Bournville Birmingham factory was the largest, most modern and most efficient cocoa and chocolate factory in the world. Using mass production techniques Forrest thoroughly endorsed, Cadbury had in fifteen years quadrupled the volume of chocolate sold in Britain by using the benefits of modernisation and mechanisation. And by cutting prices. Dairy Milk by fell by 70% from its pre-First World War levels. No one could compete with it on chocolate bars: six out of every ten chocolate bars sold in Britain were Cadbury's Dairy Milk. The company had taken over its arch-rival, J. S. Fry & Sons, while the only other major player, Rowntree's, had been driven to the brink of bankruptcy.

Forrest clearly needed Cadbury inside the tent peeing out. So, recalling his experience in sourcing Frank's chocolate from Hershey, he did a deal with Cadbury's industrial sales department to supply him with its chocolate, found other suppliers for malt, sugar, glucose and other ingredients, and in August 1933 the first Mars Bars appeared on the shelves. Paradoxically, the very strength of Cadbury's Dairy Milk was his opportunity. People were eating so many of them - just about time anytime an occasion arose where confectionery could be eaten – that they welcomed something that was both very different and, because of its size, more suitable to eat in place of a missed meal.

With Mars Bars selling well – two million bars were sold in the first year and the workforce had increased to a hundred – Forrest realised that offering more alternatives to Dairy Milk – selling a million bars a day – was a winning strategy, so he borrowed the Three Musketeers recipe, sweetened it up a bit, and cheekily named it Milky Way. Soon after, Forrest, never shy to copy and improve a good idea, produced his own version of an American brand called Whoppers and launched it in the UK under the name of Maltesers. He did have his failures – a pineapple-flavoured version of the Mars Bar brought on by a fall in the price of pineapples was a typical example – but his successes occurred often enough to form be the basis of a successful and growing business.

Incredibly, in the midst of getting his British chocolate company off the ground, in 1934 Forrest bought Chapple Brothers, a struggling British dog food company, even though most British dog owners fed their pets scraps from the table. Forrest, a keen observer of industry in general, had noticed the emergence of a dog food category in the US before he left prior to his leaving and was betting the same trend could be developed in Britain. And he was right: within five years, he had increased Chapple's sales fivefold. Pet food would become the second leg of the future Mars empire.

It is at this point that it became clear where Forrest's talents lay. Although he had worked for Frank's chocolate business and studied production techniques in the Swiss chocolate industry, Forrest was no chocolatier; he was a businessman, and a unique one. He wanted to create a very different kind of company that was moulded around his beliefs on how a business should be run. He was strongly influenced by DuPont's planning system and T. G. Rose's Higher Control in Management, a book he never tired of reading. He combined these two sets of ideas with his own and the Mars way of doing things was born.

First and foremost, Forrest believed in hiring the best people, giving them clear accountabilities and empowerment, paying more than anyone else, and bawling out or firing anyone who let him down. He abhorred bureaucracy in all its forms, had no time for management perks and firmly believed in mutuality: if the business did well then everyone did well, and vice versa. He was fanatical about product quality and demanded everyone follow suit or woe betide them. Perhaps influenced by Cadbury's success, he wanted only the newest, most modern and most efficient machinery so that he could make his Mars Bars even more cheaply, not to award himself fatter profits but to reinvest those profits into giving even better value. It was so a potent a mix that, by 1939, Mars Ltd was Britain's third-largest chocolate company behind Cadbury and Rowntree's. (it would overtake them both one day). In the meantime, the pet foods company too was also going from strength to strength.

But just as everything had begun to run smoothly, the Second World War intervened and the British Government slapped a hefty tax on all foreign residents. It was a tax Forrest had no intention of paying: it would take investment money out of his precious businesses. It was also clear that the war would put the brakes on expanding his companies, so Forrest, always a good delegator, handed over control of both the chocolate and pet food companies to his British number twos and headed back to America to start up his next business.

Forrest took an idea home with him for a product that had been in the back of his mind for some time, and which he had come across while travelling in Spain in 1938. There he had noticed Civil War soldiers eating chocolate lentils with a sugar coating that prevented the chocolate from melting. A year previously, Rowntree's had also launched a similar British concept with Smarties, small pieces of chocolate in a hard sugar shell. By the time Forrest got back to America he knew what his next business would be. In starting it, he would also be up against his deceased father's own chocolate business.

After Frank's death, his company had passed into the hands of his second wife, who left the running of it to her half-brother, a salesman who had joined in 1930. Forrest, loyal to his mother, would have nothing to do with the other Ethel, so knew he would have to look elsewhere for help in setting up his new American chocolate business. And who filled the bill better than Hershey, the largest suppliers of chocolate in the country? Forrest barged his way into the office of the Hershey president, who, having sampled the prototype new chocolate, accepted an offer he could scarcely refuse: a joint venture between Frank and the president's son to make it. To show his commitment to the idea, Forrest called his new confection would name M&Ms, standing for Mars & Murrie, the son's name. The deal was sealed and M&Ms Ltd. began production in the spring of 1940.

Forrest's motivation in offering the deal was not an admiration for Murrie's business acumen – their relationship deteriorated almost immediately owing to Forrest's fury at Murrie's approach and attitude – but because Forrest wanted access to Hershey's engineers, who would help set up the new plant. Forrest had also realised that only Hershey could guarantee him supplies of raw materials during the war. It was a brilliant plan. Huge M&Ms orders from the armed forces helped him build the scale he desired for his products. After the war, however, sales settled down to about $3 million a year, not bad. But Forrest was still a small fish in a big pond. Blaming Murrie for the lack of new orders to replace the wartime ones, Forrest bought out Murrie's 20% share in the business for $1 million.

As had been the case in the UK, Forrest had barely got the M&M business off the ground before turning to yet another new venture. This one came from an article Forrest read in a patent journal about a Texas rice mill owner who had patented a new process for rice milling. By steaming the rice before the dehulling stage, the rice that resulted was more nutritious, cooked faster and was fluffier in texture. At this stage rise was mostly sold in bulk, from barrels in stores, so the market looked somewhat unpromising. But the rapid rise of the dedicated grocery store was creating huge demand for the packaging and branding of everything. Forrest could see that would apply to even the most basic products, rice included. So he bought the mill together with its patented process and, after a long lunch with the advertising guru Leo Burnett, produced a name and a pack. Uncle Ben's rice was launched in 1944. The Houston plant would eventually produce 200,000 tons of Uncle Ben's a year.

Back in the M&M business, and perplexed at the lack of progress for a product Forrest was convinced anyone and everyone should be buying, he engaged another advertising agency, Ted Bates & Co. Bates conducted a full brand audit which was supposed to point the way forwards. It did. It turned out that M&M's was young children's most popular chocolate. But how did you persuade their parents to buy it for them? The answer to both Forrest's and American house-wives' dreams came in the Bates tag line: 'Melts in your mouth, not in your hands', which by 1954 was being hammered into the nation's brains by the M&M cartoon characters. Two years later, M&M's was the best-selling choco-late product in America, grossing $40 million a year. Now Forrest had the scale he needed to accomplish his real goal: taking over his father's old company.

How International Is It?

Mars Inc. is that rarity of an American company which actually started off, at least as far as Forrest Snr was concerned, as an international business. His British collection of businesses was the testing ground for his theories on how to run a business; their success bankrolled his reverse international expansion back into the US. The UK has continued as Mars's most important foreign outpost since the day Forrest went back to America in 1939.

UK: Confectionery

Forrest missed little action in Mars Ltd, his renamed UK chocolate company: rationing controls on practically everything sweet, from 1940 until 1953, effec-tively put the whole confectionary market into a state of suspended animation. And when rationing ended, pent-up demand put sales into orbit without any need to launch new products. The only major launch was Bounty in the mid-1950s, a straight copy of the American brand Mounds. Mars however was one of the first companies to use television advertising in Britain and by 1959 had de-veloped a hugely successful campaign for Mars Bar, with a stapline that ran for decades: A Mars a Day Helps You Work, Rest and Play.

And the up-to-date and highly efficient Mars factory stood in complete con-trast to those of its key competitors, Cadbury, Rowntree's and Fry's, all of whom were saddled with pre-war manufacturing facilities. Combined with Forrest's conviction that profits were to be reinvested rather than simply squandered, this meant Mars could offer much better value for money. It built on this advantage in the 1960s, adding a slew of new brands to the product range. His US best-sellers, Snickers and M&M's, were launched under the names of Marathon and Treets, and were joined by Topic, Twix, Spangles, Tunes and Lockets. However, Mars' boldest launch came in 1960 when it launched Galaxy, a milk chocolate bar that went head against Cadbury's flagship Dairy Milk bar. Mars and Forrest saw that the Cadbury best-seller was not the invulnerable colossus it had once been.

The 1970s was another good decade, driven by innovations such as a super-size 72 gram Mars Bar, the biggest ever, which would be followed by a raft of differently-sized, best-selling Mars brands. By 1979, Mars had all but caught Cadbury up. The 1980s saw Cadbury fight back, modernising its factories and ramping up its own innovation programme. But the inspired launch, in 1989, of the ice cream versions of Mars brands took competitors by surprise and left them scrabbling to come up with ice-cream licensing deals with ice cream manufacturers. They were terrified by this interloper.

The big Mars sponsorship deals of the 1980s and '90s of Olympics and World Cups gave Mars, now a global company, a scale advantage over its regional rivals. Mars complemented this approach by sponsoring the London Marathon and the Euro '96 football tournament. The globalisation of Mars brand names saw the Snickers name replace Marathon and M&M replace Treets, with few new brands being launched. The big sellers were flavour extensions of best-selling brands. Forrest Mars's Slough-based factory is still the heart of the UK business and the company's global R&D hub, producing over 100,000 tonnes of chocolate products a year. Mars's 27% share of the UK chocolate market would have been enough to lead it in years gone by, but the merger of Kraft with Cadbury means Mars is now a strong number two.

UK: Petfoods

The Mars Petfoods business pretty much established the British market for packaged dog and cat food from scratch, and the company continues to hold a dominant share of the market. Behind the strength of its Pedigree Chum brand – the company changed its name to Pedigree Petfoods many years ago - the company has developed a reputation for both market innovation and strong basis pet science. When most pet food came in cans, the company was the first to launch the two-piece can in 1979, then transformed the market in the late 1990s by switching to pouches for greater quality, freshness and ease of use. Forrest had instilled as much an emphasis on product quality in his pet food businesses as he did for confectionery: managers had to taste test the products themselves every day.

Mars had begun studying pet nutrition in the 1950s and ten years later had a fully staffed nutrition research unit, expanding over the years from cats and dogs to fish and horses. The company now has several horse food brands and, through acquisition and internal development, now has a range of cat and dog snack and treat brands.

UK: Food

Perhaps surprisingly, Uncle Ben's was not the first Mars food product the company marketed in the UK; that would have to wait until the mid-1980s. In 1962, Forrest's eye had been taken by a new technology for freeze-drying potato. Accordingly he had set up a business, Dornay Foods, to explore the technology on the British markets. Chipples potato sticks, the first offering, soon made way for Yeoman instant mashed potato. In the 1970s, canned meat lines were added to the range and Mars, in a most unusual move for the company, bought an individual brand, Tyne, to bolster its range. The arrival of the Uncle Ben's brand in the mid-1980s signalled the change in direction, followed by moves into pasta and pasta sauces under the Dolmio brand. The pet food pouch technology was transferred over in 1999 to add new life to the range.

UK: Drinks

Having been in the vending business since 1955, the big breakthrough came with the company's invention of the Klix hot drinks system in the mid-1970s. With the dry drinks ingredients already included in every cup, vending machines could be simplified and made more reliable. The pre-filled cups could be sold to anyone who had a hot water dispenser, enabling a much wider distribution, out of the company's vending heartland in schools and workplaces. In 1982, the innovative Flavia drinks system prepared fresh, single servings of coffee, tea, and hot chocolate drinks. The 'Fresh Pack' (the actual brewing chamber), meant each drink would not be tainted by the previously sale. The technology was later further developed for in-home use.

Western Europe

Even before Forrest left for the US, he had opened a small factory in Belgium to supply the European market, just in time for the German invasion whole to stymie the whole thing. But after the war, the Belgian factory was re-opened, supplying the large French market amongst others; the first Mars Bar hit France in 1951. This marked the beginning of the Mars modus operandi. Product would initially be imported and sales and distribution networks developed until a local factory became viable. Imports of and cat food brands, for example, began in 1959; a factory was built the very next year. A similar and much more stately model followed in France: Mars pet brands first appeared 1962 but the factory took eleven years to materialize. The West German sales office for chocolate products opened in 1961; but here the factory took 18 years to follow it. The French, Belgian and German factories supplied Mars sales organisations across the rest of Europe. Mars's drinks and foods divisions soon followed.

Australia/New Zealand

In 1954, Mars signed a deal with MacRobertson's, Cadbury's main competitor in Australia. The company would manufacture Mars Bars and Maltesers under licence, a very rare instance of Mars contracting out. In 1963, however, this arrangement was dislocated: arch-competitor Cadbury bought out MacRobertson's and Mars quickly terminated the arrangement, although it was partially reinstated on later consideration: Cadbury could keep making Maltesers as they did not compete directly with any of its product range and, in any case, Forrest Mars had the sort of warm and cordial relationship with the Cadbury family (as with other chocolate dynasties) that helped smooth over such potential conflicts.

But the sale did inhibit Mars' Australian chocolate ambitions, so the company switched its attentions to pet foods, launching Pal and Whiskas in 1965 and building a pet food factory the next year. In 1967, Mars fast-tracked its way into the Australian food business by purchasing Masterfoods, a local maker of herbs and spices, a name Mars would later transfer to several other of its foods units. Then, a year after building a second pet food factory in 1978, Mars opened its first confectionery factory in Ballarat. It could now tackle the chocolate market properly. Meanwhile, exports of pet foods further south to New Zealand had gone so well that in 1993 Mars purchased a pet food factory to ramp up production there.

Today, Mars is by far the dominant pet food manufacturer in Australia and New Zealand, with around 50% of the market. The pet food factories also act as a supply hub for more than twenty markets in the Far East. Mars Chocolate has also done well, building up to number two behind a very dominant Cadbury, which has been manufacturing in Australia since 1921. The Mars Ballarat factory, like its pet food counterpart, also supplies more than 30 markets in the Far East, Africa and the Middle East.

Eastern Europe

While other companies saw acquisition as the way to enter Eastern European markets, Mars stuck to its standard approach: get distribution for your product any which way, develop demand, and only then take the final plunge. As the barriers to Western companies in Eastern Europe began to crumble in the late 1980s, Mars did exactly that. Mars chocolate products appeared in Hungary in 1989, the year of the fall of the Wall: the company simply bartered them for animal parts that could be used in the company's pet food plants.

But the real prize was the Russian market. In late 1989, Mars plastered Moscow with advertisements announcing that the first ever Mars Bars on sale (legally) in Russia would appear, on 4th January 1990, at a store created especially for the occasion. The company had bartered the product for shipping rights. Soon after the Moscow launch, distributors appeared everywhere, working flat out to get Mars Bars and M&M's into the major Russian cities. In 1991, food and pet products were added to the distribution network and the relaxation of currency controls in 1992 meant the company could now think seriously about building a chocolate factory. It opened in the summer of 1995, at a cost of $140 million, and produced nine different products. A pet food factory opened the same year. By 1997, the Russian operation recorded its first profit, survived the Russian economic crisis, and by 2000 had a 40% share of the market with an annual ad spend of $25 million. By 2012, the company had nine factories supplying Russia and the rest of the CIS.

China

But Mars would eclipse the undoubted success of the Russian venture in the Chinese market. The company opened its first sales office in 1990 and decided to focus on M&M's, because of the brand's much greater temperature tolerance: air-conditioned retail outlets were still very rare and distribution was sketchy. However, Chinese consumers had a much more upscale image of foreign chocolates and a fun brand for kids didn't fit that pre-conceptiion. Mars got the picture very quickly and switched to the Dove chocolate bar, concentrating on the more developed coastal city markets. In 1996, the first factory opened, producing Dove bars to exactly the same standard recipe, a stark contrast to Nestlé, which compromised its recipe to for lower prices, and to Cadbury, which had major quality-control problems trying to replicate its Dairy Milk recipe using locally sourced fresh milk.

Dove was ideally positioned. It was cheaper than the imported Swiss bars and much better quality than the cheap, locally produced brands and, with a wide range of sizes to suit most price points, soon became the country's best-selling chocolate bar. However, Mars was missing another substantial market opportunity: upscale boxed chocolates, an issue it tackled by producing a new product based on the Ethel M line developed by Forrest Senior. As the Chinese teenage market developed, Snickers and M&M's took a more prominent position and, by 2005, Mars was the clear market leader. It had products in 250,000 distribution points across the country and, for the first time, it made a profit. The company now has four factories in China, two for pet foods and two for chocolate, supplying both the ever-growing Chinese market and also exporting to other Asian countries.

Middle East

Once again, after setting up a sales and marketing infrastructure in 1993, Mars opened its first chocolate factory in Dubai in 1998 to service the entire Middle East. A new factory in Saudi Arabia was opened in 2013.

Latin America

Other than as an exporter, Mars was a bit late to the Latin American region: its first factory in Mexico didn't open until 1995. Very unusually, and to help catch up, Mars bought, in 2002, Lucas World, another candy manufacturer. As well as producing a step change in its Mexican market share, the purchase also provided the opportunity to import Lucas World products to Hispanic markets in the US. Mars is now market leader in both pet food and confectionery in Mexico.

Mars's global reach was greatly enhanced recently by two major acquisitions (see What Has It Done Recently? below), the French-based pet food company Royal Canin (with operations in South Africa, Brazil, Argentina, Russia, the UK, Canada, Poland, the US and China) and, in 2008, Wrigley. Apart from South America, Mars was now truly global. Wrigley, for example, had been one of the earliest American companies to globalise, setting up in China as early as 1914.

How Did It Build Its Modern Business?

When the second Ethel died in 1945, Forrest got his foot back in his father's door: half her stock in his business passed to Forrest, as had been stipulated in Frank's will. But the other half went to hers and Frank's daughter, Patricia, who turned out to be the activist shareholder from hell. Forrest, who now held a third of the company, pleaded with her to let him buy her out. He was rebuffed.

Forrest promptly began an assault on his half-sister's daughter's citadel. The shares, he claimed, not only gave him the right to an office at the company, but also access to all the financials, which he used to berate management on a daily basis. He was banned from company property. But he was a very persistent – and surely very annoying – individual and, in 1950, a weary Chairman/CEO partially caved in. Forrest was offered one-third of the board's nine positions, which he used to push for expansion, expansion and expansion. At least in he was a change in tactics: his usual agenda was to call for the sacking of the CEO and the appointment of himself as chairman.

Forrest's biggest beef was that the Chicago plant, state of the art when he left for England in 1932, was now hopelessly outdated and highly inefficient. This was anathema to Forrest, who had never stopped updating his British chocolate and pet food factories. He won. By the end of the 1950s the plant had been expanded, updated and was running along lines not dissimilar to his British outfit. The management of the company, however, was still a frustration. Forrest had finally won the chairmanship in late 1959 but was outflanked. Patricia's latest husband was installed as President and CEO, boxing Forrest in.

His new adversary, James Fleming, knew an enemy when he saw one. He started an all-out war, in which Forrest more than gladly reciprocated. The outcome was a disaster for sales but a triumph for Forrest. The in-fighting, coupled with James's unsuitability for the role – he responded to falling sales by cutting the size and quality of the products – resulted in a 20% decline by 1963. At this point Patricia bowed to the inevitable. She agreed to sell out to her nemesis, a new level of control for Forrest which he cemented a year later by buying out the remaining shareholders. He could now merge; the M&M Company would join forces with Mars Company and the whole thing would become Mars Inc. This, actually, had been a condition of Patricia doing the deal.

Forrest's first task was to remake his vastly expanded US chocolate business in the image of what was already in corporate place. He wasted no time. Senior Chicago management got new bosses transferred from M&M, saw their offices knocked down, their secretaries fired and all their perks abolished. Forrest's way was open-plan, no meetings, no memos, long workdays and the delivery of the best results. Anyone who wouldn't or couldn't fit in was despatched in short or-der. He then set about the more arduous task of restoring Frank's brands to their past glories. Product recipes were revised back to the highest standards. Even a pinhole in the chocolate of one bar would so enrage Forrest that would see the entire day's production junked - along with the career of the guy who had let the shoddy product through.

While the fortunes of the combined US confectionery operations were being rebuilt, Forrest, as ever, still found time to add new and interesting businesses. The success of his by now worldwide pet food empire encouraged him to grab a stake in the burgeoning US market, buying the Kal Kan firm in 1966. Pet foods in the UK had been very successful in growing the dog food products with brands such as Pal, and in developing the cat foods with the launch of Whiskas in 1959. Forrest saw no reason why Kal Kan, once converted to his way of run-ning things, could not achieve the same results. In the UK pet sector, Forrest had also bought Thomas's, a firm that made all manner of pet accessories: dog leads, fish food, budgerigar food, all sorts. Forrest's eye had also been taken by the drinks vending sector and in 1955 he set up a British company, Four Square. The company later moved into the technology of electronic payment systems.

Back in the US, however, Mars Inc. had been making substantial gains on a complacent and somewhat outdated Hershey, helped by Hershey's complete fail-ure to advertise, which persisted, unbelievably, until 1970. Hershey did another foolish thing: its practice of maintaining the price of the Hershey Bar at 5c while steadily reducing its weight as ingredient costs rose was beginning seriously to dismay even the most loyal of customers. Mars Inc., a prodigious user of televi-sion advertising, always offered excellent value for money and was much more aggressive than Hershey in grabbing retail display space. It was steadily chipping away at Hershey's lead. In 1973, with victory in sight, Forrest Mars, in a career full of surprising moves, did the most surprising thing of all: he turned over all his shares in his businesses to his three children and resigned from the company. His two sons, Forrest Jnr and John (who had both worked in the company from leaving college) were left in sole charge.

To their credit, Forrest Junior and John changed very little. The individual companies, by now collectively turning over $800 million a year, ran as they had always run. The principles Forrest had established – quality, individual responsi-bility, mutuality, efficiency and freedom from outside investors – remained in place, as did the unique corporate work style. The only noticeable change was that one boss (Forrest, who managed mostly from a distance) was swapped for two bosses who managed in a very hands-on style. Individual company heads, until now allowed to run things almost autonomously, (unless they missed their targets in which case they found themselves in Forrest's crosshairs), at first struggled with the new regime. But enough had remained unchanged to maintain continuing success and, in the mid-1970s, Hershey was finally overtaken, whilst in the UK, Mars would soon be on the verge of overhauling both Cadbury and Rowntree's.

The problem child of the Mars family of businesses in the early 1980s was Kal Kan, whose loss-making performance was in complete contrast to the highly successful pet foods businesses in the UK, Europe, Australia and South America. One of the key Mars's philosophies shared by Forrest Junior and John was that success ought to be transferable, so the US pet business moved to adopt UK recipes and brand names such as Pedigree and Whiskas. Changing over the Kal Kan brands to their new identities was rocky at times but ultimately successful – Kal Kan's market share doubled by the end of the decade – vindicated Forrest's original beliefs, as well as reminding Mars that how to do things properly was how to do things the Mars way.

A key theme under the Mars brothers, who by now had been joined by their sister Jacqueline, was the globalisation of what until that point had been a collection of semi-autonomous regional businesses. Their sponsorship of the 1984 Olympics in Los Angeles had been a success in the US businesses, but following decades of autonomy abroad, the company had barely any brands on Olympic hoardings that were recognisable across all markets in all countries. In addition, the US Mars Bars and Milky Ways were a completely different pair of products in the US compared to the rest of the world.

Outiside the US, Snickers was known as Marathon and M&M's as Treets. Pet food names also varied. So it was decided to harmonise the brand, ending the problem of sponsoring future Olympics and World Cups across national frontiers and reaching a global audience with global brands. The advent of satellite television in Europe had made a nonesense of national advertising boundaries, a further spur for change.

Changing brand names that had been around for decades was a bold and forward-thinking move, but in other areas the business had become a lot more cautious under the new regime. In 1982, Mars had passed up the chance to have M&M's feature in the film ET, deciding an alien was too scary to associate with a brand aimed directly at children. The subsequent runaway success of recently-launched Reeses Pieces announced that a Hershey fight-back had been launched, which indeed culminated in the company regaining leadership of the US chocolate market in 1988, much assisted by the purchase of Cadbury's struggling US business and the subsequent acquisition of US Cadbury brand rights. Mars had been offered first refusal on the Cadbury deal but had declined; it saw difficulties in converting the Cadbury way to the Mars way. There were, however, one or two new product launches in the 1980s and a handful of acquisitions, of which by far the most notable was the 1986 purchase of DoveBar International Inc., makers of a hand-dipped ice cream bar. It was a move that mystified competitors and commentators alike.

Despite grossing over $7 billion in 1988 with three of the four best-selling chocolate products in the US (Snickers, Plain M&M's, Peanut M&M's), such was the apparent inertia creeping through the organisation that Fortune magazine ran a long article asking whether or not the Mars siblings had lost the corporate plot. But intimations of the company's demise were premature. In 1989, Mars Inc. switched tack on new product development and instead of trying (and mostly failing) to invent new chocolate bars, it focused on differently flavoured brand extensions that greatly reduced the financial risk of innovation but still benefited from the company's ability to persuade its consumers to give the developments a try. New lines like Peanut Butter Snickers and a host of new M&M variants were soon hitting the shelves. A much bigger surprise came in the same year when the Dove subsidiary launched ice cream versions of 3 Musketeers, Snickers and Milky Way. It was a move that would create an entirely new and profitable category in markets around the world for the now globalized range of Mars range brands.

The company was in the ascendancy again. By the end of the 1990s, the company was still neck-and-neck with Hershey in the US but had grown enormously around the world, operating over 40 factories globally, 25 of which were outside the US. Now it began to focus much of its energies on finding new markets for the Mars range of confectionery, pet food, rice and vending machine drinks. And with an eye to the future, particularly issues it could see down the line surrounding the ethical sourcing of crops - not least its own key ingredients of cocoa and rice - one of Mars's rare acquisitions came in 1997 when it purchased Seeds of Change, an organic seed company.

In 1999, Forrest Mars died. He had essentially been the architect of the whole enterprise, and although he had retired and left his offspring to get on with things, he hadn't completely gone away. In 1981, he had moved to Nevada and started up a hand-made gourmet chocolates business. The company, Ethel M. Chocolates, was named after his mother, its products based on recipes she herself had developed while still tolerating Frank in Tacoma. In the late 1980s, now in his mid-80s, he sold the business to Mars Inc., which continues to run it to this day. In 1992, much to the chagrin of his children, he had secretly taken it upon himself to enter into talks with Nestlé to discuss a possible merger after the retirement of his children. For once, he did not get his way; those children of his, legal owners of the business, totally rejected the idea. Even if it had gone ahead, the deal would have been complicated; in 1988, Nestlé had paid $4.5 billion for Rowntree's, so the Mars merger would have raised probably insurmountable anti-trust issues, particularly in Britain.

How Is It Structured?

The combination of unbroken family ownership and the simplicity of management structure Forrest Mars originally designed means that Mars Inc. has one of the most stable and easily understood management structures of any large company. The global head office has always been a tiny affair with fewer than 100 staff and is the least ostentatious building imaginable for a global multi-corp, When the CEO of Nestlé visited, he thought he had taken a wrong turn. Individual operating companies still have a high degree of autonomy – there is no overseas structure, for example – and there are only six levels of management between the factory floor and the family members themselves. The company has long been organised by product sector, adding more as the company expanded into new categories, and by management discipline.

In the early 1990s, management experimented with combining the various product sectors into single organisations by country, but it was not a success and was quietly abandoned in the larger markets. The next biggest change came in 2001, when the siblings retired and handed over day-to-day management to non-family associates for the first time. This led to the creation of a formal board of directors – all family members together with a small number of outside advisers. Reporting to the board is the president (currently Paul Michaels), who has under him vice presidents for People, Finance, Corporate Affairs, General Counsel and Supply, R&D and Procurement, plus the presidents of each product division. The original four divisions - Petcare, Chocolate, Food and Drinks - have more recently been joined by Wrigley, although this is run as a separate unit (beefed up by the transfer in of Mars's non-chocolate confectionery brands such as Starburst and Skittles) and what the company calls Symbioscience, the nearest Mars has to a skunk-works, a collection of development areas currently consisting of Mars Botanical, Mars Plantcare, Mars Veterinary, Mars Sustainable Solutions and Mars Biomedical. The Food and Petcare divisions have their headquarters in Belgium, the others in the US.

What Has It Been Doing Recently?

Mars Inc. is a private company, one of the largest privately owned companies in the world and one of the most private private companies to boot. It shares as little as possible with the outside world, so we cannot follow its year-by-year activities and sales performance. But although the company has reached out into new markets and launched new products, by far the most sweeping changes came, as one might expect, after the retirement of the Mars siblings and day-to-day control passed to non-family management. And the changes came soon: things were evolving rapidly on Planet Mars.

The company had made acquisitions in the past but they tended to be in either completely new areas - Uncle Ben's - or small complementary add-ons such as the UK pet treat business. In neither case would the acquisitions be large and immediately transformative. Forrests Snr, Jnr and John Mars were all convinced that large acquisitions were a bad idea, for two reasons. First, debt, which the family had a horror of, convinced, and probably correctly, that even the most liberal of lenders would impose conditions restricting the freedom to manage and invest as the mood pleased. Second, it was completely unconvinced that a large organisation with its own entrenched culture, though bought by Mars, could ever be converted to the Mars ways of doing things without falling apart at the seams in the process.

The new regime thought differently, and soon put its plans into action. Just a year after the management handover, Mars purchased the Royal Canin pet food business for €1.5 billion. While the company could cover the asking price without going into debt – although it would take money that was needed for updating plant and funding an advertising campaign – the bigger concern was the task of embedding that very strong Mars culture in a sprawling, long-established business. Other new factors to deal with were the private label brands Royal Canin supplied – Mars had avoided the area completely – and the need to drop some brands from both companies to stay competitive. Mars had never believed that brands were something you bought and sold; every brand carried too much of the company ethos to trade it with other companies.

But these were nettles that had to be grasped if the company was to get into new, faster-growing categories in a commercial environment that was changing much faster than it had at the time those celebrated unwritten rules were first formulated. Royal Canin products – breed- and age-specific dog and cat foods prescribed by professional vets – were sold primarily to a speciality area from which Mars' own pet foods were almost completely absent. For Mars to build up an equivalent position in the same market space would have been a long process, cost a great deal of money, and even then stood a serious chance of failure. So the move was a sound one and overall deemed a success despite some post-acquisition blues, not least the 2007 major product recall, followed by another in 2009. To the quality-obsessed Mars management, such disasters were both horrifying and, until now, unheard-of.

Indeed, so traumatic were they that Mars made three significant further acquisitions to bolster its under-performing US pet food business. In 2006, it acquired the Doane Petcare, a largely private label company but with an excellent manufacturing and distribution set-up that could be immediately deployed to improve the Kal Kan operation. A year later, it added Nutro Products Inc., a manufacturer of high-nutrition, high-performance natural dog and cat foods sold in pet speciality and farm and feed stores, followed closely by Banfield Pet Hospital, a chain of some 800 veterinary pet clinics.

The mother of all deals, however, and one that surprised competitors and commentators alike came in 2008. Mars would be acquiring the mighty Wrigley chewing gum company. The surprise lay not in the fact that two chocolate and gum companies were coming together. After all, in 2003, after a decade of small, local acquisitions, hadn't Cadbury splashed out $4.2 billion to buy Adams gum from Pfizer? And overtaken Mars as the world's largest confectionery company? It had. No, the logic behind the move was compelling: chewing gum was both more profitable and growing faster than chocolate. And since the two categories were sold side-by-side in most stores, selling them side-by-side was easy. It was similarly unsurprising that Wrigley saw a future combined with a chocolate company. In 2002, when Hershey was up for sale (but then withdrawn) Wrigley's bid of $12.5 billion was a full $2 billion more than the next highest, a joint bid by Cadbury and Nestlé.

So the logic of combining a large chocolate company with the world's largest gum company was unassailable. The only surprise was the debt. Mars had spent the previous 70 years entirely in the black – one of its five core principles – but it was now deeply in the red: the $23 billion acquisition had taken a lot of funding. But what it also bought, as well as a corporate giant, was global number one in confectionary for Mars. The deal had an unusual structure too: in addition to financing supplied by Wall Street investment banks, Warren Buffet's Berkshire Hathaway was also in for several billion. There was also some structural change: a new subsidiary of Mars Inc. was created, combining the Wrigley business with the Mars non-chocolate confectionery brands, with Mars holding 81% share in the new division and Berkshire Hathaway 19%.

The Mars family was deeply involved in the deal, negotiating directly with the Wrigley family. It also insisted that Berkshire Hathaway structure its input to suit the Mars family's concerns. For which 'foibles' might have been another description.

Wrigley was over 100 years old, with iconic brands such as Doublemint and Juicy Fruit generating annual sales of over $5 billion from over 100 countries. To maintain control, the Wrigley Executive Chairman, William Wrigley Junior, would continue to oversee the new division, reporting to Mars's President, Paul Michaels. But the company's concern over the challenge of changing a deeply conservative Wrigley culture to the equally long-established Mars way was revealed in an add-on to the deal: if William Wrigley resigned within one year of the deal closure, he would receive a further $19.7 million. William's CEO, William Perez, didn't last three weeks before jumping ship, watching his executive suite in Wrigley's Chicago HQ ripped out for a Mars-style 'no office, no memo' culture.

Perez's replacement, Dushan Petrovich, a 30-year Wrigley man, reported directly to Paul Michaels, leaving William Wrigley somewhat under-employed. He managed to hang on for fifteen months before taking the not-too-subtle hint and the still available $19 million. Petrovich retired in mid-2011 to be replaced by the then head of the Mars drinks division; the Marsification of Wrigley could now be brought to a conclusion.

More recently, Mars has focused increasing focus on health, balanced diets and sustainable sourcing. The dietary issue is a substantial shift for a company whose historic successes have included the 'Biggest Mars Bar Ever' and the introduction of the pioneering the king-size chocolate bar format. But the issues are being taken seriously. The company has partnered with the US Healthy Weight Commitment Foundation in putting Guideline Daily Amount information on packaging. Its recipes have reduced sodium levels by 25% and, by the end of 2013, it has committed to shipping no chocolate products that exceed 250 calories per portion. The company has even published a series of academic papers on the risks of obesity in dogs.

What Is Its DNA?

Of all the companies considered in this book, Mars' DNA is by far the most visible, not least because it has infused every aspect of its business since first being isolated in 1947 by the original Forrest Mars, and the company shares these 'Five Principles of Mars' at every opportunity. It is these principles, the company says, that 'set us apart from others, requiring we think and act differently towards our associates, our brands and our business. These principles have always been demanding and are an essential part of our heritage. We believe they are the real reason for our success'. You cannot turn a corner in a Mars office or factory without seeing the principles on prominent display, supported by live data screens showing how the company is fulfilling them. And what Mars doesn't share with the outside world, it more than makes up for internally. Few if any corporate workforces are so widely, so frequently appraised, in so detailed a fashion, of how and what and where their companies are doing business. Mars' 70,000 associates are extremely well-informed.

Quality

The consumer is our boss, quality is our work and value for money is our goal.

Every company in this book would nod their heads at that, but few, if any, follow it through to the extent Mars does. From his earliest days in his start-up British factory, in a style perhaps best described as management by apoplectic fit, Forrest Mars Snr impressed on every single worker that they were actually consumer representatives inside the factory. Every single employee was empowered to stop production for any product quality reason, no matter how big or how small. Anyone who let a problem pass would find themselves rounded on by an incandescent Forrest and accused of trying to bankrupt him. A day's production would be junked for the slightest problem. Any new machinery that could improve quality would be green-lighted with no questions asked. The factory floor would be cleaner than the average household kitchen surface. After Forrest Senior retired, the Mars siblings, visiting a factory unannounced, made it a habit to climb onto the roof. Woe betide a factory manager who hadn't had that day's bird droppings cleaned off. More recently, the commitment to quality has showed itself in the company's refusal to introduce outsourcing in order to lower costs- an increasingly common practice. It manufactures itself over 95% of the products it sells: only 5% are practices it maintains as a legacy from acquisitions. This gives the company the level of control it needs to deliver both on its quality promise and, latterly, its environmental footprint.

The Mars commitment to value for money is also legendary. The Mars Bar sold outside the US is not a difficult product to make – it has no secret ingredients or proprietary processes – but no competitor has ever been able to make anything like a similar product, offer the same value for money and still make a profit. Of course, Mars benefits from economies of scale – it produces three million Mars Bars a day at its UK plant – but the product was always designed to offer superior value for money. Nowadays, with brand benefits evolving away from grams per penny towards values that are perhaps more emotional benefits, the value-for-money commitment has become more complex to manage. But a commitment it remains, and one lies at the core of the company and across every one of its brands. Whatever the trends, Mars seems to be insisting, value for money will never really die. Who's to say it's not absolutely, well, on the money?

Responsibility

As individuals, we demand total responsibility from ourselves; as associates, we support the responsibilities of others.

Mars puts as much responsibility as possible as close as possible to the impact of the decision; that is how the company is structured and run. The minimalist head office structure is the minimum required to run a global organisation and every business unit is fully responsible for its own results in the short, medium and long terms. Within a Mars company, there are no multiple layers of management to diffuse direct responsibility and no committees to hide behind. Memos are banned and fancy Powerpoint decks tantamount to a manager's suicide note. Everyone has the authority, and so is empowered to do their own job. But no man is an island. Every Mars office around the world is the same: explicitly designed to foster team working. No one has an office: everyone sits at identical desks in one large open space; so, if you need someone's input, at any level in the company, you walk over to their desk and ask. Meeting rooms are few and far between, and generally reserved for external visitors.

In its most recent rewrite, presumably reflecting the views and concerns of the next generation Mars family - all of whom co-signed the principles document - this responsibility has been explicitly extended to include the company's responsibility both to the environment and the communities in which it operates. Very demanding goals determine attitudes and behaviour towards issues such as carbon footprint and energy and water consumption, irrespective of the impact on short-term profits.

Mutuality

A mutual benefit is a shared benefit; a shared benefit will endure.

Although in different ways, this is a principle that applies to associates, suppliers and the planet in general. For associates, the symbols of mutuality are very striking. They start in the car park, where there are no reserved spaces for management of any kind: the earlier you arrive, the closer you can park. At the entrance, even the president clocks in and there is a 10% salary penalty for lateness or a corresponding bonus for timeliness. The salaries are attractive. Mars aims to be at least a top-quartile payer; more usually it's top-decile. There are as few pay bands as there are management levels and salaries are relatively transparent: there are no individual salary awards for individual performance, so when the company does well, everyone does well. And when it does badly, everyone tightens their belts. Staff is paid broadly the same at each level, so lateral career moves into different job functions – a Mars speciality – are salary neutral, even between divisions.

There are no share option awards, because there are no shares. There is no fat-cat-favourable company pension scheme: Mars believes it pays enough for everyone to sort out their own pension arrangements. There is no executive suite with Picassos on the walls. It is, in short, a uniquely egalitarian workplace. Further there has been a recent move towards acceptance of variable work–life balances at varying stages of life, perhaps a reflection that the Mars work ethic has tended to be very hard-driving. But given the arrival of Warren Buffet on the scene, there has had to be a nod towards the need for shareholders to receive a fair but not excessive return on investment.

When it comes to suppliers, Mars always drives hard bargains to get the best ingredients and services, but never does deals that may ultimately damage suppliers' businesses. Given that much of the Mars business depends on primary crops such as cocoa and rice, much more emphasis is nowadays placed on the company's responsibility to millions of small growers in poor parts of the world. Mutuality has now been redefined as 'doing business in ways that are good for Mars, good for people and good for the planet'. In this regard, the company been eager to work with the US Government and IBM to sequence and annotate the cocoa genome, which it then shared openly so as to provide the best long-term benefit to African cocoa growers. Mars has set itself the challenge of sequencing genomes of 100 other African farm crops, whilst Mars Symbioscience is developing rice varieties that will provide greater nutritional value, taste better, produce emit fewer greenhouse gases and require less water. The company is also committed to entirely eliminate greenhouse gas emissions from its operations by 2040.

Efficiency

We only use resources to the full, waste nothing and do only what we can do best.
Since that distant day that the first Forrest Mars first read Higher Control in Management, the key driver amongst the Mars's efficiency principles has been - and remains - return on assets. This is the company's prime financial measure and, as it rightly believes, rightly vitally important growth driver. In simple

terms, Mars measures its profitability against the value of the assets employed in the business: standard enough.

Where Mars differs is that it does not measure total assets by calculating the actual capital that has been invested in existing plant, buildings, infrastructure etc. but by the replacement cost of the assets now. This is a double-edged sword for managers. On the downside, if both they and a competitor are selling a similar product at the same price and competitor costs calculations are using a similar but 20-year-old machine, the competitor will be recording a higher percentage ROTA – his machine's price will be lower than the Mars price. This might well encourage, for example, a bigger advertising spend. On the other hand, the benefit over time for the Mars manager is that, as the machine is valued not at what it cost twenty years ago but what a new one would cost today, he has every incentive to replace the machine. His ROTA will remain unchanged but he will benefit from a more modern, more efficient machine, and essentially improve his product's quality and value at no cost. Which is why Mars is always investing in newer and better machinery than its competitors.

ROTA also explains why there are no office fripperies, why managers fly economy and why Mars tends to steer clear of businesses it does not thoroughly understand. At this very moment (early 2011), ROTA is the tool that is upgrading and improving the Wrigley set-up far further and faster than Cadbury ever did with Adams. ROTA as a performance measurement means Mars has to be the most efficient company in the industries in which it operates.

Freedom

We need freedom to shape our future; we need profit to remain free.

It is a common conceit, when competitors' managers explain away their own inability to compete with Mars, to claim that as a private company Mars doesn't need to show a profit. To some extent, this is true. Mars can and does think in decades - the extension into China is a good example - rather than obsessing about quarterly earnings as a city-driven company might. But the Mars family didn't become one of the richest in America by never making a profit. The company sets itself very high operating profit targets – usually well above industry norms – but reinvests most of it back into the business. The Mars family has always paid itself modestly and rarely taken significant dividends, except in extremis: a divorce, for example.

However, there can be no doubt that the focus on profit – always intense – has been greatly magnified since the Wrigley takeover. The company now finds itself not only with a shareholder – albeit a benign one – but in mountainous debt to Wall Street and the need to pay back the debt back is the company's currently paramount wish. Profit (= freedom) is after all one of those five principles. It's made a change to a company wholly unused to balancing investment opportunities with debt repayment, but absolutely needing to. How the company navigates this tricky course will almost certainly determine whether the Wrigley acquisition is a one-off in scale terms of scale or whether Mars gets more of a taste for making the big deals. But since Mars has not, and almost certainly will never, see itself as a holding company with mixed bag of ever-changing businesses, our view is that such temptations will be resisted unless a particularly appropriate combination offers itself: another Wrigley-type deal in either confectionery or pet foods. Ferrero, for example, should the Ferrero family ever decide to sell. That, we suggest, would also be a Mars unmissable.

Summary

Mars Inc. has annual sales of over $30 billion, operates 401 factories and offices in 73 countries and employs over 70,000 associates. By any measure it is a global company, but one that acts very locally. The company has eleven brands with annual sales revenues of over $1 billion (Pedigree $4.7bn, Snickers $3.6bn, M&M's $3.5bn, Whiskas $2.8bn, Dove $2.6bn, Orbit $2.5bn, Milky Way/Mars Bar $2.4bn, Extra $2.2bn, Uncle Ben's $1.6bn, Royal Canin $1.5bn, Twix $1.5bn). Three of these came from acquisitions. Over 90% of company sales come from three categories: Pet Care, Confectionery and Gum. It is the world's largest confectionery company, Snickers and M&M's are the world's best-selling confectionery products and it is America's third-largest private company (behind Cargill and Koch Industries). So it is probably fair to say that the business model developed by Forrest Mars Senior and the brands developed by successors Frank and Forrest have been resounding successes.

Mars isn't an unstoppable machine – it can be and has been beaten locally and for long periods – but over the long haul it has proved to be an exceptionally strong and consistent performer. The Wrigley deal took Mars Inc.'s annual turnover close to $30 billion, a level that now been exceeded, and double the level at which the family handed over control in 2001. As the world's largest confectionery and pet food company – with a small range of other interests in food, drinks and science - it's fair to say the transition from family day-to-day management to something that resembles the corporate has been successful.

Looking forwards, it is highly likely it will retain its prized independence and continue to do well in most countries and most categories. Very appealingly, even charmingly, it is also pretty certain that it will continue to operate a corporate culture that is absolutely all its own.

Nestlé

Where Did They Come From?

Heinrich Nestlé was born in 1814 in Frankfurt-am-Main, but fled after a serious bout of rioting in 1833. Moving to the small town of Vevey in French-speaking Switzerland, he called himself Henri from then on. As a scientifically-minded man, Henri had trained and gone into business as an apothecary. This was a career involving a lot of work preparing formulations and experimenting for new and better ones - there were then few packaged, pre-prepared products available.

Henri had long been conscious of the high mortality rate for infants whose mothers were unable to breast feed, and, by 1847, he was devoting significant laboratory time to try to develop a substitute. Henri had a wide range of other interests; in 1857 he set up in business with other Vevey businessmen to manufacture a liquid fuel of his own invention and an artificial fertilizer. But Henri kept coming back to the problem of malnourished babies. He experimented with a mix of cow's milk, wheat-flour and sugar to find a way of overcoming the twin problem: keeping most of the nutrition while not curdling or spoiling the milk.

By 1866, Henri was convinced he had found a solution. Farine lactée was made, he claimed, from 'wholesome Swiss milk and a cereal component baked by a special process of my invention'. So Henri had a product, but needed publicity. The next year, the mother of a premature baby fell seriously ill and was unable to feed the child herself. The infant boy was too young to tolerate any of the usual foods, so was fed on farine lactée. He survived, and the news spread like wildfire.

Henri cashed in on this PR by calling his business Farine Lactée Henri Nestlé. He added to the level of personal branding by creating a logo based on the meaning of his surname – little nest. Unfortunately, 'little nest' also describes the size of the Swiss market. Virtually any manufacturing business based there had to develop internationally to have any chance of surviving at all. So Henri opened a London office, soon to be followed by sales offices in France, Germany and the United States. By 1872 he was exporting as far as South America and Australia. However, having no children and nearing his 60s - considered old in those days – Henri began turning his mind to putting his feet up. His answer came in the form of an offer of a million francs. The purchasing consortium was headed by Jules Monnerat, president of the Company Simplon Railway, and he would be chairman of the Nestlé Company for the next 25 years. Henri took a well-earned retirement.

One of Jules Monnerat's first tasks was to build upon a new product Henri had launched in 1874: condensed milk. Condensed milk was patented in USA by Gail Borden in 1856. After Borden's first two companies failed to market his miracle product, he struck a partnership with a financier on a train, and founded the New York Condensed Milk Company. The breakthrough came with the American Civil War. The Union Army placed huge orders for a nutritious, compact foodstuff its troops could all but live on. Borden could not build enough factories to meet the exponential increase in demand, so he licensed his patent far and wide. Millions of troops got a taste for condensed milk, and returned home after the war to hook their families as well. By the late 1860s, what was known as *conny-onny* in some later markets was one of America's fastest-growing foods. Borden's train-ride investor's $100,000 stake was worth $8 million at his death.

Condensed milk's dramatic growth inspired the American consul in Zurich, Charles Page, to found the Anglo-Swiss Condensed Milk Company in 1866. He saw Switzerland, with its large milk production, as being the ideal manufacturing base, particularly to target Britain, at that time the largest concentrated consumer market in the world. Anglo-Swiss had had a free run at building this lucrative new market until Henri Nestlé moved into condensed milk, seeing clear manufacturing synergies between this product and farine lactée. Nestlé's new chairman Jules Monnerat, also saw the threat in Anglo-Swiss' expansion into cheese and instant formula feed.

As well as branching out into condensed milk, Nestlé became involved in another booming new category, milk chocolate. The cocoa business had been industrialised since the 18th-century and the first chocolate bars invented in the mid-1850s. Yet, the Holy Grail for chocolatiers was to develop a milk chocolate bar that, being less bitter, would have far greater appeal. Daniel Peter, had laboured for twenty years trying to crack the secret, but it was only in 1875 when he compared notes with his friend and neighbour, Henri Nestlé, that Daniel achieved his breakthrough. Using Henri's newly launched condensed milk, he solved the problem of combining fat-rich cocoa powder with water-based milk.

Daniel and Henri didn't form a joint chocolate company to exploit the breakthrough. Instead Daniel teamed up with his father-in-law, who ran Switzerland's first chocolate maker, the Cailler Company and bought in Nestlé's condensed milk as an ingredient. As the Swiss cocoa companies rapidly consolidated, Peter-Cailler-Kohler became the world's leading manufacturer of chocolate, relying on Nestlé not only for condensed milk but also marketing and selling expertise in various foreign markets.

The growth in milk chocolate sales persuaded Nestlé themselves to enter the game in 1904. They reached agreement with the Swiss General Chocolate Company to produce Nestlé branded products. Nestlé's head-to-head battle with Anglo-Swiss may have delayed their entry to the chocolate market. Run by Americans, the Anglo-Swiss Condensed Milk Company, was international in outlook from the start. They were itching to confront the Borden firm head on in their homeland. Nestlé didn't want to miss out either and by 1900 had opened a US factory. (This was not Nestlé's first overseas venture: in 1898 they had purchased the Viking Melk (milk) company in Norway.) It became clear that the Nestlé/Anglo-Swiss battle was consuming more time, money and effort than benefit it was adding for both players, so in 1905 they agreed to merge.

Called, somewhat unimaginatively, the Nestlé and Anglo-Swiss Milk Company, it began life as a truly international company. Factories operated in the United States, Britain, Germany and Spain in addition to their Swiss base. Australia, the company's second-largest export market, got its first Nestlé factory in 1907. Exports boomed as the company set up local subsidiaries in other markets, to replace sales agents, and soon opened warehouses in Singapore, Hong Kong and Bombay. The core of the product range - baby formula and condensed milk - was perfectly suited to export, being compact and with long shelf lives. They proved particularly popular in countries where, for logistical or heat reasons, fresh milk was a rare commodity. In 1911, the company built the world's then largest milk condensing plant in Dennington, Australia.

However most of the company's manufacturing infrastructure was in continental Europe and Nestlé's supply infrastructure was severely dislocated by the outbreak of the First World War. Not only were exports across Europe and over to Britain and elsewhere almost impossible, virtually all the milk coming into Nestlé's factories had to be sold to meet the needs of milk-starved local towns. On the other hand, just as had been the case in the American Civil War, government orders for condensed milk sky-rocketed. Rather than leave this demand to be fulfilled by American competitors and risk losing their hard won sales forever, Nestlé went on a factory buying spree in America. This made Nestlé even more international in focus, operating a semi-global supply chain. By the end of the war Nestlé had forty factories across the world, producing double the company's pre-war output. And, because the Swiss head office had been essentially cut off, the overseas subsidiaries operated with near total empowerment. Thus, two key defining aspects of the Nestlé Company - global operations and highly decentralised decision-making – were in place by 1920.

However, the end of the war brought a company crisis. Government orders dried up and supplies of fresh milk resumed to the population in general. Demand for condensed milk plummeted. The situation was exacerbated by rapidly rising prices for raw materials, a worldwide economic slowdown, adverse exchange rates and hyperinflation in the German economy. In 1921 the company recorded its first ever loss. Senior management thought the situation so bad that a Swiss banking expert was brought in to restructure the company. Factories were closed, debt was paid down and the company worked through the crisis.

By 1929 Nestlé was sufficiently back on its feet to acquire the Peter-Cailler-Kohler company. This merged with their own much smaller scale chocolate set-up to make chocolate the company's second-largest category.

The company's basic focus was on milk dried to varying levels as the key ingredient for its main product lines of baby formula and condensed milk (for sale and as an ingredient in chocolate). Therefore, the science of drying water-based ingredients was Nestlé's core competence. It was always looking to develop improved methods and new uses. A scientist in Nestlé's Australian business, Thomas Mayne, was motivated by much the same concerns that had led Henri into the business in the first place - that children were receiving insufficient nutrients from their daily diet during the Great depression. Mayne developed Milo in 1934. I was, described on the label as Nestlé's Fortified Tonic Food. Simultaneously t, the main laboratories in Vevey were also working on a project that would transform the company.

In 1930, Nestlé were approached by the Brazilian Coffee Institute to find a better use for Brazil's huge coffee surpluses in the reduced markets of the Depression. Nestlé, known throughout the world for its expertise in evaporation and drying processes, was asked to come up with an improved means of creating an instant coffee. This could be sold for a premium, year-round, rather than the year's surplus being dumped onto the coffee bean market, reducing prices yet further.

The idea of instant coffee was not new. Several inventors claimed first rights to both powdered and concentrate versions and the product was commercially available by 1910. But it wasn't very good. Much flavour was lost during the drying process. Nestlé's top evaporation expert, Max Morgenthaller, assembled a team to work on the problem. He was given a long leash by today's standards, taking seven years to come up with a new process that preserved nearly all of the flavour and could be industrialised. The answer lay in spraying a fine mist of a treated coffee solution into a heated tower. The droplets evaporated almost instantly, leaving a fine powder to float down.

Nestlé introduced Nescafé in Switzerland on April 1st, 1938 and geared up their main UK factory for mass production. However, timing was not on Nestlé's side. The outbreak of war pretty much put a stop to the export of Brazilian coffee beans to Europe. Even more disruptively, company profits plummeted in 1939, down to $6 million from $20 million the year before. Vevey, in neutral Switzerland, became increasingly cut off. Many of the top executives relocated to company offices in Connecticut to run the still functioning parts of the business from the US.

Coffee beans were imported into the USA, and Nestlé began constructing drying towers. As had been the case a generation earlier, they got huge military orders for a compact, almost ever-lasting foodstuff that would help sustain the bodies and morale of tens of millions of servicemen. The Second World War was the making of Nescafé and the remaking of Nestlé.

Nescafé became the company's leading product. Production reached a million cases a year by 1943 and by 1945, even with the devastation of many of Nestlé's markets, annual sales were more than double the 1938 level at $225 million. The company had changed into a global instant coffee business, with other categories in addition. As exports from the company's many European factories had been stopped by the war, the company had used Nescafé profits to open subsidiaries and build factories in as many countries as possible unaffected by the conflict, primarily Latin America. The US business went from strength to strength.

By 1946, with Nestlé's European factories restored to raw materials and were getting back up to speed, the company was operating 107 factories spread across five continents. It was already the world's most global food company. Production was still concentrated in four large and growing categories: milk products (primarily sweetened, condensed milk), baby foods (where the postwar baby boom did wonders for sales of infant formula), chocolate and instant beverages (Nestea joining the range in 1946 to be followed by Nesquik instant hot chocolate in 1948, both developed in the US).

With the company being run once again from Vevey, the focus switched to beefing up the war-damaged European parts of the business. In 1947 a merger was agreed between Nestlé and the Swiss food company, Alimentana, whose large range of soups, bouillon cubes and spices was sold under the Maggi name. Their common link was the evaporation processes for soups and drying processes used to make the bouillon cubes. The company name evolved once again to the Nestlé Alimentana Company. They would stay that way following the 1950 acquisition of Britain's Crosse & Blackwell, a manufacturer of soups and canned foods.

The company was now a broadly based in foods, with varying degrees of dependence on the evaporation technologies in which Nestlé was a world leader. In 1952 they kept their technical lead by improving the coffee evaporation process: the spray was now made from 100% roast coffee beans. Nestlé had a geographic spread second to none and their core food categories would benefit greatly both from the rise of the supermarket format, and the growing importance of convenience foods. The coffee business went into overdrive, as instant coffee became the beverage of choice for countless millions. During the 1950s sales of Nescafé tripled, helping Nestlé quadruple their sales from 1945 to the 1960 level of $2.5 billion without making a single acquisition during the 1950s after that of Crosse & Blackwell.

As the 1960s began, Nestlé was well positioned compared to many of its competitors. Yet it was looking to widen its category participation (although dry goods categories did well with the supermarket boom) and also its technological base beyond the drying of instant products. What would be the Next Big Thing in the food industry? In 1963, Nestlé invested in the US version of their British Crosse & Blackwell subsidiary, Libby, McNeill & Libby. A canner of fruits, vegetables and meats might not have sounded like the Next Big Thing. Their next acquisition seemed more like it: Nestlé entered the emerging frozen foods sector with the purchase of Findus International, who operated primarily in Britain and Scandinavia.

Not that Nestlé completely ignored their base business at this stage. In 1965 the company's Swiss laboratories perfected a revolutionary freeze-drying method for instant coffee. This enabled the creation and launch of a whole new premium instant sector with Tasters Choice in 1966. In 1968, Nestlé entered another new category. It involved no evaporation whatsoever and yet would, in time, become not just the Next Big Thing but the Next Huge Thing – bottled water They bought a 30% stake in Vittel, the French mineral water company.

Nestlé had become Switzerland's largest company operating over 200 factories around the world. The primary mantra of the business world in the 1970s was diversification and Nestlé was no exception to the trend. As eating out became more popular at the expense of home-prepared family meals, Nestlé got into the restaurant business. It founded Eurest, a joint venture with Compagnie Internationale des Wagon Lits et du Tourisme, and then bought into the Australian restaurant chain, Cahills. The rise of the Californian wine industry also took Nestlé's eye: it bought Beringer Wines plus a host of vineyards. The American part of the business was simultaneously bolstered by the acquisition of Stouffer in 1973. The company consisted of three divisions: frozen foods, restaurants and hotels. In France, Nestlé started an ice cream business in partnership with France Glaces, and a German water business was acquired a year later.

Sales, through organic growth and acquisitions, quadrupled between 1960 and 1974, from $2.5 billion to $9.9 billion – a respectable figure even today, so huge back then. The company was now operating in eleven product areas: the seven new ones being canned goods, ice cream, frozen foods, chilled foods (including yoghurt), mineral water, restaurants and wineries. However, their first real participation outside the food sector came in 1974 when the owner of the L'Oréal hair care and beauty business, Liliane Bettencourt (daughter of the founder) approached Nestlé. Fearing nationalisation from the incoming socialist French government, she proposed swapping 30% of her L'Oréal stock for an equivalent amount of Nestlé stock. Nestlé, appreciating the growth potential of both the category and the company, took the deal. It would turn out to be one of the most lucrative investments in Nestlé's history.

1974 also saw the first organised protests against the company's marketing practices, especially in developing countries, for infant formula. Nestlé sued, and lost a case against the Bern Third World Action Group and their pamphlet, Nestlé Babies. The judgement decreed that Nestlé had to change their approach to the subject. Matters got worse as the oil crisis occasioned Nestlé's first major slowdown since it restructured after the First World War. Economies, particularly in developed markets, stagnated. The Swiss franc strengthened against many currencies, driving down company earnings. Finally, the price of two of Nestlé's two main raw ingredients, coffee and cocoa, rose four-fold and three-fold respectively between 1975 and 1977. It wasn't a full-blown crisis for Nestlé, but it flagged up that the days of easy growth were over.

A consequence of the economic changes was that growth for Nestlé slowed down in the developed markets while continuing to power ahead in developing countries. These were less stable through either bouts of hyperinflation, military coups, or both. This made Nestlé refocus its acquisition strategy and look harder for growth markets in the developed world. An inspiration was their investment in L'Oréal, which continued to pay healthy dividends. The company made its second strategic investment outside the food and beverage categories by acquiring Alcon Laboratories in 1977. Alcon was a manufacturer of pharmaceutical and ophthalmic products (contact lenses, for example). Nestlé Group chairman Pierre Liotard-Vogt explained the acquisition as being an example of the company having 'a very wide range of activities, all of which have one thing in common: they all contribute to satisfying the requirements of the human body in various ways'. This was a strategy that ruled out very little.

But one part of the business that had failed to convince everyone that it satisfied the requirements of the human body - particularly the requirements of babies in the developing world - was infant food. A US-based protest group, Infant Formula Action Coalition, initiated a boycott of all Nestlé products. This was successful enough to bring the company into negotiations with the World Health Organisation to try and lance the boil.

The business was still growing, reaching sales of $13.2 billion by 1979. However, this was nothing like the rate of growth Nestlé had become accustomed to. The company was now essentially a conglomerate administering a vast collection of highly decentralised businesses. Too many seemed to be going nowhere and Nestlé seemed to have little to offer these other than being banker and collector of earnings. As the earnings had now declined to a paltry 2.8% of sales, something needed to be done.

How Did They Build The Modern Business?

The emergence of the modern Nestlé from the cumbersome conglomerate of 1980 happened under the watch of one man, Helmut Maucher. He had joined Nestlé's Frankfurt office in 1951 and rose through the ranks to become one of the three-person executive committee in 1981. Helmut would be the driving force of change in Nestlé for the next two decades. He came into the role with some firmly held beliefs. Firstly, that all major food companies had essentially the same technical and managerial capabilities. What made the difference was clarity in direction and speed of execution. Secondly, the company was operating in categories where, if they weren't global in scale, they probably wouldn't even survive, let alone thrive. And thirdly, Nestlé was in too many categories where it simply did not have the capability to be great. Only in food production and marketing did Helmut see Nestlé as having a competitive advantage. Early in his reign he told his team, 'We want to serve the whole world, but we do not want to be the same as the rest of the world. We want to be in a business we actually know something about.' At the time, this was a surprisingly novel attitude.

The strategy was pretty simple. Improve the bottom line by getting rid of the dogs, and then use the increased financial muscle to make some transformative food acquisitions. Thus, the early 1980s saw Nestlé selling many of the more questionable fruits of its 1970s diversification phase. They made only a few small acquisitions, mainly of European roasted coffee companies and American specialist candy companies. The bottom line improved substantially and even the Nestlé boycott was lifted in 1984. The two non-food interests, L'Oréal and Alcon, were kept on simply because they were so profitable and growing so consistently. Their earnings would be needed to help fund a breakthrough acquisition. This was of the Carnation Company in 1985 for $3.4 billion, at the time the largest acquisition ever outside the oil and gas industries. Nestlé had signalled they were changing and meant business.

Nestlé chose Carnation for several reasons. Firstly, Nestlé's US business was not huge by American standards. The big retailers in the States did not see Nestlé as a major player, beyond Nescafé and Stouffer's. Secondly, Carnation had some key product synergies with Nestlé's core strengths. 40% of their sales came from dairy related products, particularly dried and evaporated milk. Thirdly, Carnation had interesting products whose marketing Nestlé thought they could improve: such as Contadina tomato products, Coffee-Mate coffee creamer and Friskies cat food. Fourthly, the company was buyable, being family-controlled with key members looking to cash in. The deal doubled Nestlé's US sales and catapulted the company to the world's number one food company ahead of Unilever. It still did not make Nestlé a top five US food company. They rounded out the year by purchasing the American coffee roasters, Hill's Brothers.

While big acquisitions, by their very nature, were infrequent, the Nestlé's direction was clearly discernible by their smaller moves. They bought single market companies in categories where the company was interested in expansion, such as the Canadian pet food company Dr. Ballard, and the roast coffee company, Club Coffee in 1987. The same year, Nestlé flagged another increasingly important category when they built on their minority stake in Vittel to take full ownership.

1988 was a defining year for the new Nestlé. They made two major acquisitions. First, they purchased Italy's third-largest food company, the Buitoni-Perugina Pasta Company, for $1.3 billion. The deal proceeded along the normal Nestlé acquisition lines of being agreed with the principle owners of the company. Nestlé's policy was never to embark on hostile acquisitions, believing the benefits of having existing management on board during the integration outweighed the occasional missing of a good target. The next target, however, was to blow that policy out of the water.

By 1987, Nestlé's chocolate business was the sixth largest in the world with a 4% global share. It was the company's fifth largest product category with sales of around $2 billion. If chocolate was going to be an advantaged category for Nestlé, they had to be bigger than sixth in the world, but the list of possible takeover targets was small. Mars, the largest player, was a private company whose owners showed no signs of wanting out. The second largest, Hershey, was controlled by a trust which again was not interested in selling. This left Cadbury and Rowntree, both with around 7% global share, as the only real candidates for a transformative confectionery acquisition. Cadbury were in the throes of fighting off interest from US firm General Cinema. Involvement would only suck Nestlé into an unwanted bidding war, so instead they approached Rowntree, suggesting a minority stake and the beginning of a long-term relationship. The British firm refused. Nestlé took the hint and walked away.

Things changed in April 1988. Nestlé's arch rival in the European chocolate market, Suchard, bought 14.9% of Rowntree shares in a dawn raid. Nestlé approached Rowntree again, offering a friendly bid to head off Suchard's unwanted takeover. Rowntree again declined, leaving Nestlé no option. If they did not bid ($2.1 billion) Nestlé risked losing out on the only realistic option to change their fortunes in confectionery. This in turn prompted Suchard to buy more Rowntree stock, increasing their holding to 29.9%. This battle for Rowntree suddenly unleashed a wave of anti-takeover protests in Britain.

Rowntree's response made it clear Nestlé was going to have to stay hostile or go home, 'Nestlé has nothing we need, not its money, not its research and development, not its marketing, and not its distribution'. Not much wriggle room there.

Suchard now owned 30% of the shares and submitted a new, higher bid at the end of May. The odds were against Nestlé forcing through a takeover, so they returned to the negotiating table to see what it would take to get an agreed bid. The answer from Rowntree was essentially a reverse takeover of the Nestlé chocolate business. They wanted a global chocolate unit created within Nestlé, run by Rowntree senior management and with a Rowntree man on the Nestlé board. This was unacceptable. Nestlé had remained structured geographically and would not countenance the creation of a business unit that crossed national boundaries. Rowntree executives were told that, just as had been the case with all their acquisitions, Rowntree would be broken up to fit into Nestlé's geographical zone structure. This was unacceptable to Rowntree executives, who had no intention of being the turkeys that celebrated Thanksgiving.

The battle finally ended on June 24th, 1988 when Rowntree reluctantly accepted an improved $4.5 billion offer. Nestlé were propelled to being the second largest confectioner in the world, with around an 11% global share and 18% in Europe. A key benefit of the acquisition, apart from the usual cost-saving synergies, was the roster of brands. Nestlé could take brands such as Kit Kat, Smarties, Rolo, Lion Bar and Black Magic into more international markets than British-based Rowntree had done. These brands, widely and frequently bought and consumed, could also be used as powerful vehicles for building and promoting the Nestlé name. The battle had changed the company for good. Everyone now knew that, in its selected categories, Nestlé was serious in its quest for scale.

Although deal-making was the name of the game now at Nestlé, the company still pursued a range of different paths to growth. The company research labs were still at the party. The Nespresso encapsulated espresso coffee concept, once developed, was test marketed in the office coffee sectors of Switzerland, Japan and Italy in 1986. By 1989, the system had been introduced into the Swiss household market in partnership with Turmix, who manufactured the machines.

In 1990, Nestlé looked outside of R&D and acquisitions for growth by forming three joint alliances. The first was with General Mills - the somewhat insular American breakfast cereal giant. The deal was that General Mills would provide their cereal brands such as Cheerios, while Nestlé would provide the distribution and marketing in countries around the world. This gave Kellogg's a wake-up call in markets such as Britain and Australia, which they had had to themselves for decades. A key part of the deal, which was a 50:50 joint venture company called Cereal Partners Worldwide, was that the Nestlé brand name would go on all the packs, giving a further huge hike to awareness.

The second tie up, with Coca-Cola, under the unsurprising name Beverage Partners Worldwide, would ultimately prove less successful. It was limited to ready-to-drink tea and coffee lines in twenty-four countries. The third deal was one that really only a company of Nestlé's global size and reach could pull off: a partnership with the Walt Disney Corporation. Not only would Nestlé be the exclusive seller of food and drinks at Disney resorts, but would also have exclusive rights to use Walt Disney characters on its packaging and advertising in a range of categories in Europe, the Middle and Far East.

These arrangements set the tone for the rest of the 1990s: large-scale moves that used and strengthened Nestlé's position in its focus categories. In 1992 Nestlé became world leaders in the bottled water category, adding the Perrier Company, with its range of brands, to their existing waters portfolio. Contrary to their earlier negotiating stance with Rowntree, Nestlé organised bottled water globally under the name Nestlé Sources International, headquartered in Paris. The acquisition of San Pellegrino soon added to this empire. Pet food became the next product sector to increase global scale, with the acquisitions of Alpo in 1994 and Spillers in 1988, making Nestlé the second largest pet food company in Europe.

The first half of the 1990s also saw Nestlé move into the newly opened markets of Eastern Europe and China. In the latter half of the decade, more acquisitions were made to strengthen their ice cream and pet food categories. So far, in the water business, the company had been solely focused on spring-based waters. However, Nestlé could not ignore the approach being taken by both Coca-Cola and PepsiCo, which both developed water brands – Dasani, for example - that did not depend on output from one particular spring.

In 1997 the Nestlé labs created a formula to add mineral salts to completely purified water and give the taste profile Nestlé felt would have greatest appeal. This was handed over to Perrier Vittel in France to develop a production process capable of being installed anywhere worldwide (subject to the availability of acceptable water). The product was tested in mid-1998 in Pakistan, Thailand,

Mexico and Brazil. Nestlé Pakistan was the first company to launch it for real, in late 1998, under the brand name Nestlé Pure Life.

Within a year, the product, now selling well from 15,000 retail outlets, was rolled out to markets such as Brazil, China, Mexico and Argentina and launched in Europe under the name Nestlé Aquarel. This was a striking example of how Nestlé maintained the principle of local autonomy. Brand essences might be sacrosanct and managed centrally, but local businesses had freedom to change brand names and tweak recipes to suit local conditions. Similarly, Nescafé had a different flavour profile in almost every country in Europe. Many other large companies sacrifice local adaptability for the cost savings of regional production and supply. Nestlé firmly believed this strategy to be a short-term measure that would cause long-term harm – it could open doors for local competitors to come up with more locally targeted products.

The main event of the late 1990s was a handing over of the CEO position from long-time occupant, Helmut Maucher to his chosen successor, Austrian and lifetime Nestlé man, Peter Brabeck. The transition had been planned years in advance. Initially, Helmut moved to an executive chairman role before handing over responsibility completely. On first taking over, Brabeck defined his priorities as follows:

- Innovation and renovation
- Efficient operation
- Greater accessibility of Nestlé products: Whenever, Wherever, However
- Improved consumer communication

Brabeck also flagged up that he saw the future as Nestlé moving from being an agro-alimentary business into one focused on consumer wellness. To that end Brabeck created a Nestlé Nutrition Division on his very first day as CEO.

Efficient operation went in two directions: the disposal of businesses deemed past their peak, such as the Findus frozen foods unit; and the outsourcing of base ingredient processing. So cocoa beans were handed over, along with a collection of Nestlé factories, to industry specialist Barry Callibaut. The combination of this portfolio cleansing and processing outsourcing netted Nestlé $1 billion; and resulted in the sale or closure of fifty-four factories. Nevertheless the company still owned and operated well over 400 factories, spread around the globe.

By the end of 1999, sales had increased from the 1980 conglomerate days by over 200%: and net profits had increased almost six-fold, up from 2.6% of sales to 6.3%. Such had been the turnaround that, for five years in a row, Fortune magazine named Nestlé the Most Admired Global Food Company. Although now more streamlined, there was no real change to Nestlé's acquisition strategy.

Pet food giant Ralston Purina was acquired in 2001 for $10.3 billion and merged with the Friskies business to form another global entity, Nestlé Purina Pet Care. This had annual sales of over $6 billion, making Nestlé the world's leading pet food company. The North American ice cream business was fluffed up in 2002 with the acquisition of Dreyer's: as was the microwave snacks segment with the purchase of Chef America Inc. the same year.

By 2002, Nestlé had six global brands: Nestlé, Nescafé, Nestes, Maggi, Buitoni and Purina. They also managed a vast portfolio of around 8,500 national and regional brands. This would have been an impossible task without the company's high degree of emphasis on local operating autonomy. Even with what seemed such a bloated portfolio, around 70% of sales came from brands either number one or number two in their respective markets. Beverages accounted for 28% of sales; Milk Products, Nutrition and Ice cream 27%; Culinary Products 25%; Confectionery 13%; with Alcon and the L'Oréal investments bringing up the rear.

How Global Are They?

Nestlé has been globally focused since its second year of operation when Henri opened a sales office in London. The whole company story is one of a food company going global; so we will not laboriously list out each market entry here. The Swiss market was never a major focus for the company, because it simply wasn't large enough to sustain a business for any length of time. It now accounts for barely more than 1% of company sales. By 2002 Nestlé was the world's biggest food producer, operating in over 450 factories and employing nearly a quarter of a million people in 84 countries. Its biggest market, the US, accounted for 12% of sales (notably, the company's entire top management were all non-US expatriates). Its next largest market, France, did not even account for 5% of sales.

Nestlé is the most global of companies in span, but at the same time one of the most local in operation. In a large European market, Nestlé sectors will have around 4,000 products for sale across all its product range, of which 99% will be regional or local brands. The world's largest food company passionately believes that the world market for food is made up of small local markets. Consumers in many countries believe Nestlé to be local – for example, 95% of Japanese consumers believe it to be a Japanese company.

How Are They Structured?

Because Nestlé went so global so early, local operating autonomy was the only practical choice to manage the company. Communications and travel were then so restricted. The company's conglomerate phase further emphasised the local and regional operating model. Again, there were no real practical alternatives for grouping together restaurants, wineries, contact lenses, condensed milk and the like. It was only when Nestlé began to concentrate its portfolio in the 1980s and '90s that it became in any way practical to start to assemble teams with global category responsibilities. Even so, acquisitions were made at the local level. When Nestlé bought Stouffer's, for example, it was actually the Nestlé USA legal entity that did the buying, and it was into the local US company that Stouffer's was absorbed.

The structure in the late 1980s was still very much driven by regionalism: five regions were the key operating units of the business:
- Zone 1 – Europe
- Zone 2 – Asia & Australia
- Zone 3 – Latin America
- Zone 4 – North America
- Zone 5 – Africa & Middle East

There was one board-level operation - Product Direction and Marketing Service – tasked with looking ahead unencumbered by profit responsibility and supporting/advising the regions and their operating units.

Major change first came in 1993 with the acquisition of Perrier. The latter was managed in a global manner. This prompted Nestlé to combine all its water interests into one globally managed division, Nestlé Waters. Even though this broke the habit of a lifetime, it made sense. The water category is somewhat unique because there are no local tastes to tweak the product and, certainly for spring brands, no scope to tweak. If you manage the Perrier brand in China or San Pellegrino in Chile, you can't just invent a new serving size to suit some under-served local retail channel, because you have no factory.

Once the core categories became fixed, Nestlé could develop systems and structures that would progressively enhance global capabilities: yet, without removing profit responsibility from local operating units. As is always the case, the first step is to get everyone talking the same language and looking at the same numbers. Nestlé tackled this challenge in 2000 with the launch of the GLOBE initiative (Global Business Excellence), which included group-wide, standardized best practices, plus data standards and information systems. This created the organisational basis for Nestlé's to embark on its transformation into a nutrition, health and wellness company with global capabilities and local operating excellence.

In 2005, the Nestlé Nutrition division, set up in 1998, was made an independent entity within the group. This assumed global responsibility for the areas of infant nutrition, healthcare nutrition, weight management and performance nutrition. By this time, other strategic business units had been set up for the other core categories, making eight in all: beverages (excluding waters); milk, nutrition and ice cream; chocolate and confectionery; prepared dishes and cooking aids; pet care products; health care and nutrition and out-of-home catering (now professional food services), along with Nestlé waters.

Three of the eight units have profit responsibility and report directly to the CEO - Nestlé waters, Nestlé health care nutrition and Nestlé professional. Health care nutrition and professional food services had quite different routes to market than the usual Nestlé set up, which is why they have full operational responsibility. Health care nutrition aims to pioneer a new industry by developing science-based and personalized nutritional solutions in the areas of gastrointestinal health, metabolic health and brain health. It is thus primarily distributed through hospitals and pharmacies. Professional food services goes through specialist food service distributors.

The remaining five strategic business units - beverages; milk, nutrition and ice cream; chocolate & confectionery; prepared dishes and cooking aids; pet care products - report into one board member, who also has responsibility for marketing and sales. These units are not profit-responsible, having a remit to operate over a longer timeframe, usually 3 to 5 years ahead. They are tasked with forecasting both how the categories will evolve and developing global category strategies. From these, market entry strategies, acquisition targets, global brand strategies and innovations and renovations can all be discerned. As so many of Nestlé's brands are either local or regional, it would make no sense at all to have profit responsibility at this level. To cope with this increased level of complexity at the corporate level, the five regional zones were reduced to three: Europe, the Americas and Asia/Oceania/Africa.

What Have They Been Doing Recently?

2004

Although Nestlé reported a slight decline in sales during the year, this was primarily due to a strengthening Swiss franc and disposals exceeding acquisitions (in what had been a quiet year). Underlying organic growth was decent at above

323

4.5%, of which 3% came from volume growth. Performance had been muted by a relatively poor year in Europe where volume declined by 1.6% and prices could not be increased to compensate. While Eastern Europe was performing well, with organic growth of nearly 8%, it was still a small part of the pie for Nestlé. These sales were not quite 10% of the total European region. Nestlé's problems lay in its two biggest European markets, France and Germany. This was partly due to the rise of discount retailers such as Aldi who carried very few Nestlé brands. Elsewhere performance was much stronger: organic growth in Zone Americas was nearly 8%, and 7% in Zone Asia, Oceania and Africa.

Within the product categories, as understandable with a diversified company such as Nestlé, performance was mixed. Waters achieved volume growth but partially through dropping prices in the key North American market. The other driver of growth was the continued rollout of Nestlé Pure Life and Nestlé Aquarel (now in 34 markets), with their combined volume up 45% to over two billion litres. Waters was now almost as important to Nestlé as soluble coffee: the latter barely moved forward in the year despite re-launches of Nescafé and Nescafé Cappuccino. As world market leader, the task in hand was to find ways to grow the category. Therefore, Nestlé had begun working with coffee associations to better understand the positive effects on the body, and also increasing a long-term sustainability agenda.

Milk products and nutrition both had good years. Condensed milk was re-launched in its largest market of Brazil; while Carnation Instant Breakfast and the rolling out of Clinutren helped drive Nutrition. Ice Cream however was becalmed despite a good year for Haagen-Dazs in North America (the only territory in which Nestlé held the license for the brand). Slow Churned Dreyer's Gar- and Light was launched in the USA using a patented technology to deliver a product as creamy as normal but with half the fat.

Cereal Partners Worldwide was proving to be an excellent partnership: entering more markets and launching new products was proving a source of steady profitable growth. But Nestlé's chocolate business was lagging behind the company average. A continuing slew of Kit Kat variants - such as Kit Kat Editions in the UK, Kit Kat Green tea in Japan and Kit Kat Chunky Peanut Butter in Canada - provided only short term growth and would need replacing early. Pet care rolled out their new strategic tagline of Your Pet, Our Passion across multiple markets. The food services division eagerly embraced the company's wellness agenda, launching fortifying soups for the elderly in France and Maggi Wellness in the Netherlands.

The performances of Nestlé's investments outside food and drink showed why it had been a good idea to hang onto them. Alcon, by far the world's leading eye care company (of which Nestlé owned around 75%), had organic growth of 11% and grew EBITDA by an impressive 17%. It is hard to get those growth rates in mature food categories. L'Oréal chipped in with a not too shabby 6.2% like-for-like increase. The two Nestlé/L'Oréal joint ventures, Galderma skincare and Laboratoires Innéov, continued to progress and provide joint research benefits.

Operationally, Nestlé were pursuing a succession of cost-saving efficiency programmes. Target 2004+, a factory efficiency initiative, was closed at the end of the year having been declared a success. It saved over 3.2 billion francs, and, as usual with such things, was immediately replaced by an even more ambitious programme, Operation EXCELLENCE 2007, to extend the same cost-cutting eye upstream to suppliers and downstream to customers. Meanwhile, administration was kept under the microscope of Project FitNes, also extended to run until 2007.

2004 also saw the nutrition agenda took firmer shape organisationally. Nestlé Nutrition was created as a stand-alone global business organisation and a Corporate Wellness Unit was formed. Nestlé Nutrition consisted of pulling together product categories characterised as ones in which the consumers' primary motivation for purchase is nutritional claims made by the product. The categories involved - infant nutrition, health-care nutrition and performance nutrition - had shared characteristics of high-level research supported both by clinical trials and by regulatory expertise. The unit was targeted to be fully formed and profit accountable by January 2006. The corporate wellness unit was a different beast, with a remit to drive the nutrition, health and wellness agenda across all the strategic business units. This included driving cross-category initiatives, such as a company response to obesity concerns and to the nutritional needs of an ageing population.

2005

Organic growth was over 6%, of which 4.2% was due to volume increases. These came from pretty much all categories and regions, and drove sales to a new high of nearly $73 billion. Again, it was mostly an acquisition-free year (along with a few small disposals), so the focus had been on embedding new structures and processes. Nestlé Nutrition was up and running by the year-end. It operated in more than 100 countries, with approximately a quarter of its 10,000 employees building close relationships with medical professionals. This unit had been expanded during the year by the acquisition of Protéika, a French wellness firm dedicated to providing solutions for weight management and metabolic disorders. The unit also set up an exclusive relationship with a company specialising in sterile filling technologies.

The Wellness unit also had a few early feathers in its cap. It drove the rollout of the Nutritional Compass on-pack labelling across 50% of the entire product range, and the inclusion of more Branded Active Benefits (BABs) on products in all categories. BABs had first been introduced in 1999 with the aim of increasing the nutritional content and health benefits of existing products. Sales of products with BABs now amounted to over 2.9 billion Swiss francs, and had grown 20% in the year. Nestlé now had a wellness champion in each zone, strategic business unit and market. The champion was charged with rolling out the 60/40 decision, tool for new products or variants. Each new recipe must not only beat the nearest competitor in taste preference 60/40, but also have more nutritional or health benefits.

Implementing these changes didn't stop the CEO, Peter Brabeck, from plotting more structural and operational changes. He wanted to get the best of both global and local worlds, and to use the size advantage of the world's largest food company - yet still remain as close to customers and consumers at a local level. Peter described his vision of Nestlé as 'a fleet of agile, fast-moving businesses'. (Exactly how how Unilever had described themselves thirty years earlier). The businesses would remain fast moving by staying focused on consumers, innovation and communication. The fleet aspect required they head in the same direction, and be linked by shared consumer insights, R&D and back office scale benefits, which in turn flowed from the strategic business units. The fuel for the fleet would come from what were more encouragingly named 'efficiency initiatives'.

All this sounds quite obvious, but it represented a significant change in operational style. Nestlé were moving away from a decentralised multinational company towards a global, and ultimately a global multifocal company. Some categories, such as water and nutrition, would be resolutely global while others, such as culinary and chocolate, would keep a strong local focus, where local tastes varied so much. The link between the operating companies and the global structures would be 'clusters', essentially category- or brand-specific teams drawn from both local and global units.

2006

In what was the company's 140th year of operation, sales increased by over 8% to a shade under 100 billion Swiss francs. , Henri would have found this mind-boggling. It was also the eleventh year in a row the company had delivered the somewhat pompously named, Nestlé Model. This was a high level of organic growth - 6.2% - with a sustainable increase in profit margins (EBIT up 12%). Such models only tend to get a mention during the good times.

The company was still pursuing the same two basic strategies. To make a transition to a nutrition, health and wellness product platform; and to make a transition to being selectively global, where scale was a competitive advantage. The portfolio transition stepped up a notch with two significant acquisitions. The first was the Jenny Craig weight management business. This consisted of over 600 Jenny Craig centres in the US, Canada, Puerto Rico, Australia and New Zealand. Here consumers received tailored support on nutrition, weight management and exercise; and were supported by personalised menus made up of Jenny Craig-branded foods. It was positioned in a fast-growing, profitable category and had been enjoying double-digit growth rates, where annual sales reached $400 million. The second acquisition, Australia's Uncle Toby's, was a little more mainstream with its range of breakfast cereals, nutritious snacks and instant soups.

While all major categories grew, some were riding positive consumer trends. So beverages were up 8% and pet care 7%. Others, such as confectionery, had less going for them and grew only 2.6%. The company now had thirty brands, each generating sales of over 1 billion francs: but only one of them, Kit Kat, was in confectionery. The current stars of the show were Nespresso, which had grown over 40% to join the billion franc club and the combination of Nestlé Pure Life and Nestlé Aquarel, which grew 30% in the year. Below those stars, old-faithfuls like Nestea (up 20%); Coffee Mate (up 17%) and Stouffers (up 11%) were contributing to the party. As per usual, the external investments continued to bring in above-average performances: Alcon up 12% and L'Oréal up 10%.

Regional growth reflected the relative weighting of emerging markets in the three zones. The one with the biggest such markets, Asia, Oceania & Africa, grew fastest at nearly 8%; second came Americas at 6% and Europe was last, at 2.3% (the latter included a double digit increase from Eastern Europe). Nestlé, which had been built mostly by acquisitions, was conscious that using the potential of emerging markets involved more than providing 'beads to the natives' i.e. rolling out developed market brands. Nestlé had instituted the concept of Popularly Positioned Products, made in local factories. Some were purpose-built, combining affordability in emerging markets with high levels of nutritional value and great taste. Availability was not left to inefficient or non-existent local networks: Nestlé invested in direct store delivery networks and had some impressive levels of distribution - 70% in Indonesia and a staggering 90% in India.

The move towards using global scale without sacrificing local commercial focus continued apace. GLOBE was now rolled out to 80% of the businesses. It was cutting a swathe through an almost ludicrous amount of complexity that had come from having hundreds of stand-alone businesses - Nestlé had 481 operational factories. Before GLOBE, the company had over a hundred data centres with no connectivity; now it had four. Almost every company used to compile its income statements differently; now there was one single Nestlé way. GLOBE was not just a standardisation tool. In Chile it identified 342 different sales channels for Nestlé products, some of which, such as cruise ships calling at Chile's ports, had fallen between the cracks. While schemes such as Operation EXCELLENCE had reduced the company's average cost of goods (from 51.8% of sales in 1996 to 41.3% in 2006), the next level of cost savings was coming from the GLOBE-enabled Global Nestlé Business Services. The latter was busy outsourcing various back office activities. Another key organisational change implemented was the integration of the concept of business executive manager. Each market now had a profit-responsible manager for each category in which they were competing.

2007

Chairman Peter Brabeck signed off his final year in the CEO role by announcing two things. First, the major steps in the transition to being a nutrition, health and wellness company were now complete. Secondly, and due to this transition, Nestlé would not only match the demographic growth opportunities of emerging markets – i.e. growing populations, increasing wealth and longer lives - but would 'clearly outpace that growth'. So no pressure then, on the new CEO, promoted from running Zone Americas, Paul Bulcke.

The major steps referred to were the acquisitions: from Novartis by its Medical Nutrition Division, and also the Gerber baby food business. These made Nestlé global number two and clear number one in each respective category. Nestlé nutrition was now an 11 billion franc turnover division operating in over 100 countries, comprised of four business units:

- Infant nutrition accounted for around 70% of the unit's sales and, in a tacit acceptance that Gerber had been ahead of Nestlé in the field, Nestlé had adopted the Gerber concept of Start Healthy. Stay Healthy across the entire Nestlé portfolio. There was also an admission that Gerber's R&D laboratories had been ahead, particularly in developing products for toddlers, such as the Graduates from Gerber product range. Gerber had also been more innovative in developing services such as Gerber Life, North America's leading provider of juvenile life insurance.

- The new healthcare nutrition unit met the needs of people with specific nutritional deficiencies, particularly the elderly: cancer and digestive illnesses plus chronic conditions such as diabetes
- Performance nutrition was perhaps a slightly exaggerated classification for products such as energy bars and sports drinks
- Weight management via the Jenny Craig came in fourth

There was little doubt that the beefed-up Nestlé nutrition was seen as the future of the company - it called itself the leader of the Nestlé fleet. However, it only accounted for just over 10% of company sales and its organic growth rate in 2007 of 9.7% was eclipsed by much stronger gains in less fashionable parts. This included Milo, Lean Cuisine, Nestea, Nan, Dog Chow, Nedo, Coffee Mate, Pure Life and Nespresso. All these were driving much higher growth rates and contributing to an overall company organic growth of 7.4%.

This growth was driven slightly more by volume than by pricing and came across all product groups. Powdered and liquid beverages grew by over 10% and prepared dishes and cooking aids brought up the rear at above 4%. Performance by zone followed the pattern of previous years - double-digit increases in Latin American and Asian emerging markets and Eastern Europe outweighed gains in developed markets. The Nestlé Model seemed well and truly entrenched.

2008

A more difficult year. Huge variations, both up and down, in raw material costs didn't stop the Nestlé Model doing its thing. Although reported net sales were only up by 2.2%, currency movements were masking organic growth of 8.3% in an acquisition-free year. Slightly worrying was a slowdown in real internal growth - volume in other words - which increased only 2.8%, with nearly double that rate of increase attributable to pricing. Great if the retailers and consumers are happy to pay, something which usually only becomes apparent over time.

Other slight causes for concern were the low growth of Gerber, a business trumpeted on acquisition as having double-digit growth rates. This increased by less than 3%, while total Nestlé Nutrition grew by less than the company average – not what was advertised at all by the previous regime. In contrast, the stars of the previous year were still storming ahead: Nespresso up by nearly 40%, Coffee Mate and Nani around 25% and Dog Chow nearly 20%. Within the categories, the big news was the poor performance of Nestlé waters: volume declined by nearly 4% and margin went down too. The reasons given, 'consumer downtrading due to the economic environment and the somewhat emotional debate about the perceived environmental issues around the category', perhaps showed a somewhat dismissive attitude to a previous growth driver which was suddenly floundering. On the plus side, the cereal and beverages joint ventures racked up an amazing 20% real internal growth. This made up for the first real slowdown in Alcon in living memory, up only 2%, and a sedate 3% growth at L'Oréal.

The big news of the year, unsurprising given a new CEO at the helm, was the introduction of a revised strategy. With the identity shift towards nutrition health and wellness company apparently complete, key questions emerged: what was management going to do with it and how? The new strategy was given, as these things usually are, a somewhat forced brand name, the 4x4x4 Roadmap. This embraced a suspiciously forced realisation that the company had four competitive advantages, four growth drivers and four strategic pillars. Theuy were outlined as follows:

Competitive advantages: Unique Differentiators

- **Unmatched product and brand portfolio.** Without doubt Nestlé has the largest portfolio of brands in the food industry but whether this is a feature or a benefit is arguable
- **Unmatched R&D capability.** Nestlé certainly has one of, if not the biggest R&D functions in the food industry. It spent 2 billion francs in 2008, employing 5,000 people in 50 countries, plus the usual open innovation links. But, as the biggest food company, so they should. Whether it is the best - it didn't seem to have been with infant nutrition – or the most intensive - as measured by % of turnover or PhDs employed per brand or whatever - is much more questionable
- **Unmatched geographic presence.** Can't argue with that. Marketing their products in around 130 countries and the longevity of their presence, particularly in emerging markets, is a huge plus; no-one else can claim to have been in China, Brazil, India and Mexico for a combined 370 years
- **People, Culture, Values and Attitude.** Every large company says this: the only real difference Nestlé has is the level of local autonomy

Growth Drivers: Enhanced Growth Potential

- **Nutrition, Health & Wellness.** Every food company was busily reducing bad-for-you ingredients such as sodium, sugars, trans-fats etc. Nestle did so in over 3,000 products in the year, and was more forward looking -- increasing the nutritional density of another 2998 products. Plus, Nestle had been an industry pioneer in adding probiotics, which were included in products that generated sales of 3 billion francs

- **Emerging Markets and Popularly Positioned Products (PPP's).** While the percentage of Nestlé's sales coming from emerging markets was not particularly earth-shattering, at circa 30%, the absolute level of sales at 35 billion francs was. Growth was also a healthy 15% in 2008. PPP products accounted for around 20% of sales in emerging markets and grew at 27% in the year. These were not just low prices out of the factory, but with an engineered low-cost route to market using micro-distributors and financed with micro-loans

- **Out-of-Home leadership.** Nestlé professional was nearly through its transition to a globally managed unit across 97 countries. It was already the world's leading company in this highly fragmented category encompassing all manner of routes-to-market. However, it was not clear what lay behind the company's goal of doubling the 6.2 billion francs sales within the next ten years

- **Premium-isation.** Premium food sectors were not new: everyone knew they were growing faster than average and delivering higher margins. The question was, was Nestlé uniquely positioned to benefit from this trend? While they owned some good premium brands, the vast bulk of Nestlé sales still came from good, basic everyday products.

Strategic Pillars: Core Competencies with Excellence Potential
- Innovation & Renovation
- Operational Efficiency
- Whenever, wherever, however
- Consumer communication

Of these, only whenever, wherever and however could be said to be a genuine, competitively-advantaged competence. Nestlé's combined and uniquely global reach, a vast collection of non-global brands and local operational autonomy did the rest.

The final leg of the Nestlé strategy lay not in the what but in the how: a way of doing business the company called 'creating shared value'. This focused on three areas:

- **Nutrition.** The company mission, in a nutshell, was to improve global nutrition: an action standard against which every management action could be measured
- **Water.** While water was a huge category for Nestlé, it was less than clear why this was a key focus in creating shared value
- **Rural Development.** This was more like it. Nestlé is a huge player in the global rural economy through coffee, cocoa and other key ingredients. The company's work with 600,000 rural farmers to increase their productivity was laudable

The bottom line on this newly laid out 4x4x4 Roadmap was that, according to Nestlé, it 'positioned us as winners regardless of the environment . . . by giving the Group excellent defensive characteristics, but also by creating a platform for profitable growth'. It would soon get a good workout.

2009

A strong Swiss franc made the top line look a bit sick, with reported sales down over 5%. The market context was: weak consumer demand, rising raw material costs and intensive price competition from both branded and non-branded competitors. An organic sales increase of over 4%, of which nearly half came from increased volume, was a good performance. As usual, Alcon and the L'Oréal ventures did better than the Nestlé food and drink business, up nearly 7% compared to 3.9%. The largest operating zone, the Americas, had a very good year considering the turmoil affecting the US consumer market. Sales there increased by nearly 3% in local currency. The region was goosed by a 10% sales increase in Brazil. Europe was essentially flat with an impressive 6% sales increase in the UK wiped out by a very poor 6% decline in Germany. This was partly due to Nestlé's continued relative lack of presence in the booming hard discounter trade channel. Asia, Oceania and Africa grew by nearly 7% with the greater China region growing double-digit.

Business within the zones was conducted with a high level of local operating autonomy. This is an ideal strategy in times of great economic uncertainty, where fast and creative responses were required. So it comes as little surprise that the monolithic global operating units within Nestlé had much less successful years. Waters had negative organic growth of -1.4%, despite growing double digit in emerging markets and the Nestlé Life brand up 14%. Nestlé nutrition, the lead ship in the fleet a mere two years earlier, was wallowing with nil growth, and going backwards in Europe and the Americas. The situation in the newly-created Nestlé professional must have been even worse. Its results were shrouded from view, with a commentary that the unit had been 'focused on establishing its strategic priorities' – management speak for a real stinker of a year.

So was the new strategy working? A look at the performance of the billion-franc brand club, accounting for 70% of company sales and up nearly 6% during the year, shows that Nestlé's growth was coming pretty much as it had been the last few years. Nespresso was seemingly unstoppable, up over 20%, Pure Life, Beneful, Dog Chow and Galderma were up double digit, Nescafé, Nana, Purina, Purina One and Friskies up high single digits. The laggards, which declined, were the likes of Nestlé Ice Cream, Herta, Stouffer's and Lean Cuisine.

2010

In 2010, Nestlé got back to making some strategic moves via mergers and acquisitions. It started with the purchase from Kraft of the DiGiorno brand of frozen pizzas, the market leader in the US. This, when combined with Nestlé's frozen meals, snacks and Ice cream, made the company the clear leader in the US frozen sector. Priced at $3.7 billion, it was good value, as Kraft was in somewhat of a fire sale situation (having to sell one of its crown jewels to finance a bid for Cadbury). Nevertheless, it is difficult to see how the acquisition in any way aided the nutrition agenda, other than perhaps pushing some more business Jenny Craig's way. This $3.7 billion was small change compared to the sum that came into Nestlé's war chest when they sold the Alcon ophthalmic business in August 2010 for an eye-watering $41 billion (including previous share divestments). This was not a bad return on an investment of $280 million in 1997. The company also made smaller acquisitions in water in China, culinary in the Ukraine, confectionery in Turkey and pet food in North America.

Organisationally, Nestlé accepted the reality that the previously much-vaunted Nestlé nutrition unit was not living up to expectations. The fit between infant nutrition, healthcare nutrition and so-called performance nutrition was to say the least forced. Infants eating bottles of pureed pears, cancer patients having bags of enteral feed infused, and joggers munching on a Powerbar don't really have a lot in common. Danone's unit in the marketplace was trouncing the healthcare nutrition business so something had to be done. The answer was to split off healthcare nutrition, along with its recently acquired metabolic disorders arm, Vitaflo, into a standalone Nestlé Health Science unit. The newly created Nestlé Institute of Health Sciences would support this.

Elsewhere, the 4x4x4 strategy trundled on its merry way, more as a convenient mnemonic for what the company had been doing anyway and was continuing to do. Emerging market sales were now up to 39 billion francs, around 36% of company sales and growing 11.5%. Nestlé now had thirteen emerging markets in which their sales exceeded one billion francs and five that exceeded two billion. 47% of the company's 449 factories were now located in emerging markets. Maggi, the leading food enhancement brand in Africa, sold 90 billion bouillon cubes, each fortified with key micronutrients to address market-specific deficiencies. This was just one of the 4860 popularly positioned products now in the range.

This emerging markets performance contributed to an overall 6.2% organic growth, of which nearly 5% was volume, another demonstration of the power of Nestlé's country-by-country capabilities. The US, which was by far Nestlé's single largest market with sales of 31 billion francs, grew by 4.5%. This performance was driven by Purina PetCare's innovations in the new and fast-growing pet treat category e.g. the launches of Purina ONE Shreds and the rather delicious-sounding Fancy Feast Gray Lovers. Whilst the new pizza business showed its strength by gaining market share, the weight management category struggled. Both Lean Cuisine and Jenny Craig had to tighten their belts during another lean year.

Brazil, where Nestlé had been for 90 years, grew another 11%. Not only was Brazil the company's third-largest market, but it was also closing quickly on the number two, France. Zone Europe had a better year, growing almost everywhere, although the problems in Germany continued with another sales decline. Zone Asia, Oceania and Africa had a predictably good year, with Greater China accelerating to a near 15% increase. Waters began to get its act together, but if you can't sell bottled water in what was, for the northern hemisphere, the hottest summer in living memory, then there is no hope.

2011

The year when the percentage of sales for emerging markets hit the magic 40% mark! Nestlé achieved 13% organic growth from those markets, with highlights like India 20%, Africa 18%, and Mexico 14%, boosted by acquisitions, China 23%. The two Chinese businesses in which Nestlé acquired 60% ownership positions were: Hsu Fu Chi (makers of sugar confectionery and traditional Chinese snacks with a strong route-to-market network); and Yin Lu (a Nestlé co-packer who also made ready-to-drink peanut milk and ready-to-eat canned rice porridge). The company also bought a host of smaller businesses, all located entirely within emerging markets.

The top line from the north was down from 110 billion francs to 84 billion. This was due to a combination of Alcon's sale and an ever-strengthening Swiss franc. Nevertheless, that reduced number contained impressive organic growth of 7.5%, split evenly between volume and pricing. To complement the 13% organic growth in emerging markets, developed markets grew by over 4%, with Europe in total finally returning to a decent, 5% level of growth. PPPs in Eastern Europe grew at twice that rate. In Asia, Oceania & Africa it was all about PPPs, as the company set a goal to reach a million more retail outlets within the next two years.

Waters had a better year, in a very warm but not exceptionally hot summer in developed markets. One trend was the continued growth of the global brands, such as Nestlé Life (up double digit again), Perrier and San Pellegrino: the large collection of regional and local brands fared less well. Nestlé Nutrition, now the baby food unit that accounted for 90% of sales (plus a few bits and bobs), generated over 7% organic growth at a company-leading operating margin of 20%. This was helped by innovations such as BabyNes, which essentially translated Nespresso machine and pod technology into the baby nutrition arena. The professional unit was getting its act together by expanding distribution of the new Nescafé Alegria machine to catering operators. Nespresso, of course, continued its dizzying climb, growing more than 20%, according to its annual norm. The concept was now supported by a holistic sales system. This included boutiques, e-commerce and call centres that gave it an exceptional competitive edge. Its strong innovation programme now embraced the first ever-global launch of a new machine, PIXIE, that reduced the pre-heat time to less than 30 seconds.

Elsewhere, under the catch-all Other sales heading, the company's three joint ventures all continued to perform well. Cereal Partners Worldwide (Nestlé and General Mills) had now garnered a global market share of over 20% in the breakfast cereal category, and grew double digit in Asia and Latin America. Beverage Partners Worldwide (Nestlé and Coca-Cola) had evolved into a sales vehicle for Nestea, which was restructured to focus on Europe and Canada. The third joint venture, Dairy Partners of America, formed with Mexican dairy company Fonterra, delivered another year of double-digit growth. Nestlé Health Science had been set up as a distinct and separate company within Nestlé, with its own board of directors and headquartered outside of the Vevey head office. It wasted no time in its first year, making some early acquisitions to add new areas of expertise, such as metabolic disorders, inflammatory bowel disease, colon cancer and oncology.

What is Their DNA?

The Nestlé DNA is very simple and consists of two complimentary elements: global and local.

Global

Nestlé is as near to being everywhere in the world as one food and beverage company can get (with the exception of the two cola giants). It has factories in 83 countries: ranging from the 81 in the United States to 29 countries, such as Bangladesh and Zimbabwe, that have one Nestlé factory. Nestle has been established for over a hundred years in at least a dozen countries. It has some gigantic brands: 4,000 cups of Nescafé are drunk every second somewhere in the world. The Vevey headquarters houses over 100 different nationalities. You cannot progress up the ranks at Nestlé without charting some of its far and wide outposts. The Nestlé name is ubiquitous; appearing on most of the billion products sold each day.

The company is managed globally in many ways. Its buying power is staggering. The forty or so billion franc brands are managed from headquarters in terms of brand positioning, quality standards and design styles. Yet Nestlé is far from a cumbersome, lumbering industrial behemoth. With the exception of tinkering with Nestlé Nutrition, the company does not spend its time endlessly redrawing boundaries of responsibility, or wrestling with the who-does-what debate that can preoccupy other global giants.

Local

The answer at Nestlé to the who-does-what question is simple: what gets done at head office is only what needs to be done at head office. Everything else is done at the local level, tightly managed by the Nestlé zone business units. The local operating autonomy, originally put in place through necessity, has been protected and nurtured to become a genuinely powerful and unique competitive advantage. This is especially so in terms of local economic performance. The rules are simple: if you are a Nescafé brand manager in Paraguay, you have no authority whatsoever to change what the brand stands for or alter any of the brand iconography. But you might get fired if the product formulation has not been tweaked, so that it was preferred, at least 60:40, against the best-selling Paraguayan competitor Likewise, your colleague managing the Kit Kat brand should have brought out a variant containing a locally popular ingredient. It is this mix of local entrepreneurialism, combined with a light but firm hand of global consistency that makes Nestlé such a successful company.

Summary

Ever since Peter Brabeck became CEO in 1998, Nestlé could not have made it clearer that it considered itself not a food and beverage company but a nutrition, health and wellness company. If we ran Nestlé, that's what we would be telling the shareholders and the analysts too. It promises higher growth and higher margin. Current CEO Paul Bulcke concisely explained the Nestlé approach to nutrition, health and wellness: it had three elements, Nestlé Health Science to pioneer critical illness nutrition solutions, the addressing of specific consumers' nutrition needs via Nestlé Nutrition and offering consumers healthier and tastier choices through the day via the remaining 85%-plus of the business.

But our contention would be that Nestlé is still a food and beverage company with a nutrition, health and wellness agenda, simply because too much of the company portfolio would not be classed as nutritious, overly healthy, or a key part of a wellness regime by the man or woman in the street. Consider the following categories and their 2011 sales in Swiss Francs:
- Soluble coffee9.2 billion
- Confectionery9.1 billion
- Frozen/chilled meals8.0 billion
- Ice cream4.5 billion

Over a third of company sales are accounted for by categories where the link to a positive nutrition agenda is tenuous, despite the fact that the company may be improving its nutritional components. Nestlé has not made serious M&A moves towards a total commitment to nutrition, health and wellness by, for example, selling its confectionery operations. Acquisitions have by no means been directed clearly towards the nutrition agenda. The purchase of DiGiorno was a smart, opportunistic move for a food and beverage company to make, but definitely not an acquisition driven by a nutrition crusade.

Having said all that, Nestlé is an extremely strong and very well run food and beverage company with a unique footprint, gigantic product range and entrepreneurial operating culture. These qualities combine to make it a formidable competitor in every market where it has a presence. Nestlé seems not to fail in markets or cut and run when they encounter problems. It is difficult to imagine that their reign as the world's biggest food and beverage company ending in the foreseeable future.

Procter & Gamble

Where Did They Come From?

The founding of great empires often becomes the stuff of legend. Rome owed its origins to two boys suckled by a she-wolf and Athens to a competition between Poseidon and Athena as to who could bestow the best gift upon the residents of the Acropolis. Procter & Gamble's was heralded by the descent of a host of angels with blond hair, playing harps and clutching boxes of Tide. Well, not quite. In fact, the beginnings of the greatest packaged goods empire the world has ever seen are a little – or shall we say a very great deal indeed? - more prosaic.

Alexander Norris, a Cincinnati candle-maker, was concerned for the financial well-being of his two daughters, Olivia and Elizabeth, during an economic downturn precipitated by a banking crisis, so he suggested to their respective husbands that they combine their struggling businesses to better weather the storm. Thus, Irish soap-maker James A. Gamble and English candle-maker William Procter dutifully pooled their collective business assets of $7,192.24 to create the firm of Procter & Gamble (P&G) on 31st October 1837. Banking crises are perhaps more useful than we may currently think.

As with virtually all businesses founded at a time before modern consumer markets, who sank and who swam was determined as much by luck as by business acumen. Which put both men Cincinnati remains unknown, but as soap- and candle-makers they were definitely in the right place: raw materials and markets were both plentiful. In 1837, Cincinnati was not known as Porkopolis for nothing. The early meat-packing capital of America, it was processing around one quarter of the hogs slaughtered annually in the entire country. Their surplus fat made a lot of candles and soap, prodigious volumes that the uncomplaining Ohio River could ship all the way down to New Orleans and thence to the major markets on the Eastern Seaboard.

Thus, the business prospered for four decades driven by a happy combination of advantaged location and ease of distribution serving a growing and increasingly affluent population. But the firm's biggest breakthrough also nearly led to its demise. And it forced P&G to develop a capability that has served it well since: to swiftly change direction when needs must or new opportunities arise. The American civil war prompted huge demand for candles. Procter & Gamble, given its location, backed the winning side and was soon shipping vast quantities of candles and, to a lesser extent, soap to the Union armies. Drawing on the mass production techniques developed by its Porkopolis suppliers, P&G ramped up the business such that, at the end of the war, Dun & Bradstreet estimated it to be a million-dollar enterprise.

How Did It Evolve?

The end of the war brought a sudden end to gigantic orders for candles from the one colossal buyer that had driven the company's growth: the Union army. This short-term disaster – candles the accounted for three-quarters of the company's sales – was compounded by two other insidious but just as disruptive changes. John D. Rockefeller's Standard Oil had begun using its scale to market cheap kerosene so the kerosene lamp was rapidly replacing candles as the night time illumination of choice. Simultaneously, Chicago was well on the way to putting Cincinnati out of business in the meat-packing trade. Thus, a firm that had specialised almost exclusively in turning local excess pork fat into tallow candles now faced the loss of its biggest customer, a rapidly shrinking market for its number-one line and diminishing raw materials at increased cost. P&G needed to get out of the animal fat candle business. Its saviour was to be Ivory soap.

Contrary to the company's own subsequent lore, Ivory did not come about solely because a gormless workman left a soap-mixing machine switched on all weekend (although he may well have done). Ivory's genesis was actually driven by three features of how the early company's business style that have become entrenched into its very core then and live on to this day: a focus on base science, an embrace of open innovation and a drive to reinvent premium luxury products as product anyone could buy.

James Norris Gamble, son of the co-founder, had studied chemistry and was an obsessive experimenter, always keeping his results in a journal. He was also a student of the soap industry at large. The animal-fat soaps turned out by P&G and its many competitors were in reality little better than the lye soaps many women still made at home; the manufactured versions were simply more convenient. But the elite used a different kind of soap altogether, Castile soap, an expensive luxury that used olive oil as the fat component. James Norris had long dreamt of producing soap as fine as Castile but making it affordable.

His breakthrough came when he met a young man who had been experimenting with vegetable oil soap. Procter bought the formula and, playing around with it, decided to combine it with another soap feature he had been experimenting with himself: floatability, which stopped the bar getting lost in murky bathwater. The outcome, launched in 1879, was Ivory. For the next 30 years, P&G concentrated most of its efforts in developing an unrivalled competence in soaps,

340

and a related activity which would again stand it in good stead for the entirety of its subsequent existence: consumer advertising.

Its initial marketing for Ivory was neither different from nor better than the norms for the time. It focused on the fact that the soap floated: the first slogan proclaimed It floats! and went on to suggest that this floating soap could, moreover, could be used for anything from fine lace to the family dog: you only need one soap. Not expensive. Will wash anything. No chapping. Segmentation would be a skill P&G developed later. But it was good enough to get by on until James Norris, having conducted multiple tests to compare Ivory soap with Castile soaps, came up with the fact that informed the company's most famous advertising slogan: 99% Pure.

P&G could have remained as one of America's hundreds of soap companies and would almost certainly have been swallowed in the great series of interwar industry consolidations with, for example, James S. Kirk & Co. They had been Chicago's leading soap manufacturer until P&G acquired them in 1930 to cement its national leadership. What made the difference, and gave P&G the extra leverage it needed, was that it had already moved from being just a bar soap company into a broad-based fats company, giving it much greater scale and scope. This was the beginning of another P&G definitive skill-set: the ability to manipulate its core ingredients and skills into new product categories.

Its first foray beyond bars of soap came in 1901 when, to protect its supplies of cottonseed oil - the increasingly difficult to obtain core raw ingredient for Ivory - P&G formed the Buckeye Cotton Oil Co. to acquire and/or build cottonseed oil mills. Six years later, in one of the most dramatic examples of avoiding Not Invented Here syndrome, a scientist, E. C. Kayser, literally walked into its office with the technology for hydrogenation, which enables liquid oils to be solidified at room temperature. P&G bought it in short order, patented it four years later and launched of Crisco, the world's first shortening made entirely from vegetable oil. The Crisco launch demanded a much more considered and disciplined marketing approach; after all, the company was building an entirely new category, something it would need to do many times in the future, from disposable diapers to Febrezing the sofa.

At the same time, P&G had been expanding laterally in the soap market. The days when one brand such as Ivory could be sold to meet all washing needs were ending: hundreds of companies were piling into the market. In 1890, P&G had 577 direct soap competitors, which kept prices low and profits elusive. So, in 1903, P&G entered laundry powder. It acquired Shultz & Company, and it particularly acquired Star, its leading brand, a well-known and successful product. P&G immediately improved it by adding naphtha. Until then, P&G's second-biggest brand after Ivory had been Lennox, a laundry bar that needed shaving into flakes to be used. Brands like Star and Lever Brothers' Lux were just boxes of soap shavings - Lux had been invented to make use of the waste from the machines that cut its Sunlight bars into shape. P&G was learning that competitors, consumers or even external forces could prompt shifts in demand that adversely affected P&G's sales.

As the soap industry began to consolidate, P&G, bolstered by the success of Crisco, was able to lead the charge, swallowing up many local, regional and even national players. It was closely followed by Lever Brothers and Palmolive, although Palmolive, having finished a distant third in the race for scale, had joined forces with Colgate. But the outcome for P&G was mixed, literally and metaphorically. It had acquired scale, but in the process a vast portfolio of undifferentiated soap brands, many launched as copies of each other. The result was chaos. The product range was mostly generic and the supply chain through America's vast army of wholesalers, jobbers and drummers made production planning a nightmare. The twin solutions to this problem in the 1920s would be P&G's greatest gifts to the world of packaged goods: in-store merchandising and brand segmentation, although both came about serendipitously.

P&G had been experimenting with direct distribution to retailers as a means of smoothing out its manufacturing peaks and troughs since a 1913, when it ran kind of distribution test in New York City. The results were promising but New York and its geographic concentration made it probably the easiest part of the country to try work in. So, in 1919, the same idea was tried across New England with similarly encouraging response. In a un-P&G-like fit of haste, the company rapidly rolled out the idea nationally in 1920 to pre-empt Lever Brothers copying the plan; the outcome nearly sank the company.

The implementation of direct order taking and fulfilment on a national scale was staggeringly complex. The number of accounts shot up from 20,000 to 400,000 overnight. Hundreds of warehouses and thousands of transportation agreements had to be set up. All this was difficult enough, but the hammer blow was organised resistance by the nation's wholesalers, who not only boycotted P&G products but did their best to persuade their customers, who still relied on the wholesaler for everything but P&G products, to do exactly the same. The results were catastrophic. Pre-rollout sales of $188 million in 1919 fell to $106 million by 1922 and did not reach their original level until 1926. Perhaps it was this drive to direct distribution that forged P&G's famous tenacity.

The goal of going direct had been to remove the production inefficiencies of wholesaler orders: vast, random and unannounced. But the true value of the move would came from P&G's realisation that the salesmen it now sent into every store could not only report demand in the form of orders but also influence sales on the ground through personal focus and in-store merchandising- much more than any wholesaler could do. The value of this breakthrough would be further enhanced by P&G's other great contribution during the interwar period: brand segmentation, administered by brand management and informed by market research.

The essential idea was simple but revolutionary: focus each brand on serving a well-defined consumer need. General Motors had first adopted this approach first. The folly of taking on Ford with a single model was apparent to all, whilst the structure of GM as a conglomeration of manufacturers and brands made it an obvious marketing gambit, boosted by the fact that Ford itself, constrained by the need to make and sell ever-cheaper Model Ts, was unable properly to respond to advances in automotive engineering. The soap market had neither of these stimuli. All the manufacturers were employing exactly the same strategies, with the soap technology of the time a technical backwater. So it was a brilliant insight for P&G to segment soap category. Now the company could market a range in which each brand was aimed not at different buyers, as had Chevrolet, Buicks and Cadillac had done, but at different cleansing tasks or differing water conditions, as opposed to Ivory's historic claim to be the Model T of soap – ideal for all needs.

A profound by-product of segmentation is an increase in overall demand, as P&G soon found: it was only when brands began to compete with each other by staking out a relevant point of difference that increases in per capita demand were stimulated. Until that point, soap had grown largely in line with population growth. Such segmentation encouraged the consumer to buy not just one large slab of generic soap at a rock-bottom price but also a whole range of higher-priced branded offerings, each of which performed a different task. And once all that soap was in the house, washing frequency unsurprisingly increased. Thus differentiated, the brands could coexist on the shelf without competing head-on with each other, retaining the benefits of vertical integration and avoiding price competition while minimising the wastefulness of internal overlap.

As a one-off exercise, this would have been impressive enough, but it was followed up by an insight of equal importance. Rather than having one internal management group supporting a mass of competing products, the range of now segmented, non-competing products could be supported by a Darwinian internal competition for resources and focus. This system developed into the brand management structures with which we are familiar. The development of brand management at P&G was an organic process, but one that fit perfectly in a segmented world. Once brands were targeted at different market segments, the currency of success shifted from low input costs and prices to data: about markets, consumers, consumer behaviour and channels of distribution – brand manger fodder.

P&G had also made a head start in building a market research capability when, to fill a sales forecasting assignment in 1924, it hired a PhD economist who had been quick to realise his sales forecasts would be a lot better if he understood what was truly driving demand. He soon rewrote his job description: bringing consumer understanding into the business. From a springboard of market research, the brand management finally coalesced as a function in 1931, driven by the initiative of the company's promotion department manager and future CEO, Neil McElroy. The initiative had been prompted by P&G's launch of Camay, a perfumed 'beauty' soap developed as a response to the launch of Palmolive. It soon became apparent that Camay could only succeed if it was allowed to compete against not just Palmolive but also Ivory itself, against which Palmolive was making big inroads.

It is no exaggeration to say that brand management is the management of segmentation, together with some implementation tactics. It would become the bedrock of P&G's subsequent success. It invented brand management at just the right time and the concept of internal competition would never be more tested than in P&G's defining moment: the launch of Tide.

The technology behind Tide, a synthetic detergent rather than a soap, had come to P&G's attention in the same year McElroy was defining the brand management. But it had languished for years - no-one had been able to find a way to make it work and it had been looked upon as a potential niche brand better suited for washing clothes in hard water areas: it was just not effective enough to cope with heavily soiled clothes. Worse, the more the formulation was strengthened, the more deposits it on the clothes, making them unacceptably stiff. By 1939, it was firmly on the back burner, kept alive by one maverick P&G chemist working in secret to avoid upsetting his bosses. But by 1945, he had actually solved all the problems and revealed its vastly superior cleaning power to his dumbfounded colleagues.

Normal P&G product launch disciplines at that time would have called for six months' worth of blind tests in a few cities, another six months for test-driven tweaks, then another year of shipping tests and advertising development before a test market lasting another couple of years. But in the sure knowledge that Lever and Colgate-Palmolive would get hold of blind test samples, figure out the technology and quickly develop their own versions, P&G decided to bet the farm on an immediate national launch to steal as much of a competitive march as it could.

But fast tracking the launch in 1946 was not the limit of P&G's boldness. Within three years, Tide had shot to a market share of over 25%, more than twice as big as the previous best seller, growth limited only by P&G's ability to build production capacity. Nevertheless, P&G faced a twin dilemma: Tide was stealing share from all brands, including its own, and was based on a completely different technology from its existing brands. In other words, Tide was busily making redundant brand assets and manufacturing assets built up over decades. But the genie was out of the bottle. By 1948, both Colgate and Lever had launched their own synthetic detergents, so there was no turning back. P&G put everything it had behind Tide irrespective of the damage to its existing brands. As a company, it never looked back

How International Are They?

P&G's first operation outside of the United States had been as early as 1915, when it opened a manufacturing plant in Hamilton, Canada, and it was another fifteen years before its first venture beyond North America, when it purchased the UK's Thomas Heldey & Co., primarily to compete against Lever Brothers in its home market. Having set up an International division in 1946, the next baby step came in 1948 with an acquisition in Mexico, soon to be followed by Venezuela and Cuba. P&G's experience in Mexico turned out to be an object lesson in what would be required to operate successfully in new and culturally distinct markets.

As it turned out, P&G was very slow to understand the very different attitudes and behaviours of Mexican housewives: it was also up against an entrenched competitor in Colgate, who had been in Mexico for decades. Its early product launches flopped and it would be a full decade before it had its first success there, with Rapido and another decade again before P&G entrenched itself, via the launch of Ariel. But the effort proved to be worthwhile for two reasons: first, what it taught P&G about how to compete in lower-income markets and second, the fact that it required P&G to build a very robust, broadly spread Mexican operation. By 1990, it was operating in sixteen product categories. Today it has a share of around 25% in the $4 billion and rapidly growing Mexican household products market, among other sectors.

It looked as though Tide would provide the leverage P&G needed to establish a bridgehead in Europe, where it would be competing against a dominant Unilever (in 1930 Lever Brothers merged with Margarine Unie to create Unilever), who, in the absence of Tide as a competitor, had been slow to bring its synthetic detergents into the market as they would devastate its own dominant nonsynthetic brands. Through the 1950s, P&G built detergent plants in France, Belgium and Italy but steered clear of the largest market, West Germany, preferring instead to extend its technology-sharing agreements, which had led to the initial development of Tide with Henkel, Europe's detergents giant.

But Tide had proved to be of limited appeal to Europeans, whose smaller, front-loading high-temperature washing machines were quite different from those in the US. It was only when P&G recognised it would have to develop brands designed for the euro-wash that it really broke through, initially with a low suds detergent called Dash but then with Ariel, first launched in West Germany in 1967 and its first brand to use enzyme technology. (P&G had terminated its non-competition agreement with Henkel a few years earlier). Ariel became P&G's power brand in its overseas markets, and strong enough to overtake Tide and become the company's largest detergent brand. Elsewhere, Pampers too became a very big brand for P&G across most of its European markets.

P&G's next major learning experience in globalism came with its 1970s experience in Japanese, by then second only to the US in market size, but dominated by two very well established local players, Lion and Kao, who had already given both Unilever and Colgate something of a trouncing. By now, P&G had a fairly standard approach to entering markets: research the consumer and retail trade, form an alliance with a local player as a quick access route and a conduit for P&G technologies and brands until a critical mass for a P&G local operation was achieved. Japan was to show P&G this would not be good enough.

By 1985, thirteen years after entering the market, P&G still hadn't turned a profit and pulled together a last-ditch attempt to make a success of its venture. It gave the project a name Ichidai Hiyaku, The Great Flying Leap, a very fair description of the task in hand. But rather than see the market as an opportunity for US-centric brands and formulations, P&G started from the ground up, designing products exactly to Japanese consumers' habits: detergents needed to perform in cold-water washes, Pampers needed to be slimmed down and advertising had to be locally developed and culturally spot-on. Finally, distribution needed to be efficient.

The plan worked three ways. Over time, P&G developed a large and profitable business in Japan, an experience that would inform its subsequent forays into Eastern Europe and the emerging BRIC markets (Brazil, Russia, India, China). And the new technologies developed for the exacting Japanese consumer, such as cold-water cleaning power and ultra-thin diapers, would become powerful brand developments in both new and old P&G markets. By the end of the 1970s, P&G had finally established itself as a genuine global company with one-third of its sales coming from outside the US. P&G entered many, mostly small new countries during the 1980s but the ones that would prove most significant to its business today were in Eastern Europe and China.

P&G was also determined to win first place in the race into the crumbling Communist markets of Eastern Europe. Even before the fall of the Berlin Wall, plans were being kicked around. As soon as it became apparent that major change was afoot, P&G sprang into action, eschewing its normal careful, country-by-country approach and coming up with a rapid rollout plan, prioritising the various markets according to based commercial attractiveness, perceived stability, availability of commercial television and government openness to free markets. On that basis, Czechoslovakia, Poland, Hungary and Russia's two major cities became top priorities. The company also prioritised its categories, aiming to launch with its big guns of laundry, diapers, hair care, feminine care and dental care while allocating region-wide responsibilities for the production and marketing of each category to specific countries. Thus, Poland focused on hair care and diapers, while Czechoslovakia handled laundry. Acquisitions played a key role in cutting market entry lead times; P&G's purchase of the Czech firm Rakona meant it was already manufacturing Ariel for the entire region by August 1991, a mere 21 months after the fall of the Berlin Wall.

Following the collapse of the Soviet Union, most Western companies found Russia was a more difficult nut to crack, especially after the economic collapse of the late 1990s. Up to that point, P&G's Eastern European business had looked very rosy indeed, with annual revenues well over $1 billion in 1997. But the Russian economic crisis was in danger of leaving the company high and dry. An army of expensive expatriate managers pushed costs and therefore prices well above those of an emerging group of local competitors. P&G slashed wherever possible, replacing many of its expats with locals and emphasising the value, as opposed to price, of its products. The storm was eventually weathered but it taught the company valuable lessons in how to manage in crisis-ridden markets. P&G is now the number-one player in the Russian household products market.

P&G was also very quick into China, opening the biggest consumer products factory in the country in 1991. Only three years later it was shipping four million cases of product a year, already making China one of P&G's top-ten markets. From an initial three – city focus on shampoo, skincare and personal cleansing, P&G again leap-frogged its global competition. It decided to attack every significant city in China, all 570 of them. In these cities, P&G would face stiff competition from local firms such as Nice, who had been rapidly upgrading its products and up-scaling its operations while keeping its costs extraordinarily low.

Having learnt from its experiences in Mexico and Japan, P&G progressively extended into fabric care, feminine care, oral care and baby care, eventually building China into its second-largest market, generating sales of $6 billion in 2012. The rate of growth in China for P&G products has been breath-taking. When Pampers was launched there in 2000, the sector size was around $200 million; ten years later, it had increased fourteen-fold to $2.8 billion. P&G sales in China are now more than double those of Unilever, P&G having mastered the distribution complexities that follow from no single retailer accounting for more than 3% of market sales and with the majority of sales going through an endless network of distributors.

P&G's growth in developing markets has become the growth engine of the entire company. Sales of $8 billion in 2001 had grown to $21 billion by 2007 when they accounted for 29% of total company sales; two years later, that was up to 32%. In the decade since 2002, P&G's compound annual growth has been 17% in China, 25% in Russia and 27% in India. But the potential is still mind-boggling both in terms of market size and market share. The per capita spend in China on P&G products is now around $4 whereas in Mexico it is nearly $20, and in 2007, P&G's market share in developing markets was only 19%. By 2012, developing markets were accounting for 38% of P&G's sales (44% of unit volume) – a $32 billion business in its own right, making P&G the world's largest consumer goods company in developing markets, an amazing achievement given how uncertainly it started off.

How Did It Build Its Modern Business?

Procter & Gamble came into the post-war period better equipped than any other packaged goods company to benefit from the twenty-year consumer boom that was about to take place. It had the best marketing organisation and was comfortable entering new categories, especially at a time when the annual GDP growth rate doubled and the baby boom accelerated population growth. It was the country's biggest advertiser at a time when television dramatically enhanced the ability to reach and influence consumers. And the Tide experience had changed the company culture to one where disruptive innovation became the over-arching goal, no matter how long it took, how much it cost and how much it made redundant its existing equities.

In the post-war era, what P&G manufactured and sold and how big it became would change the company beyond recognition – sales would increase 30-fold between 1945 and 1980 – but the attributes of how the company operated remained remarkably consistent. Tide and other detergent brands still drove P&G's growth in the 1950s as household ownership of washing machines continued to rise, but the seeds of the next great breakthrough were sown in 1957 when P&G acquired a middle-of-the-road tissue manufacturer called Charmin. It would have been natural for P&G, following the breath-taking success of Tide, to have seen itself as the leading marketer to housewives, which it was. So to extend into other housewife-domain categories such as kitchen rolls and bathroom tissue would have seemed logical. Those markets were relatively unsophisticated so perhaps P&G thought that it could simply out-market the competition. Not so.

It would be a decade of intense effort before P&G finally got to grips with paper products and learnt the technical skills required to replicate Tide in paper form: similarly breakthrough products with breakthrough performance that could command premium prices and a large market share. Several of today's billion-dollar P&G paper brands - Charmin, Bounty, Pampers and Luvs - were children of this era, powered by a technical breakthrough which dramatically increased absorbency, known in the company as Confidential Process F. But during its initial decade in the paper products business, P&G seriously considered exiting as it struggled to accommodate an entirely different business model. However, once the technical boffins had come up with Confidential Process F, P&G doubled down on its investments to reap ultimate reward.

Simultaneously with its paper business struggles, in 1955 P&G had decided to tackle Colgate head on with the launch of Crest toothpaste. The technical breakthrough behind the brand – fluoride, which prevented cavities – came not from P&G itself but from a research partnership with Indiana University. But P&G's biggest challenge came on the marketing side: persuading an initially hostile American Dental Association to come on board and vouch for Crest's key benefit. They were perhaps wary of seeing toothpaste, not their fee-earning members, deal with the cavity problem.

As Tide, Bounty, Charmin, Crest and other breakthrough brands such as 1961's Pampers surged ahead year after year, driven by colossal advertising budgets, P&G focused on developing its skills in product enhancements. Acquisitions made during the 1960s into coffee (Folgers) and peanut butter (Jif), although decent businesses in themselves, failed to become springboards for the breakthrough innovation the company sought. Hence there were no major acquisitions through the 1970s. Why should there be? The company seemed more than capable of meeting its goal of doubling in size every ten years just by keeping on keeping on, doing what it was doing. In fact, in the 1970s it tripled its sales to reach the heady heights of $10 billion.

But it had become apparent that for a $10 billion turnover company to double in size in the next decade, P&G would have to relearn and enhance its skills in making, absorbing and growing acquisitions. So the company formally analysed every single category in the grocery store to seek acquisition targets that met with P&G's needs. It looked for higher-margin, higher-growth categories that depended on innovation and branding for their success, which attracted to the soft drinks arena. It bought Crush International Ltd in 1980, followed by a citrus-processing firm the next year. But, despite much effort, P&G's belief that it could win in this category through superior flavour technology proved unfounded, although its acquisition of the Sunny Delight brand in 1989 kept it interested for a while. It left Soft Drinks Town for good in 2004.

In 1982, P&G, already dabbling in the OTC drugs market, paid a massive $371 million for Norwich Eaton Pharmaceuticals, primarily for its Pepto-Bismol and Chloraseptic brands. This move was followed up by a blockbuster deal: the purchase in 1985 of Richardson-Vicks Inc. for $1.2 billion, by far the biggest acquisition ever made by P&G. While it had purchased the company primarily for OTC brands like Vicks VapoRub, Sinex and DayQuil, Richardson-Vicks also brought into P&G an interesting range of personal care brands -Oil of Olay, Pantene shampoo and the Vidal Sassoon range. These personal care brands would eventually be the main benefit flowing from the acquisition.

On the home front, however, life had become tougher. While the 1983 launch of Always, based on Pampers' stay-dry lining and absorbency technologies, had provided the company's next blockbuster, P&G had been losing its commanding lead in its core categories of laundry and paper products. While efforts were made to shore up these areas, P&G invested further in building scale and expertise in personal care by acquiring brands such as Cover Girl, Clarion, Old Spice, Max Factor and Giorgio. P&G was now changing rapidly into a maker and seller of brands rather than having any specific category focus. It was also, somewhat more painfully, becoming a global company.

How Is It Structured?

As P&G became ever larger and more complex, how it structured and managed itself became a major part of its strategy. To keep up with the goal of doubling the size of the business every ten years, larger and larger acquisitions needed to be made. As those acquisitions took the company into new and different categories, new skills had to be learned and new management structures adopted. The issue became not just achieving growth but also coping with growth.

P&G had first structured itself into divisions as early as 1955 and it subsequently initiated occasional bouts of restructuring and downsizing as acquisitions created inefficiencies and overlaps. But as the scale of the acquisitions increased, so did the structural issues. The purchase of large, already complex companies such as Tambrands in 1997, Iams two years later, Clairol two years after that and Wella in 2003 meant that the company was in a state of constant realignment, a process not really eased by selling off some of its by now less attractive foodstuffs business. After the Wella purchase, P&G was employing nearly 100,000 people in over 80 countries. In addition to the problems of scale and scope, P&G was dealing with the added complexities of doing business with the emerging retail giants, having formed a joint customer team with Bentonville-based Walmart Personnel as early as 1998. This followed on from P&G's streamlined of its supply chain in the mid-1990s and its subsequent move away from cash discounts offers to everyday-value pricing.

The P&G/Wal-Mart initiative would become a benchmark for the rest of the packaged goods industry, with P&G employees from sales, finance, marketing, IT and logistics working as one team with their Wal-Mart counterparts. Integrating information systems to achieve joint, real-time information share was a huge challenge: the companies had different financial years and different measures of sales and profitability. But the initiative was a clear success and by 2004 P&G had teams embedded in over 50 retail customers.

In 1998, P&G launched its most sweeping re-organisation ever: Organisation 2005, the aim to with cope with the twin challenges of a truly global company trading in multifarious many market conditions on the one hand, with operating across a large number of product segments on the other. The outcome was a three-pronged matrix. Along one axis were seven global business units (GBUs), each responsible for the strategy, development and brand management of individual product sectors: tissue and towel, food and beverage, fabric and home care, baby care, feminine protection, beauty, and health care along with a separate New Ventures Group. On the second axis were eight market development organisations (MDOs) – geographic regions – that were responsible for market/customer development and local marketing execution. The third axis was a global set of corporate functions.

This change was to be an implementation nightmare. P&G was now more concerned with looking inwards than looking outwards, at a time much when competitors were out there fighting back and the company's own new product initiatives were lying fallow. P&L accountabilities were unclear, which created morale issues in the MDOs. Information to support the new structures lagged far behind the organisational changes. And the new structures themselves seemed to be fundamentally flawed, with increased overhead costs as each GBU had been set up with its own full set of functions: R&D, IT, and HR in addition to more operationally-focused activities. To avoid the impression that P&G wasn't taking the global nature of its business seriously, two of the GBUs had been headquartered outside the US, the Feminine Protection GBU drawing the Japanese short straw. Lastly, it seemed that every subsequent acquisition and disposal created fit and size issues within the GBUs. Either an acquisition didn't really fit under any of the headings so was shoehorned into somewhere essentially inappropriate or a significant disposal took a chunk out of a GBU's turnover without reducing its overheads. The outcome was an average growth of 6.7% in net sales in the eight years leading up to 1998 dropped to a miserly 2.6% for the next three years with net earnings declining each year. It was a slump that cost the CEO his job.

P&G needed to find a way to get back to the basics: focusing on consumers and customers while making its highly complicated structure work. This was to be achieved by the incoming CEO, A. G. Lafley, who was continuing the decades-long tradition of company man P&G CEOs who had started off in brand management. Lafley's first priority was to ensure every manager had a dose of hard reality: the company was losing share on key brands with key customers in key markets while delivering insufficient innovation and incurring costs that were excessive.

Focus was the answer. By merging baby care, feminine care, and tissue and towel into one new baby care and family care unit, the number of GBUs was reduced by two. Overseas GBUs were repatriated back to Cincinnati, and the matrix structure was given an external focus with Lafley's brilliantly simple Two Moments of Truth. The first moment of truth occurred in the store when shoppers decided, or not, to buy a P&G product. This was the accountability of the MDOs: making the sale. The second moment of truth occurred whenever a consumer used a P&G product. This was strictly down to the GBUs: they had to deliver the promise. Lafley also demanded a laser focus on winning with top brands, top customers and in top markets. P&G could only win if it consistently made its big brands bigger.

Lafley's new approach also came just in time to also benefit from some new and more exciting innovation coming out of the pipeline. Swiffer, Febreze, Crest Whitestrips and the recently acquired Spinbrush were all classic P&G innovations that mirrored its historical strengths in either creating premium products in previously commodity-driven categories (Swiffer) or in bringing hitherto unaffordable luxuries into the mass market (tooth bleaching and powered toothbrushes). P&G was getting back to what it did better than anyone else. In 2003, P&G's top-ten brands grew by an average of 8%, its top-ten customers by 13% and its top-ten markets by 11%. The machine was humming, or beginning to.

What Has It Been Doing Recently?

2004

This was the year that Lafley's strategies really kicked in. Net sales increased by 17% to break the $50 billion barrier, driven by 10% organic growth, with the balance due to a full year's benefit from the previous year's acquisitions, primarily Wella. Global market shares in P&G's core categories all increased to historic highs: 36% in baby care, 35% in feminine care and 31% in fabric care. The company now had a historic high of sixteen brands with sales of over $1 billion, Pampers by far the largest at $5 billion. Crucially, market shares in the US and Europe had also improved significantly.

In addition, P&G was benefiting from the upside of new product launches in its pharmaceuticals sector. Actonel, its osteoporosis brand, originally developed by leveraging its oral care calcium expertise, became the fastest-ever P&G brand to reach sales of $1 billion, whilst its Prilosec OTC brand achieved market leadership in the heartburn treatment category in a staggering five days. Indeed, healthcare and beauty care were the darling categories for P&G, showing above-average growth of 18% and 40% respectively. These higher margins and below-average market shares thus left plenty of scope for further growth and rather overshadowed more sedate growth rates in P&G's paper products and Fabric and Homecare sectors.

The orphan of the organisation was snack and beverages, which by now had been reduced to two brands: Folgers coffee and Pringles. With only $3.5 billion in sales next to $17.1 billion in beauty care, for example, it made little sense to continue carrying a separate GBU overhead, which prompted another change to the GBU structure, the sort of change that would become an almost annual habit. Snacks and beverages GBU was folded into household care, while healthcare was merged with baby and family care, leaving beauty care as the third remaining GBU. With only three GBUs, the precise synergies between Folgers and Tide, Iams and Actonel, and Tampax and Hugo Boss was not easy to discern other than as simple overhead reduction. But this simply reflected the fact that, with such an aggressive acquisitions strategy, P&G's brand portfolio was perpetually a work in progress.

2005

The rate of sales increase softened slightly but was still impressive, increasing by 11% to $57 billion: after all, without a blockbuster acquisition on the Wella scale, slowing down was inevitable. True, the announcement of the forthcoming Gillette deal gave promise of better days to come. But organic growth also slackened off a couple of points with only Dawn, the single new brand, joining the elite list of 17 billion $ brands. (22 once Gillette had been acquired). By this point, fully half of P&G's sales were coming from outside North America and the company now had four customers who sold more than $1 billion a year of P&G products. At the other end of the economic spectrum, P&G's success in growing sales by 50% over the previous four years through High Frequency Stores (mostly neighbourhood independents) made that sector larger in sales for the company than Wal-Mart. Store like these accounted for 80% of sales in the developing markets.

Within the GBUs, Tide Coldwater - developed to match the Japanese housewives' washing method of choice - made its successful transition into the Eanuropean and North American markets, where housewives took to it for its potential to save on energy bills. The company also launched Tide with a Touch of Downy, in the first of what would become an almost habitual strategy of combining the incidental benefits accrued from developments across its now vast 300-plus brand portfolio. Febreze also made its first move from the furnishing spray it had been into the larger air freshener market. The company also launched products aimed at lower-income consumers - Blendax tooth-paste in Russia, for example - but also introduced similar products into developed markets with Bounty Basic and Charmin Basic, a response both to a growing part market of lower-priced secondary brands and particularly to private labels.

The company mission was also clarified: the creation of sustainable advantages in branding, innovation, go-to-market capability and scale. With seventeen billion-dollar brands, an R & D spend of $2 billion a year, number-one supplier ranking with US retailers and $57 billion in sales, P&G was well placed on all fronts. It is clear how well the Gillette acquisition fitted in; it was a prime example, as Wella had been, of the company shifting its focus to a faster-growing, higher-margin and more asset-efficient businesses. And although Steady-Eddy paper towels might pay the bills, P&G was determined to take its skills upmarket in relatively developed markets while simultaneously taking its products into lower-income sectors in developing markets.

The Gillette deal was ratified by Gillette shareholders on 12th July 2005, costing P&G a whopping $57 billion and increasing the size of the company by 20%. As well as the Gillette brand with its 70% global market share, the deal also brought Duracell, Braun electric shavers and Oral-B toothbrushes into the fold. Short-term benefits took Gillette brands much deeper into China and P&G brands into sales channels where Gillette had been stronger - home improvement, for example - and also enabled around $1 billion in annual cost savings. Longer term, P&G, buoyed by its success in achieving dramatic growth for new brands like Pantene and Clairol, looked to broaden the Gillette franchise. As the annual report acknowledged, 'We are confident the Gillette brand can stand for more than blades, razors and pre- and post-shave products in the minds of consumers'. The initial plan was to run the Gillette business as a fourth GBU, headed by the existing Gillette CEO.

It was a blockbuster deal that made the rest of the packaged goods world - retailers and other manufacturers - sit up and take notice. P&G was driving a stake into new territory proclaiming a clear message: that acquisition capability would be a defining success factor for the future. Warren Buffet, a substantial stakeholder in both companies, unsurprisingly described it as 'a dream deal'. Not entirely un-noticed by, nor insignificant to, P&G management was that the fact the deal had created the world's biggest consumer goods company, leapfrogging Unilever: a pivotal year for P&G

2006

Unsurprisingly, the Gillette deal boosted reported net sales by 20% to $68 billion, with Gillette integration problems more than counterbalanced by the launch of Gillette Fusion, the year's best-selling new product in the consumer products industry. Organic sales increasing by a still respectable 7%, mostly powered by Actonel and Prilosec, which both seemed unstoppable? The annual GBU restructure took place in April 2006 when the family health GBU was dissolved and the component parts split between the other groups, the I-ams pet business going into household and the rest into beauty, now renamed beauty and health.

The Gillette GBU at 9% of company net sales - oral care and personal care components had already been hived off into the other GBUs - was clearly now on borrowed time as a stand-alone GBU. Sales of Gillette, Braun and Duracell had crept up by 1% in the year, increases from Fusion offset by customers taking the chance to reduce inventory as distribution shifted over to the P&G system. Overall, it was a satisfactory outcome, given the scale and complexity of an extensive integration process completed in 26 countries during the year.

It was also a year in which a change to P&G's historical approach to innovation reached a significant milestone. As with Ivory, Crisco and Tide, the company had not been shy in leveraging ideas from outside the business, although in the post-war period it had become more focused on generating new products from within the company - successfully it must be said. The mantra Connect and Develop had underpinned a particular strength: leveraging its own areas of technical expertise had led to Pampers, Actonel and Always. In 2006, around 35% of the company's new products included features or technologies sourced from out-

GREG THAIN & JOHN BRADLEY

side the company, whose explicit goal was to raise such sourcing to 50%. Given that P&G possessed, amongst packaged goods companies, undeniably the best scientific capability in the post-war period, this switch to an external focus would need to be carefully managed. It needed to exploit, not compromise, the company's scientific lead.

2007

This was the third year in a row that the rate of increase in organic sales had slowed, this time down to 5%, while acquisitions helped prop up the top-line increase to more than 12%. Tide Simple Pleasures, Febreze Noticeables and Crest Pro-Health were the main innovations and compensated for the complete absence of growth from the company's food brands, both human and canine. The acquisition of Dolce & Gabbana to bolster the company's vibrant prestige fragrances business further highlighted how much the company was changing: exactly what were the commonalities between high-end fashion brands and Pringles? The good news was that sales of blades and razors increased by a very healthy 8%, though whether this was due to synergies from the acquisition or fortunate timing - Fusion had just come on stream - remained to be seen. Margins also increased for the fourth year in a row to exceed 20% for the first time, reflecting of an acquisition policy whose job was to achieve exactly that result.

The Herculean integration of Gillette was declared complete just in time for the next round of GBU musical chairs. Gillette and Braun were moved into the Beauty GBU and reunited with their branded shave prep products, feminine care products making way by being shifted into the newly named health and well-being GBU, while Duracell went into household care.

With Gillette now integrated, Lafley defined the next big goal - looming for some time -as 'How do we keep a business the size of P&G growing?' A good question. The company now had 23 billion-dollar brands, which were almost all leaders in their categories, twelve billion-dollar countries and seven billion-dollar customers. And while much emphasis was placed on the vast resources ploughed into innovation – 8,500 scientists beavering away with seven years and a billion dollars' worth of consumer data - the answer was not clear.

2008

It seemed the answer to Lafley's question would be innovation. After all, P&G was the industry's largest innovator, churning out more new products across more categories and brands than any other, and spending more on R&D – $2 billion a year – than anyone else: double that of Unilever and more than Avon, Clorox, Colgate, Energizer, Henkel, Kimberley-Clark, L'Oréal and

356

Reckitt Benckiser put together. But then the absolute growth that P&G had to generate each year – target 6% of sales – was by now a mind-boggling $5 billion on sales of $83 billion. So the drive towards open innovation was continuing and, having reviewed and evaluated over 5,000 external innovation opportunities, the 50% target for new products with an external component was met.

On the other hand, organic growth had slowed again, down to 4% with a bigger increase in net sales coming from the foreign currency lottery. Within the GBUs, the largest organic growth came from household care, specifically within the US-centric category of family care where Charmin Ultra-strong, Bounty Basic and Bounty Extra Soft all enjoyed strong growth. Pampers, aided by the Pampers Baby Stages of Development, exceeded sales of $8 billion for the first time. Within fabric and home care, detergents had a good year helped by the rollout of new liquid detergent compaction technology across several brands. In beauty, Olay Regenerist was leading the way, aided by double-digit growth in the company's premium fragrances, as Dolce & Gabbana was fully absorbed. In grooming, the continued Fusion rollout increased brand sales by 40%, making it P&G's 24th billion-dollar brand.

But there were some warning signs that there were troubled waters ahead. The timing of P&G's year-end is 30th June, so 2008 sales did not really reflect much of the coming collapse in consumer spending provoked by the 2008 banking crisis. Most of P&G's developed market growth in its 2008 report was pre-crash, and taking place in premium categories or behind premium innovations. More bad news was that two of its recent growth and profit goldmines, the pharmaceutical and OTC brands Actonel and Prilosec, both lost volume. Worse, it seemed that this might not be just a blip: Prilosec had lost its marketplace exclusivity as an OTC version of a by now off-patent Rx (prescription) drug. Elsewhere, P&G's Folgers, Pringles and Iams brands were becalmed, with Folgers - a brand P&G had owned since the 1960s and one of the company's vaunted roster of billion-dollar brands - hived off to the J. M. Smucker Company in June 2008.

Other more insidious trends were also beginning to nibble away at the margins. Although the above-average growth in developing markets continued, driving the P&G share up three percentage points from 27% to 30% and in many respects good news, it wasn't helping gross margins: a much greater proportion of sales in these markets was in lower-priced, lower-margin products. For example, it was not Fusion that lead the charge in those markets but PrestoBarba 3, a three-bladed disposable that was essentially a cheaper version of Sensor 3 superseded by Fusion in developed markets. A combination of the inexorable shift of business to developing markets plus increasing commodity and energy costs, pushed P&G's gross margin downwards by almost a full percentage point to a lower level than 2006. To mitigate this shift, an aggressive approach was vital; isolating and exploiting cost synergies from the Gillette acquisition succeeded in knocking a full percentage point off SG&A costs while consumer marketing investment relative to sales was flat for the second year running.

2009

The economic crisis hit P&G hard. Reduced demand in many of its more premium categories was compounded by a $2 billion hit in increased energy and commodity costs, combined with a $4 billion hit on sales from foreign exchange as the dollar strengthened against most currencies. To mitigate these impacts, P&G pushed pricing ahead by around $4 billion, which helped protect gross margins and reduced advertising expenditure primarily in the fourth quarter, all of which looked suspiciously like an effort to make the numbers. To increase prices by 5 or 6% in the middle of consumer spending falls certainly looks questionable, especially as in the developing markets - up another full percentage point - P&G was increasingly competing against fast-moving, very low-cost local players with no real currency exchange problems to worry about. Clearly, the question was: could P&G afford to price-lead in these markets in difficult economic times?

P&G was also hit by negative product mix changes, because its more expensive, more profitable brands were declining the fastest. There were disproportionate volume declines for Braun appliances, prestige fragrances, Wella, Duracell batteries and the pharmaceutical brands - consumers were cutting back or trading down on luxury purchases. Even Tide and Downy declined, while their cheaper fabric care brands grew. P&G's acquisition strategy in the previous decade, going after higher-priced, higher-margin product categories, was fine when consumer markets were booming, but a P&G built upon the steady reliability of sales of bathroom tissue and diapers – baby care and family care were its only two categories to report growth – was not used to dealing with double-digit declines in what were now core categories. Overall, net sales declined by 3% to $79 billion.

More worryingly, P&G was now starting to lose global share in key categories such as fabric care and OTC, where the Prilosec declines continued. Despite a 4% boost from price increase, P&G's total Healthcare sales were down by 7%, a decline P%G aggravated by exiting its pharmaceuticals business altogether, dumping former star brand but now problematic Actonel on Warner Chilcott for $3.1 billion. Iams and Pringles had an even worse year, with net sales down by 3% despite a whopping 10% added on through price increases. Perhaps both brands were having their margins juiced for disposal. Overall, P&G lost share in categories covering two-thirds of its sales. But despite such tough marketplace conditions, there still seemed to be time for moving the deck chairs around in the GBUs. Female-grooming brands - Venus, for example - joined female beauty brands. Male brands such as Old Spice and Gillette pre- and post-shave products went the other way, splitting the Beauty/Grooming segment by sex rather than by product type.

A far bigger change came from the fact that chairman Lafley, in preparation for his retirement, had been replaced as president and CEO by another P&G lifer, Bob McDonald. New man at the helm meant changes to the company strategy. Here is McDonald's mission statement: 'We will grow by touching and improving the lives of more consumers in more parts of the world... more completely'. Which being translated meant:

- Increasing our presence in developing markets
- Extending our distributions systems to reach more consumers through underserved retail channels

Specifically:
- Drugs, pharmacy and perfumery
- High-frequency stores (neighbourhood stores in developing markets)
- Export operations (to the approximately hundred countries that did not have a P&G operation on the ground)
- E-commerce (the first time this had been mentioned as an explicit growth strategy)

'We are expanding our brand and product portfolios,' McDonald added.

This was the most far-reaching change as it entailed P&G expanding its portfolio in every possible direction: upmarket into premium, downmarket into economy and horizontally into adjacent categories. The danger with a strategy like this is it sounds suspiciously like, 'We will sell more stuff to more people in more places more often', which could easily lead to anything that might accomplish even one of these goals being judged a good idea by default. Unilever had achieved good results by making swingeing cuts to its own range of brands.

2010

P&G returned to growth, although a more than 3% increase in net sales would have been considered a failure in the earlier part of the decade. The year was notable for a certain amount of backtracking on the previous year's decisions: some of the aggressive price increases, particularly in developed markets, were rolled back and advertising were expenditures increased to try to address the market share losses. The increased advertising was affordable: gross margins jumped a whopping 250 basis points in the year from 50 to 52.5% of sales, driven by a downturn in commodity and energy costs, whose increases the previous year had prompted the aggressive price increases. However, pricing benefit was retained: prices went up in many developing market sectors to cover further adverse currency impacts. The increases seemed to have no effect on consumer interest, however. Developing market growth continued unabated and now made up to 34% of sales. The company now claimed 4.2 billion customers, an increase of 200 million in the year.

It is interesting how this return to growth was achieved. The growth in developing markets could by now be taken as a given, the margin challenges it posed mitigated by price increases that seemed to have been successfully pushed through. But in the developed markets, the acquisition boom of the late 1990s and early 2000s – P%G had averaged one increasingly massive acquisition every two years - had ground to a halt. Gillette had been the last biggie and that was five years ago. The purchase of Ambi Pur from Sara Lee in July 2010 for $470 million was 100 times smaller than the Gillette acquisition. Much of the growth this year came from a ramped-up range of innovations, although the fact that most appeared in the fourth quarter again suggested that perhaps the timing included an element of making the year-end numbers. However, Fusion ProGlide, with a larger-than-ever range of pre- and post-shave accessories, represented a significant step forward, as did Pampers with DryMax, claimed to be the biggest innovation for the brand in 25 years. Crest toothpaste added 3D White. All three products seemed very promising.

Interestingly, only a year after the 'Sell more of everything to everyone everywhere' strategy was announced, there was a new focus: simplification of what had become a staggeringly complex business. The company used over 16,000 product formulations and over 4,000 different colours in its packaging and although this was not particularly unusual - virtually all companies would reduce the complexity in manufacturing and procurement if they could – it was perhaps another sign that P&G was becoming more internally focused.

2011

The 2010 fourth quarter innovation did the trick. Slight though they were, the improvements were visible. Organic sales rose by 4%, although organic volume increased faster at more than 5%, indicating a residual underlying mix problem: it was doing better in its lower-priced, usually lower-margin products. Gillette Guard, for example, was a cheap, disposable razor system designed for the half a billion Indian men who still shaved with double-edged razors an affordable but improved shave. At 15 rupees a unit with refills for 5 rupees (1 rupee per shave), the product, launched in October 2010, was the biggest-selling razor in India just three months later. Fusion margins at one rupee a shave were much tougher to achieve.

With P&G's developing markets businesses surging ahead - P&G Brazil, for example, had grown seven-fold over the previous decade - the pressure was on to return the developed markets to significant growth. Acquisitions were no longer providing the easy options, and innovations, while strong, were not in the Ivory, Tide, or Pampers league of long-term blockbusters. And non-innovated brands in developed markets not also had to grow, so it was very encouraging when P&G showed a formerly very well-hidden skill in creative and engaging advertising, and used it to accelerate brands. The company brought home a record-breaking 32 Lion awards from the Cannes Lions International Festival of Creativity, an event it historically had paid little heed to. The best example of its new-found creative skills, in both advertising and social media, was the Smell like a man, Man campaign for Old Spice, which increased sales for Old Spice Body Wash (the first focus of the campaign) by 40%. Not bad for a seemingly moribund brand that had just turned up in the same bag as the Shulton purchase.

But P&G would need many more such successes. It needed to stem the margin drift inherent in the cheap and cheerful developing markets. For example, as its $20 billion beauty category declined in developed markets - particularly in core North America - it grew in high single digits in developing markets, thus skewing the average. But the year had its successes, principally in fabric care, home care, baby care and family care, where most of the previous year's innovations had been launched. Grooming performed adequately, growing net sales by 5%, although, as with beauty products, volume was down in developed markets, generating an overall global share loss of around half a percentage point. At the tail end of the portfolio, Braun also showed a global share loss and the snack and pet care sector had an awful year with a 5% organic sales decline, due partly by a product recall on Iams. Nor did the acquisition of the Natura pet business help much: it contributed a net sector growth of just 1%. The company also divested itself of the annual Prilosec volume losses by merging its OTC business with Teva Pharmaceutical Industries.

McDonald had now also assumed the role of chairman, and under the new management regime, P&G was changing fast, in some ways undoing many of the Organisation 2005 GBU changes. Seven were now down to two: grooming and beauty, and household care, each of which was a colossal global business in its own right. The original notion of having GBUs focus on specific segments was now long gone. Under McDonald, the focus was on integration which, he believed, would best leverage the one attribute on which P&G couldn't be matched: scale. As McDonald said, 'Integrating to operate more fully as a global company is the way we turn our size into scale and our scale into faster growth and cost advantage'.

There was much logic to the approach. The key to maintaining success in developing markets was to roll out as many P&G product categories as fast as possible; this could be done far more effectively with cohesive multi-category strategies, not unlike those employed in the company's initial rollout into Eastern Europe. Equally, there were previously untapped opportunities in multi-brand commercial activities such as the Olympic Games' sponsorship and also in direct marketing activities, with initiatives such as P&G Brand Savers. There was also integration in the supply chain, as the company moved away from gigantic, regional, single-category factories to more localised, multi-category operations. McDonald's simplification drive continued beyond formulations and colours to the product range itself, which now amounted to a startling 50,000 SKUs. The target was set to reduce this by 30% over three years, though how this would be squared with another of his goals, 'more offerings to more consumers in more retail channels' was not made clear.

There was nothing in these strategies that had not been accomplished before, at some time in the past and in some part of the world. But on a company-wide basis it was a far cry from the initial driver of P&G's success: internal competition generated by a segmented range of products guided by dedicated brand management.

2012

This was a year when the US economy returned to growth, as did many of the world's developed markets. But P&G did not. While the reported plus 3% organic growth in the twelve months ending on 30th June seemed acceptable, if a little uninspiring, it masked a much more worrying position. When acquisitions and disposals were excluded, the figures were depressingly flat. The continuing shift of business towards developing markets, now up to 38% of total sales, had a 1% negative effect on sales' value, which meant that the single driver of increased sales was a 4% average price increase. Even worse, the company was losing market share on almost every front: in beauty, dry shaving, fabric care, pet care, oral care and feminine care. Only in home care, hair care and wet shaving did it manage to hang on and only in two did it grow, batteries - where competitors declined even faster than P&G - and the ever-dependable baby care, thanks to Pampers. The only notable innovation was Tide Pods. Pringles, an iconic

P&G innovation in its day but increasingly anachronistic given the company's full tilt into beauty and shaving businesses, was sold to Kellog's. No transformative acquisitions took place. And surely it cannot have been in the plan to lose share in both shaving and batteries only seven years after paying $57 billion for Gillette purchase? Where were all the growth synergies from the mega-deal?

The response of management was to retrench, after yet another change to the GBU set-up. Once again, previous changes were undone, with the male/female split in beauty and grooming changed back into a product split. The proposed bigger solution to P&G's woes was to focus on the core, focus on the short-term, radically cut costs and hope and pray that the innovation pipeline would recover its mojo. And the focus would be a quantifiable 40/20/10: focus on its largest 40 businesses that delivered 50% of sales and 70% of profits, being primarily in the US – where P&G had lost volume almost across the board after too many price increases and not enough innovation – and China.

The second focus was on its top-twenty innovations which history had shown to usually turn out ten times bigger than other initiatives, although history had also shown that most of P&G's most successful, disruptive innovations looked anything but big and successful in their first few years. Tide, Bounty, Pringles and many more had either languished unloved or been financially underwater for years before finally coming good. Given the year's other changes, whether P&G 2012 would have the patience to indulge a rogue researcher, or a paper company that lost money for ten years, or a potato technology that took twenty years to become a billion-dollar brand, that was certainly open to question. Rather more prosaically, the company did commit to delivering by a $10 billion in cost savings by 2016 in cost of goods, marketing efficiencies and non-manufacturing overheads, while aligning management targets on short-term sales, profit growth and cash-flow. The last focus would be on the ten most important developing markets while the plan for innovation was plainly stated: 'We need to get back to this level of (discontinuous) innovation in a meaningful way'.

That is very true. P&G is now facing many of the issues that had confronted Lafley ten years ago:

- Declining sales and share in developed markets
- Prices too high
- A patchy innovation record
- Costs that needed a severe pruning

The question is whether the company can solve these problems all over again.

What Is Its DNA?

As we have seen, P&G has been through many transformations: the products it markets, the countries it markets them in and how it interfaces with its retail customers to name but three. But although James A. Gamble and William Procter probably didn't expect their company to be selling shaving aids, dog food and designer perfumes in every corner of the world, we believe they would probably still recognise some of the key ways in which P&G did, and continues to do, its business. Here is Current Chairman, President and CEO Robert A. McDonald's description of the company as follows in the 2012 annual report:

'Our long track record of success is based on a time-tested business model – we discover meaningful insights into what consumers need and want; we translate those insights into noticeably superior products focused on those needs; we communicate that superiority through advertising that includes compelling claims, performance demonstrations, and superior visual benefits; and we price our products at a point where consumers experience overall value'.

We would argue this description is a little too narrow and, to at least some extent, not truly reflective of today's P&G. Dolce & Gabbana and Old Spice advertising talks little of true product superiority and Bounty Basic is not a superior product, although it may be a better-value one than those offered by competitors. In our view, P&G's DNA is:

P&G Is In the Business of Building Brands

Since the launch of Ivory, P&G has built brands. Across the branded goods era, there can be no question that P&G has not only been the biggest but also the best at building, reinforcing and cashing in on branded properties. Not only has it been the largest packaged goods advertiser for more than a century, but it also invented, refined and perfected many of the inherent processes and capabilities of brand building.

It was not only the first company to produce half-hour television serials, it was also the first company to align every function in the business around the sole goal of building brands. It holds massive global shares in most of the categories in which it competes and has far more billion-dollar brands than anyone else. Nor does it restrict itself to building its own brands. P&G has been an extremely acquisitive company and many of its greatest successes have come from creating much more growth and value from brands and technologies than previous owners were able to. Its market capitalisation of around $180 billion is more than $100 billion greater than the book value of the company's tangible assets, so it doesn't just build brands: it builds brand value, $100 billion of it, out of every-day products that slightly improve the lives of billions of people.

The Appliance of Science to Brand-building

While all consumer goods companies would claim to be in the business of building brands, where P&G has been most noticeably different in its approach to brand building has been its focus on and expertise in core science. P&G spends hundreds of millions of dollars researching billions of consumers and more often than not its biggest successes have come from deriving new consumer benefits from scientific advances.

This emphasis on the science that underlies consumer products has been a feature of the company since James Norris Gamble reverse engineered his competitors' products and experimented on how to improve them further. By 1890, Gamble had recruited university chemistry graduates to populate one of the first corporate laboratories in the emerging consumer goods industry. The company was a pioneer in building dedicated pilot plants rather than utilising unwanted or unused bits of kit. By the 1920s, P&G was employing hundreds of science graduates in a multi-faceted chemical division where the Research Department worked on base science, passing on its discoveries to the process department, which would find ways to leverage them into a mass production environment to deliver clear, demonstrable, product usage benefits.

It also mastered the skill of cross-fertilisation, where scientific advances in one part of the product range could be used to enhance or create completely new benefits in another part of the business. Thus, its original expertise in fats and oils in soaps led directly to the creation of a new kind of shortening and later to peanut butter and potato chips. Its post-Tide skills in detergents provided openings in other kinds of cleaning such as hair and teeth. Its understanding of cellulose that came from the Charmin acquisition led straight to Pampers and Always; the combination of Tide and Charmin knowledge led to Bounce, and so on and so on.

No other consumer goods company has P&G's breadth and depth of scientific expertise; it spends $2 billion a year on R & D across 150 different sciences. Data showed that P&G had had 132 products on the Top 25 New Product Pacesetters list over the past sixteen years – more than its six largest competitors combined. Its move towards open innovation continues a long tradition of being open to and incorporating ideas from outside the business, but its skills have always predominantly been in what it does inside its business that its competitors don't. Open innovation is, well, open to everyone else, so the required attributes shift from having the most and best science to finding and nurturing the best external science. It is unclear whether P&G will be as competitively advantaged at that as it has been in doing the science itself.

Rigour and Tenacity

It perhaps shouldn't be a surprise that a company which has thousands of scientists in the building would be a believer in methodical and rigorous analysis, experimentation, testing, tweaking, retesting and rollout. P&G has built an empire demonstrating that product is king and the world will wait for a great idea. It has also demonstrated Edison's mantra that genius is 99% perspiration. Tide came about because of one researcher's perspiration over years, Charmin was a money pit for a decade, Pampers failed in its first three test markets, Crest was initially poo-pooed by the dental establishment and Pringles looked like it was never going to break even.

Pringles is an excellent example of P&G's tenacity. It began as a project in the mid-1950s as P&G had close links with the potato chip industry, being a leading supplier of fats and oils to it at the time. Potato chips have a short shelf life and are mostly delivered by a dedicated rapid distribution system, which P&G did not have or want. So the product had to be packed in nitrogen to extend the shelf life and packaged much more space efficiently to keep packaging costs down. So the tube and the stackability were driven by P&G's desired means of distribution rather than some underlying consumer need. It wasn't until ten years later that the basic formula and production process was finally cracked, at which point $70 million was pumped in to take the concept to test market stage by 1968. After rollout, the brand peaked with sales north of $100 million, but by the end of the 1970s sales had dropped by two-thirds. Pringles were expensive, the flavour and texture were sub-optimal and the brand was slated for discontinuation. The product was re-engineered to be cheaper and better and, just as importantly, P&G realised that competing in the snack category was not only about demonstrable product benefits: other features such as variety and fun were equally important. The brand first made an annual profit in the early 1980s, a quarter of a century after its genesis, and went on to reach billion-dollar brand status by the late 1990s, almost half a century on!

However, it must be said that tenacity has its downside. Olestra, its patented fat replacement food ingredient, was laboured over for far too long. In the face of overwhelming evidence that the public would not accept a food ingredient that did nothing but give them a better chance of a stomach upset, it should have been dropped. In any case, it had been discovered by accident during research for a fat that could be better digested by premature infants. It was first considered as an anti-cholesterol-drug, but the FDA disagreed. Only at the end was the idea born to use Olestra as a food additive replacing 'bad' fats. It was simply a very expensive idea looking for a use. However, it must also be said that two of the greatest successes came when caution was thrown to the winds. The trick is not to let the rigour get in the way when the idea really is great and not to let an idea continue without a use – literally useless – run forever, or far too long.

Summary

The combination of these three attributes, applied over different times, in different product sectors, in different geographies and countries, has resulted in a company ranked Number Six in Fortune's World's Most Admired Companies, Number Two in Fortune's Top Companies for Leaders, Number Three in Barron's World's Most Respected Companies and Number Twelve in Business Week's World's Most Innovative Companies. How long it will maintain these kinds of rankings depends to a very large extent on its current strategies.

Its growth in developing markets will undoubtedly continue. P&G learnt the hard way how to apply its DNA successfully in markets very different from its US/Europe heartland, and with $32 billion in sales already from these markets, it is better positioned than anyone else to capture the further growth that will come from hundreds of millions of new consumers entering the middle classes and extending the consumption of its products.

P&G currently sells 40 billion products a year and it expects to increase that to 60 billion in the next few years. But, as we have seen, this inexorable growth in developing markets is for cheaper products and lower margins than P&G has become accustomed to in developed markets, which is why it is currently looking to get $10 billion of costs out of its business.

After protecting margins, its second challenge is to return to growth - and above-average growth - in the developed markets. Since the economic crisis, P&G has suffered volume and market share declines in many categories. It has been taking on heavy price increases, has produced no blockbuster innovations and has completed no transformative acquisitions. Not a pretty sight. Turning this around while simultaneously cutting costs savagely, with all the internal navel-gazing such an exercise entails, will be its biggest challenge.

PepsiCo

Where Did It Come from?

Two American men, 25 years apart, invented drinks that would bestride the world – as Coca-Cola and Pepsi-Cola have done - and both died in obscure penury, knowing nothing of their ultimate success. John Styth Pemberton mixed and drank his first glass of Coca-Cola in 1866, the year before Caleb D. Bradham was born.

Caleb became a North Carolina pharmacist and drug store owner and he was not one to accept for a moment Coca-Cola's dominance over the soft drinks market. Caleb mixed prescriptions and also new concoctions to be sold at his store's soda fountain. Sometime during the early 1890s he was selling a drink consisting of sugar, vanilla, oils, spices and extract of the African kola nut. Caleb was alert to feedback from his enthusiastic customers about what they called Brad's Drink. Caleb became convinced his drink relieved upset stomachs and the pain from peptic ulcers, so, by 1898, he had christened it Pepsi-Cola. Its success caused him to expand his distribution base. Caleb hired a manager to run the drug store while he set up a syrup factory in the back room. He set about finding more soda fountain customers for his newly patented drink.

Business boomed surprisingly quickly. In 1902, the first year of operation, he shifted around 2,000 gallons of syrup and the next year ran advertising campaigns - Exhilarating, Invigorating, Aids Digestion - which quadrupled sales to almost 8,000 gallons. This volume was 1% of Coca-Cola's sales in the same year. Caleb had started a long, arduous and tortuous journey. Could Pepsi-Cola become a serious rival to Coca-Cola? He made a good start: the speed of his subsequent growth was astounding. Within eight years, mostly due to an enthusiastic pursuit of bottled sales, he was selling 100,000 gallons of syrup a year. These came from a combination of his own factory, thousands of soda fountains and 280 bottlers across 24 states. For all Coca-Cola's dominance, it seemed there were absolutely no barriers to entry into the category.

However, in 1920/21 the price of sugar first rocketed and then collapsed. This almost bankrupted the mighty Coca-Cola, so little Pepsi-Cola had no chance. Its assets of well over $1 million were not insufficient to withstand a $150,000 loss on sugar when the 1920 price of 25 cents/lb. collapsed by 90% the year after. Caleb sold off everything not nailed down and got a mortgage on what was. It wasn't enough. In January 1922, with liabilities five times assets on the balance sheet, Caleb lost control to a Wall Street firm and left the beverages business for good.

The all-but-broke company changed hands more than once for peanuts and lost money throughout the 1920s, even though Prohibition did wonders for the soft drinks industry in general. Pepsi-Cola was in no fit state to survive the Great Depression so, in 1931, it was declared bankrupt once again.

How Did They Evolve?

Pepsi-Cola's saviour was, ironically, a Coca-Cola customer. Charles C. Guth, the president of the Loft Inc. chain of confectionery stores, was a mercurial chancer. He was as stubborn as a mule with a temper to match. Loft Inc. ran 200 stores, which sold over 30,000 gallons of Coca-Cola a year from its soda fountains. This made Charles a substantial Coke customer, who was accounting for around 1% of their syrup sales. Yet his request for a bigger discount was turned down flat. An outraged Charles recalled a bankrupt drinks firm he had been offered for a song three years earlier.

Determined to show Atlanta they couldn't push Charles C. Guth around, he bought the Pepsi-Cola firm for around $12,000 and kicked Coke out of his stores. To misquote Don Corleone, this move was personal, not business. It made no sense. Coca-Cola was already a national institution and its availability drove the traffic of soda fountains. Hence Loft Stores' takings plummeted in the aftermath of the switch. In the following few years, Loft's purchases of Pepsi syrup declined by 30% compared to their earlier volumes of Coke. Charles' initial hope that he could substitute the syrups and nobody would notice had been stymied – partly because he liked the taste of his Pepsi drink even less than did his customers.

Charles commissioned his confectionery expert, Richard Richie, to reformulate Pepsi to taste something like Coca-Cola. Richard achieved this feat in a shade under three weeks. But it still wasn't Coca-Cola and Loft's customers drifted away.

Loft stores were purchasing around half of all Pepsi-Cola syrup, making the drink little more than the store's private label cola. Charles needed new outlets for his drink. His breakthrough came in 1933 in the form of a used bottle dealer. He suggested to the ever bargain-conscious Charles that he put Pepsi in used beer bottles. These were twice the size of Coke bottles but cost next to nothing. Like a drowning man grasping a lifebelt, Charles was all over this idea. He had been struggling to come up with a proposition for bottled sales that stood a chance against Coca. After some experimentation and following a suggestion from his head candy salesman, Charles had discovered the only chink in Coke's armour: value.

The price of Charles' 12 oz. bottles of Pepsi was 5 cents, the same as charged for the 6 oz. bottle of Coke. This would be the saving of the brand, if not of Charles' career. This bold tactic demonstrated two things. First, that Charles had been right to demand a discount. If he and his bottlers could fill and sell a 12 oz. bottle for 5 cents and both still make money, then Coca-Cola was abusing its brand monopoly and gouging its customers. Secondly, the move demonstrated something that remains true to this day: every brand has its price. If you can undercut a brand leader by a big enough price gap with a good enough product, then a significant number of consumers will switch.

Charles was a bright enough to realise the vulnerability of Pepsi's own position. If he could sell twice as much cola for the price of a Coke, then so could anyone else. He had a limited window of opportunity to make the most of this opening and solidify his position as the low cost supplier. His first move was to call all the bottlers he knew personally and plead with them to tool up for the 12 oz. bottle, promising to cover any losses should it not pan out. Within six months of agreeing, the first Pepsi bottler to do so was shifting a thousand cases a day. Charles used this evidence to sign up as many new bottlers as quickly as possible.

The 12 oz. bottle was a runaway success. Within four years Pepsi was making over $3 million profit a year, through a network of over 300 bottlers covering the nation. Throughout this time, Charles C. Guth had been double-hatting. He was head of Pepsi-Cola (of which he owned 91%) while still managing Loft Stores. He had not run it very well. Loft lost money throughout the time he was resurrecting Pepsi from the grave. Loft and Charles fell out in spectacular style. The Loft owners sued him for his stake in Pepsi, claiming he had used their assets and people to build it up. Outside investors, seeing a juicy prize if the case was won, bankrolled Loft's lawsuit, which they won. In 1935, ownership of Pepsi was transferred to Loft by the courts.

Guth, who clearly had the skin of a rhino, stayed on as general manager hoping for a chance to win Pepsi back. He was finally kicked out in 1939 when he purchased another cola company to try the same trick. Loft paid him $3 million to go away and no doubt felt it a bargain. While Guth was a loose cannon (to put it mildly) and was perhaps not the man to take things forward, the fact is Pepsi would have died without him. If he hadn't picked a fight with Coke and then latched onto the 12 oz bottle for 5 cents, Pepsi-Cola would have gone the way of all the others Coke had put out of business. Instead, by 1940, Pepsi-Cola was the market number two, slightly ahead of Seven-Up with sales around 20%

of Coke's. They had a network of over 400 bottlers, earning the company over $8 million in profit a year; an amazing figure for a brand on its uppers seven years previously.

Coca-Cola was hugely dominant in fountain sales where there was usually only one supplier. However, when it came to bottle sales in stores where there were many suppliers, Pepsi's 12oz was accounting for an impressive 26% of sales. Coke bottlers and franchises, already living high off the hog with a license to print money, were not keen to wipe out the capital invested in the 6oz size. A bigger bottle was not introduced for another fifteen years, giving Pepsi the time to become a firmly entrenched competitor.

Guth had been succeeded at the head of Pepsi by Walter Staunton Mack Junior, who would put his own indelible mark on the evolution of the Pepsi-Cola brand. Even though Pepsi was now well established, it was still very much the David to Coke's Goliath. With an advertising budget one-thirteenth the size of Coca-Cola's, Pepsi had no choice but to be creative. Mack endlessly encouraged a risk-taking approach. So when what looked like a couple of deadbeats walked into his office claiming to have the answer to all his problems, he did not throw them out. They immediately burst into song with a Pepsi jingle they had written. Mack couldn't wait to sign them up. Most radio commercials at the time, including Coke's, were five-minute-long, cover-all-the-bases eulogies to the endless benefits of the brand. A thirty-second ditty, sung to the tune of Do Ye Ken John Peel, while not unique (Wheaties had run something similar), was certainly in the margins of advertising practice. Radio stations didn't want to sell airtime in 30-second chunks, when they could save 90% of the work by selling it in five-minute slabs. Nor was the advertising agency thrilled to be cut out of the creative process.

Mack approached small radio stations, which were grateful to get any advertising sales. He started spending. Within two weeks the results were promising enough to take to other stations. By the end of 1941 it had been broadcast 300,000 times across nearly 500 stations. The jingle not only built sales, but also began a unique personality for the brand. Mack built on this by abandoning the old beer bottles and adopting a unique Pepsi bottle. This became famous for its baked-on label: it was designed by the man responsible for the interior of Tiffany's Fifth Avenue store.

The move to build uniqueness into the brand was not before time. Pepsi-Cola's value positioning would soon begin to dissolve. The price of sugar shot up after the Second World War. This put tremendous strain on Pepsi's price positioning: Coke was big enough to absorb the increases for far longer than Pepsi. And to maintain such a discounted value proposition long term, you needed to be the lowest cost producer. Pepsi was not, and they could hold the line no longer than 1948. They tested putting the price up to 6 cents, and launched a smaller 8oz., bottle for 5 cents. Both bombed. Sales growth completely stalled, which prompted a cabal of disgruntled bottlers to force Mack out and introduce another strongman who would shake things up.

Next in line was Alfred N. Steele. He saw straight away Pepsi's value positioning was doomed. It was seen as quirky and cheeky, the cheap cola you served to your kids and their friends. Mindful of his predecessor's fate, he also realised that the bottler network - a rougher, tougher bunch than Coke3's - needed hauling back onboard the good ship Pepsi. Steele, the ultimate schmoozer, promised the bottlers if they followed him he would 'take them out of their Fords and put them in Cadillacs'. Coke bottlers spent their lives on the golf course. Too used to having no direct competition, they were flabby and lazy, he told them. They're there for the taking,

For Pepsi to take on Coke, it had to match Coke standards. When the selling point had been twice as much for the same price, no one had paid much attention to product consistency. Pepsi varied in taste between different bottlers and even different production runs. That, Steele said, had to change. He sent mobile laboratories around the country. If bottlers couldn't get the product right, they had no place in Pepsi's system. Steele hired ex-Coke employees in droves. With the ability to deliver a consistent product, he could build a national brand, differentiated along dimensions other than price. The chosen dimensions were packaging, product and target market.

As above, the flabby Coke bottling system was highly resistant to investment and change. Steele saw that his rival could always be out-innovated on packaging. So during the 1950s, Pepsi introduced a range of sizes that met different needs. For example, the 26oz Hostess bottle in 1955 was loved by the rapidly expanding grocery chains, which Coke were slow to embrace. On the product side, Steele also saw two vulnerabilities in Coke's overwhelming strength. First, the brand was targeted to absolutely everyone, i.e. no one in particular, and secondly it was tied to the same recipe. Coke couldn't change its product to appeal to specific segments of the buying population and wouldn't introduce variants that could do the same job. So the Pepsi management reached for the nuclear button: they reformulated their product with the specific aim of making it more appealing to women. Prompted also by the high cost of sugar, Pepsi adopted a lighter taste with fewer calories. Their advertising emphasised benefits such as looking smart, keeping up-to-date and being fair and debonair. Previously a copycat of Coke, Pepsi now had a differentiated product in a range that sold in the prime trade channel for reaching women - grocery stores. Pepsi had achieved a cohesive, segmentation-based approach to the market, allowing their price to creep up to-wards that of Coke. Steele's marriage to movie star Joan Crawford, who was immediately dragooned into brand spokesperson, accentuated the difference between modern Pepsi and staid old Coke. Pepsi couldn't beat Coke overall, but they could beat them with women.

The results of this approach were outstanding. By the time Steele died in 1959, Pepsi's sales had tripled while the market only increased by 30%. The company's profits increased five-fold while Coke's only doubled. Steele had also ramped up Pepsi's overseas operations, going from three concentrate plants located abroad to twelve. The bottlers were not only driving around in Cadillacs, they believed where the company was going. They were also contributing an unheard of two-thirds of the total Pepsi advertising budget. Having Joan Crawford come open your new bottling line in the middle of nowhere did wonders for bottler commitment and morale.

The key to the Pepsi strategy was always to keep one step ahead of Coke - to do what they couldn't, or wouldn't do. While Coke had Eisenhower as its man in Washington, Pepsi signed up Richard Nixon. He helped engineer the publicity coup of having Nikita Khrushchev drink a Pepsi when Nixon visited Moscow. When diet drinks became a realistic possibility for mainstream companies, Pepsi was first out of the gate with Diet Pepsi. And as the grocery chains continued an inexorable growth, Pepsi brought out new sizes and plenty of promotions. But the making of the Pepsi brand came from what seems in hindsight an almost inevitable evolution of Steele's approach. From targeting women to the Pepsi Generation, Pepsi was already in the right territory, but the genius was to take a demographic positioning - moms with young kids – and turn it into an attitudinal positioning: people who think young, who look forward, who are positive, curious and want more out of life. The first manifestation of this thinking came in 1961 with a campaign which carried the punch line Think Young. It reached fruition two years later with the slogan, Come alive – You're in the Pepsi Generation. This was perfect for the times and was everything Coke was not.

Pepsi-Cola was used to having dynamic, forceful leaders. After something of an interregnum, order was restored in 1963 with the appointment of Donald M. Kendall. He had worked his way up from a lowly fountain salesman and was Pepsi through and through. Kendall would lead the company into its modern manifestation as not just an American drinks brand, but also a global food and beverage company.

How Did They Build The Modern Company?

Kendall did not wait long in flagging up that things were changing. Within a year of his appointment, Pepsi made its first acquisition, that of the small Virginia-based Tip Corporation and its brand, Mountain Dew. The management mantra of the 1960s was diversification and the corporate vehicle of choice was the multi-category conglomerate. Pepsi, as a highly focused soft drinks company with high margins, was a tempting target. Kendall was keen to remain master of his own fate but hampered by the fact Pepsi was too small to make major acquisitions of its own. So he engineered a merger in 1965 with another company also keen to keep out of conglomerate clutches: Frito-Lay.

Frito-Lay was itself the product of a 1961 merger between the Frito Company and the H.W. Lay Company. Herman W. Lay became chairman of the newly created PepsiCo Inc. with Kendall as president and CEO. The new company had sales of just over $500 million, made up of around one-third snacks sales and two-thirds beverages. The merger had a lot of logic:

- Both companies did most of their business with the same customers – grocery chains
- Both product sectors used a system of direct store delivery by their own or their bottlers' trucks
- Salty snacks made you thirsty: soft drinks quenched thirst

Even though the two companies essentially operated as separate divisions of PepsiCo, the deal attracted the ire of the Federal Trade Commission. The regulator was suspicious that their combined might would create unfair competition in the snack food business, particularly in the buying of advertising. A compromise was finally agreed in 1968: PepsiCo would not buy and run ads for each division back-to-back, and would not acquire another beverage or snack food company for the next ten years. So, with no acquisition prospects within their existing categories, the company sought to expand beyond snacks and beverages. In 1964 Kendall had established the Pepsi-Cola Equipment Corporation, to lease vending machines and trucks to bottlers. This sideline became so profitable that the company deepened its trucking activities, progressively buying trucking and transportation companies. An abortive bid was made for the Miller Brewing Co. and in 1970 Pepsi spread even further afield by purchasing Wilson Sporting Goods, makers of tennis rackets and golf balls among other sporting paraphernalia.

While the snacks side of the business stuck to its knitting by introducing Doritos in 1966, mistakes began to be made on the core Pepsi USA business. Kendall was now at one step remove, focused on building the company's international presence (see below). In the meantime, mainstream Pepsi became envious of a successful milk-based brand called Yoo-Hoo, and set about developing a challenger called Devil Shake. They discovered too late that the Yoo-Hoo Chocolate Beverage Corporation held the rights to the only technology at the time, which could give the product a decent shelf life. Pepsi had to write off $5 million development costs. Even worse was the 1967 decision to move away from the Pepsi Generation-themed advertising. The reversion to the more product-oriented Taste That Beats the Others Cold (Pepsi Pours It On) was a mistake only corrected after two years of flat sales.

The early 1970s saw strategic thrusts which quickly doubled the size of PepsiCo from the high of $1 billion annual sales reached in 1970. The sales powerhouse of the 1970s would be the massive expansion of the Frito-Lay direct store delivery system. This opened a new manufacturing plant every year as it extended its reach to over 700,000 sales calls a week in over 300,000 stores. Deliverymen had the scope to put Frito-Lay products front and centre of every snack display. On the Pepsi side, the emphasis switched from innovating new brands (most of which had flopped), and back to what had helped build the brand - innovating packaging formats. This culminated in the industry's first two-litre bottle in 1974. The mantra of the drinks division became one of marketing package and price ahead of taste and flavour, and exploiting the greater flexibility of their bottling system. As grocery stores were getting ever larger, there was more shelving to be occupied; so more sizes were welcomed with open arms. From October 1971 Pepsi gained market share for seventy-two consecutive months, and pulled level with Coke in grocery stores. It was an impressive achievement.

However, Pepsi wasn't doing well everywhere. In Texas it had a pathetic 6% market share and was a distant number three behind Coke and the home-grown Dr Pepper brand. Local bottlers found the Pepsi Generation thematic advertising useless against entrenched competitors and demanded head office help. An executive was sent and concurred with the local view that, outsold eight-to-one as they were, they needed an ad campaign with real balls. Moving the sales needle meant risk-taking. Seeking to understand the appeal of Dr. Pepper, the executive conducted taste tests of the three brands. He was amazed to find that Pepsi consistently outscored Coke. Even more amazing was the fact that neither Coke nor Pepsi's head offices had ever conducted blind taste tests of the two brands, presumably because they are never bought blind (this is the main argument against blind taste tests). Hence was born the Pepsi Challenge.

More acquisitions later in the 1970s changed PepsiCo's make-up. While Pepsi was consistently gaining on Coke in the grocery chains where all brands were stocked, it had made little to no headway in Quick Service Restaurants

(QSRs). There only one cola would be served, which was invariably Coke. Kendall's answer harked back to Charles Guth's style - to buy the restaurant chains and kick Coke out. They acquired Taco Bell in 1977 and Pizza Hut a year later. When combined with the meteoric progress of the snacks division - Frito-Lay sales had increased six-fold since the 1965 merger - over 60% of company sales were now coming from categories other than beverages. The next year, international sales of snacks were greater than had been Frito-Lay's entire sales at the merger.

By 1981, PepsiCo was a $7 billion a year company and the clear number one in take-home sales of cola. Their fountain business, which had been given a shot in the arm with the acquisitions of Taco Bell and Pizza Hut, improved further when Burger King also decided to switch from Coke to Pepsi. Then, in 1986, PepsiCo acquired KFC. The company solidified around three divisions: soft drinks, snack foods and restaurants, selling off the transportation and sporting goods companies in 1984. But the big Pepsi event of the early to mid-1980s was not something PepsiCo did, Coca-Cola. At last, old-fashioned, conservative Coke responded to a whole series of Pepsi moves over time. The something was New Coke.

It's not often in business your competitor makes a move you thought they would never or should never do. When it happens, what counts is how quickly and forcefully you respond. Pepsi-Cola had been steadily gaining on Coke from 1977 to 1982, partially thanks to the national rollout of the Pepsi Challenge, but progress had slowed. So Pepsi turned up the heat. Pepsi Free, the caffeine-free cola introduced to challenge the newly launched diet Coke, exceeded all expectations - shipping 150 million cases in its first year. Also in 1983, Pepsi signalled a move away from the Pepsi Challenge. That November, it signed the biggest advertising contract in history: $5 million. Michael Jackson would appear in two commercials to add a new level of awareness to the resurrected Choice of a New Generation advertising theme. The launching of a gut-busting 3-litre bottle in May 1984 once again broke new ground. There was a lot going on with Pepsi, and Coke was left trailing.

Coca-Cola got new leadership. The long-time president Robert W. Woodruff had had a strategy of 'do today what we did yesterday only better'. As Pepsi was changing everything all the time, Woodruff's strategy was deemed old-hat and misplaced. A new president, Roberto Goizueta, was given the mission of shaking up Coca-Cola to increase its fizz. What better way to start than slaughter the most sacred of cows – the secret formula locked in the Atlanta bank vault. On April 19, 1985, Coca-Cola committed a major blunder: indicating they would make a major announcement the following Tuesday. Forewarned Pepsi executives could scarcely believe their luck when they got hold of a smuggled preview six-pack of the new flavour. They had three days to craft a response. They declared a company-wide holiday. They booked a full-page ad in The New York Times trumpeting that Pepsi-Cola had won the cola wars. They fed questions that the press could throw at the hapless Goizueta. Coke's biggest moment for a hundred years had been turned into Pepsi's best haul of favourable PR in its history. That was the disastrous something that Coca-Cola did.

Coke eventually announced 'discovering' this new, even better Coke formula while developing Diet Coca. This sounded less plausible, and a lot less interesting, than the idea, followed by the plain fact, that Pepsi had psyched them out and Coke had pressed the panic button. The consumer response, as we all know, was to desert the Coke brand in droves. Brand share fell off a cliff and within three months the old recipe was back, escorted by the distinctly implausible claim that the fiasco had been a success by reawakening the consumers' love for Coke.

Pepsi did the better of the two in 1985 by growing 5%, increasing to 7% in the first quarter of 1986. It had been a masterful performance by Pepsi management. They even developed their own version of original Coke to launch - Savannah Cola. Pepsi only pulled back when they realised bulk buying of spent coca leaves (used in the Coke formula) would alert Coke's executives, who could then bring back Classic Coke sooner than they did.

Following this triumph, corporate attention once again turned to M&A activities, and a huge move to bolster its soft drinks division. PepsiCo arranged to buy Seven-Up from Philip Morris for $380. PepsiCo were buying America's third-largest soft drinks brand. This alone added seven share points to the company, and took them within striking distance of Coke. They would also have got a very strong international organisation plus almost an entire new bottling network (as only 20% of Seven-Up bottlers also bottled Pepsi).

Unfortunately, the Federal Trade Commission voted unanimously to oppose the deal. PepsiCo were left to buy the international unit of Seven-Up Co. for $246 million in cash. In 1987, PepsiCo's total sales of over $11 billion were almost 50% greater than those of The Coca-Cola Company and twenty-two times greater than the year PepsiCo had been formed.

The early 1990s saw PepsiCo broaden its beverages product range by latching onto emerging trends. A range of ready-to-drink teas developed in tandem with Thomas J. Lipton was launched in 1992, followed a year later by the test marketing of Aquafina water and the overseas launch of Pepsi Max. Frito-Lay continued to extend its DSD system, with new offerings such as Wavy Lays Original and Au Gratin flavours. On the restaurants side, East Side Mario's was acquired along with the D'Angelo Sandwich Shops chain. In 1994, following the success of the Lipton deal, new partnerships were agreed with Starbucks to develop ready-to-drink coffee beverages, and with Proctor & Gamble to use the Citrus Hill trademark.

By 1996 sales had reached $20 billion. The national rollout of Aquafina and the purchase of the Cracker Jack snack brand added more. A year later, the top-line took a hit as the restaurants division was spun off as Tricon Global Restaurants Inc. - soon to be renamed Yum! and locked into a lifetime contract to sell Pepsi beverage brands). The money from the spin-off was almost immediately put to good use with the acquisition of Tropicana (at $3.3 billion, the largest in PepsiCo's history). Pepsi's Tropicana could take the orange juice fight to Coca-Cola's Minute Maid. PepsiCo was now such a large beverages and snacks company that it contributed more to the 1998 sales growth of America's supermarkets, mass merchandisers and drug stores than any other packaged goods company.

The 21st-century began with more of the same. The Pepsi Challenge was revived, and a host of new products in fast-growing categories introduced. The standout development was a $13 billion share swap merger - a takeover in all but name - with The Quaker Oats Company, primarily for its Gatorade brand. Gatorade had a massive 84% share of the sports drink category that PepsiCo had tried and failed to crack. PepsiCo rounded out its beverage portfolio by purchasing a majority stake in the South Beach Beverage Company, for its SoBe brand. By 2003, PepsiCo was the fourth-largest food and beverage company in the world, behind Nestlé, Kraft and Unilever.

How International Are They?

Given the company's precarious early existence, it was not until 1934 that Pepsi opened its first bottling plant outside the US, Montreal serviced French Canada, where Pepsi holds the lead over Coca-Cola to this day. Their next plants, in Cuba and the Dominican Republic, were typical of a 'baby steps' approach (i.e. keeping close to the US) by an American company expanding abroad. In 1940 Walter Mack poached William B. Forsythe from the Coca-Cola Export Corporation. He immediately expanded Pepsi's overseas footprint, heading for markets where Coca-Cola was either absent or had not yet become firmly established. Thus Latin America, the Philippines, South Africa, the Middle East and the Far East all became strong markets for Pepsi. Between 1945 and 1950, Forsythe opened up fifty-six foreign markets for the Pepsi-Cola brand. This increased export sales by 45% in 1946 and another 70% the year after.

Future president Donald Kendall made his name during the 1950s pushing the company's export side. He put into action Alfred Steele's strategy of expanding massively Pepsi's overseas business. During Kendall's first three years, Pepsi International opened a new bottling plant abroad at the staggering rate of one every 11.5 days. The outcome was that an international bottler network numbering 70 in 1957 had risen to 278 by 1962. Pepsi was now available in nearly a hundred countries and international sales accounted for half of Pepsi-Cola's total revenue. Having run out of places to go where Coke wasn't, attention turned to Europe and bottling partnerships with big local players such as Britain's Schweppes, France's Perrier and the Netherland's Heineken.

In 1966, Pepsi entered the large Japanese market followed by deals negotiated with Communist governments in Rumania and Yugoslavia. These were achieved soon after head cheerleader Richard Nixon poured Pepsi down Soviet leader Khrushchev's throat in Moscow. But Kendall's crowning glory came in 1972 when, following up on Richard Nixon's Kremilin tasting, he negotiated Pepsi-Cola as the first foreign product sold with official approval in the USSR. It was a massive coup and gave Pepsi a huge advantage in what would become one of the world's fastest-growing soft drinks markets. The only downside was that Pepsi got paid in vodka! They were given the exclusive rights to import Stolichnaya Russian vodka into the US.

In 1973, Richard Nixon, now promoting Pepsi from the Oval Office, got the brand into Nationalist China and Cambodia ahead of Coca-Cola. However, a million-dollar bottling plant in Saigon did not survive long enough to pay back its somewhat optimistic investment. The company got serious about building an overseas business for its snacks division, setting up Foods International to markets snack foods abroad. Unlike many companies, Pepsi International took a hands-on role in marketing their brands overseas. They worked with one advertising agency, J. Walter Thompson, for all the various markets, but did not mandate the use of global ads everywhere. Footage from ads shot in various major markets was pooled together and local operating companies could make their own ads by using whatever snippets took their fancy.

International expansion continued apace for the next decade. A highlight was the agreement with China to begin production of Pepsi-Cola in 1982. Three years later Pepsi beverages were available in nearly 150 countries while company snack foods had expanded at a rather more sedate pace - to ten international markets. The firm's growing complexity prompted the first of several reorganisations: beverage operations were combined into one structural entity, PepsiCo Worldwide Beverages, while snack foods were combined under PepsiCo Worldwide Foods.

After signing a joint venture agreement in India in 1988 to bottle Pepsi, international expansion focussed more on the snacks side. Partnerships and acquisitions were the preferred method rather than the difficult task of snack foods start-ups. They signed a partnership with Hostess Foods in Canada. In 1989, they acquired two of Britain's leading snack food companies, Walkers Crisps and Smiths Crisps. While Smiths had seen better days, Walkers would become the leading light in the PepsiCo snacks empire, building up a dominant position in the British salty snacks category. The next year PepsiCo acquired a controlling interest in Mexico's largest cookie company. In 1991 they entered the chocolate business, with the purchase of Poland's leading local firm, Wedel SA, soon after the fall of the communist government. The same year PepsiCo and General Mills formed a joint company, Snack Ventures Worldwide, to tackle jointly the mainland European market.

In 1995 PepsiCo began the process of making Lay's a global brand. They introduced it into twenty markets around the world, although still met local needs, for example by producing a cheese-less version of Cheetos in China. More acquisitions achieved leading snack positions in several South American markets. Meanwhile the Tropicana brand, already significant in China and twenty-one other overseas markets, was rolled out into the huge Indian market. Due to the acquisitions of North American-centric companies such as Tropicana, Quaker Oats and SoBe, by 2003 the percentage of total sales coming from outside North America was down to a surprisingly low 32%.

How Are They Structured?

The evolution of the structure of PepsiCo has been driven by the company's acquisition and international expansion policies. In 1984, when transportation and sporting goods were sold off, the company adopted a three-division structure: soft drinks, snack foods and restaurants. Each division had its own international unit. When the restaurants were spun off in 1997, the structure was reduced to two global divisions - snacks and soft drinks, each of which accounted for approximately 50% of company sales. 25% of beverages sales, compared to 33% of snack food sales, came from international markets.

Following its acquisition, Tropicana was initially run as a third division, alongside the now renamed Pepsi-Cola and Frito-Lay soft drinks and snacks divisions. The next structural change came in 1999, when the company spun off 60% of its North American, Canadian, Russian, and other overseas bottling operations as the Pepsi Bottling Group. The combination of decades of above-average growth from Frito-Lay, strong snacks acquisitions and the spin-off of bottling meant that: the Frito-Lay division was contributing 62% of sales, Pepsi-Cola 26% and Tropicana 12%. While Pepsi-Cola was still sub-divided into Pepsi-Cola North America and Pepsi-Cola International; the greater size and greater complexity of the snacks side meant Frito-Lay was structured into Frito-Lay North America, Frito-Lay Europe/Africa/Middle East and Frito-Lay Latin America/Asia Pacific/Australia.

Following its 2001 acquisition, Quaker Oats was effectively split into three. Frito-Lay North America created a unit dedicated to opportunities in the broader $50 billion market for convenient foods, combining Frito-Lay's cookies, crackers, nuts, meat snacks and Cracker Jack treats with Quaker's granola bars, fruit and oatmeal bars, energy bars and rice snacks. This unit generated nearly $1 billion in revenues.

Gatorade was eagerly snatched up by the Pepsi-Cola division, which had also subsumed Tropicana. The remainder of Quaker, consisting mostly of breakfast cereals, grain products and the Aunt Jemima brand was run as a separate division. In a cosmetic change, the two main divisions were renamed worldwide snacks and worldwide beverages. In 2003, just to keep it interesting, all the business's international components were consolidated into a new division, PepsiCo International, leaving Frito-Lay North America, PepsiCo Beverages North America and Quaker Foods North America to tackle the North American market.

What Have They Been Doing Recently?

2004

Management's challenge in 2004 was to move from a collection of acquired businesses to one cohesive new PepsiCo. Strategically, the new company defined its three distinct competitive advantages:

- Big, muscular brands. Muscular was an interesting choice of words for an assortment of soft drinks, potato chips and granola brands. And PepsiCo did have a lot of them: sixteen with sales of over $1 billion, which was more than any other food and beverage company
- Proven ability to innovate and create differentiated products. While this was undoubtedly true, it's hard to demonstrate PepsiCo was better than any of their peer companies. The company divided its innovation efforts into three distinct types
- Type A – flavour extensions, including seasonal in-and-out products such as Mountain Dew Pitch Black for Halloween

- Type B – New sub-brands of existing brands, delivering additional benefits or meeting niche needs, such as Tostitos Scoops and Tropicana Light'n'Healthy
- Type C – Completely new platforms such as Quaker Milk Chillers and Tropicana Fruit Integrity

The pipeline would be skewed towards Types B and C (due to their greater longevity), although there was a higher failure rate, particularly in Type C's powerful go-to-market systems. The new PepsiCo, thanks to its recent acquisitions, now had the full range of go-to-market systems. The crown jewels were the direct store delivery (DSD) capabilities in the US, UK and Mexico for the salty snack products. Nobody else in the category had anything this powerful: the Sabritas organisation in Mexico called on over 700,000 outlets, almost every store in the country.

Naturally, given the acquisitions, benefits were sought in collaboration - between categories - within the retail environment and in back-office harmonisation. The in-store component, called PepsiCo's Power of One, involved anything from joint Superbowl Sunday promotions between Pepsi and Frito-Lay, to Breakfast Bundling tie-ups between Quaker and Tropicana. Behind the scenes, the Business Process Transformation project was launched. This wide-ranging initiative aimed to harmonise billing, purchasing and logistics and also encompassed best practice harmonisation of sales and marketing processes, together with a consolidated approach to gleaning insights into consumers and customers.

The new PepsiCo had a good 2004, growing volume by 6%, with revenues were 8% up to $29.3 billion. The new PepsiCo International division, operating in over 200 countries, was now marginally the largest in the company at 34% of sales. It delivered over 50% of the growth, justifying management's faith that the majority of its future growth would come from abroad. However, margins would need to improve as the division only contributed 22% of operating profit. Frito-Lay North America was the goldmine, contributing nearly 40% of the profit from 33% of the sales. Within the total product portfolio, over a hundred lines displayed the Smart Spot logo, identifying products that contribute to healthier lifestyles. This range grew at double the rate of the remaining fun for you products. It was slated to provide over 50% of new product revenues from the North American market in the coming years.

Within the divisions, Frito-Lay North America grew revenue 5% (coming on top of 6% in 2003). PepsiCo International's revenue grew by 14%, (snacks volume up 8%, beverages up 12%), both product categories doing best in the Asia/Pacific region (growing 14% and 15% respectively). PepsiCo Beverages

North America increased volume by 3% and revenue by 7%. These increases were driven by double-digit increases in Gatorade, Aquafina and Propel, together with the launch of a range of Tropicana branded fruit juices distributed via the bottler system. Within the US beverages business, nearly 70% of profit came from the 37% of sales accounted for by the non-carbonated brands. These accounted for almost all the division's growth. Bringing up the rear, with a turnover of only $1.5 billion, was the Quaker Foods North America rump business, which had managed only a cumulative 4% growth over the previous two years.

2005

With volume up 7% and revenue by 11% (both boosted slightly by taking a 53rd week into its accounting year), progress in the new PepsiCo was more than satisfactory. Encouragingly, progress was made on all nearly all fronts - no division recorded less than a 4% volume increase. Pepsi International again led the way, growing snacks volume by 7% and beverages by 11%. A series of acquisitions in the European region boosted the company's snacks presence in markets such as Poland and Germany. PepsiCo took full ownership of Snack Ventures Europe, Europe's largest snack food company, from their partner General Mills. This gave more latitude to develop the European snack foods strategy as it saw fit. Snacks and foods now made up nearly three-quarters of PepsiCo International's revenues.

The three divisions operating in the US market encountered starkly different issues. The previously slumbering Quaker Foods North America was star of the show. It recorded a 9% volume increase on the back of growth in Oatmeal, Aunt Jemima, Rice-a-Roni, and Cap'n Crunch rising Kraken-like from the depths to record a high single-digit increase. Frito-Lay North America had another good year, helped by the addition of another 475 new distribution routes to the DSD system, the biggest increase for a decade.

In PepsiCo Beverages North America, however, all was not well. The 4% sales increase was made up of a 16% increase in the non-carbonated range, compensating for a decline in the carbonated brands (although diet formats were still growing, in an above-average warm summer). The core brands of Pepsi-Cola and Mountain Dew were in decline, despite a host of innovations. While Pepsi was still the number two US supermarket food brand behind Coke, the acquisition strategy that had brought in the numbers three and four brands, Tropicana and Gatorade, was looking smarter by the day. Senior management shrugged off charges that they were competing in a declining soda category by switching attention to a 2.5% increase in a category they called Total Liquid Refreshment

Beverages. As its definition excluded coffee, alcohol, trap water and bulk water, it really wasn't all that total.

Elsewhere, the Business Process Transformation project was ready to go live in January 2006. The Smart Spot initiative, applied to over 250 lines thanks to health-based product reformulations, also extended into the activity side of the calorie equation. PepsiCo was the first major food and beverage company to promote more active lifestyles via its S.M.A.R.T. programme: five steps for healthier living supported by a major television advertising campaign.

2006

With volume gains of over 5% and revenue up 8%, PepsiCo was a growth machine. It averaged 8% top-line growth over the previous five years, better than any other major food and beverage company. PepsiCo now had number one or number two positions in eighteen categories of snacks, beverages and foods. However, it was not all sweetness and light. Not only had the declines in the core US carbonated brands not been reversed, they had accelerated, down 2%. The booming non-carbonated side was bolstered by the acquisition of Naked Juice and an agreement with Ocean Spray to market, bottle and distribute single-serve cranberry juice products.

In contrast to the US woes, beverages were doing quite nicely in PepsiCo International. They were up another 9% due mainly to double-digit increases in markets such as China - where Pepsi was the leading soft drink - Russia, Argentina and Venezuela. With the snacks side also growing 9% in many of the same markets, PepsiCo International now had 18 countries with revenues of at least $300 million. It was generating 41% of company sales and an improving 36% of operating profit. Gatorade was now in 42 markets. Tropicana, which was more difficult to extend internationally as it was not shipped to bottlers as a concentrate, was in 27 countries. This was only five more than when PepsiCo had bought it.

Frito-Lay North America had a poor year by its standards, growing volumes only by 1% due to declines in both the Lays and Doritos brands. This was counterbalanced by growth in healthier offerings such as SunChips and Quaker Rice Cakes. The launches of Tostitos Multigrain and Flat Earth vegetable and fruit crisps showed which way the wind was blowing in the salty snacks category. PepsiCo was promoting a healthier eating agenda but Lays' switch to sunflower oil was an unconvincing support. PepsiCo's new initiatives in 2006 - working with the Clinton Foundation and the American Heart Association to develop policies for selling beverages and snacks in American schools - probably were not likely to drive growth of Lays or Pepsi. Two-thirds of the company's growth in North

America came from Smart Spot products. This prompted the company to target achieving 50% of total North American sales from such lines by 2010.

PepsiCo had multiple routes-to-market. This meant they were not as dependent on their major retail customers as more traditional American food companies such as Kellogg's and General Mills. Wal-Mart was their single largest customer, accounting for 9% of total sales and 13% of sales in North America. Their next four biggest customers accounted for another 13% between them. Overall this represented a fairly healthy position for PepsiCo.

2007

While 12% growth looked amazing given the beginnings of the global economic crisis, the underlying figures were a bit more realistic. Only 3% of the growth came from volume. Robust price increases, particularly in North American beverages, added 4%. 3% came from a slew of small and mid-sized acquisitions while currency movements contributed the final 2%. Cause for celebration was a new addition to the list of $1 billion-plus mega-brands: Fritos Corn Chips.

A change of CEO heralded the usual corporate restructuring in November 2007. PepsiCo International was shorn of its booming Latin American components. PepsiCo Americas Beverages was created to combine the North and Latin American businesses, as was PepsiCo Americas Foods, which brought together Frito-Lay North America, Quaker Foods North America, and the Latin American foods and snacks businesses. Despite being somewhat dismembered, PepsiCo International still managed to be the largest contributor to the company's sales and profit growth (even when the numbers were recalculated into the new structure for the entire year). However, a shift took place. PepsiCo International's biggest individual components, Sabritas in Mexico and the UK's Walkers, both suffered declines. Walkers' downturn was attributed to 'market pressures', something which shareholders might think their executives were paid to manage. However, double-digit growth in Russia, Turkey, China, India and the Middle East more than covered these losses. International beverages continued their usual trajectory, growing another 8%.

In North America, both Frito-Lay and Quaker had decent years, growing their volume by 3% and 2% respectively. However, another mid-single-digit decline in Lays compounded worries that there was an underlying market shift taking place. Fortunately, the company seemed well stocked with healthier snacks and had significant growth from both Doritos and SunChips. The worry in PepsiCo Americas Beverages was an accelerated decline in sales of carbonated soft beverages, this time 3% down. Pepsi was the main culprit as Mountain Dew held steady and Sierra Mist grew slightly. The good news was a booming still beverages portfolio. A double-digit increase for Lipton's Tea prompted an extension of the contract with Unilever. Aquafina, Propel and SoBe Life Water enjoyed similar growth. There was much excitement with the Gatorade brand. This not only grew double digit but also developed an exclusive deal with Tiger Woods for a signature line of sports performance beverages, beginning with Gatorade Tiger. One hopes they employed a good contracts lawyer.

2008

Even more than the previous year, the impressive top-line growth of 10% masked a less appealing story. The business had mostly stagnant volumes (up 1%), and had pushed prices up (6%) well ahead of the overall inflation rate. They took the opportunity of the crisis to pick up some well-priced acquisitions (up 2%) and benefited slightly from a strengthening dollar (up 1%). Six percent price increases in the middle of the worst recession for decades are nice if you can make them stick and hold onto the volume, but it was definitely risky.

In November 2007 PepsiCo had been re-organised into three divisions. One of these, PepsiCo Americas Foods, contributed nearly half the company's sales. Most of the company's performance monitoring happened at a lower level. This led to the suspicion that all the re-organisation had done was to add another layer. The six divisions that actually did the work were:

- Frito-Lay North America
- Quaker Foods North America
- Latin American Foods
- PepsiCo Americas Beverages
- UK/Europe
- Middle East/Africa/Asia

Within the year, none of the Americas-based divisions managed to grow volume whereas UK/Europe – just as affected by the recession as North America – grew by 4%. Walkers enjoyed a turnaround, while the emerging markets (dominated by Middle East/Africa/Asia) grew volume by 13%, albeit heavily acquisition assisted. So what was going on at PepsiCo Americas Beverages? Volume again declined a depressing 3%. This performance, perhaps unsurprisingly, was made up of a reasonable-looking 4% growth in Latin America, offset by a somewhat shocking 5% decline in North America. Pepsi sank another 5% while the normally reliable Sierra Mist also fell back slightly. The non-carbonated range had previously been seen by the company as good for double-digit growth. But it actually declined by 6%. This was despite a complete brand makeover for Gatorade. Maybe such makeovers (also rolled out for Pepsi, Mountain Dew and Sierra Mist), were meant to make brand managers look busy whilst failing to understand the underlying problems. Similarly within Frito-Lay, the Lays brand was now in a rut of continued mid-digit declines. In this it had been joined by Doritos. Moves into nut products and dips were all well and good, but you cannot let your biggest brands keep declining year after year.

Fortunately, all was in relatively good shape abroad. UK/Europe snacks volume grew by 16%, led by a double-digit increase in Russia. Beverages powered forwards 17%, of which half came from acquisitions. The most important of these was of Russia's leading juice company, Lebedyansky, and the UK's V Water. Within Asia/Middle East/Africa, both snacks and beverages grew volumes double digit with little to no help from acquisitions made within the year. The bad news for shareholders was that, despite an increase of 6% in the division's operating revenue, total company operating profit was down 3% (thanks to PepsiCo's share of a major restructuring charge within the Pepsi Bottling Group).

2009

The big news, coming only ten years after spinning off a majority stake in Pepsi Group Bottlers, was the announcement of the merging into PepsiCo of the two anchor bottlers, Pepsi Bottling Group and PepsiAmericas. This was at a cost in cash and shares of around $8 billion. The usual management-speak explaining the move, 'to create a more agile, efficient, innovative and competitive beverage system', can be read as, 'given an even worse performance by PepsiCo Americas Beverages which declined 6%, if you can't sell Pepsi-Cola then we will'. The merger, once finalised, would make PepsiCo a $60 billion company, although one that would now have to grapple with an asset-rich, margin-poor bottling empire.

In anticipation of the deal being approved, a new strategy was outlined. It consisted of six key elements:

- Expand the global leadership position of the snacks business. Right from day one of the original Pepsi and Frito-Lay merger, snacks had been the key category and by now beverages accounted for barely a third of sales. The snacks business had long been the more vibrant: with an ideal mix of global capability and the ability to tailor products to meet local tastes. Potato chips do not lend themselves to regional or global sourcing, given the short shelf life and transportation inefficiencies a fact PepsiCo had been leveraging to the full).

- Ensure sustainable, profitable growth in global beverages. The key element to this part of the strategy was the hope that the bottling merger, plus the brand makeovers, would turn around a now slumping US business. Developing markets, emerging categories and positive nutrition beverages were seen as opportunities. Everyone else thought the same. So this element of the new strategy was more a hope than a clear path to growth.

3) • Unleash The Power of One. Coming a mere 48 years after the original Pepsi / Frito-Lay merger created the potential for The Power of One, it was overdue for this be turned to a competitive advantage.

4) • Rapidly expand the Good for You category. As less than 25% of the annual sales was accounted for by such products, this was another strategic thrust that was not before time. Key to its success was the newly announced R&D revamp. Here a new team of clinicians, epidemiologists and food scientists were recruited to take the company beyond formulation of new flavours into the actual underlying science of nutrition.

5) • Continue to deliver on environmental and sustainability issues. Not new for PepsiCo and not market-leading, more the avoidance of negative press than a genuine growth strategy.

6) • 'Cherish our Associates and Develop the Leadership to Sustain Our Growth'. Generic stuff.

The announced acquisition of the two main bottlers, together with a new strategy, raised the stakes for PepsiCo after a not very inspiring year. Total volume was down with another 5% piled onto pricing (which were eaten up anyway by adverse currency movements). Frito-Lay North America, by far the company's largest profit contributor, inched volume ahead by 1%. This was entirely due to new ventures, including dips and the joint venture with Sabra. Lays was still in decline while Ruffles was down a high single-digit. PepsiCo Beverages North America had a dreadful year. Non-carbonated beverages portfolio fell off a cliff, down by a massive 11%. Chief culprits were Aquafina and Gatorade, both down double digit. Pepsi seemed to be coming off worse in the US water market, up against Danone, Nestlé and Coke's Dasani while Gatorade was in the midst of a brand re-launch. The brand's name was changed from Gatorade to the G series - GI, GII and GIII. Changing a brand name, especially such a well-established one, is always a big risk in a category with a lot of impulse purchasing. If busy consumers don't see it or recognise it, they won't go looking. One hopes the marketing department knew what they were doing. The only bright spot was in Asia/Middle East/Africa where snacks volume grew 9% and beverages 8%. Even this contained the worrying nugget that business in China had basically stalled.

2010

The impact of the bottling acquisitions - which cost the company the thick end of $1 billion in merger and acquisition charges and fees – was immediately apparent, and in several ways:

- Top-line sales shot up 33% to nearly $58 billion
- Operating profit margin percentage shot down from 18.6% to 14.4%, reflecting the lower margins made by bottling operations
- Beverages now accounted for 51% of total sales
- The US market now accounted for 53% of sales
- While PepsiCo Americas Foods was still the largest division at 37% of sales, PepsiCo Americas Beverages was now not far behind at 35%
- The move lowered the margin and made the company more dependent on the US soft drinks market, which had been in the doldrums since 2007. Where were the upsides?

Looking into the divisional performances, the eye was drawn to PepsiCo Americas Beverages, where top-line sales had more than doubled. Three key components made up this growth pattern:

- Inclusion of the bottled sales rather than concentrate sales in the acquired bottlers.
- The sales volume of brands distributed by the acquired bottlers and not owned by PepsiCo.
- The organic sales volume performance of PepsiCo brands.

Leaving aside the sales benefit of bottling brands - just a transfer of the bottlers' net sales - total volume for the company increased by 10%. The bad news was that the inclusion of other companies' brands more than accounted for the entire growth, meaning PepsiCo's own brands had declined by 1%. Not exactly what the doctor ordered. Digging deeper, carbonated beverages did just as badly in the first year of PepsiCo running the bottling, as they did when the bottlers had been in charge - a 3% decline. But at least the rot was stopped on non-carbonated volumes. These grew 1%, although barely making a dent on recovering the cataclysmic losses of 2009. Gatorade, or G as we must learn to call it, recovered around half of the previous year's losses, while Aquafina continued to go down the drain. A good increase in Lipton's Teas was balanced by a poor year by Tropicana.

Frito-Lay North America, now shorn of the Quaker snack bars, which were sent back to the Quaker Foods unit, slightly declined. For once this was not due to Lays, which had its first year of growth in a while. The unit was looking becalmed with brands taking turns to have good and bad years, plus the problem besetting Quaker Foods North America, which was going nowhere fast. Other divisions seemed to be able to do a better job with snacks. Latin America Foods grew by 4% while snacks in Europe grew by 2%. In Asia/Middle/East/Africa a 15% growth was due to strong performances in India, China and the Middle East. A similar story existed for beverages. They grew, net of bottler acquisitions, by 5% in Europe. This was driven by Russia (where PepsiCo acquired WBD, Russia's largest food and beverage company) and Turkey, and by 7% in Asia/Middle/East/Africa. The company was gaining new traction in India and China.

If sales performance after the bottling acquisition was debatable, it was clear the strategic issues facing the company were now mounting. One only has to look at some of the commitments the company made to see that their brand portfolio - bulging with nineteen $1 billion brands – was facing some strong consumer headwinds. A number of what were hoped to be key decisions were made:

- Reduce the average amount of sodium per serving in key global food brands, in key countries, by 25% by 2015, compared to a 2006 baseline
- Reduce the average amount of saturated fat per serving in key global food brands, in key countries, by 15% by 2020, compared to a 2006 baseline
- Reduce the amount of added sugar per serving in key global beverage brands, in key countries, by 25% by 2022, compared to a 2006 baseline
- Display calorie count and key nutrients on food and beverage packaging by 2012
- Advertise to children under 12 only products that meet our global science-based nutrition standards
- Eliminate the direct sale of full-sugar soft drinks to primary and secondary schools around the globe by 2012
- Increase the range of foods and beverages that offer solutions for managing calories, like portion sizes
- Invest in our business and R&D to expand our offerings of more affordable, nutritionally relevant products for under-served and lower-income communities

Only a couple of these could be classified as growth strategies rather than decline preventatives. But leaving that aside, PepsiCo was late to the party compared to companies such as Nestlé. Re-segmenting a portfolio that in past times had been cheerfully labelled Fun for You into three categories: Fun for You, Better for You and Good for You did not change the fact that the company's core sales and profitability rested on salty snacks and sugary beverages. The announcement of an increased R&D investment in sweetener technologies, next-generation processing and packaging and nutritional products was several years overdue.

2011

The acquisitions of the bottlers, WBD and the enhanced agreement with the Dr Pepper Snapple Group gave a good gloss to the top-line numbers, up almost $9 billion. In truth, it was hard to see much was changing at the operational level of the pre-existing businesses. The most important unit, Frito-Lay North America, finally got a bit of traction: growing volume by 3% and sales by 6%. Still this was no return to the heady days of earlier times. Quaker Foods North America, despite having more than its fair share of the nutrition products, lost a depressing 5% volume. This was partly because of its disadvantaged position in ready-to-eat cereals where it faced the much larger General Mills and Kellogg's.

How much longer Pepsi wanted to stay in this category was a question that perhaps the company should answer. Latin America Foods pushed forwards in its advantaged markets of Mexico and Brazil. In Europe (discounting the huge impact of the WBD acquisition that added 31% to the division's volume), underlying snacks grew volume by 4%, thanks to the huge Walkers UK unit and 1% in beverages (when the 20% volume increase attributable to WBD was factored out). In Asia/Middle East/Africa, snacks were doing better than beverages, up 15% versus 5%.

But still, the big question: how was the bottling acquisition in the US working out? Its raison d'être was to kick-start the core bottling brands back into life. Unfortunately, carbonated volume, which was the prime business segment of the bottling operation, fell back again by another 2%. That non-carbonated volumes increased by 4% to leave the unit largely flat on company-owned brands was not helpful, considering that $8 billion of shareholders money had been splashed out on buying up the bottlers. The good news for the marketing department was that the Gatorade re-launch was finally paying off, with the brand up double-digit. This essentially took it back to where it had been before the bright idea of a G Series had come along.

What is Their DNA?

If Coke is the American Southern Gentleman, courteous, polite and well-mannered, then PepsiCo is the brawler from the Bronx, brought up on the wrong side of the tracks, parents of questionable morals, had to fight for everything it has and anything it wanted. While this may seem an odd way to view the world's second-largest food and beverage company, we believe its DNA does derive from a toilsome life committed to permanent struggle against a dominant and dominating competitor.

Acts Like a Challenger

For almost its entire corporate life, Pepsi-Cola and then PepsiCo has been the underdog, and even when it hasn't been, has acted like it was. This mentality is still fed by its global number two cola position in a world where there is often only really room for one. While Coke sponsors World Cups and Olympics, PepsiCo is in the trenches battling it out on Superbowl Sunday. Even where the company is completely dominant, such as in the UK with the Walkers brand, or in Mexico with Sabritas, PepsiCo has kept those businesses at the top by never getting complacent or taking its success for granted.

Irreverent

PepsiCo has a history of not taking itself, or its product categories, too seriously. It has demonstrated a good sense regarding where their products sit in people's lives, yet combines that with a fierce pride and passion for what it does. The company response to New Coke probably did more than anything to establish itself as both fun, but deadly. Similarly, PepsiCo's marketing activities for the Walkers brand have been ground-breaking: capturing the fun and irreverence of the product category and turning them into powerful drivers of sales increases. PepsiCo still manages to make huge brands feel warm, friendly and approachable, no mean feat in modern, global vastness.

Good Acquirers

There is no doubt the original merger between Pepsi-Cola and Frito-Lay was one of the most harmonious and successful mergers of the latter half of the twentieth century. The subsequent success, particularly on the sales side, has been astounding. Similarly, the acquisitions made at the end of the century of Tropicana and Quaker gave the beverages portfolio a breadth and a strength that lifted the company away from being Coke's Mini-Me. On the snacks side, Walkers and Sabritas have succeeded far beyond any potential apparent in the brands in the days before joining PepsiCo. This is in no small part due to the DSD business model for salty snacks, a model pioneered by the Frito-Lay Company before the original merger but taken to new heights by PepsiCo: they pioneered technologies such as nitrogen filled bags to improve freshness. The company has barely missed a step in its acquisition strategy.

Summary

The rise of PepsiCo within one person's lifespan from serial bankrupt to the world's second largest, and North America's largest, food and beverage company is one of the business success stories of the modern era. While we are no fans of the heroic CEO idea, it cannot be denied that a series of bold and aggressive leaders successively remade the company. Each took PepsiCo to a new level, rather than the success stemming from the brand portfolio or the business model. It was only after the Frito-Lay merger that the company's success became less dependent on the whims of forceful leaders.

Since the merger, success has been inexorable, but perhaps too much so. As we have seen, at the core US market the company has latterly stalled, with a brand portfolio seemingly out of step with market trends towards healthy eating and hydration. The company has done little to get ahead of such trends. The bottler acquisition is in danger of looking more like an act of hubris than a sound use of $8 billion of shareholders' funds. We fear that, of late, the company has actually drifted away from its DNA. It seems to regard being the second-largest food and drinks company in the world as a pinnacle of success, whereas the old Pepsi would have considered being the second-largest cola company as a grievous wrong to be righted. And are Nestlé looking over their shoulders and reacting to PepsiCo's initiatives, as Coca-Cola was made to do? Quite the opposite. Nestlé have made health and wellness a core value, while PepsiCo sets modest targets to reduce bad ingredients by 2020. Nestlé's water business is booming while Aquafina is floundering. Even Coca-Cola has stopped dancing to PepsiCo's tune. PepsiCo needs to get back to the attitude that got it to where it is today.

Reckitt Benckiser

Where Did It Come From?

The creation of Reckitt Benckiser in 1999 was more than just another merger: it was the deliberate creation of a completely new company with no nationality and a unique style of operating. But a better understanding of its subsequent impressive success can be gleaned from understanding the salient parts of the history of Reckitt & Colman Ltd and Benckiser NV.

First out of the gate was Jeremiah Colman, a miller by training, who managed a mill in Norfolk, England before buying his own mill in 1803. In an asset utilisation exercise to get the most out of his fixed investment in mill and millstones, in 1814 he bought a mustard business and added the crushing of mustard seeds to that of wheat kernels. By 1829, he had extended his reach to London and, by 1854, three years after Jeremiah's death, Colman's had constructed Britain's first mill dedicated entirely to mustard. Jeremiah's nephew James (Jeremiah being childless) had taken over the firm, having been co-opted as a partner in 1823 and, clearly sharing his uncle's partiality for asset-driven expansion into new categories, he took the firm into the manufacture of starch, laundry blue and corn flour, all leveraging the company's investment and expertise in milling.

Entry into the starch category brought Colman's into competition with another trained miller, Isaac Reckitt, who, after twenty years of unsuccessfully running a series of flour milling businesses and losing all his capital, borrowed enough from his obviously loving relatives to rent a starch works in the north of England. There he yet again failed to make his mark, until his four sons, including a chemist and a salesman, took over the key roles. For the first seven years, the business lost money and it was only when the product range was extended beyond starch that the business became viable. Unlike Colman, the Reckitt expansion strategy was not asset-led but category-led, moving beyond starch products into other emerging household product categories such as black-lead for polishing fire grates and ovens, synthetic ultramarine and washing paste. It took the business a full eighteen years to pay back Isaac's relatives, whom he only outlived by four years.

The third 19th-century industrialist involved in the genesis of Reckitt Benckiser was Johann Adam Benckiser, who founded an industrial chemicals manufacturing business in Pforzheim, Germany in 1823. Johann was a dyed-in-the-wool heavy industrialist, initially manufacturing ammonia, hydrochloric acid and ammonium chloride and subsequently acquiring a gold plating factory and setting up a pottery. In 1851, Johann co-founded a chemical plant with chemist Ludwig Reimann, seven years later relocating the business to Ludwigshafen, where it also began the production of phosphates, citric acid and other commodity chemicals.

This unlikely trio of mustard cook, household products manufacturer and chemical industrialist would bring something different to the Reckitt Benckiser party. The mustard maker's great nephew would be one of 19th-century Britain's most innovative advertisers, building leading-edge marketing skills in selling a product half of which was scraped off plates uneaten at the end of meals. The household products maker's sons recognised that a huge business could be built on the insight of making the homemaker's life easier, and embarked on a late-19th-century acquisition spree of all kinds of household goods brands while internationalising the business as early as 1864. The German industrialist's descendants, who would spend well over a century in the commodity chemicals sector, were exceptionally astute business strategists who knew how to revolutionise a business.

How Did It Evolve?

By the turn of the 20th century, Reckitt & Sons and J & J Colman were both very well established British consumer goods companies that had done well out of the ready markets of Britain's great industrial cities and from the far flung markets of the British Empire. Although J & J Colman was primarily a food company and Reckitt & Sons a household goods company, they were both still in the starch market and continually bumping up against each other in markets all over the world. In an era when trusts were seen as being eminently good business sense, the two firms finally buried the hatchet in 1913 when they formed a joint company, Atlantis Ltd, to distribute both companies' product ranges in South America.

This arrangement worked so smoothly that in 1921, when rising tariff barriers in many of their main overseas markets were choking off demand, the two companies combined all their overseas businesses in order to generate the critical mass to run manufacturing operations in key markets such as Australia, Canada and South Africa. This was a common arrangement at the time by British firms, who competed with each other tooth and nail in the British market but cooperated to the point of partnership in overseas ventures. In this instance, the working arrangements became progressively closer, culminating in the setting up in 1938 of Reckitt & Colman Ltd to manage both businesses as one, while each kept a separate stock market listing. The full financial merger did not take place until 1953, at which point the newly merged firm was joined by a major boot polish company, Chiswick Products, in which Reckitt & Sons had held joint ownership.

By this time, Reckitt & Sons had either acquired or invented for itself a number of own-brands that would go on to form the backbone of the company, such as Harpic lavatory cleaner, a booming brand acquired in 1932 when indoor toilets were fast becoming the norm, and Dettol, launched a year later. Dettol had begun as a project in 1929 to develop an antiseptic disinfectant that could be safely applied to open cuts and wounds. It was successfully tested in a maternity hospital in 1932 and launched to the general public a year later, its trump card being an endorsement by the medical profession. Further acquisitions such as the denture cleaner Steradent in 1938 had taken Reckitt & Sons further out of the kitchen and into all household products.

While the newly merged Reckitt & Colman went from strength to strength in the 1950s thanks, amongst other thing, to the advent of commercial television in Britain, it wasn't until 1956 that Benckiser, now run by the Reimann family, made the decision to diversify into consumer goods and industrial cleaning products, beginning with the launch of Calgon water softener the same year.

So, as both companies entered the 1960s, both were diversifying. For Benckiser, moves into chemically driven new consumer goods such as automatic washer and dishwasher detergent - Calgonit in 1964 and Quanto fabric softener in 1966 - made complete sense. For Reckitt & Colman, on the other hand, the trajectory was positively whimsical. It bought into the leisure industry, for example, particularly in North America. As the company mushroomed, it was constantly undergoing disruptive reorganisations with 'sprawling' being one of the kinder descriptions of the business. However, at its heart, it still had thriving businesses in food, household goods and pharmaceutical items, all sold around the world: 70% of the company's revenues came from overseas.

By the end of the 1970s, both companies faced strategic choices. Within Reckitt & Colman the decision was finally made to concentrate on the core product ranges, so it set in place a divestment strategy to rid itself of its leisure interests and various commodity-type businesses, such as its American potato-processing factory. Simultaneously, the company looked for big brand name acquisitions in its chosen areas of operation, picking up Airwick Industries, Durkee Famous Foods, with its North American-leading French's mustard, and Gold Seal, which made a range of laundry aids and bath additives. In 1989, it picked up Nenuco, a Spanish baby care company, as part of a European drive to better prepare the company for economic unification.

During the 1990s, it also made the big decision to prioritise household goods over food, beginning with the $1.3 billion transformative acquisition in 1990 of the US Boyle-Midway household goods arm of American Home Products Inc., bringing in such brands as Woolite fabric care, Wizard air fresheners, Easy-Off oven cleaner, Sani-flush toilet cleaner and Old English furniture cleaning products. This deal made Reckitt & Colman the seventh-largest household goods company in the world and fifth-largest in America, significantly shifting its business centre of gravity. This deal would be bettered in 1994 when Reckitt & Colman paid Eastman Kodak $1.55 billion to for L&F Products, half of whose turnover was accounted for by the Lysol brand. The deal catapulted Reckitt & Colman into the top four globally, but to fund it the company had to sell off the bulk of the food business, including the iconic Colman's mustard brand, sold to Unilever in 1995 for £250 million, which left only the US French's unit on the food side. But it continued to acquire strong brands such as Spray 'n Wash, while selling off weaker products without strong market share positions. Despite these sound strategic moves, there was still much investor doubt about the quality of the company's management, compounded by a disastrous 25% decline in 1998 profits owing to poor handling of the Latin American and Asian markets that generated 30% of company sales.

Meanwhile, over at Benckiser, the company was taking something of a hammering on the industrial chemicals side of the business, now a global industry dominated by huge multinationals: Benckiser had become a relative minnow, with annual sales of only $250 million. So in 1981 the still family-owned business recruited a Harvard MBA to lead the full transition out of chemicals and into a more commanding position in household goods. Over the next decade, following the chemicals divestment, the company would make 26 acquisitions, the first of which was the French firm of St. Marc in 1985. In 1987, a more transformative acquisition came with the purchase of the worldwide branded division of Ecolab Inc. for $240, which, although loss-making, Benckiser expertise would soon turn round.

Benckiser continued to acquire strong local brands, such as Italy's Mira Lanza and Panigel together with Spain's leading detergent company, S.A. Camp Group, with its memorably named leading brand, Colon. Benckiser competed with the multinational giants such as Unilever and P&G through a combination of aggressive cost cutting in the non-essentials combined with marketing strategies aimed at meeting local needs, heavily funded by big marketing budgets. In 1990, the company significantly increased its US presence with the acquisition of SmithKline Beecham's North American household products division for $106 million, which it followed up with a somewhat radical departure from household goods, buying the Margaret Astor and Lancaster cosmetics businesses for $380 million, also from SmithKline.

Almost immediately, Benckiser set about expanding its new cosmetics arm, picking up the Jovan, Germaine Monteil, Bogner cosmetics and Joop! perfumes. In 1994, Benckiser became US market leader in mass-market cosmetics with the $440 million purchase from Pfizer of the Coty business, which included brands such as Emeraude, Exclamation, Lady Stetson, L'Effleur, Sand & Sable and Wild Musk. This pushed the company cosmetics and fragrances sales of $3.4 billion to 45% of turnover, with household products and detergents accounting for the remainder. The cosmetics play finally came to a halt in 1996 when Benckiser was outbid by L'Oréal after a short but intense bidding war for Maybelline Inc., the third-largest cosmetics business in the US.

With annual sales now over $3 billion, helped by Benckiser's aggressive forays into the newly opened markets of Eastern Europe and China during the early to mid-1990s, the extended family owners began to plan for at least a partial transition to public ownership as part of a major estate and inheritance tax minimisation strategy. In 1996, Benckiser organised all its cosmetics businesses into one single holding company, Coty Inc., which it spun off with the family retaining outright ownership. In the following year, the remaining household goods and laundry division was firstly relocated to the more beneficial tax regime of the Netherlands, where it adopted the name Benckiser NV. The same year 40% of the firm went on public sale on the New York and Amsterdam stock exchanges, which brought in a handy $704 million, with Coty and other privately-held investments organised under a Benckiser holding company still owned 100% by the family.

By 1999, Reckitt & Colman and Benckiser NV were both very large companies – but each had a significant problem. Reckitt & Colman had, over a prolonged period, innovated or acquired a peerless collection of worldwide best-selling household goods brands but had questionable management, widely acknowledged not to be making the most of their portfolio. Benckiser's management, on the other hand, had the mirror-image of the problem, a management widely admired for their strategic and operational capabilities but a company which, after the Coty spin-off, had no particularly inspiring collection of brands management to practise on, beyond the exceptions of Vanish, a miracle stain removal product, and Finish dishwashing powder.

Geographically, the same was true. Reckitt & Colman was very strong in the US, Britain, the old British Empire countries, Latin America and some of the Far East, precisely where Benckiser was weak. Benckiser was strong in Continental Europe and the emerging markets of Eastern Europe and China, precisely where

Reckitt and Colman had little or no influence. A merger seemed quite a good idea from everyone's point of view. It was a marriage made, if not in Heaven, then in the boardroom of some prescient and very-well informed coporate match-maker. Or a very happy accident.

How International Is It?

Reckitt Benckiser came into being as an international company thanks to the joint efforts of the pre-merged entities, so international expansion was low on the management agenda. Much more important was launching their powerbrands into as many markets as possible as quickly as possible. By 2003, Reckitt Benckiser was selling its products in some 180 countries and had operations in 60 countries. In 2003, sales were split by region as follows:

- Western Europe – 47%
- North America – 27%
- Asia-Pacific – 12%
- Latin America – 4%
- Rest of World – 10%.

Clearly, Latin America and Asia-Pacific were relatively under-developed, particularly in comparison with a competitor like Unilever. But Reckitt Benckiser, by avoiding the large but intensely competitive laundry products market, prioritised its international strategy more by regional and local levels of category development than by the number of pins in a map.

How Did It Build Its Modern Business?

On 27th July 1999, the merger of Reckitt & Colman and Benckiser created a business with sales of more than £3 billion, making it the world's fourth-biggest manufacturer of household cleaning and personal care products behind only Procter & Gamble, Unilever and Colgate. The brand list included the likes of Harpic toilet cleaner, Mr Sheen furniture polish, Cherry Blossom shoe polish, Disprin, Dettol, Immac hair remover, Finish, Calgon and Vanish. Although 59% of the shares went to Reckitt investors - Reckitt & Colman was the substantially the bigger of the two - the new company was biased very much in Benckiser's favour, even though the merged company was based in London and had Alan Dalby, chairman of Reckitt for the past four years, continuing in the role.

But the key CEO role went to Benckiser's Bart Becht. His entire executive team, apart from one outside hire, were also Benckiser managers.

Right from its first day, Reckitt Benckiser had three overriding priorities:

- To focus the brand portfolio into five categories: Surface Care, Fabric Care Dishwashing, Home Care, and Health & Personal Care
- To reduce costs
- To deploy the Benckiser strategy and operating style on everything in the Reckitt & Colman brand portfolio that survived the category cull

A disposal programme was immediately instigated, which by 2001 had got rid of virtually all the unwanted elements of the portfolio. An acquisition programme ran in parallel to fill in geographic or product gaps in the five categories, such as an Indonesian pest control business (pest control having become a Reckitt & Colman strength) and Oxy, the leading Korean household goods business.

Much more crucial to the future success of Reckitt Benckiser than portfolio tweaking would be the second and third priorities. Reckitt Benckiser was set up from the outset as a lean, no-frills organisation in a Spartan and anonymous office block on the outskirts of London. In the first two years, the company created two permanent hit teams, Squeeze and X-trim, dedicated full time to cutting costs across the business. The remit of Squeeze was to look at the detailed design of products and find ways to squeeze out costs without adversely affecting the utility or efficacy. In the new Reckitt Benckiser, product costs were far too important to be left to the whims of individual brand management teams. By having one dedicated team working across the business, synergistic cost savings could be found and applied across a variety of brands and categories. The X-trim team focused on saving costs elsewhere in the business, from global materials sourcing to reducing the number of office photocopiers.

The Benckiser strategy applied to the new business had not changed since first formulated in the mid-1990s and it was deceptively simple:

- A disproportionate focus on brands that were either number one or two in categories with above-average growth prospects
- Grow categories and brand share via an unrelenting programme of incremental improvement innovations, executed with great speed, and above-average marketing spends
- Focus mainly on organic growth. Acquisitions, as had been the case soon after the merger, would only be considered if targets had a great strategic fit, either regionally or within the portfolio, if Reckitt Benckiser could

clearly add value beyond the capabilities of existing owners and if there
was a clear path to enhanced shareholder value

The implementation began in 2002 with the introduction of the concept of
'powerbrands', defined as leading global brands in high-growth categories with
disproportionately high margins. Powerbrands would receive disproportionately
high marketing spends – well above category averages – and would be the priorities for management and resources across all markets. They would be managed
centrally in terms of brand image and strategic direction, but each market would
be allowed to push for local tweaks in order to make the brand more relevant and
successful at the local level: kitchen surface cleaning products would be formulated differently in India than in Italy to cope with the different kinds of food spills.
The company also believed strongly in growing the categories in which they
competed and so spent substantial sums promoting the ownership of dishwashers, which it did not sell, as that would drive sales of dishwasher tablets, which it
did.

Behind the powerbrands would be a constant stream of incremental innovation, usually aimed at offering more convenience for consumers for which hefty
brand premiums would be charged. An example was the launch of Finish Powerball 2-in-1 dishwasher tablets with an integrated rinse aid. The follow-up, Finish
Powerball 3-in-1, also included the salt consumers were adding to their dishwashers. The research effort was primarily consumer research with a big emphasis
on in-home studies, rather than technical R&D research. Reckitt Benckiser had a
fairly low level of R&D investment, 1.8% of sales or less, believing that growth
came from multiple small improvements based on studying products use rather
than rare but big improvements based on the discovery of some wonder new ingredient. At the time of the merger, around 20% of sales were derived from
products launched in the previous three years: this would quickly rise to 30%
and then reach 40% by 2003.

The company also believed in operating with great speed. Innovations in a
country would be evaluated within weeks and either quickly taken off the market
or scaled up for launch in multiple countries before competitors even knew what
was happening. Products would be rolled out even before product costs had been
optimised - the Squeeze team could look after that later. To facilitate such speed,
the company operated with an extremely flat organisation and had a culture of
making decisions and moving to action in the first meeting in which any topic
was discussed. This required a certain type of manager which the company took
great pains to find, often freely admitting that it would rather leave a post vacant

rather than fill it a candidate who was only half-right. Reckitt Benckiser was not a company for shrinking violets or office politics.

It would be this unique strategy and style that drove performance in the first few years of operation, when no major acquisitions were made or new brands launched. By 2003, net sales revenue stood 28% above the 1999 level, while operating profit had increased by 90%, pushing a 12% margin to above 18%, despite marketing spends as a percentage of sales that were increased every year.

Sales in 2003 were split between the five product categories as follows:

- Fabric care: 27%. Number one worldwide in fabric treatment and Wwater softener categories
- Surface care: 20%. Number one worldwide in disinfectant cleaning and lavatory cleaning.
- Home care: 15%. Number two worldwide in air care, shoe care and pest control.
- Health and personal care: 15%. Dettol was the world leader in antiseptics bought for use at home; Veet was the world leader in depilatories.
- Dishwashing: 14%. Number one worldwide in automatic dishwashing.

How Is It Structured?

Reckitt Benckiser began life in 1999 with a regional management structure in which country managers reported into regions or sub-regions. For example, the United Kingdom would report into Northern Europe, which reported into Western Europe. In 2003, as the company got a handle on the different issues in the different markets, it moved to a hybrid regional/market development structure. Thus, the Eastern Europe region was combined with Western Europe to create one European area. To combine all of the company's lesser-developed markets into a single management entity, it created the developing markets area covering Asia, Africa, the Middle East and Latin America. The remaining regions of North America (household and food) and Australia/New Zealand were combined to form North America and Australia Area. Alongside the regional structure there was also a category development function, which managed the categories and powerbrands at a global level. There were subsidiary management roles within each region.

What Has It Been Doing Recently?

2004

Reckitt Benckiser celebrated five years of unbroken success since its formation with 10% growth in the year at constant exchange rates. The growth was fairly evenly spread around the world, with Europe growing by 8%, North America and Australia by 9% and developing markets by 16%. Operating margins expanded a full 1.3 percentage points up to 19.6%, the company having almost tripled its annual operating profit since 1999. Much of the increase in margins came from increases in gross margin, up from an industry-trailing 46.4% in 1999 to an industry-leading 54.8%.

This dramatic expansion had come from the combination of robust pricing of the many innovations together with the Squeeze team's reduction of product costs, an annual £2 million alone coming from a redesign of the Harpic and Lysol bottles, with plastic and shipping costs going down as on-shelf visibility and squeezability went up. Wider margins had also enabled the doubling of media spend over the previous five years. But as usual, there were profitability challenges in developing markets: the company delivered only 7% compared to more than 20% elsewhere.

With no significant acquisitions or new brand launches in the year, growth had come from the business-as-usual application of the strategy: focus on the powerbrands, backed by huge numbers of incremental innovations, rolled out to as many markets as possible. Within fabric care, which grew by 9%, the highlight was the patented new formulation behind Vanish Oxi Action Max, which was more effective against greasy stains than chlorine bleach. The brand was also extended by the launches of Vanish Oxi Action gel and Vanish Carpet Cleaner, which gained leadership of the European market, tripling the size of the category in Germany. Vanish was now sold in more than 40 countries; it had been launched in the UK in 1999.

Elsewhere in the portfolio, health and personal care led the way, growing by 15% in the year with multiple successes including the launch of Veet Rasera, a hair removal cream that acted in only three minutes and required no shaving. This doubled the brand share in North America, 60% of sales coming from consumers who had previously shaved, which grew the category. Also doing well was the antacid brand Gaviscon, which was being rolled out across Europe, and the patented opioid-dependency treatment Suboxone. Foods, the Cinderella of the company, with sales of less than £200 million, made up almost entirely by French's mustard and Frank's Red Hot Sauce, spiced up the year by growing by 9%.

This was a performance that showed the strength of the company's basic consumer philosophy: 'to understand everyday irritations that drive you nuts. We want to develop even better household cleaning, health and personal care products that solve those problems, make your life easier, and earn your trust and loyalty'. Why hadn't Reckitt Benckiser's competitors thought of this one?

2005

In what was a mildly disappointing year by Reckitt Benckiser's standards, sales grew by 8%, but only by 6% at constant exchange rates. The usual round of innovations hit the market and powerbrands, now eighteen in number, accounted for 60% of total sales. New to the elite club was Bang, sold under the Cillit brand in Europe and Easy Off in the rest of the world. Bang, a multi-purpose cleaner, was launched in 68 countries during the year, giving the company global leadership in the category. This new standard in brand rollouts meant that Bang was now sold in more countries than any other single Reckitt Benckiser brand: the venerable Vanish being had a mere 48.

By product category, the only real problem was in the largest category, fabric care, where revenues grew by a mere 2%, the continued success of Vanish Oxi negated by competitive pressures in the laundry detergent and fabric care markets. This is not that surprising as laundry was a segment where Reckitt Benckiser was toe-to-toe with the industry giants of P&G, Unilever and, in Europe, Henkel, whereas in most other categories the company's powerbrands competed in what were secondary sectors for the laundry behemoths. On the cost side, the company SWAT teams had to work ever harder than to negate some substantial increases in raw material costs, particularly plastic, steel and tinplate, but negate them they did, growing gross margins by ten basis points to 54.9%, via innovations such as glossy labels, cheaper than printing directly onto packs.

However, the big news in the year was the largest acquisition in the company's short history, that of Boots Healthcare International for £1.9 billion. Reckitt Benckiser had been looking for a major acquisition within OTC healthcare that met their fairly ruthless specifications: outstanding long-term growth prospects in aging populations in the context of European government trends to curb healthcare costs by encouraging more self-treatment for less problematic conditions. All angles covered beautifully there. Reckitt Benckiser also felt that its rapid, incremental innovation model worked well in the OTC arena, as it had shown in its stewardship of Lemsip and Gaviscon. The particular attraction of BHI was its roster of three powerful multi-national brands: Nurofen, Europe's number-two analgesic, Clearasil, the world's number-one anti-acne brand and Strepsils, outside North America the world's leading over-the-counter sore throat medication. BHI brands and infrastructure would be absorbed into Reckitt Benckiser's health and personal care category, bringing with it a strong route-to-market in medical detailing and pharmacy channels, complementing the company's existing strengths in grocery and mass-market distribution.

2006

With eleven months of BHI sales in 2006, overall revenues grew by 18% to a shade under £5 billion, while like-for-like sales grew by a still impressive 7%. Performance highlights included the prescription drug Suboxone, which Reckitt Benckiser owned and had the US distribution rights for, and its related drug Subutex, which grew by 30% in to £165 million with the high profit margins of on-patent drug. However, the year was dominated by the BHI integration into Reckitt Benckiser, a process that took place remarkably quickly. By mid-year, overlapping functions had been downsized and BHI products were appearing on Reckitt Benckiser invoices. By the end of the third quarter, systems in all countries had been integrated and by the end of the year no visible trace of BHI organisation remained: it was all Reckitt Benckiser now. Remarkably, sales of BHI brands managed to grow by 3% during this process and cost synergies were 15% ahead of target.

But it was not just about integration; it was also about preparing the ground for the Reckitt Benckiser growth model. One difference in the OTC market is the regulatory factor in new products approval, especially their efficacy claim, a process which significantly increased the route-to-market times compared to rest of the company portfolio, where innovations could invented and launched within weeks. So while the innovation pipeline was being primed to start delivering in 2008, much of the 2006 preparation had been to improve in-market execution the following year, in particular on-shelf displays in pharmacies and the advertising campaigns behind which increased media spend tests could be run. The Reckitt Benckiser growth model would still be applied, but essentially with a one-year time lag for the incremental innovations to come to market. As consumer loyalty generally gave OTC brands higher profit margins, the three big brands acquired from BHI were going to get a lot of focus and investment. The European bias of BHI further increased the area percentage of Reckitt Benckiser sales, up to 53%, and, by doing so, presented the company with plenty of opportunity to do what it was good at: rolling out brands to new markets.

2007

A 7% increase in reported revenues, with 10% on a like-for-like basis, yielded an eighth consecutive year of above-average industry growth: proof that the BHI acquisition firstly had not distracted Reckitt Benckiser management from its day job and secondly had demonstrated the growth prospects within BHI, whose product sales grew by 10% in the first full year of Reckitt Benckiser ownership. Most of the BHI growth came from the three powerbrands of Nurofen, Strepsils and Clearasil, helped along by substantial increases in media support and some early innovations such as Nurofen Express, which promised express relief from pain: its blood-stream absorption rate was twice as fast as the generic ibuprofen products.

This was an excellent start in a year when all but one of the eighteen Power-brands gained market share, accounting for 61% of total sales. Growth came through the usual mix of new products - Air Wick Freshmatic Mini and Vanish Oxi Action Multi – and geographic rollouts that had now taken Veet into 73 countries, Air Wick into 70 and Vanish into 57. High media spending - 12.4% of total revenues and more like 15% on the powerbrands – also made its contribution.

With the BHI acquisition fully integrated, the new, improved Reckitt Benckiser now had 75% of its revenues from brands that were number one or two in their markets. Together with numerous leading local and regional brands and categories, the company was now worldwide number one or two in the following categories:

Number One

- Fabric Treatment
- Water Softeners
- Surface Care
- Disinfectant Cleaners
- Automatic Dishwashing
- Topical Antiseptics
- Depilatory Products
- Medicated Sore Throat Products

Number Two

- Garment Care
- Air Care
- Shoe Care

Across the regions, the North American pharmaceutical unit was having such an impact on the numbers for the total area that it was being treated almost as a discrete entity, the Buprenorphine Business Group. A loosening of the regulatory rules for the heroin addiction treatment meant that doctors could prescribe it to more patients, so Reckitt Benckiser had substantially increased its sales infrastructure and received an immediate payback: 42% sales rises delivered a staggering 56% margin, when the area average for all other products was just 21%. There was also some movement on the M&A front. The BHI Hermal prescription skincare business sold for £260 million. The company also announced its intention to acquire Adams Respiratory Therapeutic Inc. for £2.3 billion, which would bring Reckitt Benckiser into the US OTC market via Mucinex, the clear US market-leading cough relief brand, which was slated to become powerbrand number 19.

2008

The Adams acquisition not only added to the top line but grew by 12% in the eleven months it was owned by Reckitt Benckiser. Thus the company posted a 25% increase in sales to £6.5 billion, its core business having grown by 13% and its powerbrands by 17%. The powerbrand list had also been lightly culled: two brands were dropped while Mucinex was added. Seventeen powerbrands were now going forwards:

The 2008 Powerbrands

Fabric Care	Surface Care	Dishwashing	Home Care
Vanish	Lysol	Finish	Air Wick
Calgon	Dettol	—	Mortein
Woolite	Bang	—	—
—	Harpic	—	—
Health Care	**Personal care**	**Food**	—
Strepsils	Dettol	French's	—
Mucinex	Veet	—	—
Nurofen	Clearasil	—	—
Gaviscon	—	—	—

Of these seventeen, fifteen were number one or two globally. Similar regional brands were now being awarded powerbrand status, the US's Electrasol and Jet Dry would be re-branded as Finish, starting with the launch of Finish Quantum.

The usual regional trends applied during the year with Europe and North America and Australia growing like-for-like by 7% and 6% respectively, while developing markets powered ahead by 16%, where the operating margin was now well into the double-digit territory at 13.7%. Overall, the company yet again increased its gross margin by a full percentage point to 59.3%. There were three factors driving this increase:

- Better-than-average performances by the higher-margin categories
- Continued 'Squeeze' cost savings such as the £1 million that came from a redesign of a French's mustard dispensing cap that also eliminated drips
- The continued explosive growth of the now renamed pharmaceuticals unit, whose sales increased another 45% up to £341 million, delivering an eye-watering £193 million operating profit which added nearly two whole percentage points to the entire company's operating profit margin

The pharmaceuticals unit was turning into a backyard oil well, although it might not gush forever. Subutex, for example, was marketed by Reckitt Benckiser in the US and Australia but principally by Schering Plough in Europe, where permission had just been granted to market the drug in 27 member states of the European Union. However, in America, the drug had Orphan Drug status (enhanced patent protection rights) until September 2009, beyond which point exclusivity would lapse and generics could decimate both sales and margins. It would be a big gap to plug.

2009

The big question in 2009 was how the Reckitt Benckiser growth strategy would cope with the deep recession into which many of its key markets had plunged. With over 80% of sales coming from developed markets, the company was more vulnerable than many to the slowdown. The answer is that the organic growth model coped well but the past acquisition and focus strategies worked better.

Overall, the company grew by an impressive 18%, 8% at constant exchange rates, to reach £7.8 billion – a top-class performance in the economic circumstances. If we dig a little deeper we see that, unsurprisingly, Europe struggled, growing only 1% with margins wilting slightly. Developing markets, largely untouched by the crisis, grew across all regions by a still impressive 16% to nearly £1.5 billion, with the margin creeping up once again. The star of the show, though, was the backyard gusher of pharmaceuticals, which put on another 50% of highly profitable revenue. Without this, total company performance would have shown a 6% top-line growth and a 4% increase in operating margin, good but not stellar. And the company was getting naturally very nervous about what would happen after the loss of Orphan Drug status in October 2009: US revenues of £502 million could decline by up to 80%.

While treatment of heroin addiction was clearly recession-proof, perhaps even recession-fed, the company had deliberately added some areas of the portfolio in recent years specifically tp protect against economic downturn as well as to make money in healthier times. Thus, while not one of fabric care, surface care, dishwashing, home care and food could put on more than a 5% growth, health and personal care zoomed ahead by 14% driven by Nurofen, Strepsils, Gaviscon and Mucinex: headaches, sore throats, acid reflux or nasal congestion take scant notice of the economy. And more cost savings had pushed the gross margin over 60% for the first time in the company's 10-year history, an increase of almost fifteen percentage points over the period. But the much vaunted media spend as a percentage of sales was more subdued, declining from 12.4 to 11.1%, partly because of the almost exponential sales increases of the unadvertised Suboxone but also because of the company, whose business model was not completely recession-proof.

2010

Another 9% on the top line took sales to nearly £8.5 billion, like-for-like growth of 6% and still a respectable 5%, excluding pharmaceuticals. Once again, health and personal care performed strongly, helped by a good piece of cross-category innovation with the surface care brands Dettol and Lysol each launching the No-Touch Hand Soap System. Coming a year after the H1N1 scare, this was the right product at the right time. Not to be outdone, home care increased by 8%, driven by a slew of innovations in the Air Wick brand, Air Wick Aqua Mist and Air Wick Ribbons, for example. Dishwashing, fabric care and surface care had uneventful years, while food, justifying French's newfound status as a powerbrand, grew by 9% in the year, driven by the new variants its new status allowed.

The once-again newly named RB Pharmaceuticals continued to perform. It was not really news that sales had increased again, but the rise to £737 million was impressive, while the 37% increase in operating profit to £531 million was even more so, both clear signs that oil from the company well was not being siphoned off by no-name competitors. A development that kept such creatures at bay was the regulatory approval and subsequent launch of a patented and user-preferred film version of the drug to supplant previous tablet versions. The film, developed via an exclusive agreement with Mono-Sol Rx using its proprietary technology, already accounted for 25% of sales and, by dissolving faster and tasting much better, was keeping patients in treatment longer. Although the film diluted margins slightly, the long-term beneficial effect of continued treatment patent protection in the US was of huge value. Reported sales in RB Pharmaceuticals had also been boosted by the company's £100 million re-purchase of the European distribution rights. The new rights began to bite on July 1st. Reckitt Benckiser was now most definitely in pharmaceuticals; the unit contributed 9% of the year's total sales..

The other big news in the year was the July announcement of the acquisition of SSL International, maker of sexual wellbeing brand Durex and foot-care brand Scholl. The £2.5 billion deal was completed on 29th October. The addition of SSL would increase the size of the health and personal care category by 36% and add two new brands to the powerbrand list. The acquisition also transformed Reckitt Benckiser's previously somewhat limited presence in the crucial Chinese and Japanese markets. And the company's reputation for innovations in the field was beginning to intrigue, if not excite, the world's lovers. Reckitt Benckiser also made another significant acquisition, the Indian company Paras Pharmaceuticals, which now gave the company a viable health care business in that other great emerging market. Partly helped by these acquisitions, total sales in developing markets had increased by 18% during the year and now accounted for 22% of company business.

2011

By far the biggest news in the company's short history was the shock April announcement in of the retirement of Bart Becht, the only CEO the company had ever had. To say the news was unexpected was the understatement of the year. Becht was still in his fifties and had shown no signs whatsoever of reaching for his pipe and slippers. Rumours in the investment community, denied by both Reckitt Benckiser and Becht, suggested that he had stormed out following a major strategic bust up with the board.

While more plausible than the company's party line, it would have been an ironic way for Becht to go. Becht, more than anyone, had been responsible for, and very proud of, the curious Reckitt Benckiser operating style: meetings were essentially shouting matches. But they were always resolved within the meeting itself, with a course of action agreed that everyone would thereafter religiously support. For someone to flounce off because he didn't get his way would have been a sackable offence for anyone else in the company but Becht. Maybe it was for him too, judging from the annual report's single sentence on the matter; one would have expected rather more for the man who had taken Benckiser from obscure European packaged goods bit-part player to one of the best-performing companies on the London Stock Exchange: the send-off was not a gushing epitaph marking the well-earned retirement of one of the world's best-performing CEOs. But then Becht didn't retire. He was immediately snapped up by

Reimann – the previous owner of Benckiser – to co-run its multi-billion-dollar investment company Joh A Benckiser Sarl, which had a seat on the Reckitt Benckiser Board Becht had just left. Which it retained.

What happened afterwards was another indication that Becht's departure had not been entirely amicable. Although the company promoted 25-year veteran Rakesh Kapoor to the CEO position, the new man wasted no time in introducing a dramatically different strategic direction for the company. There would be no smooth continuation of the Becht ways. The first shift in direction came in a restructuring of the portfolio. There were to be three powerbrand groupings: health and the OTC brands, hygiene and the cleaning and pest control brands and finally home, with utilitarian brands such as Vanish, Woolite and Air Wick. There was to be an exaggerated focus on health and hygiene, food would be run as a stand-alone business (making it easy to dispose of at some stage), as would RB Pharmaceuticals, giventhat it was essentially a one-product division with a unique route to market and management agenda.

The powerbrand concept was still central to the company's way of operating, but with more focus, attention and resources given to the health and hygiene powerbrands. The company's identity would shift from household cleaning-centred on to health, hygiene and home. The rationale was clear. First, Reckitt Benckiser's M&A strategy had got the company into higher-margin categories such as OTC while, at the same time, the vaunted innovation/high media spend strategy had not been performing as it used to in servicing the more mundane product areas. The days of double-digit growth in dishwashing and surface cleaning were long gone - more recently, the company had been delivering decidedly average performances in those categories. Also deemed past its sell-by date was the company's habit of measuring brand investment levels purely in media spend as a percentage of net income. Under the new regime, that would be expanded to cover digital and social media, education programmes and medical marketing.

The second strategic shift was geographic. Under Becht, Reckitt Benckiser had been far more focused on taking more powerbrands into existing Reckitt Benckiser markets than in opening up new markets for all the company's brands. Consequently, it had long lagged behind its major competitors in sales percentages from emerging markets. This was now going to change. Three new reporting regions were put in place to replace the old structure, each grouping together markets the company saw as having similar consumer and retail dynamics:

- LAPAC – Latin America, North Asia (i.e. China), South East Asia (India down to Borneo), Australia and New Zealand
- RUMEA – Russia & CIS, Middle East, North Africa, Turkey, Sub-Saharan Africa

- ENA – Europe and North America

While the company insisted that developed markets were 'still important', the focus would turn from ENA towards the other two regions, with particular emphasis on what Reckitt Benckiser had identified as sixteen powermarkets. This emphasis would involve a migration of management away from developed markets, which currently had 64% of staff looking at 900 million consumers, towards the powermarkets, where 36% of staff serviced six billion consumers. KPIs were set on both strategic shifts: 72% of 'core company revenues' (excluding food and pharmaceuticals) coming from health and hygiene by 2016 (currently 67%), and 50% of core revenues from LAPAC and RUMEA by the same year (currently 42%). The numbers involved in the targets were not revolutionary, but the shift in emphasis was. Reckitt Benckiser would now be a quite different company than it had been in the first thirteen years of its life. Would it be as successful?

2012

In the first year of the new strategy, it seemed that the Reckitt Benckiser machine had adjusted well to its new settings. Although top-line sales were up by barely 1% to £9.6 billion – all coming from RB Pharmaceuticals – this masked a more robust like-for-like increase of 4% when exchange rates were factored out. The strategy, remember, was to grow the health and hygiene categories faster, along with the LAPAC and RUMEA regions, and here the company succeeded. Health grew by 6%, helped by the Durex brand increasing its reach in China, a growth rate matched by hygiene in which Dettol Daily Care, Lysol No-Touch Kitchen System and the Quantum brand all made significant gains. The deprioritised home and food sectors all still managed like-for-like growth, but in the 1–2% range. RB Pharmaceuticals put on an additional 10% revenue with strong volume growth in the key US market, tempered by the switch from Suboxone tablets to lower-margin film. The film, patent protected until 2020, now accounted for 64% of sales and was progressing so well the company felt comfortable enough to announce the planned withdrawal of the tablets during 2013, not least because they were coming under pressure from generic manufacturers. Within the regions, LAPAC led the way with an 11% like-for-like growth as the powerbrands continued their market rollouts and distributions gains; RUMEA was up by 8%, primarily because of Russia and the rest of the CIS; while ENA still managed to inch ahead by 1%.

Strategically, the company made two significant shifts during 2012. After a review early in the year, the company set about terminating its contracts to supply private label products, primarily laundry products, to European retailers. This was followed in the last quarter by an announcement of the $1.4 billion acquisition of Schiff Nutrition International Inc., the leading US vitamin, mineral and supplement brand, which opened up a new $30 billion category for Reckitt Benckiser. A second acquisition, this time of China's Oriental Medicine Company Ltd, reinforced the sense that Reckitt Benckiser was moving rapidly away from its more prosaic, home cleaning brands heartland.

What Is Its DNA?

Until the day Bart Becht left the building, Reckitt Benckiser had been the most consistently managed of all the world's major packaged goods companies, applying its own idiosyncratic style year in, year out. There were no secrets in how Reckitt Benckiser delivered its results, not least because Becht never tired of telling anyone who would listen what the strategy was: focus on the brands that were advantaged in both profitability and growth prospects, churn out exceptional numbers of innovations and advertise the hell out of them. Everyone knew what the company was doing but no one could stop or even match it. The key elements of the company's DNA that facilitated this strategy are, we believe, as follows:

Consumer Focus

It may seem odd to include this; after all, doesn't every company in this book have a consumer focus? They are all consumer packaged goods companies, after all. However, we believe it is a particular strength of Reckitt Benckiser's. The company has had an obsessive focus on getting under the skin of how consumers use its products and how they feel about every fine detail of the consumption experience. The vast majority of the company's countless innovations have been fine-tuned improvements to its own offerings; it launched very few new brands, even fewer me-toos and no completely novel products. While P&G predominantly relied on technical breakthroughs like Febreze and Swiffer, Reckitt Benckiser relied predominantly on a succession of incremental improvements to the consumer experience. To do this over such a prolonged period requires an obsession with getting into people's homes in different markets, seeing how they use the products and asking plenty of questions about how they feel about it. There are no desk-bound marketers in Reckitt Benckiser.

Speed

Reckitt Benckiser doesn't just do things quickly. Compared to its competitors, it does everything at warp speed. Cillit Bang was launched in Hungary. Its potential for scaling up was agreed within weeks, with a global launch following within a couple of months. Facilitated by a very flat organisation, a cultural style that prohibits procrastination beyond a single meeting for any issue, a 'you snooze, you lose' attitude to taking products to market and an evaluation process that takes weeks not months to pick the winners and losers, the company sets a pace of market activity its competitors are structurally and culturally unable to get anywhere close to. What some purists may consider a 'throw stuff at the wall and see what sticks' strategy, Reckitt Benckiser made into a highly successful reality. Most company meetings are less than productive. Office politics are destructive. The best market research is whether or not something sells after you launch it: Reckitt Benckiser actually did something about these business truths rather than just grumble about them.

Creative Tension

Working at Reckitt Benckiser isn't for everyone. The company's leaders would be first to admit that new employees either love or hate the place, and the business does little to work with the ones who hate it: the sooner they leave, the happier everyone will be. Core to the day-to-day operating style is a culture that not only encourages but also actively demands conflict. Opinions must be aired at all times and need to be done so forcibly to have any chance of making them heard, let alone acted upon. Managers from small markets must shout up for what their market needs for the powerbrands to succeed there. The company believes the coming together of strongly held views, passionately argued, results in better outcomes. Rank and seniority count for nothing in the discussion phase; those closest to the consumer are expected to fight tooth and nail to get what their consumers want. Right from the beginning, the company moved managers around different countries and had a nationally neutral culture; English was made the operating language of the company in every meeting in every country. Outright anarchy is avoided by an equally strong belief in backing absolutely whatever decision a meeting arrives at; you may get outvoted or shouted down, but you are required to support the outcome as though it were your own idea. It is a powerful approach that does indeed get everything out on the table.

Summary

Reckitt Benckiser has been one of the biggest consumer goods success stories of the early 21st century. During its first twelve years, its share price increased five times more than Unilever's. The combination of a set of somewhat tired-looking Reckitt & Colman brands with the Benckiser approach to strategy and management has been little short of spectacular. The company has been the subject of countless case studies in its approach to innovation; not surprising, as it has set new benchmarks for the level of innovation sustainable by a large packaged goods company. But the company has recently undergone its first transitions of both CEO and strategy, which raises several questions.

Just how much was the success of the company driven by Bart Becht himself? We are instinctively not believers in the concept of the heroic CEO but there can be no doubt that Reckitt Benckiser was created and moulded in his style. And while there can be no arguing with the direction of the new strategy – most future growth is coming from emerging markets and OTC brands are generally more profitable than cleaning or household brands – here is the question: is Reckitt Benckiser as advantaged in those two areas as it has been in doing what it has been doing?

Unilever, P&G and Henkel have been more active in emerging markets for decades than has Reckitt Benckiser and they no longer regard Reckitt Benckiser as a cheeky upstart on the fringes of their businesses. Also, while Reckitt Benckiser has largely operated off the giants' radar, it is coming up against indigenous firms in emerging markets who are even more agile and quick than they are.

A key factor in the growth of Reckitt Benckiser has been its unique culture, one that developed fast and then embedded itself strongly. And, as the company was so focused on organic growth for so long and made so few acquisitions, it stayed that way. But nothing dilutes a management culture quicker than big acquisitions and the purchase of SSL conceivably falls into that category. SSL was a long-established company with its own culture operating in a multitude of different countries, some of which were to be spearheads for the Reckitt Benckiser brands. It is difficult in those circumstances to turf out the incumbent management who operate very differently, as happened with the Reckitt & Colman merger.

In short, this is a crucial phase in the brief history of Reckitt Benckiser. Will history show it to have been an enduring business phenomenon that can outperform its competitors ad infinitum? Or a passing phase where the stars aligned to create a set of ideal conditions for above-average growth: under-exploited brands, easy geographic expansion opportunities, and complacent competitors? As we all know from the stock market, past performance is no guarantee of future returns, especially in periods of great change. The new regime has the toughest of acts to follow.

The Estée Lauder Company

Where Did They Come From?

In 1920s New York City, John Schotz, a Hungarian chemist, was working tirelessly in the kitchen of his brother's house to develop the perfect face cream. His hairdresser niece, Josephine Esther Mentzer, bombarded him with suggestions. She thought one of his face creams was amazing, as did all of her friends. She devised a name for the cream, the somewhat catch-all Super-Rich All Purpose Crème, and gave samples to her customers at the Florence Morris Beauty Salon.

Josephine Esther married young, to a Mr. Joseph Lauter, whose father, on moving to the United States, had had his original name - Lauder – mis-spelt by the immigration officer. The couple decided to re-adopt the original family and Esther took the opportunity to nuance her own name. Estée and Joseph Lauder would between them rewrite the rules of the beauty business and create a global empire generating $10 billion a year sales.

Estée continued her uncle's work in her own kitchen with Joseph's support. She was a born saleswoman, in touch with the needs and wants of her target market - women - and with an unshakeable faith in her own judgement. Now, promoting a range of four products, including her uncle's original cream, she used her salon job to sample the miracle cream to her customers while they were under the hairdryer. In most cases, she made a sale by the time their hair was done. It was in the salon she hit on the big idea that would live on in the company to this day: the free gift with a purchase. Every woman who bought something from her in the salon would also get a sample of one of her other make-up products.

Estée Lauder's added-value hairdressing experience was a hit and she was soon asked to demonstrate her products at another beauty salon. Estée's reaction was, why stop at two? She immediately realised that while she had great products, sales were more down to her personal touch. To expand she needed to recruit and train saleswomen moulded into her own style. Right from the beginning, Estée set her standards high. Of the first twenty applicants to demonstrate and sell her products in salons, only one was deemed good enough. Next came the packaging. Estée reasoned that her products would sit in the bathroom, where she wanted the face cream jar to look special. It could not have a label that would peel off in steam from the shower. So her name would be engraved on the bottle, its pale turquoise colour chosen to match by Estée after an exhaustive survey of as many bathrooms to which she could gain access.

While business through the two salons was good, Estée realised that her sales were limited by her reliance on unplanned purchases. In an era before credit or debit cards, she was losing sales because many clients simply didn't have enough money with them. She needed to be in the big department stores where many customers came planning to buy cosmetics and could pay on their store charge cards. Most of all, Estée wanted to sell her products in Saks Fifth Avenue. She was determined to break down the barriers specifically designed to stop people like her reaching Saks buyers. The Saks cosmetics buyer eventually wilted under the human tornado that was Estée Lauder. They gave her an order for $800 worth of merchandise. Based on this one order, Estée pulled out of the two sa-lons and, with Joseph's full support, invested their entire savings into buying a former restaurant as their first factory. Joseph and Estée prepared the creams on the restaurant's gas burners (one of which she kept for the rest of her life) and then set about talking the buyer into a promotional campaign. This was unheard of from Saks' more traditional suppliers. Everyone with a charge account at Saks was sent a card announcing *Saks Fifth Avenue is proud to present the Estée Lauder line of cosmetics: now available at our cosmetics department.* And of course, every item sold came with that all-important free gift.

Her business grew steadily at Saks and, on the back of the reputation that a Saks listing bestowed, it was soon expanding into any and every department store she could talk her way into. Estée realised from the beginning that where her products were sold would dictate what her name stood for. Department stores capable of lending her products exclusivity and a premium aura were cultivated: those precious attributes would surely be lost if Estée found herself on the shelves in the local drugstore. She formulated four golden rules from this early depart-ment store experience:

- She would open every new concession herself, spending a week in the store to get everything absolutely right
- Her salespeople needed to be not just walking advertisements for her products, but be gushing enthusiasts for their efficacy
- The counter had to be a turquoise magnet, a 'tiny, shining spa'
- The gift with purchase was mandatory, whatever the store's policy re-garding other cosmetic counters

All this was revolutionary for the time.

Always one to think big, Estée approached New York's advertising agencies. She was rebuffed, no-one wanted to know. So she ploughed her advertising budget into more free samples, this time to department store customers whether they had bought a product or not. Postcards were sent out saying, Madam, because you are one of our preferred customers, please stop by the Estée Lauder counter and present this card for a free gift. Estée also insisted that the free gift was prime merchandise, not last season's failures. But she soon realised that, good though her face cream was, it would not cause women to make a special trip. Face cream was at the more mundane end of the cosmetics spectrum. What they would beat down the doors for was a brilliant new lipstick colour, and this became the subsequent giveaway of choice. In 1947, The Estée Lauder Company Inc. was formed.

How Did They Evolve?

Although Estée had a growing business built around a miracle face cream and some good lipsticks and blushers, it was at this stage still a niche business. All around her counters in the major department stores were the counters of the French perfumers. If Estée was to make it big, she needed a killer perfume. Her opportunity came via an insight from her still obsessive safaris through the nation's boudoirs: that makers made their money from perfume that evaporated away while sitting rarely used on the dressing table. In those days, perfume was then the perfect gift from the man to his loved one(s), but Estée saw this little piece of sociology as a market killer. She wanted women to buy their own perfume and use it every day. She would sell it like lipstick, not like rarely proffered diamond rings or large boxes of chocolate.

For her scent, she went back to one of her uncle's early concoctions and tinkered with it until she was happy she had the ideal aroma. That was the easy part: the trick was in persuading women to buy and use it frequently. Estée's first step was to not call it a perfume at all. Her Youth Dew was called a perfumed bath oil. Next came the packaging: she opted for a screw top rather than the more usual cellophane wrapping: she wanted browsers to unscrew and sniff in-store. Indeed Estée was not beyond splashing some on the floor near her counters, prompting shoppers to ask, what was that marvellous scent?

Youth Dew, launched in 1953, was immediately a huge success for the Estée Lauder Company. Selling 5,000 units a week, it became a long-term best-seller, still clearing $30 million a year in the 1980s. It also gave the company a caché for scent that could be used to launch actual perfumes. Estée and then Azurée were launched with names conjuring up the appeal of the French perfumes but packaged and sold with none of their stuffiness. In Saks, Estée Lauder was now number three behind Helena Rubinstein and Elizabeth Arden and consequently,

Estée was now coming to her rivals' attention. Meeting Helena Rubinstein for the first time, Estée made an impact by telling Madame R that her neck would benefit from Estée's Crème Pack. She didn't trust her local competitor, Charles Revlon, in the slightest. She was constantly on her guard against industrial espionage, and insisted that either she or Joseph, personally and in secret, add the last few secret ingredients to every batch of perfume produced in her factory.

While Joe ran the business side of things, Estée was constantly on the road: opening stores and cementing relationships with store buyers. In 1958, annual sales hit the magic $1 million, which was all achieved through Estée's vision and force of personality. The US cosmetics market was booming – sales would nearly treble between 1955 and 1965. Estée Lauder was now a leading name in the American cosmetics industry, a position she had cemented with the launch of Re-Nutriv in 1957, selling for a heart-stopping $115 a jar. As the business grew, seasoned industry executives were recruited into the business, particularly anyone who had fallen out with Charles Revson. There was no love lost in either direction. In the ten years from 1958, company sales grew at an average of 45% a year, helped by two of its biggest successes. These would transform the company into an industry powerhouse.

How Did They Build the Modern Business?

When the Estée Lauder Company finally adopted advertising in 1962, their different approach changed the industry. The existing industry convention was to use a variety of models in ads. This made sense: the product was the hero and the model's role was to accentuate the benefits of whatever product was being advertised.

Estée Lauder took an obverse view. She would use only one model, who would be the face of the company. She would appear on every product over several years. The first face of Estée Lauder was Karen Harris. Estée took the precaution of not naming her in the ads in order not to divert attention from the brand. Indeed, many assumed that Karen was Estée Lauder herself. Karen lasted throughout the 1960s before a new face of the brand, Karen Graham, took over duties.

Estée Lauder's second revolution was in the area of men's fragrance. This was the orphan of the industry. It was dominated by Shulton's Old Spice, a brand ageing as rapidly as its customer base. Even the more upmarket brands failed to excite Estée. She found Joseph's preferred after-shave brand to be less than pleasing, and the lotions slapped on in the barbershop to be positively nauseating. Ignoring the advice ringing in her ears to stick to what she knew – women's cosmetics - Estée ploughed on. She believed she was a skin expert rather than a cosmetics expert. Roping in every male employee in the company, i.e. Joseph and eight others, she spent months trying out an endless stream of concoctions. The outcome was Aramis, launched in 1965.

Sales results were uninspiring. It was launched as a fragrance, a cologne and an after-shave lotion. It featured a large dollop of Estée Lauder branding across the otherwise plain brown packaging, Estée decided she had made the mistake of pulling her punches. For this to work, she had to reinvent men's grooming. That meant the product and not a house name that was known for high end female cosmetics. The outcome, in 1967, was a brand re-launch. Estée now presented an entire range of products: after-shave, eye pads and a face mask. Although clothed in the now familiar brown and gold tortoiseshell livery (taken from one of Estée's oriental fans), the Estée Lauder name was relegated to small print and soon dropped altogether. The first advertisement for the brand ran in The New Yorker featuring the All-Weather Hand Cream – Estée was selling to metrosexuals thirty years before the term came into common parlance.

The significance for the company of this successful re-launch cannot be overstated. It showed that Estée Lauder was no one-trick-pony. They were now a fully-fledged cosmetics company, which had moved beyond one brand aimed at a subset of one sex. They could appeal to both sexes and all ages by developing products that did not rely on the Estée Lauder brand equity. The sky was the limit.

The next major initiative that would transform both the industry and the company was, for once, not powered by Estée, but by her son. Leonard had joined the business in 1958, fresh from completing his Columbia MBA. Leonard was an adherent of Schumpert's creative destruction. He constantly told his parents that if ever there was to be a concept that could knock an Estée Lauder brand off its perch, he wanted the Estée Lauder Company to introduce it. That concept, although it would not quite deliver a knockout punch to Estée Lauder, was Clinique.

Major brand cosmetics companies had long understood that their products sometimes caused allergic reactions in some customers. But it was seen as a niche area. Several companies had tried to capture the market but the strategy of eliminating known sensitising ingredients also eliminated most of the appeal and allure of the category itself. Charles Revson kept his Revlon company out of it altogether, declaring hypoallergenic cosmetics to be 'a drag'. Leonard thought differently. Rather than just be watered down version of the real thing, if properly developed from the ground up, it could be even bigger than Youth Dew. His insight was that, while relatively few had genuine allergic reactions to cosmetics, most women believed that skin, particularly their own, was a sensitive and delicate thing.

Leonard accepted that some of the glamour and allure of high-end cosmetics would be lost with a hypoallergenic claim. But the concept was grounded in the appeal of something else: medical reassurance. This reassurance would infuse every aspect of the brand. The products themselves were developed in partnership with Dr. Norman Orentreich, a widely acknowledged expert in the field of skin sensitivities, and in his laboratories. Estée Lauder herself conjured up the name, out of her fertile brain and intuitive understanding of customers. Very few American women might speak French, yet they would all appreciate that Clinique persuasively recalled images of salons where one went for a facial.

Leonard's wife, Evelyn, made Clinique the complete family effort. She equipped sales staff with penlights in their white lab coats. Clinique's counter was not just easily up to the standards expected in a department store: it stood out not just for its bright, clean lines; the artist's lamp for examining customers' skin; and a question-and-answer board (later a computer) to take the guesswork out of the process. The packaging was deliberately not too clinical; this still had to sit comfortably on the nation's dressing tables. The boldest moves were to go 100% fragrance-free when sold in a part of the store primarily selling fragrances; and to position Clinique as being completely separate from Estée Lauder. It had its own counter, its own staff and would compete for customers with Estée Lauder as would Elizabeth Arden.

Launch day approached for what had been codenamed Project Miss Estée. Then a trademark search turned up a product sold by the little-known firm of Jacquet and Jacquet called Astringent Clinique. Lawyers informed Leonard that if they came to court, they would lose. Leonard saddled up and went to the Jacquet and Jacquet's owners with a $5,000 offer. He came back with the name but was $100,000 poorer. He declared it the best deal he had ever made. Not that those early sales justified Leonard's assertion. Launched in 1968, the brand lost $3 million in its first seven years; no mean sum for a company with a $40 million a year turnover. Also, competitors piled into the category, led by the man who had declared the whole thing to be a drag. Revlon quickly launched Etherea, as did another 179 competitors around the world. But the competition all missed the point. Clinique would be the driving force behind a ten-fold expansion in Estée Lauder sales in the coming years.

The 1970s saw much change in the industry, and two of Estée Lauder's main competitors suffered badly. The deaths of both Elizabeth Arden and Helena Rubinstein in the mid-1960s cost a loss of drive. More fundamentally, these firms lost direction when acquired by pharmaceutical companies (Elizabeth Arden in

1970 by Eli Lily; Helene Rubinstein by Colgate Palmolive in 1973). Despite many offers to follow suit, the Lauder family, now increasingly led by Leonard (who became President in 1973), decided to keep control. This gave them a definite edge as the others floundered in the grip of conglomerates.

While Clinique powered on, increasingly the company saw its main competition as being Revlon and Avon - both much larger companies with differing distribution strategies - and French fashion designers who were moving their brand equities into cosmetics. Estée passionately believed that the department store was the only place to be, whereas Revlon's heartland was the more downmarket, yet much more numerous, drug stores. By 1973, Estée Lauder had only 2,000 points of distribution in the United States while Revlon had 15,000. Avon had countless more due to selling in customers' homes. There they were able to outdo Estée Lauder in personalised selling, which had been a core company strength.

Revlon had a big hit in 1973 with the launch of Charlie. This made the Estée Lauder brand seem behind the times - what your mum wore. Then, from the top end of the market, Yves Saint Laurent's Opium launched in the US in 1978. Estée Lauder was being squeezed, and, for the first time, the company was on the back foot. It showed when the launches of Soft Youth Dew and Cinnabar were rushed, and both fell well short of past standards of success. Still, by 1978, annual sales had reached close to $250 million, with Clinique and Aramis together accounting for almost half the total. On the back of Clinique's runaway success, the concept was taken even further in 1979 with Prescriptives. Here every customer got a full one-hour consultation, in which a custom-coloured make-up was developed to exactly match skin-type and tone. However, Prescriptives gave Estée Lauder a long and deep financial haircut, soaking up $40 million of investment and losses before finally coming good in the late 1980s. More immediate success came from White Linen, launched in 1978 as part of a trio of fragrances called New Romantics. These were designed to be worn in tandem, with advertisements urging Wear one. Wear two. Wear all three together. Customers were quite happy wearing just White Linen.

The company returned to its skin care roots in 1983 with the launch of Night Repair, trumpeted in ads as a biological breakthrough. Unfortunately, the message was undermined by the Clinique collaborator, Dr Orentreich, going rogue, and debunking the whole idea in the press. Estée herself had mostly taken a back seat, and the company powered its fragrance new-product pipeline with a well-staffed and funded R&D function. Their Beautiful, launched in 1985, was a blockbuster that became another long-term success. Estée Lauder were now undisputed kings of the department store cosmetics floor, and second only to Avon in sales of fragrances.

In 1990, Leonard Lauder recruited a new head of the company's domestic US division. Robin Burns had been the brain, which propelled Calvin Klein from nowhere to become a major competitor, with launches such as Obsession and Eternity. Under Burns' leadership, the now slightly ageing portfolio and advertising was updated. A notable development was Origins, which was run as a separate entity and headed by Leonard's son, William. Origins was a range of botanically based products aimed at heading off the threat posed by the rise of Body Shop. It was sold either through stand-alone company-owned stores, or stores-within-a-store in selected major outlets. William described Origins' mission as 'trying to rewrite the book on how a cosmetics company operates and thinks in the 21st-century'. Then, in 1993, the company responded to the rise of the designer-fragrance phenomenon and signed a deal with Tommy Hilfiger to license his name on cosmetics.

Pro-active thinking was at the heart of the company's strategy during the 1990s as it made the precarious transition from being family-run to being run as a corporation. Joseph was deceased, Estée in semi-retirement in an advisory and figurehead role, and other family members uninvolved. Transition to being publicly owned was now seen as essential for the long-term health of the business. A November IPO raised more than $450 million, while the family kept much of the common stock and most of the voting stock. Many family-owned businesses struggle in these transitions, but the Lauders had, from their earliest days, recruited the best and most experienced people they could. So business continued to prosper without skipping a beat. In 1996, sales, which had grown every single year since the company's inception, rose to nearly $3 billion.

So far, the company had been hugely successful developing its own brands, but around the IPO, they ventured into acquisitions. They targeted distinctive brands that would complement the company's portfolio, and take it into areas difficult to develop internally. The first was Make-up Art Cosmetics Ltd. (M•A•C), aimed at professional make-up artists. This was followed by another professionals' beauty line, Bobbi Brown Essentials.

Estée Lauder were still wary of Revlon's success in drug stores, supermarkets and even Wal-Mart, yet were unwilling to take their own brands there. So Sassaby Inc., with its Jane brand, was unashamedly purchased for its populist appeal to teenagers.

The next deal took the company into a new product field; Aveda was purchased for $300 million - 85% of their sales coming from the channel where Estée started, hair salons. Then, the La Mer brand of high-end moisturisers was purchased. In 1997, another licensing deal was struck, with Donna Karen International Ltd., for use of the Donna Karen New York and DKNY trademarks. In

1999, another professionals' line, Stila, was acquired, as was a British brand, Jo Malone. Another five deals soon followed, adding the Bumble and bumble, Kate Spade, Michael Kors, Darphin and Rodin & Fields brands to the portfolio.

Estée Lauder assumed an industry leadership role in selling its products over the Internet. In 1998, it formed a separate division, ELC Online, to coordinate the web activities of all the brands. While other cosmetics houses recoiled with horror at the thought, Estée Lauder had always been about in-depth interaction with its customers. The Internet was recognised as providing an ideal environment for one-to-ones, in a new and even more engaging way. In the space of a decade, the company had been transformed. From a handful of brands sold exclusively through department stores, Estée Lauder had become an industry giant covering a wide variety of channels and consumers. It was also by now a global company, with sales in the billions and promotional and advertising budgets that exceeded $1 billion. Not all the acquisitions worked – the Jane brand was sold in 2004 and Stila would soon follow – but most were contributing to the impressive growth of the company.

How Global Are They?

Estée saw no reason why her products couldn't sell anywhere in the world and had set about ensuring they did so, beginning in 1960. Following the success of her Saks first policy in the United States, Estée was in no doubt where her international empire should start: Harrods' of London. Given that she was no longer a hairdresser selling products in two salons, but the head of a successful and well-known American cosmetics firm, it is surprising that her request for a meeting with Harrods' met with a blank refusal. Undeterred, she went to London for a full month, schmoozing every beauty editor in town and getting rave write-ups for her brands. Still to no avail.

The next year Estée was back and Harrods' cosmetics buyer, worn down by the incessant requests and the avalanche of positive publicity for her brands, grudgingly gave Estée a tiny order. It would be displayed in the general toiletries section, far away from the main cosmetics brands. And oh, just for good measure, they wouldn't do the gift-with-purchase. Far from being deterred, this was Estée's opening. On the back of 'now listed in Harrods', she pitched herself once again to the beauty editors. It took a few more such forceful visits from Estée before her brands were getting their due prominence in the flagship store. And this in turn helped get her brands into Harrods' competitors, Fortnum & Mason and Selfridge's. At first Estée was given even shorter shrift from Paris's great department store, Galaries Lafayette. So she resorted to surreptitiously spilling some of her Youth Dew on the shop floor, which got customers clamouring to know what was the marvellous aroma?

For much of the 1960s, Estée carried her sales bag around the world, opening up concessions wherever she went: Hong Kong, Canada, Austria, Italy and Germany. Estée then handed over the task to an international sales manager. This role soon morphed into a separate division within the company, Estée Lauder International Inc. Their first store in Moscow opened in 1981 while it was still the capital of the Soviet Union. By the mid-1990s, the company was selling in over 100 countries and when Estée Lauder passed away in April 2004, 45% of annual sales, amounting to $5.7 billion, and over half of operating income, was coming from non-US affiliates.

How Are They Structured?

For much of its life, the company structure's role was to disseminate the ideas flowing from Estée's fertile brain. The early decision to run Clinique completely separately from the Estée Lauder brand put in place a new structure. Each brand had its own president to drive sales and marketing. The International Division was similarly structured. A matrix-type complex of manufacturing, finance etc supported these units. When the international business became too unwieldy to run operationally as one entity, heads of individual regions were put in place. This added complexity did not impede the growth of the business. Indeed, the company upheld its exceptional feat of growing sales in every single year of its existence well into the twenty-first century.

In 2009, William Lauder handed over his chairman's role to then CEO, Fabrizio Freda, and the two announced a major change in company structure to simplify the bloated mix of brand, regional and functional heads. Henceforth, the brands would now fall into one of four groupings, organised according to the channel and consumer segmentation of the individual brands

- High-end prestige brands and make-up artist brands
- Estée Lauder, M•A•C, Bobbi Brown, Prescriptives, La Mer, Jo Malone, Tom Ford Beauty
- Prestige skin care and alternative channels
- Clinique, Origins, Ojon
- Fragrance licensing
- Aramis and designer fragrances
- Salon and Pharmacy channel
- Aveda, Bumble and bumble, Darphin

In addition, regionally, the North American business, together with Canada and Puerto Rico - where many of the brands had been operating fairly autonomously - was conjoined into one North American affiliate, providing a single point of contact for its customers. With 42% of sales coming from this one unit, it was a huge multi-billion dollar enterprise in its own right.

What Have They Been Doing Recently?

2004

The 58th successive year of sales growth saw a company-record increase of $700 million, making the top line up to $5.8 billion. Five of the company's brands - Estée Lauder, Clinique, Aramis, Donna Karen fragrances and Tommy Hilfiger fragrances – were available in over 120 countries, Clinique in over 130. Estée Lauder and Clinique were growing rapidly in China, Aveda was launched in Japan and M•A•C was growing fast in Brazil via its own stores. Darphin, a high-end botanical beauty brand sold primarily through independent European pharmacies, was acquired. The company set up BeautyBank, an internal, new concept think-tank, as a separate division. BeautyBank's initial output was three new brands, which were launch through the Kohl's chain of 600 department stores. With Ashley Judd signed up as a brand face and P. Diddy as the latest licensed fragrance, the machine was humming.

The scale and scope of the Estée Lauder business with over 8,000 product lines was now vast. Innovation was a core part of the strategy: 400 scientists were working in six research centres around the world, churning out 300 new product launches in the year. The Estée Lauder Beyond Paradise launch, utilising essential oils developed exclusively for the company, was a huge success. It reached the top five best-selling fragrances in US Department stores, and contributed to the company having five of the top ten.

However, with about one-third of sales coming from products launched in the previous three years, the company was on something of an innovation treadmill. A percentage of the new products each year needed to make good, to compensate for the percentage of the earlier introductions that didn't make the grade. Once companies find themselves on this treadmill, it is very hard to get off.

2005

Sales reached a new high of $6.3 billion. Growth was coming from around the world. In the US, where sales increased by a quarter billion, Estée Lauder had four of the top five best-selling fragrances in department stores. But the fragrance market was getting tougher all the time. The company was now marketing a range of over 90 prestige fragrance brands with over 200 new ones being launched by the industry each year. Fragrance marketing was now much less about a manufacturer's credentials, and mostly about the marketability of the attached celebrity name. By focussing on here today gone tomorrow celebrities, the life span of the average new fragrance had plummeted; and so had profitability, as a large wedge of the profits was handed over to the name.

Overall, Estée Lauder's portfolio was in good shape. The range of brands had expanded over the years, and now stood at 26 with the addition of fashion designer Tom Ford's name. Yet, 70% of sales was coming from the five core brands the company had developed themselves: Estée Lauder, Clinique, Aramis, Prescriptives and Origins. A key reason for the health of the core brands was their now almost ubiquitous global reach. Clinique was launched into Vietnam during the year, soon followed by Estée Lauder. Not that the other brands were having bad years. M·A·C launched into both India and China during the year, both countries where the core brands had paved the way. They were growing strongly: Clinique and Estée Lauder, launching in another 23 Chinese cities, almost doubled sales.

However, the trend in the portfolio was clear. Skin care and make-up were now the key categories, with sales of approximately $2.4 billion each. These numbers were almost double the size of the difficult fragrance business, and nearly ten times the size of the small but rapidly growing hair care category. While fragrance sales crept up only 3% on the year, the other categories all grew in double digits.

2006

The sales increase was below par, at just 3%: signs that the company was entering choppy waters. Management questioned some of the previously unshakeable icons of the business model. Despite all the diversification of two decades, Estée Lauder was still heavily reliant on US department stores, which accounted for around a third of total sales. The problem was that this trade channel was in trouble, being squeezed at either end: by category killer chains and by Wal-Mart. This lost footfall meant a huge struggle for the company to keep growing sales. A second problem was the slow but inexorable decline in the effectiveness of the gift-with-purchase promotional technique. This had been expensive at the best of times, but now was so widely copied as to be ubiquitous. It was becoming more a cost of doing business than a driver of increased competitiveness.

All this was coming on top of continued challenges in the fragrance category. Sales declined, despite makeovers for the venerable Youth Dew, White Linen and Pleasures brands. The saving grace in the year was the make-up category, which drove most of Estée Lauder's growth. M•A•C was the company's fastest growing brand, launching into Russia as well as China and India. Elsewhere in the portfolio, the super-premium skin care brand, La Mer, had quadrupled sales since 2002.

The management's strategic review resulted in the development of five strategic imperatives to negotiate the more difficult trading conditions, viz.

- Optimising the brand portfolio. Already the modernisation of some of the iconic brands was begun, and the M•A•C and Bobbi Brown brands were accelerated in their global rollout.

- Strengthening product categories. The eighth of the company's global R&D facilities had opened during the year in Shanghai. This resource promised to be a key competitive edge in the future, as appropriate for the world's largest, single-focus prestige cosmetics company.

- Strengthening and expanding global presence. Given the troubles besetting the American department store retail channel (unlikely to improve anytime soon), an increased rate of expansion overseas - particularly in China, Russia, India and Brazil - would be the cornerstone of the future growth strategy.

- Diversifying distribution. Internet, travel retail (duty free), and the company's own stores represented the fastest areas of growth, and would be given incremental focus and resources going forwards.

- Achieving operational and cost excellence. The business had come a long way since Estée and Joseph had cooked up four products in a converted restaurant kitchen. Now over one billion a year individual units were manufactured across 8,000 stock keeping units (SKUs). Surely scope existed for improvement to be facilitated by the implementation of SAP business enterprise software throughout the company, starting with Aveda.

2007

A 9% increase drove sales over the $7 billion barrier, with success across the board. It was a stellar year for new product launches, with four new brands added to the existing roster of 27. The mergers and acquisitions arm disposed of Rodan & Fields, and acquired the Ojon Corporation. Tom Ford Beauty added to Estée Lauder's range of brands in the ultraluxe niche. Two Daisy Fuentes fragrances were launched exclusively in Kohl's and a Coach-branded fragrance was introduced through distribution in Coach stores. Finally, at the lower end of the market, Estée Lauder collaborated with the Ford Motor Company to launch Mustang onto the mid-tier retail channel.

This variety of launch channels reflected the strategy to reduce reliance on department stores and reach a wider range of customers in new and different ways. Internet sales grew another 25% with the expansion of the online business to the UK, Australia and France. Certain brands were listed in Sephora, Canada's Shoppers Drug Mart and ULTA's 450 beauty superstores. Estée Lauder now had more than 450 free-standing stores around the world for its prestige brands, and Origins was available in the European pharmacy channel. No channel was deemed unworthy; Bobbi Brown's debut on QVC resulted in the shopping channel's most successful beauty launch for twenty years. This was clearly an expansion out of Estée Lauder's department store heartland. Yet, because it was driven by new brands with different target markets, it in no way diluted the equities of the still very profitable original brands.

Internationally, the Americas were the most sluggish region, creeping forwards only 3%. Sales elsewhere increased by mid-teen percentages - albeit this was somewhat exchange-rate-assisted. Even after stripping out currency effects, business outside the Americas moved ahead by a full 10%. The company now had 35 international affiliate organisations, including a newly opened one in Brazil and the acquisition of a distributor in Turkey. These supported sales in over 130 countries. Eight brands were now available in China with Estée Lauder leading the way in 32 cities.

2008

Estée Lauder added almost a billion in top-line sales, a 12% increase that seemed to belie the global economic crisis. True, a third of this growth came from favourable currency movements, but it was still an impressive performance. Meanwhile, sales in their largest market, the US, didn't grow at all - the consumer spending malaise was hitting the department store trade harder than most other channels. Skin care was again the best category, and generated almost $3 billion in sales. Their performance was driven by the Asia/Pacific region's very strong sales of skin-whitening products and a continued fast growth in China. Make-up, another $3 billion category, grew 10% with around two-thirds of the growth coming from the make-up artist brands, M•A•C and Bobbi Brown. These two inspired acquisitions of the mid-1990s had prospered under Estée Lauder's guidance.

The Estée Lauder Companies were now truly global. All growth came from outside the United States. In 2003, the company had sales of $5 billion of which over half, $2.7 billion, came from the US. By 2008, while the US business had grown by a stately but still respectable 20% to $3.2 billion, international sales had doubled to nearly $4.7 billion - impressive by any standards. This was due to three factors:

- The company's core product range was well aligned to the aspirations of the fast-growing middle classes around the world. In most of the Asian and European markets in which it competed, Estée Lauder was the fastest growing luxury brand; and sales increased 22% in the Middle East.
- The company was flexible in positioning itself. In Asia, where beauty equated to radiant complexions, they focussed upon skin care products that brighten and protect the skin (La Mer's top two international markets were Japan and Hong Kong); whereas in Russia and Brazil, two of Estée Lauder's fastest growing markets, they appealed to classic fragrance brands and the latest innovations in make-up.
- Emerging markets, by now accounting for 9% of sales, had vibrant and fast-growing high net worth consumer segments, ideal for the company's brands. Both China and Russia were now $100 million markets and two core brands, Estée Lauder and Clinique, became the company's fifth and sixth brands there - both opened their own stores.

Another significant factor behind the continued good news was the company's success in positioning itself not as a reactive victim of the changes in how their consumers were reached, but as proactive beneficiaries. Other than its tradition of iconic advertising, Estée Lauder's touchstone had always been a close interaction with its customers, typically in department stores. In the US, that channel was in trouble - slipping from being worth 41% of sales in 2003, to 30% in 2008. This malaise was unlikely to ease soon, although the company upgraded its in-store Clinique customer experience.

While US department stores were becalmed, international department stores, more than doubling sales to over $2 billion in the previous five years, were Estée Lauder's fastest growing channel. This was due in no small part to its long-term strength in that environment. So, taken together, total department stores still contributed half of total sales. Otherwise, the company was most excited about the potential offered in four up-and-coming channels:

The Internet. Fifteen brands were now available for sales online in a growing number of countries - Korea being the latest - and total online sales leapt up 40% in the year. But the channel was much more than another outlet. Brands with limited distribution now had the chance to reach a much wider audience. In line with Estée Lauder's trademark personal touch, Clinique, M•A•C, Bobbi Brown and Origins all offered live chat, with real make-up artists providing personalised advice.

Direct Response TV. This was another arena where a prolonged interaction with the audience played to company strengths. It was now a significant route to market: in 2008 sales of cosmetics and toiletries on direct response TV channels exceeded $500 million. Clinique, Origins, Bobbi Brown and Ojon had all been big hits. Indeed, Ojon had been acquired primarily because it was primarily a direct response TV brand.

Company Stores. Here the personal touch was taken even further - no constraints from department store rules and no presence of competing counters. Estée Lauder now operated 577 stores, which acted as advertising billboards in some of the world's most prestigious real estate.

Travel Retail. Estée Lauder brands had always been well featured in duty-free outlets. Now, many new airport terminals had opened which emphasised the development of the high-end retail component - a very helpful trend. As well as featuring in upgraded duty-free areas, stand-alone company stores were part of the strategy, and helped drive sales in this channel up by 20% in the year.

This combination of routes to the consumer also gave the company the opportunity to develop ground-breaking, multi-channel launch strategies for new products. For example, Tri-Aktiline Instant Deep Wrinkle Filler was launched internationally in 2008 via speciality cosmetics stores, direct response TV, the internet and travel retail.

2009

The mid-year timing of the company's financial year end could no longer insulate it from the global financial downturn; the company's first ever annual sales decline was recorded. Yet, the reported decline of 7% to $7.3 billion was more due to currency fluctuations than to volume decline (only 2%). Estée Lauder reduced its SKU count by 16% and cut merchandising, advertising and sampling budgets. This was simply a very strong company enduring some difficult market conditions.

Estée Lauder focused on driving the higher margin parts of the portfolio and the fastest growing regions; whilst propping up the brands and markets most badly hit by the downturn. Customer experience was enhanced at the Bobbi Brown counters and in the Origins stores, whilst, for the traditional fragrance brands, smaller, less expensive pack sizes were introduced. Department stores were for once allowed to display prices, discretely. Internet sales increased another 20% with Bumble and bumble going online. Estée Lauder and Clinique websites were launched in China. In local currency, company sales of skin care products powered ahead 17% in the Asia/Pacific region, with acceleration in China more than making up for a slowdown in Japan.

2010

Estée Lauder showed its resilience, bouncing back with a 6% sales increase to $7.8 billion. Indeed, but for the effect of currency changes inflating the record 2008 figures, this was the company's best year yet in real terms. As the American market was still becalmed, Asia and Europe drove the growth. Sales in China increased by almost 30%, with e-commerce chipping in a 23% increase.

One company strength was to repair the visible signs of ageing. New product launches in this area added nearly $250 million during 2010. The launch of Estée Lauder's Advanced Night Repair was the most successful in the company's history. The make-up artist brands were still driving ahead, 79 M•A•C stores opened around the world and the Bobbi Brown line was launched into Poland. The fragrance category slightly declined, as sales of the franchise name brands such as DKNY, Hilfiger and Sean John fell off. The unpredictability of this sub-category, and therefore its lower profitability, prompted the company to switch focus onto their own fragrance brands. They were rewarded with growth – even the venerable Aramis had a good year.

Organisationally, the major acquisition was the Smashbox Beauty Cosmetics company, a prestige brand sold primarily in speciality beauty channels in the US and 40 other countries. A decision to discontinue the Prescriptives brand was partially withdrawn due to a social media campaign by its core followers. Estée Lauder made the formerly best-selling line available for sale online while transitioning some products into other brands.

The company was a year into its new four-year strategy, which involved a significant restructuring (see above) and resizing of the company. The number of SKUs was reduced again, this time by 10%, and a programme to trim the workforce by 2,000 was put into place.

2011

A record year added over a billion to the top line, a 13% increase which was three times the growth rate of the total industry. A third of this increase came from the US market. Here increased footfall in department stores met Estée Lauder's revitalised counters, which now boasted special lighting, interactive touch screen tools and a host of new products. Business also grew in other US channels, particularly fast-growing multi-brand beauty retailers like Sephora, where Bumble and Bumble launched in 298 stores. Further expansion and investment in digital selling tools saw online sales rise yet again by an impressive 28%. Skin care products again led the way, increasing by 15% to almost $4 billion (almost a billion had been added in only two years). Even fragrances had a good year, helped by the launch of Estée Lauder Pleasures Bloom.

On the international front, the company became leaders in China in the prestige beauty category. They were now selling 11 brands in 38 cities through a variety of department stores, company stores and multi-brand specialist retailers. Estée Lauder had recently opened a larger R&D facility to focus on new products, designed around local needs. La Mer grew by 55% through increased distribution and the launch of an E-Commerce site. Combined sales in China, Hong Kong, Taiwan and Korea grew by $181 million.

In Brazil, the world's third-largest beauty market, company growth was spearheaded by Clinique and M•A•C, the country's leading brands. To make up for the relative lack of Brazilian department stores, focus was placed on opening company stores and expanding e-commerce.

2012

The luxury consumer was back. Spending in the prestige beauty market outpaced growth in the lower-priced offerings. This trend was very much to the company's advantage. Indeed they outperformed the competition: their 10% record increase grew at double the sector rate. For the first time the eponymous Estée Lauder brand became the largest prestige beauty brand in the world.

As was becoming familiar, the high growth categories were skin care, with a large range of new products, and make-up, primarily the make-up artist's brands. The work done improving the attractiveness and customer experience in their department stores counters continued to pay dividends: US sales grew by over $250 million. Clinique consolidated its position as the number one overall beauty brand and new products in the Estée Lauder range brought many new customers into the brand.

Outside the United States, another 50 company stores opened and online business increased by 24%. The company had by now 340 marketing and e-commerce sites across more than 50 countries. The Estée Lauder Companies were now the clear leaders in the online beauty business, a fact confirmed in an internal benchmarking study. In the past decade, online sales had increased almost tenfold, and showed no signs of slowing down. Online was now the fastest growing sales channel for beauty sales, especially in countries lacking full department store coverage. In China the company estimated it accounted for fully half of all beauty market purchases. Opening more company stores helped drive up brand availability to 58 cities.

Store opening was also a priority in Brazil with seven new M•A•C stores cementing the brand's number 1 position in the beauty market. Jo Malone and Bobbi Brown also opened stores in the Middle East, a fast-growing market. In

Latin America, the company assumed market leadership in Mexico, Venezuela and Peru.

What is Their DNA

Perhaps the biggest strength of Estée Lauder is that its DNA can be traced directly back to its founder. There is no doubt Estée Lauder herself would completely recognise the business today. Its key strengths now were her strengths then, although updated and adapted for the challenges of today.

Consumer Contact

Estée Lauder said of the business that, in its earliest days, the most important aspect was making human contact. She knew who was buying and her customers knew who was selling. When she expanded to two salons, she ingrained this attitude into the fabric of her business. What she did so successfully is still a unique cornerstone, now updated into the company's High-Touch model. The outcomes are the same today. Product selection is personalised. Consumers are educated about their own skin and how to look after it. The high involvement creates strong emotional connections and ultimately builds brand loyalty. The secret has been to evolve the method, over time and into new channels, beyond the department store. Computer touch screens have replaced Estée's question-and-answer sheet, and the pushy saleswoman is now a beauty consultant. Perhaps the company's greatest achievement has been to translate its USP (unique selling point) into areas such as company stores, direct response TV and, most successfully, the internet.

Global

Estée knew right from the start, as she was barger her way into Harrods's, she was helping to meet basic needs applicable across all races, countries and languages - albeit that the more precise issues and solutions would differ. The company has stuck to those beliefs and runs a highly successful global operation. Indeed, there is not a country of note where the company has failed, been beaten to the punch or misread consumer needs. It has not gone to each market with a global template. Rather, the great variety amongst the biggest brands has eased access to the various markets. Estée Lauder is in an ideal position to benefit hugely from the rapidly increasing new middle classes in emerging markets - having powerful, leading positions in the BRIC markets (Brazil, Russia, India and China) and elsewhere.

Innovation

Innovation has always been at the heart of the company, both in what the products did and how they were sold. Throughout its existence, Estée Lauder has been a trendsetter more than a follower. Estée's sales techniques, through Aramis and Clinique right up until the present day - when eight global R&D laboratories provide an endless stream of hundreds of new products a year – has been a permanent bench-marking process for the rest of the industry. The company's prowess in innovation is perhaps best illustrated by the Forbes' 2012 lists: The Estée Lauder Companies ranked number 933 in sales, number 716 in profits, number 348 in market cap and number 23 in Innovative. This is one place above Google.

Brand Management

If a class of MBA students sought paragons of brand management, they might start with the usual suspects: P&G, Unilever and so forth. But brand management has also been an unmistakable core strength of Estée Lauder. All of the original brands that built the company have been so nurtured and adapted that they remain relevant today. Take Estée Lauder and Clinique, for example. Virtually every acquired brand has gone on to much greater heights under company stewardship: M•A•C. Brand equities have been zealously protected, in particular through managing the process of expanding beyond the department store core of the business. That process continues today. Which brands should appear in which retail environments has always been a company obsession - iron discipline in this area is the key reason why the Estée Lauder brand itself is now the world's leader.

Summary

It is difficult to see anything but continued success for The Estée Lauder Companies. Of course, they are as exposed to spending downturns in the economy and currency fluctuations as any other global company selling high-end products. Yet, their strengths in brand portfolio, consumer contact, innovation, emerging markets and E-Commerce mean that any such problems will be more bumps in the road than major derailments. They have strong competitors but they are exceptionally well-positioned competitively. They have never been a company to slavishly follow what someone else is doing.

Although the company has been publicly quoted for almost two decades, it is still in the control of the family. It deserves much credit for cherishing the company's heart and soul, while bringing in outside expertise to keep it up-to-date and relevant. They are a case study of how a family firm should evolve over time. Estée Lauder is immune from hostile takeover so can continue to take a more balanced view between short-term and long-term. This has always been one of the company's defining characteristics: Aramis and Clinique would never have made it in a next-quarter-results culture. Estée would be proud.

Unilever

Where Did They Come From?

Unilever came into being on 2nd September 1929 when the British firm Lever Brothers and the Dutch-owned Margarine Unie signed an agreement to create Unilever. Both companies were at that time long-established - the merger created one of Europe's largest companies – but many of the attributes of Unilever were to derive from the personality of the founder of Lever Brothers, William Lever.

William was born into the grocery trade, his father owning a small wholesale grocery business in the North of England, and in 1867, despite his mother's wishes he train to be a doctor, William entered the family business at the age of sixteen. As the owner's son, William did not have an easy ride; he was put to work in the warehouse preparing orders for delivery to local shops, a job that included the onerous task of cutting soap to each retailer's requested quantity, the soap having been delivered to Lever's in large unwrapped chunks for William to cut and wrap in greaseproof paper. Surely there must be a better system than this, thought William, his first business lesson: there had to be potential in improving things.

William soon talked his father into giving him a travelling salesman's job, sealing the deal by offering to forego the salesman's salary and stick to his existing arrangement of bed, board and pocket money. That William was a natural salesman was apparent from the off. He was also a hard worker, his favourite book being Samuel Smiles' Self Help, a series of biographies of famous and successful men from humble beginnings who succeeded through determination and hard work. William applied its lessons diligently, expanding his sales territory far beyond its existing boundaries and taking customers from other wholesalers. This was William's second business lesson: expansion brought success.

William's third business lesson came several years later when he and his brother James, both now effectively running the business, put in a big order for eggs from Ireland and were dismayed at the Liverpool dockside to find them largely broken and cracked. Between them they designed a crate to keep wholesale orders of eggs intact and took it to the Liverpool Patent Office. Following the passing of the Trademark Act in 1875, the office also handled the new area of trademark applications, which prompted William, on a whim, to trademark the name Lever's Pure Honey. He then began stamping it on the cut down bars of generic soap (still being processed in his warehouse), which he sold at a price premium. He had discovered the power of a good brand name.

By 1884, William, now the dominant partner in charge of a large, successful wholesale enterprise, albeit still owned by his father, when the lessons he had learned all came together. His own business told him that soap was booming - indoor plumbing was becoming more common - and he wanted a bigger piece of that cake. So he went back to the Liverpool Patent Office to discuss possible new brand names for a soap he did not yet have the facilities to manufacture. Taken by one of the patent agent's suggestions - Sunlight - William's first idea was to source a range of quality soaps from several suppliers and package them all under the Sunlight brand name – a concept not dissimilar to a retail private label brand, but at the wholesale level of the supply chain. In reviewing the candidate soaps, he was taken by one, which he thought stood head and shoulders above the others.

However, once the supplier heard the term 'exclusive supplier' and started talking up his price, William realised he would forever be at the man's mercy. For the plan to work, he had to buy the recipe. But the Lever brothers, as mere employees, still had little to no capital, so they tapped up their father who, after much grumbling, handed over a lump sum which, augmented by the brothers from other sources, was enough to buy the recipe and lease a soap works in the town of Warrington. Two soap-making experts who came with the factory tweaked the recipe to solve a few issues and soon had a winning formula based on Copra oil (derived from coconuts), tallow (from American and Australian sheep and cattle), cotton oil, and resin (from pine trees). The resulting mix was scented by citronella imported from Southern Asia but came without the usual industry filler of silicate of soda: William wanted to market his soap as 'Pure'. The next step in his USP was to cut the bars to size in the factory, wrap them not only in parchment paper but box them, using the newly accessible litho printing processes to create a powerful full-colour visual on the box. This was revolution-ary stuff for 1885. Production started in January 1885. Two years later, his facto-ry was bursting at the seams, making 450 tons a week. William bought a site for a gigantic new factory, and called it Port Sunlight.

William had immediately realised the future of Sunlight soap was not to grow the wholesale business, but to make a soap business. He would sell Sunlight to any and every wholesaler and retailer he could find, a novel approach in an in-dustry where the leading soap-makers carved up the country cosily between themselves on a regional basis. By the mid-1890s Sunlight sales were at a stagger-ing 40,000 tons a year, a level that encouraged the ever-frugal William to find uses for the waste that came from the various production stages. Thus Lifebuoy was launched in 1894 and made from waste from the boiling pans plus a large helping of an antiseptic. Then followed by Sunlight Flakes - waste from the bar cutting machines soon to be rebranded as Lux Soap Flakes in 1900. As business continued to boom, the Lever Brothers product range expanded, and not just in soaps. As well as a good number of toilet soaps at prices higher than Sunlight, it moved into other emerging cleaning needs: scouring powder with Vim in 1904 and laundry powder with Omo – first conceived simply as a bleaching powder - in 1908. William never forgot the lesson as a salesman, driving his horse and trap far and wide to expand the business's reach: scale was a big benefit.

In the meantime, his key ingredients were now coming from all corners of the globe and he worried endlessly about securing their supply. One way to solve this was to be as big a buyer as possible, which he set about in two ways: acquisition and international expansion. He had no time for the soap makers' cartel and took great delight in buying out as many of its members as possible as they were crushed under the Sunlight bandwagon, his greatest triumph being the snaring of the famous Pears soap company in 1915. But perhaps the most significant acquisition came in 1919 with Crosfield of Warrington, with which came the rights to sell in the UK a German washing powder brand developed by Henkel: Persil. With over 60% of the UK soap market, William was a big believer in the power of internal competition to keep everyone on their toes, so most of his acquired companies happily competed against each other while Lever Brothers benefitted from the increased economies of scale. This sowed the seeds of a Unilever operating style that would prove very troublesome in later years: a very high degree of operational independence at the operating company level, with head office being more administrators than managers.

William Lever was also an early internationalist, and by this time had set up operations in several countries including the United States, Switzerland, Canada, Australia and Germany: more scale, which meant, however, more worry over his raw materials, which need integration back up the supply chain. But he had already begun the process in 1892, when emerging margarine companies began competing for his precious copra oil: he himself had made the arduous journey to Fiji and Samoa to see the industry for himself. But by 1909, his eye had turned to palm oil and the company began developing its own palm plantations in the Solomon Islands. It had not escaped his notice that the Dutch margarine companies, Jurgens and Van den Bergh, had set up a palm plantation joint venture in Germany's African empire (both companies had several factories in Germany). A year later Lever Bros opened its own African company to do exactly the same.

Lever Brotherss venture into Africa would have profound effects at two points in the company's future. After further investments in the Congo, in 1920 the company made an investment in Nigeria that was near disastrous and terminal for William's leadership. Lever Brothers massively overpaid for the Niger Company, which produced 100,000 tons of oilseed a year, at a time when a post World War One depression had badly impacted demand for soap in most of Lever's key markets. The net result was the company could not finance the acquisition and were rescued from possible bankruptcy only by their bankers, in return for a large proportion of the company voting stock, until this point 100% owned by Lever himself.

Despite having built one of Britain's largest companies from scratch, the fact is that the banks and some of his senior management had been losing faith in the great man. William was a somewhat unique and polarising leader. His management style took the word autocratic to new levels: 'We won't argue, you're wrong' was his favourite response to any discussion. His own ideas were railroaded through by referring the decision to the shareholders: himself. Yet despite his autocracy, his company had become so vast and convoluted that it had become impossible for him to control. Diversification had followed diversification to the point where, he discovered to his own surprise, he owned a saw-mill, a coal-mine, a limestone quarry, a paper mill and an engineering firm.

The outcome was that William's effective sidelining by the new majority banker shareholders, who, appalled at the near catastrophe the Niger Company purchase had precipitated, installed one of the company's accountants, Francis D'Arcy Cooper, as the new managing director. Cooper went through the company like a dose of salts, questioning every penny of expenditure, trying to restructure the convolutions along more logical lines and selling off anything he thought didn't fit in. The moving of the company's head office from Port Sunlight to London in 1921 removed any lingering doubts that things had permanently changed.

Even after William's corporate demise, his influence was still significant. In the last few years of his reign he had branched out on his own and purchased a whole raft of companies including a fishing fleet and a chain of fish shops. These, along with a sausage company, T. Wall & Sons, that now sold ice cream during the slow summer months, were taken over by Lever Bros and would form the nucleus of their future Foods Division. The Niger Company would also form the nucleus of The United African Company, the subsidiary whose profits would be virtually propping the company up fifty years later. However, William never recovered from this hammer blow to his pride; he passed away in 1925 having just informed the AGM that the company had made a profit for the first time in five years since the Niger Company debacle.

Even before William's fishing and sausage businesses joined, the company had actually been in the food business for more than a decade. In 1914, to utilise its expertise in using fats, the company had been asked by the British government to manufacture margarine when the German invasion of France and the Low Countries cut off supplies. This of course meant that Lever Brothers was bumping heads with the likes of Van den Bergh, a friction amplified by the Dutch margarine companies' diversification into soap. As both sets of industry giants continued to expand internationally during the 1920s, the sources of friction multiplied. A series of margarine industry mergers in Holland in the late 1920s created Margarine Unie, a company every bit as monolithic as Lever; both soon realised that perhaps cooperation might be more productive than competition for sales, new markets and raw materials.

Jurgens and Van den Bergh, the component companies of Margarine Unie, had been in business since 1872, even longer than Lever Brothers. By 1888, both had set up factories in the much larger German market. In 1908 the two companies did a deal to share profits while still nominally competing against each other; in the 1920s, following the collapse of a German economy beset by hyper-inflation, set up in Britain, competing against Lever's brand, Planters. So, when Jurgens and Van den Bergh officially merged in 1927, the competitive threat to Lever Brothers was greatly magnified, which brought both companies to the ne-gotiating table. At first the plan was for a cooperation agreement but, as both companies had been built on the premise of scale and plenty of it, a full merger was the obvious conclusion.

How Did They Evolve?

The form the newly merged company took was unique at the time and al-most remains so to this day. Unilever was two holding companies: a British Uni-lever Ltd, listed on the London Stock Exchange and capitalised in sterling and a Dutch Unilever NV, listed on the Rotterdam Stock Exchange and capitalised in guilders. The two companies also had different shareholders. An Equalisation Agreement between the two ensured that both sets of shareholders would always be paid equivalent dividends. There were two boards with the same members but for a joint chairman, and the boards sat in London and Rotterdam respectively. A Special Committee was established to manage the affairs of the joint compa-nies, reporting to both boards.

The timing of the merger - in the same year as the Great Depression - was not propitious, neither was the news the next year that the mighty American firm, Procter & Gamble, was finally moving into the British market with the acquisition of Thomas Hedley Ltd., one of Lever's few remaining soap competitors. But even though William Lever was gone, his approach of growth through acquisition and overseas expansion plus a decentralised operating culture continued regardless. Some acquisitions were by design, such as that of the largest U.S. manufacturer of tea, the Thomas J. Lipton Company, while others were through necessity: Nazi restrictions on exporting dividends meant the large profits from Unilever's substantial German assets had to be reinvested into whatever German companies they could buy, taking Unilever into cheese, ice cream, transportation and public utilities.

During the war years the company's decentralised style became even more accentuated as businesses in German and Japanese occupied territories were cut off from head office, as indeed was the Rotterdam head office itself. But during the war, business continued wherever it could. In Britain, Lifebuoy soap provided a free washing and bathing service to bombed-out civilians. Acquisitions were still being made too, the most notable being the 1943 purchases of Batchelor Foods and a majority stake in Frosted Foods, who owned the U.K. rights to the Birds Eye frozen foods brand. The purchases were followed by the 1944 acquisition of the Pepsodent toothpaste. And thanks to the 1919 Crosfields acquisition, Unilever was also big in silicates, plastic and paint, all of which were ramped up during the war.

After the war, the company decided to continue its high wartime levels of decentralisation as a matter of policy, leaving its many operating companies to get on with their own business, Head Office operating more as a central banker, with local operating companies making cases for local acquisitions and pitching head office for the funds. Thus, the American arm of the business, still called Lever Brothers, bought a Chicago-based margarine manufacturer and America's oldest cosmetics firm, Harriet Hubbard Ayer, to prop up a soap business that was struggling to keep up with P&G.

The purchase of the not very modern-sounding Harriet Hubbard Ayer brand awakened Head Office to the potential of personal care brands. It was a growing category, highly responsive to innovation and advertising, and delivered higher than average margins and identified as a category that suited the company's soap brand-building skills. Thus, Sunsilk was launched in the UK in 1954 and by the end of the decade was selling in eighteen countries. Sunsilk had arrived just in time to benefit from the 1955 launch of British commercial television, Unilever running the very first television advertisement in the country for its Gibbs SR toothpaste. The French soap and toothpaste company, Thibauld Gibbs, was purchased in 1956, the product range being slowly moved into transitioned over to hair-care products under the more alluring-sounding name of Elida Gibbs. In 1957 the US operation acquired the rights to a toothpaste tube technology that enabled the squeezing of stripes, and then immediately launched the brand Signal, marketed as a breath-freshening toothpaste with the magic ingredient in the little red stripes. The same year, the US Lever brothers also launched Dove, containing 25% moisturising crème and sold at twice the price of Lux.

During the 1950s, it became readily apparent that the decentralisation strategy was a mixed blessing. On the plus side, many innovations that would later have global significance sprang up seemingly spontaneously from local business units grasping local opportunities. Thus, in 1955, the fledgling British frozen food arm borrowed the idea of fish fingers from America and within a decade was accounting for 10% of the nation's consumption of fish. The German operation, which had survived the war largely unscathed (the economy for consumer goods having continued far longer in Germany than in Britain during the war), came up with the idea in 1959 of selling margarine in tubs, the extra cost of the tub being more than mitigated by the consumer benefits softer, spreadable fats. Netherlands Unilever bought an ice cream company and in Africa, the Niger Company that had almost everything, and now renamed the United Africa Company, was buying into a whole range of industries in multiple countries during the de-colonisation phase. By the mid-1950s, it was earning 15% of Unilever's entire profits.

However, there was a downside to all of this local entrepreneurism. Unilever had an excessive number of brands, most of which only sold in one country, and the company struggled to come up with a coherent response to P&G's regional approach to its European entry, a situation highlighted by Unilever's piecemeal and feeble response to the arrival of Tide. Tide, launched in the US in test market in 1946 and fully national by 1949, was a synthetic detergent not made of soap at all which had decimated the American soap brands of not only Lever Brothers but P&G itself. Unilever executives understood the technology - pre-war relationships with its inventors at Germany's I.G. Farben saw to that - but they were shy of bringing out their own version in Europe: no national company had the nerve to decimate their own soap brands to ward off a threat that might never arrive. In any case, there was no over-arching management structure to impose a region-wide response once Tide did arrive. Consequently, Unilever's dominant shares of many of Europe's markets - 80% in Britain in 1955 – went into a prolonged decline that took decades to reverse. The 1957 reformulation of the UK's Persil – it remained a soap powder - was a typically inadequate response given that Tide had halved their US market share, resulting in an 80% share bottoming out in the 1970s at 25%. Not too bad, actually: the company's share in the much larger German market would fall by three-quarters. The re-launch of Omo in 1957 as a synthetic detergent was simply too little, too late.

Unilever's response to the unfolding soap opera was to encourage a focus on the foods side, currently less than 10% of company sales. This became a third leg of the business alongside detergents and margarines, although in truth the company's leg count was almost centipede standard, ranging from advertising agencies to roll-on roll-off ferries. Thus, in 1957 Unilever in Britain bought out its junior partner in the UK Birds Eye franchise, the American parent General Foods, as many of the European companies got into the rapidly expanding category. While increasing home ownership of refrigerators with freezer compartments was driving consumer demand, setting up in the business required a huge investment in frozen manufacturing, transportation and retailing equipment, an area where the huge scale of Unilever gave the company an advantage; they could easily afford to invest ahead of demand.

The 1960s continued in much the same way as the latter part of the 1950s. Faced with tumbling market shares in detergents – even in a growing market, Unilever would lose one-third of its total European market share during the decade – and a margarine business that had benefited from rising edible fats markets that had now stalled, the company was forced to compete much more aggressively for its butter brands share. So it ramped up its diversification and innovation efforts. It was a big enough brand in many countries, and could afford to pursue its expansionist strategy with little fear of takeover or running out of cash.

Two areas where both parts of the strategy came together were in ice cream and frozen foods, which of course shared the need for frozen storage. With both Wall's in the UK and its enforced German diversification, the company had been in ice cream since the early 1920s, upgrading and expanding capacity in both. The first major additions came in 1960 with the purchases of Streets in Australia (who would later invent the Magnum bar) and Frisko in Denmark. A year later the becalmed US operation bought the Breyer's Good Humor brand, but were singularly inept at managing it, driving it into loss in 1968 and for the next sixteen years. Success would come with the 1962 acquisition of Italy's Spica, with Cornetto in its portfolio. There followed several more European acquisitions, several of which were juiced up by a partnership with Nestlé to share infrastructure costs.

One advantage of the Unilever operating model now and then is that companies were not shy to borrow a good idea from another market, so just about every Unilever ice cream company ran with Cornetto, some too early: the company had not yet perfected the means of keeping the cone crisp. Other innovations that quickly spread around the Unilever Empire were Cif/Jif, the first liquid abrasive household cleaner. The Dove cleansing bar made its way across the Atlantic into several European markets albeit with a different formulation and the 1968 launch of Persil Automatic helped stem detergent market share losses. However, Unilever's overall innovation record was patchy. The US launch of Dove washing up liquid, soon marketed as a cut-price budget brand, was a flop that harmed the brand image of the soap, and Comfort fabric conditioner, launched in Germany in 1966, failed to put much of a dent into P&G's Lenor. Unilever was first to market dishwashing liquids in Europe, but soon lost their lead to P&G.

On the diversification side, the company was already the biggest fish British retailer and owned of a fully integrated German fish operation from trawler fleet to fish restaurants. The company moved into salmon farming too, then set about expanding its slaughterhouse businesses for the Walls and Hartog meat brands. Anything that looked even remotely like the Next Big Thing was snapped up, a German-owned Ceylon-based tea company experimenting in an instant tea, for example. The company was also expanding its operations in animal feeds, chemicals, paper, packaging and transportation (sold mostly to other Unilever companies). The in-house Unilever advertising agency, Lintas, was by now in over twenty countries and taking on work from any non-competing advertiser.

Meanwhile The United Africa Company seemed to be following a strategy all of its own. It was the main African agent for Caterpillar heavy earth-moving equipment and Africa's largest brewer through joint ventures with Heineken and Guinness: Nigeria was Guinness's second largest overseas market after the US due to a long-running marketing campaign claiming aphrodisiac and performance-enhancing properties qualities (in stark contrast to amateur European and American bedroom-based market research). UAC was even expanding beyond Africa, opening up operations in the Middle East and Pacifica Islands, mainly to provide ongoing career opportunities for its vast army of professional expat managers.

It was indirectly due to UAC's involvement in the beer business that Unilever almost merged with Allied Breweries in the late 1960s. One member of the Unilever Special Committee had spent most of his a career in UAC and pushed the company to the very brink of amalgamation after an Allied approach in 1968 intended to leverage Unilever's immense grocery distribution capabilities on the deregulation of alcohol sales. However, few outside a handful of senior executives were convinced by the logic. The move fell through following a collapse in the share price of Unilever Ltd during consideration of the deal by Britain's Monopolies and Mergers Commission.

By the end of the 1960s, Unilever, with its vastly extensive range of categories and brands, was truly immense, with more sales than P&G, Colgate Palmolive, Nestlé and Henkel combined. In market share terms, it held around one-third of the global market for detergents, its relative weakness in Europe and the US made up by being first mover in many other markets and a much greater geographic spread than its main soap and detergent competitors. In edible fats, Unilever enjoyed a 12% global market share, 50% accounted for by butter. In personal care, however, the company was barely beginning: its global share was a measly 4%. But the biggest issue was the never-ending tension between decentralisation and central control. But whilst decentralisation had hurt the detergents business, it was a positive advantage in the food sector, where tastes remained resolutely national. In this much more fragmented food market Unilever had many category strengths, not least the world's second-largest soup manufacturer in a subsidiary of T.J. Lipton. And it was expert in opening new markets, making acquisitions and marketing locally, all keys strengths. Two-thirds of turnover was accounted for by detergents, edible oils and foods.

Although business seemed to be proceeding as normal with the 1970 acquisition of the Dutch meat business Zwanenberg's, the launch of Impulse deodorant by the South African business and the purchase of Lipton International (combined with the US's Lipton & Son the acquisition made Unilever one of the world's largest tea businesses), all was not well. The lack of central direction hit home when the company was hit by a cash flow crisis that accelerated dramatically between 1968 and 1970, caused primarily by a rapid decline in margins. Many of its key markets suffered rapidly rising costs and price controls and return on capital dropped from 8.2% to 6.8% during the same two-year spell. The company had not foreseen the problem, which was exacerbated by a fall-out between the Dutch Head Office and the British Finance Director. Sales had kept growing, but profit performance was well off the pace.

An accounts system where each operating company submitted detailed and accountable forecasts was now a necessity, a more disciplined approach to cash allocation of cash for new investments, previously doled out to whoever marshalled the most convincing arguments. Times were suddenly getting tough. Struggles in detergents, margarine and the US business combined with the 1973 world oil crisis made them worse. Europe, previously the business cash cow, stalled and then declined, due mainly to a precipitous drop in the yellow fats market in Britain and Germany - around 25% during the 1970s and early 1980s. Across Europe as a whole in the first quarter of 1975, the company actually made a loss. The year after, fourteen out of thirty-one Netherlands operating units were also making a loss.

In detergents, Unilever was still being steamrollered by P&G, whose 200-plus global detergent portfolio compared to a ludicrously large Lever Brothers portfolio of 665 spread across 42 markets. Even worse, while Tide was being launched everywhere, Unilever's strongest brand, Persil – the UK's largest grocery brand - was only available in relatively few. Henkel, its original inventor, had kept a grip on its star performer. Henkel. Frozen foods were little better as other companies piled into the market, reducing Birds Eye to a loss by the end of the 1970s. Ice cream did little better, although the company was still having some personal care successes. Rexona (Sure in the UK and South Africa) became the world's number two deodorant, whilst the launches of Timotei and Signal were fighting Colgate hard for the top European toothpaste slot.

In the US Lever Brothers was by now almost a byword in that country for management incompetence. It had declined to a paltry 12% share in detergents and was losing money on everything apart from Lipton's tea and its sideline in soups, forcing the company to rely on its largely unchallenged detergent and personal positions in Asia, Latin America and Africa for the generation of any growth at all: around 26% of its detergent sales were coming from these markets compared to single digit levels for P&G and Colgate-Palmolive. A further 25% in the 1970s originated from the combination of UAC, plantations and chemicals, hardly the sign of a vibrant packaged goods business. UAC was the most profitable component of the sprawling Unilever empire: Nigeria accounted for up to 60% of total sales outside of Europe and the US: in addition to 13 breweries, UAC was into textiles and importing GM trucks and cars.

The only solution to its US woes looked like some kind big acquisition, and from a long list of luminaries - Chesebrough-Ponds, Gillette, Heinz, Quaker Oats, Gerber and CPC -they settled in 1978 for the chemicals company, National Starch and bought it for a then whopping $487 million, a record for a foreign-based company investing in the US. While the deal would not be transformative in the long run, it did send a signal that the company was serious about building a viable operation in the world's largest market. But the 1970s effectively remained a write-off: sales increases barely kept pace with inflation and over 50% was wiped off the stock value of the joint holding companies. Things were so bad, McKinsey were summoned to cast their beady eye over the sorry state of affairs.

One of McKinsey's first observations was that the company wasn't seeing much of a return from its 7,000 R&D employees scattered around the world. Many of the better innovations, such as Cornetto, had come with acquisitions.

All too often the company was second best, or took so long bringing break-throughs to market the advantage was lost. A case in point had been with the company's development of Tetra-Acetyl Ethylene Diamene (TAED), which enabled bleaching action at lower temperatures, which is precisely what most Europeans were doing: coloured fabrics could not be boiled. It had been the biggest advance in the category since Tide. Work had begun in the mid-1960s but Unilever were not able to bring a product to market until the patent had almost expired. Result? Competitors followed quickly and any long-term gain was lost.

McKinsey, unsurprisingly, also homed in on the failing US business which, amongst its many other troubles, had been progressively slashing its R&D spend for years trying to protect its worsening bottom line. Following the review, a 1980 R&D spend of $9.6 million rose to $42 million two years later with the emphasis on personal care. McKinsey also recommended the company withdraw from the US margarine market, but the company decided differently, closing its manufacturing facilities and sourcing from a third-party supplier, immediately boosting margins whilst they waited for a better idea to come along, which it duly did. In 1983, the supplier launched a brand of its own, a low-fat spread called Country Crock, which was an immediate success. Unilever promptly bought the supplier, secured a much lower than their own factories and a stronger brand in the market. On the downside, the fact that a primarily private label supplier had shown Unilever how to innovative proved McKinsey's point about Unilever's feeble innovation capabilities.

Whether due to McKinsey's promptings or simply a blocked pipeline, the company actually came up with some winners in the early 1980s. A bright spark in the ice cream R&D team was Vienetta – an affordable luxury ice cream dessert, with a production technology protected by patent with many years left to run. The French personal products division created Axe body spray (branded Lynx in the UK), by the end of the decade was Unilever's largest deodorant. Dove had been re-launched in the United States and was on its way to becoming the country's best-selling soap bar. But just when the R&D director was feeling confident enough to look his colleagues in the eye, the company walked into the disaster that was New System Persil, the changing of the brand from soap to enzymes. It was a catastrophe: widespread reports of skin irritation caused brand share to plummet, forcing the company to execute a New Coca-style about face and reintroduce the old version as quickly as possible. By 1984, the company had had enough; a dramatic change was required if it was going to prosper.

How Did They Build the Modern Company?

By the early to mid-1980s, many companies who had taken their consultants' advice to diversify were beginning to regret the experience, so diversification on the Unilever was old-fashioned to say the least. Focus and core competences were the new buzzwords, which Unilever needed to adopt more than anyone. The company had to decide what it wanted to be and the fact that money could be made (occasionally) from trucking, fishing, car dealing, advertising and packaging was insufficient reason to be in those businesses. So, in 1984, Unilever embarked on what it called its Core Business Strategy.

As a first stage, Unilever identified a set of businesses it identified as being core to the company which were to be strengthened and grown, mainly through transformative acquisition. Unfortunately, as well as including some clear long-term packaged goods growth categories such as foods, detergents and personal products – the three legs of two decades ago – the list also included elements deemed core for other reasons, such as too big or too profitable to let go, in particular speciality chemicals and some chunks of UAC. It would be another ten years before Unilever took the steps to become a fully-fledged packaged goods specialist, but it was a good start. First on the chopping block were the transport companies, soon to be followed by market research, advertising, animal feeds, packaging and the non-African components of UAC. The next step was to go out and buy some businesses that were capable of transforming the shape and growth prospects of what was still one of the world's largest companies.

Unilever had initially been attracted to Richardson-Vicks but alerted that Brooke-Bond might soon be in range, switched attention to the British tea and food giant. Unilever had thought previously about bidding Brooke Bond but the company's substantial tea plantations, then a bridge for even for the sprawling Unilever had put it off. However, the attraction of becoming the world's largest tea company plus a few other trifles like Fray Bentos and Oxo convinced Unilever it should not let slip the prize this time. The company embarked on its first-ever hostile takeover bid, winning through in in September 2004 at a price of £390 million.

Attention then turned to personal care where there were successes but little further capability to grow organically. So it began looking at some mostly US-based industry giants, with Richardson-Vicks at the top of the pile. A hostile bid was launched: it went spectacularly wrong. The Richardson family took great exception to Unilever's straight out of the gate hostility, a dislike that sunk to new depths when a family member keeled over with a fatal heart attack in a meeting with Unilever executives and advisors. The Richardson family were more than happy to spurn Unilever's $60 a share offer; they accepted a white knight bid from P&G.

Unilever were re-buffed. But hearing that Chesebrough-Ponds was being stalked by American Brands, they moved in with a white knight offer of their own and acquired the company in January 1987 for an eye-watering cash pile just a shade under £2 billion. Brands such as Vaseline and Pond's catapulted Unilever from nowhere to the fourth-largest global skincare company, with the added bonus of food brands such as Ragu sauces. By now the secret was out. Companies were approaching Unilever suggesting with acquisition offers – them not Unilever - most notably Elizabeth Arden-Fabergé who made their pitch in October 1988 (Fabergé had only acquired Elizabeth Arden the year before). This deal was consummated in 1989 for £996 million and soon followed by Calvin Klein with its highly successful Obsession and Eternity brands. As the chemicals division was still on the expand and grow list, acquisitions were made in that area too making the company one of the world's top fifty chemical companies and one of the top two makers of adhesives. One small acquisition that would pay back many times over was that of a small US margarine manufacturer, J. H. Filbert. Filbert was bought primarily bought for its production facilities, part of the deal being the purchase for one dollar of a brand by the name of I Can't Believe It's Not Butter. By the end of the decade, the butter substitute would have US sales of $100 million.

Within the core businesses, fortunes began to improve. The Becel margarine brand was proving a success, as was the subsequent extension of the brand into cooking oil and beyond. Sunsilk was selling in over 30 countries, with particular success in South America, giving the brand 12% of the world shampoo market in 1985. Signal was sold in eighteen countries and had 5% of world toothpaste sales. The company's Unipath subsidiary developed a highly successful pregnancy testing kit called Clearblue. The Dove brand began its European rollout in 1989, the same year that the Magnum brand appeared as a response to the entry of Mars into the ice cream category. The company had also started the long and tortuous process of adding some global discipline to its local entrepreneurship, with baby steps such as a single logo for Lipton's Tea, the company's largest global brand with annual sales of £600 million, pretty good for the highly fragmented Unilever but less than a quarter the size of Nestlé's Nescafé. The problematic US market had begun to turn around, but the pursuit of market share at any price on detergents lost the company over $70 million between 1985 and 1987. Head Office gave the US a year to turn around the chronically loss-making Breyer's Good Humor. A further acquisition solved that problem.

By the end of the 1980s, Unilever was a very different company from six years ago. Over seventy mostly low margin commodity businesses had been sold; a staggering 197 acquisitions had been made. Three-quarters of these were small - less than £10 million each - and overwhelmingly single country, single category companies that could be bolted onto a Unilever operation. The majority were in Europe. While sales in real terms were still well below the level of fifteen years ago, the company was now much more profitable, with a return on capital employed better than P&G. The Core segments of food, detergents, personal care and chemicals were now accounting for over 90% of sales and the company had built up some strong global market share positions: 10% in personal care, 50% in margarine, 14% in ice cream and just a shade behind P&G in detergents.

Two consequences to the make-up of the business from this unprecedented acquisition and disposal splurge were, firstly, that the marketing to sales ratio had risen substantially, partly because most of the disposed businesses had had little or no marketing spend but also because the company had simply increased what it spent by a considerable amount: 50%. A more negative consequence was that the brand portfolio was now almost grotesque: 1,500 brands were being actively marketed. Half were in food, there were over 300 in detergents and a paltry 170 personal products. But even the company's biggest brands were relative minnows compared to the market leaders. Omo was one-third the size of Ariel and Tide; Sunsilk was smaller than any one of five P&G personal care brands. Unilever's two biggest toothpaste brands combined, Close-Up and Signal, were still not as big as P&G's Crest.

The early 1990s saw some major restructuring within Unilever along category lines, the company having finally decided to grasp the decentralisation issue so that finally some global strategies for brands could be put in place. Axe became the world's largest global male toiletries brand through following a disciplined rollout of new products into new markets. Signal was repositioned as the company's key brand to fight tooth decay. And Organics shampoo was a global brand two years after its introduction in Thailand. Further divestments followed as what was considered core was redefined to exclude firstly the remaining portions of UAC - finally sold by 1994. Agribusinesses followed in 1995, the meat processing and fish businesses in 1997, the same year that the chemicals division, despite its 15% contribution to company sales, was sold to ICI for a hefty £4.9 billion.

But Unilever wasn't just trying to shrink its way to being a pure packaged goods company. Significant acquisitions were also being made, including the Helene Curtis hair-care business, Breyers ice cream (which made Unilever America's largest ice cream company), Ben & Jerry's, Slimfast, and in 2000 the company's biggest acquisition by far, Bestfoods, which took total company sales to $52 billion a year. Bestfoods brought some leading brands into the fold too: Knorr and Hellman's and, with 40% of its sales from outside North America, it was an ideal fit with the globalised Unilever. Now the company could combine all its disparate food companies to form one distinct entity, Unilever Bestfoods. The company also had second thoughts about its moves into upscale cosmetics – recognizing these as a different category altogether - so it sold both Elizabeth Arden and Calvin Klein. By 2000, the company was now beyond a shadow of doubt a packaged goods company. But one nettle remained to be grasped – the brand portfolio.

The same year as the Bestfoods acquisition, Unilever announced it would reduce its range of marketed brands from the then current 1,600 to just 400: 1,000 of the brands delivered only 8% of total company sales. The collateral damage was that 100 of the 350 factories would go along with 25,000 employees. Only a year later the company portfolio was down to 900 brands as 87 businesses were sold off. However, by 2003 it became clear the plan wasn't quite working: sales, which had been growing quite nicely, turned south. The long tail of products contributing little to the top line is a seductive and compelling argument, but the devil was in the detail: many brands, minute though they may have been in the overall company scale of things, tended to sell in one country only, where they were quite significant. Cancelling or selling them was no guarantee that Unilever's other brands would pick up all the slack, which indeed was the problem. The extra management and financial focus on the 400 brands wasn't making up the 8% of chopped-down sales. 2004 needed something of a tweak to the plan.

How International Are They?

Both the original Unilever companies had been enthusiastic exporters almost from the very beginning. Scale was an advantage in the sourcing of the key raw materials, especially when it led to vertical integration back to the sources of supply. Also, for the Dutch companies, Holland may have been a small market but it had Germany market on its doorstep, so it was only natural that attention was soon focused beyond national borders. Lever Brothers, like most British manufacturers of almost anything, saw the British Empire countries of Canada, Australia, South Africa and New Zealand as almost one contiguous market with the UK, so salesmen were sent wherever the Union Jack fluttered.

William Lever differed somewhat from most other British businessmen in having an early and prolonged enthusiasm for selling his products, always led by Sunlight Soap, in continental Europe and the United States. By 1889 there were thriving Lever Brothers sales agencies in Belgium, Germany, France, Switzerland and Holland, each led by an indigenous manager due to William's own personal belief that the biggest barrier to international trade was the inability to understand the needs, habits and desires of people in another country. In Holland Lever happily locked horns with the companies with which his own would eventually merge.

Lever also appreciated early on that the scale advantage in soap lay in the certainty of supply and price paid for raw materials rather than in factory manufacturing efficiencies so, although Port Sunlight was a vast and efficient enterprise, as soon as a sales office abroad had built the business to a sufficient size, he would build a factory there to increase the local responsiveness of the business. Thus, by 1906, 25% of the capital employed was in six overseas factories: Belgium, Germany, Switzerland, Canada, Australia and the US with every carton of Sunlight Soap boasting it was the largest selling soap in the world.

Lever had first visited North America in 1888 when he set up sales offices in New York and Toronto. His attention was soon back on the New York sales office as his sales figures showed him that the best-selling brand there was not Sunlight, but Lifebuoy. If there was one thing William believed in, it was the selling power of his beloved Sunlight Soap, so any salesman who couldn't sell it no matter where was branded either useless or up to no good. With his American office manager his suspicion was the latter, so much so that William hired a private detective to follow the man's every move, which only showed the man and his team were putting in all hours. After visiting for five years in a row to grow sales of Sunlight through the force of his personality, a dejected William Lever finally gave up in 1899 and bought an American manufacturer, Benjamin Brooke & Co., makers of the popular Monkey Brand soap. The factory was also geared up to make Sunlight and Lifebuoy but Sunlight never did make the grade, and was withdrawn a few years later. As the business prospered post World War One, Lever green-lighted the purchase of a margarine company in 1920, one of his last acts as leader of the company. Following William's demise, the new regime at carried on exactly as before, opening up operations in Thailand, Indonesia, China, Argentina, Brazil and, in what would be the best example of any western company cracking an emerging market, India.

India, as a leading part of the British Empire, had been an export market from the earliest days, with Sunlight first sold there by 1888. This was soon followed by Lifebuoy in 1895 and then other Lever bestsellers such as Pears, Lux and Vim. Vanaspati, a brand of hydrogenated vegetable fat used in place of butter in Indian cooking was launched in 1918 and was the first Unilever brand to be manufactured in India itself, starting up in 1932. Two years later a modern soap factory was up and running in Bombay, followed by the setting up of third subsidiary, United Traders Limited. These three companies merged to form Hindustan Unilever Ltd. (HUL) in 1956, by which time they also had a Calcutta-based factory making a range of personal products such as shaving cream and talcum powder.

HUL had a local flavour from the start, having offered 10% of its equity to the Indian public, the first foreign-owned company to do so. It continued in this vein by appointing the first Indian chairman of an overseas-owned Indian company. The company would need all the local influence it could get in later years. By 1967 HUL was one of the top five companies in India, its 7,000 employees and 6 factories producing a highly diversified product range including dehydrated peas, baby foods, dried milk curd and, at the government's request, condoms, of which it sold more than all its convenience foods put together.

Many western-owned companies who had set up in India did not survive the 1970s when oppressive government restrictions drove the likes of Coca-Cola and IBM away. But Unilever was renowned for not giving up anywhere, always believing that if there was a way to hang on, they would be in pole position when matters improved. It was an attitude that kept them in many politically unstable African countries. HUL's Indian chairman mostly spent his time in negotiation with government officials trying to influence policy toward foreign-owned companies, or delay implementation of new measures, and he succeeded in keeping Unilever as the majority owner of HUL where most others either failed or gave up and left.

The acquisition of Chesebrough-Ponds gave HUL's faltering personal products business a major boost, the Unilever brands being rolled into their portfolio, whereas Brooke Bond, when acquired, was kept separate: combining the two would have created monopoly problems with the government of the time. Although a dominant force in the country, HUL did not have the Indian market to itself, as local competitors sprang up to grab a share of markets HUL had largely created. A major attack on their detergents business from a low cost competitor in the mid-1970s decimated the leading Surf brand, prompting HUL to successfully launch its own range of lower-priced brands, such as Wheel in 1987, which six years later had a market share of over 20%.

Government economic policy softened in the early 1990s, enabling a merger between HUL and Tata Oil Mills Company in 1993. In 1996, HUL formed a 50:50 joint venture with another Tata subsidiary, Lakme, to market Lakme's leading cosmetics brands, which HUL bought outright two years later. HUL, as India's leading packaged goods company, was in big demand as a joint venture partner, forming another in 1994 with Kimberly Clark to market Huggies Diapers and Kotex Sanitary Pads. HUL also set up a subsidiary in Nepal, Unilever Nepal Limited (UNL), to manufacture soap, detergents and personal care products both for the domestic market and exports to India.

In 1994, Brooke Bond India and Lipton India merged to form Brooke Bond Lipton India Limited (BBLIL), which immediately launched the Wall's range of frozen desserts along with acquiring distribution rights for other leading brands. Finally, BBLIL merged with HUL, with effect in 1996, followed by the merger of Pond's (India) Limited with HUL in 1998. In 2000 the government decided to award 74 per cent equity in the government-owned bread business, Modern Foods to HUL, HUL acquiring full control two years later.

In the immediate post-war years, while the Indian business was becoming well-established, Unilever opened up subsidiaries far and wide across Africa, Asia and South America, determined to be in on the ground floor of developing countries, with a range of brands that were among the first to be bought in any great quantities by newly emerging consumer classes -soap, shampoo and detergents - and confident it could ride out any political storms in the meantime to keep its treasured first-mover status, a position from which it could later add on more of its product categories as economies expanded, even if somewhat erratically.

A case in point is the company's development in Brazil. Unilever's first soap powder brand to be sold in any great quantity in Brazil had been the cheap and cheerful Rinso, which, in 1959, was supplanted by Brazil's first synthetic brand, Omo. With the Brazilian economy, population and degree of urbanisation all booming, in 1960 Unilever bought their main local detergents competitor, trebling their business at a stroke, and, as in India, had local managers running the company. Unilever's famed resilience would be sorely tested by Brazil's high-inflation economy, running at 20% a year in the 1960s up to a hyper-inflationary 2,500% by the end of the 1980s. But the company learned how to cope in this environment; a lesson that would prove useful elsewhere. During this time, the company had been adding extra divisions as new categories were opened up. Thus Elida Gibbs, Van den Berghs and the acquired Gelato ice cream company all ran semi autonomously alongside Unilever in developing their own categories. Further acquisitions followed, most notably the Henkel Brazilian subsidiary, such that by 1990 Unilever sales in Brazil were approaching £700 million, the company making close to a million tons of detergents a year.

By 1970, Unilever had 22 operating companies with annual sales of over £30 million a year, of which 14 were based outside the U.K. and the Netherlands. Of total Unilever sales from the rest of the world excluding North America and Europe, India was accounting for 24%, South Africa 11% and Turkey 7%. A rare failure was Mexico, where a 1960s joint venture in margarine turned rancid, forcing the company to pull out in the mid-1970s before entering again via the National Starch and Chesebrough-Ponds acquisitions.

Japan had also been a rocky road for the company. Lever had built a soap factory there in 1913, but it was sold ten years later after a decade of heavy losses. As early as 1947 a manager had been sent to prospect the war-ravaged country but it would not be until the 1960s that Unilever entered another margarine joint venture. Despite two decades of losses, Unilever persisted, slowly reaching 80% ownership in 1977 at which point the company name became Nippon Lever. The breakthrough came with the ever-dependable Sunsilk, launched in 1977, which sustained the company through failures such as Surf Sachets, Port Sunlight boffins not having realised that most Japanese housewives did their laundry in cold water, which did not dissolve the sachets to release the detergent. The storm was weathered and the company boomed in the mid-late 1980s, growing at an average of 23% a year.

The Japanese experience demonstrated that by the 1980s, Unilever's best weapon of attack in new markets had become personal care products, Sunsilk having supplanted Rinso as the company's storm trooper. Sunsilk initially be targeted at the rich elite who used hairdressers, positioned as a woman's indispensable beauty aid, before being cascaded down to meet the increasing mass market of new consumers. Consequently, Unilever built up some commanding market share positions in shampoo before P&G had even entered the market. Sometimes toothpaste would be added to the initial range of brands, the deodorant Rexona following on behind. Unlike other Unilever categories such as higher-end detergents, margarine and ice cream, the advantages of these brands was that they did not depend on reliable supplies of household electricity. Margarine depended on a local culture that ate buttered bread.

Of course, the emerging market to crack was China. Unilever's large pre-war operation there had been wiped out by a combination of the Japanese invasion of Manchuria and the coastal cities followed by the communist revolution. By the early 1980s Unilever wanted to return but was extremely nervous of a joint venture, fearful their proprietary technologies would leak through their partner to appear in a local start-up. Amazingly, Unilever's pre-war soap factory in Shanghai, although somewhat rundown, was still going, making 125,000 tons of soap a year, a third of the nation's supply. So Unilever formed a 50:50 joint venture, Shanghai-Lever, with the factory's new owner in 1985, beginning with the production of Lux in 1987. This was soon followed by two more joint ventures with the same partner - a conglomerate of sorts - with Shanghai Pond's and Shanghai Van den Bergh easing the company into the Chinese personal care and edible fats markets. By 1990, Unilever's sales in China had reached a respectable $32 million a year, although they were still small in comparison to the company's total overseas sales (excluding Europe and North America) of nearly £5 billion a year, Brazil now ahead of India and the single largest component. Following the fall of the Berlin Wall, Unilever completed its global rollout, opening up in 1992 in the Czech Republic, Hungary and Russia, where by 2001 the company had seven manufacturing sites including a margarine factory in Moscow, dressing, tea, home and personal care factories in St Petersburg, and food and ice cream factories in Tula and Omsk. They were employing 6,500 people with a total investment in the Russian economy that was close to $1 billion.

How Are They Structured?

An entire book could be written about the evolution of Unilever's convoluted management structure. As described at the beginning of this chapter, Unilever was set up with two distinct, capitalised entities, which shared the same board of directors, had separate chairmen, with agreements in place to ensure dividends were paid equally. Some of the operating companies were owned by Unilever PLC, some by Unilever NV and some jointly, giving each entity around half the assets. The first board meeting of each year in each country delegated executive to the Special Committee, usually both chairmen plus one other, usually the vice-chairman of Unilever PLC. Thus, for the most part, the special committee had two British and one Dutch member who collectively acted as the CEO. There was an understanding that the Dutch side would run continental Europe and the British side the rest of the world, although as we have seen, 'run' is perhaps too strong a word: 'administer' would be more appropriate.

By the mid 60s, the boards were large - approximately 25 company executives, all Unilever lifers - and met weekly: a company with hundreds of subsidiaries required a lot of administering. Their central banking role took up a lot of time, adjudicating on new factory or acquisition proposals from any of the hundreds of operating companies, the spoils going not necessarily to the most deserving cases but to those either best argued or with the board most allies. It was a unique operating style, often bemusing to the executives themselves, who vacillated between seeing themselves as a conglomerate or a linked set of operating companies. The company wrestled endlessly to balance centralisation and decentralisation in terms of empowerment and between geographies and product groups in terms of management direction.

The free-for-all could not last forever and by 1960 there existed a structure beneath the special committee and the boards to manage around five hundred operating companies. This consisted of six management groups: UK Committee, Continental European Group, Overseas Committee, Plantation, UAC and North America. Virtually every country had a national manager who gradually accrued operational and profit responsibilities for the operating companies within his remit. The UK and North America were exceptions. Due to the number and size of operating companies there, there was no one figurehead.

However, as we have seen, the combination of geographic management centralised at the country level was proving a big restriction on Unilever's ability to respond to competitors such as P&G, who operated regionally and furthermore had nothing like the spread of categories that Unilever had to worry about. So the 1950s and 1960 saw the setting-up of product groups - co-ordinations - whose roles were to develop strategies for their product areas. By 1960, product committees had been set up for detergents, foods, toiletries and edible fats, all based in Rotterdam. Their primary task was to identify from the vast portfolio products with international potential, then develop their specifications. Implementation was a different matter: as the co-ordinators had virtually no staff and even less executive authority. Persuasion was their only weapon.

This was looking like the worst of all worlds, so in 1966 the co-ordinators were given sales and profit responsibilities for their categories in a number of key markets, beginning with Great Britain, Netherlands, Germany and Belgium. As the shape of the company changed through acquisition, so did the number of co-ordinators: packaging and then chemicals acquired a couple. In 1972, McKinsey had recommended extending co-ordination to all the other European countries, keeping national managers in place but with reduced responsibilities. But Lever felt that the main issues in those markets were best managed by a strong local leader, influencing the political agenda, dealing with hyperinflation and so on. Post-McKinsey, the company structure looked not simpler, as it should have done, but a lot more complicated. Dotted lines ran every which way. But in fact it was a start. Unilever was beginning to move from chaos to national management, to product field-management where product-based competence could be accumulated and strategies developed.

The next stimulus for change came in the mid-1980s with the EEC Single Market programme, which would clearly make management on national lines somewhat redundant. The detergents co-ordination group pushed for a high degree of centralisation, not surprising given what they were up against, whereas the foods group were less keen on the idea, as the brands they managed were mostly national. The only co-ordination with global sales and profit responsibility was chemicals. In 1989 a new foods executive was formed in Rotterdam, its remit to develop a global foods strategy. The three foods co-ordinations were replaced by five new product groupings: spreads, oils and dressings; meat and meal components; ice cream and sweet snacks; beverages and savoury snacks; and professional markets. A year later, as a clearly necessary step to combat the ever-powerful P&G, Unilever Europe - headquartered in Brussels - was formed at the urging of the detergents co-ordinator.

Once the acquisitions and divestments had finally settled Unilever down into a form recognizable at last as a simple packaged goods company, the next step could be taken: structure the business along category lines. In 2001 Unilever was organised into two global divisions, food and home and personal care, with the aim of optimising synergies across the product portfolio. Within the two divisions, the majority of the categories were managed at the regional level, the exceptions being the fragrance business and Unilever food solutions, the food service arm. In early 2005, this was simplified into a matrix structure, with the two divisions responsible for strategy and brand development. The regional groups of each division were merged, with the regional level responsible for go-to-market execution.

What Have They Done Recently?

2004

Here is a selection of comments Unilever's two chairmen made about their company:
- We are not where we set out to be
- We do not end this period of Unilever's history with the level of growth we wanted
- We have not been fast enough in reacting to toughening market conditions and competitive challenges

It's fair to say that the Path to Growth laid out in 2000 had taken a wrong turn along the way, although it had not all been bad news:
- Twelve brands had sales in excess of €1 billion, and approximately two-thirds of total sales derived from brands larger than €0.5 billion, no mean feat given a starting point of 1,600 brands
- Knorr, the company's largest brand, was sold in over 100 countries
- Dove, Signal and Pepsodent were all re-launched
- The Pro-Activ cholesterol-lowering spread was extended into other dairy categories
- The ever-reliable Sunsilk grew by double digits

- The €1 billion+ R&D programme had been realigned behind the new Vitality agenda to fast-track incorporating health and wellness benefits into foods and beverages, registering 370 patents in the year
- The Latin American region had an underlying sales growth in the year - mostly through volume – due to successes with Vitality initiatives for the well-to-do and low unit price offerings for the monetarily challenged

But overall there was still more bad news than good, not least a feeble increase in underlying sales of 0.4%. All the unwanted brands and businesses were being sold off - 70 in the previous two years with a combined turnover of over €1.8 billion – but the components that were kept on weren't making up the difference. The entire Unilever foods category had an underlying sales decline in the year. Beverages were the worst culprit, with a 4% decline as Slim-Fast didn't Change-Fast in the light of shifting consumer attitudes towards its carbohydrates (i.e. sugar) content. Ice cream was almost as bad, losing 3.4% of underlying volume with a bad summer being blamed. If you want to be the world's largest maker of ice cream, which Unilever is, you are going to get bad summers: the onus is on the market leader to de-seasonalise and temperature-proof the category. The best excuse was in the spreads and cooking products category: 'Overall growth in the category was held back by lower sales of 'tail' brands which are being managed for value and where investment is low'. No, overall growth was held back because the big brands that had the investment didn't grow enough.

The chairmen had clearly seen enough of such poor performance and embarrassing excuses: change was needed. The long-running sore of too many levels and committees muddying the waters with unclear responsibilities would finally be addressed under new CEO, Patrick Cescau, currently chairman of Unilever NV. For the first time since its formation, Unilever would have one chairman, one board, one CEO with one executive team. There would be two category presidents, one each for foods, and for home and personal care (HPC), responsible for R&D, brand development and category development. Alongside would be three regional presidents (Europe, The Americas, Asia/Africa, Middle East and Turkey) responsible for country and customer development. The company would support this new structure with increased brand investment, paid for out of the new One Unilever efficiency programme. No more excuses.

2005

It was perhaps a sign of the times for Unilever that holding market share in the year would count as a success. The new CEO had set the focus on stopping the rot in Europe, (the company's largest region accounting for 41% of sales), accelerating growth in developing and emerging markets (long a strength for Unilever with over half their employees working outside of Europe and the Americas), spreading the Vitality programme across the portfolio (especially in personal care) and pushing structural reorganisation down through the company.

Overall results were positive, kind of. More disposals, primarily of the prestige fragrances business (Unilever Cosmetics International) to Coty Inc. for $800 million, put a big dent in the underlying sales growth of 3.1% But that sales increase had been driven by volume, supported by an extra €500 million in advertising and promotions and combined with some price decreases, particularly in Europe where the company's value offering, failing to understand then respond to hard discounters like Aldi, had got badly out of line. In Europe volume was very slightly positive but the price decreases meant that there was another annual decline in cash sales. And there were still issues in France, Germany and particularly the UK where sales declined, mostly in personal care, which wiped out an excellent year in Central and Eastern Europe where Russian sales had grown by 20%. The Americas, however, driven by a US recovery, grew by 3%, Asia/Africa etc. grew by 9% with China up by over 20% and a strong recovery in the key Indian market. For the first time, sales in all the developing and emerging markets exceeded those in Europe.

The driver of most of the good regional performances was the personal care, up over 6%. The combination of strong global brands such as Axe, Dove, Sunsilk and Rexona, combined with Vitality-based programmes such as the Dove Campaign for Real Beauty, Omo's Dirt is Good and Lifebuoy's regular handwashing campaign in the poorer parts of Asia was Unilever working at its best. And now such initiatives could be quickly rolled out regionally or globally. The Foods Division was having more challenges, with a more fragmented brand portfolio and substantial challenges in implementing the Vitality programme. The company also assessed the nutritional profiles of over 16,000 products in the year and found many in difficulties: fast-evolving consumer attitudes to saturated fats, sugar and sodium were seriously compromising sales. Developed-world initiatives such as Knorr Vie mini shots and developing world affordability initiatives such as Knorr Cubitos were all well and good, but a couple of decades of acquisitions had bequeathed a huge list of products not designed for success given modern-day sensibilities.

Organisationally, much had happened quickly: merged One Unilever single-country organisations accounted for 80% of total turnover by the end of the year and had also delivered savings that more than paid for the extra €500 million in marketing spend. The remainder would start the merging process in 2006. At the board level, in the light of the organisational changes made at the beginning of the year, a six-month project had reviewed Unilever's unique PLC/NV dual list-ing share structure, concluding that it still offered more benefits than a single structure, particularly in terms of financial flexibility and the company's unique multi-cultural operating style.

2006

Now Unilever was finally a pure packaged goods business with a structure that enabled rather than hindered its global scale and reach, the company could, for the first time in its history, define a clear mission for itself:

- Our mission is to add Vitality to life. We meet everyday needs for nutri-tion, hygiene and personal care with brands that help people feel good, look good and get more out of life

It was something that hadn't been really possible when running breweries, an ad agency and selling GM trucks. And the company had a global balance: only one-third of sales coming from Western Europe, it had built up via growth and acquisition a substantial personal care business and had a raft of €1 billion-plus brands joined most recently by Rexona. It was leaner and fitter after the sales of most of their European frozen foods businesses. There was a clarity of purpose and a toolkit it had never enjoyed before. But how good would the company be at exploiting its new persona?

2006 didn't really answer that question. Top line sales grew by 3.8%; about on par given a strong U.S. economy and booming emerging and developing markets. But Unilever hadn't gained share for four years now. Personal care was still making the running, growing at over 6% again while food was limping along. In personal care the brands were more concentrated - Omo was now over €2.5 billion – and the Vitality programme seemed to have more, well, vitality. Domestos, an unexciting brand if ever there was one, launched Domestos 5x which killed germs in the toilet bowl for five times longer than anything else on the market, as consumers could see for themselves with a helpfully supplied test strip to dunk in the bowl. Small and Mighty super-concentrated detergents were being rolled out. And Surf Excel in India, with its unique low-rinse formulation, was reducing the water needed for a wash-load by two-thirds. Meanwhile the foods division was wrestling with removing 37,000 tons of fats, 17,000 tons of sugar and 3,000 tons of sodium from its products without altering the flavour, initiatives which begged the question as to what all that unhealthy stuff was do-ing there in the first place.

Nor had the European malaise had yet been cured: volume was going no-where again. Whenever gains were made in ice cream, soup, deodorant or body care, there was bad news in detergents, hair care and tea. A second problem was that new, rapidly growing markets for many of the company's less international competitors were mature markets for Unilever. In Brazil, they had been big for over fifty years, in Mexico for forty. Yet the company was not growing distribution or pushing forward by acquisition, but struggling to fend off the companies who were doing precisely these things. In Asia/Africa, the company's underlying sales growth of over 7.7% was not significantly better than GDP growth. China was really the only market where Unilever was growing at a new entrant's pace, through a mix of strong global brands such as Lux, Omo and Pond's, together with some local brands such as Zhonhua toothpaste.

As befitting a company of Unilever's size, it was now doing what was normally expected of a global player. On the cost side, large chunks of IT, Finance and HR were being outsourced. On the opportunity side, the company was investing €350 million in venturing activities to develop the winners of tomorrow. However, the real challenge was to make the combination of unique heritage and newly coherent structure work to achieve competitive advantage: to, in point of fact, consistently gain market share.

2007

With an underlying sales growth of over 5% and even Europe pitching in with more than 3%, it looked like the hard work in restructuring Unilever was finally paying off. The company was now able to do what it had never been able to manage before: launch with breadth and speed. Clear, a new shampoo with enhanced proprietary ant-dandruff technology was launched simultaneously in some of the largest hair care markets in the world, including China, Russia and Brazil. Unilever had also sharpened its execution capabilities: Axe became the best-selling male deodorant brand in Japan just six months after its launch.

The continued direction of resources into Vitality, personal care and developing and emerging markets was also providing a consistent focus that the company had previously lacked. Personal care grew by almost 7%. Rexona was the world's largest deodorant brand and Axe the largest male deodorant. Knorr was now almost a €4 billion brand. The top 25 brands accounted for almost 75% of turnover and 44% of company sales came from developing and emerging markets.

Most crucially, success was now becoming more widespread throughout the portfolio, including the less glamorous parts. The company's roster of household cleaning brands, including Domestos and Cif, grew by an impressive 9%. Vaseline grew by 8% and Dove's Campaign for Real Beauty was partnering with organisations in over twenty countries. In foods, while the Nutrition Enhancement

Programme continued to root out fats, salt and sugar, a more focused R&D pro-gramme was delivering increasingly relevant breakthroughs. Hellman's Extra Light was using citrus fibre to deliver a very low-fat content and a very high prof-it margin, Lipton's was meeting each region's differing healthy beverage needs via Lipton Green Tea in the U.S., Lipton Linea slimming teas in Europe and Lipton Milk Tea in Asia. Most interestingly, a range of nutritious snacks and drinks spe-cifically designed to assist mental development was launched in Turkey under the take-no-prisoners brand name, Amaze Brainfood. These were all examples of the new foods R&D focus on delivering one or more of functionality, lighter, and naturalness and authenticity.

Within the regions, Europe's more than 2.8% underlying sales growth was based on a stronger performance in all the key markets which reflected general improvements in execution capability rather than one or two new and block-buster products. This was exactly the kind of improvement Unilever had been striving to achieve. Two developments of high potential were the extension to all European markets of a 50:50 partnership with Pepsico to sell Lipton ready-to-drink teas and the announcement of the acquisition of Russia's leading ice cream company, Inmarko. The Americas did somewhat better too, with an underlying growth of 4.1% thanks to a reasonable balance of pricing and volume increases, while Asia/Africa set a new standard, growing by over 11% with volume and contributing two-thirds of the growth. Areas of strength were India, the Philip-pines, South Africa and Turkey, which all grew double digit. The company had a good category balance of growth, with laundry and personal wash tending to lead in the lower income groups whilst ice cream - led by the Moo brand rolled out throughout the region - and deodorants led with the more affluent.

A year in Unilever wouldn't be complete without the announcement of more structural changes: the latest being the regionalisation of head office functions to jointly serve several country markets, a rationalisation which arrived in the same year that some countries - Brazil, Argentina and Mexico, for example - were still catching up with the One Unilever single-head-office-per-country notion. More global and regional overheads were slated for the chop, along with more than fifty factories. The disposal programme was also getting ramped up again, not only including brands that didn't fit in with the new laser focus but also those ones deemed structurally disadvantaged. Thus the company's North American laundry business was put on the auction block, over a century since William Lev-er himself put it on the too-difficult pile and went the acquisition route.

2008

For the third year in a row, Unilever increased its rate of underlying sales growth, this time to an impressive sounding 7.4% increase. While all of this came from price increases to cover raw material cost increases, it was very encouraging that volume was not lost given the scale of the pricing changes. The sales growth was spread fairly evenly across all the product categories; home care charging ahead at more than 9.8% and ice cream and beverages bringing up the rear at more than 5.9%. Savings from One Unilever and elsewhere provided over €1 billion to protect both the marketing budget and the margin, although new CEO Paul Polman, previously chief financial officer and head of North America for Nestlé, still felt there was more fat to be shed.

There were big changes on the R&D front, where the nearly €1 billion budget and 6,000 staff were finally brought together into one organisation. This was a consequence of another structural change, as the company's two product sectors were combined into one cohesive group. That there were synergies to be had by combining expertise across product groups was demonstrated with the launch of Signal White Now, the world's first toothpaste that whitens teeth instantly by adopting the detergents' trick of including a blue dye to make yellow teeth look white, a ruse that had been pioneered by P&G's Daz with its Blue Whiteness decades ago. So now, brands were managed under four sub-groups: savoury, dressing and spreads, ice cream and beverages, personal care; and home care. Another reorganisation was the detachment of Central and Eastern Europe from the Europe region for the more similar markets of Africa/Asia.

By removing the fastest-growing part of the European region, Western Europe was now looking poorly once more, with underlying growth of only 1.3% versus 6.5% for the Americas and 14.2% for Africa/Asia. Prices increases of 3.8% also dug deeply into European performance and volume slipped by 2.5%, choking off the company's recovery in the region. While this kind of performance was quite typical for a packaged goods company in 2008 - cash-strapped shoppers were looking more to private label and deep discounters - it was encouraging that in the countries where the One Unilever integration of separate business units and multi-country back-offices was more accelerated, the UK and Netherlands for example, performance had been better. But the nature of growth across categories was varied: innovation led deodorants and oral care whereas in spreads and dressings it was driven by deep discounting.

In the Americas, the US business grew by 3.8% whereas – the usual story for everyone - Latin America steamed ahead by 12%. Campaigns like Dirt is Good were proving particularly effective global rollouts in Latin America. The newly named Asia, Africa and Central and Eastern Europe region (AACEE) seemed to be recession-free: underlying sales grew by an impressive 14%. Unilever's top five developing and emerging markets in the region also grew by approximately 20%, with both prices and volume moving ahead and the region was further bolstered by the acquisition of Indonesia's Buavitaq brand of fruit-based vitality drinks. It was a busy year for disposals too: for a €3 billion total, the Boursin cheese brand, Lawry's and Adolph's brands of seasoning and marinades and Bertolli olive oil and vinegar joined the North American laundry business (sold to venture capitalists) in leaving the company.

Also evident was an increasing focus on social and environmental issues, a logical consequence of the Vitality programme, which as well as adding Vitality to Life at the individual and family level, also needed to do so at the corporate, impact-the-planet level if it really a true operating philosophy and not just a marketing flavour of the month. This the company proudly boasted of in its 10 years as a of the Dow Jones Sustainability Indexes sector leader, although it accepted that more needed to be done on emissions, water usage, waste production and the nutritional profiles of its food brands.

2009

The top priority for the year, despite dire economic conditions in many countries, was to get Unilever back to volume growth without sacrificing margin. Growing only through price increases, as had been the case the previous year, was neither desirable nor sustainable in the eyes of the new CEO. Although turnover was down slightly at €39.8 billion - a level at which it had hovered for some years as divestments wiped out organic sales – underlying growth excluding divestments and currency impacts was a more healthy plus 3.5%, two-thirds of which was the result of volume increases.

As had recently become the norm, performances within the three regions were starkly different. Africa, Asia, Central and Eastern Europe were now the largest of the three at nearly €15 billion and also delivered the biggest operating profit, nearly €2 billion. The region had had another excellent year with underlying sales growth of more than 7.7%, with volume up 4.1%. As economies had begun to recover during the year, so had Unilever's rate of volume growth, which had reached nearly 10% in the fourth quarter. Market share gains were made in most markets and categories, the exception being the huge Indian business, under intense attack from low-cost local competitors and failing, in the eyes of the CEO, to respond quickly or aggressively enough. Not good to be on the new chief's radar so early in his reign.

The Americas, second-largest with sales of nearly €13 billion and with the highest operating margin of the three, delivered an underlying sales growth of more than 4.2%, volume accounting for more than 2.5%, rising to more than 5.5% in the fourth quarter. The two key markets in the region, the US and Brazil, were the strongest performers, helped by increases in advertising and promotional spending paid for from cost savings. As had been the case for several years, Western Europe was still the sick man of the triumvirate with a 2% decline in underlying sales to €12 billion. Volume slipping very slightly, although with some marginal share gain. The downward trend on the top line, which happened in most of the key markets, reflected rising sales of private labels and price decreases, which were dialling back some of the previous year's increases that had proved unsustainable in the tough economic conditions.

Overall it was an improved performance in the circumstances. Unilever was now gaining share in two-thirds of its business compared to one-third a year previous, it was global number one in seven categories, and ten of the thirteen €1 billion-plus brands were gaining share. Four reasons were highlighted for the improvement:

Bigger and better innovations were rolled out faster, facilitated by the One Unilever reorganisations

Dove Minimising Deodorant had been launched in 37 markets. Clear shampoo was now in 35 markets, Signal White Now in 21 and Knorr Stockpots (using a proprietary gel formula) in 12. With a new innovation centre opened in Shanghai and a doubling of projects in the pipeline - sales potential of greater than €50 million – the pace could only keep increasing.

More discipline throughout the organisation

Unilever was now acting more like a global company doing things the Unilever way than a loose collection of affiliates of varying entrepreneurial abilities.

A more competitive cost structure

One ironic advantage of Unilever's long-term structural complexity was that it now reaped huge cost savings each year as it simplified and went global. As an example, the company appointed its first ever chief global supply chain officer during 2009, a role long common elsewhere. Another €1.4 billion had been thrown into the pot in 2009 which had enabled a substantial increase in marketing spend while covering input cost increases. Unilever's competitors were now having to choose between maintaining ad spend, putting up prices or taking a hit on margins.

Driving a performance culture

The delayering, simplification and clarification of the organisation meant that there was now a much greater emphasis on individual target-setting and performance. There was also a shift from divestment to acquisition, with the purchase of the TGI professional hair care brands to boost the company's hair care business, a Russian ketchup business and, most crucially, the announcement of the impending purchase of Sara Lee's personal care brands, Sanex, Radox and Duschdas, which Unilever would be able to take more global.

The company's global environmental and sustainability agenda received a further boost with the appointment to the board of Louise Fresco, the Professor of International Development and Sustainability at the University of Amsterdam. While the company was improving the sustainability aspect of its ingredients, with 2 billion people using a Unilever product every day, Unilever had the reach to change things for the better in how its products are used. One aspect of Unilever's unique sales footprint in developing and emerging markets is that it sells its laundry products in some of the more water-challenged parts of the world. So the company was actively developing more products like Comfort One Rinse fabric conditioner, which required dramatically less rinsing. Even more impressively, since 2002 the Lifebuoy disinfectant soap had been running a campaign in India encouraging frequent hand-washing to decrease transmission of water-borne illnesses to children. Expanded to Bangladesh, Sri Lanka, Pakistan, Indonesia, Vietnam and South Africa, the campaign was grown to include backing of Global Hand-washing Day, and reached over 133 million people. Lifebuoy was voted one of India's most trusted brands.

While it seemed that all was coming together quite nicely, new CEO Paul Polman was clearly not a man to rest on his laurels He announced a bold new strategy that would really drive the new Unilever hard. The new vision – to double the size of the business while improving its environmental footprint - was both simple and stretching, although it did sound just a little generic:

- Winning with brands and innovation
- Winning in the marketplace
- Winning through continuous improvement
- Winning with people

Who could say no to any of that? However, the unique aspects though were in the detail and they all stressed the same theme: overlaying world-class performance standards on Unilever's unique global footprint:

- Now the company finally had one integrated R&D function, it could act like a global innovator through its somewhat Star Trek-sounding Genesis Programme
- Now the company had one integrated go-to-market organisation, it could lead the development and growth of its categories with the 5.9 billion people living in developing and emerging markets, where the company had a presence second to none
- Now the company had a global supply chain, it could source globally
- And now the company understood the critical importance to its Vitality strategy of its environmental footprint, it could set ambitious goals: reducing wash temperature and water usage in the 125 billion wash cycles a year its products made and, for Lifebuoy, changing the personal hygiene of one billion people by 2015

Exciting times for Unilever.

2010

Turnover finally left the €40 billion mark, rising 11% to over €44 billion. While 7% of the rise was due to currency changes, the remaining 4% hid an impressive story of an underlying volume increase of nearly 6% - the highest for more than thirty years – coupled with a pricing decrease of 2% as protection against low price and private label competition. That this could be done while increasing the underlying operating margin, was due once again to another €1.4 billion in savings, mostly from global sourcing.

Within the regions, the same three-tiered performance standards were still in place. Asia, Africa, Central and Eastern Europe excelled with an increase of 18% on the currency-enhanced top line, underpinned by a 10% volume increase - close to amazing given the absolute size and spread of the region. Every major unit delivered at least a 5% volume increase with China, India, Turkey and Vietnam being well into double-digit territory. Indian management in particular will have been delighted to move themselves off the CEO's problem pile, showing what they could do with initiatives such as re-launching the Wheel detergent brand across 25 Indian states in just 49 days and expanding their direct delivery network to another 630,000 stores in 110,000 new villages during the year.

In the Americas, Latin America, in particular Brazil, Argentina and Mexico once again drove the volume increase to nearly 5%, with even the USA managing modest volume growth to maintain overall market share and gaining share in the hair and skin cleansing categories, although losing it in spreads and weight management. Western Europe once again brought up the rear, although it did return to an over 1.4% volume growth: not bad, given the basket cases of Ireland, Greece and Spain, all substantial Unilever markets. The company grew volume by at least 2% and grew market share in the UK, France, Italy and the Netherlands.

Such broad-based success was clearly a result of the improving condition of the Unilever organisation. More than forty innovations in the year were launched into more than ten markets and some, such as Magnum Gold and Dove Men+Care rolled out to thirty. There was also great progress in retail customer management, with the development of more joint business plans, pro-active use of an increased number of the company's Customer Insight and Innovation centres and much improved in-store execution, particularly in emerging markets, with the development of agreed perfect store standards. One recognition of the progress Unilever had made in the whole area of customer management was their Global Supplier of the Year award from both Wal-Mart and Tesco.

Unilever's great advantage was, however, its sheer size in developing and emerging markets, now over 50% of business. Performance in each of their four product categories correlated directly with the exposure of the category to such markets. Savouries, dressings and spreads had only 35% of its turnover in the developing and emerging markets and delivered an over 2.5% volume increase; ice cream and beverages had 45% exposure and grew by 5.9%, whilst personal care had 61% of sales and grew 7.9%. At the top was home care: 78% of developing and emerging turnover grew by 8.2%. And William Lever's initiative in getting into these markets decades before P&G was now paying off in spades. In 2010, Comfort gained 5.7 million new users in China while Rexona deodorant lotion picked up 5.3 million in Indonesia. The future of Unilever would be decided in these markets, where brands and categories were being built with staggering numbers of new consumers.

The Unilever sustainability agenda also took another step forward with the announcement of the Unilever Sustainable Living Plan, which committed to help more than a billion people take action to improve their health and well-being, halve the environmental impact of company product use and manufacture and source 100% of agricultural raw materials sustainably. With some tidying up of the brand portfolio through divestment and the announcement of the blockbuster purchase of the Alberto Culver Company for $3.7 billion, Unilever was, as the CEO proclaimed, 'now fit to compete'.

2011

Given the renewed economic uncertainty in many of Unilever's key markets, it would have been hard to match the 2010 performance. And so it proved. Underlying volume growth dropped back to 1.6%, although significant cost-driven price increases totalled €2.4 billion, driving the underlying sales growth up to a recent high of more 6.5%. As ever, performance differences between emerging and developed markets were marked. India, China, Turkey and South Africa again grew double digit, powering an 11.5% sales increase across all emerging markets: the company's developed markets trod water. The combination of price increases and a further €1.5 billion in cost savings protected the operating margin and enabling a modest increase in the company's €6 billion advertising budget (Unilever are the world's second-largest advertiser). Dove became the company's first €3 billion personal care brand and more than three million shops signed up to the Unilever perfect store programme.

The speed with which Unilever now operated was light years ahead of the days of the special committee and the convoluted organisation chart. Axe Excite was launched in 100 markets in the year, seventy innovations were launched into more than ten markets, and within nine months of completing the Alberto Culver acquisition, TRESemmé had been launched into Brazil, Simple into the U.S., and Motions into South Africa. The Genesis programme was now producing some genuine breakthroughs, including a process to preserve the essence of freshly picked tea leaves - incorporated into PG Tips and Lipton Yellow Label - and the Motionsense technology that greatly prolonged the efficacy of Rexona deodorant: tiny bundles of fragrance were released during the day as the wearer moved around. Unilever had also joined the herd of big companies embracing open innovation, working with five hundred external partners during the year.

The categories were again reflecting the differential exposure to emerging markets. Personal care led the way with an underlying volume growth of over 4%, home care delivered 2.2% more volume, and refreshment (the newly-named ice cream and beverages category) grew volumes by only 1.4% while the beleaguered foods division dropped 1.2% by volume: spreads, dressings and soups were not developing and emerging favourites.

2012

But 2012 was strong year. Despite increasing commodity costs, the core operating margin increased to 13.8%, boosted by Magnum and Sunsilk. Unilever now have 14 brands with sales of more than $1 billion per year and these key brands accounted for almost 50% of the 2012 growth. The launch of TRESemme in Brazil was also one of the company's most successful ever, adding €150 million to turnover, which increased by 10.5% and took Unilever above the €50 billion barrier for the first time, although the emerging markets continued to be the prime engine for growth. They now account for more than 55% of total business

What is Their DNA?

There can be no doubt that Unilever is a unique company. And much of that uniqueness can be traced back to the company's three key formative elements: William Lever himself, the 1929 merger that created a multi-category, multi-national company and the company's remaking into a focused packaged goods company.

Making Acquisitions Work

William Lever saw almost from the very beginning that acquisitions were the path to success in the soap and detergents battlefield. Anybody could make soap; indeed, when he started his business, most housewives did. But it was only scale that could provide the security of low cost ingredients and the resources to create entry barriers by bringing in ever more complex science. Lever acquired his way to complete UK market dominance and his successors were equally enthusiastic participants in the great inter-war shakedown of the US soap industry. Similarly, the company's Dutch margarine barons employed the same before the big the merger. Afterwards, and for almost all of Unilever's history, it has been a serial acquirer of businesses, buying at least a thousand. It may have bought the wrong ones sometimes, like prestige cosmetics that didn't fit their strengths, and it may have purchased the occasional dud, but along the way it built unparalleled experience and expertise at absorbing what it bought. It is a strength that was not much needed during the prolonged divestment phase, but we forecast it will play an increasingly important role in the drive to double the size of the business.

Emerging Markets

That this is a unique strength of the business has been apparent throughout this chapter. The scale of Unilever's emerging markets business, accounting for 54% of the sales and rising, is impressive enough: Nestlé clock in with around 40% and P&G with 36%. Second comes organic sales growth, which Unilever has been achieving ever since emerging markets hit the radar. It has averaged a 9% underlying sales increase over the past twenty years in these very fertile markets. Put perhaps most important is the depth of engagement the company has with retailers and consumers. Unilever has not simply acquired its way to an emerging market presence as have many of its packaged goods peers, but has been building brand equities and retail relationships for many decades. The company has unparalleled experience of operating in sometimes extremely basic and volatile economic conditions, which give it an expertise often absent elsewhere. Lifebuoy, for example, is the hand-washing soap of choice for countless millions rural poor. Who amongst Unilever's global competitors would possibly devote the resources needed to distribute and then displace this fantastic brand that William Lever invented? Unilever's primary competitor in emerging markets is emerging local companies, so it is important Unilever can act locally enough to head off these threats. But Unilever has been managing local talent for decades. In virtually every emerging market of note it is number one and the most sought-after packaged goods employer. The huge advantage of emerging markets is only Unilever's to lose rather than someone else's to supplant.

Local Roots with Global Scale

The divestment of non-packaged goods businesses followed by the creation of a global operating structure has created a new and recent addition to the Unilever DNA: a superb balance of global and local capabilities. In the past it must have seemed to the likes of P&G that competing with Unilever was competing with a loose association of extremely local companies, an advantage that enabled P&G to decimate Unilever's detergent market shares in Europe. Today however, P&G are in effect facing a new global competitor with strong global brands being rolled out - seemingly effortlessly - into almost every market by a strong, very well established, ear-to-the-ground organisation. Somewhat ironically, this is the very model William Lever envisaged as he took Sunlight soap to as many countries as possible. The sharpening of Unilever's somewhat lax historical performance culture by the current CEO looks like being the final piece of a now-complete puzzle that should make Unilever the very best global-local packaged goods business.

Summary

Unilever is perhaps the best example of how understanding a company's formation, roots and early evolution helps us to understand it both today and tomorrow. The company seems to have been evolving since the day of the merger and is only now emerging from its chrysalis. Not that such a prolonged evolution has been a major problem; along the way, the company has built skills and market positions that now simply cannot be replicated.

The single major question mark over Unilever is the role of the foods division, which doesn't really fit in with today's company. Skippy has already been sold and surely Slimfast can't be far behind. We believe the rest of the foods division should be added too, and for four key reasons:

- The logic that brought margarine and detergents together in the first place no longer applies: their technologies and ingredients have diverged too far

- As the company becomes ever more global in what and how it operates, many of the foods brand are more local in strength, with thousands of differing recipes. 65% of sales are outside emerging markets where the company is strategically advantaged. Instead they operate in developed markets where Unilever perennially struggles to gain momentum

- While the benefits of green tea in the company's Unilever Sustainable Living Plan are plain to see, it's hard to see how the planet will benefit from the sale of more Hellmann's Mayonnaise.

- We believe the Unilever of today would not buy Bestfoods if it were still independent and up for sale. It doesn't leverage its strengths or strengthen its powers and abilities. If P&G bought those brands today Unilever wouldn't lose any sleep.

- The tea and ice cream businesses have global scale, with global and regional brands and a much clearer role in the company's strategy. Margarine, stock cubes and salad dressings don't. They need to go and the sooner the better

And with that, Unilever would be unstoppable.

Emerging Markets

China

We may live in a global economy but the eighteen businesses we have looked at so far embrace just six locations: twelve American, two French, one Swiss, one German, one British/Dutch and one British/Dutch/German based in Britain. Of the CEOs on April 17th, 2013 there was a little more diversity: seven Americans, two French, two Indians, a Turkish-American and one each from Italy, Australia, the U.K., Belgium, Holland, and Denmark. And every company except Estée Lauder Company predates the Second World War, although several - Dean Foods and Reckitt Benkiser are good examples of those who have radically transformed themselves into their current guises more recently.

So is it the case that today's biggest FMCG companies, most of who have been big for a very long time, will remain the biggest? How likely is it that new global giants will arise from the emerging markets in which virtually all packaged goods growth is taking place? After all, there are plenty of giants in other markets: India's Tata group is now a global player in steel, soda ash, cars and, in a formerly exclusive packaged goods fiefdom, tea. Lenovo was established in China in 1984 to conduct quality checks on computers. Then it developed a circuit board that allowed IBM-compatible personal computers to process Chinese characters. Twenty-one years later, it bought out IBM's personal computer division to become the world's third-largest PC manufacturer.

However, virtually all the companies we have looked at have already built up substantial businesses in the key emerging markets, firmly establishing their brands and usually setting the performance benchmarks for the categories in which they compete for business. Does this mean they are invulnerable to a new generation of competitors? Are they not big enough and global enough to buy any emerging markets players before they are powerful enough to pose a threat? And would it really matter if a local Indian firm took on Hindustan Unilever Ltd and beat it? When Hindustan Unilever itself is already a huge, successful and thoroughly Indian business, what difference would it make to anyone other than Unilever employees and shareholders?

There are many reasons to believe that there will be no big new players joining those we have already covered, at least for the next ten or even twenty years. But that's the way it often seems; the reasons for decline and fall only become obvious in hindsight. Nineteenth century giants included Lydia Pinkham's Vegetable Compound and Brandreth's Purgative Pills, yet they and others like them were comprehensively undone by a long-running campaign against the patent medicine industry by the deceptively benign-sounding Ladies Home Journal. No doubt the Pinkham and Brandreth managers thought of themselves as both invincible and immortal. But they had been cheating the consumer for many years; their products' lavish claims were exposed as illusory -temporary and palliative at best - and their corporate cynicism and greed led to ignominious oblivion. Today's products, undoubtedly as well equipped in the cynicism and greed departments, do at least deliver the benefits they claim: the law says they have to. So we are inclined to forgive them the rest.

But new technology can radically change the existing order: Nestlé was founded on the invention of infant formula and Kraft on processed cheese. Might such watersheds happen again? Or will the tens of thousands of R&D professionals working in the large firms, and backed by hundreds of millions of dollars, permanently maintain the upper hand? The answer is no. The unlikely pairing of Chaleo Yoovidhya and Dietrich Mateschitz beat the combined brains of the world's largest soft drinks firms with the product they devised: in 2011, Red Bull shifted 4.6 billion cans.

The rise of Red Bull, and the many similar drinks riding on its coat-tails - including some from the established giants - is a good example of an inherent weakness in the large packaged goods firms, the desire to perpetuate the brands that made them giants and kept them that way. While many companies preach disruptive innovation, they are very selective about where the disruption should take place: in other peoples' brands. Huge chunks of every company's R&D budget go not to innovation but to perpetuating existing products' status quo, improving profitability by cheaper ingredients with the same functionality or improved production processes. No real innovation there, and certainly no disruption.

But many of the giants will also feel that diversification itself protects against disruptive innovation. If some brash new idea makes Swiffers redundant overnight, P&G have enough other businesses to make this a problem to be solved in time rather than a catastrophe to be weathered at all costs. But diversification can itself become a weakness. Is Dolce & Gabana a stronger brand for being owned by P&G? Is P&G stronger for owning it? Are the executives running Estée Lauder quaking at the thought of a shoot-out with P&G? Or are they relishing the opportunity to use their industry expertise to teach the makers of Pampers a lesson about perfumes?

In fact, many of the companies we have looked at remain complacent, despite the fact that their annual reports increasingly chart a private label growth that is beginning to restrict their ability to pile on the price increases. In the glory days of television advertising, retailers could be and were treated like second-class citizens and their cheap, poor quality, private label offerings dismissed as jokes. However retailers today arecomplex modern businesses, with both manufacturing capacity and resources that are greater than some of the companies we have looked at in the preceding pages. If you analyse the world's top 20 FMCG, manufactures, you will find that seven of them are retailers.

And the world is changing. Asia and South America are driving the growth of a global middle class, which means that these days, the giants cannot afford to be anything like so laisser-faire. The possibility of being taken on and beaten by upstart companies in emerging markets is all too real. How? Let's take three developments in China as our examples.

Inherently Local Industries

Whether the multinationals like it or not, there are some key packaged goods categories in which being global gives few, if any, advantages beyond cash resources. PepsiCo, for example, sets great store by its ability to offer local flavours of potato chips. This is possible because it is more economical to disperse potato chip manufacturing, than to set up colossal regional or global factories, whose efficiency is compromised by short product life and the product's high volume. When you have only six weeks to distribute and sell a product whose packaging is mostly air, you make more money by having smaller factories as close to the market volume as possible. But this reduces any would-be competitor's entry costs dramatically. And China, the world's largest potato producer, already has over fifty companies in the market.

Mengniu

An industry that demands even greater localisation is dairy. The Mengniu Dairy Group was founded in 1999 by Niu Gensheng who began his career in 1978 working for a dairy in Hohhot, capital of the Inner Mongolian Autonomous Region in north-central China. By 1998, Niu worked his way up to become the Vice CEO of Inner Mongolia Yili Group, one of the largest dairy manufacturers in China. But Niu Gensheng would not be the first manager in the dairy industry to think he could do things better than his employer. Like Dean Foods' Ted Best, Niu Gensheng set out on his own, took over a small dairy producer, Mengniu Dairy. In five years Mengiu was a listed company on the Hong Kong exchange.

In this case, scale was the key. The dairy chiller, perhaps the least glamorous part of the grocery store, has a huge turnover per linear inch compared to the darker recesses of the dry goods aisles, yet it depends mainly on local, relatively small suppliers, dairy even more than potato chips, since it is mostly commoditised and so does not usually come to the attention of the large-scale branded companies. But when you buy up a lot of dairies, you also buy the scale to invest in the production of other dairy products where brands play a greater role - such as yoghurt and ice cream, and an equally scaled-up retailer relationship for your branded products.

Following this pattern, by 2005, Mengniu was operating 14 production sites, processing 2.8 million tons of liquid milk and selling three categories of products: liquid milk products (UHT milk, milk beverages and yoghurt), ice cream and other dairy (milk powder and milk tablets). Turnover had reached $1.3 billion, only $200 million behind his old employer Yii, the market leader.

If the highly fragmented nature of the Chinese dairy industry had made the achievement possible in the first place, it took two further ingredients to catapult Mengniu to the number one spot: better technology enabling more differentiated products and effective branding. The technology came through a 2006 joint venture with the European dairy giant, Arla Foods, a Danish, Swedish and German-owned dairy co-operative. Together, the companies established Mengniu Arla (Inner Mongolia) Dairy Products Co. Ltd. The goal was to build the best milk powder brand in China by adding high- value nutrition products. That such a product could also continuously improve the health and life-quality of Chinese people did no harm at all, and, within one year, Mengniu Arla opened one of the world's most advanced dairy R&D centres, simultaneously launching a full series of milk powder products catering for practically every group you can thinks of, from babies to adults, milk powder for pregnant women, newborns, 7-year-olds, students and seniors. The company advertised hugely throughout China, sponsoring the Chinese space programme via campaigns announcing 'special milk for Chinese astronauts' on and after the launches of the manned Shenzou 5 and Shenzou 6 spacecraft.

Not all joint ventures proved so productive, however. Mengniu signed a series of contracts with Danone in December 2006 to set up three yoghurt joint ventures in Inner Mongolia, Beijing and Ma'anshan with ownership split 51:49 in favour of Mengniu, with a one-year get-out clause in case of corporate fire. Some progress was made, but the partnership failed, due primarily to local governments failing to grant the required approvals and consents, and parties agreed a termination in December 2007. Some cooperation continued - co-packing and distribution of yoghurt under the BIO brand, for example – but that too came to nothing, as Danone reconsidered its China strategy following a huge legal battle with the Wahaha group.

The trouble with going the branded route is that your business increasingly depends on the brand reputation. So when the Chinese tainted milk scandal broke in 2008, Mengniu, by no means at the centre of the problem, still found itself in difficulties. The chief culprit was Sanlu, a cut-price producer that had been adding melamine to milk to boost its apparent protein levels. But the practice spread to dairies that supplied both Mengniu and Yili with almost disastrous consequences. Even though the company immediately recalled the products involved, it suffered mass de-listings by supermarkets and found its export markets in Malaysia, Singapore, Taiwan and the Philippines suddenly closed. The company's shares took a hammering on the Hong Kong Stock Exchange. Only an injection of capital from state-owned COFCO Ltd., China's largest food importer and exporter, plus with private equity cash in return for 20% of the equity, kept Mengniu afloat.

But the storm passed: by the end of 2009 Mengniu was again one of the top 20 global dairy companies, a year later made number sixteen in the world and, both in volume and value terms, number one in China. In 2011, sales reached a new high of just over $6 billion, with 90% in liquid milk products, 9% in ice cream and 1%. In liquid milk, UHT accounted for a steadily declining 61% with the more strongly branded beverages making 25% and yoghurt 14%. Milk Deluxe, Champion, Future Star, Fruit Milk Drink and Youyi C all enjoyed strong double-digit growth, moved from 17% in 2008 to 27% in 2012. It was this strong, branded portfolio that decided Arla to take a 6% stake in mid-2012, a closer cooperation it is hoped will increase Chinese five-fold by 2016. Nor need these sales come at Mengiu's expense: the company's market shares in all main product categories are still below 30%, leaving plenty of room for further organic growth through nationally advertised brands and superior NPD capability.

The next big question is how aggressive the company will be in looking beyond China once homeland growth flattens out. It will certainly have the scale to make significant acquisitions and both the technical and the branding capabilities to do so. We should watch that space: by 2020, China is likely to be should be the world's number one economy, with India at number three and Russia at number five by PPP.

Expansion from Other Areas of the Value Chain

It is often forgotten today that one of the main stimuli for brands and branding was the never-ending struggle between producers, middlemen and retailers for a greater share of profits. Before the emergence of modern brands in the mid-19th century, the key player in the value chain had been the middleman, whose access to capital and credit gave them the ability to strong-arm the subscale pre-industrial manufacturers of the day. But the scale of industrialization enabled the early mass production barons to reverse this position and encroach upon the banking and credit facilities previously controlled by the merchants, thus largely squeezing them out of the picture.

Branding was born both to compete with other manufacturers more effectively for sales and to squeeze better profits from the retailer and it did so by talking directly to the consumer about superior quality. The process was enhanced by packaging, which protected products from adulteration by retailers and provided a better canvas from which to communicate brand identity. Middlemen were now much more transporters and distributors, and were squeezed even there as companies saw the merchandising benefits of delivering direct themselves. Branding strategy was so successful that we now tend to see it as the natural preserve of the manufacturer. The recent crumbling of that edifice, as evidenced by the remarkable rise of retailers' private labels from the 1990s onwards, should not have come as the shock that it did Had manufacturers looked more carefully, they would have seen that the economics and technologies which underpin branding were changing.

This shift of brand power from manufacturer to retailer does illustrate that there is no natural and permanent locus of branding in the value chain; from the industrial perspective, the locus of branding can be different. Any player in the value chain -producer, distributor or retailer - could be the predominant force in the right circumstances. Occasionally, the middleman became the brand owner himself: two such examples being bananas and port wine.

For its entire history, Chiquita has been an expert in the transportation of bananas which largely grown by independent farmers. By transporting bananas for many producers and retailers, it was able to lead the value chain by unlocking benefits of scale: the larger the warehouses and refrigerated ships, the cheaper the bananas. The little Chiquita label gives assures the consumer that his bananas are not only good value, but trustworthy. Which gives the company the power to squeeze at both ends, growers and retailers alike. Sherry and port are very similar cases: Harvey's in sherry, and Sandeman's in port, also hold the whip-hand.

Brands that flow to the product from the middleman has breathed new life into the role and function of the middleman and almost certainly changes the developed market manufacturer-retailer dynamic The rise of the Chinese economy as supplier to the western world presents new opportunities for a new kind of competitor which follows this model. Li & Fung is a very good example.

Li & Fung

Li & Fung is a Hong Kong company whose roots go back to the early 1900s, when it became one of the first Chinese-owned export companies in a market dominated by foreign-owned trading houses. Li & Fung began by exporting porcelain and silk products, mostly to the US, but soon expanded into jade, bamboo, rattan furniture, fireworks and handicrafts. It filled a valuable and hence profitable role: in most cases in those days, American buyers spoke no Chinese and Chinese manufacturers spoke no English, so the company could charge high commissions. But the Second World War was forced the company to cease trading for several years. Then the 1949 communist takeover of China delivered a second and almost fatal blow, cutting off all suppliers in the Chinese hinterland. So Li & Fung reoriented itself to source from the Hong Kong itself, where the manufacture of labour-intensive products - toys, plastic flowers, garments and electronics – had begun. Li & Fung became Hong Kong's largest exporter of these new products.

The company began its change from exporter to supply chain expert in the 1970s, when it started acting as a regional sourcing specialist, matching overseas buyers with sellers not just from a nascent Chinese manufacturing industry but also Singapore, Korea and Taiwan. By now managed by the Harvard-educated brothers William and Victor Fung, the traditional broker role was nevertheless being squeezed from both ends (as had happened in western markets fifty years earlier). The Fung brothers decided to restructure; whilst the traditional middleman role of matching buyers to sellers was shrinking, there were many other value chain processes to consider. So the company spread its net, sourcing from countries closer to the buyers: Mexico, Honduras and Guatemala for the US and Turkey, Egypt and Tunisia for European markets. The business achieved true global scale when it tripled its size by acquiring Inchape Buying Services in 1995, giving it a substantial network in India, Pakistan, Bangladesh and Sri Lanka.

Li & Fung now had the ability to source essentially anything from whichever low-cost country most suited to the needs of its client and this it used as a springboard into more value-added activities. The company disaggregated the value chain into what it called 'dispersed manufacturing', designing product itself and then outsourcing the manufacturing to the appropriate country. It manufactured in China, for example, but managed quality control in Hong Kong. All the client had to do was specify the product requirements and Li & Fung did the rest. To achieve shorter order to delivery cycles, Li & Fung would extend its value chain reach upstream by managing production runs in its suppliers and further dis-aggregating production processes, so customers like Levis could have delivery only four weeks after passing colour sales trends to Li & Fung. The company also developed its IT: information between supply and demand was usually far better than anything its customers could do.

During the late 1990s, as private labels became the leading but still fragmented component of growth in developed markets, Li & Fung was perfectly placed to manage the rapid growth in SKU's and supply chain complexity, cementing its position as the leading consumer goods trading company. It understood better than the rapidly evolving packaged goods value chain, saw where the value lay and how to increase its share.

Over the next decade sales grew seven-fold, reaching $14.3 billion by 2008 and giving the company enough scale to use acquisitions to extend its reach. In 2009 alone, Li & Fung acquired a British footwear company, a manufacturer of technical equipment for Nike, a major handbag maker along and the in-house sourcing divisions of Liz Claiborne and Talbots. It entered branding business via a recently launched U.S. division, LF USA. Royal Velvet, Cannon and the company that makes Vera Wang clothes for Kohl's are some of the brands the company now either owns or licenses. The company claimed it intended simply to add the front end of design onto the back end of sourcing, but the real reason was to grab the brand, the most valuable part of the value chain. An early exposure to the benefits of being the brand owner was Black Cat. This fireworks brand was introduced into the US in the 1940s, became a registered trademark in 1952, and is now the oldest and most highly recognized fireworks brand in the world, having gobbled up competitors such as Standard Fireworks, Britain's long time market leader, in 1998.

In 2011 Li & Fung (Trading) Limited had a turnover of around $20 billion and employed about 28,000 people worldwide. It is a member of the Fung Group of companies, which also includes privately held retailing and publicly listed consumer-goods distribution businesses in Asia such as Toys R Us and the Circle K franchises. Today, Li & Fung sources from 45 countries, up from 13 in 1994, and is developing supply arrangements in new markets such as Sub-Saharan Africa, which it believes could one day replace China as the world's lowest-cost maker of consumer goods.

The company, whilst being highly decentralised (in effect, a business unit for every customer) is basically divided into three: Trading, Logistics and Distribution. Within the Trading arm, Li & Fung is the world's leading consumer goods sourcing company across a wide range. The company is increasingly used by its customers to take an initial design idea all the way through to the finished product. With the product made, Logistics kicks in, offering warehousing, transport, repacking, customs brokerage, freight forwarding, hubbing and consolidation. Distribution, based primarily in the US and Europe, means much more than simply trucking product. It too is divided into three: private labels, proprietary brands and brand licensing. For private labels, Li & Fung takes on all aspects of the value chain apart from retailing, the second two the company develops exclusive lines of branded merchandise for brands owned either by itself or outside entities. Added to all this is the Fung business intelligence centre which, thanks to its enormous global reach, collects and analyses market data on China's economy and other Asian countries.

While Li & Fung has not yet become a major brand-owning company, it may represent their next logical step. The company has all the capabilities needed to be a successful brand owner; top-notch knowledge of market trends, world-class capabilities in product design, sourcing, logistics, retailer relationships and distribution. Were they to buy a major brand, or several, here is no reason why they could not or should not succeed in developing them. Their turnover already approaches that of Kellogg's and Heinz combined, a clout that would leave a sizeable footprint in both major and emerging economies.

Head-on Competition

While many of the companies examined in this book are used to competing with local players in emerging markets, they are not accustomed to new competitors in these markets taking on their core brands. Although this is a commonplace in categories such as consumer electronics, it has hardly ever happened in packaged goods. But when it does, it comes as a major shock to the leading manufacturers. Senior executives in Coca-Cola and PepsiCo, marvelling at the annual sales increases from China in the latter part of the 20th-century, had no idea that their toughest new competitor for decades would come from a middle-aged salesman whom the cultural revolution had re-cast as a rural peasant for 15 years and who started in business delivering goods to retailers on his tricycle.

Wahaha

Zong Qinghou founded Wahaha in 1987, selling ice cream, soda drinks and school exercise books, all delivered by tricycle, in Hangtzhou, Zhejiang Province. In 1988 he moved into oral tonic and did very well. But he also realised that although the nutritional drinks category was swamped with competitors, none of them was targeted children. A year later he had set up the Hangzhou Wahaha Nutritional Foods Factory to make the Wahaha Nutrient Beverage for Children. Wahaha means 'to make children happy' and with an advertising campaign aimed squarely at China's state-enforced one-child families - nothing was too good for these little emperors - it was an immediate success. Sales hit $65 million by 1990.

In 1991, Wahaha merged with an ailing foods business, which greatly enhanced its market capabilities. It wasted no time, launching a fruit-flavoured milk drink in 1991, soon followed by Wahaha Milk, enriched with vitamins and minerals, and this during a period when a staggering 3,000 companies had entered the children's beverage market. Wahaha fended them off not by being the innovator, but the best and quickest, backed by a distribution network that extended deep into China's rural hinterland.

Wahaha had more than its fair share of failures but maintained an increasing scale by buying up insolvent food and drink companies. The company's finances were stretched, but the watershed came with the realisation that world-class production technology was needed, both to triumph over the tidal wave of local competitors and, more importantly, the multinationals now entering the Chinese market. After a prolonged courtship it decided to partner with the French giant, Groupe Danone. The two companies established several joint ventures, Danone owning 51% of the equity and Wahaha controlling local management, sales and marketing. The new venture's key launch was Wahaha Pure Water (bottled water was a major product in Danone's portfolio), which rapidly became the number one brand in the market. On the back of this success, Wahaha acquired over 40 companies in 22 provincial cities to become one of the country's largest beverage companies. While the Danone relationship would later turn spectacularly sour, the relationship and the profits from Wahaha Pure Water would finance the company's most ambitious move to date: into the cola market.

By 1998, both Coca-Cola and PepsiCo were well established in China. Coca-Cola, there before the communist takeover, was in 1979 the first western brand to re-enter the market; by the time Wahaha was contemplating entering the market, it had over 20 bottling plants. PepsiCo was only two years behind, establishing a joint venture bottling plant in Shenzhen in 1981, with ten plants running by 1998. Coke and Pepsi accounted for a quarter of China's rapidly growing soft drink market and 80% of the cola category. The two companies had focused on snatching market share from local cola manufacturers even at the expense of their bottom lines.

So why would Wahaha even think of entering this market and risk the wrath of these two global titans with their bottomless pockets? Zong Qinghou, after years of exile in the countryside, was something of an expert on the country's rural market and he knew very well that the cola giants had thus far restricted their efforts to the major cities where they could access large and well-established distribution networks and retailers. The hinterland was still mostly virgin territory. And it contained 1.1 billion people who, despite their lower per capita income, still accounted for two-thirds of consumer spending. As might be expected from a man who started his business delivering products on a tricycle, Zong Qinghou had by now established a superb distribution network to the smallest Chinese towns and villages. He saw multinational firms as nothing to be scared of, believing that local knowledge and expertise, a good enough product, great marketing and distribution, could trump global reach He also had a healthy disregard for the Chinese market research industry. Feedback from his village-visiting sales people was what counted.

Wahaha spent two years developing the product, consulting with the best R&D and flavour houses, and conducted thousands of taste tests worldwide. The product was as close as possible to Pepsi and Coke but tweaked sweeter and stronger to suit Chinese tastes. Wahaha Future Cola was launched during the 1998 World Cup, 25% cheaper than the major brands and exploited the company's widespread distribution outside the Coke and Pepsi big city heartlands. The brand was marketed as a patriotic cola, packaged with symbols of happiness and good luck - crucial in appealing to traditional rural families - and the company negotiated preferential advertising spots and rates. Demand soon outstripped supply. Wahaha approached third-party bottlers. Coca-Cola and PepsiCo strong-armed their bottlers and distributors to say no, threatening them with dire consequences if they took on Future Cola and its new line extensions, a caffeine-free children's cola and Future Coffee Cola.

Wahaha's big advantage was the unique set of relationships its sales offices had developed in over thirty provinces where over 1,000 local distributors delivered its product to the remotest corners of the country, where 70% of Future Cola's sales were taking place, mostly in rural areas where Pepsi or Coke had yet to appear in any great strength. Between 1998 and 2001, sales of Future Cola increased almost ten-fold giving it a market share of 14%; a year later share was up to 18%, with the extra 4% coming straight off Coke's leading market share of 47%. In some provinces, Future itself was the market leader.

By this point Wahaha was China's largest soft drink producer with sales of around $1 billion. Over forty subsidiaries operated over 60 modern production lines in fifteen of China's twenty-two provinces and five autonomous areas. On the success of Future Cola, the company launched Future branded tea and fruit juice lines which, when combined with the company's water sales, meant that in 2002 Wahaha's total soft drink output in China exceeded that of The Coca-Cola Company. Wahaha was also one of the top ten advertisers in China, outspending Coca-Cola by around 20%, as they increasingly pushed their products into the supermarkets and hypermarkets of the major cities.

As might be imagined, this finally caught the attention of the two giants who began undercutting the selling price of Future in their original big-city key markets and taking a more localised approach to their marketing against what was firmly seen as China's cola. Coca-Cola belatedly took the fight to Future in the rural areas, which slowed, but did not stop Future's growth, which reached 650,000 tons by 2005. Tit for tat, Wahaha cheekily launched Future in the US, selling through small convenience stores in New York City and Los Angeles. By 2008, Wahaha's Future Cola was a firmly established number three player in the Chinese cola market with a market share not far behind that of Pepsi. Wahaha in total was ranked the number five global beverages company.

Even after a somewhat acrimonious split from Danone, with Wahaha winning the argument that the Wahaha name never belonged to the joint water venture, Wahaha is still China's biggest beverage producer with sales approaching $10 billion. The company now has 30,000 employees and has expanded way beyond its water, dairy, tea, juices and cola drinks into children's clothing. It has even built a shopping complex and a Future Cola factory in Indonesia. It exports not only to other Far Eastern countries but also to France, Germany, Italy, Spain and The Netherlands and has recently signed a sponsorship deal with Manchester United. The fact that the founder and CEO, Mr Zong Qinghou, is now China's richest man shows what can be achieved when an enterprising local business in an emerging market dares to take on the global giants.

In summary, the unique scale of the Chinese market and its speed of growth is creating a hothouse; new competitors can appear seemingly from nowhere, in rapidly conditions last seen in the latter part of the 19th-century and long since forgotten. Mengniu seems to be well on the way to joining Dean Foods and Arla at the pinnacle of the global dairy industry. The domination of Li & Fung in those major parts of the value chain that were previously the domain of the branded giants might well be a Trojan Horse containing a global competitor with all of the advantages and none of the drawbacks. And the success of Wahaha in competing head on with the most powerful brand in the world shows that no one is guaranteed an easy ride when faced with a Chinese packaged goods manufacturer. However, and as we shall see below, it is not just in China where new players are emerging

Emerging Market Companies: The Rest of World

Will new packaged goods giants rise from the emerging markets? That is not the question: they are already doing so, in countries whose development just preceded archetypal emerging markets like China and India. Here we consider three companies from three different countries, each of which has taken a very different approach on their path to greatness.

Brazil: BRF-Brasil Foods SA

Where Did They Come From?

In 1934, two Italian immigrants, Saul Brandalise and Angelo Ponzoni opened a grocery store in Vila das Perdizes, in the far south of Brazil, almost equidistant from São Paulo and Buenos Aires. The partner's first aim was to establish a fledgling retail empire simply by merging with a store in a nearby town. However, within a year they had switched careers and were in meat production. This decision was aided by their location - the state of Santa Catarina was awash with livestock farms run by European settlers. In 1941 the firm of Brandalise, Ponzoni and Cie launched their first pork products under the Perdigão brand name.

How Did They Evolve?

Under Saul and Angelo's energetic leadership, the company rapidly expanded into adjacent business sectors. They acquired a tannery to process their own pig skins, then branched into flour milling and even bought a saw mill. During the 1950s, the company, by now renamed Brandalise, Ponzoni SA Comércio e Industria, concentrated its expansion efforts on vertical integration. This would become an enduring hallmark. By the mid-1950s the company was farm-rearing its own pigs and its chickens were fed from its own feed mills. The resulting products were distributed by its own subsidiary, which included two Douglas DC-3 aircraft to get fresh produce to the São Paulo markets 1100kms away. Their Perdigão brand name (meaning partridge) became so popular the company adopted that as its official name in 1958.

The 1960s saw the company's establishment in the large Brazilian cities of São Paulo and Rio de Janiero, and during the 1970s they developed a national presence across Brazil. Soon after, Perdigão made its first foray into a production of branded processed meat products such as hamburgers and salami. They were also steadily increasing investment in R&D capabilities. R&D came up trumps in 1981 when the company launched chickens under the Chester brand name. These had been specially bred to have a greater proportion of meat in the breast and thigh portions, and were quickly followed up with low fat versions. In the mid-1980s Perdigão withdrew from a number of what were now non-core operations, such as the saw mill and retail outlets. By expanding into the beef category, they became a dedicated food producer. The company increasingly added brands to its portfolio through: a combination of its own efforts, the use of established children's characters such as Turma da Mônica, and acquisitions such as that of Swift canned vegetables in 1989.

Unfortunately, the apparently irresistible force of Perdigão's constant expansion hit the immovable object of the Brazilian economic crisis of the early 1990s. It very nearly bankrupted the business. In 1994, the Brandalise and Ponzoni families sold out to a consortium of pension funds. They wasted no time in seeking to turn around their investment.

How Did They Build the Modern Business?

The transition from being a family-run to professional manager-run business can be a slow and tortuous process. Not so with Perdigão. The new owners had a clear out at the top and hired a team of seasoned executives to embark on an extensive restructuring of the company, both operationally and financially. This resulted in a tighter definition of what were the core operations, with the outcome that non-core activities like the animal feed divisions were sold off.

The new regime then concentrated on the underlying problem: Perdigão was not well equipped, in either facilities or strength of product range, to withstand a flood of cheap meat imports from the Far East. Therefore, more than $260 million was spent on modernising and upgrading manufacturing facilities while the product range moved towards higher margin, added-value categories. Here branding could play a greater role.

In 1997 the company launched the Healthful Choice brand of frozen foods, initially a range of vegetables and then fish products. Next came the launch of a range of ready-made meals under the Toque da Sabor brand, which was quickly followed by the Apreciatta range of frozen pizzas. Perdigão acquired the Batavia brand of turkey products, which they quickly extended into a range of low-sodium products. Sales grew so rapidly that Perdigão became the number two meat products company in Brazil behind Sadia. The company's success enabled a 2001 investment of $250 million to construct Latin America's largest pig and poultry facility. By 2002, Perdigão had got into the cheese business. Their total annual sales were R2.8 billion ($1.4 billion), almost half of which was exported.

Pursuing essentially the same strategy nearly doubled sales between 2002 and 2006. A takeover bid from rival Sadia was promptly rejected. The next year Perdigão changed gear. They agreed with Unilever to create a joint venture to manage the Becel and Becel pro.activ heart health brands in Brazil. As part of the deal, Perdigão acquired Unilever's Doriana, Delicata and Claybom margarine brands, together with the associated production facilities. Perdigão soon overtook Sadia as Brazil's biggest food company, helped by the acquisitions of poultry and dairy producer Eleva Alimentos SA; and the meat-processing unit of Cebeco Groep BV. By now Perdigão had more than 55,000 employees and was selling its poultry, pizza and lasagne in more than 110 countries (see next section).

However, Perdigão's big break came in 2009 when they launched a bid for their great rival. Sadia had lost more than R3 billion in ill-advised derivative bets on the Brazilian Real currency and made a whopping loss in the year. Perdigão agreed to take over Sadia in a share-swap transaction, thus forming the world's biggest poultry processor. Its value, at about $5.3 billion, had overtaken the US's Tyson Foods. The new company would be called BRF Brasil Foods SA and was forecast to generate anywhere from R2-4 billion cost savings in distribution and production. This would give them a significant cost advantage over other major global players.

However, the deal, in which Sadia would be run as a wholly owned subsidiary of Perdigão, had to be considered by Brazil's anti-trust body, Cade. Their approval came with strings attached. The company was required to sell off a host of processing plants, farms and abattoirs, plus thirteen brands and the suspension of the Perdigão and Batavo brands in certain categories. These disposals brought in R1.7 billion, while the brand suspensions decreased combined revenues by R1.2 billion. These seemed an extremely tough set of conditions, but in recompense BRF received the entire shareholding of Quickfood SA, owner of Argentina's leading hamburger brand, Paty. During this convoluted and highly complex integration process, management kept their eye on the ball. Sales rose from R20.9 billion in 2009 to R25.7 in 2011 - making BRF the world's seventh-largest food company - and contributing to an average total shareholder return of over 30% since the merger had been announced.

Even after the enforced shedding, BRF still had a portfolio of over thirty brands spread across 3,300 product lines. An average of approximately 300 new products launched each year helped earn the company a place in the Forbes list of the world's 100 most innovative companies. The company now had one of the most impressive supply chains in Brazil, reaching over 150,000 distribution points, and giving access to their products to 98% of the country's population. The new company's mission was 'To be a part of people's lives by offering tasty foods with high quality, innovation and at affordable prices anywhere in the world'. This mission was being realised: over 40% of sales were being exported to over 120 countries.

The International Dimension

In 1975 Perdigão had been the first Brazilian poultry company to export its products when it sent its first shipment to Saudi Arabia. This led Brazil to become one of the world's leading poultry-producing countries. In 1985 Perdigão set up a partnership with the Mitsubishi Corporation to export its products into Japan and in 1990 EC permission was granted for the company to import into Europe. The next step change had come in 2001. Perdigão and Sadia joined forces to create an export joint venture, BRF Trading, with the aim of exploiting new markets in Russia, Africa and the Caribbean. When the partners fell out Perdigão took over the entire operation.

By 2012, they had amassed 19 commercial offices overseas and owned, in addition to 61 plants in Brazil, five in Argentina, and two in Europe (UK and The Netherlands). Another was under construction in Abu Dhabi. Perhaps the most promising was a joint venture with Dah Chong Hong Ltd to distribute the company's products in China through both retail and food service sectors. In 2012 export sales reached R11.6 billion off a volume of 2.5 million tons. This was up nearly 10% year-on-year. With the exception of North America, they enjoyed a good global spread: 33% going to the Middle East; 20% to the Far East; 16% to Europe; 13% to South America; 9% to Eurasia and 8% to Africa. Africa had previously been a Sadia strength. Now, the latter's products were rebranded under the Perdix name. The Sadia brand itself was repositioned as a premium brand and as such was re-launched into fifteen African countries. This was the first leg of a new international strategy. Their processed foods were to be branded upmarket, regionalised to meet local tastes and supported by the acquisition of local producers and distributors.

How Are They Structured?

After Sadia's acquisition, the latter operated as a stand-alone subsidiary, in parallel with the company's other main Brazilian businesses. The international divisions were consolidated under one holding subsidiary, Crossban Holdings BmbH (which was registered in Austria). By the end of 2012, Sadia SA had been fully absorbed into the main business.

What Have They Done Recently?

The merger with Sadia was one of the most complicated anywhere in the world. From 2009 onwards a huge number of activities were necessary: absorbing and divesting facilities and brands; and also managing brand transitions where their names had been forced to take a hiatus. All this was accomplished while still driving the business forwards.

The enforced transfer of assets and suspension of brands knocked an eye-watering one-third off the company's domestic sales. Even so, it still managed to move ahead by 10.9% in 2012. Even more impressively, like-for-like domestic sales in the second half of the year were up 50%. The company quickly replaced the lost sales. It rolled out new lines under the Sadia brand to replace the suspended Perdigão products, and launched new lines under the Perdigão brand into categories not affected by the suspension. In total the company brought out 99 new products into the Brazilian market. These were principally ready-to-eat meals, pizzas and the Meu Menu brand of frozen pasta meals. They contributed an additional 8.5% to the top line.

The company had built up some very impressive market shares:

2012 % Share
Speciality meat56.6
Margarine59.9
Pizzas64.6
Frozen meats68.3
Pastas72.7

Only in dairy was the company a minor player. There, 10.6% represented the third largest share. The food services unit grew its sales to 62,000 customers while in the overseas markets the company grew by over 30% in South America and Eurasia and over 10% in the Far East and Middle East. The company capped off a fine year by investing over R100 million in a new technology centre. This brought together the 250-strong R&D teams.

What Is Their DNA?

Given a complete clean sweep of management and strategy in 1994 and the mega-merger with Sadia in 2009, it is fair to say that the BRF DNA is still evolving. A cause of their recent success must be the level of professionalism and dynamism they have brought to a historically somewhat staid category. They are a match for anyone in the food business and a competitor to be feared.

Summary

With a 2012 turnover of over $13 billion, BRF is already a bigger company than some of the venerable first world leviathans covered earlier in this book. And they are growing faster than many. Their background and a substantial chunk of their existing business is in fresh and frozen meat and poultry. Yet, their shift into more branded categories is inexorable. Plus, it should not be forgotten that many of today's brand giants, for example General Mills, started off in commodity-type areas and transitioned into branded portfolios over time. With their expertise, scale and cost advantage in meat production and processing, BRF have plenty of growth left in them.

Mexico : Grupo Bimbo

Where Did They Come From?

Panificadora Bimbo started life (July 1945) already thinking big. Its founder, Lorenzo Servitje, had worked part-time in his father's bakery, El Molino, since 1928. When the father died in 1937, Lorenzo abandoned his accountancy studies to join the business fulltime, working alongside his uncle, Jaime Sendra. However, running a bakery was never going to be enough. With a childhood friend, José T. Mata, Lorenzo established an import/export company and employed his cousin, Jaime Jorba as sales manager.

Together, in 1943, these four began planning a mass market, packaged bread business; they would deliver freshly baked, wrapped bread to small stores. Jaime Jorba mapped out distribution routes in Mexico City. Lorenzo recruited a master baker. Alphonso Velasco was not only the son of the founder of Mexico's first bread baking company but also a graduate of Chicago's American Institute of Baking. Alphonso designed the factory and devised the recipes for four types of bread - large and small white loaves, rye bread and toasted bread – planned for the company's launch. Lorenzo recruited 38 employees and hired five delivery vans.

The final pieces of the puzzle were the company's unique selling point and logo. The USP was that the bread would be cellophane-wrapped: a first in Mexico on this industrial scale. The logo was a bear cub made to look like a baker, drawn by Jaime Sendra's artistic wife, and initially tried as a Christmas card. The Bimbo name had already been decided at an early planning stage, two years previously. The hygienically wrapped bread, enriched with milk and vitamins and delivered to the smallest of Mexico City's local stores, was an immediate hit. The product range was soon increased to nine lines with the addition of a range of buns and pound cakes. Only four years after launch, the company expanded outside Mexico City. They opened a depot in the city of Puebla and by 1950 the company's music-playing delivery vans were announcing the arrival of fresh bread in rural villages throughout Central Mexico.

How Did They Evolve?

In 1952 Bimbo began a decade of innovation. They introduced the Bimbollo and Medias Noches Bimbo hamburger and hot-dog buns, thus initiating a craving for American-style eating amongst Mexico's young. This craze was compounded by the launch of Donas del Osito doughnuts, which became one of the company's best sellers. By 1955 Bimbo had a fleet of over a hundred delivery trucks. To these was added a dedicated distribution network of customised Vespa scooters. They were known as Ganseras and distributed Bimbo's new Gansito range of cellophane-wrapped cupcakes, the first to be produced on an industrial basis in Mexico.

In 1964 Bimbo began to think internationally. (Perhaps they were prompted by one of their founders, Jaime Jorba, who returned to his native Spain in 1961. There he employed the same concept and also called it Bimbo). Aided by its newish plant in Monterrey (adjacent to the US border), Bimbo acquired the Mexican rights to the Sunbeam brand of bread from Quality Bakers of America. Further expansion across Mexico was Bimbo's prime agenda during the 1960s and early 1970s. This culminated in the opening of Latin America's largest bakery, which was also one of the ten largest in the world in 1972.

Expansion into new categories was also taking place. Bimbo established a new division for confectionery in 1971 and launched jams and marmalades in 1973. This range sprang out of the supply of ingredients for the cupcakes. These newcomers were soon followed by ranges of sweet breads, salty snacks, tortillas and, in 1978, the Bubulubu brand of candies and chocolates.

By the end of the decade, Bimbo had twelve plants and 15,000 employees with almost full coverage of the Mexican market. This prompted the company to offer 15% of its stock on the Mexican Stock Exchange in 1980. The fact that Bimbo's expansion so far had been financed entirely without debt meant they survived the 1982 Mexican economic crisis relatively unscathed. It did slow their expansion plans, by delaying the opening of another major plant until 1987.

How Did They Build The Modern Business?

Grupo Bimbo approached global scale as an international business with two developments in the mid-1980s. First, they began shipping long-shelf-life cakes, under the Suandy brand name, into the southern United States. Then, they purchased the Wonder Bread brand, which took them into milling for the first time.

By the late 1980s the company had a wide range of products organised under eight main brands:

- Bread and Sponge Cakes - Bimbo (by now the generic name for packaged bread in Mexico), Sunbean, Suandy, Tia Rosa.
- Cakes and Cookies – Miranela.
- Confectionery – Ricolino.
- Snacks – Barcel.
- Jams – Carmel.

With 25,000 employees and a contract to supply McDonald's with hamburger buns, Bimbo was now a major Mexican company. Yet, it had little corporate structure and was still run as the personal fiefdom of the remaining founders. In 1991 it turned up the gas further. Bimbo launched a $400 million investment programme (again internally funded), to open new plants in ten more cities and upgrade several more. The secret of Bimbo's success was its vast fleet of delivery trucks - now 11,000 and counting – which serviced over 200,000 family-run, stores which acco. These accounted for over three-quarters of its sales. The company was still short of its maximum potential in Mexico. All this success had been achieved despite the fact that only around 20% of the population bought packaged bread. Bimbo was the dominant player, with over 85% share, in a category that had much room for growth.

Bimbo diversified further in 1993 with the acquisition of a 40% stake in Mexico's leading ice cream company. These two companies later formed a joint venture with Unilever for Latin America. As in the early 1980s, Bimbo survived the 1994 Peso crisis relatively unscathed and the next year reported sales of over 10 billion Pesos ($1.5 billion) - Mexico accounted for 89% of this volume. They overhauled their Mexican direct-store delivery system by moving to a just-in-time process. Afterwards, the main thrust of Bimbo's continued growth would come in the international arena.

The International Dimension

Although Jaime Jorba had set up another Bimbo in Spain in the early 1960s, that company ran completely independently from the original Mexican enterprise. It achieved a similar level of success, becoming Spain's leading bread company before Jaime sold out to the American firm Campbell Taggart. Bimbo's first international operation came in 1989 when it purchased a small bakery in Guatemala City. The company geared up for further expansion in Latin America when it set up Bimbo Argentina and a separate Latin America management structure. Companies in Chile, Venezuela and El Salvador all mirrored the development of Bimbo in Mexico: they launched a packaged bread business, delivered direct to store, and then progressively added to the product range,.

By the early 1990s Bimbo had also greatly expanded its export business into the United States, reaching as far as New York, Chicago, Los Angeles and Miami. A joint venture with the Sara Lee Corporation was established to distribute Sara Lee products in Mexico. The same subsidiary, based in Texas, then entered the US tortilla market via an acquisition. By the end of 1994, Bimbo had a sizeable import operation into the US, with 23 products being delivered by over 100 trucks in California alone. The American tortilla business was a goldmine. The company sold more than quadruple the volume managed in Mexico, even though the Mexican market was many times larger. The difference was that in Mexico countless stores, making their own, offered competition, whereas in the US Bimbo had much more of a free run.

In 1998 Bimbo sent a clear signal that it intended to become a serious US operator when it acquited the ninety-year-old Texan bakery, Mrs Baird's. Bimbo moved its US headquarters from Carrollton, Texas, to Mrs Baird's head office in Fort Worth. There they created a newly enlarged division, Bimbo Bakeries USA. Bimbo wasted no time expanding Mrs Baird's. They moved into Oklahoma with eleven delivery routes in September of the same year, supported by television advertising and radio promotions. This was the first stage of an ambitious national expansion strategy. That strategy would get a huge boost in 2002 with the acquisition, for $610 million, of the Western US baking business, George Weston Limited, along with its Oroweat brand.

Bimbo expanded its category participation in Mexico with its 2005 acquisition of the El Globo chain of pastry shops. They looked further afield in 2006, buying the Beijing Panrico Food Processing Center for 9.2 million euros. This subsidiary of Spanish company Panrico meant Bimbo got a company with 800 employees, one production plant and a wide portfolio of baked products. These were formulated and developed for the Chinese market, and had broad distribution in Beijing and Tianjin. In 2008, the company turned its attentions back to Latin America with the purchase of the Nutrella bakery in Brazil. This was merged with the Plus Vita and Pullman businesses, which were acquired there in 2001.

In early 2009 however, Bimbo pivoted northwards once again. They secured the transformative acquisition of Weston Foods Inc., the only American bakery with a national presence. Purchased for $2.4 billion from George Weston Ltd., the acquisition made Bimbo the largest bakery in America, with 22 factories and 4,000 delivery trucks. Weston Foods had sales of over $2 billion from the Boboli, Brownberry, Entenmann's, Freihofer's, Stroehmann and Thomas' brands of breads, rolls, muffins and bagels. The acquisition was expected to help lift Bimbo's total sales to $10 billion during 2009. Bimbo spent two years digesting the Weston purchase before making three international acquisitions in 2011. These made the company the largest bakery in the world. Bimbo Iberia, the largest in Spain and Portugal, was finally brought back into the fold while Argentina's market-leading Fargo bakery business strengthened the company's South American presence.

However, Bimbo's breakthrough deal was to acquire the Sara Lee brand for bakery products in the US and selected overseas markets along with regional US brands such as Heiner's and Rainbo. These cost nearly $1 billion. Sara Lee kept its frozen desserts and meat products businesses under the same name. The Sara Lee business came with 13,000 employees, 41 plants and 4,800 distribution routes. Bimbo planned to invest $1 billion into this infrastructure, over the next five years, to improve manufacturing and distribution efficiencies.

This deal meant that Mexico now accounted for less than half of the company's sales. The US now constituted 40%, and Latin America 14%, of the total sales of 133 billion Pesos (around $13 billion.) The international business now looked as follows:

RegionCategoriesBrands
USABreads, BagelsSara Lee, Mrs Baird's,
Earthgrains, Heiner's
Central AmericaBreads, Pastries,Bimbo, Marinela, Monarcha
Latin AmericaBreads, CookiesPullman, PlusVita, Nutrella, Fargo
AsiaBreadsBimbo
EuropeBreads, SnacksBimbo

How Are They Structured?

Grupo Bimbo has always believed in keeping organisational matters as simple as possible. Indeed, after being founded, eighteen years passed before it had a head office structure at all. By 1991 the Wall Street Journal described Grupo Bimbo as a pillar of conservatism, with neither corporate offices nor annual report, but unlimited ambitions. Two years later the company was reorganised on a divisional basis. Eight divisions were each run as a semi-autonomous subsidiary. They included an International Division and Altex, a division servicing the other seven with raw materials, machinery, supplies and services (some of which they also sold to external companies). During 2000 Bimbo spun off the flour mills and processed jellies units which formed the bulk of the Altex division. However the new Grupo Altex agreed to continue supplying Grupo Bimbo.

Today the company is organised into two divisions: Baked Goods, which is further subdivided, and Salty Snacks and Confectionery which are organised under one company, Barcel S.A. de C.V. The latter operates exclusively in Mex, where the company is number two in both salty snacks and confectionery. The baked goods division is organised regionally as follows:

- Mexico – Number one in packaged baked goods, cookies and crackers, and pastries.
- United States – Number one in premium breads, muffins, Hispanic brands.
- Central and South America – Number one in packaged baked goods in fourteen countries.
- Portugal & Spain – Number one in packaged baked goods.
- Asia – Number one in packaged baked goods in Beijing and Tianjing.

What Have They Done Recently?

Over recent years, Grupo Bimbo has had two major priorities: to make and integrate acquisitions and to re-engineer their product range towards a health and wellness agenda. Through the above acquisitions and strong organic growth in Mexico (where it averaged just under 10% in 2011 and 2012), company sales increased by 14% in 2011 and nearly 30% in 2012. At 64 billion pesos, the US is now Grupo Bimbo's single largest market. They are four times larger than just four years earlier: the company now had 75 production facilities there.

The process of integrating major acquisitions brought about a rethinking of the company's growth strategy. Grupo Bimbo defined its strategic priorities as follows:

- Innovation and deep consumer understanding
- Creating deep connections with consumers
- Creating value for customers
- Building efficiency and scale to achieve a low-cost operation

The significant change reflected in these priorities is that, until quite recently, numbers 3 and 4 would have been 1 and 2, while the latter might not even have made the list.

The key to delivering these priorities is the R&D platform. This is built upon six innovation and nutrition institutes: two are located in Mexico, three in the US and one in Brazil. Their remit is to develop products that are innovative, healthy and of the highest quality (using new technologies that enable the company to act like the industry leader that it now is). The first stage, completed in 2011, was to define a company-wide, consumer-focused innovation process, named the Grupo Bimbo Model. The second stage was to develop a points rating system to categorize all the company's SKUs into one of four ratings: healthy, better, good, and indulgent. Innovation plans would then target the launch of two products, in the better and healthy ratings, in each brand/region every year. The brand renovation agenda aimed either to move products up a rating or to increase the average score. Actions to date have focused on re-engineering the existing product range: specifically reducing levels of sodium, sugar and fat, and/or increasing the fibre content. In 2011 the company went for low hanging fruit. It improved the nutritional profiles of the 700 products, which it was easiest to do. They eliminated nearly 10,000 tons of sugar, 3,600 tons of salt and 1,300 tons of fat. In 2012 the focus shifted to working on the biggest brands in each category: here the challenge to maintain taste appeal was more crucial. On the fibre task, Grupo Bimbo won an award from the Whole Grains Council for the introduction in 2011 of forty-two new whole grain products, each bearing the seal of the Council.

Aside from implementing a consumer-driven strategy and beginning to re-engineer their product range, Grupo Bimbo returned to the acquisition trail in 2013. They paid $31.9 million for the purchase of the Beefsteak brand of rye breads, acquired as part of the Hostess Brands bankruptcy proceedings. Beefsteak is one of the largest volume selling brands of rye bread in the United States. Its strong, established presence in the Midwest and Mid-Atlantic regions offered BBU a significant opportunity for national expansion, given its much strengthened distribution capabilities.

What is Their DNA?

There is no secret formula in a bank vault. Nor is there an army of PhDs in laboratories. Grupo Bimbo's success is based on a superior business model for the bread and sweet treats industry, relentlessly and consistently applied over time and geography. They are an extremely focused company who have, for the most part, stuck to what they do best. They put their efforts into doing it better, and in more places.

Summary

Thanks to the major acquisitions, plus some minor ones, Grupo Bimbo more than doubled its size between 2008 and 2012: from a turnover of 82 billion pesos to 173 billion ($13.1 billion). It has 103 brands consisting of over 8,000 products produced in 156 factories, sold in 19 countries by 127,000 associates and delivered to over 2 million points of distribution by a vast fleet of over 50,000 trucks. Interestingly, it is almost exactly the same business model first envisioned by the founders in the early 1940s, a mass-market packaged bread business reliant on a superior distribution system. They were going to get fresh product into pretty much every store in the land. With few if any transformative acquisition opportunities left in the Americas, it will be interesting to see what Grupo Bimbo does to expand its footholds in the European single market and in China.

The founders deserve tremendous credit for envisioning and creating a superior business model in the fresh bread business. The company is fully deserving of its status as the world's most successful bakery company. Reflecting its colossal size and status, Grupo Bimbo is now undergoing its most dramatic transformation since being founded. They need to change from being a sales-led company, dependent on its best-in-class delivery systems, to a marketing-led company. Here the product range has to do more of the heavy lifting to drive growth. Grupo Bimbo is at a crossroads, and we shall watch its progress with great interest.

Taiwan

Uni-President Enterprises Corporation

Where Did They Come From?

Kao Ching-yuen was born into poverty in Syuejia, a small town in the south of Taiwan. He worked as a labourer on leaving school, and joined Taiwan Spinning, a textile company, in 1954. During a stay of twelve years he rose into the managerial ranks. Seeing opportunities in the emerging industrialisation of Taiwan, in 1967 he joined forces with an acquaintance, Wu Hsiu-Chi, to set up a flour mill and an animal feed factory. From the very beginning, Uni-President was run with Wu Hsiu-Chi's philosophy of Three Good and One Fairness: good quality, good credibility, good services, and a fair price.

Within three years, annual sales of Uni-President Animal Feed exceeded 20,000 tons. The company invested in food for humans with the launch of Tong Yi Noodles. Aiming to open a new plant every year, the next, in 1971, was a cooking oil and fats factory. At this point the company consisted of four divisions: Flour, Food Products, Animal Feed, and Oil and Grease. Each factory was equipped with the latest mass production manufacturing equipment.

How Did They Evolve?

By now the Taiwanese economy was growing rapidly, with a consequent surge in consumer spending power. Uni-President's goal was not to be confined to its existing product fields, but to get into those higher added-value consumer markets it saw as having potential. So in 1974 the company launched a range of canned beverages. They followed up by taking over a dairy company and set up its own dairy division. Always alert to the latest technologies, the company was the first in Taiwan to offer its milk and juice products in Tetra-Pak packaging for increased freshness and shelf life.

Having got into the production of baked goods and confectionery, Uni-President ventured much further afield in 1979. It signed a deal with America's Southland Corporation to bring its 7-Eleven retail concept to Taiwan: they opened fourteen stores in the first year. Uni-President, never shy about seeking alliances, also signed a bottling deal with PepsiCo and in 1981 became the General Electric Company's distributor in Taiwan for semi-conductors. They expanded their food and beverage businesses with a host of new product launches into categories such as coffee, sports drinks and soy sauce.

Uni-President was now well on the way to becoming a consumer goods/retail/industrial conglomerate, with a diverse range of initiatives and activities. In 1985 alone, they launched such delights as Tong Yi Imperial Sausage and Tong Yi Pickled Cabbage and Duck and won numerous awards for new products and advertising. In addition, the company became the Taiwanese distributor for Meiji's high protein milk powder; placed over 1,000 vending machines, and opened Taiwan's first branch of Kentucky Fried Chicken along with the hundredth branch of 7-Eleven. Distribution rights for Budweiser beer soon followed, as did moves into meat and shrimp processing, infant formula and a chain of bakery stores. By the end of the 1980s, Uni-President was Taiwan's leading food manufacturer.

How Did They Build the Modern Business?

At this point, it becomes almost impossible to keep track of the number and spread of developments. Uni-President was by now a sprawling, but still tightly managed $1 billion turnover conglomerate, seemingly active on all fronts. If it wasn't the grand opening of the 300th franchise bakery or the 500th 7-Eleven, it was the launch into a new product category, such as dog food or the importation of fresh tulips from Holland.

Nevertheless fundamental changes were afoot regarding the company's investment in science and technology, which it increasingly saw as the way forward. In 1993 the company invented a process for the manufacture of low-cholesterol refined lard and its Kikkoman brand soy sauce manufacturing facility was rated the best of its kind in the country. No product category seemed off limits, from drinkable yoghurt to aquarium food via the Starbucks licence for Taiwan.

Uni-President in the twenty-first century was uniquely positioned to benefit from its vertical integration - from flour-mills to retailing via its distribution companies - and its horizontal integration into dozens of categories. There was no emerging trend the company did not have its eye on. They instigated online shopping and delivery for the 7-Eleven chain. This now had 2,000 branches and was the subject of a perpetual licensing agreement with Uni-President. In 2001 the company established its Life Sciences Research centre. This focused on the development of health and wellness food options from a unique combination of health foods, traditional Chinese herbs and genetic technology. An early output was the development of technology for extracting chicken essence through hydrolysis, and a host of patents of immune system enhancement products.

In 2004, Uni-President instituted a brand management system throughout the company. Its pivot towards being more consumer-driven and health-focused led to a garnering of a multitude of National Healthy Product certifications. A year later, on the fortieth anniversary of the company's founding, it received the award of Most Admired Company in Taiwan for the eleventh year in a row.

Their R&D team came up with proprietary manufacturing technology for instant noodles and Taiwan's first low temperature Pasteurised milk. The logistics arm got into the running of department stores and building a shopping mall. Next, a joint venture was signed to bring the British retailer Marks & Spencer to Taiwan. But Uni-President's success, stunning though it had been, was not just restricted to Taiwan.

The International Dimension

Uni-President's first international venture came only five years after the company's foundation, with the building of an instant noodles factory in Thailand. Just three years later the company expanded into the US, building a similar noodles factory in Los Angeles. During the 1980s the company established a process in which they built a sufficient scale of export business in markets, before then localising production. In Australia, the lead product line was tomato paste, launched in 1984. The US venture was expanded two years later with the importation of canned fruit juices. This presence was dramatically increased in 1990 with the $335 million acquisition of America's third-largest cookie manufacturer, Wyndham Foods. Wyndham had 8,000 employees, eight baking plants across the country and the iconic Girl Scout Cookies business.

Further investments in Indonesia, Thailand, Vietnam and the Philippines followed, before Uni-President made its first venture into mainland China in 1992. While beginning as usual with noodles, Uni-President thought big from the start with its China operation. It analysed each region in depth - for consumer income trends, purchasing power, spending preferences and growth categories - before deciding in which categories to invest. The company rolled out along the coast (taking advantage of special economic development districts), while also venturing inland by building factories in population centres along the Yangtse River. Just three years after entering the market, Uni-President opened its seventeenth Chinese factory, importing the latest Taiwanese and Japanese noodle-making equipment. By 2000, the company's Chinese operations had moved into profit. Its first R&D centre on the Chinese mainland was opened a year later and by 2012, fifty-one of Uni-President's four hundred subsidiaries were operating in China. These ranged from seventeen food businesses to running the Starbucks franchise. The company is currently building factories in the second- and third-tier cities with the aim of having a food factory in every significant population centre. Elsewhere, Uni-President is currently evaluating its entry strategy for the Indian market, along with the pan-Indian ocean market for shrimp. It has thriving export markets in over thirty countries on five continents.

How Are They Structured?

Good question. With over 400 subsidiaries covering a very wide range of products, services and activities, a notable feature of the company is its multi-dimensional management approach. One level below the total company, there are what Uni-President calls 'sub-conglomerates'. These group together subsidiaries based on their characteristics and the nature of their operations: food manufacturing, logistics, retailing and investment.

Within food manufacturing, there are six groups:

- Dairy and beverage group: This was the largest group in 2008, accounting for 38% of total sales, primarily in Taiwan, and covers a wide range of products from fresh milk to tea and bottled water.

- Provisions group: The second-largest at 35% of 2008 sales, this was the first "virtual company" to be set up in Uni-President. I was established in 2001 to manage the five core businesses of foodstuffs, animal feed, flour, edible oils and aquatic products on a global basis. Its current agenda is to increase an international reach, implement regional production and marketing, increase the differentiation of the product range, and diversify marketing across more media

- Instant food group: This manages the noodles business on a global basis. It accounts for 10% of sales, and the key markets are Taiwan, South East Asia, China and the United States. There are exports to over 30 other countries. The group essentially uses two brands: Tong Yi Mein in Chinese-speaking countries and Unif elsewhere

- General food group: A bit of a mixed bag with four divisions: Meat Products, Sauces and Seasonings, Frozen Prepared foods, and Ice cream. These account for 8% of sales

- Consumer health group: This is the newest and smallest of the groups, contributing 7% of sales. It was established in 2003 to bring together bakery, health products – split into longevity and preventative products - and the organic products division (which was established in 1999 to sell a combination of internally developed products and many overseas brands on licence)

Supporting all of the food products divisions, the Central Research Institute has facilities in Taiwan, Shanghai, the Philippines, Thailand, Vietnam and Indonesia. It has a triple remit, to develop new products, new technologies and quality improvement technologies and processes. Outside of the food products sub-conglomerate is the logistics sub-conglomerate. This includes 51 wholesalers and 133 retail chains spread across Taiwan, distributing the products not only of Uni-President but of 30,000 other manufacturers through the country's largest route-to-market system.

What Have They Done Recently?

There are two ways of looking at the performance of the Uni-President business, because it reports two levels of operating income. In 2008 the business generated nearly NT$ 50 billion of revenue ($1.7 billion) but if the revenues of the retail and wholesale businesses are consolidated, the size of the business rockets to nearly NT$300 billion ($10 billion). As the business grows organically, making very few major acquisitions, recent annual progress has been steady rather than spectacular. The one bad year was when the global financial crisis was at its height:

Year-on-year % Change
Consolidated operating revenue Operating Revenue
2008+3.9+7.4
2009-3.2-9.4
2010+18.3+9.3
2011+13.0+5.9

The bounce-back year of 2010 took the business to highs on new sales and market share in all its major markets. This feat was subsequently exceeded in 2011. The potential in China for instant noodles and beverages has encouraged Uni-President to commit to building another seventeen factories there over the following two years. Of the eighteen major food categories in Taiwan in which the company competes, it has over a 40% market share in five of them and over 20% in another six. This level of concentration results from the company's focus on its megabrands: nearly fifty brands and hundred SKUs that each generate NT$100 million in annual sales.

In 2012, the company targeted the sale of a million tons of foodstuffs: nearly half a billion packets of noodles, 100 million cases of dairy and other beverages, nearly 100 million bottles of soy sauce and 200 million loaves of bread. This excludes activities in categories away from the food business.

What is Their DNA?

Uni-President has focussed heavily on building its brand management and R&D capabilities. Yet, at its heart, the company is run as a conglomerate rather than as a product-driven enterprise. High profit, high potential categories and businesses are pursued, while low profit, low potential businesses are sold, de-emphasised or given R&D focus to re-energise. We believe this gives Uni-President a quite different DNA to the other companies in this book. This is a company of business and market analytics.

Summary

Uni-President is in some ways a role model for other companies in this book who seek growth more through the selection and refinement of the categories in which they compete rather than through excellence in R&D, marketing or route-to-market. Uni-President enjoys nearly $13 billion in consolidated sales, generated across a host of business types, product categories and geographies.

With such a business model, management does not get too excited at the short-term ups and downs of either the economy or particular product sectors. Uni-President operates in mature product sectors like Taiwan, where it is the largest food company. Yet it has only a 10% total market share of total food, which offers plenty of scope for growth. In China, fully one-quarter of all consumer spending goes on food. This too provides almost limitless potential for growth.

It is an interesting business model and one we predict will become increasingly prevalent, as category-specific manufacturers struggle to cope with enormous and powerful retailers and seek scale through breadth rather than depth.

Global FMCGs:
Money, Mojo or Marketing?

In the introduction to this book, we commented: 'It has become fashionable in some quarters to regard the FMCG category as old hat: yesterday's manufacturers of humdrum products populating the boring centre aisles of yesterday's bricks-and-mortar retail outlets'. We went further, and accused a few of the perpetrators of this ridiculous idea face to face: 'MBA course attendees,' we observed, showing no compunction at all in identifying the principal culprits and their modish preoccupations, 'want new and they want exciting: Apple, Facebook, Google. Yet the biggest four companies in this book – Nestlé, Proctor & Gamble, Unilever and Pepsico – each have combined revenues larger than Facebook and Google combined, and by some distance'.

With the benefit of hindsight, which the concluding chapter of any book of hard fact often confers, especially a book so well furnished with the commodity as this one, we didn't go far enough by a long way. Given the histories of the big eighteen we chose, and the less detailed tales of another six – for sure the tip of the ice-berg – already moving onto the global stage, what perhaps we should have said was something much more definitive: that FMCGs were now as entrenched in the story of humanity as the drive to procreate, as fixed as government, and as bound to evolve into fitter states as life itself. Come to think of it, that last point is probably why we discussed their DNA.

But didn't some of the giants we've just examined come close to failure? Didn't Coca-cola almost never start at all? Didn't it almost fall of the edge of the world twice more? Wasn't Kimberly-Clark on its uppers before the unlikely white knight of menstruation saved its bacon? Didn't Pepsi go bust on a regular basis? Didn't 'the world's best FMCG' (Unilever) get almost fatally lost twice? Or possibly three times? Wasn't Kraft rather finely sliced?

Admittedly, these were threats brought about by relatively sudden and deeply radical shifts in what looked like a status quo built on granite. Or fabulously bad decisions, gross miscalculations or terminal complacency. So are we saying that such things don't happen anymore? We are not. Because they do. And one of those relatively sudden and deeply radical shifts is happening right now.

But before we examine more closely what is certainly the 21ˢᵗ Century's watershed, two themes stand out from the welter of entrepreneurial drive, genius, failure, hubris, nerve, stamina and extremely hard work that have gone into the making of our chosen companies. Those two themes are firstly what everybody does and secondly what everybody is looking at. Marketing is what everybody does, and the spends easily reach into the billions, with the spend online permanently on the increase. Bart Becht, Rekitt Benckiser's no-nonsense supremo until his wholly unexpected and wholly no-nonsense departure, summed it up: you get yourself a product, you get it on the market and then you 'market the hell out of it'. Which brings us to the second theme: what is everybody looking at? The emerging markets are what everybody is looking at; and it is this combination of marketing and emergence that is driving the watershed.

Why? Let's look at the mature markets: Europe, America, Canada, and Australasia. Here, even if more and more mistakenly, it is still perfectly possible to pursue consumers through what have become known as the traditional media: the push media. Companies can still take out newspaper ads, put expertly designed and expensively produced bill-boards on busy street corners, run even more expensively produced TV commercials on a variety of national networks and broadcast their cheaper cousins on the radio.

However, how does this mature market approach fare in the emerging markets? Not well, and sometimes not at all. Lake Tanganyika, for example, has no TV, radio, billboards or newspapers. But it's a wi-fi zone, and its fishermen use their internet-enabled mobiles not only to see who's paying the best fish prices but whose consumer goods do they want, or need, to spend their fish-money on. In emerging markets – FMCG's next gigantic honey-pot – marketing is mobile-based and digital, because it has to be: there is effectively no over-arching media infrastructure to exploit. So one way of looking at the shape of the FMCG future is to look at how well the world's best-known brands are keeping pace with this new, and immensely powerful, sales and marketing technique? How are they responding to the revolution in consumer expectations, interests and behaviour? And is digital marketing not simply the emerging markets' future, but everyone's?

One: Coca-Cola

Coca-Cola's range of innovative sales and brand-awareness campaigns gives the company a leading position in the Modern Marketing landscape

It may not surprise you to learn that one of the world's most iconic brands is also one of the world's virtuoso exploiters of Modern Marketing. Coke's early entry onto the digital landscape and its rapid implementation of best-practice Modern Marketing tactics has resulted in a catalogue of impressive achievements and ROI right across the product range. This case-study will look at three imaginative and highly successful campaigns that show how very effectively Coca-Cola has picked up the digital baton and run with it.

Before we look at specific campaigns, however, it is worth analyzing how and why Coca-Cola has embraced Modern Marketing, in particular one of its absolutely key elements: Social Media.

Coca Cola and the Social Media

Coca-Cola employs 150,000 employees in more than 200 countries, who together help to promote and sell over 500 branded beverages. And one thing it has come to understand very clearly is that not only are its employees talking to each other online every hour of every day, they're also talking to their friends, who are talking to *their* friends, who are talking to . . . well, you get the picture. The world's largest beverage company wants to be a part of that global conversation, to share its values and, of course, to promulgate its own, 'to inspire moments of optimism and happiness' as it builds its brand image.

To this end, Coca-Cola has invested heavily in building global communities. To date, its achievements include:

- Some of the largest online communities in the world, ranking in the Top 10 global brands, across all social media platforms and across all industries
- 63 million fans on its main Facebook page, which is focused on maintaining the brand image and raising awareness of its ad campaigns
- Facebook pages for other products, such as Diet Coke and Coke Zero. Such brands have far fewer fans than the Real Thing, but they effectively advance a key supporting strategy: niche platforms for niche products with niche consumers.
- One of the most active brands in the Twittersphere, a main-product Twitter feed with more than 700,000 followers and a 75,000 Tweet history
- The maintenance, like Facebook, of separate Twitter feeds for each of its local markets

The Campaigns

Coca Cola's understanding of the power of social marketing is impressive. Even more impressive is the apparent ease with which it has been able to integrate that insight into the bigger picture, an integration which has been the key to its success. The Share A Coke campaign is a perfect example, showcasing how an FMCG brand can best use social media – Facebook in this case – to drive consumer engagement and thus achieve a real and clearly attributable improvement in global product sales.

The Share A Coke campaign offers consumers the chance to order personalized Coke cans via a Facebook app. Once people receive their bespoke Coca-Cola product, they are then encouraged to share their enjoyment of their very own Coke product online via the Coke Facebook page. This 2011 campaign increased global sales by a full 7 per cent. It created worldwide attention for Coca-Cola, amassing18 million online media events and fuelling a huge, 870 per cent rise in traffic on the Coca-Cola Facebook page, with page likes increasing by 39 percent.

Now let's look at a second Coca Cola online success story, the **Coca-Cola Happiness Machine**. Here, Coca-Cola actually customized its popular vending machines; not only did they dispense the drink, but offered consumers extra treats like free drinks, pizza, sandwiches and even flowers. In Singapore, for example, physically hugging the machine itself would get you a free drink. In Belgium, you had to dance with it. Coca-Cola then videoed people's reactions and put the footage on their specially branded YouTube channel, amassing millions of views and tons of brand goodwill. This highly imaginative campaign required relatively low investment, yet made brilliant use of the social media at a point-of-sale level to communicate the key brand values of fun and sociability.

A third campaign, this time exploiting Coke's long-term sponsorship of global sports and music events, centred on the 2012 London Olympics. The campaign, Move to the Beat, is arguably one of the company's very best, using both music and sport to help the company communicate with its thirsty teenage market. Coke recruited London-based producer Mark Ronson and singer Katie B, then took five Olympic hopefuls, recorded the sounds of their respective sports and combined the results to create a song. The campaign involved five key elements: a feature length documentary, the song itself, TV commercials, Beat TV, and a series of digital/mobile apps called *The Global Beat*. Move to the Beat was a master class in integration, and it achieved impressive results:

- More than 25 million video views in total across desktop and mobile
- 1,220 subscribers
- It made Coke the Games' second most talked-about brand
- It prompted 242 million social web responses, 39 million on Facebook and 546,000 on YouTube and Beat TV
- Move To The Beat itself was mentioned 246,000 times on Facebook

Coca-Cola attracted an additional 1.5 million Facebook fans and 21,000 Twitter followers.

The campaign prompted 245 million searches, 461,000 clicks and a CTR of 0.2%.

Share a Coke, The Happiness Machine and Move to the Beat show perfectly how well Coca-Cola understands the power of social media and how well it is able to integrate that understanding into broader campaigns in both digital and traditional worlds, with the digital dimension now an indispensable part of its marketing strategies. The company understands exactly what its values are and with whom it needs to communicate them. Digital analyst John Furrier writing for Forbes.com said: 'Successful brand marketers like Coca-Cola understand that traditional marketing disciplines must be supplemented with new models rich with content, engagement, conversation, and analytics – the essence of social commerce. As big brands need to create an even better brand experience and empower their marketers with tools that will allow them to do so simply and effectively, more and more companies are turning to social software solutions to provide them the advantage they need to stay ahead of the curve.'

Coca-Cola has shown the world how revolutionary the company can still be, how creative, and how the imaginative deployment of Modern Marketing techniques forges fresh, long-lasting and essentially emotional ties between consumer, company and brand.

Two: Colgate-Palmolive

In the last few years, Colgate has been criticized for its lack of 'bite' in responding to the growth of Modern Marketing. This may be about to change.

In 2012 Jack Haber, Colgate's vice-president for advertising and digital, admitted his company was 'not where it should be' given consumer appetite for mobile phone marketing. Speaking at the GroupM What's Next conference, Haber said: 'It will take some time to get mobile fully woven into the fabric of the company's marketing activities.' The reasons for the omission are common enough: resistance to change both within companies and within the larger advertising and marketing community. Colgate-Palmolive was a typical case in point, still spending 80 percent of its ad budget on TV. But Haber saw the problem: 'We're all behind. The industry is not as focused as it should be, especially among the creative ranks. People talk about integration, but it's still TV first at many ad shops. We need to change that.'

And it's true that consumers have embraced mobile devices far faster than the FMCG industry anticipated; many brands are still trying to catch up. Colgate, however, has now made the development of a coherent, integrated and global mobile strategy one of its top international marketing priorities.

The company began its marketing makeover with **There's Something in Your Tweet**, a pro-active entry into the social media launched via Twitter in 2013. The Canada-based campaign encouraged Tweeters to send Twitter alerts to Colgate's Twitter account giving details of friends, family or colleagues who had food stuck in their teeth, with Colgate thoughtfully providing a menu – ranging from pop-corn to 'super-healthy' kale – to help distinguish precisely what was stuck. This social media-led campaign was designed to raise the consumer profile of Colgate's Slim Softy/MC toothbrush's 17x slimmer tips tapered bristles – ideal for removing foodstuffs from teeth – and played on the embarrassment of a social faux pas to do so. Both sender and 'shamed' associate were rewarded with a $1-off coupon for – yes - a new Colgate's Slim SoftTM/MC 17x slimmer food-removing toothbrush.

Colgate has also turned to Facebook . The Smile Facebook campaign, supported by a Facebook mobile app, asked users to upload photographs of themselves smiling. The brand was now learning fast. By creating both a positive sense of community and a sense of fun, it has learned the lesson that positive impressions made on a second social medium lead to positive effects on purchasing decisions.

Much more dramatically, Colgate proved conclusively how big an impact online campaigning can make. In the summer of 2013, the company launched Brushswap, a promotion that encouraged existing consumers to trade their old electric toothbrushes for the new Colgate ProClinical A1500 toothbrush worth £170. A promotional stall first set up at London Waterloo station was swamped; too swamped, in fact: organisers were forced to close it. Colgate promptly moved the campaign online, asking all interested consumers to register at ColgatePro-Clinical.co.uk and from there begin the full promotional journey via the internet: a clear case of the virtual world managing consumer demand, promotional delivery and campaign metrics from the more logistically manageable dimension of the web and thus achieving an outcome that no-one could swamp.

Unlike the agile Coca Cola, Colgate-Palmolive is one FMCG still in the process, if not the early stages, of making its transition from the old style of marketing to the new. But campaigns like Brushswap, and the company's somewhat tentative move to mobile, are teaching them the hard way that consumers have changed both in how they get their information and how they interact with new products.

Three: Danone

Danone shows how data collected via Modern Marketing can drive people to engage online and buy offline.

Like Colgate-Palmolive, Danone is another brand slow to adopt Modern Marketing techniques but keen to pick up the pace. The French food-products multinational has launched a number of online campaigns to help boost its marketing success and move with the times. One such initiative was a sponsorship deal in early 2012 with the food-related FMCG website Foodie.com, whose tagline For the Love of Food suited Danone perfectly. The aim was the vertical promotion of Danone's Activia yogurt brand. But where online or offline display advertising might once have been the natural choice, using the foodie.com website gave the company the ability to tailor much more precisely both its ad content and its on-page placement, thus creating a far more consumer-friendly means of reaching its target audiences.

Modern Marketing ' . . . is new for us,' said Michael Neuwirth, senior director of communications at Danone. 'We were not really an early adopter in terms of the shift to digital and, in particular, vertical. As the opportunities like Foodie.com shape up with very focused consumer interest areas, we now see a much clearer opportunity than previously.'

Danone have also begun to understand and exploit digital's ability to gather high-value consumer information. The company was one of a number of FMCG market leaders to use a new data service from Dunnhumby to connect their consumers' online engagement and in-store shopping habits with their brand. Dunnhumby are able to track the effectiveness of a Modern Marketing campaign by comparing the behaviour of Tesco Clubcard customers who respond to Danone's online loyalty campaigns and those who do not. By doing so, Dunnhumby can measure the effect of online loyalty campaigns on brand trials, loyalty, sales uplifts and ROI, an information set which allows Danone to improve the relationship between its online and offline activities. What is clear is that Danone, like Colgate Palmolive, is also learning fast, as other recent digital campaigns for Evian, Volvic and Activia yoghurt have successfully demonstrated: the company is moving with the times.

Four: Estée Lauder

How cosmetics giant Estee Lauder leverages social media on a global scale by understanding how consumer word-of-mouth sells products in the beauty sector.

If conversation is king with online communities, then Estee Lauder has surely made the connection: 'women buy what their friends and family recommend'. And the company that owns Clinique, MAC, Bobbi Brown, Aveda and Estee Lauder proper is justifiably proud to be one of the most digitally forward in its sector, where consumers typically seek quality content and quality information before they commit to buying quality cosmetics. As Estée Lauder's online president Dennis McEniry confirms: 'Social plays a huge role. The number one influence on beauty consumers in every market around the world is advice from friends. With social media, not only are they able to get timely brand information directly from brands, but also all of the validation from authorities and friends. In addition to Facebook and Twitter, we also have country-specific networks that are important, local players like Orkut in Brazil and RenRen in China. And because social media allows for two-way communication, it's also valuable for getting great feedback. We can use it find out what consumers like and don't like, how we can get them the latest information, how we can improve our products.'

Whilst the key metrics of success for Estée Lauder are customer engagement and consumer loyalty, the company takes great care to monitor traffic and sales conversions, showing a truly Modern Marketing perspective in developing online business and recognizing then exploiting the current trends that help reach their audience. And once again, one such trend is social media. As McEniry observes, 'Right now social media are delivering in the top five traffic sources for every one of our brands, and . . . consistently over index in terms of conversions.'

A leading factor in social's success is that it reaches Estée's 'influencers', whose value to a business reliant on word of mouth recommendation, online or offline, is immense. In McEniry's words, Estee is constantly looking at 'what [influencers] do in terms of education and influencing people in their network, how they interact with each other and their overall impact on the business.'

One thing influencers are certainly doing is using their mobile phones. And, whilst most of the FMCG producers are but slowly realizing the power of the medium, this FMCG super-brand is watching this growing trend like no other, as McEniry confirms: 'The biggest trend we're watching is mobile. For some of our brands in bigger markets like Japan half of our sales are on mobile devices, and generally speaking we're seeing unbelievable growth rates around the world. We're also researching how mobile is affecting real-world retail, [particularly] how consumers are using mobile phones for interacting with and getting product knowledge at the point of sale, both at counters and in salons. We want to know how to make that mobile-enabled experience as good as possible and how to market to consumers in mobile. After all, no one leaves home without their mobile phones anymore.'

Estée Lauder now vies with Coke as one of the best Modern Marketers in the whole FMCG marketplace.

Estée Lauder and China

Whilst the company's success has been global, perhaps no territory on earth has been a bigger surprise than China. In the 2012 Digital IQ Index on China (released by L2 Think Tank), the luxury beauty brand was ranked as Genius in four key areas: site, digital marketing, social media and mobile. The brand earned its rating by inspired brand specialization, targeting its products specifically at young, affluent Chinese consumers and thus utilizing the key digital platforms the upwardly mobile visit. Additionally, and also crucially, the company implemented highly effective online search strategies across the major Chinese engines. But perhaps most importantly, Estée Lauder saw the worth, the effectiveness and the beauty of Modern Marketing and invested very significantly. In the meantime, China is just one example of a territory where Estée Lauder enjoys digital dominance. The brand's future looks bright indeed.

Five: Heinz

When asked to name a brand, any brand, 17 percent of the UK public choose Heinz. For a brand that is such a household word, this major FMCG producer had never enjoyed a unified view of all its customers, across all its numerous varieties, until it embraced Modern Marketing. Finally, if belatedly, Heinz created a new website to host a community of loyal but previously dispersed consumers: a good example of how digital can be integrated into existing marketing strategies to bring consumers together.

Heinz Offers was launched in 2013, and the site now sits at the core of the company's UK Modern Marketing strategy. Heinz Offers asks consumers to provide data on themselves, rewarding their commitment with a quarterly email newsletter containing money-off vouchers and product news. 'We set out to integrate all consumer touch-points,' said Peter Ebsworth, marketing manager at Heinz. 'What excites me is that we can start to build a picture of our consumers across our entire product range, from baby food to soups to frozen meals,' he adds. 'If we can identify consumers who are loyal to Heinz in certain areas, but not in others, we can persuade them to buy into other areas of our portfolio.'

Immediately after the site launch, the first money-back coupons were sent out to registered consumers for new the brand variant Top Down Tomato Ketchup. While Heinz was still tracking redemption rates, some two-thirds of email recipients printed off the coupon, indicating at least the intention to use it. The July newsletter also contained hyperlinks to various Heinz sites so that the company could track who had clicked on what. A second newsletter went out in October and included a coupon for 20p off Heinz Microwaveable Soup Cups, another new launch. 'As a result of the success of the first coupon, we decided to repeat the idea,' says Ebsworth. 'It's only a trial at present, but the results look very promising.'

It's now policy at Heinz to consider the role of digital with every new marketing campaign it launches. Through supporting websites, the company believes every product can be marketed actively online, even when there is no activity offline. And it doesn't stop within the brand's own sites. Heinz has forged content partnerships with other relevant high traffic websites, whether or not they feature Heinz products. All that matters is the relevance of the link and the act of communication with Heinz. Ebsworth sums up: 'Digital is all about turning a monologue into a dialogue.'

Six: Henkel AG

Although e-commerce changed the way people buy books, clothes and electronics, shopping for household items such as detergent still largely takes place offline. Discover how Henkel now uses social media to stimulate sales for its domestic goods.

For the German FMCG maker of such household brands as Dial soap and Purex detergent, the first key realization was not that the internet affected direct product sales positively or negatively, but that it transformed how consumers interacted with their brands. As Henkel chief executive Kasper Rorsted observes: 'Digital and social media have an enormous impact on how people are viewing fast-moving consumer goods, from the way they are being talked about to the way they are being perceived. Consumers also are giving feedback on what is working and what isn't. You've now got to create a community online in the digital environment that you didn't have before, and that has a big impact on how people actually go shopping. We are very much focused on engaging online with consumers.'

Yes despite the fact that e-commerce is changing the FMCG consumer industry, Henkel have not quite moved their full advertising spend to digital, since consumers in its sector still use traditional media for product information. Rorsted explains: 'People are spending more time online, but they are continuing to spend, in absolute terms, more time watching television. As digital use has gone up, TV use hasn't really been going down. TV advertising still is the predominant vehicle for advertising. The consumer is still fairly traditional in the way he or she is exposed to most of our products. But if you take some of our youth-oriented styling brands, such as the hair-care got2b, that's largely digital, because that's the only way you can engage with that group.'

However, as more FMCG brands target the younger consumer, the future points definitely to an online approach. Rorsted and Henkel, optimistic but cautious about their own advertising spend, are still moving inexorably in the direction of Modern Marketing. Says Rorsted: 'Our media spend is growing in digital, but at a slower rate than I would say we thought five years ago. Digital a couple of years ago was a high single-digit percentage of our budget, and now it is low double-digit.'

Seven: Kellogg's

Another FMCG brand focusing on mobile as part of its Modern Marketing mix is Kellogg's. The company has launched a number of landmark campaigns.

In 2010, Kellogg's launched its first-ever mobile virtual store app. Consumers could use their phone to choose Kellogg's brands - Special K or Crunchy Nut, for example - and then add them to the cart of their favourite retailer for their next online shop, all without leaving the portal. Results were encouraging: Kellogg's reported 20,000 actively-engaged consumers since the launch, with early figures showing that 3 percent of site visitors had added products to their carts. But sales were not the only bottom-line. Insights on online consumer purchasing behaviour enabled the development of new e-commerce opportunities for all Kellogg's brands, providing vital information for future campaigns As Kellogg's digital manager Leanda Falcon said in 2010: 'The e-commerce activity we're developing at the moment is about giving our consumers choice in how they interact with us. Online grocery sales are set to double in the next five years and we want to be able to capitalise on this by setting up a framework across all digital channels for our customers now.'

In 2012, Kellogg's remained true to the strategy, releasing an updated app for its Special K product that allowed users to manage their weight loss personally via mobile and desktop. The app is supported by a website, where personal weight loss accounts can sync with mobile or computer devices, with promotion via social media, print and TV/radio campaigns. Yuvraj Arora, senior director of

Special K at Kellogg's in the US, provides an example of how this works: 'The Special K brand is asking women to think about their New Year's resolutions differently. Rather than focusing on numbers on the scales, the Special K brand is challenging women to reshape their thinking by answering, 'What will I gain when I lose?' such as confidence, moxie, pride or energy.'

Kellogg's is another FMCG brand that is responding to the meteoric rise in smart-phone ownership; as a result the FMCG giant is branching into mobile. Add this to cross-platform social media support from such sources as Facebook, Twitter, Google Plus and Pinterest and it is evident that Kellogg's are among the leaders in the creation of interactive, consumer-convenient campaign planning.

Eight: Kimberly-Clark

The classic consumer goods company is using social media to target its diverse range of audiences and is looking into e-commerce to direct-sell its products.

Kimberly Clark may be over 140 years old, but the company has been by no means 19th Century in recognizing the advantages of digital, nor been shy at investing in a Modern Marketing strategy. The makers of Kleenex, Huggies, Scott and Cottonelle have been involved with online marketing and digital outreach for a number of years, continually evolving the effective use of these channels to reach consumers. Consequently, Kimberly-Clark invests in most areas of digital marketing, understanding that this is where consumers now tend to connect both with peers and their favourite brands. The company favours social media as a core means to communicate, build relationships and drive participation and has shown itself adept at tailoring the right social media platforms to its products and its consumer demographic.

As Jeff Jarret, vice-president of global digital marketing explains: 'We facilitate conversations between consumers and give them interesting content to share with each other. This is especially true among our baby-care brands like Huggies. We see high engagement from moms. They are very willing to share ideas and help each other. With our other brands, especially the adult brands (Depends, GoodNites), we have different strategies because social in these areas requires a lot more discretion.'

The FMCG producer has also noted the supremacy of video over written content in driving sales. 'Videos - online video product recommendations - are key for driving commerce sales. We've even done some testing on this and found it leads to much stronger conversion rates. Our YouTube channels are really important to us,' said Jarret. Another strand of the company's multidimensional approach is the practically omnipresent social media. Jarret says, 'Social is core to our digital marketing strategy. For many of our brands, it is a cornerstone. We use it as a means to communicate to fans but also as a platform to build relationships and drive participation. We facilitate conversations between consumers and give them interesting content to share with each other. This is especially true among our baby-care brands like Huggies. We see high engagement from moms. They are very willing to share ideas and help each other. With our other brands, especially the adult brands (Depends, GoodNites), we have different strategies because social in these areas requires a lot more discretion. We use Facebook, Twitter, Tumblr and YouTube.' Once again, the central planks of effective digital marketing mean relevant, shareable content, the initiating and then leading of online conversations and the use of the right technical platforms for the right brand audience.

Kimberley-Clark has also joined the growing group of FMCG companies - GSK, P&G, Kellogg's and Diageo, for example - who have invested in direct-sell e-commerce websites. The trial launch of the virtual Kleenex Shop in the UK allowed the company not only to sell the full Kleenex range, including products not available elsewhere in the UK, but to gain useful insights into consumer preferences, which went on to inform future product, packaging design, and online and retail strategy as well as marketing. As Adrian Percival, senior manager of ecommerce at Kimberly-Clark UK, confirms: 'We're seeing significant growth in the online channel through our retail partners and we're determined to win in this channel so we need to know what influences their behaviour, that's the goal of this shop.'

Yet whilst online selling can certainly be a money-spinner for FMCG producers, it may well be even more important for brands to manage their presence in the marketplace and reputation online than to sell products directly. What Kimberly-Clark UK has shown through trialing and testing the marketplace is that they can almost certainly do both.

Nine: Kraft Foods

The FMCG global leader recommends the ingredients needed for effective digital marketing.

Kraft was an early adopter of Modern Marketing tactics and today understands better than most brands just what the parameters of digital are and what it can offer its practitioners. The company believes the focus lies on engagement, user experience and customers' completion of high-value tasks to measure these processes. Such tasks could be opting into an email newsletter, entering personal information to customize the user experience on the KraftFoods.com website, or interacting with particular parts of the site. 'If you know what you want [users] to do and you can track it, then you can quantify it and show the value of the interaction,' said Kathleen Olvany Riordan, VP of global digital marketing strategy at Kraft Foods.

At KraftFoods.com, the strategy is to empower online consumers with information or content relevant to them, such as recipes and nutrition information, as well as demonstrating the values and attributes of Kraft's brands in interactive ways that cannot be achieved offline. Such interaction involves consumers in each brand and encourages them integrate the brands that particularly suit them into their everyday lives. A good example of such a tactic was Kraft's targeting of 'millenials', young adults born between 1979 and 1994. Since many of the millenials had not learned to cook at home, Kraft created the Kraft Cooking School, featuring on-demand video content that explained basic cookery tasks and preparation methods. It proved an ideal way to reach this web-savvy target audience and involve them in the Kraft brand.

To guide it towards achieving the best online consumer experience, Kraft builds into every campaign three 'marketing imperatives': Insights, Ideas and Integration. It also makes sure that it co-ordinates the wide variety of multimedia marketing platforms and tools available by optimising its Modern Marketing consumer experience across multiple touch points by the tailored support of its own stable of product websites via Facebook Pages, Twitter, and Tumblr. Kraft has learned to curate the 'voice' or message of its content to particular consumer groups' particular needs.

Yet it's not only niche products or the youth market that benefit from Modern Marketing. Kraft claims that 80 percent of its new brands benefit from online consumer interaction. But perhaps the key takeaway message is less the actual content than the Modern Marketing strategy. Julie Fleischer, director of Content Strategy & Integration at Kraft Foods sums up the vital issue: 'We don't chase every bleeding edge technology, but we do pay close attention to the technologies and platforms our consumers are using and, when the time is right, then we look to introduce our content.'

Knowing where the next effective online 'space' is to catch your consumers is a big part of getting it right for the future. But beyond getting the right space for your message, Kraft, like other successful FMCG brands, well understands that it may not be a purchase that online consumers first have in mind but simply an interaction. 'We're not designing a banner ad, or rich media, or a Web site,' Riordan says, 'we're designing consumer experience.' And in Kraft's view, it all flows from there.

Ten: Nestle

Looking after your brand reputation is vital in today's busy marketplace. Nestle show how Modern Marketing helped combat negative PR from web users.

No brand in the world is exempt from damaging online PR. But when the $200 billion food giant Nestle faced a wave of negative online publicity, it fought back with its own ethical customer involvement program: online.

Although many FMCG brands outsource their social media management to third-party agencies, Nestle has set up, at its US nerve centre in California, an internal social media global response centre to deal internally with the problem of negative consumer coverage. This is what Nestle calls the Digital Acceleration team. 'With 1.5 billion searches on the Internet, food products are in a quite different category from computers and technology products. Especially in this area, people are looking for transparency and integrity,' says Dr. Alexander Decker, Head of Consumer Relations at Nestlé Germany.

The Digital Acceleration team is responsible for the daily monitoring of, and rapid reaction to, potential PR crises. So, instead of viewing the internet public as a potential threat, the brand views it as the world's greatest focus group. 'When there is a high number of comments, it alerts you that you need to engage,' explains Pete Blackshaw, head of digital marketing and global media at Nestle. 'This can mean a real-time response from a member of staff or the issue may be escalated.'

In 2010, as a first step, Nestlé began by rewriting its social media engagement principles, developing a code of ethics promoting open, honest engagement and distributing it to all staff. Backing up this ethical stance, the Digital Accelerators team is ready to post positive reactions and an ethical defence of their brands and company whenever the need arises . Such responses might explain why Nestlé has been accused of purchasing social media followers and celebrity endorsements, or paying bloggers for pro-Nestlé posts, charges it strenuously denies. And the results have certainly been highly beneficial, creating a new and positive ethical framework, using data and online insights to guide social media activity in the future and helping to generate successful campaigns.

There is nothing particularly revolutionary at work here. Nestlé's transformation is simply one further example of how social media have changed the online marketing landscape, providing new pathways for connections between brands and consumers. Nestlé's catalysts here were confidence, vision and humility: to drive forward innovative new strategies, among them the Digital Acceleration Team, and to learn from past mistakes the company undoubtedly made in protecting its reputation online. Consumer communication and open collaboration are now the way ahead.

Eleven: Pepsico

Even a global giant can target local consumers with current Modern Marketing tactics. Discover how Pepsi Beverages hopped on the newest trend in social: SoLoMo.

SoLoMo, or Social, Local, Mobile is one of the newest trends in social marketing and Pepsico are just one FMCG producer who are embracing it. SoLoMo allowed brand Pepsi to integrate social media with location-based mobile marketing to establish a geo-local reach-out to a key consumer audience, 18-25 year olds. The company used content taken from their Live For Now campaign on Pepsi.com, targeting consumers in specific geographical locations and following through on the company's firm belief that cyberspace, rather than traditional television, print, radio or billboard advertising, was the best way to achieve its goals.

Local customer data came from platforms like Facebook, where Pepsi has a more than 8 million strong community. George Smith, senior manager for social strategy and execution for Pepsi Beverages, says: 'With digital, you end up with a lot of extra data, and you end up with a lot more understanding of who your consumer is. By comparison, marketers can't deduce nearly as much about customer behavior through other forms of advertising, such as TV and billboards. Like many companies . . . Pepsi monitors what people say online about its products and sometimes steps in to refer disgruntled consumers to its customer-service team.'

Pepsi is a good role model for anyone interested in using the social media to get demographic information, engagement and brand opinion from an audience. Techniques like newsletter submissions, contest entries and other supporting or relevant promotions automatically amass data invaluable to a marketer, a tech-enabled power shift that has effectively neutralized many traditional forms of outbound, or push, marketing. Today's savvy consumers want to be listened to and courted, with channels of communication that go directly to the brands. Finding and targeting consumers in their own locations, as Pepsico has, keeps these customers focused on the brand like never before.

Skilfully deployed, Modern Marketing is a win-win for both brands and consumers. Smith recognizes the mutual benefit of this direct consumer interaction: 'It's nice to be able to have that direct conversation with [consumers], and not have to rely on a specific media channel to push this, or buy TV constantly to push that message.'

Twelve: Procter & Gamble

As many FMCG producers move into the digital space, the two key questions are Where and How Much? What have Proctor and Gamble's answers been? How much does the FMCG giant spend on digital and is it paying off?

At the end of 2012, Procter & Gamble estimated an allocation to digital of 35% of its massive marketing budget in the US. The company recently cut $10 million from their traditional marketing budget to re-focus on digital and mobile advertising. All this from a FMCG conglomerate which once leaned heavily on TV and magazine advertising in the past, but has now long been behind the broader market in digital.

A variety of estimates by industry analysts put P&G's current digital spend at somewhere between $1.2 and $4.8 billion, with The Interactive Advertising Bureau estimating a total US digital of $36.6 billion, to which the entire US FMCG industry contributes 7% or $2.5 billion. Plainly, exact amounts remain unclear. But whatever they are, P&G has certainly emerged as an extremely heavyweight digital investor. But the bottom-line is that Modern Marketing is working for P&G. Figures suggest the company is ahead of its competition. Even the conservative estimate of $1.2 billion in digital spending amounts to 3.8% to 5.6% of total US sales, compared to an average 2.8% spent on digital marketing by other manufacturers in the survey. Nor does P&G show any sign of retrenchment in either spend or digital commitment. When questioned on the future of digital marketing, P&G's Roisin Donnelly was quick to defend her employer's strategy and its more intangible advantages: 'Fundamental from a marketing standpoint, though, is the opportunity that digital provides you to truly connect people to your brand. The age of one-way, push-only communications is over as digital gives us the chance to build real, emotional and long-lasting connections with people in the spaces they choose. Our ultimate vision is to be able have 1:1 conversations between our brands and all our consumers, tailored to them and their needs and preferences. We're not there yet, but the pace of developments in digital makes it a real possibility in the future.'

P&G clearly recognizes that consumers are spending more time in digital media. 'They are getting entertainment, news and views, and doing shopping online.' Donnelly adds. 'People have access to information anytime and anywhere they want it, and it's not just what you say about your brands that they can find.'

With consumer access to brand information better today than ever before, and likely to do nothing but grow, the issue of brand trust is at the forefront. However, Donnelly realizes that traditional and Modern Marketing can work together to build that relationship: 'Brands need to find the right mix of digital and traditional media for their consumers. But not every brand needs to have presence in every media. You need to make choices driven by your consumers. They key is to be present and effective with the right message, at the right time and in the right place-based on where your consumers want and expect you to be.'

Thirteen: Reckitt Benckiser

Find out how the company used an online social media platform only to launch a new consumer product.

As 2012 marketing campaigns went, it surely ranked as bold: offering consumers the chance to buy the Reckitt Benckiser (RB) Cillit Bang All in 1 Dish & Surface Cleaner exclusively via Facebook. The washing up liquid product that comes with an automatic dispenser was made available to RB's Facebook Fans only and preceded its rollout in shops. Dubbed f-commerce, FMCG brands like Reckitt Benckiser, plus others Heinz and Asos, have been curious to test the marketing and e-commerce potential of the world's largest social network.

Reckitt Benckiser's UK marketing director Stefan Gaa was quick to defend his company's campaign at a time when social commerce had and still has its critics. Gaa said: 'RB prides itself on trying new stuff and this Facebook activity is another example of the company trying to push boundaries and try things out. In the end a business is about sales so to make it viable, you need to make sales but the beauty of social commerce is you're putting commerce into people's homes and bringing products to an environment consumers are already spending a lot of time.'

As our case-studies have already indicated, FMCG companies and consumers already have high levels of online engagement. But many see the next stage as social commerce. This is certainly true of RB, who want to join the likes of Heinz and Asos and encourage customers buy directly through Facebook. For now, however, return on investment is unclear. A study last year by Havas Media Social and Lightspeed Research found that 44% of people remain unconvinced and only 11% have actually bought anything at all.

Nonetheless, Reckitt Benckiser believes that because so many of its customers are spending so much time on social media sites it is important to target marketing energies in the same place. Gaa is optimistic: 'You never know before you do something how it will turn out. The world doesn't stand still - no one expected mobile phones or text messages to be the mass communication that they are. Our responsibility is to experiment because often in marketing you don't know, so you just do something and then the next time around you know a bit more.'

Another Reckitt Benckiser campaign, which may just indicate a company tip towards Modern Marketing, was Lysol Power & Free. The household bleach cleaner was marketed in 2013 via Facebook in the US, predominantly to reach female consumers aged between 24-54 years old, and promoted especially to appeal to ethical shoppers because of the product's positioning as a kinder alternative over harsher chemicals. The results were impressive. The Facebook campaign achieved 310 million page impressions - three-quarters of which were generated via earned rather than paid media. And although the company did use TV advertising in support, Laurent Faracci, US chief strategy and marketing officer for RB, confirmed both that the Facebook marketing results were similar to those RB typically achieves on TV in a similar time frame, and, given Facebook's low cost-per-thousand rates and the campaign's emphasis on earned social media impressions during the campaign, that the investment was almost certainly less.

In many ways, Lysol Power & Free campaign was an ideal online campaign, able to tap into the ecological concerns of the kind of culture-driven customer base that social media sites make it relatively easy to locate and then speak to. The resultant 30 percent boost to brand seems to clinch the argument.

Fourteen: Unilever

Modern Marketing means 1:1 marketing. The results Unilever has seen – and the FMCG industry as a whole - suggest the company is betting digital as the key to brand building.

Digital and mobile are the key components of Unilever's communications strategy. Jay Altschuler, Unilever's director of global media innovation, put the point bullishly to attendees at the Internet Advertising Bureau's annual Engage conference in 2013: 'For brand marketers, technology has made a 1:1 relationship with customers a reality. The most important value for brands to pursue is trust, because if you don't have that, then customers won't let you use their data.'

Unilever trusts its consumers so much that it puts company money where Altschuler's mouth is, as its Knorr brand launches an online portal to recruit food enthusiasts to act as advocates in a wider £12m marketing push to raise its profile in the UK. The campaign will unashamedly promote both the quality and taste of its products, as well as continuing to highlight convenience as a key selling point. The move aims to tap into the popularity of TV cookery shows such as Masterchef and Come Dine With Me.

The launch entails the effective creation of an online community to spearhead the charge and introduce new shoppers to the full Knorr product range. The portal will further serve as a hub for the brand's digital activity, providing an opportunity for consumers to interact with the brand's 230-strong team of Knorr Chefs who are responsible for making every single Knorr product. Visitors will be able to share recipes both from the experts and the celebrity chef Marco Pierre White as well as using a Buy It Now feature to purchase products such as stock cubes and gravy pots. Alongside print advertising, sampling and PR supporting the hub, the company will use Facebook to recruit fans for the brand's Kitchen Academy, which will offers members' recipes tailored to their preferences. A TV campaign will launch later this year to extend the push.

Earlier in 2013 Unilever launched its own social network with the aim of increasing trust and fostering collaboration between its in-house international marketing staff and external agencies. The move allowed marketers to share campaign knowledge and best-practice insight using Salesforce's Chatter technology. With the launch imminent, Marc Mathieu, Unilever's senior vice president of marketing gave details: 'The platform provides our team with the tools they need to develop and build our brands in local markets. It also frees up time for our team to create more magic - that is, to engage with consumers and create more effective marketing, which will be key to delivering our ambition to double the size of our business.'

So, if brand trust is the key universal that Unilever believe lies at the heart of Modern Marketing, the future of marketing is changing for all FMCG producers, with versatility also illuminating the way forward in the Unilever scheme of things. As Unilever's Paul Polman concludes: 'We are looking at more dynamic ways of involving the consumer and, no doubt, social networks are part of that. However, I don't think you want to make big statements. Otherwise, all of a sudden, everything is about Facebook. . . . TV [still] has a role to play and it will for a long time, but you first need to really talk about the brand, what it stands for and the message.'

Managing the Digital Marketplace

At the beginning of this chapter, we asked whether Modern Marketing was simply the emerging markets' future or everyone's. The answer must now be clear: everyone's. This heralds another interesting change. When the marketing media were traditional – the so-called push media – managing them was a simple matter: you had some agency think of fancy ideas, you booked the space or the slot, chose when and where it would be seen and heard. If your product could be written about, you had some journalist plug it. If it just looked good, you got a friendly film director to leave a pack of it in Sean Connery's Aston or Brigitte Bardot's bath (vary car, bath, actor as appropriate. Or product, or course: where was Lurpak in Last Tango in Paris?). This was simple stuff: you could make a list of it all. You knew where it was, and what it was, and what it said, and what you hoped it would do. But digital is different. Out there in digital there is a tsunami of information that is growing larger every second. We genuinely are at a threshold moment; over the next few years, the world and everyone in it will be digital and be connected. To the companies we have highlighted in this book, this will throw out both massive challenges and massive opportunities.

But this is not merely because digital is a new medium. It is not simply a case of local radio taking over from local papers in late 50s America, or TV taking over from them both. We have just pointed out the essential controllability, and in a sense predictability, of the traditional media: the simple stuff you could jot down in a cheap notebook. The digital media are both far more subtle, but far more powerful, than anything that has gone before. It's as if you'd put a couple of billboards in a town, and the billboards had suddenly started talking to each other, and then one or two more billboards joined in, some of which, as prominently displayed at the first two you'd commissioned, violently disagreed: rogue billboards, bigger than your own. Suddenly your company has a billboard footprint that can walk anywhere it wants to, and leave its grubby footprints all over that pristine brand image you've been striving for. That's digital. And a campaign on digital works in exactly the same way, but on a scale of billions and billions of conversations about you and your product. That is neither essential controllability nor in any sense predictability, but a digital footprint– and almost everyone has a DF these days - that can be a law unto itself. It's not a couple of actors with the ad agency's lines to read, it's a gigantic auditorium of interested parties with an axe to grind, all talking at once, and without a script. And your Facebook page – you chose Facebook instead of the billboards – set the whole thing going.

The Threshold Moment

Near-saturated mature markets groaning with infrastructure are going digital as fast as a technology that operates at light speed can allow. Very much bigger and very much hungrier markets – the emerging markets – are probably going even faster. And because they are infrastructure-light, there is, for example, no nostalgia for the printed word that slows them down. Digital is in a sense what mature markets must learn to understand: its powers of communication, its social influence, its links to everywhere and everyone and the fact that it fits in your pocket, whereas it's a reality that emerging markets – everybody's target – takes absolutely for granted. The consumers of the emerging markets – every operator's brightest future – grew up with digital – every future consumer's link to the markets, the market-places and the products. Remember, current growth rates predict that by 2020 – six short years away as we go to press - China will the world's number one, India number three and Russia number six by PPP. In marketing terms, the consumer has become an individual. Unhappy consumers now have the opportunity via viral interaction to damage brands and thus companies. But such bad news has an equal and opposite potential for good news: benefits, new products, new trends, new fashions, consumer approval and consumer brand enthusiasm, all will travel faster and grow faster than ever.

The Future

There is nothing so foolish or (future) scorn-provoking an activity as predicting the future. Nonetheless, we're going to try. We predict:
- That global FMCG companies are here to stay
- That their relative positions in the world league tables will reflect to a very large extent their relationships between the digital world and their continued success in the world's emerging markets
- That seven of the world's top twenty consumer goods manufactures are already retailers, who themselves are looking to develop prime relationships with the consumer
- That these league tables will change substantially – not quite beyond recognition – in the years to come as companies from emerging markets begin to make their presences felt: by huge acquisitions, for example
- That the takeover and major acquisition process will continue, because size improves not only buying power but also strength of negotiation with the retail trade

- And, finally, that the biggest and the best, using principally new digital technology, will be *the* personal marketers *par excellence*

And now, since we have to end the book somewhere, this seems as good a place as any, although, as endings go, it is not really final. This book's website will be updated at least twice a year, with all the latest figures and the latest, most relevant changes. We will almost certainly be adding new in-depth analyses of more companies. And later this year we will be publishing E-Retail. But that is another story.

To be continued, then.

Greg Thain and John Bradley

FMCG – Background Reading

Brandon, R. (2011). *Ugly Beauty*. New York: Harper

Bucher, A. & Villines, M. (2005). *The Greatest Thing Since Sliced Cheese: Stories of Kraft Foods Inventors and their Inventions*. Northfield: Kraft Foods Holdings Inc.

Dienstag, E.F. (1994). *In Good Company: 125 Years at the Heinz Table*. New York: Warner Books Inc.

Dyer, D., Dalzell, F. & Olegario, R. (2004). *Rising Tide: Lessons from 165 Years of Brand Building at Proctor & Gamble*. Boston: Harvard Business School Press

Enrico, R. & Kornbluth, J. (1986). *The Other Guy Blinked: How Pepsi Won the Cola Wars*. New York: Bantam Books

Foster, D. R. (1975). *The Story of Colgate-Palmolive: One Hundred and Sixty-Nine Years of Progress*. New York: Newcomen Society in North America

Gray, J. (1954). *Business Without Boundary: The Story of General Mills*. Minneapolis: University of Minnesota Press

Heinrich, T. & Batchelor, B. (2004). *Kotex, Kleenex, Huggies: Kimberly-Clark and the Consumer Revolution in American Business*. Columbus: The Ohio State University Press

Jones, G. (2005). *Renewing Unilever: Transformation and Tradition*. New York: Oxford University Press

Lauder, E. (1986). *Estée: A Success Story*. New York: Ballantine Books

Louis, C.J. & Yazijian, H.Z., (1980). *The Cola Wars*. New York: Everest House

Macqueen, A. (2005). *The King of Sunlight: How William Lever Cleaned up the World*. London: Corgi Books

Mason, R. & Foley, J. (1972). *The Food Makers. A History of General Foods Ltd*. Banbury, U.K.: General Foods

Mattern, J. (2011). *The Kellogg Family: Breakfast Cereal Pioneers*. Edina: ABDO Publishing

Potter, S. (1959). *The Magic Number: The Story of 57*. London: Max Reinhardt

Prendergast, M. (1993). *For God, Country & Coca-Cola*. New York: Basic Books

Schwartz, F. (2002). *Nestlé: The Secrets of Food, Trust and Globalization*. Toronto: Key Porter Books

FMCG: What You Didn't Know

Coca-Cola
Coca-Cola . . . 'was far from making Pemberton either rich or even debt free. When he fell ill the next year, he sold two-thirds of his joint-ownership of his company for the princely sum of $283.24. The tired and disillusioned Pemberton would almost certainly have taken his drink to the grave.' As it is, Coke's founder went without it. He died penniless a year later.

Danone
Danone was founded by a man more interested in curing orphans than keeping the middle classes healthy. He named his extremely unpopular product – and so the company – after his son.

General Mills
General Mills, world famous as the creator of Wheaties, Cheerios and Betty Crocker, was once the world's biggest toy company

Kimberley-Clark
Kimberley-Clark invented Cellucotton by accident, and although it found a highly valuable use for the material as a constituent of dressings for servicemen in the Second World War, when the war ended, it was deemed surplus to requirements. In fact, it rescued the company in true breakthrough style. How? See inside.

PepsiCo
Essentially, PeposiCo went bust three times and the man who first devised the drink left the business in disgust. PepsiCo became America's biggest food and beverage company

Unilever
Once owned a saw-mill, a coal-mine, a limestone quarry, a paper mill and an engineering firm.

Who are the CEOs

Coca-Cola Company	Muhtar A. Kent, born in 1952, is a Turkish-American business executive. He is the Chairman and Chief Executive Officer of The Coca-Cola Company. He was appointed to the position in 2008 and became Chairman of the Board in 2009.
Danone	Franck Riboud Chairman and Chief Executive Officer of Danone since May 2, 1996.
Dean Foods	Gregg A. Tanner Serves as Chief Executive Officer for Dean Foods, a role he assumed in October 2012.
Estée Lauder Companies	Fabrizio Freda is President and Chief Executive Officer, a position he assumed on July 1, 2009.
General Mills	Kendall J. Powell In 2006, Powell was elected President and Chief Operating Officer of General Mills with overall global operating responsibility for the company. He was elected Chief Executive Officer in September 2007 and Chairman in May 2008.
Henkel	Kasper Rorsted Chief Executive Officer since April 2008.
HJ Heinz	Bernardo Hees On the merger on June 7, 2013, in accordance with the Merger Agreement, Bernardo Hees was appointed as Chief Executive Officer of the Company.

Kellogg Company	John A. Bryant John A. Bryant has been President and Chief Executive Officer of Kellogg's since January 2011.
Kimberly-Clark	Chairman and CEO Thomas J. Falk. Falk was elected Chief Executive Officer in 2002 and became Chairman in 2003.
Kraft Foods Group	Tony Vernon became the first CEO of the new Kraft Foods Group upon its founding on October 1, 2012.
L'Oreal Group	Jean-Paul Agon is the current Chairman and CEO of L'Oréal since March 17, 2011.
Mars	Paul S. Michaels is Mars' current President.
Nestle	Paul Bulcke is a Belgian businessman who was appointed Chief Executive Officer of Nestlé on 20 September 2007 but assumed his new role officially in April 2008.
PepsiCo	Indra K. Nooyi Mrs. Nooyi was named President and CEO on October 1, 2006 and assumed the role of Chairman on May 2, 2007.
Reckitt Benckiser Group	Rakesh Kapoor became CEO in September 2011.
The Colgate-Palmolive Company	Ian M. Cook In 2005, Mr. Cook became President and Chief Operating Officer, responsible for all Colgate operations worldwide and was elected President and Chief Executive Officer in 2007. He became Chairman in January 1, 2009.

The Procter & Gamble Company	Alan George 'A.G.' Lafley, born June 13 1947, is the Chairman of the Board, President, and Chief Executive Officer of Procter & Gamble. Originally retired in 2010, he rejoined the company on May 23, 2013. Lafley previously served as P&G's President & CEO from 2000 to 2009.
Unilever	Paul Polman has been Chief Executive Officer since 1st January 2009.

Financials

Company	Country of HQ	Employee Numbers	Financial Year	Sales	Net income	Net Margin	Total Assets	Current Assets	Current Liablts	Market Cap
Coca-Cola	USA	146200	31/12/2012	48017	9019	18.8%	86174	30328	27821	171911
Colgate-P	USA	37700	31/12/2013	17420	2241	12.9%	13876	4822	3562	57990
Dean Foods	USA	21915	31/12/2012	11462	158	1.4%	5697	3980	2410	1390
Gen Mills	USA	35000	26/05/2013	17774	1855	10.4%	22658	4298	5293	31160
HJ Heinz	USA	31900	29/04/2012	11649	923	7.9%	11983	3882	2647	23240
Kellogg's	USA	31000	28/12/2013	14792	1807	12.2%	15474	3267	3835	21790
K-Clark	USA	58000	31/12/2013	21152	2142	10.1%	18919	6550	5848	41980
Kraft	USA	23000	29/12/2012	18339	1642	9.0%	23329	4823	3606	32050
P & G	USA	126000	30/06/2013	84167	11312	13.4%	139263	23990	30037	215290
PepsiCo	USA	278000	28/12/2013	66415	6740	10.1%	77478	22203	17839	119760
Estee L	USA	38500	30/06/2013	10181	1019	10.0%	7145	4297	1934	26330
Danone	France	101885	31/12/2012	26817	2336	8.7%	37959	8892	10987	38010
Henkel	Germany	46610	31/12/2012	21215	1999	9.4%	25090	9763	7435	47879
L'Oreal	France	68900	2012/12/31	28864	3818	13.2%	40221	12015	8468	121767
Nestle	Switzerland	339000	31/12/2012	98279	11791	12.0%	134572	37532	41314	224371
Unilever	UK / Neth	173000	31/12/2012	65951	6358	9.6%	59323	15609	20322	144357
R-Benckiser	UK	37800	31/12/2012	15164	2905	19.2%	23902	4845	10282	56616

All financials figures are in $US millions. Figures correct as at 17/02/2014

INDEX

Brazil, 4, 26, 29, 31, 32, 52, 54, 66,
67, 69, 77, 78, 79, 80, 83, 109,
118, 122, 144, 147, 154, 155,
182, 218, 224, 240, 247, 248,
274, 276, 294, 312, 320, 324,
330, 332, 334, 346, 361, 392,
429, 431, 432, 433, 436, 438,
457, 459, 461, 467, 468, 471,
473, 475, 491, 492, 493, 494,
495, 500, 502, 518
Brazil SA, 154
Brazilian, 312, 313
Brazilian Coffee Institute, 312
Bref Power, 160
Breyer's Good Humor, 448, 454
Breyers, 455
BRF, 491, 493, 494, 495, 496
BRIC, 346, 438
BRICIT, 218, 219, 220, 221, 222
Brie, 230
Britain, 41, 42, 108, 131, 139, 217,
238, 239, 286, 287, 289, 299,
310, 311, 313, 314, 318, 319,
380, 381, 395, 396, 397, 399,
444, 445, 446, 447, 448, 450,
479, 486
Britannia Biscuits, 64, 67, 78
Britannia Industries, 53
British, 4, 39, 131, 151, 188, 217,
234, 238, 239, 256, 286, 287,
289, 290, 291, 295, 296, 303,
314, 317, 318, 381, 396, 427,
441, 445, 446, 447, 449, 450,
453, 456, 461, 479, 486, 506
British Colonies, 4
British Empire, 131, 151, 238, 254,
396, 399, 456, 457
British Government, 287
British Royal Navy, 151
British Unilever Ltd, 445
Bronx, 393
Brooke Bond, 453, 458
Brooke Bond India, 459
Brooke Bond Lipton India Limited,
459
Brooke-Bond, 453
Brownberry, 500

Brushswap, 516
Brussels, 463
Bryant, John A., 195, 197, 537
BSN, 60, 61, 62, 63, 64, 65, 66, 80,
82
BSN-Gervais Danone, 61, 62, 67
Buavitaq, 470
Bubulubu, 497
Buckeye Cotton Oil Co., 341
Budget Gourmet, 136, 237
Budweiser, 505
Buenos Aires, 491
Buffalo, 229
Buffet, Warren, 301, 305, 355
Bugles, 108, 111
Buicks, 343
Buitoni, 317, 321
Buitoni-Perugina Pasta Company,
317
Bulcke, Paul, 328, 337, 537
Bulgaria, 63, 67
Bulgarian Activia Breakfast, 76
Bumble and bumble, 427, 428, 434
Buprenorphine Business Group,
407
Burger King, 377
Burma, 25
Burnett, Leo, 129, 179, 180, 238,
288
Burns, Robin, 426
Business Process Transformation,
383, 385
Business Week's World's Most
Innovative Companies, 367

C.J. Root Company of Indiana, 13
Cabbage Patch Dolls, 121
Cacharel, 266, 268, 271
Cadbury, 53, 243, 253, 254, 255,
256, 257, 258, 286, 287, 289,
290, 292, 293, 297, 301, 306,
317, 333, 600
Cadbury Brothers, 286
Cadbury India, 53
Cadbury, George, 229
Cadbury's Dairy Milk, 286
Cade, 493

Cadillac, 343, 373
Cadmun, 42
Caffeine-Free Diet Coca, 23
CAGR, 31
Cahills, 314
Cailler Company, 310
Calcutta, 458
Calgon, 397, 400, 408
California, 103, 284, 499, 525
Californian, 314
Callard & Bowser, 242
Callibaut, Barry, 320
Calvin Klein, 426, 454, 456
Camay, 156, 344
Camay and Fairy, 156
Cambodia, 380
Camel, 284
Camels, 284
Camembert, 230, 234
Campbell Taggart, 499
Campbell's, 128, 131
Can and Steel Institute, 20
Canada, 15, 16, 21, 25, 26, 30, 32,
    64, 69, 98, 109, 110, 112, 113,
    116, 122, 127, 131, 137, 157,
    181, 182, 183, 190, 196, 216,
    218, 238, 239, 241, 245, 247,
    251, 252, 255, 256, 268, 294,
    324, 327, 335, 345, 379, 381,
    396, 428, 429, 432, 443, 456,
    457, 512, 516,600
Canada Dry, 24
Canadian, 48, 107, 130, 133, 138,
    181, 202, 217, 218, 229, 241,
    249, 283, 317, 381
Candler, Asa Griggs, 10, 11, 12, 13,
    14, 16, 23
Cannes Lions International Festival
    of Creativity, 361
Cannon, 486
Cantonese, 108
Cap'n Crunch, 384
Capital Magazine, 161
Capri Sun, 242
Capri-Sun, 244
Carasso, Daniel, 3, 57, 58, 59, 65, 75,
    80

Carasso, Issac, 57
Care Bears, 111, 121
Cargill, 307
Caribbean, 191, 192, 494
Carmel, 498
Carnation, 316
Carnation Company, 316
Carnation Instant Breakfast, 324
Carraso, Daniel, 59
Carrefour, 49, 59, 72
Cascadian Farm, 116
Cashmere Bouquet, 39
Castile, 340, 341
Caterpillar, 449
Cebeco Groep BV, 493
CEE, 32, 33
Cellucotton, 3, 203, 205, 206, 212,
    217, 224, 225, 226, 535
Cellucotton Products Company, 204,
    206, 207, 208, 209, 212, 218, 451
Cellucotton Products Company
    (CPC), 204
Celta, 95
Central America, 26, 46, 182, 217
Central Europe, 44, 133, 155, 168,
    465, 469, 470, 473
Central European, 253
Central Research, 161
Central Research Group, 162
Central Research Institute, 508
Centrale Laitière du Maroc, 80
Cereal Partners Worldwide, 4, 107,
    109, 116, 118, 119, 120, 183,
    198, 319, 324, 335
Cescau, Patrick, 464
Ceylon, 449
Champion, 483
Chapman, Charles, 232
Chapple, 286
Chapple Brothers, 286
Charlie, 425
Charmin, 212, 349, 365, 366
Charmin Basic, 354
Charmin Paper Company, 212
Charmin Ultra-strong, 357
Chattanooga, 11, 24
Cheerioats, 107

Dove, 293, 294, 298, 307, 447, 449,
452, 454, 463, 465, 467, 475
Dove Campaign for Real Beauty,
465
Dove Men+Care, 474
Dove Minimising Deodorant, 471
DoveBar International Inc., 298
Dow Jones Sustainability Indexes,
470
Downy, 358
Dr Pepper, 254, 376, 392
Dr Pepper Snapple Group, 254, 392
Dr. Ballard, 317
Dr. Mitchell's Cola-Bola, 9
Dr. Pepper, 16, 24, 376
Dr. Tucker's Specific, 9
Dreyer's, 321
Dry Idea, 163
DS Waters LP, 69
DSD, 89, 94, 95, 97, 98, 183, 188,
190, 192, 195, 378, 383, 384, 394
Dubai, 7, 276, 294
Dudley Do-Right, 237
Dumex, 73, 74, 79
Dun & Bradstreet, 340
Dun's Business Month, 135
Duncan Foods, 19
Dunlap, Albert J., 216
Dunlap, Chainsaw Al, 216, 281
Dunnhumby, 517
DuPont, 287
Duracell, 237, 238, 240, 354, 355,
356, 358
Durex, 411, 413
Düsseldorf, 149, 150, 153, 155, 156,
164
Dutch, 73, 96, 131, 151, 441, 443,
445, 450, 456, 461, 476, 479
Dyson, James, 208

Earth's Best, 136
Earthgrains, 500
East Asia, 27, 29
East German, 63, 158
East Germany, 67
East Side Mario's, 378
Eastern Bloc, 63

Eastern Europe, 26, 31, 63, 82, 132,
155, 162, 163, 168, 169, 259,
271, 272, 275, 279, 324, 327,
335, 346, 347, 362, 399, 403,
465, 473
Eastern European, 63, 277, 293
Eastern Europeans, 63
Eastern Seaboard, 339
Eastman Kodak, 398
Easy Off, 405
Easy-Off, 398
EBIT, 327
EBITDA, 88, 325
Ebsworth, Peter, 519
EC, 494
Ecolab Inc., 398
e-commerce, 335, 435, 436, 520,
521, 522, 523, 528
E-Commerce, 436, 438, 600
Edam, 230
Eddie Bauer, 110, 111
EDLP, 139
EEC Single Market, 462
Eggo, 184, 185, 186, 189, 190, 196,
198
Eggo Blueberry Frozen Waffles, 184
Eggo French Toast, 184
Eggo Pancakes, 191
Egypt, 109, 132, 485
Eisenhower, Dwight, 17
El Globo, 499
El Molino, 496
El Reno, 103
El Salvador, 499
Electrasol, 408
Eleva Alimentos SA, 493
Elf Aquitaine's Sanofi, 272
Elida Gibbs, 447, 459
Elizabeth Arden, 20, 421, 424, 454,
456
Elkhorn, 229, 230
Emeraude, 399
ENA, 413
Energizer, 356
Energy Cosmetics, 275
Engels, Gregg, 99

IntoguSeal, 222
Interedi-Cosmopolitan, 265
International Association for Dental
  Research, 54
International Delight, 88, 90, 91, 92,
  93, 94, 95, 97, 98
International Millers' Exhibition,
  103
International Olympic Committee,
  28
Internet, 427, 431, 432, 433, 434,
  525, 529
Internet Advertising Bureau, 529
iPad, 122
IPO, 97, 99, 426
Iran, 25
Ireland, 42, 60, 71, 155, 181, 182,
  183, 193, 441, 474
Irene's, 254, 256
Irish, 43, 45, 47, 129, 339
Irish Spring, 43, 45, 47
Isdell, E. Neville, 26, 27, 28, 30
IT, 351, 467, 486
Italy, 29, 42, 62, 65, 66, 71, 73, 108,
  111, 131, 137, 142, 154, 182,
  193, 216, 223, 225, 239, 267,
  317, 318, 346, 398, 402, 428,
  448, 474, 479, 490, 491
Its Healthy Management, 174
Ivory, 40, 340, 341, 343, 344, 355,
  361, 364

J & J Colman, 396
J. M. Smucker Company, 357
J. S. Fry & Sons, 286
J. Walter Thompson, 380
Jack's, 242, 255
Jack's Frozen Pizza Inc., 242
Jackson, James Caleb, 174
Jackson, Michael, 377
Jacobs, 239, 241, 245, 250, 255, 256
Jacobs Suchard, 245
Jacobs, Joseph, 9
Jacquet and Jacquet, 424
Jamaica, 157
James S. Kirk & Co., 341
Jane, 426

Japan, 2, 27, 30, 31, 51, 52, 78, 127,
  131, 154, 155, 158, 163, 164,
  167, 170, 182, 193, 217, 268,
  270, 273, 279, 318, 324, 346,
  347, 429, 433, 434, 460, 467,
  494, 518
Japan Tobacco International, 2
Japanese, 13, 65, 66, 108, 267, 270,
  321, 346, 352, 354, 380, 411,
  446, 460, 506
Japanese Lion Corporation, 154
Jarret, Jeff, 522
Javex, 48
Jell-O, 240, 242
Jell-O No Bake, 244
Jell-O Yoghurt, 242
Jenness, Jim, 197
Jenny Craig, 327, 329, 333, 334
Jerky Treat, 134
Jersey City, 39
Jet Dry, 408
Jewish, 58
Jif, 349
JLFoods, 133, 136
Jo Malone, 427, 428, 436
John Labatt Ltd, 133
John West, 138
Johnson & Johnson, 206, 209, 211,
  212, 214
Johnson, Caleb, 40
Johnson, William R., 137
Johnston Coca-Cola Bottling Group,
  24
Joop!, 399
Jorba, Jaime, 496, 497, 499
Joseph Crosfield & Sons Ltd, 151
Jovan, 399
JTL Corporation, 24
Judd, Ashley, 429
Jugos del Valle, 29, 34
Juicy Fruit, 302
Jurgens, 443, 445

Kal Kan, 296, 297, 301
Kansas City, 39
Kapoor, Rakesh, 412, 537

4

KFC, 377
KGF Commercial Products, 241
KGF Frozen Products, 241
KGF International, 241
Khrushchev, 380
Khrushchev, Nikita, 374
Kiehl, 270, 271, 275, 278, 279, 280
Kikkoman, 505
Kimberley, John A., 201
Kimberley-Clark, 3, 170, 215, 217,
  218, 220, 221, 223, 356, 523, 535
Kimberly, 5, 7, 201, 202, 203, 204,
  206, 208, 209, 210, 211, 212,
  213, 214, 215, 216, 217, 218,
  219, 223, 224, 225, 226, 458,
  511, 522, 523, 534, 537
Kimberly, Clark & Co., 201, 202
Kimberly, John A., 201
Kimberly-Clark, 5, 7, 201, 203, 204,
  206, 208, 209, 210, 211, 212,
  213, 214, 215, 216, 217, 218,
  219, 223, 224, 225, 226, 511,
  522, 523, 534, 537
Kimberly-Clark Business-to-
  Business, 218, 219
Kimberly-Clark Consumer Products,
  218
Kimberly-Clark Consumer Tissue,
  218, 219
Kimberly-Clark de Mexico, 217
Kimberly-Clark Personal Care, 218,
  219
Kimberly-Clark Personal Care and
  Healthcare, 220
Kimberly-Clark Taiwan, 218
Kimbies, 212, 213, 214
Kit Kat, 318, 324, 327, 336
Kit Kat Chunky Peanut Butter, 324
Kit Kat Green, 324
Kitchen Aid, 237
Kitchens of Sara Lee Company, 233
Kix, 107
Kleenex, 206, 207, 208, 209, 210,
  212, 213, 214, 217, 219, 225,
  522, 534
Kleenex Anti-viral, 219
Kleenex Boutique, 210

Kleenex Cleansing Tissues to
  Kleenex Disposable
  Handkerchiefs, 207
Kleenex Facial Tissue with Lotion,
  222
Kleenex Huggies, 214
Kleenex Shop, 523
Kleenex Tissues, 206
Klix, 291
Knorr, 456, 463, 465, 467, 529, 530
Knorr Chefs, 530
Knorr Cubitos, 465
Knorr Stockpots, 471
Koch Industries, 307
Kohl's, 429, 431
Kohl's, 486
Kolynos Oral Care, 44
Kool-Aid, 240, 244
Kool-Aid Jammers, 244
Korea, 137, 193, 217, 433, 436, 485
Korean, 401
Kotex, 204, 205, 206, 207, 208, 209,
  210, 211, 212, 213, 214, 216,
  459, 534
Kotex Lightdays, 212, 215, 219
Kotex Lightdays Panty Liner, 212
KPIs, 413
Kraft, 230, 231, 232, 233, 234, 235,
  236, 237, 238, 239, 240, 241,
  242, 244, 245, 246, 247, 248,
  249, 250, 251, 252, 253, 254,
  255, 256, 257, 259, 290
Kraft Caramels, 233
Kraft Catalina French Dressing, 235
Kraft Cheese, 230
Kraft Cheese and Macaroni Dinner,
  233
Kraft Cheese Slices, 235
Kraft Cheese Sticks, 246
Kraft Cheez Whiz, 235
Kraft Company, 233
Kraft Cooking School, 524
Kraft Dairy, 245
Kraft Dairylea, 239
Kraft Developing Markets, 253
Kraft Dinner, 242
Kraft Europe, 245, 253

Murray, 188
Mustang, 431
Myanmar, 25

Nabisco, 4, 62, 238, 239, 242, 243,
    245, 250, 251, 253, 255
Nabisco 100 Calories Packs, 247
Nabisco Brands, 240
Nabisco Group Holding Corp., 242
Nabisco Holdings, 242
Naked Juice, 385
Namibia, 275
Nan, 329
Nana, 333
Nani, 329
Narang Beverages, 78
National Association of
    Broadcasters, 211
National Cancer Institute, 186
National Dairy, 231, 234, 236
National Dairy Products
    Corporation, 231, 234
National Healthy Product, 506
National Socialist, 153
National Starch, 164, 166, 168, 451,
    460
National Starch's Adhesives and
    Electronic Materials, 164
Natura, 361
Natural & Pure, 164
Natural Elements, 164, 166
Nature Valley, 111, 114, 115, 116,
    117, 118, 119, 120, 122
Nature's Purest and Most
    Wholesome Drink, 16
Nazi, 263, 446
Nazis, 263
NBC, 105, 208
Neenah, 7, 201
Neenah Paper, 216
Neenah Paper Inc., 219
Neiman Marcus, 270
Nelson Peltz, 257, 259
Nenuco, 397
Nepal, 459
Nescafé, 312, 313, 314, 317, 320,
    321, 324, 333, 336, 454

Nescafé Alegria, 335
Nescafé Cappuccino, 324
Nespresso, 318, 327, 329, 333, 335
Nesquik, 108, 313
Nestea, 28, 313, 327, 329, 335
Nestlé, 5, 1, 2, 4, 7, 28, 62, 64, 65, 69,
    82, 107, 108, 109, 112, 114, 119,
    183, 246, 255, 265, 266, 269,
    271, 276, 282, 285, 293, 298,
    299, 301, 309, 310, 311, 312,
    313, 314, 315, 316, 317, 318,
    319, 320, 321, 322, 323, 324,
    325, 326, 327, 328, 329, 330,
    331, 332, 333, 334, 335, 336,
    337, 379, 389, 392, 394, 448,
    450, 454, 469, 476, 480, 511,
    525, 534, 537
Nestlé 2011 Annual General
    Meeting, 282
Nestlé Alimentana Company, 313
Nestlé Aquarel, 320, 324, 327
Nestlé Babies, 315
Nestlé Company, 310, 311
Nestlé Group, 315
Nestlé Health Science, 333, 335, 337
Nestlé Ice Cream, 333
Nestlé Institute of Health Sciences,
    333
Nestlé Model, 326
Nestlé Nutrition, 320, 323, 325, 335,
    336, 337
Nestlé Nutrition Division, 320
Nestlé Pure Life, 320, 324, 327
Nestlé Purina Pet Care, 321
Nestlé Sources International, 319
Nestlé USA, 322
Nestlé, Heinrich, 309, 310, 312, 321,
    326
Nestlé/L'Oréal, 325
Nestlé's Fortified Tonic Food, 312
Netherland's, 380
Netherlands, 7, 26, 69, 96, 127, 144,
    154, 182, 324, 399, 447, 451,
    459, 462, 469, 474, 490, 494
Nevada, 298
Nevex, 49
New Coke, 23, 377

Shanghai, 7, 139, 163, 166, 168, 431, 460, 471, 508
Shanghai Longfong Foods, 139
Shanghai Pond's, 460
Shanghai Van den Bergh, 460
Shanghai-Lever, 460
Shattuck, Frank, 201
'She's a Jazz Baby', 105
Shenzhen, 488
Shenzou 6, 482
Shoppers Drug Mart, 432
Shredded Wheat, 108, 177
Shu Uemura, 270, 271, 274
Shu Uemura Cosmetics, Inc., 270
Shulton, 361, 422
Shultz & Company, 341
Sichel-Werke AG, 155
Sierra Leone, 25
Sierra Mist, 386, 387
Signal, 447, 451, 454, 455, 463, 469
Signal White Now, 471
Sil, 152
Silk, 90, 91, 92, 93, 94, 95
Silk Fruit & Protein, 97
Silk Kids, 91
Silk Live, 91
Silk Pure Almond, 98
Simply White Gel, 44
Sinex, 350
Singapore, 198, 311, 483, 485, 514
Skinceuticals, 271
Skippy, 478
Skittles, 299
SKU, 54, 92, 93, 138, 140, 434, 486
SKUs, 51, 139, 362, 431, 435, 502, 508
Slimfast, 455, 478
Slim-Fast, 464
Slough, 285, 290
Slow Churned Dreyer's Garand Light, 324
Small and Mighty, 466
Small Planet Foods, 112, 113, 119
Smart Ones, 134, 142, 143
Smart Spot, 383, 385, 386
Smart Start Healthy Start, 191
Smarties, 287, 318

Smashbox Beauty Cosmetics, 435
Smith, Carl, 106
Smith, Darwin, 211, 212, 213
Smith's Crisps, 107
SmithKline, 398
SmithKline Beecham, 398
Smiths, 381
Smiths Crisps, 381
Snack Ventures, 108, 115, 384
Snack Ventures Europe, 108
Snacking, 188, 236, 251
Snickers, 285, 289, 290, 294, 297, 298, 307
SoBe, 379, 381, 387
Social Media, 513
Societa del Plasmon, 131
Société d'Electro Chimie, 151
Société Européenne des Brasseries, 60
Société Francaise des Teintures Inoffensives, 261
Sodiaal, 119
SoFine Foods, 96
Soft & Dry, 163
Soft Drinks Town, 350
Soft Sheen, 269
Soft Youth Dew, 425
SoftSheen-Carson, 270
Softsoap, 44, 45, 49
Softsoap Kitchen Fresh Hands, 47
Softsoap Shea Butter, 47
Sojinal, 96
Solomon Islands, 443
Solvite, 155
Somat, 155, 166, 168
Somat 7, 163
Somat 9, 166
Sony, 23
Soreal, 268
Souchon-Neuvesel, 60
South (United States Civil War), 10
South Africa, 52, 154, 182, 197, 198, 276, 294, 396, 451, 456, 459, 468, 475
South African, 450
South African Pulp and Paper, 217

Suchard, Jacob, 241
Sugar Smacks, 193
Suiza, 87, 88, 89, 90, 93, 95, 98
Suiza Dairy, 85, 87, 88
Suiza Foods, 87, 88, 89, 95
Suiza-Dean, 97
Sun Soy, 88
Sunbeam, 497
SunChips, 385, 386
Sunlight, 342, 442, 443, 457, 477, 534
Sunlight Flakes, 443
Sunlight Soap, 456, 457
Sunny Delight, 350
Sunsilk, 446, 454, 455, 460, 463, 465, 475
Suntory Group, 69
Superbowl Sunday, 383, 393
Super-Rich All Purpose Crème, 419
Sur, 65
Surf, 458, 466
Surf Sachets, 460
Surgeon-General, 203
SWAT, 405
Sweden, 42, 182, 600
Swedish, 32, 482
Swiffer, 352, 414, 480
Swiss, 95, 285, 287, 294, 309, 310, 311, 312, 314, 315, 318, 321, 323, 326, 332, 334
Swiss General Chocolate Company, 311
Swiss Premium, 95
Switzerland, 4, 7, 42, 137, 151, 154, 182, 218, 225, 234, 265, 309, 311, 312, 313, 314, 443, 457, 479
Sydney, 181
Symbioscience, 299, 305
Synthélabo, 265, 272
Syoss, 159
Syria, 25
Syuejia, 504

T. G. Rose's Higher Control in Management, 287
T. Wall & Sons, 444
Tab, 19, 21, 23

Taco Bell, 377
Tacoma, 7, 283, 298
Tacoma, Washington, 283
Taft LYCRA, 162
Taiwan, 116, 218, 436, 483, 485, 504, 505, 506, 507, 508, 509
Taiwan Spinning, 504
Taiwanese, 504, 505, 506
Talbots, 486
Tambrands, 212, 215, 351
Tampax, 207, 209, 353
Tampax Sales Corporation, 208
Tang, 248, 255, 256
Tanner, Gregg A., 536
Target 2004+, 325
Tassimo, 247, 256
Tasters Choice, 314
Tata, 53, 458, 479
Tata Beverages, 53
Tata Oil Mills Company, 458
T-Bird, 20
Ted Bates & Co., 288
Tenderich, Gertrude, 208
Tennessee, 89
Terra Activ, 166
Tesco, 474
Tesco Clubcard, 517
Tetra-Acetyl Ethylene Diamene (TAED), 452
Tetra-Pak, 504
Teutonic, 149
Teva Pharmaceutical Industries, 361
Texas, 101, 173, 288, 376, 499
TGI, 138, 140, 143, 147, 472
TGI Friday, 138, 143, 147
Thailand, 31, 42, 51, 132, 183, 276, 319, 455, 457, 506, 508
Thanksgiving, 318
The Betty Crocker Cooking School of the Air, 105
The Body Shop, 274, 275, 277, 279, 280
The Breakfast of Champions, 105
The Coca-Cola Company, 37, 378
The Coke Side of Life, 28
The Danone Group, 83

286, 289, 291, 294, 295, 296,
297, 298, 299, 301, 303, 309,
311, 313, 314, 315, 316, 317,
321, 322, 327, 332, 333, 334,
336, 345, 346, 352, 353, 354,
357, 362, 363, 367, 379, 380,
383, 384, 385, 389, 390, 392,
394, 398, 399, 406, 408, 409,
410, 413, 414, 419, 422, 425,
426, 427, 428, 429, 430, 432,
433, 435, 436, 443, 446, 447,
448, 449, 450, 451, 452, 453,
454, 456, 457, 465, 466, 468,
469, 471, 475, 476, 485, 486,
487, 490, 493, 497, 498, 499,
500, 501, 502, 506, 507, 522,
525, 527, 529
United States Patent Office, 178
United Traders Limited, 458
University of Amsterdam, 472
University of California, 284
University of Minnesota, 110, 534
Unsweetened, 91
Urals, 4, 158
Uruguay, 268
US Bimbo, 499
US Boyle-Midway, 398
US Department of Agriculture, 126
US Government, 234, 305
US Healthy Weight Commitment
Foundation, 302
US Morning Foods Kellogg's, 196
US Snacks, 189
USA, 7, 52, 77, 95, 126, 136, 137,
138, 144, 145, 241, 310, 313,
324, 473, 486, 499
USABreads, 500
USP (unique selling point), 437
USP (Unique Selling Point), 437,
442, 496
USSR, 380

V, 72
V Water, 388
V. Pearl, 108
Van den Bergh, 443, 445
Van den Berghs, 459

Vanaspati, 457
Vandemoortele, Philippe, 96
Vanilla Coke, 24
Vanish, 399, 400, 404, 405, 407,
408, 412
Vanish Carpet Cleaner, 404
Vanish Oxi Action, 404, 407
Vaseline, 454, 467
Veet, 403, 404, 407, 408
Veet Rasera, 404
Vegemite, 238
Vegetable Compound, 480
Velasco, Alphonso, 496
Velveeta, 231
Velveeta Cheese, 239
Velveeta Creamy Potatoes, 244
Venezuela, 131, 133, 157, 182, 190,
191, 345, 385, 437, 499
Ventures Worldwide, 381
Vera Wang, 486
Vernon, 103
Vernon, Tony, 537
Very Vanilla, 91
Vespa, 497
VetEssentails, 51
Vevey, 7, 309, 312, 313, 335, 336
VIA, 256
Vichy, 264, 270, 271, 272, 273, 274
Vichy Thermal Spa Water, 264
Vicks VapoRub, 350
Victorian Butter Creams, 283, 284
Vidal Sassoon, 350
Vienetta, 452
Vietnam, 67, 274, 276, 430, 472,
473, 506, 508
Viking Melk, 311
Vila das Perdizes, 491
Vim, 443, 457
Virginia, 375
Vitaflo, 333
Vitalinea-Taillefine, 71
Vitality, 464, 465, 466, 467, 470,
473
Vittel, 314, 317
Volvic, 62, 65, 517

Waco, 103

Authors

Greg Thain has over 35 years of senior international business experience across a number of business areas: real estate, investment, property funds, agricultural consultancy, the internet, market research, retailing and publishing. For the last 20 years, in Russia and the emerging markets, he has been chairman or CEO of eight public companies and a director of companies in the UK, Australia, India, Russia, Ukraine, Romania, Hungary, Sweden, Hong Kong, Cyprus, Turkey and Greece.

Greg has also linked his commercial experience to the academic world. He is Adjunct Professor of E-Commerce, E-Retail & Marketing in International University of Monaco, and, throughout the last two decades, he has been a regular speaker at major events and conferences on the emerging markets, property, agriculture and marketing, with particular reference to how traditional marketing must now respond to the pressures and opportunities posed by the internet.

He is a co-author of *Storewars: The Battle for Mindspace and Shelfspace*, a major work now considered a must-have for every retail guru. Greg's new book, *FMCG: The Power of Fast-moving Consumer* Goods, also co-written with John Bradley, is published in June 2014. It will be followed later in the year by *E-Retailing*.

John Bradley held international marketing positions in Cadbury for 24 years before becoming a consultant and writer. John is the author of two business histories, *Cadbury's Purple Reign*, and *Fry's Chocolate Dream*, and the co-author, with Greg Thain, of the updated version of *Store Wars*. John now lives and works in Canada.

CPSIA information can be obtained at www.ICGtesting.com
Printed in the USA
BVOW02s1901260716

456932BV00029B/260/P

9 781622 876488